BUSINESS PLANNING AND POLICY

BUSINESS PLANNING AND POLICY

The Late Dr. C.B. Mamoria
Ex. Prof. & Head of Department,
Department of Commerce and Management Studies,
University of Udaipur,
Udaipur.

The Late Dr. Satish Mamoria
Ex. Reader in Commerce,
P.G. Department of Business Studies,
S.P. University,
Vallabh Vidyanagar,
Gujarat.

Dr. P. Subba Rao,
Professor and Head
S.K. Institute of Management,
Sri Krishnadevaraya University,
Anantpur — 515 003.
(E-mail: pulapas@rediffmail.com)

Himalaya Publishing House

MUMBAI • NEW DELHI • NAGPUR • BENGALURU • HYDERABAD • CHENNAI • PUNE
LUCKNOW • AHMEDABAD • ERNAKULAM • BHUBANESWAR • INDORE • KOLKATA • GUWAHATI

First Edition : 1987
Reprint : 1996
Reprint : 1997
Reprint : 1998
Reprint : 1999
Second Revised Edition : 2001
Reprint : 2003
Reprint : 2006
Reprint : 2013

Published by : Mrs. Meena Pandey for **Himalaya Publishing House Pvt. Ltd.,** "Ramdoot", Dr. Bhalerao Marg, Girgaon, **Mumbai - 400 004.** Phone: 022-23860170/23863863, Fax: 022-23877178
E-mail: himpub@vsnl.com; Website: www.himpub.com

Branch Offices :

New Delhi : "Pooja Apartments", 4-B, Murari Lal Street, Ansari Road, Darya Ganj, New Delhi - 110 002. Phone: 011-23270392, 23278631; Fax: 011-23256286

Nagpur : Kundanlal Chandak Industrial Estate, Ghat Road, Nagpur - 440 018. Phone: 0712-2738731, 3296733; Telefax: 0712-2721215

Bengaluru : No. 16/1 (Old 12/1), 1st Floor, Next to Hotel Highlands, Madhava Nagar, Race Course Road, Bengaluru - 560 001. Phone: 080-32919385; Telefax: 080-22286611

Hyderabad : No. 3-4-184, Lingampally, Besides Raghavendra Swamy Matham, Kachiguda, Hyderabad - 500 027. Phone: 040-27560041, 27550139; Mobile: 09390905282

Chennai : No. 8/2, Modley 2nd Street, Ground Floor, T. Nagar, Chennai - 600 017. Phone: 044-28144004/28144005; Mobile: 09345345051

Pune : First Floor, "Laksha" Apartment, No. 527, Mehunpura, Shaniwarpeth (Near Prabhat Theatre), Pune - 411 030. Phone: 020-24496323/24496333; Mobile: 09370579333

Lucknow : House No. 731, Sehkhupura Colony, Near B.D. Convent School, Lucknow -226024.Mobile : 09307501549

Ahmedabad : 114, "SHAIL", 1st Floor, Opp. Madhu Sudan House, C.G. Road, Navrang Pura, Ahmedabad - 380 009. Phone: 079-26560126; Mobile: 09377088847

Ernakulam : 39/104 A, Lakshmi Apartment, Karikkamuri Cross Rd., Ernakulam, Cochin - 622011, Kerala. Phone: 0484-2378012, 2378016; Mobile: 09344199799

Bhubaneswar : 5 Station Square, Bhubaneswar - 751 001 (Odisha). Phone: 0674-2532129, Mobile: 09338746007

Indore : Kesardeep Avenue Extension, 73, Narayan Bagh, Flat No. 302, IIIrd Floor, Near Humpty Dumpty School, Indore - 452 007 (M.P.). Mobile: 09301386468

Kolkata : 108/4, Beliaghata Main Road, Near ID Hospital, Opp. SBI Bank, Kolkata - 700 010, Phone: 033-32449649, Mobile: 09910440956

Guwahati : House No. 15, Behind Pragjyotish College, Near Sharma Printing Press, P.O. Bharalumukh, Guwahati - 781009, (Assam). Mobile: 09883055590, 09883055536

Printed at : New Offset Printers, New Delhi

PREFACE TO THE SECOND EDITION

Information technology has brought dramatic shifts in business operations during the last ten years. These shifts have ranged from creation of a new ventures like software solutions to new products like cellular phones which enable managers to be in contact with their field staff to computers that can design products and handle inventory control and help employees to communicate with each other via e-mail.

Information technology enabled the multinational companies to produce various parts of the product in more than ten countries, and finally to produce/assemble the product in the eleventh country through on-line instructions. Thereafter the MNC could sell the product in a number of countries at a superior speed due to the contribution of information technology. Further, information technology changed the way of business process through Business Process Re-engineering (BPRE), Enterprise Resource Planning (ERP) and Supply Chain Management.

Added to this, organisations shifted their structures from tall to flat and from rigid structures to flexible structures. Job designs drastically changed from individual designs to team design organisations.

The widespread trend towards globalisation by liberalising the economies and privatising the public sector has erased national political boundaries for the purpose of business. This shift made the industry of various advanced countries to spread its operations throughout the globe. This process magnified the domestic competition and turned the domestic competition into international competition. These trends of information technology and globalisation changed even the product design from standard to customised.

Ultimately, these developments changed the nature and scope of Business Planning and Policy. The old concepts and beliefs have become redundant and the new concepts of 'structure follows the strategy,' 'culture follows the strategy' and 'to-day's competitor is tomorrow's collaborator and vise-versa' have emerged.

This background forced the Publishers to think of revising the book. But the death of both the previous authors i.e., Dr. C.B. Mamoria and his son Dr. Satish Mamoria made the publishers to search for a third author. At this juncture, I have taken up the responsibility of revising this book thoroughly.

The second and revised edition of the book contains the material on the economic liberalisation and the following new chapters on information technology, economic liberalisation and global business, as also the latest developments in area and strategic management.

- Business Process Re-engineering and Enterprise Research Planning
- E-Commerce and Policy Implications
- New Economic Policy
- Major Macro Policies
- Multinational Corporations
- Total Quality Management
- Strategic Decision-Making
- The Strategist
- Social Accounting and Social Audit
- Managing Strategic Change
- Strategic Management in Non-Profit Organisations.

In addition, the information in other chapters has been thoroughly revised and concepts are provided lucidly with the help of exhibits and figures.

Shri. D.P. Pandey of Himalaya Publishing House persuaded and encouraged me to revise this book. My special thanks are due to him. Shri Niraj Pandey has been a continuous source of monitoring the progress of this revision. I thank him immensely.

I thank my wife, Mrs. P. Rama Devi, daughter Hima Bindu and son Venkata Rama Tej Kumar for having put up with the inconveniences caused during the period of revising this book.

Anantapur, **DR. P. SUBBA RAO**
May 2001.

PREFACE TO THE FIRST EDITION

Business policy is relatively a new concept in the history of management literature. It monitors managerial behaviour in terms of decision-making throughout the organizational hierarchy. It specifies the manner in which a firm should deploy its resources, overcome competition, exploit opportunities and minimize threats. By providing a unified theme for all activities, it facilitates management to optimize enterprise effectiveness.

In the present century, due to the unprecedented pace of S & T changes, business environment has become more hostile and uncertain than before. Consequently, organizations are finding it difficult to fulfil their mission. In such an environmental dilemma, the Darwinian maxim, "the survival of the fittest" will hold good too for the business organizations. Therefore, there is every reason to believe that not only survival but growth and development of business enterprise, too, is intimately linked with dynamism and pragmatism of its policies. This requires that the top brass of the organization should be well-versed with this important tool of management.

It has been noted that most books on business policy are primarily case books and the need has now arisen for a comprehensive and detailed text material in the field. Keeping this in mind, the book is presented. The book examines in depth the diverse aspects of business policy along with a host of related issues. To be specific, it deals at length with the concept of business, goals of business, business environment, social responsibilities of business, the planning process and different types of management policies, besides a thorough treatment of corporate strategies.

Needless to say that the book is the outcome of teaching the subject to post-graduate classes for a decade. In the preparation of the present work, the authour has heavily drawn upon standard literature, both Indian and foreign, for which he is highly indebted to the authors, editors and publishers of the works cited in references.

The book is largely the outcome of writings of my father, Dr. C.B. Mamoria, who unfortunately died when the final touches to the manuscript were in progress. The author finalized the remaining portion of the book. Hence its publication is delayed a bit. The author is deeply indebted to Dr. A. Dasgupta (Delhi), Dr. C.D. Singh (Bhagalpur), Dr. T.N. Kapoor (Delhi), Prof. M.M. Shah, Vallabh Vidyanagar, Dr. H.P. Chowksi (Baroda), Prof. U.M. Shah (Poona), Dr. V.L. Shrivastava, Dr. L.D. Joshi (Lucknow) and Dr. N.S. Rathore whose valuable views/guidance have immensely helped him in elucidating some controversail aspects of business policies.

I am also thankful to my departmental colleagues for their constant help and encouragement in pursuing my economic work.

I am very much obliged to Prof. D.R. Shrivastava for taking a keen personal interest in the preparation of the book.

My sincere thanks are also due to Mr. D.P. Pandey of the Himalaya Publishing House for taking pains to get the manuscript typed and for its publication.

The author sincerely feels that this comprehensive volume will meet the genuine needs not only of students of Business Administration but would also be equally useful to the top executives, corporate planners, government officials and all those concerned with corporate planning.

Suggestions for the further improvement of the publication are most welcome from all concerned quarters.

SATISH MAMORIA

P.G. Department of Business Studies,
S.P. University
Vallabh Vidyanagar (Gujarat)

CONTENTS

CHAPTER 1

BUSINESS SYSTEM

- **Introduction**
- **Goals of Business**
- **Business is a Social System**
- **Business and Economic Systems**
- **Forms of Business Firms**

INTRODUCTION

The term 'business' typically refers to the development and processing of economic values in society. Normally, the term is applied to that portion of economy whose primary purpose is to provide goods and services for society in an effective manner. It is also applied to economic and commercial activities of institutions having other purposes, such as the business office of an opera, association or Tennessee Valley Authority.[1]

"Business comprises all profit-seeking activities and enterprises that provide goods and services necessary to an economic system. *It is the economic pulse of a nation*, striving to increase society's standard of living. Profits are a primary mechanism for motivating these activities."[2]

"Business is any enterprise which makes, distributes, or provides any article or service which other members of the community need and are able and willing to pay for." [3]

Business may be defined as "the organised effort by individuals to produce goods and services, to sell these goods and services in a market place, and to reap some reward for this effort."[4]

Functionally, we may define business as "those human activities which involves production or purchase of goods with the object of selling them at a profit." In essence, business represents an organised effort by an individual or individuals engaged in making a living. Each firm furnishes goods and services to others, and each operates with the aim of furnishing some return to its members.

Characteristics of Business

Business possesses the following characteristics :

1. It is the *business of 'business' to provide goods and services to the people*. It provides the public with the things it needs and wants in order to survive, enjoy life, and improve in a material sense. From the point of view of the consumer, business is the satisfier of needs and desire. What the customer demands is what business should provide.
2. Goods which have been produced or procured for sale in return for price enter the realm of business. This activity of selling results in the production of wealth for the society. In satisfying demand, business uses the resources of land, labour, and capital. These resources when taken separately have little value; but business combines, structures, and refines the resources to produce useful goods and services, which are an addition to the value of society. Further, business employees people who exchange their talents for wages and salaries. These people, in turn, exchange their compensation for the desired goods and services

1. Davis, Keith and Robert L.Blomstrom, *Business and Society Environment and Responsibility*, McGraw–Hill Book Co., New York, 1975 Third Edition, p.19.
2. Boone, Louis E. and David L.Kurtz, *Contemporary Business*, Dryden Press, Hinsdale, Illinois, 1975, 2nd edition, p.7.
3. Urwick and Hunt, *Handbook of Business Administration.*
4. Davis, Keith, *The challenge of Business*, McGraw-Hill Book Co., New York, 1975, p.5.

3. *Business is a profit-seeking activity*. It supplies goods and services to satisfy demand and adds to society's value by earning a profit. Profit is the biggest stimulus for maintaining the continuity of business and its future development. Society permits business to earn this profit as a reward for assuming the risks of operating a business.
4. *Business is also a participant in society*. In satisfying demand, supplying goods and services, and earning profits, business is deeply involved in the most fundamental activities of society. As a result, society looks to business for something more than products, services, and profits. It looks to business for leadership and direction in helping to achieve society's objectives. It expects business to assist in the establishment of a better society.

Components of Business

Business includes the total enterprise of the country in industry and commerce. Business activity has two branches :

(i) the production of goods and services required in the market. This activity is referred to as 'Industry', and

(ii) exchange or distribution of goods and services to the customers. This is called 'Commerce'.

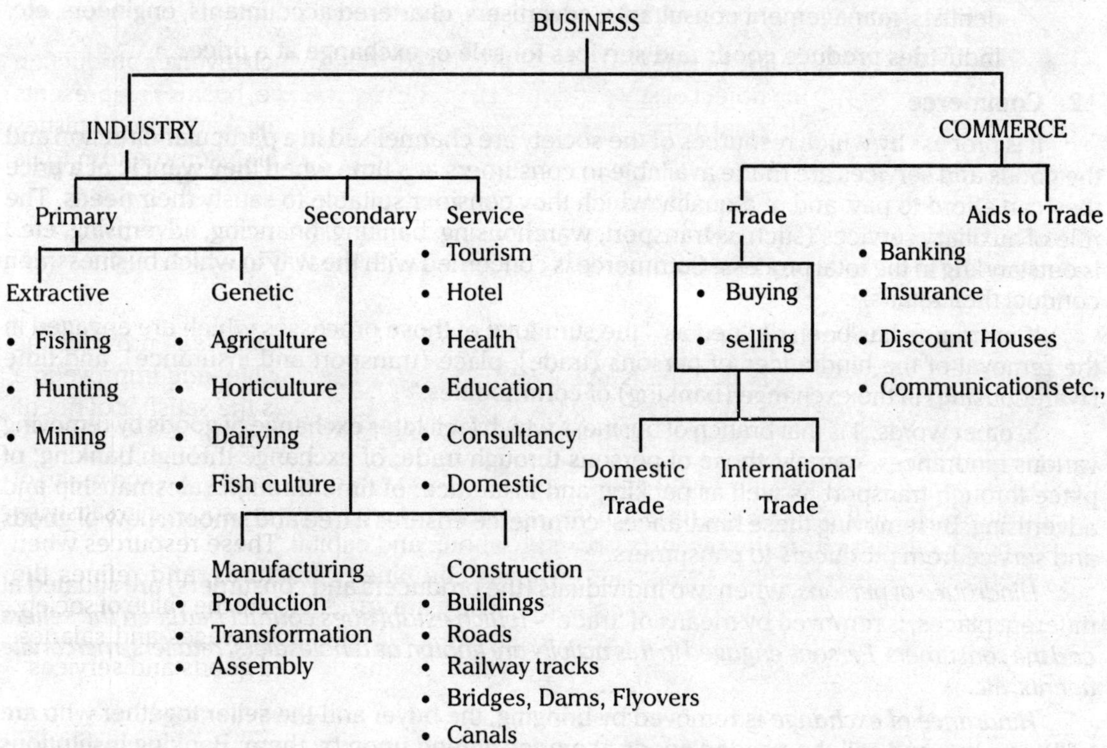

Fig. 1.1 Components of Business.

1. Industry

Industry is concerned with the production of goods and rendering of services to the final consumer or the industrialist for further production of goods and services. Industries are generally subdivided into five main categories :

(a) *Extractive industries*, which are engaged in raising from the soil resources or extracting from the bowels of the earth various forms of resources (wealth), *e.g.*, hunting, fishing, mining, fruit-gathering, agriculture, etc.

(b) *Genetic industries*, which require for their raising better human skill and knowledge such as poultry, and dairy farming, cattle-breeding, breeding plants, horticulture, pisci-culture, seri-culture, arbori-culture, etc.

(c) *Manufacturing industries*, which are engaged in the conversion and processing of raw material – through separation, combination and transformation – to finished goods for direct consumption by the consumer or to be used as raw material for other industries, such as machinery and plants of all types, iron and steel, sugar, paper, cotton cloth, electrical appliances, zinc ore, paper – pulp, water power, etc.

(d) *Construction industries* are concerned with the construction of roads, railways, dams, canals, buildings, bridges, etc. They are mainly concerned with the manufacture of non-movable items.

(e) *Territory or Service industries*, which produce intangible goods – those which cannot be seen or touched. Included in this category are banking, transport, insurance, communication and services of a professional nature such as of lawyers, doctors, dentists, management consultants, advertisers, chartered accountants, engineers, etc.

Industries produce goods and services for sale or exchange at a price.

2. Commerce

It is process by which resources of the society are channelised in a particular direction and the goods and services are made available to consumers at a time when they want it, at a price they can afford to pay, and of a quality which they consider suitable to satisfy their needs. The role of auxiliary services (such as transport, warehousing, banking, financing, advertising, etc.) is outstanding in the total process. Commerce is concerned with the way in which businessmen conduct their affairs.

'Commerce has been defined as' "the sum total of those processes which are engaged in the removal of the hindrances of persons (trade), place (transport and insurance), and time (warehousing) in the exchange (banking) of commodities."[5]

In other words, it is that branch of business which facilitates exchange of goods by removing various hindrances, namely, those of persons through trade; of exchange through banking; of place through transport as well as packing and insurance; of time through salesmanship and advertising. By removing these hindrances, commerce ensures a free and smooth flow of goods and service from producers to consumers.

Hindrance of persons, when two individuals (the producers and consumers) are situated at different places, is removed by means of 'trade' – *which establishes contact between the sellers and the consumers. Persons engaged in this activity are known as wholesalers, retailers, mercantile agents, etc.*

Hindrance of exchange is removed by bringing, the buyer and the seller together who are willing to buy and sell the needed goods at a price agreed upon by them. Banking institutions facilitate this payment.

Hindrance of place, i.e., the barrier of distance between the place of production and market, is removed by different means of transport – trucks, railways, boats etc. The risk involved in

5. Stephenson, James, *Principles and Practice of Commerce*, Sir Isaac Pitman & Sons Ltd., London, 1965.

transportation of goods can be covered by insurance, so also the loss incurred during storage and packaging and damage and pilferage.

Hindrance of time. Goods are produced in anticipation of demand and, therefore, they have to be stored before use. So creating of storage and warehousing facilities removes this hindrance and insurance removes the risk of loss or damage through fire or theft during storage.

Hindrance of knowledge. The consumer may not be aware of the goods produced, of their quality and price, but this hindrance is removed by such activities as advertising and salesmanship undertaken by the sellers.

3. Trade

It means sale, transfer or exchange of goods and services, through certain ancillary functions, such as packaging, warehousing, banking, transportation, insurance, and advertising.

Trade may be (i) *home of domestic*, it may be *local or regional* or *inter-state*: or (ii) *external* or *foreign* popularly known as *international trade*, and may comprise export, import, entrepot or re-export trade.

GOALS OF BUSINESS

Peter Drucker has emphasised that the only one valid purpose/goal of business is to "create a customer". In support of this statement, he argues that "Business enterprise aims to earn profits through serving the customer demand. It thinks more in terms of profitable sale rather than more sales volume for its own sake. Today, marketing in the firm begins and ends with the customers. First, we have to identify customers, then we offer our output of goods and services primarily to secure continuous customer satisfaction. Repeat sales are possible only on customer satisfaction. The firm's profits, indeed its very survival, are linked to the satisfaction of customer need and wants."

In other words, the business undertakes to fulfil the following economic and social goals :

I. Economic Goals

These comprise :

1. *High Standard of Living*, which means an abundance of goods and services available for consumption by the people and a substantial amount of leisure which such abundance make possible. This goal requires the achievement of high productivity.
2. *Increase in Productivity and Efficiency*, which goal indicates that good businessmen are aware of the fact that they have an overriding obligation "to be a productive and creative force in society"; and that they "must build, expand and put forth goods and services in abundance." To achieve these expansions, they undertake research and development (R & D) programmes, invest profits in the purchases of new tools and equipments; adopt aggressive sales promotion schemes, provide extra incentive and motivation to workers, and lower prices by the use of modern production techniques.
3. *Economic Progress*, which can be achieved by making an optimum utilisation of the material and non-material resources of capital by developing inventiveness, administrative skills,

craftsmanship, education and training of workers; and conserving energy of the employees so that the natural resources are properly utilized.

4. *Economic Stability*, which is and can be achieved by framing and adopting economic and fiscal policies, making accurate sales forecasts, preparing production schedules, diversifying products, and stimulating sales in off-season so that frequent fluctuations in economic activity, prices and cost of living are restricted.

5. *Discipline in Economic Life*, which requires the regular flow of goods and services to the market, the systematic equalization of demand and supply in the market and the absence of industrial strifes.

II. Social Goals

Social goals include the following :

1. *Justice and Equality* : Business tries to equitably distribute wealth and means of production and a wide diffusion of opportunity for personal development and economic growth.
2. *Community of Relations* : Business tries to maintain good relations with the community. Since the company is regarded as a citizen and a neighbour in the community in which its plants are located, it must fulfil its obligations of a good citizen and neighbour.
3. *Community Improvement*, which can be achieved by arranging the location of factories and markets at proper places: disposal of smoke and waste, removing ugly appearance of buildings, slum clearance, sanitation schemes, etc. So that the living environment of the community is made healthful and aesthetically satisfying.
4. *Conservation of National Resources*, which means that the non-renewable resources of Nature should not be ruthlessly exploited but utilised economically with an eye to the future requirements.
5. *Educational Programmes*. In the words of Paul G. Hoffman, "Businessmen should be torch-bearers of economic literacy." Education is directed towards stockholders, employees, consumers, government officials, and the general public. Education is imparted to achieve the following objectives: (a) to quicken the interest of the shareholders in the company they own and in the enterprise system generally; (b) to achieve better labour-management relations and greater labour productivity; (c) to develop better public relations and (d) to develop more favourable attitude towards the individual enterprises.
6. *Improve Personal Integrity of Business*, which is to maintain high standards of honour in all economic activities and transactions. This includes truthfulness in advertising and selling, faithful observance of contract; fairness in relations with competitors; avoidance of questionable financial manipulations and unfair trade practices; compliance with government policies, honest payment of taxes and duties; and general adherence to the 'rules of game', both in letter and spirit.
7. *Development of Individual Person*, which means that individual personality should be developed by providing: (i) a healthy work environment to the employees; (ii) mutual respect and consideration in the relationship of individuals, (iii) increased opportunities for creative activities; and personal advancement.
8. *Personal Security*, which means that certain contingencies of life which are beyond the means and control of an individual because of old age, physical disability, illness, accident,

poverty, and other hazards of life like unemployment, maternity etc. are provided for by such economic and social security measures/assistance as provident fund and pension benefits, welfare and medical facilities, leave with wages for a certain specified period, free hospitalisation, etc.

9. *Human Dignity and Relations*. This means that businessmen should make efforts to establish face-to-face relationship and a friendly atmosphere within the company.

Decisions of Businessmen are Indicative of their Goals

However, it may be noted that it is on the basis of economic and social goals stated above that the (social) performance of a business is judged. These are the pivoted points which businessmen are expected to consider, along with their own interests, when they are making decisions on production, pricing, selecting personnel, making inventories, and searching for funds and their investments. The questions a businessman must ask himself while taking a decision are: What this decision will mean in terms of the standard of living of the people? Will it increase their income and raise them above the poverty line to a comfortable level? Is it consistent with the economic policy of the state and progress? Does it promote economic stability and bring economic discipline among the employees? Is it good for personal security and bringing about the development of individual personality? Does it help to preserve and strengthen the law and order situation? Is it just and fair? Does it bring freedom to the employee? Does it help people toward self-realisation? Is it good for the community? Is it good for and helpful towards national integrity and security? Is it hourable?

When a businessman decides :

1. Whether or not to produce a new product or service, *his aim is to decide the range of products available to the consumers;*
2. Whether or not to purchase new plant and machinery, *his aim is to determine the rate of economic progress and to influence the level of employment and prices;*
3. To build up or reduce inventories, *he contributes to inflation or accelerate recession;*
4. To change his wage or dividend policy, *his aim is to influence both the level of employment and the degree of justice achieved in the distribution of income;*
5. To close down a plant or to move it to another location, *his aim may be to affect the economic future;*
6. To use the newspaper, radio, television for advertising or public relations, *he may be influencing moral and cultural standards;*
7. To introduce new personnel policies, *he contributes towards co-operation and understanding between labour and management or he may be aggravating existing tensions and factions between them;*
8. To transact business in foreign lands, he may be contributing to international tensions or international understanding;
9. To provide for community services, he may wish to fulfil his social responsibility towards it or to get its image improved.

BUSINESS IS A SOCIAL SYSTEM

A business is a complex economic and social entity, which has interactions with other parts of society. Every action of business is related to the external environment surrounding it and, in turn, everything which occurs in this external surrounding is related to business. If this significant relationship of business with its environment could be identified, it will be noticed that business is effectively related with the larger framework known as the 'social system'. Through this the contributions which business and society make to each can be better understood. Further, by having this knowledge, the managers may utilise the inputs more effectively for making better judgements. The society also stands to benefit in so far as it can evaluate whether and how well the objectives of the business have been achieved.

Chief Characteristics of Business As a Social System

1. *Sub-systems make an Inter-related Whole*. Business is here seen as a 'whole', each part of which has its own function, i.e, 'doing its own thing'. It can be compared to a human body in which the eyes perform the function of seeing while the hands do the work. But the parts in the system are *inter-related*, affecting each other in various ways through their inputs and outputs among themselves. Similarly, business is also a part of a larger system, which again is a part of an even larger system, and so on, until all related parts have been joined in terms of the largest known system. Thus, something is a 'whole system' from one point of view, but a 'sub-system' from a larger point of view. The 'sub-system' is also called a 'lower-order system' compared with a 'higher order system'. Systems exist in hierarchies from the lower order to a higher order.[6]

2. *Dynamic and Stabilising Tendencies* : The social system is not static but dynamic. This dynamism is due to the fact that people are living, thinking and active beings. This characteristic of theirs adds to the variability and uncertainty making social systems a difficult challenge for the managers. However, with this dynamism is also found a certain degree of accommodation and harmony, both among its parts and its external environment, i.e., it operates in some degree of *equilibrium*. Keith and Blomstrom compare this equilibrium with a quiet ocean filled with moving sea life and waves – all of which operate in a balanced manner. If and when a typhoon builds towering waves that are destructive or the water becomes so polluted that sea life begins to die, disequilibrium occurs. Similarly, a *business needs to maintain satisfactory equilibrium*, both internally and externally, *in order to survive and make reasonable progress to achieve its objectives*.[7] If internal parts or external factors do not work in the same direction, disequilibrium in business results, leading to its partial or total failure in achieving its objectives.

Therefore, business maintains an effective equilibrium by keeping a co-operative relationship between the internal and the external factors and by remedying the inconsistencies. This tendency of self-correction has been termed "homeo-statis" by Davis and Blomstrom. This situation is essential for a business to keep itself in existence for a long time.

6. Davis, Keith and Robert L. Blomstrom, *Business and Society: Environment And Responsibility*, McGraw-Hill Book Co., New York, 1975. p.13.
7. *Davis, K, and Blomstrom, Ibid.*, p. 14.

3. *Viability*. This implies the "drive to live and grow", "to accomplish a probable potential objective", and "to achieve all that a living system is capable of becoming", This drive for growth is accomplished by improving the quality and quantity of services it renders, and by meeting competition through a better sales campaign.

4. *Business Viability*. This means adaptability to change when circumstances so demand. Improvement in technology, working conditions and international development are instances whose viability has been more easily responded. To be a viably entity, business must contribute its share of forces to its environment rather than merely adjust itself to outside forces. Every business needs a drive and spirit, all of its own, to make it a positive actor on the societal stage rather than a reactor or a reflector,[8]

5. *Public Visibility*. This refers to the extent that an organisation's activities are known to persons/public outside the organisation. The activities of the organisation may be directly observed, such as polluted atmosphere when smoke is seen coming out of a mill-chimney or a smokestack or purchase of a product which is adulterated or of short weight or measure. Incidentally, these activities may be communicated by news media, neighbours and other sources. The idea of public visibility is that it makes business activities subject to public examination, discussion, and judgement, for unless the activities are known, they cannot be judged.

6. *Social Values*. Business normally operates in an environment of social values, both of society and those of the business itself. For business, such values are derived from various sources such as the mission of the business as a social institution, the country in which the business is located, the type of industry in which it is active, the nature of its employees, the management philosophy, the customs and traditions of society and normal practices of other business. In course of time, these values become institutionalised, i.e., they are accepted by a large number of people in the organisation and also the society and consequently, they take the shape of an official policy of the business.

Social values perform certain important functions. One, they become guides for employee decision in the interests of business and its environment; and, two they become strong motivators for people in a business. Thus, they become a key factor in the system relationship of business with society.[9]

7. *Interface with an External Environment*. An individual business cannot work in isolation and is, therefore, related to other businesses and social groups. This area of contact between one system and another system has been termed as 'interface'. Areas of interface are of vital significance because they are sources of inputs into the system. These inputs give it additional resources from which outputs are produced, and the system is provided with information feed-back which enables it to take corrective action to maintain equilibrium with its environment.

Thus, it should be noted that *business* organisations are open systems interconnected with such external groups as customers, trade unions, government, community agencies, and others.

8. Davis, K., R.L. Blomstrom, *Ibid.*, p.15.
9. Davis, K, and R.L. Blomstrom, *Ibid.*, p. 19.

BUSINESS AND ECONOMIC SYSTEMS

By "economic system is meant the *different forms of economic organisations that arise in the community from the organisation or mode of product.*" In other words, it is a set-up which comprises various institutions and bodies, with the ultimate purpose of satisfying the wants of the people living within a particular territory and in the way in which those people want.[10]

Basic Features of Economic Systems

The basic features of an economic system are that:

(i) They are not static, they are relative to the needs of the people and, hence, are of a changing nature.

(ii) They have fundamental uniformity of problems within a mechanism of great diversity.

(iii) They are all evolving patterns of human relations. With the help of institutions, (such as property, money system, labour organisation, government agencies, production unit, etc,), they try to secure maximum production from scarce human and natural resources.

(iv) Their goal is to satisfy individuals and public by production of goods and services required by them.

Factors influencing Economic Systems

Economic system arise and are modified, from time to time, by various factors, such as :

(a) the laws of the land;

(b) the decisions of the judicial agencies;

(c) the contractual arrangements people set up among themselves in order to carry on exchange;

(d) the customs, habits, set of beliefs that people develop within the social and political set-up of the country; and

(e) the public opinion about the wages and means through which people wish to satisfy their wants.

Loucks has observed that "The economic system of a country is determined by these forces (i) the historic-cultural resources of its people's ideals, desires and attitudes; (ii) its natural

10. Some definitions of 'economic system' are: "An economic system is an evolving pattern of complex human relations which is concerned with the disposal of scarce resources for the purpose of satisfying various private and public needs for goods and services" (M. Gottlieb, *Theory of an Economic System*, p.8.)
– "An economic system consists of those institutions which a given people, a nation, or a group of nations has chosen or accepted as the means through which their resources are utilized for the satisfaction of human wants", (W.W. Loucks, *Comparative Economic Systems*, p.5.)
–"An economic system is the sum total of devices which through their interaction give effect to economic choice, i.e., which translate choice from an idea into action. Action in this context means the actual movement of resources towards the intended uses". (Jan Prybla, *Comparative Economic Systems*, p.10)

resources, including climate; (iii) the philosophies which some or many of its people possess and advocate; (iv) the present and past theorizing of its people about how to achieve chosen ideals and goals; and (v) the trials and errors of its people in seeking economic ends." [11]

FORMS OF BUSINESS FIRMS

The stage of economic development and the level of economic activity determine the suitability of a form of business firm. In fact, a particular form of business firm play a dominant role in the economic activities at a particular stage of economic development. In other words, all forms of business firms play their due roles in the economic activities.

Forms of Business firms.

Private sector
- Sole proprietorship
- Partnership
- Joint stock companies
  - Private limited
  - Public limited

Public sector
- Departmental undertakings
- Statutory corporations

Cooperative sector
- Co-operative societies

Fig.1.2

The total business activity in the country is carried out in three sectors *viz.*, private sector, public sector and cooperative sector. Private sector plays major role in capitalist or market economies. Public sector and cooperative sectors play significant roles in communistic or socialistic economic systems.

Private Sector

Private investment, management and control dominate in private sector. The forms of business firms in private sector include: sole proprietorship firms, partnership firms, private limited companies and public limited companies.

Sole proprietorship

The sole proprietor or sole trader is an individual who invests, owns, manages and controls the business. The individual invests his own and /or borrowed capital, manages the business, bears all the risks alone, enjoys all the profits and suffers from all the losses. Thus the sole proprietor is the sole owner, manager, controller, strategist, policy maker, risk-bearer, financier all rolled into one.

Advantages

The advantages of sole proprietorship form of businesses include : ease facility of formation, quick decision-making prompt, action, establishment of maximum personal contact with customers, confidentiality of business decisions, flexibility, lower costs of management etc.

11. Samuelson, Paul A., *Economics,* McGraw - Hill Book Co., New York, 8th Ed., 1970, pp. 15-16.

Disadvantages

Sole proprietorship form of business suffers from the following disadvantages. They are : limited capital, limited abilities of management, unlimited liability when the business form incurs losses, absence of legal status, absence if specialisation and economies of scale due to small size and the like.

Partnership Firms

The limitations of sole proprietorship firms particularly, availability of limited capital, limited scope for expansion and small size of the business, partnership type of firms have emerged. A partnership is usually formed to combine capital, labour and varied specialised skills and knowledge. The term partnership is defined by the Indian Partnership Act, 1932 as, "the relation between two or more persons who have agreed to share profits of a business, carried on by all or any of them acting for all."

Features

The features of partnership include : (i) It is a form of business firm (ii) It is a result of agreement between two or among more than two partners (iii) the object of starting a partnership is sharing of profit among partners. (iv) a partner can act simultaneously as principal/owner and an agent of the firm, (v) the essence of partnership is the spirit of cooperation. (vi) the minimum number of members of a trading partnership firm is 20 and of a banking partnership firm is 10, (vii) the liability of partners is unlimited, joint as well as several. In other words, partners are jointly and individually liable for the payment of complete debts even from their personal assets, (viii) partners are not permitted to sell or transfer their shares to others without the consent of all partners.

Advantages

The advantages of partnership firms include : (i) high capital raising power of the firm (ii) higher and varied managerial skills, (iii) easy formation of partnership firm (iv) simple dissolution (v) maintenance of business secrecy and (vi) partners do the business continuously without taking much risk as the liability of the partners is unlimited, joint and several. However, the partnership also suffers from some disadvantages.

Disadvantages

The disadvantages of partnership firms include : (i) limitation on capital (ii) managerial skills of the partners may be limited (iii) absence of separate legal status and stable life (iv) dangers of unlimited, joint and several liability (v) problems of non-transferable shares of the partners and (vii) absence of public confidence.

Joint Stock Companies

Neither the sole proprietorship firms nor partnership firms can normally mobilise large amount of capital required by large scale industries. Similarly these firms also can't provide necessary managerial skills for the large business houses. Another major problem of these two forms of business firms is unlimited liability. Added to this, is the emergence of large scale business firms resulting in the formation of Joint stock companies.

A joint stock company "is an incorporated association which is an artificial person (an association of natural persons) created by law having a common seal and perceptual succession." The joint stock company is a limited company because the liability of the owner/shareholder is limited to the extent of unpaid amount of the face value of the share.

Features

The features of a joint stock company include : (i) compulsory incorporation (ii) company is an artificial person, (iii) company has a common seal (iv) company has perpetual/continuous life, (v) the company can enjoy expert and professional managerial talents and skills due to separation of ownership from management, (vi) company enjoys lower tax liability as it is recognised as an independent legal person (vii) the shareholders of a joint stock company have a privilege of limited liability. Their liability is limited to the extent of unpaid amount of the face value of the share (viii) wide distribution of risk of loss due to large number of shareholders (ix) easy transferability of shares. Members of the company can transfer their shares easily (x) The capital of the joint stock is contributed by a large number of members. Thus the joint stock company has a large number of shareholders (xi) capital mobilisation : The features of limited liability, large number of shareholders and easy transferability of shares enables the joint stock company to mobilise huge capital resources.

The joint stock companies are of two types *viz.*, private limited companies and public limited companies.

Private Limited Companies : The features of the private limited company include : (i) limitation of membership : The minimum number of share holders are two and the maximum number of shareholders are 50, (ii) Restriction on transfer of shares : Restrictions are imposed on the sale and transfer of shares. First preference for buying the shares should be given to the existing share holders at a fair price to be determined by the directors in consultation with the company auditors, (iii) prohibition on the public issue of shares : A private company cannot invite the public to subscribe to its shares or debentures through prospectus or any such open market offer (iv) private company cannot issue share warrants.

Public Limited Company : Features of a public limited company include : (i) number of shareholders. The minimum number of shareholders are seven and the maximum number is unlimited, (ii) the shares are freely transferred (iii) public limited company can approach the public by means of prospectus and other open market operations to issue the shares (iv) public limited company can issue share warrants.

A comparative analysis of public limited company and a private limited company is presented in exhibit.

Public Sector

Public sector firms are organised differently for purposes of management and control. They are departmental undertakings, statutory corporations, central boards and companies.

(i) Departmental undertakings : The departmental form of public enterprises is the oldest form. The characteristics of this form include.

(a) Enterprises under this form are run by government department with a minister at its helm. For example, Indian Railways, Defence, Posts etc.

(b) They are financed from the treasury.

(c) Their day-to-day management is run by the civil servants.

(d) They are under the direct supervision of the parliament.

(e) The ministry concerned of the department is directly responsible to parliament for the efficient running of the firm.

(ii) Statutory corporations

A corporation is a body corporate created by a separate law, independently financed and vested with autonomy in managing its activities. For example : Life Insurance Corporation of India, Reserve Bank of India, Industrial Finance Corporation of India, Oil and Natural Gas Commission, Air India, National Textile Corporation etc.

The characteristics of the corporations are :

(a) Each public corporation is established separately by a statute with a separate legal entity.

(b) They are free from parliamentary control in its day-to-day management. Parliamentary control is limited to the business policies and strategic management

(c) These corporations do not have shareholders, but they can raise loans with the approval of the minister and the consent of the treasury.

(d) The employees of these corporations are not civil servants.

(iii) Central Boards

These are common in river valley projects which involve huge capital investments. These are normally set up with the help of both central government and state government concerned. Examples are Nagarjuna Sagar, Bhakra Nangal, Hirakud etc. Box 1.1 provides Public Sector reforms.

(iv) Companies

According to Section 617 of the Companies Act, 1956, is that in which not less than 51 percent of the paid up share capital is held by the central government, state government (s) or by the central government and state governments jointly. A subsidiary of a government company is also a government company. The characteristics of a government company are :

(a) The capital to the extent of 51 per cent and above is held by the government.

(b) All or majority of the directors are appointed by the government.

(c) It is created under the provisions of the companies act, 1956.

(d) Its funds are obtained from the government and private shareholders.

(e) It has freedom and functions on commercial lines.

Cooperative Sector

In cooperative forms of business firms, people voluntarily associate together, as human beings, on the basis of equality for the promotion of furtherance of their common economic interests. Cooperative organisations prefer (i) service maximisation rather than profit maximisation, (ii) joint action instead of keen competition (iii) self help and self-reliance rather than undue dependence on external bodies and (iv) development of moral values of their members.

The different types of cooperative firms are : cooperative industrial firms, cooperative retail organisations, cooperative distribution agencies, cooperative banks etc.

Features

The distinctive features of cooperative organisations include :

(a) spirit of cooperation under the motto "each for all and all for each".

(b) united and joint action.

(c) common interest.

(d) economic democracy and democratic management : Individual members are recognised as human beings but not as capitalists. Every member has only one vote irrespective of amount of his investment or the number of shares he holds.

(e) membership is open to all adults without caste or colour or creed.

(f) emphasis is laid on moral values of the members.

(g) dividend hunting element is absent and the fixed rate of return on the capital is assured.

(h) cooperative organisation has to be registered under the separate legislation.

Advantages

The advantages of cooperative organisations include :

(a) cooperative organisations help the poor people who do not have other means.

(b) it is a judicious compromise between radical communism and extreme capitalism.

(c) capitalism provides for removal of the evils of capitalism.

(d) emphasis on the development of moral values and character.

(e) cooperatives provide the advantage of limited liability to the extent of the face value of the share.

(f) government provides different kinds of help to cooperatives as they are social organisations.

Disadvantages

Despite the advantages, the cooperatives suffer from certain disadvantages. They are :

(a) the absence of cooperative spirit among the members is the greatest disadvantage.

(b) cooperatives cannot raise huge financial resources

(c) cooperatives cannot appoint specialised and professional managers due to their poor financial position.

(d) excessive government involvement discourages the voluntary character of the cooperatives.

(e) the politics among the members weakens the functioning of cooperatives.

Cooperative organisations failed in India due to these disadvantages.

Power Sector reforms

THE ENERGY SUMMIT held in Chennai last week under the aegis of the confederation of Indian Industry (CCI) focussed attention on some worrisome features of the so-called "reform process" in the energy sector. Ambitious power generation targets visualised in the Five Year Plans have not been matched by achievements. During the Eighth Plan period, the capacity addition was far short of the revised target of 30,000 MW. Resource constraints do not adequately explain the disappointing performance. Free supply of power has become a politically competitive and sensitive issue among the States and few have the will to take a realistic stand on pricing electricity for different categories of consumers. Without proper pricing, the State Electricity Boards (SEBs) and other power generating agencies are unlikely to regain their financial health.

The Central law envisaging regulatory outfits to determine the power tariff was indeed a bold step but most States are still dragging their feet on restructuring their generation and distribution systems. Private investors find the situation understandably "frustrating" despite the ministerial assurances that the reform process is in place. The summit has served to highlight their problems. While the private sector has to play an effective role in the creation of additional power generation and distribution capacities in the country, inordinate delays in clearances will only drive the investors away to more lucrative areas.

Given the incentives, foreign investment in the power sector may increase substantially in the years ahead. During the Eighth Plan period, the private sector's share in power generation showed a marked increase. If the projects in the pipeline are completed soon, the private sector's share will increase further in the Ninth Plan. It is unfortunate that bureaucratic delays have led to cost and time over-runs in several key projects. Unless the thermal and hydel power mix is improved, the power generation utilities will be faced with an acute shortage in meeting the peak demand. For this the hydel resources should be harnessed more effectively to raise their share in power generation. But this is easier said than done.

Ironically, although Chennai and its neighbourhood continue to experience persistent power cuts disrupting normal life, both the Tamil Nadu Chief Minister, Mr. M. Karunanidhi, and the Union Power Minister, Mr. P. R. Kumaramangalam, have held out high hopes for the future. Tamil Nadu plans to double its existing power generating capacity to meet the projected demand of 13,000 MW in less than a decade from now. The Central power agencies are expected to add 6,000 MW. The prospect of surplus power in Tamil Nadu will be a major incentive to private investors. But restructuring of the overmanned SEB to cope with the emerging situation is still way off. Also the process of setting up the electricity regulatory agency is yet to be completed.

As the independent power producers and foreign financial institutions continue to insist on "guarantees" and "escrows" to cover their investment risks – they seem to overdo it on some "hypothetical" considerations – the Centre should expeditiously issue appropriate guide lines to give more teeth to the contracts. There is also the urgency to cut the high transmission and distribution losses to the SEBs, estimated at over Rs. 11,000 crores. Such huge losses have further strained the resources of the SEBs. Firm steps are needed to cut these losses and for the reforms to be effective. For competition to be meaningful, power should be reasonably priced and supplied to the consumer. That is the message of the summit.

CHAPTER 2

BUSINESS PLANNING

Introduction

Benefits of Business Planning

Significance of Business Planning

Steps in Business Planning

Process of Business Planning

Limitations of Business Planning

Methods of Making Business Planning Effective

INTRODUCTION

Business planning has become a very important part of the top management function due to the influence of external environmental factors and systems approach to the business management. Business planning is strategic planning because it is concerned mainly with the designing of business. According to Scott, long range business planning is a systematic approach to decision-making about issues which are fundamental and of crucial importance to its continuing long term effectiveness. Long range strategy is designed to provide information about an organization's vision, mission, purpose, direction and objectives.

Implementation planning, in contrast to business planning, explains the details of the policies and procedures, which are required to accomplish the strategies of the firm. These plans produce immediate and tangible results in relatively shorter period. However, the business planning is concerned with:

(a) The direction in which the company should move.

(b) The implementation of the plan for the subsequent period and

(c) The alternatives which are to be sacrificed, if the plan is accepted and implemented.

Business planning involves more than one strategy. In other words, the strategies relating to different functional areas are involved in business planning. An activity rather than a form of organization, is at the core of business planning.[1]

Business planning provides a means to deal explicitly and systematically with matters of fundamental importance. Business planning is, "the process of selecting an organization's goals, determining the policies and strategic programmes necessary to achieve specific objectives en-route to the goals and establishing the methods necessary to assure that the policies and strategic programmes are achieved."[2]. Thus, business planning is derived from strategic planning and strategy.

According to Stoner, business planning is different from implementation planning. According to him, business planning, "is not only planning activity of an organization; however, it is one in which the top management's role is most critical. Planning at lower levels is called operational planning. It focuses on present operations and its prime concern is efficiency rather than effectiveness. In the sense that strategic planning provides guidance and boundaries for operational management ...... Effective management must have a strategy and must operate on the day-to-day level to achieve goals."

The differences between operational planning and strategic planning are presented in the Exhibit 2.1. It is clear from the exhibit that there is a great deal of difference between strategic planning and operational implementation planning.

1. Scott, "Long - Range planning in American Industry", American Management Association. 1965, p. 31.
2. Stoner, "Management", Prentice - Hall, 1982, p. 101.

Exhibit 2.1 : Differences Between Operational Planning and Strategic Planning

	Operational Planning	*Strategic Planning*
Focus	Operational Problems	Long term, survival and Developmental
Objectives	Present Profit	Future profit
Constraints	Present Resources, Environment	Future Resources, Environment.
Rewards	Efficiency, Stability	Development of future potential
Information	Present Business	Future opportunities
Organization	Bureaucratic / stable	Entrepreneurial/Flexible
Leadership	Conservative	Inspires Radical changes
Problem-solving	Relies on past experience Low Risk	Anticipates, finds new approaches. High Risk

BENEFITS OF BUSINESS PLANNING

The systematic business planning helps the business to derive its advantages and get benefits out of them. The Benefits of business planning include

1. Business Planning helps the Company to formulate objectives and goals clearly. The company formulates objectives after discussing thoroughly with superiors, colleagues and sub-ordinates. These objectives help the company to achieve stability of business and maximise profits.
2. Business planning helps to avoid piece-meal approach and to have integrative approach.
3. Business planning helps to view the organization in total rather than department-wise.
4. Business plan aims at the long-range plan rather than short-range plan.
5. Business plan integrates the company plan with the national plans and priorities.
6. Business plan takes into consideration the environmental factors. Technological factors influence the business plan significantly. Technology has been upgraded continuously. The changes in technology are pivotal, resulting in high technology.

   Announcement of economic liberalizations, globalization and privatization policies by the Government, in 1991, changed the economic scenario of the country. The changing scenario influences the economic environment. Added to this, significant changes have taken place in social and political environment.
7. Liberalization, Privatization and Globalization not only brought significant changes in the economy, but they have intensified the competition. Globalization allowed many MNC's to enter and operate in India. This resulted in tough competition between domestic and foreign companies.

The liberalizations policy of the Government allowed for the establishment of a number of companies. It resulted in severe competition even within the domestic companies. Business plan should take into consideration, the competition levels among the companies.

8. Business plan helps the company to anticipate the political changes and developments in the national and international scenarios and their possible impact on the business.
9. Effective business plan helps the company to achieve its objectives and goals.
10. Effective business plan certainly contributes for the achievement of high rate of profits and increases in earning per share.
11. Business plan helps to determine potential growth and profit.

SIGNIFICANCE OF BUSINESS PLANNING

Business planning plays significant role in the corporate governance. The significant role played by the business planning can be attributed to the benefits which can be derived. The main reasons for the increasing importance of business planning, according to George Stoner, are:

1. The increasing rate of technological change : Technological changes witnessed significant growth particularly during the last quarter of the 1990s. The revolution in the information technology, Enterprise Resource planning, Business process re-engineering, e-commerce, paper less office, on-line marketing and the like, brought phenomenal developments in the operations of business. Globalization policies announced by various governments resulted in severe competition, which in turn led to heavy spending on R & D by the corporate giants. This, in turn, brought strides in technology. Technology upgradation, in turn, accelerated the growth rate of business and economy.
2. The long term business plan orientation from the corporate world's angle is clearly evident through the changed view of the business firms. Business firms were concentrating on the short-run profits in the past. But, they are busily engaged in building relationship business which can produce long-run results.
3. Increasing Complexity of External Environment: External environment is becoming increasingly complex. Governments are tending towards capitalist economies from communistic or socialistic economic systems. Added to this, the economy is liberalized and globalised. Thus there is significant change in the economic environmental factors. Further, the technological factors have become complex due to the sudden shift in the technology from the traditional, to high-tech. Added to this, the revolution in the information technology has complicated the environment for the business.

   The shifts in the economic, political and technological factors brought remarkable changes in the way of life and other social factors. Customer/consumer behavior changed predominantly. Other significant changes include increasing awareness and concern towards the nature and ecology, decreasing government interference in the business, increasing concern of the workers towards quality of life at work place, challenging work, and changed management. The shift from rule-bound industrial relations to human relations, is another area which complicates the business environment.

The more complex the business environment is, the more significant is the business planning.

4. There has been a significant shift in human resource. Employees of the new melliennium concentrate on productivity, management challenges, quality, service and the like. Business plan foresees the management challenges, plans for and formulates the strategies and tactics to meet the challenges with the commitment of the employees.
5. Short term plans and operational plans are based on the long term and business plans. The company should formulate long range and business plans in order to achieve short range and operational objectives/goals.
6. Business plan provides the top management with a better basis for making judgements about the overall balance among the different parts of the company. Business plans provide a starting point in the analysis of the proposed programme.
7. Business planning is a continuous process. This process is aided by modern sophisticated computers. Fig. 2.1 presents the broader aspects of business planning.
8. As mentioned earlier, the change in environmental factors particularly social and political increase the significance of business planning. Fig. 2.2 presents the changes in social and political factors and their influence on the significance of the business.
9. The model of business planning does not signify one -time-dimension but many dimensions.

STEPS IN BUSINESS PLANNING

The steps involved in business planning include.

1. Establishing verifiable goals or set of goals to be achieved: The business plan is based on the enterprise objectives. These objectives are mostly formulated by the top management, The values and beliefs held by the top management are reflected in these goals.
2. Establishing planning premises: Planning premises include certain assumptions about the future on the basis of which the plan will be ultimately formulated. Planning premises include:
   (a) Internal and external premises
   (b) Tangible and intangible premises
   (c) Controllable and non controllable premises.

(a) Internal premises include sales forecasts, policies and programmes of the organization, capital investment, managerial competency, human resource skills, other organizational resources. External premises include general business and economic environment, technological changes, Government policies and regulations, population growth, political stability, and social factors.

Management would identify the objectives/goals to be achieved or 'where should we go?' 'where are we?' The gap between these two is termed as 'gap analysis'. Many companies have used gap analysis by setting the objectives and identifying the gap between them and the prospective growth of the present. The firms should achieve high performance in order to fill the gap. Fig. 2.3 represents the gap-filling analysis.

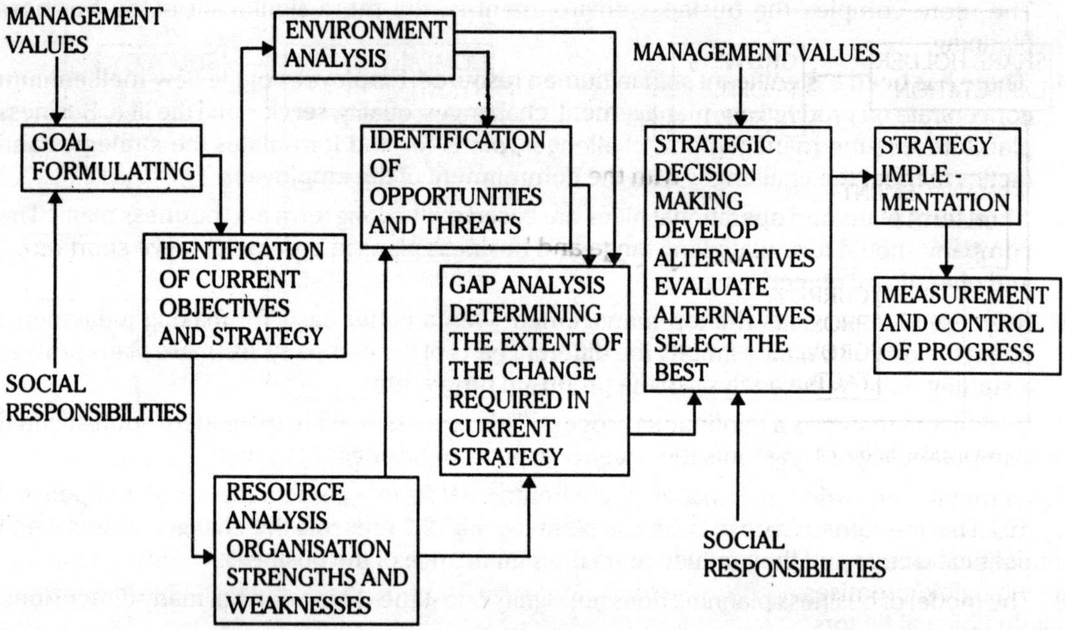

Source : Nanjundaiah, *op. cit*, p. 32.

Fig. 2.1 Broader Aspects of Business Planning.

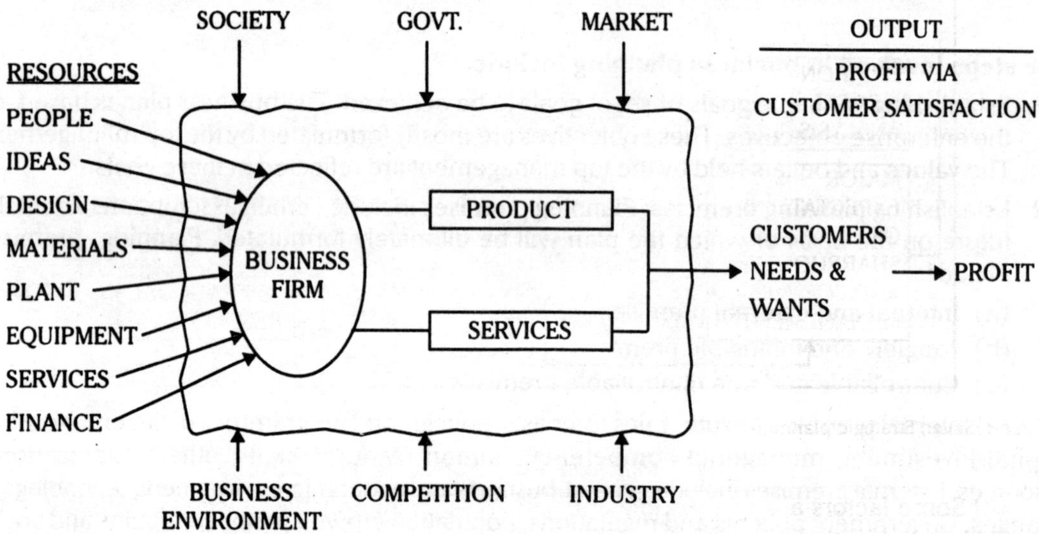

Source : Nanjundaiah, *op. cit*, p. 37.

Fig. 2.2 Changes in social and political factors.

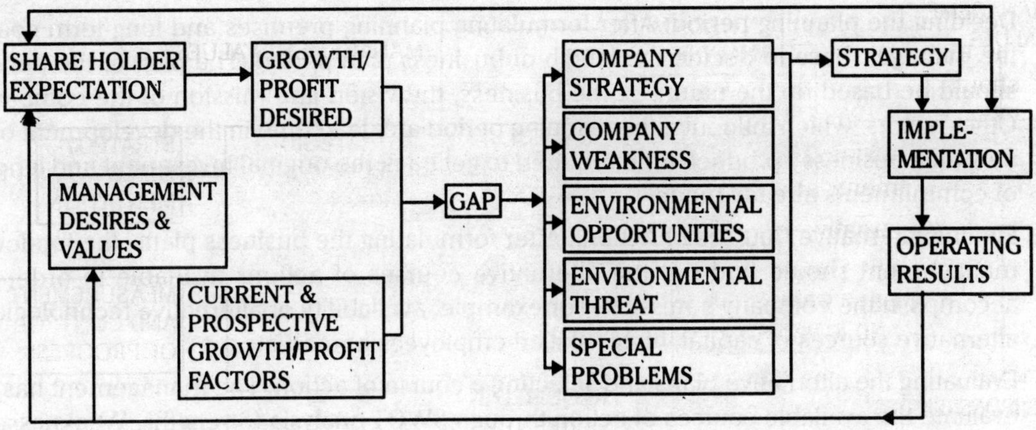

Source : Nanjundaich, *op. cit.*, p. 45

Fig. 2.3 Gap Filling Analysis.

(b) The premises which can be quantifiable are called tangible premises. The tangible premises include population growth, product demand, past sales, capital invested and the like. The intangible premises are those which cannot be measured quantitatively. These premises include political factors, social factors, technological factors, natural factors etc.

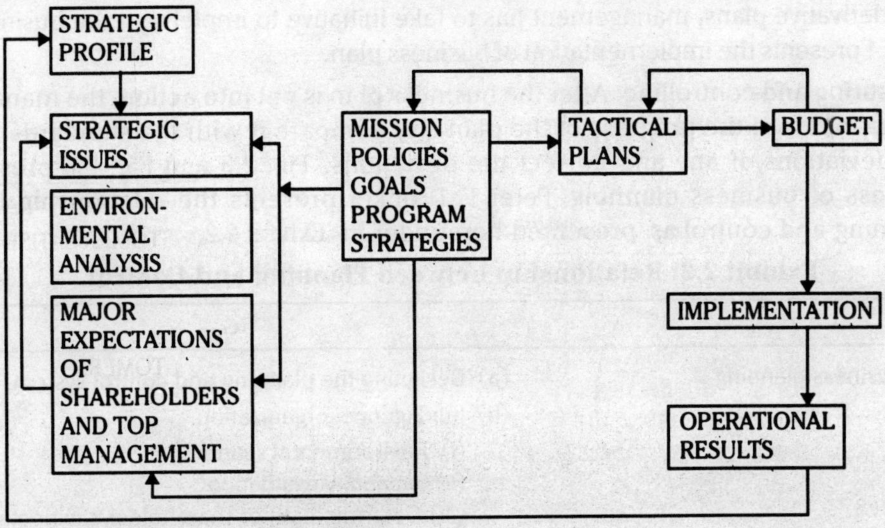

Source : Stiver, Strategic planning, 1979, p-26

Fig. 2.4 Implementation of Business Plan.

(c) Some factors are controllable and some are uncontrollable. Business plans are to be modified and sometimes reformulated due to the presence of and interaction of uncontrollable premises. Uncontrollable premises include strikes, lockouts, wars natural calamities, emergency situations etc. Controllable premises include company's labour policy, investment policy, advertising policy , level of technology competency of managerial personnel, quality of human resources, availability of financial resources etc.,

3. Deciding the planning period: After formulating planning premises and long-term goals, the manager have to decide the length of business plan period. The plan of the period should be based on the nature of the business, the vision and mission of the company. Other factors which influence the planning period are: lead time in the development of a new idea business / product, time required to get back the original investment and length of commitments already made.
4. Finding Alternative Courses of Action.: After formulating the business plans, the top-level management should find out the alternative courses of actions available in order to accomplish the company's mission. For example, availability of alternative technologies, alternative sources of capital, highly skilled employees abroad etc.,
5. Evaluating the alternative plans and selecting a course of action: The management has to evaluate the available courses of action through SWOT analysis (Strengths, Weaknesses, Opportunities and Threats) and rank the alternatives. After ranking the alternatives, the management has to select the best business plan.
6. Developing Derivative plans. The management after selecting the best business plan, it should formulate the other policies and plans which are the sub plans to the main plan. Management should involve and consult the lower level managers while formulating the derivative plans.
7. Implementation of the Business Plans: After the development and selection of the plans and derivative plans, management has to take initiative to implement the business plan. Fig.2.4 presents the implementation of business plan.
8. Measuring and controlling: After the business plan is put into action, the management has to measure the progress of the plan and compare it with the standards, observe the deviations, if any and correct the deviations. Fig. 2.5 and Fig. 2.6 presents the process of business planning. Peter F. Drucker presents the relationship between planning and control as presented hereunder in Exhibit 2.2.

Exhibit 2.2: Relationship between Planning and Control.

Cycle	*Step*
1. Business planning	(a) Designing the planning and control system
	(b) Intelligence organization.
	(i) Environmental scanning
	(ii) Capability evaluation
	(iii) Determination of shareholder's expectations
	(iv) Analysis of past performance
	(c) Formulation of statement of strategic mission
2. Programme planning and Resource allocation	(d) New programme generation and intelligence
	(e) Programme evalution and resource allocation.
	(f) Specification of long range plans
	(g) Responsibility planning
3. Responsibility Unit Planning and control	(h) Responsibility Unit performance control
	(i) Systems evaluation, adaptation and review.

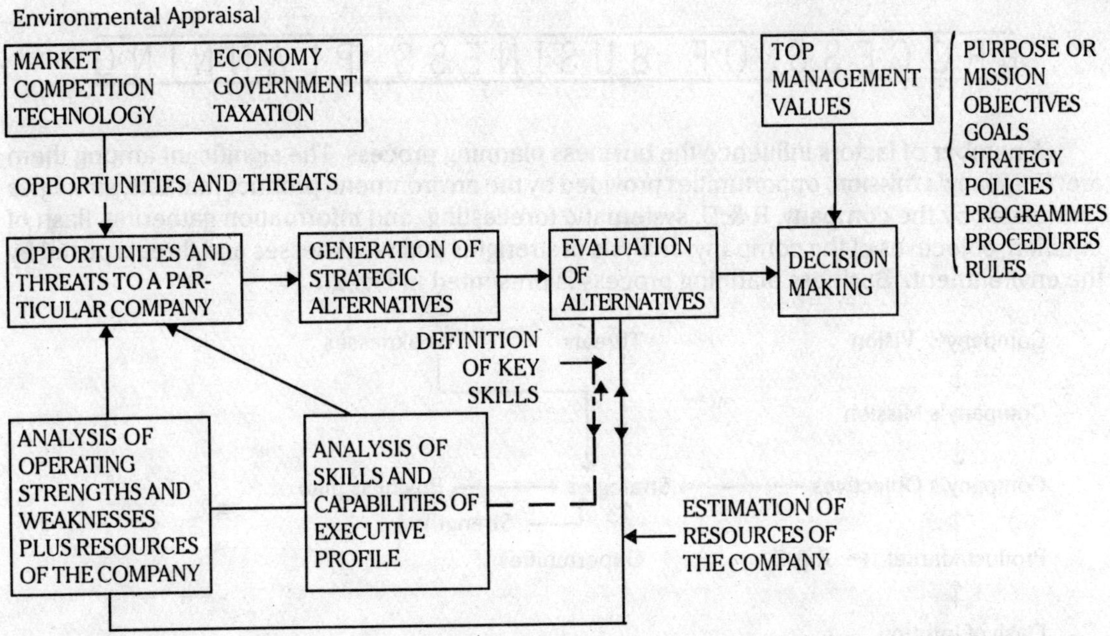

Source : Ibid., p. 80

Fig. 2.5 Process of Business Planning.

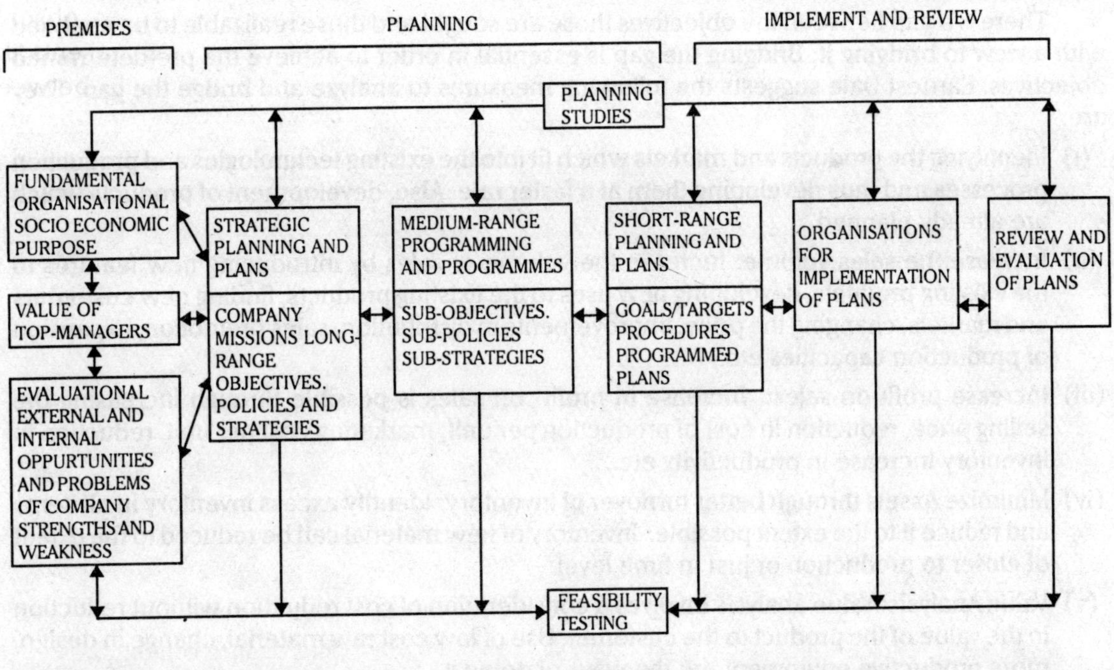

Source : G. A. Steiner, "Top Management Planning". p. 33.

Fig. 2.6 Process of Business Planning.

PROCESS OF BUSINESS PLANNING

A number of factors influence the business planning process. The significant among them are: Company's mission, opportunities provided by the environment, product/markets, strategies formulated by the company, R & D, systematic forecasting and information gathering, flash of intuition, objectives of the company, analysis of strengths and weaknesses and threats posed by the environment. Business planning process is presented in Fig. 2.7.

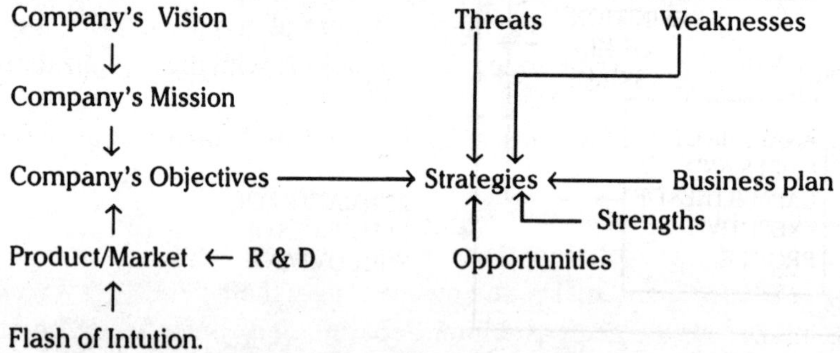

Fig. 2.7. Business Planning Process.

Gap Analysis

There is a gap between the objectives those are sought and those realizable to be analysed with a view to bridging it. Bridging the gap is essential in order to achieve the pre-determined objectives. Earnest Dale suggests the following measures to analyze and bridge the gap. They are:

(i) Identifying the products and markets which fit into the existing technologies and production processes and thus developing them at a faster rate. Also, development of products which are already planned.

(ii) Increase the sales volume: Increase the volume of sales by introducing new features to the existing products, developing new uses to the existing products, finding new customers and markets, changing the price, improvements in distribution, sales promotion, expansion of production capacities etc.,

(iii) Increase profit on sales: Increase in profit on sales is possible through increasing the selling price, reduction in cost of production per unit, marketing cost per unit, reduction in inventory increase in productivity etc.,

(iv) Minimize Assets through better turnover of inventory: Identify excess inventory in all items and reduce it to the extent possible. Inventory of new material can be reduced to the extent of closer to production or just in time level

(v) Value Analysis: Value analysis involves a consideration of cost reduction without reduction in the value of the product to the customer. Use of low cost raw material, change in design, more productive equipment are the ways of doing it.

(vi) Reducing the Fat: This involves reduction of unnecessary, available and controllable costs. These are labour costs, general wastage, non-performing assets etc.

LIMITATIONS OF BUSINESS PLANNING

Though the top management formulates the business plans, sometimes they fail in producing results due to the uncertainties in the implementation stage. The limitations of the business planning include:

(i) Implementation of the strategic plan should be pre-planned and based on detailed action. Many times managements fail to monitor the implementation process.

(ii) Some managers are reluctant to formulate objectives for their departments or jobs.

(iii) Managers are sometimes afraid of failure, to achieve business plans.

(iv) Managers fail to integrate the plans of their departments or jobs with the organizational / company plans.

(v) Some managers do not have required skills to understand and analyze the external environment.

(vi) Forecasting often becomes misleading due to wrong premises.

(vii) Managers due to their deficient and inherent nature, fail to plan efficiently.

(viii) The uncertainties in the environment, makes the business plan inefficient.

(ix) Inter-group conflicts: Inter group conflicts and inter-departmental conflicts are the other important limitations of business plan. These limitations are also due to

- Lack of understanding about the objectives of the firm.
- Lack of a constructive approach to objectives
- Different values and personalities of individual managers.
- Competition for scarce resources.
- Built-in conflict between a young manager and an experienced Manager.

METHODS OF MAKING BUSINESS PLANNING EFFECTIVE

The Management at different levels should take measures to make the business plan effective due to the possibility of limitations. These measures include :

(i) Establishment of co-ordination between long-term plans and short-term plans.

(ii) Bringing co-ordination among all the departments in the organization in formulating and implementing plans.

(iii) Formulating a comprehensive plan linking all the departmental plans with the corporate level plans.

(iv) Giving proper attention to the departmental level plans.

(v) Ensuring the commitment and involvement of all managers at all levels in the organization.

(vi) Ensuring the free-flow of communication particularly the bottom up communication.

(vii) Train and develop the managers in analyzing and understanding external environment, formulate the plans effectively.

(viii) Foresee the environmental changes, feed the information forward to all the levels in the organization.

(ix) Ensuring effective team work and empower the managers to formulate effective plans.

CHAPTER 3

BUSINESS POLICY - CONCEPTUAL ANALYSIS

- **Business Policy - Meaning and Definition**
- **Chief Features of Business Policy**
- **Essentials of an Effective Business Policy**
- **Importance of Business Policy**
- **Scope of Business Policies**
- **The need for Business Policies**
- **Mechanism of Policy Making**
- **Classification of Business Policies**

BUSINESS POLICY-MEANING AND DEFINITION

Policy-making is one of the most important components of business planning. Policies are a guide to action. They provide broad guidelines as to how objectives of business are to be achieved. While objectives are a goal or an end to be sought, policies are a general rule of action or guideline which helps in attaining the goal. The objective sets a long-range target; a policy provides guides which assists the company in achieving this target.

Policy does not tell a person exactly what to do, but it does point out the direction in which to go. Familiar policies are summed up in these statements: "We sell only for cash and allow liberal discount thereon". "We insure all property worth more than Rs. 50,000/- against loss by fire or burglary". "Our motto is to serve the customers in all possible ways in matters of quality, price, weight and contents." In each instance, some important aspect of a recurring problem has been singled out, and a guide established for dealing with it.

On the other hand, some policies provide only board guidelines, such as; "Preference will be given to goods produced by union labour" does indicate the intention but leaves the purchaser to decide whether the preference comes first or whether it should be considered only when all other considerations are equal.

Yet, some policies can be much more specific. For example, an investment banking firm makes the following statement about the duration of vacation to its employees:

"Employees shall normally be entitled to vacation according to the following schedule:

On pay roll 6 to 18 months prior to March 1, 2000 – one week.

On pay roll, 6 years to 15 years prior to March 1, 2000–Three weeks.

On pay roll over 15 years prior to March 1, 2000– Four weeks.

Policies may be defined as "the mode of thought and the principles underlying the activities of an organisation or an institution." Policies are plans in that they are general statements of principles which guide the thinking, decision-making and action in an organisation.[1] They guide the management in the conduct of business/enterprise operations; and offer a ready-made or standing answer to a recurring question. They are, therefore, sometimes considered as a substitute for common sense. However, policies cannot answer every potential problem situation. One can hardly refer to all policies as statements, since they are implied in the actions of managers.

We give below some of the definitions of business policy:

Terry says, "A business policy is an implied overall guide setting up boundaries that supply the general limits and direction in which managerial action will take place."[2]

Thus, according to this definition, policy reveals the **management's** intentions for the future. They spell out clearly the sanctioned general direction and areas within which work has to be done.

According to Peters and Wotrube. "A business policy is nothing more than a well-developed statement of directions and goals. *Goals* involve the definition of precisely what the business is

1. Koontz, Harold, Cyril O' Donnell and Heinz Weihrich, *Management*, McGraw Hill Kogakusha Ltd., Tokyo, Edition, 1980, p. 164.
2. Terry George, R. *Principles of Management*, Richard D. Irwin, Inc., 1972.

or should be, and the particular kind of company it should be. Direction guides the action of the firm to accomplish these goals."[3]

These authors regard business policy as a well-developed statement of directions and goals, i.e., what is to be achieved and how it is to be achieved.

To Rodgers, "A business policy is one which focusses attention on the strategic allocation of scarce resources: human, financial, physical or intangible. Conceptually speaking, strategy is the direction of such resource allocation while planning is the timing of allocation."[4]

According to this author, a business policy is concerned with developing the general management point of view which demands that the manager sublimates his departmental, functional or specialist perspective in order to take a balanced company-wide look.

Haner has defined business policy as "a statement – verbal, written, or implied–of those principles and rules that are set by executive leadership as guidelines and constraints for the organisation's thought and action. Their purpose is to enable the management to relate properly the organisation's work to its objectives."[5]

Newman and Logan observe that, "A business policy is often used to cover both the objectives and the general rules of action for an enterprise...The purpose of such a policy is to resolve any conflict there may be between the several objectives. The policy guides the action of the company along a path toward the objectives; it represents the best thinking of the company management as to how the objectives may be achieved in the prevailing economic and social conditions."[6]

Says Flipps, "A business policy is a man-made or predetermined course of action that is established to guide the performance of work toward the organisation's objectives. It is a type of standing plan that serves to guide subordinates in the execution of their tasks."[7]

Yoder observes, "A management policy is a predetermined, selected course established as a guide towards accepted goals and objectives. Policies establish the framework of guiding principles that facilitate delegation to lower levels and permit individual managers to select appropriate tactics or programmes...Such policies are developed by working organisations to keep them on course, headed and directed towards their organisational objectives. These define the intentions of the organisation and serve as guidelines to give consistency and continuity to total operations...They provide a base for 'management by principle' as contrasted to 'management by expediency'.....In fact, *they serve as a road map for managers.*"[8]

In the opinion of Miller, "A policy is a statement or a commonly accepted understanding of decision-making criteria or formulae, prepared or evolved to achieve economy in operations by making decision relatively routine on frequently occurring problems and, consequently, facilitating the delegation of such decision to lower managerial levels."[9]

3. Gray Edmund (Ed)., *Readings in Business Policy,* 1968, p. 17
4. Rodgers, David C., *Business Policy and Planning; Text and Cases,* 1977, Preface p. ix.
5. Haner, F.T., *Business Policy and Planning,* 1976, p. 71.
6. Newman, William H., and James, P. Logan, *Business Policies and Central Management,* D.B. Taraporewala Sons & Co., Pvt. Ltd., Bombay, 1970 p. 82.
7. Flipps, Edwin P., *Principles of Management.*
8. Yoder, Dale, *Personnel Management and Industrial Relations,* Prentice-Hall of India, New Delhi, 1972, pp. 26.28
9. Miller, Ernest C. "Personnel Policies–Framework for Management Decisions," in *The Management Review* January 1960. p. 20.

According to this definition, a policy by providing decision-making criteria gives assurance that decisions made will be consistent, fair and in keeping with the objectives and interests of the business. A policy permits decisions to be made on similar problems without repetition of the closely-reasoned and expensive analysis required initially to state the policy to make the decision.

Observes Thomas, "Policy is the study of the nature and process of choice about the future of independent enterprises by those responsible for decisions and their implementation."[10]

We may define business policy as a principle or a group of related principles, along with their consequent rule (s) of action that provide for the successful achievement of specific organisation/business objectives. Accordingly, a policy contains both a "principle" and a "rule of action."[11] Both should be there for the maximum effectiveness of a policy. One or the other, when omitted, is implied.

CHIEF FEATURES OF BUSINESS POLICY

Analysing the definitions, certain special features of a business policy may be noted thus:

1. *Policies are a general statement of principles for the attainment of objectives* which serve as a guide to action for the executives at different levels. In other words, they are a broad path along which the subordinates move towards their objectives.
2. *Policies have an hierachy,* i.e., for each set of objectives at each level of management, there is a corresponding set of policies. For example, *basic overall corporate policies* determined by the central management (or the board of directors); the corporate executive policies determined by the top management; *divisional and/or departmental policies* determined by their managers; and *sectional policies* determined by the middle managers, and so on, right up to the first line supervisors.
3. *The policies delimit the area within which a decision is to be made and ensure that the decision will be consistent with and contribute to the objectives.* However, they do allow some discretion on the part of the man on the firing line, otherwise, they would be mere rules. Too much discretion in matters on policy may prove harmful to the accomplishment of organisational objectives. Hence, it is generally within limits. The amount of discretion allowed depends upon then policy, which in turn reflects the position and authority in the organisation. In most policies, the discretion area is very broad, but in others, it is extremely narrow.
4. *Policies in general are meant for mutual application by subordinates.* They are framed to suit a specific situation to which they are applied, for they cannot apply themselves.
5. *Policies tend to predecide issues, avoid repeated analysis and give a unified structure to other types of plans,* thus permitting managers to delegate authority while maintaining control.

10. Thomas, R.E., *Business Policy,* Heritage Publishers, New Delhi, 1983, p.1
11. A *"Principle"* may be defined as a fundamental truth while a *"rule of action"* is a restrictive statement of this principle for a given situation.

6. In a well- managed organisation, *policies are found in all functional areas and at various levels within these areas.* There are policies for corporate planning, marketing, research and development, engineering, manufacturing, inventory, purchasing, physical distribution, accounting, financial, costing. In a typical manufacturing firm, within the marketing area, advertising, personal selling, and special promotion policies, among others, are found.
7. Policies serve an extremely useful purpose. *They avoid confusion and provide clear-cut guidelines at all levels to subordinates*; and therefore, they enable the business to be carried on smoothly and often without break. They also lead to better and maximum utilisation of resources, human, financial, and physical, by adhering to actions for conservation.

Thus, it should be noted that the *business policy is the keystone in the arch of management and the life-blood for the successful functioning of business,* because without well-laid down policies, there cannot be lasting improvements in the economic condition of the firm and labour management relations. It indicates an agreement to a general cause of action, telling specifically what the business proposes to do and suggest the values and view points which dominate the top executives' and organisations' action.

Finally, a policy is a positive declaration and a command to its followers. It translates the goals of an organisation into selected routes and provides the general guidelines that prescribe and proscribe programmes, which in turn, dictate practices and procedures.

Purpose of Business Policy

A business policy to be effective should permeate all functional areas of management. *Their main purpose* is to: (i) clarify objectives, (ii) guide planning, (iii) help subordinates in reaching operating decisions; (iv) facilitate an overall coordination and control; (v) act as a yardstick for evaluating the quality of executive decision-making and action; (vi) build up employee enthusiasm and loyalty; and (vii) seek to ensure consistency and uniformity in decisions as problems that "recur frequently and under similar, but not identical, circumstances."

Examples of Business Policy

We give below the corporate policy on social responsibility of three companies:

CORPORATE POLICY ON SOCIAL RESPONSIBILITY

1. We are actively concerned with maintaining a healthy environment, not only with the physical environment around us, but also with the environment of the mind and spirit of the people in the company, and in communities where our plants operate. We will endeavour our employment practices to ensure equal opportunity for all qualified persons, irrespective of caste, creed, or sex, who are now employed or may seek employment hereafter in plants and offices of the company *(A Textile Concern).*
2. It is out company's policy to dispose of air-borne and water borne wastes in a manner which: (a) will not adversely affect the health, safety or property of the company's employees and neighbours; (b) will not create unreasonable or unnecessary pollution problems in the surrounding community; and (c) will not interfere with reasonable and necessary use of public waters. *(An Oil Company).*
3. It is our policy to manufacture and market useful, safe, and high-quality products for.... people around the country; adhere to good manufacturing standards and practices; and guard against abuse or misuse of our products *(A Phamaceutical Company).*

The motives cited for formulation of such policies include: assurance of a persistent favourable climate for subsequent company activities; (ii) a desire for positive and consistent responses to social responsibility issues throughout the company; and (iii) a need to do something that would be visible to external and internal participants, such as minority groups, consumer advocates, environmentalists, and employees.

ESSENTIALS OF AN EFFECTIVE BUSINESS POLICY

For policies to be effective, they should be sound. For any business, such policies properly elucidated and correctly understood by all concerned in it are a pre-requisite for efficient programme designing and its effective implementation.

One expert lays down certain criteria for judging whether a business policy is sound or otherwise. He maintains that policies to be effective, should be:[12]

1. based on organisation objectives;
2. capable of relating objectives to functions, physical factors, and company personnel;
3. in conformity with the accepted ethical standards of business;
4. stated in definite, understandable terms, preferably in writing;
5. stable and flexible;
6. sufficiently comprehensive in scope;
7. complementary to co-ordinate policies;
8. supplementary to superior policies.

We would discuss the essentials of a sound business policy under the following heads;

1. *Relationship to Organisation Objectives:* The policies should be based on organisation objectives, i.e., what purposes and objectives the business has in view to achieve and how these can best be achieved. It should clearly reflect the principles, concepts, practices and philosophies of the organisation.

Further, the policies should be capable of relating organisation's objectives to other factors. It should be noted that when a policy fails to take into account inconsistencies between organisation objectives and personal objectives of individuals and groups, the firm will find itself seriously hampered in trying to achieve its objectives than the company's personnel in trying to achieve theirs...For this reason, a harmonious integration of these objectives is particularly important.

2. *Simple and Easily Understandable:* The policy should be stated in definite, positive and clear understandable terms. Unambiguous statement of policy is necessary for a clear understanding of it on the part of those affected by it. *Clarity is the essence of a good policy* so that everyone in the organisation knows what it proposes to achieve.

Clear-cut policies should minimise the number of situations in which decisions must be based on personal opinion and hastily collected information. Regardless of the size of the firm, policies should be reducible to the point where they have significance for each individual in the organisation. Such policies are more easily formulated and applied if they are reduced to writing.

3. *Written Policies:* Preferably, policies should be written so that they can be integrated within systems and policy manuals. Henry Carl has rightly observed that "A policy, conceived as

12. Davis Ralph C., *The Fundamentals of Top Management. Harper and Brother,* New York, 1951, p. 179.

a management tool, does not exist unless it is in writing."[13] Written policies make a commitment on the part of management, employees and others that "the top management does what it says." They ensure uniformity of application, and assure continuity of action even when the top management is changed. They limit the freedom of action on the part of the management, for the foreman cannot go off half-cocked and come up with his personal interpretation of the organisation's intent. They help to ensure that professed policies are 'right', for an organisation tries to put its best foot forward.

4. *Stable but not Rigid*: The policy must be reasonably stable but not rigid. Stability implies firmness and constancy. Such a stable policy inspires confidence in the minds of the employees, customers and dealers. It should not be altered frequently, but should be stable for a fairly long time, say two to three years. Frequent changes in policies often create confusion in the minds of those who are to follow these. The policies should be periodically reviewed, evaluated, assessed, and revised and should be in tune with the challenge of circumstances, needs and urgency of the company and changes in the environment. If modification is to be made successfully, the management must constantly study economic trends within and outside the community, and of the effects of changes on the suitability of prices.

'*Flexibility*' refers to the ability to adapt to short-run changes. It should have an in-built resilience for adjustment from time to time. An example of the long-run change is the increase in hiring of women and minority groups, while the short-run change would be seasonal and cyclical that might affect the hiring of these groups for a short run.

5. *Comprehensiveness*: The policy should be sufficiently comprehensive in scope and should cover, as far as possible, all issues that are of interest to the firm. The comprehensiveness of a policy can be checked by listing the organisation's major functions and sub-functions along with its managerial functions and sub-functions, all of which should be covered by policy statements. If there are no policies stated for some of these areas, a deficiency in comprehensiveness may be said to remain in them.

6. *Complementary to one another:* All policies in the functional areas of business must be complementary to one another. An example is the manufacturing policy that complements the production policy so that these two functions can be coordinated effectively.

7. *Supplementary to overall corporate Policies*: Supplementary policies add to and extend the overall organisation policies from which they are derived. Overall policies that are directed towards the achievement of economic service objectives can be broken down into supportive policies, which can further be separated as lower-level policies. A firm's advertising policy, for example , should supplement the overall marketing policy which, in turn, should supplement the economic service objective. Thus, lower-level policies are supplementary to the highest or superior level policies.

If the policies are not supplementary, there might be a conflict between the departmental policy and the overall policy, and that would be tantamount to insubordination. Peter Drucker has observed; "The policies of an enterprise have to be balanced with the kind of reputation an enterprise wants to build up with special reference to the social and human needs, objectives and values."

8. *Consistent with Public Policy:* The business policy should also be consistent with the public policy, i.e., with the spirit rather than the letter of the law, so that the intentions and settled course of an organisation are appreciated in terms of public opinion from the standpoint of national, economic and social justice for the employees and for the community at large.

13. Carl, Henry, *Reading Courses in Executive Technique: How to Think About Management Problems, Solutions to Specific Problems and Development of Labour Turnover Policies*. Fune and Wagnalls Co., New York, 1948, p. 25.

The principle of consistency, for example, should be followed in the selection and training of employees. In choosing sales people, the personnel manager should hire individuals who not only know the merchandise they will sell, but also have the capability to meet customers and being at ease with them. Then all employees should be trained in such a way that customers may receive substantially the same type of treatment from every representative of the firm with whom they come into contact, whether he be credit manager, salesperson, or deliveryman.

9. ***Fair, Just and Reasonable:*** The policy should be fair to all, offering equity and justice to those who are affected by it. Besides, it should be reasonable, i.e., capable of being implemented.

10. ***Ethical Standards:*** The policies to be effective should be in accordance with the accepted ethical standards of business, i.e., they should not only avoid what is "wrong", but also what is "bad or immoral". In other words, the policies should be indicative of the intention that the business is aware of its social responsibility towards the concerned people and the institution.

11. ***Planned Development*:** The business policy must be a planned development rather than the result of opportunistic decisions on the spur of the moment. Naturally, not every problem arising from the functioning of a firm can be foreseen or solved on the basis of an established policy. But though there will usually be a very large and important area in which judgement of management will be the only guide, yet routine activities should be carried on in a manner specified the policy.

12. ***Individuality:*** The general business policy should lead to the development of a clear-cut character or responsibility for the establishment. Having individuality offers several competitive advantages. For one thing, it enables the firm to build up a strong clientele whose patronage does not depend on a constant promotional barrage. Further, it tends to reduce the vulnerability of the firm to direct price competition, although individuality may be acquired through a policy of low and competitive prices.

In brief, it should be noted that a good policy is: (1) Directly related to an objective of the organisation; (ii) stated in understandable, written terms; (iii) translatable into the practices and specialities of every department/division of the organisation; (iv) subject to change, but still relatively stable with a high degree of permanency; (v) reasonable, feasible and effectively communicable to all concerned; (vi) founded upon facts and sound judgement; (vii) should be able to cover all reasonably anticipated conditions; (viii) consistent with other policies and allows discretion to the manager responsible for its implementation; and is in conformity with the economic principles, statutes and regulations and compatible with the public interest.

Effects of Inadequate Policies

Business policies are inadequate to the extent that they do not meet the requirements stated above. The effects of such inadequacies as well as of the absence of policy, become apparent in many ways. Eventually

(i) They cause unprofitable operation and subsequent failure.

(ii) Business mortalities attributed to insufficient capital, poor location, overbuying and competition in many instances actually result from the adoption of improper/faulty policies for a particular business situation or due to lack of definite policy.

Features of the Policies:

(i) Policies act as guidelines to managers to resolve recurring problems, so as to attain predetermined objectives.

(ii) Policies help the management to delegate duties to subordinates with full confidence that these duties will be carried out strictly as per the policy decisions.

(iii) The effective policies help the executives to know how others will act and this will help them to have better co-ordination in achieving the well formulated objectives.

(iv) Business policies are never static and are subject to alternation or modification depending upon the business environment.

(v) Policies should be properly implemented by trained managers and executives in right time so as to attain the results.

(vi) Clear-cut policies help the organisation to have consistency in execution process and also performance of the executives.

(vii) Policies deal with the nature and process of choice about the future of the business activities. These policies are to be handled by the top level and middle level executives.

(viii) Policies are not a set of rigid of clear-cut rules and regulations instead they are living percepts guiding an enterprise to continue within the set pattern of behaviour.

(ix) They are overall guides determining the direction of managerial action subject to policy restrictions.

(x) Policies further cover the wide field of product mix and market mix guiding the enterprise as to how much and what type of products to be manufactured and its channels of distribution.

(xi) Policies provide guidelines for subordinates and are framed to suit a specific situation.

(xii) Policies are general statement of principles for achieving predetermined goals through guiding actions by executives at different levels.

(xiii) Policies are multipurpose in nature. Their functions include:

(a) avoiding confusion.

(b) providing guidelines at all levels.

(e) enabling the enterprise to run smoothly without any hiderance,

(d) helping management to achieve maximum utilisation of human resources and material resources.

(xiv) Policies decide the course of action for all other functional areas of management and they act as formal agreement to be followed strictly at all levels in the organisation before taking any decision.

(xv) Business Policies govern the planning, decision making, co-ordination, direction, control and other managerial functions.

IMPORTANCE OF BUSINESS POLICY

Policies flow from planning and are extremely useful connections between goals and action. The policies are useful day-to-day guides. As a guide for making decisions, policies provide the following advantages:

1. *They tend to serve as precedents* and thus reduce the repetitive rethinking of all the factors in individual decisions; they save time.
2. *Policies aid in coordination,* if a number of individuals are guided by the same policies, they can predict more accurately the actions and decisions of others.

14. B. K. Acharya and P.B. Govekar, *Business Policy and Strategic Management*, Himalaya Publishing House, Mumbai, 1998 pp. 10-11.

3. *Policies provide stability in the organisation.* A certainty of action is assured even though the top management may change. The policies continue and this continuity promotes stability in the organisation and thus diminish frustrations of members.
4. *Clear policies encourage definite individual decisions* in as much as each manager has a clear understanding of the range within which he can make decision and thus feels less uncertain as to whether he can give answers to subordinates without 'getting into trouble.'
5. Because they specify routes towards selected goals, *policies serve as a standard or measuring yard for evaluating performance*. The actual results can be compared with the policies to determine how well the members of an organisation have lived upto their professed intentions and to what extent goals have been achieved.
6. *Sound Policies help build up employee enthusiasm and loyalty for the organisation.* This is specially true when they reflect established principles of fair play and justice and when they help people to know that within an organisation.
7. *They set the pattern of behaviour and permit participants to plan with a greater degree of confidence* and lead to better co-operation.
8. *Policies are 'control guides of delegated decision-making'*. They seek to ensure consistency and uniformity in decisions on problems 'that recur frequently and under similar, but not identical, circumstances.'
9. *Policies, with clarity, relevance and reasonableness, enable a firm to make the optimum utilisation of scarce available resources* and thereby bring about an efficient level of operations because wastage is avoided.
10. *Corporate policies build up an image of the business in the eyes of the public* and this brings in more reputation, goodwill, sale and profits so that more and more acts of social responsibilities may be undertaken.
11. *Proper administration and implementation of policies encourage initiative in the employees* so that they act with full responsibility within the framework of the policies. This naturally improves the working environment with good labour-management relations.

Policies help the firm to clarify its objectives, guide planning for future operations, aid subordinates in reaching operating decisions, facilitate overall coordination and control and act as yardsticks for evaluating the quality of executive decision-making and action.

It is through policies that the organisation's objectives are achieved, better use of resources is ensured, social responsibility is fulfilled in an increasing manner, personal satisfaction is obtained by the employees and the management is enabled to take useful decisions.

Since policies emanate from good plans and since the actual performance of duties and activities depend upon some means of directing future actions, planning and policies are closely related in the management of an organisation.

Functions of Business Policy

The important functions of business policy are:

(i) Objectives of the company are defined and classified.

(ii) The planning function is done systematically.

(iii) Business policy clearly states the amount of authority that the subordinates have. It also specifies the limits of the authority of the subordinates. Thus it tightens the authority on one hand and provides initiatives to the subordinates.

(iv) Subordinates can use the policy directives intelligently and carefully. It also helps the managerial personnel to perform the functions of control and co-ordination successfully.
(v) Policy acts as the main foundation for evaluation and determining the quality of action and decisions taken by executives.

SCOPE OF BUSINESS POLICIES

Business policies are statements of directions, guidance for corporate thinking, corporate behaviour and action, and therefore, cover a very broad area. Such policies usually cover an approach of a business firm to its environment in general and to the various challenges and problems thrown before it in particular.

Business policies are influenced by the objectives of the business unit, its management structure, the economic and financial resources available to it at a particular point of time, the attitudes, social values and norms of the top management, local/regional traditions, customs and practises, the industrial, economic, fiscal and commercial policy of the government, the national or plant agreements between representatives of employers, managers, employees and the government, the policy of the sister concerns and business associations, government regulations and control measures, public opinion and expectations from business etc.

Therefore, the policies cover such a wide variety of subjects and are so broad-based that every possible matter that affects the interests of any one in the organisation, the community and the government are included in them. In fact, business policies cover all the functional areas of business–production, marketing, personnel and finance. These functional areas are generally covered by what may be termed as 'major' policies, and 'minor' policies,.

Major policies pertain to the overall objectives, procedures and control which affect the organisation as a whole. They cover, in a general way, nearly every phase of enterprise and its products and their marketing, methods of financing, its organisational structure, plant locations, its personnel, and issues demanding special top executive's consideration, such as merger of two concerns; expansion of the existing concern and its facilities; research for finding new processes and procedures for conducting research activities; contraction in production or personnel; settlement of executive problems relating to promotions, transfer, retirement; employment policies regarding women and minorities, and introduction of computerization schemes.

Such policies are formulated at the top level and a framework is established within which the major executives fit themselves to carry out the major objectives of the business.

Minor policies, on the other hand, cover relationship in a segment of an organisation, with considerable emphasis on details and procedures. Such policies are the outgrowth of the major policies and preserve their unity of purpose. In fact, the operational efficiency of a firm depends, to a great extent, on the effective implementation of minor policies.

Such policies are concerned with meeting day-to-day requirements of the departments and are generally decided at the sectional and departmental levels. Such policies may cover: rules of promotion (by seniority, merit or by both); relations with dealers, agents and lines of relationship with these; leave rules; package incentives to employees; rates of discount or cash payment; terms of credit to be given to the dealers, rate of interest and term of credit, etc.

Business policies, thus, cover a wide range of subjects, including policies on product-mix, market-mix, promotion-mix and policies are directly concerned with their administration, particularly the aspects of policy formulation, policy promulgation and its acceptance, its intepretation, its implementation, control and review and feed-back and adjustments therein.

THE NEED FOR BUSINESS POLICIES

Establishing and operating a business firm is a complex activity. It involves the coordination of numerous and varied activities requiring special knowledge and skills on the part of promoters/ sponsors.

Before a business firm comes into actual operation, the management or proprietor must consider a variety of factors which determine its proper location and size, the kinds and amount of equipment, fixtures, plants, machinery, building structures, etc., the legal form of organisation–whether sole proprietorship, partnership, company or a corporation–and the most suitable methods of production and/or selling the product dealt in. The prospective market has to be analysed to locate the potential customers, their nature and what kind of goods and services they will need, when they will want them and how and where they will wish to make their purchase. The management will also be required to search out the sources from which finance can be obtained, the labour market from where to recruit personnel needed for specific jobs and expertise. It must also be conversant with many aspects of business such as market analysis, business law, accounting procedures, the country's legal requirements, the means of transportation facilities available, the nature and extent of competition in the same product and must be able to make skilful application of such knowledge at its disposal.

But the ability to take care of the day-to-day problems involved in the business does not in itself constitute effective management. There is a need for a basic underlying guide which the proprietor/manager can follow in directing all activities toward the same goal, and by means of which the various business operations are and can be integrated. The coordination of the various phases of business operations is facilitated by the selection and application of "*policies*–those settled courses of business procedures which are designed to lead to the attainment of specified objectives.

In the absence of clear-cut objectives and related business policies, the management is liable to become lost in a maze of details to the extent that the overall management of the business may be impaired. For example, failures attributed to inadequate management or insufficient capital occur because the capital and other resources and efforts of the personnel have been dissipated in inconsistent, conflicting practice which were/are not properly related to the goals of the business. Similarly, managements spend much of their time and energy on details which could conveniently be handled by the subordinates, if a proper explicit policy is in vogue.

Policies provide a guide and a framework for subordinates' decisions. Strong and clear policies encourage the delegation of the power of decision-making. Good policies provide a definite and clear direction by top management and at the same time, allow subordinates to make their own decisions within the clearly-stated limits.

Though formulation of policies is important for business and management, they may have certain limitations:

1. They are formulated by the top management to relieve subordinates of the necessity of rethinking about the factors upon which the policy is based. In short, a policy eliminates

thinking about repetitive matters. If subordinates develop the habit of referring to company policy as the only reason for their actions, they may use policies as crutches and defeat the intent of the policies themselves.

2. Policies provide stability and direction to the action of the members of the firm; yet, if a policy remains in existence for long after conditions have changed, it can have the effect of retarding and hindering progress.
3. If policies are not stated in broad and definite terms, they may tend to encourage a subordinate to avoid responsibility for making his own decisions.

MECHANISM OF POLICY MAKING

1. *Identification of the situation:* Policy generation is a complex process, calling for the help of experts. The policies are required to be so designed as to reflect the good practices in society. *The first step* in the mechanics of formulating a policy is the identification of the situation/problem. Policy-making involves all levels in the working organisation. The formulation of a policy is not a job for an ivory-tower specialist. The person preparing a draft of it must be thoroughly familiar with the subject from personal experience and involvement.

2. *Development of Policy*: In the second stage, the draft should be given wide publicity among all who may be expected to operate it because their constructive criticisms and suggestions would be very valuable. Policies are developed after a thorough discussion so that the top and the middle management involved in their related areas of responsibility, are personally committed to them. Developed in this manner, these policies will stand the test of time, and will hold even 'under conditions of stress'.

3. *Dissemination of the Policy*: After the policy has been formulated, i.e., set forth systematically, in clear, precise simple statements in accordance with some principle, and rule(s) of action, it must be disseminated (announced or promulgated) to those who are responsible for its application. In some cases, the policy is promulgated by word of mouth, sometimes at meetings and seminars. In other situations, written memoranda, posted bulletins, revised policy manuals, and company hand-books disseminate the policy.

4. *Explanation of the Policy*: In the next stage, the exact meaning of the policy must also be explained (education) i.e., the person concerned should be explained, in clear terms, all aspects of the policy thoroughly–its purpose; contents/components; significance; its relevance to the business environment in which it is to be operated; the role of the persons who are to impelement it; and the relationship of the policy with the goals of the company. This education may be given through any or all of these techniques–elucidation, explanation, illustration, demonstration, experimentation, verification, simulation, role planning and case studies.

5. *Acceptance of the Policy*: Before a policy can be accepted, the company personnel must understand the principle underlying it and its rule(s) of action. Once the policy is operative (application), questions generally arise as to its specific points. These questions require interpretation by managers who have authority over and responsibility for the policy. This interpretation gives an opportunity to the policy-makers to modify/improve the policy, as per the situation.

Then there must be the assurance that the policy is being adhered to as originally formulated. A control mechanism which includes observation, periodic reports, and complaints is required. Control generally helps in two ways: (a) better utilization of different inputs of the various factors of production; and (ii) timely detection of the undesirable deviations so that they may be corrected promptly. This causes minimum waste of inputs and assures timely completion of work and quality production.

6. *Feed Back:* Finally, after a certain time, it may be necessary to know whether the policy has been effective in the areas at which it was aimed. The opinion, complaints, reactions, comments or suggestions are got from the person entrusted with the implementation of the policy. Effectiveness may be judged on the basis of *quantitative measurements*, such as net profits, return on equity capital, earnings per share or rates of dividend declared; or on the basis of *quanlitative measurement*, such as internal consistency of the policies implemented, consistency with the external factors, appropriateness, acceptability, and workability.

In the light of the review/evaluation, the policy may be revised or necessary adjustment made therein, in order to confirm to changed conditions operating within and/or outside the organisation.

Policy Manual

When the policies are written, they are generally compiled into Policy Manuals for all its personnel. Hand-books, house-bulletins and even booklets may be used for the purpose.

The moment a policy is written down or published, it encourages the staff to be constantly alert so that it may be properly implemented. Francis Clarence says, "If you write it (policy) down, you have got to live up to it or die trying. If you set a high standard, you will fall far short of perfection. But your performance, simply because you have pledged yourself to the standard, will be better than it would be if you lacked a special goal."

The organisation is considerably strengthened by having a Policy Manual because then the statement of policy becomes readily available for reference and guidance. Some other advantages of such a Manual are that they:

(i) reduce misinterpretation, misunderstanding, and resulting friction because policies are stated in writing.

(ii) provide a check-list of current policies which can be used to determine whether or not they are being adhered to; and

(iii) constitute useful instructional device for acquainting the personnel with the principles and procedures required to make the policies effective in the operation of the enterprise.

Precautions to be taken in Policy Framing

Essentially, in the administration of a business policy, (i) a large sum of money is involved; and (ii) an unsound decision may endanger the company's bargaining power. Therefore, thorough consideration must be given to the following issues:

(i) What purpose and objectives will it serve?

(ii) What principles, concepts, practices and philosophies of the organisation/ management will it protect?

(iii) How much would its implementation cost?

(iv) Is it administratively feasible and fair to those concerned?

(v) What areas will it cover?

(vi) Will it be acceptable and consistent?

(vii) What authority/responsibility will it give to personnel at different levels?

Skills necessary to study Business Policies:

(i) The managers should have the skills of studying quickly and accurately the situation relating to the core problems. The managers should keep in mind the policy, the responsibility of top management, financial position of the company, public expectations etc., while studying and analysing the policies.

(ii) The manager/executive should consider the internal environment of the organisation and external environment more carefully based on the facts and complete information. The study of the internal environment helps the managers to appraise organisations strengths and weaknesses. The study of external environment helps the managers to understand the opportunities provided by and threats posed by the various external environmental factors. The SWOT analysis helps for the formulation of strategies.

(iii) Policies help in formulating alternative strategies which would suit various situations.

(iv) Managers should have the skill of matching the situation and strategy.

(v) Managers should have the skill of getting the information about various functional areas like marketing, finance, human resources and production/operations.

(vi) Managers should have the skills of understanding the practical situations more accurately and indentifying the appropriate strategy and execute it.

Policy Issues

Business problems are often discussed in terms of current policy issues. A policy that works for one firm may not work for another. Some business policies apply to the entire company and may cover long periods of time. Several general policies receiving attention in recent years are:

Diversification

Large companies often guide their activities into many different lines of business to avoid having all the eggs in one basket. Diversification is employed to: (i) insulate the company against violent fluctuations in the sales of a single product; (ii) give the company more in the current share of the market; (iii) follow up discoveries made in a research and development programme, which provides new knowledge in areas not previously considered to be of company's interest.

Vertical Integration

Some companies strive to operate at all stages of production, from the raw material to the final sales to the consumers. An integrated policy gives more security to the source of supply of raw materials and more control over the quality of parts and supplies used in production. In some industries, such as oil and steel, the manufacturing process dictates that a single company handles the product at different stages in order to attain economy in operations.

Search for Niches

A firm may concentrate on looking for those areas of operation that are overlooked by its competitors. This policy stresses the development of those operations in which the firm has a comparative advantage and avoids trying 'to beat a competitor in his own backyard'.

Departmental policies may apply to personnel matters, marketing guides, financial questions, or other operational phases of business.

CLASSIFICATION OF BUSINESS POLICIES

A policy is a model of thought and principles underlying the activities of an organisation. It is a guiding decision by the management which guides the organisation in dealing with a particular situation in a particular manner. It is a code of general use which states the established procedure to follow in a recurring situation. A particular policy which may be of importance in one situation may be disregarded in another. Further, with the expansion and diversification of business and severe competition from sister businesses, not only the business policies have tended to increase in number but also in their complexity. Hence, we have various types of business policies, which differ from business unit to business unit in different situations. However, it need be remembered that these policies are flexible in application, subject to change and improvement as per the needs of the business, and subject to enforcement to be effective.

Broadly speaking, policies may be considered as those framed by the government or those formulated by the business itself. Since the government is the guardian of its citizens, it announces a wide variety of policies, from time to time, to: (i) safeguard the interests of the people; (ii) achieve the desired level of economic/industrial development; (iii) improve the economic and social conditions of the people, including the minority, the handicapped, the scheduled castes and the scheduled tribes; (iv) raise the national and *per capita* income; (v) achieve self-sufficiency in matters of food and much-needed raw materials; and (vi) to banish poverty and develop a contented labour class, etc.

To achieve these and many other objectives, the government has the power to frame requisite policies in the respective domains. Consequently, we have economic policy, industrial policy, agricultural and food policy, irrigation policy, fiscal and monetary policy, trade policy, export-import policy, health and education policy, population policy, mineral policy, taxation policy, transport policy, and the like.

But we are not concerned here with these. Our main concern is the business policies, which are framed by individual business units for the efficient and successful conduct of their business. The modern business environment demands special attention in two directions, one, the policies to be formulated should be a collaborative effort not only of the top management people but also of other executives working at different levels as well as the scientists and technicians. Two, the basic policy must reflect the concept of wider, social responsibility of management to fulfil the aspirations of customers, employees, and the community, in addition to those of shareholders or owners of the enterprises, and the government.

Basis and Classification of Policies

With the passage of time, business people have developed certain bases for having different types of policies. These are based on the nature of objectives to be achieved, on the custom and tradition of the business and on the past experience and the exigencies or needs of the time. Though basically there are three main types of policies, viz., basic policy, general policy and departmental policy, yet the present trend is to have as many policies as there are functional areas. For example, Alfred and Beatty have classified policies as[15]: (1) Top management policies, (2) Upper middle management policies, (3) Middle management policies, (4) Foremen policies, (5) Operating force policies, (6) Sales policies, (7) Production policies, (8) Research policies,

15. Alfred and Beatty, Principles of Industrial Management, p.p. 102-103

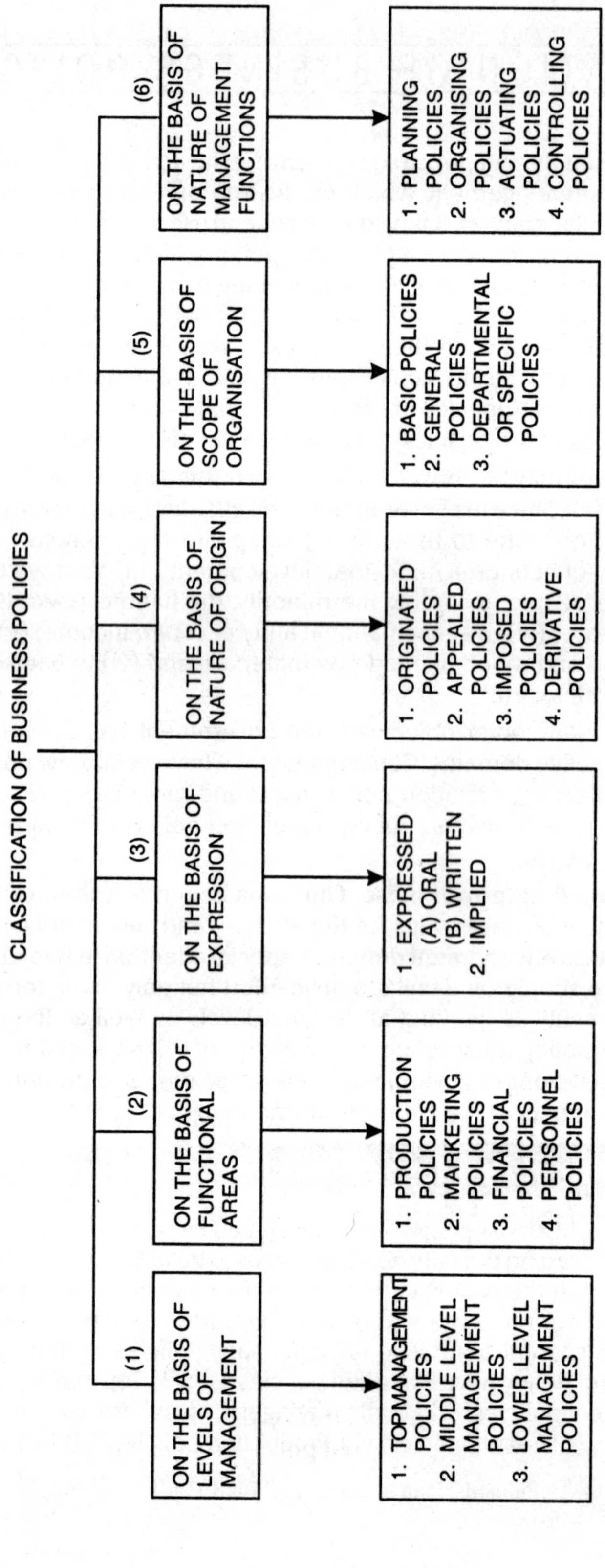

Fig 3.1 Classification of Business Policies.

(9) Financial policies, (10) Costing policy, (11) Accounting policy, (12) Marketing policy, (13) Promotion policy, and (14) Product policies. Besides, there may be policies in various other areas of management.

For the sake of convenience, we classify business policies as given in Fig. 3.1

1. Business Policies Classified According to the Level of Formulation

Business policies are framed at different levels of the management, and accordingly they may be classified as:

1. Top Management Policies: These policies are derived from the top management planning. The top management comprises of the Board of Directors, Chairman/President, Vice-Chairman/ Vice-President, Managing Director, General Manager, etc. The Top management frames the policies by themselves and it is, therefore, responsible for these. These people are the ultimate level of authority in the operation of the enterprise. They set the objectives, define the goals, establish the policies, see that these policies are put into effect and judge the results.

The Top management policies are concerned with the long-range product selection (i.e. line of product), extent of its diversification, acquisitions and mergers of two or more units, spin offs–their nature, extent and liability – sales forecasting, sizing the enterprise, process selection, machine selection, determining the site, location and needs of the plant, decisions regarding investment of available resources in capital and human research and development, settlement of problems of executives regarding their promotion, transfer, retirement etc., and accomplishment of the organisation objectives/goals.

2. *Middle Level Management Policies*: These policies are the out-come of the deliberations of the executives at the upper middle and middle level.

The *upper middle management consists* of the head of the Personnel Administration Department. Works or Production Manager, Sales Manager, Marketing Manager, Financial Manager, Dy. General Manager, Assistant Manager, etc. These executives are responsible for research, finance, accounting and marketing etc.

They lay down the policies regarding the establishment of organisation, selection of the best-suited executives, staff and employees to carry out the plans, installation of proper departments, designing of operating policies and operating routines, deciding processes, methods and techniques of production, exploration of new markets and decisions about channels of distribution, assigning of duties to each department and to each individual, deciding about sources of manpower, resources and their selection, deciding about wage, and salary and incentive plans for them, obtaining necessary finances, controlling costs, solving problems of actual sales activities. etc.[16]

Middle Management consists of the deputy heads of the various sections under different functional departments—employment and training, industrial relations, labour welfare and social security—junior executive, superintendents of departments/divisions, etc. These executives are functional, product or area specialists within the sales, production, research, finance or accounting divisions of the organisation. They frame policies on these matters; and these policies are known as *middle management policies*.

3. *Lower Level Management Policies*: The lower level management people are men who have direct supervision over the working force in office, factory, sales field, and other areas of activity of the concern. They are directly related to the accomplishment of the tasks for the small sub-divisions of the whole enterprise. They chalk out policies for the assignment of the jobs to

16. Hemple, F.H. *Top Management Planning*, p. 23

the best suited persons, the provision of adequate tools, raw materials, training the workers, issuing of orders, maintenance of quality, improving working conditions, and morale, maintaining discipline, controlling absenteeism. etc.

4. *Operating Force Policies:* These are the rules or a code for doing the job entrusted to a particular worker. These are usually written down in the notebooks of the workers, lest they should forget them. From these, the worker knows how long each job should take, what tricks of the trade are required, and what quality features are emphasised.

So far as different management level policies are concerned, it is worth noting that the *Policies framed by the top management always scan the horizon and ply in high skies in search of routes to reach the goals. In fact, they fathom the oceans.* On the other hand, policies framed by the middle management are like birds that have nests in the trees but roam in the skies. In other words, *they go beyond operations and touch the issues and the areas that are on the periphery of basic management policies. In fact, they rule the waves of the sea.*

2. Classification of Business Policies According to Functional Areas to Organisation.

Such policies are better known as *functional policies*, and are generally categorised into two types , viz., (i) *managerial functional policies,* which are formulated to guide the management in the sphere of planning, organising, directing and controlling. The policies in these areas encounter the recurring problems therein: and (ii) *operating functions policies,* which are a guide for management in the performance of specialised functions in the field of production, marketing, finance, and personnel.

We discuss in a nutshell, the policies regarding these functional areas:

1. *Production Policies*: These policies are framed and concerned with: (i) the product to be produced (product line, type of product); (ii) the type of technology, processes, equipment and tools, to be used; (iii) the selection of factory/office/plant site, location, and layout; (iv) the decisions regarding scale of production; (v) making of production budget, manufacturing costs; and deciding about total cost and cost of installation and its maintenance; (vi) the selection of junior executives; (vii) the organisation and co-ordination of their activities; (viii) inventory control; (ix) collective bargaining and labour relations; (x) selection of systems of quality, cost, and production control, and the like.

Production policies are the basic determinants of the total policy-making procedure.

2. *Marketing and Sales Policies:* These policies relate to policies in market analysis, business law, display, salesmanship, advertising etc., i.e., they are concerned with total process of marketing, covering both *'product mix'* and *'market mix'*. The *'product mix'* includes decisions regarding the type, quantity and quality of product, product design, contents shape, methods and techniques of production, etc. *'Market Mix'* covers the issues or channels of distribution, advertising policies, packaging and branding decisions, consumer phychology and behaviour, pricing of the product, etc.

Since the modern concept of market treat 'consumer as a king', every product is brought to satisfy his needs. Hence its gamut is very vast. The policies in this field, therefore, deal with: (i) spotting out of the present and potential markets, the size and nature of consumers; (ii) the degree of competition in the market and how best could it be met; (iii) the location of prospects and persuading them to purchase; (iv) fixing price of product, offering rebates, discounts, and other concessions; (v) compensating salesman adequately; and providing them with training and developmental opportunities; (vi) selecting channels of distribution or employing representatives and agents; (vii) dividing the total market into branch or dealer areas; (viii) establishing advertising policies; (ix) setting up sales control policies; and (x) establishing sales volume and expense budgets.

3. *Financial Policies*: These policies may be regarded as the most important business policies, as the entire success of failure of a business unit depends upon these. Properly framed financial policies result in prosperity and long survival, while faulty policies result in the unit's ruin.

In the area of finance, a number of policies are needed, such as: (1) the capital requirements–for short, medium and long term—and the sources from which these would be procured; (ii) the methods of raising funds and the ratio between the various types of sources of funds, particularly the ratio of owned funds to borrowed funds; (iii) utilization of the funds and the ratio between different types of assets; (iv) the credit policy and the distribution of dividend to the shareholders; how much to be declared out of the profits earned; (v) profit policy and provisions for taxes, renovations and modernisation of plants and machinery.

Costing Policy includes the policy for selecting the method of costing, the method of allocating, apportioning, reapportioning and absorbing overheads etc.

Accounting Policy includes: (i) the basis of valuation of the stock of finished goods—whether at total cost, or at direct cost, or at work cost; (ii) the issue price of raw materials—whether to follow First In Last Out (FILO) or Last In First Out (LIFO) or average cost or any other method of pricing ; (iii) Depreciation policy—the method to be followed; (iv) the treatment of deferred revenue expenditure, intangible assets, fictitious assets and preliminary expenses; (v) capitalisation of expenditure during construction period; and (iv) the policy for provision of bad and doubtful debts, investment losses, etc.

4. *Personnel Policies*: These policies are concerned with human resource utilisation, its recruitment, and selection, sources of supply, training of employees, at whose cost, for how much duration, and in what subjects, and why; the promotion and transfer policy, the issues regarding compensation to the employees, wages incentives and other perks, benefits and services, etc.

3. Classification According to Expression

Business policies may be either express or implied, which in turn may be oral or written.

1. *Express Policies*: These policies are explicitly stated in clear words, either orally or in writing.

(i) *Oral Policies* are those which are issued or stated by the management by word of mouth to its subordinates. Such policies are generally adopted when an organisation is small and face to face communication is desired. Since they are direct, they are more effective and, hence, can be better understood and implemented. They are more flexible and can be adjusted to different organisational conditions. However, the main drawbacks of such policies are that as they are not written, they can be interpreted in any way by persons receiving them. They are often not remembered for long and easily forgotten, especially when there are a number of policies and where their frequency of issue is great. Therefore, usually oral policies are not in popular use.

(ii) *Written Policies* are those which are normally put in black and white and stated in clear terms so that they are easily understood by persons whom they are addressed to. For putting the policies in writing much care has to be taken, for example, (i) Policy is always written in words which are neither vague nor unnecessarily academic, nor in any way offensive to those for whom it is meant. (ii) Words, sentences and paragraphs should be short and the statement of policy should be complete and precise; (iii) It should not contain irritating words or expressions which are antagonistic or cast aspersion on others; (iv) The tone should be warm, without use of any legalistic phraseology; (v) The frame should be convenient and handy for management reference and application.

Written policies are desirable when.

(a) the subject matter on which a policy is to be formulated is of a very controversial nature;

(b) the distance between the top and the lower levels of management is so wide as to make personal/informal contact and communication rather difficult;

(c) consistent treatment to all is needed and a certainty of action desired;

(d) Preciseness and complete understanding is needed to be conveyed to the employees at different levels.

There are distinct advantages of written policies. *In the first place*, the writing of policies makes a commitments on the part of an organisation. *Secondly*, writing ensures uniformity of application and assures continuity of action even when the management is changed. *Thirdly*, it limits the freedom of action on the part of the management, for it is to work within the bounds of the policy. *Fourthly*, writing helps to ensure that the professed policies are 'right', for an organisation tries to put its best foot forward. *Fifthly*, the likelihood of wrong interpretation or misunderstanding is very much lessened. *Sixthly*, written policies provide something concrete on which to base an appeal if there is any disagreement about what the organisation's policy is. *Finally*, written policies facilitate easy and smooth compliance. They result in greater convenience both to the policy-framers and to the implementors.

However, written policies cannot be easily changed and perfect secrecy, when desired, cannot be maintained; and writing of good policies needs fluency in English, which every person does not posses.

Even then, in all large organisations, written policies are a rule rather than an exception.

2. *Implied Policies*: These are the policies which are implied from the code of conduct or from the mode of behaviour of business executives; but they are not stated or expressed orally. They generally flow from the philosophy of the business, its social values and even traditions for examples, smoking and drinking may be prohibited not in writing but is implied by the conduct of the superior executives who refrain from these habits while on duty. Employment or otherwise of women on social, sex, and racial discrimination may be a policy which may only be implied.

4. Classification According to Nature of Origin

1. *Original* or *Originated Policies*: These policies emanate from the company objectives which are determined by the top management, who are primarily responsible for shaping business policies to guide and direct *them* and the subordinates in the attainment of organisation objectives. These are framed by the Board of Directors, the President, General Manager, etc. and passed on to the executives in the hierarchy for implementation.

Such policies are usually readily accepted by the subordinates because they have been framed by higher–ups in power who are entrusted with the shaping of business policies for a concern.

2. *Appealed Policies:* These policies are often known as "suggested policies," because they are framed on the suggestions of the subordinates or those who are to implement the policies. The idea is to make a policy more effective so that particular problems could find solutions under it. Such policies also have general acceptance as that of the originated policy because, they have already got the approval of the top management.

3. *Imposed Policies:* These policies are not voluntarily accepted by the companies but are imposed upon them by certain external forces such as: (i) government rules and regulations that effectively curtail the company executives' freedom of policy-making; (ii) agreements with trade unions and the decisions arrived there at; (iii) import-export policies of the government which may allow or prohibit trading with certain foreign customers; (iv) legislative enactments passed by the Central or the State governments; and (v) the pressure of trade unions which often dictate the policy to be followed in matters of labour unrest; and (vi) the consciousness about the social responsibilities of the business towards the community, such as keeping the environment clean, etc.

The imposed policies are required to be followed by the companies, whether they like them or not.

4. *Derivative Policies:* These policies are generally derived from the company's basic or major policies, and are operational in nature. They are guidelines for action in its day-to-day operations and are concerned with the achieving of certain specific time-bound objectives. They are framed and followed by the departments/sections in such areas as production, marketing, finance and personnel.

5. Classification According to the Scope of Organisation

Business policies may also be categorised as Basic Policies, General Policies, and Specific Policies.

1. *Basic Policies*: These policies are the very basis of the organisation and are framed by the top management. They spell out the basic approach of a company to its activities and its environment. The extent of influence of such policies is very broad in as much as they affect every unit of the organisation and hence are of the greatest importance to the organisation. For example, marketing policy of a firm may be 'customer-oriented' as against 'product-oriented', with the main purpose of competing with the products of all the major competitors in the market. Such a policy emphasises that the customer shall be the centre of the company's marketing universe.

2. *General Policies*: Such policies are generally more specific and apply to large segments of the organisation. They are mainly framed by the middle level management, e.g., purchasing policy to give first preference to local suppliers provided the quality and price of the materials are standard in comparison with other suppliers.

3. *Specific of Departmental Policies*: A departmental policy is that which is specific in nature. It is formulated by the foremen and supervisors. It applies to routine activities in the department, e.g., employees should give casual leave applications one day in advance of day they want to remain absent from work. Similarly, the marketing manager shall assure delivery to all customers in a particular area/locality, say within 3 days from the receipt of orders.

6. Classification According to the Nature of the Managerial Functions

The management undertakes four functions, viz., (i) Planning; (ii) Organising; (iii) Actuating; and (iv) Controlling. Accordingly, the policies may be Planning Policies, Organising Policies, Actuating or Directional Policies, and Controlling Policies.

1. *Planning Policies*: These policies are concerned with the paths of action which lead to company activities, and to the attainment of its objectives. Planning presupposes the existence of policies. Planning emphasises the fact that "If we know where we are going, we are more likely to get there". *It is through planning policies that good managers make things happen.*

Planning policies decide the objectives to be achieved; the policies or paths that should be followed to achieve the objectives, and how the objectives set are to be achieved through programmes and processes. Such Policies include: (i) the determination of corporate objectives; (ii) the collection and classification of relevant information relating to objectives; (iii) the development of alternative courses of action; (iv) comparison of alternatives in terms of objectives, feasibility and consequences; (v) selection of the optimum course of action; and (vi) establishment of policies, procedures, methods, schedules, programmes, systems, standards and budgets.

2. *Organising Policies*: Organisation is another management function, which is concerned with the division or allocation of necessary competent activities to members of the group so that through collective efforts, the objectives may be achieved.

Organisation policies cover: (i) the establishment and maintenance of a clear and precise organisation structure; (ii) the determination of the role of the Board of Directors, Managing Directors, and top managerial group; (iii) deciding the authority/responsibility net-work within the organisation—the degree of decentralisation or extent of centralisation; and (iv) line and staff relationships.

3. *Actuating of Directional Policies*: To carry out the physical activities resulting from planning and organising, the manager has to take measures to see that the members of the organisation continue to work till needed. The actuating policies, therefore, include; (i) providing effective leadership; (ii) integrating people and tasks and convincing them to assist in the achievement of the overall objectives; (iii) effective communication with the members; and (iv) providing climate for the subordinates' development and their motivation to work.

4. *Controlling Policies*: Controlling is the process of measuring actual results or present performance, comparing those results to plans or some standard of performance, finding out the reason for deviations of the actual from the desired result and taking corrective action when necessary.

Controlling policies involve a series of activities: (i) continuous observation and study of periodic results of performance in order to identify potential problems; (ii) selection of the best mode of control; (iii) comparison of the performance with the range of standards established beforehand; (iv) pin-pointing significant deviations; (v) ascertaining their exact causes; and (vi) initiation and implementation of corrective actions or measures.

It is through these policies that the managers accomplish and achieve the objectives of their organisation.

7. Situation and Contingency Policies

Finally, business policies are also sometimes classified according to situations prevailing in the business, i.e., which situation may be treated as normal and which as contigent.

1. *Normal Policies:* with regard normal situations, the policies are so framed that they hold good for such situations. They provide guidelines to the employees in routine day-to-day conduct of the business and its smooth running. Such policies may be termed as *normal policies*.

2. *Contingency Policies*: Contrary to normal times, there are certain events which might happen unexpectedly any time, and which if not anticipated well in advance, might adversely affect the smooth functioning of the business. Such contingencies may relate to: (i) actions of super natural power or nature such as sudden floods, earthquakes, breaking out of fire, continued draught for a number of years, market slump or (ii) changes in business, folly or whims such as declaration of war by the neighbouring country, internal revolts, general prolonged labour strikes and work stoppages, political upheavals, social boycotts and social sensitivity to pollution, etc., or (iii) business situations which are beyond the control of the business unit in the economic sphere, such as changed economic and fiscal policy of the state, unfavourable monetary or trade policy, or industrial policy; or (iv) production strategies of the competitors, their increasing budgets on Research and Development programmes, innovations in product line, quality improvement, new processes and techniques of production all of which adversely affect the firm's business.

To meet such unforeseen, unexpected situations, the farsighted companies frame *contingency policies* to enable them to meet the situations whenever they arise.

Recent Trends in Business Policies

The views of the Chief Executives : The chief executives are the linking pins. In other words they link the organisation with the external environment. In addition they link different departments with the central office within the organisation. They also relate the organisation with the changing factors or conditions within and outside the organisation.

He sees total system which includes the total organisation rather than part of it and the relevant external environment. The relevant external environment includes the competitors, technology, political parties, government and its economic policies, economic factors, social and cultural factors, customers, international and natural factors. Thus the recent trend in formulating business policy is that viewing the total system by the top management rather than mere organisation. In the past, top management used to consider the total organisation rather than the total system in formulating the policies.

Strategic management and strategic planning: Strategic management comprises of the top management which formulates policies. The middle level management is concerned with the implementation of the policies. Policy formulation and implementation are done with the help of strategy formulation and implementation. Strategic planning is concerned with the long range planning of the corporate activities.

Formulation and implementation of strategies assume greater significance in the recent times. Business policies work as broad guidelines in the running of the business where as strategies work as specific acts to be performed. In fact, the strategies are based on policy of the company. Thus the recent trend in the business policy is the shift toward strategy formulation, implementation and strategic management. Strategic Planning plays the vital role in the strategic management process. It specifies the clear direction for the organisation.

Research on Organisational Policy

Business policies vary from company to company. Further, the environment which affect the business also varies from company to company. Hence, it is viewed that the relevant environment differs from one company to the other. Therefore, it is quite essential to find out the relevant environment for each company.

The companies should conduct/organise research studies in order to find out the relevant environmental factors, internal organisational factors, evaluate the organisation, find out the organisation's strengths and weaknesses, opportunities provided and threats posed by the external environment. Further, the research is also necessary to find out the appropriate strategy that suits to the organisation's strengths and weaknesses, environment's threats and opportunities.

The research on Organisational Policy is also necessary as many variables are involved in the process of strategy formulation and implementation. The research helps to find out various factors, the nature and level of their influence etc., This research helps the organisation to find out the factors and take the steps to convert the possible negative effect of the factors into the positive effects. Hence, many organisations started organising research studies in business policy.

Non Profit Organisations

It is beyond doubt that the modern profit organisations formulate policies and implement them. Recently, the non-profit organisations have realised that the policy formulation and implementation help them to improve their efficiency.

Social Responsibilities and Ethical standards: Social responsibilities of the business and ethical standards influence the policy formulation. The recent development in the concept of social responsibilities are commercial attitudes of the managements. Therefore, managements give commercial approach to social responsibilities and ethical standards in policy formulation.

Exhibit A : Policy Statements of Labour Relations

(i) *Employees' needs, aspirations and rights*. There must be realistic, purposeful and general understanding and acceptance of the worker's needs, aspirations and rights.

(ii) *Progress and evolutionary approach towards Unions*. Such an approach requires;

(a) a recognition of the right of workmen to organise into a union and to be represented through union for collective bargaining or other issues affecting them;

(b) that all issues concerning workmen are resolved through mutual discussions;

(c) that all arguments/understanding with unions are honoured; and

(d) that there should be no interference in the affairs of the union nor should any workman be discriminated against for legitimate union activities, etc.

(iii) *Provision for adequate wages, good working conditions, job security, suitable opportunities for promotion and self-development.*

(iv) *Role of line management in labour relations.* Line management to be closely associated with evolving labour relations policies and programmes.

(v) *Setting high standards of efficiency and productivity.*

(vi) Consultation with union on matters affecting workmen.

(vii) Grievances. No grievance is to be considered small, no employee insignificant and no challenge too great.

(viii) Communicating aims and objectives of the company to all employees.

In sum, the labour relation policy may be studied thus:

(a) Promoting social and welfare amenities for the workers;

(b) Providing speedy redress of all grievances, however small.

(c) Creating a forum for discussion/consultation on matters of special interest, and

(d) Conducting negotiations with the representative unions.

Exhibit B: Labour Relations Philosophy and Goals (Public Sector N. 10)

Philosophy/Values	Goals
1. Regarding human beings as the most important human asset.	1. To achieve higher increased productivity/ better performance.
2. Boosting and maintaining morale of workers.	2. To maintain industrial peace/harmony.
3. Betterment of work and social life.	3. To serve the customer.
4. Maintaining cordial relations with the Unions.	4. To maintain good discipline.
5. Encouraging participative spirit and and motivation.	5. To produce goods and services of dependable quality at economic prices.
6. Career advancement of employees.	6. To improve the standard of living of workers.
7. Personal fulfilment of workers and their job satisfaction.	

Labour Relations Philosophy and Goals (Private Sector N. 8)

Philosophy/Values	Goals
1. To Instil in workers feelings of loyalty, commitment, belonging, importance, involvement, and recognition.	1. To reduce conflicts between employees and workmen.
2. To provide safe and salutary working. conditions.	2. To secure workers effective and willing co-operation for achieving company's objectives.
3. To have a constructive approach to men and matters.	3. To attract and retain employees of the highest quality.
4. To comply with the principle: "Industrial Relations are human relations".	4. To create an awareness for productivity.
5. To continually promote growth and development of employees.	5. To increase organisation's productivity.
6. To believe in the precept: Man behind the machine is the most important in an enterprise/ human assets are more important assets.	6. To ensure substance and growth of company.
	7. To effectively and continually contribute to the profitability of the company.

(*Source*: Suri. G.K. and Rama M. Joshi "Labour Relations: Philosophy, Policy and Strategy", *Indian Management*, New Delhi, May, 1983, pp. 9 -10)

CHAPTER 4

BUSINESS POLICY RELATED ASPECTS

- **Policy and other Related Terms**
- **Strategies**
- **Programmes**
- **Procedures**
- **Standards**
- **Rules**

POLICY AND OTHER RELATED TERMS

A policy is an understanding by the members of a group that makes the actions of each member of the group in a given set of circumstances more predictable to other members. *It is a guide for making decisions.* If a decision provides help for decisions in other situations, it is said to be a *policy decision*, but it sets a precedent and provides some guide for decision-making in future also. Policy decision provides a range to freedom within which subordinates can make single-slab decisions.

Table 4.1 clarifies the meaning of policy by defining the related terms that should not be confused with it.

TABLE 4.1 POLICY AND RELATED TERMS

Policy	:	An understanding by persons of a group that makes the actions of each member more predictable to other members. Policy is a guide for making decisions.
Rule	:	A statement of precisely what is to be done (or not to be done) in the same way every time with no permitted deviation. Rules allow no range for decision making; policy encourages decision – making by offering guides.
Law	:	A statement of an order that is invariable under given conditions. Laws are rigid statements providing a framework for policy formulation.
Creed	:	A belief or faith that lacks precision but serves as a foundation upon which policies develop.
Procedures	:	A system that describes in detail, the steps to be taken in order to accomplish a job. *Procedures emphasize details; policies concentrate on basic general approaches.*
Practice	:	The usual mode of handling a given problem. *A practice stresses expendiency and things as they are; a policy stresses direction and things as they should be.*
Principle	:	A universal statement that remains true even when conflicting statements may be claimed to be valid. *A principle is valid and cannot be good or bad; a policy may be good or bad, but it is valid only in the sense that someone has decided that it is to be used as a guide.*

Below we discuss, in some detail, the basic facts and differences between some important terms.

STRATEGIES

A strategy is a term derived from military science. It means the art of a General leading an army. It is an art of war, compelling the enemy to fight on the opponent's chosen terms and conditions. It means a skill to move and deploy the army in such a manner as to impose upon the

1. Massie, Joseph, L. *Essentials of Management*, Prentice Hall of India, New Delhi, Second Edition, 1973.

enemy the terms and conditions regarding time and place of fighting a war.[2] It is a technique of managing the war campaign by the military commanders in such a way as to make it favourable to the concerned military commanders and their army.

In corporate planning, strategy is the '*grand design*' or an overall 'plan' which an organisation chooses in order to move or react towards the set objectives by using its resources. Strategies, most often, devote a general programme of action and an implied deployment of emphasis and resources to attain comprehensive objectives.[3]

Anthony defines strategy as "Resulting changes from the process of deciding on objectives of the organisation, on changes in these objectives, on the resources used to attain these objectives, and on the policies that are to govern the acquisition, use, and disposition of these resources."[4]

And as Chandler has stated, a strategy is "The determination of basic long-term goals and objectives of an enterprise, and the allocation of resources necessary to carry out these goals."[5]

Thus, an organisation's strategies revolve round specific programmes of action that are capable of meeting competition as well as fulfilling the organisation's objectives comprehensively so as to employ the firm's resources efficiently and economically.

Strategy, in the words of McFarland is, "The executive behaviour whose purpose is to achieve success for the company or personal goals in a competitive environment, based on the actual or probable actions of others – chiefly rivals, market competitors, suppliers, customers, employees and government units – or on potential or predictable events occurring in the organisation's environment .... Strategy includes an awareness of goals, the unpredictability and uncreditability and uncertainty of events and the need to take into account the probable or actual behaviours of others, principally opponents."[6]

Strategy includes :

(i) awareness of the mission, purpose and objectives. This provides the central concept for planning, indicating what is our business, who are our customers, what goods and services we are to supply;

(ii) the unpredictability and uncertainty of events indicating economic, social, technological and political conditions which form the business environment; and

(iii) the need to take into account probable behaviour of others in general and of the rivals in particular. For instance, strategies of marketing shall take into consideration the probable behaviour of customers and competitors; and strategies dealing with employees will anticipate employee behaviour and so on.

The purpose of strategies is to determine and communicate, through a system of major objectives and policies, a picture of the kind of enterprise that is envisaged. They show a unified direction and imply a deployment of emphasis and resources. They serve the useful purpose of guiding enterprise thinking and action. These strategies are then integrated into the organisation's major and minor supporting programmes.

2. Hodgett, Richard, M., and Max S. Wortman, Jr. *Administrative Policy and Strategic Management*, 2nd edition, 1980,p. 89.
3. Koontz, Harold, Cyril O'Donnell, and Heinz Weihrich, *Management*, McGraw-Hill Kogakusha, Ltd., Tokyo, 7th Ed. 1980, p. 163.
4. Anthony R.N., *Planning and Control Systems : A Framework for Analysis*, Harvard Business School, Boston, 1965, p.24.
5. Chandler, A.D., *Strategy and Structure*, M.I.T. Press, Cambridge, Massachusetts, 1962, p.13.
6. McFarland: *Principles and Practice of Management*, Macmillan & Co., 1980.

An organisation's strategies revolve round specific programmes of action. These programmes are competent to meet competition as well as to fulfil the organisation's objectives comprehensively for which the resources of the enterprise are employed efficiently and economically. The corporate strategies can integrate knowledge about technology and social changes and the top management can formulate programmes that embrace new technology, new products, enlarged markets, higher earnings, and increased rate of growth.

Strategy covers skills such as : (i) being able to guide in time what to do in a complicated, critical and uncertain risky situation; and (ii) doing the best one can with the available resources; and dealing effectively with risk, insecurity, uncertainty, which a business has often to face. Strategy helps the enterprise to establish a useful relationship with all the present and future environmental forces in which it is to function, and thereby reduce risk and insecurity. In other words, strategic decisions help the management to develop a fine art of dealing with the unknown and the unfamiliar in an important situation. Without a strategy, the organisation is like a ship without a rudder, going round in circles. It is like a tramp, which has no particular destination to go to. Without an appropriate strategy effectively implemented, the future is always dark and hence, the chances of business failure.

Policies vs. Strategies

1. Policies are guidelines or paths of action to reach the goals, while strategies are *major* courses of action or patterns of successful action to achieve the objectives. They are intended to meet and fight against a certain competition, much larger and apparently more powerful than the enterprise itself by using its resources in the best possible manner.
2. A policy embraces both thought and action, while strategy concentrates mostly on action, i.e., *it is most action-oriented.*
3. A policy usually spells out a certain course of action/approach to reach the set objectives, the strategy outlines one's approach to meet competitive situations, uncertainties, risk and insecurity likely to arise in the future.
4. Business policy lays emphasis mainly on long-term growth, through a set path of action for achieving the goal; whereas strategy's main concentration is on meeting a competitive situation; and therefore, they have a short or medium-term target before them.
5. Business policy is an overall guide/path of action that sets the limits and the direction of managerial action; while a strategy is deployed to mobilise the available resources in a marketing campaign to explore new markets or to consolidate the existing one in the face of free competition through a vigorous advertising campaign,.
6. In business policy, some of the implementation part of the process can be delegated to the subordinates, such delegation is not possible in business strategy, nor even desirable.
7. Finally, whereas a *policy* is concerned with the estimation, availability, application, conservation, and improvement of resources of a firm to utilise them to the optimum benefit of all, a *strategy* is only concerned with the mobilization of available resources and their deployment on different aspects of competition.

Thus, it should be noted that a strategy is :

- An action plan of the firm, and action decisions in specific directions;
- A long-term design chartered to fight competition in marketing campaigns;
- An application of available resources for effectively meeting a competitor in the market;

- The result of policies; and
- A broad line of action to meet uncertainty, risk and insecurity that may arise in future so that these can be met effectively.

Policies cover the broad aspects and strategies are specific oriented. Exhibit 4.1 presents the differences between policies and strategies.

Exhibit 4.1 Difference between policies and strategies

	Policies	*Strategies*
1.	Policies are statements or a commonly accepted understandings of decision making.	Strategies are specific actions suggested to achieve the objectives.
2.	Policies are thought – oriented	Strategies are action- oriented
3.	Power is delegated to the Subordinates for implementation.	Everyone is empowered to implement the strategy
4.	Policies are guidelines	Strategies are means to an end.
5.	Policy is in general concerned with the course of action to fulfil the set objectives	Strategy is concerned with uncertainties, competitive situations, risks etc that are likely to take place at a future date.
6.	Policy is an overall guide that governs and controls the managerial action	Strategy is deployed to mobilise the available resources in the best interest of the company.

PROGRAMMES

A programme is a single-use comprehensive plan laying down the principal steps for accomplishing a specific objective and sets an approximate time limit for each stage. A programme outlines the actions to be taken by 'whom', 'when' and 'where'

Programmes are guided by the organisation's objectives and strategies and cover many of the other types of plans. They (i) are a complex of activities, resources to be employed and other necessary elements for carrying out a given cause of action; (ii) cover many goals, policies, procedures, task assignments, steps to be taken and resources to be employed; (iii) are normally supported by capital and organisation budgets; (iv) show the sequence of activities in proper order which are designed to implement policies and accomplish set objectives; (v) are the instruments for coordination; for they require system, thinking and action and involve integrated and coordinated planning efforts; (vi) give a step-by-step approach to guide the action necessary to reach the predetermined goals.

Product development programmes based on new technology, large capital expansion programmes to build new plants; long-range programmes for firing employees, training programmes, sales promotion programmes, management development programmes, etc. are examples of programmes.

A well-designed programming covers these steps:[7]

(i) Division of activities into steps needed for achieving the objectives.

(ii) Establishing relationship between steps and ensuring their sequence in operation.

(iii) Deciding responsibility for doing each activity and accountability for each step.

(iv) Determining the sources – materials, finance, personnel and facilities – that will be needed.

(v) Laying down the time-limit within which each step is to be completed.

(vi) Assigning definite date for each part of the programme.

As programmes have a hierarchy of sub-programmes and as they are complex, higher planning skill is needed. It is to be noted that a programme is only as good as its weakest sub-programme allows it to be. Poorly conceived sub-programmes always damage the entire programme.

Policies vs. Programmes

(i) While a 'policy' indicates 'why', 'procedures' tell 'how the work is to be done'; and the 'programme' tells 'what'. It consists of the entire broad course of action governing employees at all levels.

(ii) A policy is a plan of action, a programme is a 'stable plan of action' that continues over an extensive period of time. It is the end product of the philosophy, values, concepts, principles, policies and procedures.

(iii) Programmes represent simple or complex activities, presumably developed to carry out the policy. They are a step ahead of policy in that they simplify the process of decision - making and reduce it to a routine.

Exhibit 4.2 provides the distinction between policies and programmes

Exhibit 4.2 : Distinction between policies and programmes.

	Policies	*Programmes*
1.	Policies provide broad and comprehensive guidelines about the future direction of the company.	Programmes provide detailed and step-by-step course of the action.
2.	Policies provide long range plan of action.	Programme provides stable and short range plan of action.
3.	Policy is a broad direction to be followed.	Programmes represent simple or complex activities in order to carry out policy.
4.	Policy is the basis for programmes.	Programmes are based on policies.

PROCEDURES

Organisation plans, including strategies, programmes, policies, budgets, need to be supplemented with detailed specifications as to how they are to/would operate. Such

7. Adapted from W. H Newman and J.P Logan *Strategy, Policy and Central Management*, South-Western Publishing Company, Cincinnati, 1971, Chapter 21.

specifications are referred to as 'procedures'. In general terms, a procedure can be defined as "A series of functions or steps performed to accomplish a specific task or undertaking." In other words, *it is a precise means of making a step-by-step guide to action that operates within a policy framework*. Procedures are established sub-policies of an organisation. They are a guide to action rather than thinking and represent policy decisions made in advance.

Company action on even relatively small matters usually requires the work of several individuals. A procedure helps to integrate these bits of work into a meaningful whole.

Most companies have literally hundreds of such procedures – for grievances, capital expenditure; for selection, promotion, transfer of the employees; for flow of business papers, i.e., orders, bills, requests, reports, applications, etc. – most are essential for smooth operation.

Some examples of procedures are:

- Calling tenders for purchase of materials, keeping them in a stock-room and issuing them against requisition slips;
- Granting employees leave, by avoiding disruption of work, setting times of vacation, and maintaining records of leave and vacations.
- Procedure for the selection of employees may have these steps; preliminary interview, application blank, reference check, employment tests, final interview, medical check-up, appointment, and induction or orientation.

In these cases, Procedures communicate the tasks to be performed, the organisation interfaces, and the responsibilities of the individuals involved.

It should be said that a procedure is also a standing plan describing a customary method of handling a future activity. It gives a sequence of actions directed at a single goal (usually short-term) that is repeatedly pursued, e.g., procedure for purchasing materials, or preparation and despatch of invoices/accounts to the customers, or adopting budget, making procedures or granting sick leave to an employee against medical certificate, and giving from the provident fund loan/advance to an employee in case of need.

Importance of Procedures

Procedures play an important role in an organisation's daily operations. They relieve the manager of much of the details in directing the subordinates. They indicate the steps to be taken as well as the required time and order of performing certain things or actions. They help in facilitating the training of new employees. An orderly statement of 'what to do' and 'how to do' can save the new employee the expense and frustration of a trial and error method of finding an acceptable way of performing a task. As they are well-thought-out steps in carrying out the task, work operation is facilitated and better results at lower cost are ensured. Since procedures dictate a chronological sequence of doing a task and set the time limit for its performance, effective control over each operation is possible.

Requirements for Effective Procedures

If procedures are to be effective :

(i) their detailed steps and the order of their performance must be focussed on the desired objective;

(ii) they should be standardised and, at the same time, aid in placing responsibility so that accountability can be established;

(iii) their operative phases should be linked with control procedures, so that exceptions from planned performance can be reviewed.

(iv) They should, as far as possible, be stable but not rigid. With a change in objectives, or influence of external environment or some crisis in business or some expediency, procedures should be modified accordingly.

(v) They should be built with due consideration of time, cost, environment etc. and it should be ascertained that they are going to be fruitful.

(vi) Changes in the existing procedures should be made orderly in advance by putting them in writing so that all operators concerned can be well acquainted with the changes introduced.

(vii) They must be known, understood and accepted by everyone involved in following them.

In the past, those responsible for effective procedures have been, for the most part, the firm's managers. Today, the responsibility for development of new procedures has passed over to systems analysis (associated with the Computerized Management Information System), time and motion study (for production) and procedural analysis (for administrative and office work).

Before adopting new procedures, the analyst must ask some basic questions about them, such as :

1. Can the procedure be improved to realise more fully the firm's objectives?
2. Are all the steps in the procedure necessary?
3. Is it possible to simplify the procedure through modification of the existing company policies, departmental structures, practices of other departments or similar considerations?
4. Is there too much handling of a document in the procedure?
5. Does the procedure route the document through too many of the firm's personnel and departments?
6. Can the procedure be performed in a quicker and more economic manner?
7. Does the procedure make a contribution to the quality or flow of work?
8. Is the cost of procedure greater than its value to the firm?
9. Are all the forms used in the procedure necessary? Can some of the forms be combined?
10. Is there duplication of work in the procedure?
11. Are the steps of the procedure in a logical sequence for the greatest efficiency?
12. Are there any parts of the procedure that functionally belong to another activity?
13. Is the procedure really essential to the firm's operations?
14. What would happen if one or more steps in the procedure were eliminated?

Once these questions have been answered, the analyst must test the procedure of its practicability, efficiency, and economy. Generally, a procedure is not isolated, but a part of other procedures.

An effective procedure, therefore :

(i) incorporates only essential steps;

(ii) is simple and ensures quicker and economical performance;

(iii) involves minimum paper-handling work;

(iv) enhances utility and flow of work;

(v) eliminates duplication of work;

(vi) gives steps in a logical sequence; and

(vii) ensures practicability.

Policies vs Procedures

1. Policy is a guide for thinking and action, whereas a procedure is a guide for action and performance to achieve the organisation's objectives, i.e., it shows the method of doing the task.
2. Policies are the basis on which procedures are built, but procedures are a reflection of policies, i.e., *policies take the first place and procedures follow later on.*
3. Policy–making is a superior order of activity in executive responsibility. Procedures are always subordinate to policy.
4. Officers formulating procedures must work within the framework established by the policy-makers who are the high-level executives, whereas procedures are more rapid and permit less liberty in managerial decision-making.
5. A policy covers a broad area and is growth-oriented. It is a long-range thing or a basic issue, whereas a procedure normally deals with the way a policy is carried out. It is a narrow lane to operate.
6. A statement of procedure is more specific than a statement of policy as it enumerates the time-wise steps to be taken in sequence in order to achieve a stated objective.
7. Policies are directly related to goals, for goals determine policies and policies depend on goals. But procedures are indirectly connected with goals. They tell the way to do a task and thereby help the organisation in reaching the goals.
8. A policy is concerned with estimating the availability of resources, their procurement, their augmentation and their efficient utilisation. On the other hand, a procedure is concerned with the actual utilisation of resources.

A procedure is a means of implementing a policy, which is done in sequential steps. A statement of procedure is more specific than a statement of policy as it enumerates the time-bound steps to be taken in a sequence for achieving specified objectives. When a procedure for dealing with recurring problems becomes formalized, it is called a *Standing Operating Procedure*. (See Table 4.1)

Differences between policies and procedures are presented in Exhibit 4.3

Exhibit 4.3 : Differences between policies and procedures

	Policy	*Procedure*
1.	Policy is a guide for thinking and action	Procedures are guide for action. They show the method of doing a task.
2.	Policies are basis for procedures	Procedures follow the policies
3.	Policies are responsibilities of top management	Procedures are responsibilities of middle level and lower level managers.
4.	Policies are stable	Procedures can be changes in the short – run
5.	Policies give emphasis on general approach	Procedures give emphasis on stage-by-stage details
6.	Policies are broad and comprehensive	Procedures are more rigid and allow no freedom.

7. Policies are applied in long-range planning	Procedures are applied in short range planning.
8. Policies are directly related to goals	Procedures are indirectly related to goals.
9. Policy does not provide any method of doing a work.	Procedure is a standard method of doing a work

STANDARDS

A standards is a 'norm' or 'criterion' against which performance is compared and evaluated. Standards are an integral part of the control function in management.

A standard can be established on the basis of past experience, guesses or probable estimates and also scientific methods. These standards relate to quantity, quality, time and cost. Generally, managerial standards are broader than those for operatives. For example, for managers, the standard may be 'return on sales', 'return on investment', 'department or divisional expense ratios', financial ratios – such as liquidity ratio, current ratio, etc. – standards of ethical and moral conduct, and such other matters.

For operators, the standards set are quite different, i.e.,*performance standards* determined by time and motion study, e.g., based on this study, quantity standards can be prescribed, say 500 units per hour to be produced, and the standard time needed may be fixed as 5 minutes to produce one part. Qualitative and quantitative standards are set in each area of business, such as physical standards, quality standards, standards of service and conduct, etc.

Where *quantitative standards* are difficult of application, cost standards are employed. For example, the standard cost for a manufactured part might be stated in money terms, such as Rs. 7/- per piece.

For *quality standards*, devices like statistical and mathematical techniques are used, e.g., random, sampling and quality control charts.

Tactics

Tactics are used to implement strategies. To implement the strategies effectively, the management should prepare detailed programme. These detailed programmes are known as tactics. Tactics are action programmes through which strategies are implemented. Strategies must be supported by effective tactics.

Organisational decision varies from a broad master strategy at one end and minute tactics at the other. The strategists should have a clear understanding about the differences between strategy and tactics. Exhibit 4.4 presents strategy vs tactics.

Exhibit 4.4 Strategy Vs Tactics

Strategy	***Tactics***
1. **Level of Conduct:** Strategy is developed at the top level of the management and relates exclusively to decisions in the province of these levels.	Tactics are employed at and relate to lower levels of management.

2. **Regularity:** The formulation of strategy is both continuous and irregular. The process is continuous, but the timing of decision is irregular for it depends upon and is triggered by the appearance of opportunities, new ideas, management initiative, crises and other non-routine stimuli.	Tactics are determined, for many companies, on a periodic cycle with a fixed time schedule, such as the annual budget process.
3. **Subjective Value:** Strategic decision-making is more heavily weighted with subjective values.	Tactical decision-making is less weighted with subjective values.
4. **Range of Alternatives:** The total possible range of alternatives from which a management must choose is far greater in strategy.	The total possible range of alternatives from-which a management must choose is less in tactics.
5. **Uncertainty:** Uncertainty is usually much greater in both formulation and implementation of strategy. It is difficult to assess the risks in strategy.	It is usually less in tactics. Risks are more easily assessed in tractics.
6. **Nature of Problems:** Strategic Problems are generally unstructured and tend to be one of a kind.	Tactical problems are more structural and often repetitive in nature.
7. **Information Needs:** Strategy formulation requires large amounts of information desired from and relating to areas of knowledge outside the corporation. Most of the relevant data needed relate to the future are difficult to get with accuracy and are tailored to each problem.	Tactical informational needs, rely more heavily on internally generated data. Particularly from accounting system, and involve a higher proportionate use of historical information.
8. **Time Horizons:** Strategies, especially when successful, are intended to, and do last for long periods of time. However, sometimes the time dimension is very short.	Tactics cover a shorter duration and are more uniform for all parts of an operating programme.
9. **Reference:** Strategy is original in the sense that it is the source or origin for the development of tactics.	Tactics are foumulated within and in pursuit of strategies.
10. **Detail:** Strategies are usually broad and with few details.	Tactics have many details.
11. **Type of Personnal Involved in Formulation:** Strategies are mostly formulated by top management and its staff.	Tactics are formulated by lower-level executives.
12. **Ease of Evaluation:** It is difficult to evaluate strategies. It takes a number of years to evaluate strategy.	It is easy to evaluate tactics. Tactical results are quickly evident and much more easily identified with specific actions.
13. **Point of View:** Strategies are formulated from a corporate point of view.	Tactics are developed principally from a functional point of view.
14. **Importance:** Strategies are of highest importance to an organisation.	Tactics are relatively less important.

Source: Modified version from: George A. Steiner, John B. Niner and Edmund R. Gray, "*Management Policy* and *Strategy*." Macmillan Publishing Company, New York, 1986, pp. 13-14.

Tactics are applied under the following conditions.

1. **To meet competitions effectively** : Strategies are implemented through tactics. Therefore, tactics are the micro-level actions in the direction of attainment of organisational objectives and policies. Managers formulate strategies to win over the competitors, to attack the competitor's weaknesses like cost, quality, delivery, service etc. Tactics are the actual activities with which the competitor is attacked. Tactics include advertising, rendering a crucial service, attracting a key customer who in turn get many customers, getting a crucial input at less price etc. Thus tactics are useful to meet the competition effectively.
2. **Continuous efforts to curb Aggressive Firms** : Some firms react to the tactics employed by the competitors while some other firms play the leader's role and attack the follower firms through their tactics. These firms are called aggressive firms. Aggressive firms create problems for the small, weak and follower firms. Therefore, the follower firms employ the tactics continuously in order to curb the tactics of the aggressive firms. Their tactics mostly aim at hitting the weaknesses of the aggressive firms.
3. **To Retain competitive position** : Normally, the firms acquire the competitive position by competing with the competitors through their tactics. The firms acquire competitive position in the areas like cost, quality, delivery, service, convenience and the like. The firms exert all their energies to retain their competitive position, if not develop their competitive position further. Therefore, the firms employ the tactics relating the stability and sustainable growth strategies.
4. **To consolidate gains** : After retaining the competitive position, the next step of the firm is to consolidate the gains. The gains of the firm include new customers, new markets, price/cost advantage, suitability of the product features to the customer requirements, bridging the existing marketing gap by the product, superior service, delivery, and the like. The firm at this stage should employ the tactics further or intensify them in order to consolidate the gains already acquired.
5. **Tactics of Retreat** : The firms gain and consolidate the competitive position under certain favourable environmental conditions or opportunities. These opportunities would not be continuous due to the dynamic nature of the environment. Thus, today's opportunities may turn to be the tomorrow's threats and vice versa. The competitors would dominate the companies and take away the gains acquired during favourable environment, Hence, the companies should develop the tactics to retreat.

Policies and Tactics

Policies are broad guidelines which direct the future course of the business whereas the tactics are the micro-level actions which contribute for the achievement of policies and organisational objectives. Exhibit 4.5 presents the differences between policies and tactics.

Exhibit 4.5 Differences between Policies and Tactics.

	Policies	*Tactics*
1.	Policies are broad guidelines	Tactics are micro level – activities or actions. They are specific methods used to achieve the policies.
2.	Policies are concerned with thinking	Tactics are concerned with a specific area of operation. They are action – oriented.

3.	Policies are concerned with the long-range planning	Tactics deal with immediate problem like decline in sales.
4.	Scope of the policies is wide, broad and of long-range	Scope of the tactics is narrow, specific and of very short-range.
5.	Policies are over all guide for the entire business and external environment.	Tactics are developed to utilise available resources in the best possible manner.
6.	Policy implementation and delegation of authority for implementation depend upon the size of the firm.	Tactics are executed by the junior executives. Their responsibilities are clear and specific.
7.	Policies are generally mission oriented.	Tactics are goal and target oriented
8.	Policies give birth to strategies hence policies are primary	Strategies give birth to tactics. Therefore, tactics are primarily derived from policies.
9.	Policies are drawn at estimating the future availability of different kinds of resources like financial, human and material.	Tactics are concerned with the mobilisation and utilisation of presently available resources.
10.	Policies, main role is to guide and direct the future course of the business.	Tactic's role is to solve the present/existing problems.
11.	Policies are future oriented	Tactics are current – oriented.
12.	Policies are stable but not rigid.	Tactics are formulated to suit the requirements of each problem separately.

RULES

Rules constitute the simple and the most specific type of standing plans, chosen from various alternatives. *A rule is a principle to which an action or a procedure conforms or is intended to conform. In other words, it is a standard or a norm to be followed in the conduct of a business in a particular situation.* It is more rigid, and always much more specific than a policy. It demands that a specific action should or should not be taken with respect to a particular situation. It is related to a procedure as 'guides to action' but mentions no time sequence. A rule is formulated to define in advance what decision must be made. *It guides action, but it gives no discretion in it's applicability.* A rule is a rule allowing no liberty or leniency, and therefore, does not tolerate much deviation. Rules have to be strictly followed, and any breach or non compliance might amount to defiance or act of insubordination, which may entail penalty/punishment for the defaulter in the shape of a fine or even dismissal from employment. For example, 'No smoking' or 'No Spitting' in the verandahs or other places is a rule which has to be adhered to equally by the top executive as well as the operator.

Thus, it will be seen that rules are 'tenets' or 'principles' of conduct/behaviour in a particular situation; and that they reflect a managerial decision that certain actions be taken or not be taken.

Policies vs. Rules

1. Policies are concerned with ways of thinking and paths of action; whereas rules generally apply to action.
2. Policies are broad instructions, directions and guidelines, while rules are specific and definite actions to be taken or not to be taken.
3. Since policies are normally broad and general, discretion is often allowed but rules being specific, directions do not permit deviation, and failure to follow these might lead to punishment or penalty.

Table 4.2

EXAMPLE OF PROGRAMMES, PROCEDURES AND PRACTICES DEVELOPMENT

(i) By Private Sector Companies (in order of frequency of use)

Programmes		*Procedures and Practices*
Workers' participation/closer association of employees. with management	–	Involvement in achieving company goals through Joint Committees in inter-related areas of grievances, wages, housing, schools, hospitals, etc.
Well developed grievance procedure	–	Expeditious handling of individual grievances.
Training programme, specially for workers	–	On-the-job and in-company training by outside agencies and through worker's education classes.
Negotiations with Unions issues.	–	Periodic meetings with union officials and settlements with unions of inter-related
A good communication system	–	Sharing company information by establishing a two-way communication system.
Welfare and social activities	–	Off-the-job activities such as organising sports, a cooperative credit society, library service, picnics, etc.
Salary and perquisite structure	–	Giving salary increments commensurate with performance.
Charting career paths	–	Making every individual employee aware of career opportunities.
Performance review	–	Reviewing performance against job goals.
		(ii) By Pubic Section Companies (In order of frequency of use)
Workers' participation	–	Three-tier joint consultative machinery at unit, department, and Organisation level, open style of management.
Well-defined grievance procedure	–	Quick and satisfactory redress of employee grievances.
Extensive training programme for all	–	Training imparted to executives, supervisors, and in some cases, trade union officials as also to workers by organising workers' education classes.
Communication system	–	Management-employee communication meetings; organisation's policies made known to employees through communication programmes.
Social security measures and cultural and welfare programmes	–	Housing, sports, schools, recreation, free medical care, group. insurance, etc.
Fair wage structure	–	Productivity-linked incentive schemes and offer of incentive bonus.
Career plan for employees	–	———
Performance appraisal	–	Identification of key-result areas, and review of performance against objectives.

Source : Suri, G.K., and Rama M. Joshi, 'Labour Relations: Philosophy, Policy and Strategy', *Indian Management*, New Delhi, May, 1983, pp. 9 and 10.

Exhibit 4.6

Labour Relations Philosophy, Policy and Strategy (Private Sector)

Philosophy	*Goals*	*Established Policy*	*Programmes, Practices, Procedures*
"Where does the Organisation want to go"?		"How can the Organisation get there?	Actions defined to implement policies
Human Relations	Productivity/Performance	– By promoting social and Welfare amenities	– Workers' participation: well-graded grievance procedure.
Boosting Morale	Peace and harmony	– By providing speedy redressal of grievances	– Extensive training programme for all employees.
Cordial relations	– – with unions	– – –	– Bi-partite settlements with unions.
Personal fulfilment	Discipline	– By encouraging consultations on matters of special interest	– Communication meetings.
Job Satisfaction	Reputation as industry leaders	– By negotiating with representative unions	– Social welfare and cultural activities.
Motivation	Customer Service	– – –	Wages linked with Productivity Career plans Appraisal by objectives.

Labour Relations Philosophy, Policy and Strategy (Public Sector)

Instil feelings of loyalty, commitment, belonging,	Profits, Reduce conflicts,	– Understanding employee needs, aspirations and rights	– Closer association of employees with management.
Involvement, importance, achievement, recognition	secure worker's cooperations	– Progressive approach to Union	– grievance solving procedure conditions
Safe working conditions	Attracting and re-training employees	– Providing good working conditions	– On the job and in-company training.
Growth and development of employees	– –	– Providing opportunities for promotion and self-development	– Settlement with unions on interest related issues.
Constructive approach to men and matters	Productivity	– Recognising line manager's role in industrial relations	– Sharing company.
Importance of man	Sustenance and growth	– Setting high standards of efficiency and productivity	– Welfare and social activities. – Salary commensurate with performance.
Human Relations	– –	– Evolving machinery for Grievance redress	– Opening Career paths.
		– Communicating aims and objectives of the company.	– Reviewing performance against Objectives.

CHAPTER 5

OBJECTIVES OF BUSINESS

INTRODUCTION

No business firm is completely static, like a building or a machine with stationary framework and standard parts that may be replaced from the ready stock or got from outside. Instead, shifts in demand, in competition, and in other external forces call for continuous adaptation; and, the ambitions and drives of executives within the company keep it evolving. And, as changes are made in one part of the company, compensating adjustments are needed in other parts. Consequently, each company should be thought of as a dynamic, integrated entity.

Each of these business entities develops character and an individual personality of its own. This personality is shaped, not only by physical resources and technology, or financial inputs, but also by some basic objectives which may be set for it by the top management. Objectives are the ends towards which enterprise activities are aimed - the end points of planning.[1] In fact, management process begins with setting organisation objectives and ends with determining how well they have been accomplished. The setting of objectives is an essential part of the initial phase of planning. In the next phase, the organisation is structured so as to accomplish the work set forth by the firm's objectives. The third phase is of direction which is centred on the leadership and motivation of company employees towards specific objectives. Finally, the control function compares results with objectives in order to find out whether objectives set have been achieved or fallen short of achievement. In the latter case, corrective actions may be recommended that conform to organisation objectives.

To manage a business is to first determine the objectives, which will focus and guide the activities of the company. Determining objectives is like identifying the North Star in the sky at night to locate the direction. These objectives give direction to the activities of the group and serve as media by which multiple interests are channelled into joint effort.[2] In other words, *objectives give purpose and direction to the work of all employees, and they indicate the broad limits within which action is to be taken.*

Purpose/Objectives

Objectives are needed in every area where performance and results directly and vitally affect the survival and prosperity of the business.[3] These are the areas which are affected by every management decision and which, therefore, have to be considered in every management decision. *They decide what it means concretely to manage the business*. They spell out what results the business must aim at and what is needed to work effectively toward these targets.

Objectives contribute to management process and they influence the size and character of organisation, its policies, personnel interests, type of leadership and managerial control. They are the very basis of management philosophy; and it is through their adoption that Management by Objectives (MBO) could be created and practised.

1. Koontz, Harold, Cyril O'Donnell and Heinz Weihrich, *Management*, McGraw-Hill Kogakusha Ltd. International Student Edition, Tokyo, 1980, p. 188.
2. Massie, Joseph L. *Essentials of Management*, Prentice-Hall of India, New Delhi, Eastern Economy Edition, 1973, p. 33.
3. Drucker, Peter F., *The Practice of Management*, Harper & Brothers, New York, 1954. P. 64.

Besides, recognition of objectives is an important first step in planning. Objectives serve as guides in the determination of policy, in selecting resources, and in setting up programmes.

Well-recognised objectives are useful in guiding day-to-day execution because they help to avoid getting off on a sidetrack, and actions taken by different individuals and at different times are more likely to be consistent rather than working at cross-purposes.

Finally, objectives serve as a useful standard when an executive is appraising the accomplishment of a department or enterprise.

According to Drucker, "the objectives (in the key areas) should enable us to do five things:[4]

1. to organise and explain the whole range of business phenomena in a small number of general statements;
2. to list these statements in actual experience;
3. to predict behaviour;
4. to appraise the soundness of decisions when they are still being made; and
5. to enable practising businessmen to analyze their own experience and, as a result, improve their performance.

In fact, managing a business enterprise without objectives is rowing a boat in the open sea without a rudder. It is the objectives which constantly guide the organisation on the path to the destination. They have been virtually regarded as the ends towards which all organisation activities are aimed at. The objectives decide, to a large extent, "where the firm would like to be, and accordingly takes action to get there."

Criteria for Effective Objectives

Before we discuss the characteristics of organisation objectives, understanding of the criteria for effective objectives would be fruitful. The principal criteria are:[5]

1. Individuals responsible for carrying out the objectives should have a role in setting them, since they are the closest to the situation and generally have the best information concerning what is achievable. Moreover, if they help in formulating the objectives, their commitment to achieving them is much stronger.
2. Top managers, who set overall objectives, have a responsibility for derivative or lower-level objectives. They should not accept proposals on these objectives with little or no question.
3. The objectives should be realistic in the light of internal and external environmental constraints as well as future trends.
4. The objectives should be reasonable, i.e., within the reach of the organisation, and should represent a challenge to organisation members.
5. Objective of company's functional areas should be examined to see if they are mutually consistent.
6. Management must update and revise objectives once a year, at the minimum, at least as far as strategies and supporting programmes are concerned.
7. Key objectives should be stated simply, so that they can be remembered by the personnel responsible for carrying them out.

4. *Ibid.*, p. 64, and his *Management : Tasks, Responsibilities and Practices,* Allied Publishers Pvt. Ltd., Mumbai, Indian Ed. 1975, pp. 100-101.
5. Granger, Charles H., "How to set Company Objectives," *Management Review,* New York, July, 1970, pp. 2-8.

8. Some objectives should be innovative. There are occasions when the best course is to continue in the same pattern, but in today's rapidly changing environment, objectives which show no innovation can be a danger signal to an organisation.
9. Finally, objectives should be pre-determined and stated, preferably in a written form.

Other characteristics of sound objectives may be suggested thus:

(i) Objectives should make people reach a bit.

(ii) They should allow for creative methods and should not predetermine the means for achieving them.

(iii) They should be known to all employees so that they may understand the targets for their own work and how they are related to the broader objectives of the organisation.

CHARACTERISTICS OF OBJECTIVES

Objectives have certain basic characteristics such as measurability, hierarchy, net-work, multiplicity, short, medium, and long-range objectives. These are discussed below.

Measurability of Objectives

Objectives of an organisation must be measurable. Each management programme should include enough information to enable specific objectives to be verified against certain criteria. Unless the management is aware of what is to be accomplished, there can be no measure of effectiveness. Unmeasurable objectives result in violation of the efficiency and economy of the organisation. Therefore, the modern manager is anxious to know, for example, that production should be for profit, and also how much profit should be earned; how much diversification can be achieved; what should be paid to the employees; how much amount should be spent on research and development; and what should be the extent of new product development. To find answers to these questions, objectives are so stated that they are capable of being measured in terms/units of performance.

Hierachy of Objectives

Organisation objectives are structured into a hierachy, i.e., in successive grades. The hierarchy of objectives corresponds roughly to the structure of the organisation. At the top, the entire organisation aims in a given direction the objectives set are broad, fundamental and general in the form of purpose, or mission; such as:

"Our purpose is to furnish low-cost and convenient transport services to the average person;" and "our mission is to produce and market cars."

These aims are, in turn, translated into general objectives or strategies, such as designing, producing and marketing a cheap, fuel efficient and reliable motor car.

The objectives at the higher level act as ends and those at the next lower level act as means. Each level of objectives stands as an end relative to the level below it and as a means relative to the level above it.

At the next lower level, each department in turn directs its efforts toward its own sets or goals; and each subdivision of each department has its own meaningful aims. Each of these sub-goals should be consistent with, and contribute toward the goals of the next higher level.

This may be explained by a concrete example. It is generally assumed that a corporation has the broad objective of maximising profit. To aid in achieving the overall goal, it is necessary to define more meaningful sub-goals for individual departments. The marketing department may have goals in terms of certain increase in total sales (say, from Rs. 2 lakhs to Rs. 5 lakhs a year) and its subdivision may be given goals in definite geographic areas/territories or in specific product line (soap or biscuits). The production department may state its goals in terms of minimising costs and its subdivision may be given sub-goals for particular types of costs. Other departments in turn have goals redefined for them so that they can visualise exactly their part in striving for the company's broad goal of maximising profits (see Fig. 5.1).

Net-work of Objectives

Objectives and planning programmes form a net-work of desired results and events. If the objectives of a management programme are not interconnected and mutually supportive, managers tend to pursue individual goals that can often be detrimental to the firm. Hence, it is important when developing specialised programmes to recognise that they interlock and are an integral part of the total programme. In the final analysis, all programmes contribute to the total management programme. (Fig. 5.2).

A net-work of programmes that is guided by specific goals requires the utmost cooperation and coordination among managers so that the components can mesh together properly. What is needed is a net-work of mutually supportive objectives.

Multiplicity of Objectives

Every business organisation, by its very nature, has more than one objective. Multiple objectives include one or more for each of the firms, functional areas. Similarly, at each functional level, goals are likely to be multiple. For example, "A business might include among its overall objectives a certain rate of profit and return on investment (ROI)(say 10% by Dec. 2000); emphasis on research to develop a continuing flow of proprietary products; developing publicly-held stock ownership; financing primarily by ploughing back earnings in business and borrowing from banks; distributing products in local and foreign markets; undertaking vigorous advertising campaigns; assuring competitive prices for quality goods; achieving a dominant share in the industry and adhering in all respects to the value of the society."[6]

Short-, Medium-, and Long-Range Objectives

If planning is to be effective, the short, medium and long-range objectives must have an integral relationship with one another.

Short-range objectives are very specific and are generally realised within one year. They proceed from an evaluation of priorities relating to long-term objectives. Certain things need to be done first, either because they are pre-requisite to doing other things or because of lead time considerations. For example: "When a new firm is established, raising capital for fixed and operating expenses is likely to be a prime objective and may be the sole short-run objective." To achieve this objective, managers hire engineers, production personnel, and sales personnel etc.

6. Koontz, Harold, Cyril O'Donnell and Heinz Weihrich, *Ibid.*, p. 192.

Top Management

1. Represent stockholders' interest – net profit of 10% or more.
2. Provide service to consumers – provide reliable products.
3. Maintain growth of assets and sales – double each decade.
4. Provide continuity of employment for company personnel – no involuntary lay-offs.
5. Develop favorable image with public.

Production Department

1. Keep cost of goods not more than 5% of sales.
2. Increase productivity of labour by 3% per year.
3. Maintain rejects of less than 2%
4. Maintain inventory at 6 months of sales.
5. Keep production rate stable with not more than 20% variability from yearly average.

Sales Department

1. Introduce new products so that over a 10 year period, 75% will be new.
2. Maintain a market share of 15%.
3. Seek new market areas so that sales may grow at a 15% annual rate.
4. Maintain advertising costs at 4% of sales.

Finance & Accounting Department

1. Borrowing should not exceed 50% of assets.
2. Maximise tax write-off.
3. Provide monthly statements to operating Deptts. by the 25th of the following month.
4. Pay dividends at the rate of 50% of net earnings.

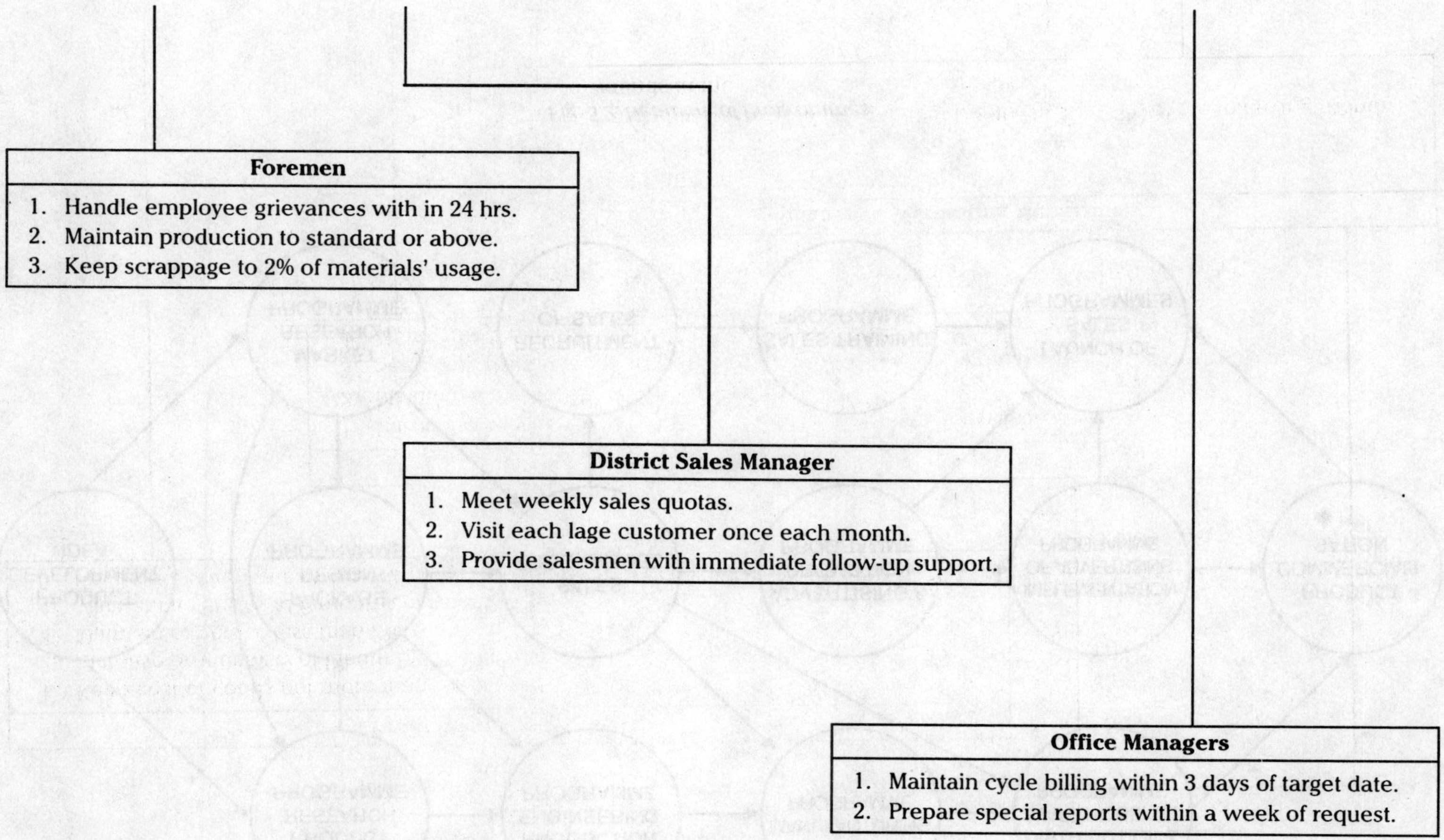

Fig. 5.1 Sample of a Hierarchy of Objectives in a middle-sized company.

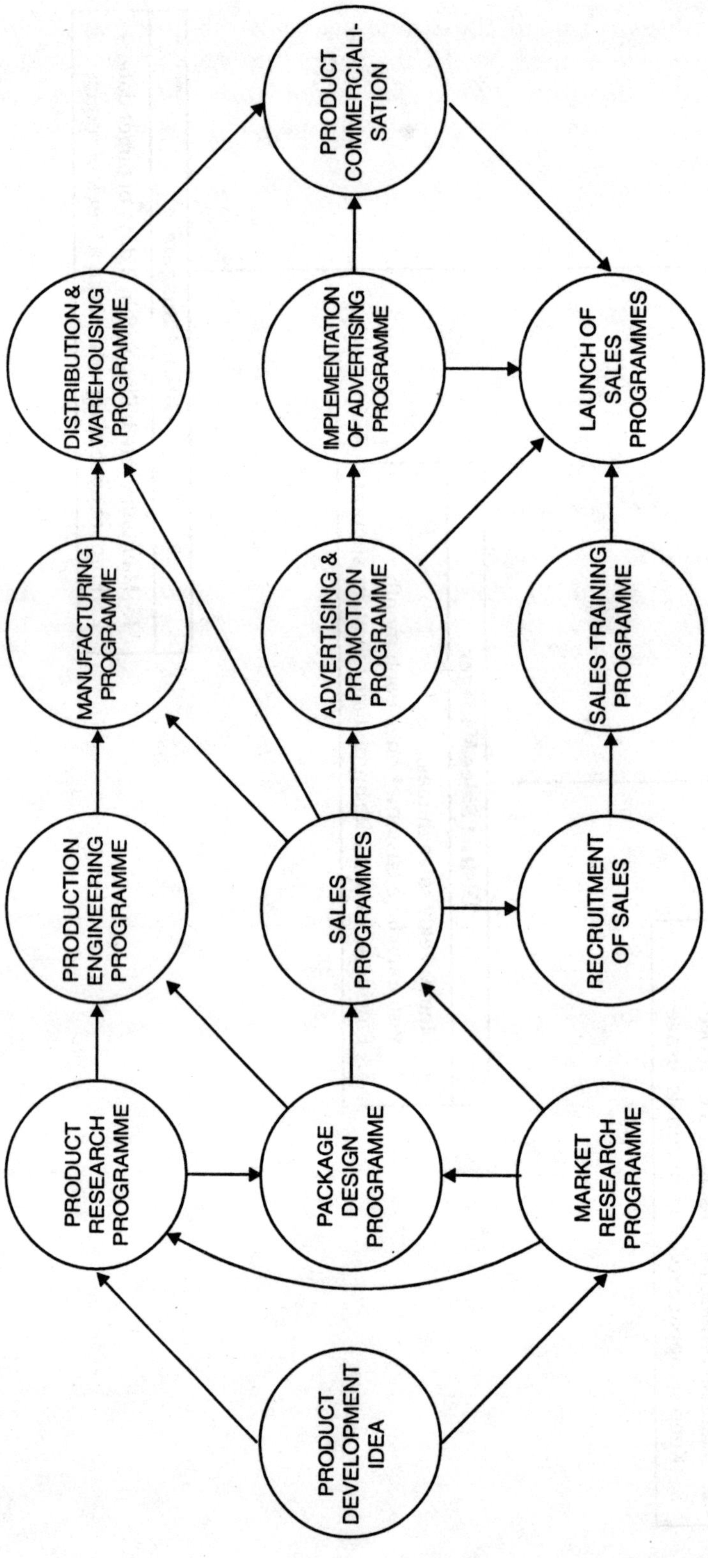

Fig. 5.2. Net-work of Programmes.

Medium-range objectives generally extend over a two-to-four year period. Long range objectives extend over five or more years; they are more speculative for distant years. In order that longer-term objectives can be achieved, they must relate to shorter-term objectives. A master plan, then, is needed to bring various time level objectives together for consistency and practicability.

PRINCIPLES OF OBJECTIVES

The underlying principles of objectives provide a logical framework for the management functions (of planning, organising, directing and controlling) and are applicable to objectives, whether qualitative or quantitative and they apply from the highest level down to the lowest level.

The basic principles of objectives are:[7]

1. Principle of the Primacy of Service Object

Management's primary aim is to create customer-value satisfaction. This objective is dictated by the markets which it serves; because it is the set of saleable values that justifies the economic existence of the firm.

2. Principle of (Collateral Secondary) Service Objectives

These objectives are values that individuals and groups within the firm, those associated with the firm, and the firm itself seek to acquire. *For example,* employees want reasonable and competitive wages, firms desire reasonable profits and the trade unions want amicable relations and good working conditions for labour.

3. Principle of Setting Objectives by Top Management

The objectives must be set by the top management so that they could be carried out/ accomplished smoothly. Objectives may also be set by lower and middle management, but this should be done in consultation with the top management so that they are easily approved and implemented willingly by the personnel and the lower level.

4. Other Principles

The other principles are: Principle of the measurability of objectives; principle of the hierarchy of objectives; principle of multiplicity of objectives; and principle of short-to-long-range objectives. All of these have been discussed in the previous section.

Management of philosophy

The interest in management philosophy and practice has steadily increased during the present century, especially since World War II. This management philosophy has been stated by R. C. Davis, thus: "The problem of greatest importance in the field of management is and probably will be the further development of the philosophy of management. A philosophy is a system of thought. It is based on some orderly, logical statements of objectives, principles, policies, and general methods of approach to the solution of some set of problems........

7. Thierauf, Robert J, Robert C. Klekamp, and Daniel W. Geeding, *Management Principles and Practices* (A Contingency Approach).

"Business objectives involve the public interest as well as the interests of customers, dealers, bankers, owners, and employees. They affect everyone in an industrial company. A managerial philosophy that is commonly accepted is a requisite for a common scale of values in an economy. Therefore, it is necessary for unity of thought and action in the accomplishment of economic objectives. We cannot have effective industrial economy without effective industrial leadership. We cannot have an effective leadership without a sound managerial philosophy.......

"Industrial leaders without such a philosophy are business mechanics rather than professional executives......."[8]

The main reasons for the continued interest in management philosophy among educators, public administrators, and progressive businessmen are:

1. The increasing trend towards decentralisation of operating responsibilities and decision-making in business and governmental organisations.
2. The increasing numbers of professional executives required in business and government for growth and decentralisation of operations.
3. The necessity for a logical framework of managerial management philosophy and practice as a basis for framing in executive-development programmes, and professional curricula.

In modern times, the starting point for either a philosophy or the practice of management seems to centre around pre-determined objectives. The entire management process concerns itself with ways and means to realise pre-determined results with the intelligent use of people. These objects may be general or specific, they may concern the organisation as a whole or a part of it within the unit.

The objectives of management would be clear from the extracts given below as culled from the writings of experts on the subject:[9].

"The goal of the business must be this – to make a better product to be sold at a lower price – profit cannot be the goal. Profit must be a by–product. This is a state of mind and a philosophy. Actually, an organisation doing its job as it can be done will make large profits which must be properly divided between user, worker, and stockholder. This takes ability and character."[10]

"It has been our (Texaco's) settled policy of thinking, first of quality of product and service to the customer, and only second to the size of its profits. To some of you, this may sound somewhat trite. But it is the starkest kind of business realism. In a highly competitive industry, the highest rewards are reserved for those who render the greatest service."[11]

"The mission of business organisation is to acquire, produce and distribute certain values. The business objective, therefore, is the starting point for business thinking. The *Primary objectives* of a business organisation are always those economic values with which we serve the customer.

8. Davis, Ralpha C., "Research in Management During the 50's", in Arthur E. Warner (ed), *Research Need in Business the 50s,* School of Business, Indiana University, Bloomigton, 1950, p. 2
7. Thierauf, Robert J, Robert C. Klekamp, and Daniel W. Geeding, *Management Principles and Practices* (A Contingency Approach).
9. Mee, John F., "Management Philosophy for Professional Executives", in Richard I. Harthman, etc., (ed) *Modern Business Administration,* D.B. Taraporewala & Co., Ltd., Mumbai, Indian Reprint, 1975, p. 22.
10. Lincoln, James F., "*Intelligence Selfishness and Manufacturing*", Bulletin No, 434, Lincoln Electric Company, New York.
11. Klein, Harry T., *The Way Ahead,* the Texas Co., New York, 1952, . 14.

The *Principal objective* of a businessman, naturally, is profit. And profit is merely an academic consideration, nevertheless, until we get the customer's dollar."[12]

The fundamental objective of the Tata Iron & Steel Co. Ltd., is to: strengthen India's base through increased productivity, effective utilization of material and manpower resources, and applied and continued application of modern scientific and managerial methods as well as through systematic growth in keeping with material aspirations.......

The Company recognises that while honesty and integrity are the essential ingredients of a strong and stable enterprise, profitability provides the main spark for economic activity. It affirms its faith in democratic values and in the importance of the success of the individual, collective and corporate enterprise for the economic emancipation and prosperity of the country.......

The objectives of the company are directed towards making the TISCO:

The best company to buy from;

A sound company to invest in;

A good company to work for;

A reliable company to sell; and

A leading company in the life of the country and the community."[13]

Numerous further examples of the objectives of modern business could be presented. However, all of them could be summarised with the conclusion that: (i) *Profit* is the motivating force for business; (ii) *Service* to customers by the provision of desired economic values (goods and services) justifies the existence of the business. *Profit and service objectives* are linked together; (iii) *Social responsibilities* do exist for business in accordance with the ethical and moral codes established by the society in which the industry resides and functions.

Establishing Objectives

The task of establishing or setting objectives involves individuals and groups within and outside the organisation. There are two schools of thought on the issue of setting objectives. The *traditional school of management* feels that the organisation's overall objectives must be determined by the Board of Directors and the top management, so that a close co-ordination and co-operation may be established whereby the company's objectives can be accomplished effectively. But it should be noted that though these objectives are posted for all members for their information, often the *stated* goals are not the *real* goals. Real objectives are the result of pressure from specific groups–shareholders, creditors, labour unions, and minority groups.

The behavioural school of management is of the view that power plays a dominant role in determining the firm's *real goal*. Who yields power in the organisational level and how much often influences the mode of thinking of others and consequently objectives are framed accordingly.

The best way is to set the objectives in consultation with the different levels of management by the top executive so that conflicts, if any, could be reduced to the bare minimum. [14]

When a subordinate and superior are involved in the process of searching for sound objectives, they have the opportunity to select the specific objectives from a number of sources.

12. Davis, Ralph C., "What the staff Function Actually is", *Advaced Management,* Vol. XIX, May, 1954, p. 13.
13. Quoted from the *Policy Manual of the Tisco,* Jamshedpur.
14. Theirauf, R.J., R.C. Klekamp and D.W. Geeding, *Management Principles and Practices,* John Wiley & Sons, New York, 1977, pp. 170-171.

First, the objectives may be built upon past experience, for example, cost will be reduced by 10% or sale will be increased by 5%. *Second,* the objective can be based upon some outside authority; for example, as a result of research, it may be discovered that a fair day's work for a reasonable standard would be 10 units of work (say, 5 metres of cloth), or Rs. 20/– in the form of profit, or Rs. 15/– as a cost or a given percentage of a total. *Third,* the objective may also be based upon an average of similar operations by other organisations. *Finally,* the objective may be based upon response from the customer or user of the output: for example, the number of complaints must be kept below 5 out of 100 sales transactions.

CLASSIFICATION OF ORGANISATION OBJECTIVES

Organisation objectives may be classified on at least *three* bases:

1. On the basis of nature of objectives:
   (a) General objectives, and (b) Specific objectives.
2. On the basis of multiplicity of objectives:
   (a) Economic service objectives: (b) Broadly-stated company objectives; (c) Survival and Growth Objectives; (d) Personal Group Objectives; and (e) Governmental and Societal Objectives.
3. On the basis of measurable goals:
   (a) Productivity objectives; (b) Budgetary objectives; (c) Quantitative objectives; and (d) Qualitative objectives.

On the Basis of Nature of Objectives

Such objectives may be *general or specific.*

(a) General Objectives. These objectives are statements which include many goals and take many directions. They should be positive, clear and self-explanatory. But often, the words used are very vague, such as "generating optimum profit; to develop a sound financial position, good, vigorous; growing; diversified;" because their meaning is not clear in the statement of objectives. Therefore, if they are to be effective and meaningful, they need be stated as specific measurable objectives.

Below are given two examples of a good general objective :

(i) "The company seeks to earn a rate of interest on invested capital each year that is at least equal to the average rate of return for its five competitors having annual sales closest to that of the company."

Or Simply:

"To obtain 15 per cent return on investment (ROI) by the end of the calendar year 2000."

(ii) "The company's objectives is to increase the number of units of products – 'Usha Fan' – by 10 per cent without an increase in cost or reduction of current quality level by December, 2000."

(b) Specific Objectives give a clear–cut picture about the goals/targets which a company expects to accomplish within a specified time period. Such objectives add to the management effectiveness by making the objectives attainable. Actual performance can be reported in relation to the measures and target values that have been set in the objectives. The planning and control functions can be served with greater utility because the 'objectives' and the 'results' are expressed in the same terms.

On the Basis of Multiplicity of Objectives

To manage a business is to balance a variety of needs and goals and this requires multiple objectives as are needed in all areas in which the survival of the business depends. The specific targets, the goals in any objective are a, depend on the strategy of the individual business. But the areas in which objectives are needed are the same for all businesses, for all businesses depend on the same factor for their survival.

A business's function is to create functions. There is, therefore, need for a *marketing objective*. Businesses must be able to innovate or else their competitors will outstrip them by their superior techniques. There is also need for *innovation objective*. All businesses depend upon three factors of production, i.e., on the *human resource*, the *capital resource*, and the *physical resource*. There must be objectives for their supply, their employment and their development. The resources must be employed productively and their productivity has to grow if the business is to survive. There is need, therefore, for *productivity objectives*. Business exists in society and community and, therefore, has to discharge social responsibility, at least to the point where it takes responsibility for its impact upon the environment. Therefore, objectives in respect of the *social dimensions* of business are needed. Finally, there is need for *profit*, otherwise none of the objectives can be attained. Therefore, *profitability objective* has also to be established.

Objectives, therefore, have to be set, according to Prof. Drucker, in these eight *key areas*: (1) market standing; (2) innovation; (3) human organisation (manager performance and development); (4) worker performance and attitude; (5) physical and financial resources; (6) productivity; (7) social or public responsibility; and (8) profit requirements.[15]

Objectives in the key areas, 1, 2, 5, 6 and 8 can be subject to quantitative measurement. These objectives have received universal recognition. These are the traditional methods of growth and well being of an organisation. However, unless these five objectives are properly supported by the other objectives, they become meaningless. If the three objectives (manager performance and development; worker performance and public responsibility) soon result in a loss of market standing, loss of technical leadership, productivity and profit, the entire edifice of business objectives will ultimately collapse.

It must be remembered that a business enterprise is a *community of human beings*. Its performance is the performance of human beings. And a human community must be founded on common beliefs, must symbolise its cohesion in common principle. Otherwise, it becomes paralysed, unable to act, unable to demand and to obtain effort and performance from its members.

To be effective in accomplishing its tasks, management should recognise that the firm has multiple objectives. Such objectives can be conveniently categorised into two groups, viz. (i) those *overall organisation objectives* which are concerned with the firm's broad goals and which focus on operating profitably in the long run for the benefit of the share/stock-holders; and (ii) *specific organisation* objectives, which look at the whole system of managing and appraising management results through measurable goals.

Overall Organisation Objectives

These comprise (a) economic service objectives, (b) broadly-stated company objectives;

15. Drucker, Peter F., *Management: Tasks, Responsibilities and Practices*, p. 100.

(c) survival and growth objectives; (d) personal group objectives; and (e) government and social objectives.

(a) Economic Service Objectives

These objectives recognise that economic service objective is *primary* and making a profit is *secondary.* Satisfaction of a customer need is the primary objective. But profits are also necessary to attract capital for investment opportunities which create further expansion in business which, in turn, provides more employment. Large investments in plants and machinery reduce the cost of manufacture, thereby making the goods more competitive; and higher profits mean more tax revenues for government programmes needing finance. Finally, *profits* are essential in meeting the real purpose of business which is that of satisfying customer needs.

Profit is the ultimate test of business performance. It is a true criterion for efficiency. The more efficient a business is, the greater are the profits it earns. It is the 'risk premium' that covers the costs of staying in business – replacement, obsolescence, market risk and uncertainty. Profits are 'costs of being in business' and 'costs of staying in business.' Under this objective, the creation and distribution of economic values – whether they be goods or services – come first and profits second and are the result of fulfilling the economic service objective in an efficient and economical manner. *Therefore,* the *service objective must be well defined and integrated for effective cooperation and coordination.*

(b) Broadly-stated Company Objectives

To meet the demands of the different market segments, the products and services to be sold must be specified in very broad terms so as not to make these obsolete in the long run.

(c) Survival and Growth Objectives

The importance of staying in business and growing is an objective which every business firm cherishes. Business enterprise is productive when it has a stable and growing earning power. Peter Drucker observes, "It is the purpose, nature and necessity of this institute to take risks, to create risks. Unless we provide for risk, we are going to destroy capacity to produce. And, therefore, a minimum profitability, adequate to the risks which we, by necessity, assume and create, is an absolute condition for survival not only of enterprise but for society too."

So a firm wants not only just to stay in business but also to grow and prosper. Growth objectives include acquiring the economic advantages that come from being of a certain size and becoming a recognised leader in the industry. Such an environment stimulates organisation members to greater heights and endures against going out of business. Desirable growth goals often lead to producing better products and service which are recognised by the customer. This, in turn, leads to higher sales and more profits, which allows the firm to pay higher salaries and offer opportunity to advancement. A successive pattern of this type leads to a desired growth rate.

According to Peter Drucker, there are five survival functions of business:

(i) It is a human organisation designed for joint performance and capable of perpetuation itself.

(ii) It exists in society and economy. Anticipation of social climate and economic policy is a business need and business is a creature of the economy – population, income, wages of spending, expectations and values.

(iii) The specific purpose of business is to supply economic goods and services. This is the only reason why business exists.

(iv) The business enterprise is an institution that is designed to create change. In a changing economy and a changing technology, every business strives to innovate.

(v) There is an absolute requirement of survival, i.e., of profitability.

(d) Personal Group Objectives

Personal objectives refer to the aspirations and goals of individual members of the enterprise, and include financial and non-financial incentives (like salaries, wages, bonus), status in society and organisation, the opportunity to advance, desire for association with other people, the need for security of employment and drive for achievement. Each individual strives for the accomplishment of these objectives. These objectives must be met by the firm to gain the cooperation of its members. Thus, goals of individuals become organisation goals which can work for the betterment or detriment of the firm. If there are conflicts between personal and objective goals, people will leave the firm and seek employment elsewhere.

It would, therefore, be in the fitness of things that the objectives of the organisation and the personal groups should be balanced. The primary responsibility of a business manager is to "reduce the areas of such conflict and to bring about harmony of interest among diverse groups." Peter Drucker remarks, "There are few things that distinguish competent from incompetent manager quite as sharply as the performance of balancing objectives. It is the job of an enlightened manager to continuously balance his objectives without allowing any conflict to arise between two or more objectives."

(e) Governmental and Social Objectives

These objectives create other economic values desired by society through government legislation and regulation. For example, the Companies Act, 1956, provides for checking concentration of economic power and promoting the spread of professional management ; regulation and regularisation of company management by infusing new discipline and introducing new sprit in the company promotion, management and administration.

On the Basis of Measurable Goals

These are the objectives which provide a measuring yard to evaluate the objectives set. For this purpose, attention is focused on these:

(a) Productivity objectives;
(b) Budgetary objectives;
(c) Quantitative objectives; and
(d) Qualitative objectives.

(a) Productivity Objectives

These objectives aim at developing productivity factors for manufacturing and non-manufacturing operations that can be utilised as a measure of operating efficiency and economy.

"Productivity is the measure not of how *hard* we work, but of how *well* we use our intelligence, our imagination, and our capital."[16] In other words, it is "to produce more with the same amount of ...... effort."

Increased productivity results from: (i) better planning and improved technology; (ii) employment of better techniques; (iii) greater efficiency of equipment; (iv) more inventiveness and more ingenuity, that is, through the better exercise of the management functions; (v) improved working conditions; (vi) removal of boredom from routine task; and (vii) attitude of workers towards their work, etc.

16. Henry Gord II, "Henry Ford speaks out on Productivity and Today's Shortages," *The Wall Street Journal*, March 14, 1974, p. 11.

An enlightened manager, aware of these factors and the relationship between the worker and productivity, uses such techniques as job enrichment, group incentives, promotion opportunities, adopts technology and improved materials and standardised equipments so that the cost is reduced and productivity increases. He also uses joint labour management productivity teams.[17]

(b) Budgetary Objectives

These objectives develop reliable financial data on a flexible or variable budget basis that can be used to establish expected performance at all levels. Budgets are translated into financial statements (Balance Sheet, Income Statement, Cash Budget, Source and Application of Funds, etc). This budgeted information becomes the specific goal towards which actions are directed. They form the basis for expected performance.

(c) Quantitative Objectives

These objectives state 'how much' the objectives can be measured in quantitative terms, for example, the objectives set may be: average five calls a day on new customers, and 10 calls a day for old and regular customers; 10 units of work per day at a fixed money cost; or set limits for labour turnover, scrappage and absenteeism during the month.

Other examples are:

Marketing objectives can be the rate of return of sale, number of new customers, number of service calls, number of different products sold, types of customers served.

In manufacturing, the objectives can be so many rupees of wages per hour, so much amount for fringe benefits, number of work stoppages, hours/days lost because of strikes and grievances, ratio of productive hours earned to productive time available.

In the field of finance, the objectives may be:

Cash to accounts payable, ratio of current assets to current liabilities, rupee cost of assets for employee, number of stockholders, the ratio of cost of money to average capital employed.

These objectives are variable in quantitative terms.

(d) Qualitative Objectives

These are the objectives which can be gauged by 'how well' they accomplish their tasks. Such tasks are generally stated in qualitative terms. Such objectives include setting long-range market objectives and specifying research and development activities. A typical example is the R & D development's objective of finishing a new product design by a certain fixed date, or the marketing department may have the objective of improving product quality as well as service to customers within a specified time.

One author has developed objectives, based on research and its evaluation. According to him, the *first* of these objectives (which he refers to as *'Bed-rock objectives'*) is to promote reasonable and improving corporate earnings through productive effort applied primarily. This objective places emphasis on 'profit motive'. This *second* is to conduct the business as a constructive and honourable corporate citizen in its relations designed to be mutually profitable - with shareholders, customers, employees, suppliers, government and the community. Both these objectives are fundamental to the long-term success of any business.[18]

The bed-rock objectives are the first step. To make them effective, some more *basic objectives* are needed for each company and also the means of accomplishing them. These *basic objectives* are termed as *Administrative Organisation Objectives* and *Operating Organisation Objectives*.

17. Logan, H. Cheek, "Cost Effectiveness Comes to the Personnel Function," *Harvard Business Review*, May-June, 1973, pp. 96-105.
18. Huston, Charles L., "Setting Corporate Objectives". *Dun's Review*, Oct. 1962, pp. 62-63 and 124-126.

Administrative Organisation Objectives

These aim at establishing and periodically re-evaluating four objectives for corporate guidance:

(a) To plan, direct , and co-ordinate the various company organisations, programmes and activities for comprehensive, balanced accomplishment.

(b) To secure a reasonable return on company investments in markets, plant facilities, products and manpower.

(c) To build good, mutually profitable relations with all those who help to make the company a constructive and successful enterprise.

(d) To develop and maintain a sound, clearly-understood organisation structure and personnel classified to meet the needs of the business.

Operating Organisation Objectives

These objectives aim at improving the business. For this, detailed standards and controls are developed to improve the quality of products, reduce costs of their manufacture and provide added insurance for ontime deliveries to customers. The purpose is:

(a) to strive for both major and minor economies in operations and procedures, for increased savings and improved earnings;

(b) to undertake developments that promise new improved products;

(c) to develop and apply human resources to stimulate recognition of employee as individual – involving his dignity, his status and service in the organisation and his contribution to the success of the enterprise.

BASIC OBJECTIVES OF BUSINESS

A business is an organisation of human, material and other intangible resources. It is a socio-economic unit and , therefore, a modern business must undertake some basic functions to fulfil human objectives such as recognition of human values in organisation, treating employees as responsible human beings (and not merely cogs in the wheel). It must ensure job satisfaction and higher employee morale through financial as well as non-financial motivation. It must recognise public and social responsibilities and promote public welfare and satisfaction. It must offer maximum consumer service and satisfaction. To achieve these basic objectives, the business enterprise is treated as a whole dynamic unit.

Newman and Logan classifies basic objectives of a company under four heads, viz.,[19]

1. The place company seeks in its industry;
2. Emphasis on stability vs. dynamism;
3. Social philosophy of the company; and
4. Management philosophy of the company.

19. Newman, William H., and James P. Logan, *Business Policies and Central Management*, D.B. Taraporewala Sons & Co., Pvt. Ltd., Bombay, 2nd Indian Ed., 1970, pp. 84-98.

1. To decide the place of the Company in the Industry

The first objective is to decide in which industry it will operate. This decision will take into consideration questions such as:

(i) What major functions are to be performed – the production and distribution of goods and service, or serving a particular class of customers or general customers and in what particular product;

(ii) Whether to concentrate in one line/type of product or to go into diversification of its activities;

(iii) What range or quality of product is to be produced – that which is in demand by sophisticated class or middle-class society; and

(iv) What should be the size of operation, because it is the size which profoundly affects the sales promotional activities, its financial structure, organisational set-up and executive personnel, investment facilities, operating procedures, and many other phases of management. Careful thought on all the four issues/objectives will give the company a better character and a place in the industry.

2. Emphasis on Stability vs. Dynamism

(i) The company has also to decide whether it seeks stability or it wants to be dynamic, because this issue influences the character and type of administration of the company. For this, the objectives have to be set whether it wants to be *progressive,* i.e., to use the modern techniques of doing business with the adoption of most modern facilities, policies and techniques; new personnel practices in regard to selection, training, salary and wage administration, employee services; adoption of materials handling equipment and continuous methods of manufacture; computerised accounting system; latest techniques of market research and analysis. "Some practical managers place greater emphasis on stability of operations. New policies and techniques naturally require changes, and there is considerable human energy and financial cost involved in introducing changes into a going enterprise. If these changes are introduced frequently, a feeling of insecurity and instability develops among the executives and employees. Moreover, the development of new methods is always accompanied by unanticipated difficulties and mistakes. Hence, progressive objectives are held in abeyance till tangible results are available from demonstrations and trial use."[20]

(ii) The other objective may be *aggressiveness* which refers to the energy, the self-assertiveness, and attack on the other company which is its competitor by adopting aggressive sales promotional measures, undertcutting of prices or by giving a handsome discount.

(iii) Willingness to take risk may be another objective. Every business involves risk, especially when changes in its objectives/policies are made.

(iv) Along with the bearing of risk, business expansion needs considerable capital resources from within or outside the company, which have to be arranged.

3. Social Philosophy of the Company

Social objectives do shape the character of a company in the minds of the people and the community. The purpose is to find out what kind of business the citizens want the company to be

20. Newman, William H., and James P. Logan, *Ibid,* pp. 87-88.

in; and to fulfil these expectations are the social objectives of a company. These generally include: (i) maintenance of the quality of the product or service; (ii) fixation of reasonable and fair prices for customers; (iii) offer of complete satisfaction to the customers through 'customer-oriented' marketing approach instead of 'product-oriented' marketing approach; (iv) a fair return on capital to the shareholders; (v) healthy working conditions, and fair pay to the workers; (vi) fulfilment of moral obligations towards the government and the competitors; (vii) make business a growing asset to the local community and the nation by: (a) controlling pollution problems; (b) creation of jobs to maintain employment and income; (c) optimum utilisation of scarce resources; (d) conservation and better use of resources; (e) minimisation of evils of monopolistic and restrictive trade practices. In other words, "Business must behave as a good neighbour, which should take part in the betterment of the community and fulfilling its responsibility as a responsible citizen in a democracy."

4. Management Philosophy of the Company

This basic objective has a profound influence on the entire administration of company. It is clearly reflected in:

(i) *Centralisation vs. decentralisation in decision-making.* This is an important objective decision, because it affects the whole way of doing business. The type and the nature of the plans needed, the selection of personnel, the building of company morale, the organisation structure, the marketing strategy, the type of control necessary, are all affected.

(ii) *Quality of key personnel.* The objective is to obtain and retain the best possible and highly competent and dependable employees–executives and workers–for the performance of various tasks in the organisation. Such persons may be considered suitable on the basis of "technical compliance, during, rugged individualism, social attitude, persuasiveness, and resourcefulness" to carry on the responsibility.

(iii) *Extent of advance planning objective.* The business operations are forecast much ahead and then the best way of dealing with the anticipated problems is tackled.

(iv) *The manager of supervision or strictness of control is another objective.* This objective deals with the internal mechanism of the company, whereas the first three principal basic objectives are concerned with external relationship.

It is pertinent to note that these basic objectives, discussed above, cut across and permeate other phases of management. They influence, directly or indirectly, the policies, the organisation, the resources, and the execution.[21]

We give below an ideal statement of objectives commonly found in all modern organisations:

A Statement of Business Objectives

1. In our Business Relations, we will

- act on all occasions in an ethical manner with honesty and complete fairness;
- direct the company's manpower resources, technological capabilities and physical facilities to the task of meeting industry's and consumer's needs successfully, economically and effectively throughout the world;

21. Newman, William H, and James P. Logan, *Ibid.*, p. 99.

- maintain the willingness to pioneer for higher quality, lower cost, better service and broader market;
- make it desirable and convenient for all customers' potential suppliers to do business with us;
- foster autonomy in the division and development under a concept which provides for decentralised operations with top management coordination and control to assure adherence to overall corporate objectives and policies;
- anticipate and develop new product responsive to changing needs to civilization;
- buy only on the basis of quality, service and price.

2. In Relations with the Government, we will

- work vigorously to obtain and to support good government at all levels – central, state and local.
- strive to meet governmental policies which encourage economic growth and preserve individual liberties.
- foster a better understanding through our employees, through representatives of government, and through leaders of critical economic and political issues that affect industry.
- keep ourselves informed on legislative and other trends in government.

3. In Relations with shareholders, we will

- provide them with an optimum continuing return on their investment.
- strive on a long-term basis to improve the investment advantages of the company's shares and to attract purchases of these shares.

4. In Relations with Plant Communities, we will

- be a good neighbour in all the terms implied.
- make our plants safe and attractive places in which to work.
- co-operate with all properly constituted authorities to reduce air and stream pollution.

5. In Relations with Our Personnel, we will

- stand pre-eminent in the eyes of all people as a desirable company for which to work and enhance our stature in the business community through the efficient conduct of our operations and our public relations.
- continue our belief that the determining factor in hiring and placing employees are the requirements of the specific job and qualifications of the individual. Company policy is to treat applicants equally without regard to race, color, sex, creed, national origin, religion or political preference.
- utilise and encourage the creativity of the individual by providing special job opportunities;
- define functions and relationship clearly but not so literally as to hamper initiative, action and growth;
- recognise and develop personnel resources within the company and maintain programmes which will ensure the successful future management of the company;
- promote from within but recruit from outside, if necessary, to assure growth or to acquire new skills;
- maintain an anti-nepotism policy in employment practices;

- maintain all employee relations in good faith;
- provide an opportunity for individuals to achieve eminent stature and high level monetary reward through technical or staff specialist routes as well as administrative routes;
- maintain the most beneficial balance, the importance and well-being of the individual employee and our responsibilities to customers and shareholders.

6. In Our Growth, we will

- recognise opportunities in any field where the company capabilities may be applied profitably through the unique skills of management science and technology, finance, production or marketing;
- grow in specific instances or in specific situations through joint ventures or acquisitions which demonstrably will provide sound economic means of entering a market or business profitably under conditions fully compatible with the law then in effect;
- provide a balanced research programme aimed at an optimum return on present capital investment and at providing a steady flow of profitable new products and processes;
- emphasise expansion in areas where the company can achieve and maintain advantages through patents, franchise, marketing, trade marks or other special strengths;
- plan and grow globally with full appreciation of current politico social movements and study opportunities in the light of these developments.

MANAGEMENT BY OBJECTIVES

Genesis of MBO

One of the most important and interesting developments that has occurred across the management scene in the last three decades has been the gaining of popularity of the concept of 'Management by Objectives', a term said to have been used by Prof. Peter Drucker in 1954. He observed that:

"Managers must set out clearly their own objectives applicable to their specific functions and must actively involve themselves in the process of determining the goals. Furthermore, the managers at every level should actively participate in laying down the objectives for higher levels also. In this process, they will be able to understand the broader nature of objectives of the organisation and how their own particular objectives should be related to overall objectives of the organisation."[22]

Peter emphasized that "Objectives are needed in every area where performance and results directly and vitally affect the survival and prosperity of business and the performance that is expected of the manager must be derived from the performance of goals of the business, his results must be measured by the contribution they make to the success of the enterprise."[23] This in turn requires 'Management by Objectives' and 'Control by self-Control.' The main purpose of

22. Drucker, Peter, *The Practice of Management,* Harper & Bros, New York, 1954, p. 63.
23. *Ibid.*, p. 101

introducing M.B.O. is to achieve an efficient and successful working of the entire organisation through the efficient working, co-ordination, and integration of its related parts, and the resources at its disposal.

Douglas McGregor (in 1957) also emphasised on "appraising people on the basis of pre-set objectives," because such a method is much better and useful for evaluating the performance of managers as it correctly lays emphasis on actual performance rather than on the personality traits of a manager. Its main advantage would be to "stimulate development of subordinates and give them means for greater motivation."[24]

Edward Schleh also contributed to the further development of MBO. He said "Management objectives state the specific accomplishment expected of each individual in a specific period of time so that the work of the whole management group is soundly blended at a particular moment of time," and "Objectives should be set for personnel all the way down to each foreman and salesman and, in addition, to staff people such as accountants, industrial engineers, chemists etc..... Delegation be by results expected appraisal geared to the same standard."[25]

Earlier than these authorities, other like Henry Fayol, Urwick and Chester Barnard also put emphasis on M.B.O. They mentioned accomplishment of objectives as one of the distinguishing features of a formal organisation and the effectiveness of the M.B.O. depending upon the ability of the management to convert organisational objectives into personal goals for all managerial levels.

What is M.B.O?

It has now been increasingly recognised that M.B.O. is an important means of integrating individual needs and organisational demands. Individuals become active participants in the managerial process, which motivate people at all levels to contribute to the success of an enterprise. M.B.O. is concerned not only with organisational goals but also with the personal growth objectives.

M.B.O. is a result-oriented process of management for effective utilisation of resources – human, capital, material, etc. – of the organisation. It relates individual aims to business goals and fits in the business unit with its environment. It is also called 'Management by Results'.[26] It involves setting yardsticks of effectiveness for each managerial position and a periodic conversion of these yardsticks into usable objectives. It tells employees the expected levels of performance from them.

Management by objectives can be described as a process whereby the superior and subordinate manager of an organisation jointly identify its common goals, define each individual's major areas of responsibility in terms of results expected of him and use these measures as guides for operating the unit and assigning the contributions of each of its members.[27]

From another point of view, M.B.O. has been defined as: (1) a systems approach to managing an organisation, where those accountable for directing the organisation first determine where they want to take the organisation; (2) a process requiring and encouraging

24. McGregor, Douglas, 'An Uneasy Look at Performance Appraisal,' *Harvard Business Review,* Vol. 35 No. 3, May-June, 1957. p. 89-94.
25. Schleh, Edward, *Management by Results,* McGraw - Hill Book Co., New York, 1961, pp. 18-19.
26. Massie, Joseph L. and John Douglas, *Managing: Contemporary Introduction,* Prentice Hall of India, New Delhi, 1977, pp. 279-280.
27. Odiorne, George S., *Management by Objectives,* Pitmans, London, 1965, pp. 55-56.

all key management personnel to contribute their maximum to achieving the overall objectives; (3) an effort to blend and balance all the goals of all key personnel; and (4) an evaluation mechanism.[28]

Its basic ideas is the joint participation of subordinates and superiors in the establishment of clear and definite objectives for each individual and unit. The usual approach is for each manager and his subordinate to get together at the beginning of the period and discuss objectives until an agreement on clear objectives is reached.

From a broad point of view, M.B.O. can be defined as an effective way of practising the basic functions of planning, organising, directing, and controlling. Peter Drucker states that it is based on the concept of human behaviour and motivation.

Factors Influencing M.B.O. Programme

The M.B.O. programme is gaining popularity due to certain factors, such as:

1. *The dynamic nature of the environment in which the business operates.* The environment is never static but dynamic and, therefore, any change in it requires changes in the policies and programmes of the business, i.e., the management should be adaptable to changes or else it will be out of existence very soon. M.B.O. is suitable for activities that are not reflective but where changes are desired to accomplish the goals.
2. *The change in the objective of business from 'profit maximisation to growth and survival'* has necessitated that the objective can be better accomplished if M.B.O. is practised, which aims at better utilisation of material, human and physical resources of the organisation.
3. *The realisation of the fact that the aspirations of the individuals should be fulfilled or satisfied if the best is to be drawn out from them.* The M.B.O. ensures accommodation of organisation objectives with those of the individual objectives.
4. The current thinking that the appraisal of the personnel against the set objectives and in which the person concerned has participated is a more reliable and positive assessment, for it leads to the improvement in the performance of the person concerned.
5. *The development of the concept of corporate planning,* which is concerned with the top management largely because it requires ability, experience, and need for maintaining secrecy and information, though M.B.O. is concerned with all levels of management by involving everyone in fixing the goals of the organisation.
6. M.B.O. has been the result of various supportive concepts, such as Maslow's hierarchy of needs; McGregor's Theory of Motivation (Theory X and Theory Y); and Herzberg's Hygiene Theory. These theories have played an important role in the development of the M.B.O. concept, since they recognise that desire of most managers is to satisfy their higher level needs on the job and to assume responsibility. Managements are achievement-oriented and desire a degree of control over their jobs.

From the point of view of the subordinates, M.B.O. places great emphasis on participation by directly involving individuals in their jobs. The underlying assumption is that involvement leads to commitment and if employees are consulted, they will be motivated to perform the jobs in a manner that will directly contribute to the achievement of organisation objectives. Hence, management by objectives develops a framework for participation, since decisions that affect individuals' jobs are made jointly by the individuals and their superiors.

28. McConskey, Dale D., "Applying Management by Objectives to Non-Profit Organisations," *Advanced Management Journal,* January, 1973, pp. 10-20.

Process and Basic Steps of M.B.O.

Management by objectives is a method by which organisation members themselves jointly establish the firm's goals. Each member, with the assistance of his superior, defines his area of responsibility and sets objectives that state expected results clearly.[29] The persons involved develop organisation performance measures that are guides for managing and serve as standards for evaluation.

The process of M.B.O. involves four steps:

1. Setting of objectives;
2. Developing action plans;
3. Conducting periodic reviews;
4. Appraising annual performance.

1. Setting Objectives: Setting objectives is a multi-stage process. In the initial phase, those areas that are considered important (critical) to the firm's long-run success by the top management are determined or identified. These are frequently referred to as *Key Result Areas* (KRA). They focus on market position, productivity, profitability, personnel development, social responsibility, etc. Other important KRA are aimed at changing the fundamental assumptions, policies and direction of the area in question. In addition, KRA are specified for each functional area and each unit in the organisation. For example:

'5% increase in production during 2000 - 01.'

'10% increase in customers in 2000 - 01'

'$7^1/_2$% position to be given to minority class'.

'Sales to be increased by 10% over the last year's performance.'

These are determined after analysing the strengths and weaknesses of the organisation, the prevailing environmental situation, and the opportunities available. Of course, the objectives set are tentative, subject to changes as per the exigencies of demand.

The next phase in this step is that performance measures for each area are determined. For example, the KRA for a production operation may be 'output as measured by quantity within a certain time period'; cost performance as measured by 'variable and fixed costs'; resource utilisation as measured by 'return on investment and turnover or inventories.'

In the last phase, standards against which performance can be measured are determined. For example, marketing objectives for a specific product line could be to increase the organisation share by 10% during 2000-01

Under this step, the objectives for the subordinates are also set in their mutual consultation by the superiors. The subordinates can help their managers in determining realistic objectives because they are the people who know best what they can do and within what time limit. Observed Koontz and others: "The superiors must listen to, and work with their subordinates, but in the end they take responsibility for approving goals by subordinates. Their judgement and final approval must be based upon what is reasonably attainable with 'stretch' and 'pull' what is fully supportive of upper - level objectives, what is consistent with goals of other managers in other functions, and what goals will not be inconsistent with the longer-run objectives and interests of the department and company."[30]

29. Thierauf, Robert J., Robert C. Klekamp, and Daniel, W. Geeding, *Management Principles and Practices,* John Wiley and Sons, New York, 1977, p. 192.
30. Koontz, Harold, Cyril O'Donnel, and Heinz Weihrich, *Management,* McGraw-Hill Kagakusha Ltd., Tokyo, 1980, p. 204.

The objectives set should be verifiable, specific and clear, should state the time when they are to be achieved, and indicate the quality of objectives and the cost in changing them. They should also be flexible enough to accommodate new ideas, and should stress individual responsibility. They should present a challenge, indicate priorities, and promote personal and professional growth and development.[31]

The first step, thus, is to integrate the organisation's objectives with the objectives of the individual managers in such a way that M.B.O. becomes an integral part of the management process. The objectives must be a cooperative venture between the parties involved. They must feel that the objectives are important, challenging and achievable.

2. Developing Action Plans: After the objectives have been set, they must be translated into action plans, i.e., programmes that give the organisation decision and unity of purpose. For this, the manager has to define and divide into steps all of the required activities. Chalking out of an effective line of action is a meaningful exercise, involving work-schedule, time-schedule and resource-schedule so that goals of realising the targets could be achieved effectively. That is, the manager has to decide the responsibility for each activity, the amount of resources needed, and the time needed for accomplishing the work. This process provides the input for scheduling and starting and ending dates for all activities. This scheduling phase is commonly referred to as "targeting" since it specifies a date for accomplishing specific objectives. Developing action plans, in effect, establishes a solid basis for M.B.O.

The last phase in this step is to give the requisite operational freedom to the line managers who are responsible for putting the programmes into realities. For this, they are often given a wide measure of discretion to devise their own line of action to achieve the objectives, of course, within the policy limitations of the organisation.

3. Conducting Periodic Reviews: The next step is to establish a control system which monitors the activities being performed through periodic reviews. The purpose is to determine whether the designers of the programmes/managers are accomplishing the stated objectives and how efficiently they are achieving them. The system not only measures performance against standards set, but also provides 'feedback' that keeps the organisation members informed of their progress toward the stated objectives.

'Feedback' is a technique which enables the management to know the reactions and results of the programmes. Significant deviations from the standards are reported for appraisal and modification or correction (if needed). Feedback is important because motivation to accomplish results tends to increase as people are informed about progress toward these results. Organisation members can be expected to perform with greater effectiveness if they are aware of the objectives sought, the purpose of their work and the degree of success they are achieving in relation to meeting those objectives.

4. Appraising Annual Performance: This is the last step of M.B.O. Annual performance appraisal is made annually. It concentrates on results–it gives both breadth and depth of treatment to all aspects of the M.B.O. programme. It incorporates all individual contributors into a composite for the organisation. This appraisal forms the basis for the next year. Mutually agreed upon objectives, for which individuals are responsible, are reviewed. Actual results are measured against predetermined standards. Any significant deviation or shortfall is noted for correction.

The MBO programmes vary widely from company to company–these may be for some sub–units or for the whole organisation. Accordingly, the methods used also differ widely. However,

31. *Ibid.*, p. 205.

the desirable method is one which starts at the top of the organisation, which has the support of the top management and which are verifiable objectives. M.B.O. programmes may be laid down with different objectives. For example, in the U.K., emphasis is placed on 'corporate planning' or 'development strategy'; and on efficiency in reaching the objectives of the organisation, where is in the USA, emphasis is laid on the 'motivation of individuals,' and on the 'participation of the subordinates in goal setting' rather than on corporate strategy. In India, the process of M.B.O. is yet in its infancy, where the objectives are generally set by superiors and these are thrust upon subordinates.

Benefits/Strengths of M.B.O.

M.B.O. is an important performance tool. Its major benefits may be set forth as follows:

1. Since the subordinates participate and are directly involved in setting goals, *there is a greater commitment on their part for performance.* People become willing and enthusiastic masters of their own fate.

2. *M.B.O. helps in more effective planning.* Actionable objectives are established with planning, and result-oriented planning makes real sense. It forces managers to think of planning by results, rather than merely planning activities. To achieve given results, the managers are also required to give full consideration to the question of the personnel and the resources needed.

3. *M.B.O. aids in developing effective controls.* The standards / yardsticks or reach-points are laid down for measurement of performance, through which actual performance can be measured and deviations corrected in time. Through these standards, performance measurement of different cadres of people can be possible.

4. *M.B.O. provides more confidence to the management in managing its task,* the reason being that the management is more sure of what it wants to do and where it wants to go. It can, therefore, communicate in a better way with different rungs of organisational hierarchy. Better communication is an important benefit of M.B.O.

5. *Managers are more likely to compete with themselves than with other managers.* This kind of evaluation can reduce internal conflicts that often arise when managers compete with each other to obtain scarce resources.

6. *M.B.O. results in a 'means/ends' chain.* Managers at succeedingly lower levels in the organisation establish targets which are integrated with those at the next higher level. Thus, it can help ensure that everyone's's activity is ultimately aimed toward organisation's goals.

7. *M.B.O. reduces role conflict and ambiguity.* Role conflict comes into existence when a person is faced with conflicting demands from two or more superiors; and *role* ambiguity arises when a person is uncertain as to how he will be evaluated, or what he has to achieve. Since M.B. O.aims at providing clear targets and their order priority, it reduces both these situations.

8. *M.B.O. Provides more objective appraisal criteria.* The targets that emerge from the M.B.O. process provide a sound set of criteria for evaluating the manager's performance.

9. *M.B.O. identifies performance deficiencies* and enables the management and the employees to set individualised self-improvement goals and thus proves effective in training and development of people.

10. *M.B.O. helps the individual manager to develop personal leadership;* especially the skills of listening, planning, counselling, motivation and evaluating. This approach to managing instils a personal commitment to respond positively to the organisation's major concerns as well as to the development of human assets. Such a manager has a far greater chance to move ahead within the management hierarchy than a non M.B.O. type.

McGregor observes that M.B.O., in most cases, does some good without costing much. He points out, "Under proper conditions, participation and consultative management provide encouragement to people to direct their creative energies towards organisation objectives, give them some voice in decisions which affect them, and provide sufficient opportunities for satisfaction of social, egoistic and self-fulfilment needs."

11. *M.B.O. provides a suitable climate for better motivation* to the people for more fruitful and better work. Fixing objectives clearly in advance of efforts, acts as a motivation for better performance, job satisfaction, etc.

Thus, M.B.O. is equally good for the subordinates and the managers. The subordinates are confident that their evaluation will be done on performance and not on personal traits. Thus feeling encourages them to perform better. So far as the managers are concerned, they know where they are and where they want to go: therefore, they are willing to take more responsibility.

Weaknesses and Shortcomings of M.B.O.

There are several weaknesses of the system, such as:

1. Effectiveness of the M.B.O. system depends on top management support, for objectives and targets are usually set by middle management and lower management in the light of the primary goals fixed by the top management. If the top management prefers a strong authoritarian approach with centralised control and decision-making, it will require considerable re-education and change in aptitude of the top management.

2. Verifiable goal-setting or framing a specific list of individual objectives and responsibilities is a difficult and time-consuming task, especially when a subordinate job is complex. Job description needs frequent review and decision within the organisation during the implementation of the M.B.O. programme, which itself may cause changes in duties and responsibilities at every level of management.

3. Confusion often arises in the minds of managers regarding challenging and realistic objectives, giving rise to problems of measuring objectives difficult, as also in setting attainable goals, and in describing the objectives in clear and precise terms. Further, considerable difficulties may be encountered in co-ordinating objectives of the organisation with those of the individual and the department.

4. The philosophy of M.B.O. is not so simple as it seems to be. The implementing of M.B.O. programme requires the full knowledge of what it is, how it works, why it is being done, what part it will play in appraising managerial performance, and how participants can benefit.

5. In M.B.O. goals are generally fixed for a short term, usually for a year. This creates the danger of emphasising too much short-term objectives, perhaps at the cost of long-term goals. The managers need to see that long-term objectives are not neglected.

6. There is often the danger that one individual's goals may not be consistent with those of another. For example, the production manager's goal for low cost might find no support from the marketing manager's goals of product availability or quality; or the financial manager's goal of low inventory. In such a situation, different individuals pursue paths that are best in their own interest but which are detrimental to the company as a whole.

7. The manager's/subordinates' appraisal and goal-setting procedure require a high degree of skill in interpersonal relations and extensive training in counselling and interviewing.

8. The M.B.O. programme takes a great deal of time, energy and form-completing on the part of managers. An individual becomes so enmeshed in performing assigned functions that he often loses sight of the goal, the reason for performance. It has been called 'the activity trap' by Odiorne.

It requires a great deal of investment of the top management's time and effort before it arrives at realistic targets and reviews the performance.

9. M.B.O. is far from a panacea. Those executives who have been in volved in it very often find it difficult to apply M.B.O. concepts to their own work habits. They find it hard to think about the results of workers rather than the work itself. They tend to over-emphasise goals that are easy to quantify, sometimes forgetting that workers often behave almost like children at play and when the game is no longer challenging, interest is soon lost.

10. In some areas, such as cutting costs or increasing sales, measuring performance is a straight forward and more or less objectives matter. But in many other areas, such as subordinate development, appraising performance can be an acute problem.

A number of pitfalls have been indicated by the researches in the way of effective working of the M.B.O. programmes. The reasons for failure in the M.B.O. process are hasty implementation; unknowledgeable users; lack of top management follow-through and support; over-emphasis on structure, treatment as another gimmick; failure to carefully monitor and encourage the M.B.O. process during the hard initial years of implementation.

The most important reason why M.B.O. fails is that many managers are unconcerned with performance, and they reward other criteria (e.g., reward people for 'looking productive', rather than for 'being productive'). More concern is shown to how actions look than to the effect of these actions. Instead of rewarding good performance, managers frequently reward other characteristics: things like getting along with people, good work habit, physical appearance, and personality. Further, organisations offer a narrow differentiation in the awards that are offered. As a result of community wage patterns, union contracts and organisational policies, salaries for similar jobs tend to bunch quite closely, irrespective of the performance that individuals exhibit on these jobs. This undermines the concept of M.B.O.

How to Make M.B.O. Effective

In spite of the shortcomings stated above, the M.B.O. system has been put into practice in the West in view of the benefits it enjoys. However, the system may be made effective provided the following requirements are fulfilled:

1. *A successful M.B.O. programme must have the backing and support of the top management.* The active involvement and participation of a chief executive officer who has both the will and capacity to manage is essential. In addition, M.B.O. must be tailored to the executives' style of managing. Ignoring this important consideration may adversely affect the M.B.O. process.

2. *The objectives set must be clear, specific, easily attainable and realistic, must present a challenge and indicate priorities, etc.* Arbitrary goal-setting is not only self-defeating but is also a folly. Objectives can be made verifiable by spelling out the elements of various objectives, time schedule and the finance required in the implementation of the programme.

3. *The M.B.O. programme should be seen as a net-work of programme elements, and the individual goals their programme should fit in the desired niche in this net-work.* This necessitates careful definition of end-result areas, dissemination of consistent planning premises, and careful review of various goals by those responsible for them.

4. The persons in charge of setting goals need some specific guidelines, e.g., what corporate goals are, and how their activity fits in with them. They also need planning premises and knowledge of controlling enterprise policies.

5. *Superiors and subordinates should have regular information available to them as to how well a subordinate's goal performance is progressing.* Superiors should regularly review progress through this information and through personal consultation, and should make themselves available for counselling to help subordinates in meeting goals.

In sum, it may be stated that M.B.O. system is not a panacea, a cure-all for organisational problems. But it can certainly improve many ills by facilitating the sharpening of the corporate goals, clarifying the corporation policy, creating new organisation structures, improving of the information and control system.

CONCLUSION

There is no single statement that explains the nature and purpose of a business. Rather, when establishing objectives, a manager must think in a plural sense. As pointed out by Peter Drucker, "Objectives are needed in every area where performance and results directly and vitally affect the survival and prosperity of the business." These statements of objectives are needed to organise, test, predict, appraise, and analyse the performance and results of business.

The objectives may be to earn profit, to offer services to customers, to undertake market innovations, etc. These objectives cannot be established in a vacuum but must be structured realistically within the framework of the competitive environment of free enterprise. Further, they cannot be established once and then stored carefully in the company's vault. Nor can the objectives of the business be limited to the single time dimension. Instead, objectives must be structured in the light of both long - and short-term factors.

The primary responsibility of management is to reduce the areas of conflict between different claimants for share in business's resulting benefits, and to bring about harmony of interest among the diverse groups (i.e., owners, stockholders, customers, employees, society). Fred C. Crawford has rightly expressed his idea thus: "Management stands in the middle of a triangle. At the lower right corner is *labour*, with a rope round management's right leg; yanking for raises. At the lower left corner is *capital* with a rope round management's left leg, yanking for dividends. The top corner, the *market corner*, is the worse. It has a rope round management's neck like a noose yanking for ever bigger bargains."[32]

It is necessary, therefore, that an enlightened management must continuously balance the diverse objectives without allowing any conflict to arise between two or more objectives.

Exhibit 1: Extracts from the Statement of Objectives of the Hindustan Steel Ltd.

Premises

The objectives of H.S.L. stem from the following major premises:

1. As a public undertaking accountable to the people of India, the company will strive in the national interest in discharging its responsibilities and will constantly seek to deserve and enjoy the highest measure of public trust and esteem.

2. In continuing its business with honesty and integrity, the company will also endeavour to function as a profitable enterprise working towards the achievement of a self-reliant and self-generating economy.

32. Reader's Digest.

3. The company will operate in the highly specialised fields of iron and steel and allied manufacturers. It will pioneer in new fields of applied science, through the pooling of the finest scientific and engineering talents in an environment which will facilitate the proper utilisation of their knowledge, interest, and skill.

4. The operations of the Company will be led by a management group which will command the respect of the whole organisation for its ability, integrity, sense of justice, and its human approach to problems.

5. A high rate of economic growth sustained over a long period, the essential pre-requisite for achieving a rising standard of living for the people. With this in view and within the limits of resources it can generate, the Company will seek to increase investments in basic production capacities and economic and social overheads so as to yield benefits, now and in future.

6. The Company will ensure good corporate health by adopting sound management practices, including the establishment and maintenance of a dynamic organisational structure suited to meet the present and future company needs; long-range planning; products diversification; strong financial control; and comprehensive research, development, engineering and consultancy services.

Objectives

Towards the People of India

As an autonomous body, the H.S.L. will be accountable to the people of India through Parliament and the government, for running a highly competent, business-minded, technologically-oriented enterprise, engaging in manufacture, research and development to meet the needs of the domestic as well as world markets for iron, steel and allied products.

The company will endeavour to earn a fair return on investment; to maximise production and to institute adequate cost control. It will be managed with such competence and skill as will inspire confidence and pride in the minds of the people.

Towards Employees

The company will seek to be model employer by:

1. Attracting competent personnel with growth potential and by developing their maximum capabilities in a working environment through the provision of opportunities for advancement and other incentives.

2. Developing and sustaining a favourable employee attitude and obtaining maximum contribution for employees through stable employment, adequate wage commensurate with the company's capacity to pay; good and safe working conditions and job satisfaction.

3. Establishing a system for redressal of employees' grievances in the shortest possible time and at the lowest possible level;

4. Providing training facilities and other opportunities for self-development in their current job and for advancement;

5. Fostering fellowship and a sense of belonging to the company as a whole through closer association of employees with the management by way of participation in various joint bodies which will also inspire them to respect and value their occupation, and tools of production;

6. By dealing fairly with recognised representatives of workers and encouraging in them healthy trade union practices.

Towards Customers

The company will serve its customers by:

1. Providing prompt, courteous, dependable and competitive service.

2. Selling products of high quality at prices determined in the best interest of the nation.

3. Establishing confidence in the customer that products and services supplied are backed by modern production and research facilities manned by the most competent men available.

Towards Suppliers

The company recognises that important role of its suppliers in providing various materials and services in its operation by:

1. Ensuring prompt dealings based on integrity, impartiality and courtesy.

2. Making available to them the benefits of research, skills and information in order to promote indigenous growth, reduce drain of foreign exchange and increase the quality of indigenous products and services.

Towards the Community

The company accepts its social obligations to the communities in which it operates by:

1. Promoting concepts of national integration in its broadest sense, through providing community services, developing and assisting democratic institutions and generally ensuring that the Company as a whole and its employees act on ideals of social justice without discrimination.

2. Providing know-how and assistance and encouraging talent and growth among members of the communities through the establishment of cooperative institutions.

CHAPTER 6

NEW ECONOMIC POLICY

- Economic Liberalisations : A Global Perspective
- Economic Reforms in India
- New Economic Policy, 1991
- Components of New Economic Policy
- Evaluation of the New Economic Policy
- United Front Government's Policy on Economic Reforms
- Economic Reforms and BJP and its Allies

ECONOMIC LIBERALISATIONS: A GLOBAL PERSPECTIVE

Many countries in the past structured their economies based on the communistic/socialistic economic systems with a view to achieve economic development with equality. This system could not result in fast economic development compared to those of capitalistic economic systems. This is true even in mixed economic systems like India. The socialistic nations including the mixed economies realised that the slow growth of their economies has been due to the nature of their economic systems. They also realised that the faster economic development is possible through the capitalist economic systems.

Most of the global economies have chosen to turn their economic systems towards the market economies. The economic reforms are being introduced by various countries like eastern Europe, Vietnam, Peru, Mexico, Brazil, India, Eritrea, Ethiopia, Morocco, Chile, Spain, Cuba etc. These countries have been discarding old economic philosophies. They have introduced ambitious reforms in their political ideologies, economic systems and economic policies. Consequently the economies of these countries have undergone dramatic changes regarding markets, institutions, social relations of production, finance, marketing, human resources and systems. Structures of the business organisations, level and nature of competition, concern for customer have changed significantly in these countries.

Initially, the countries that introduced economic reforms faced certain problems like unemployment, raise in price, increase in competition, failure of domestic business, closure of small scale industries. Later, these problems were wiped out due to inflow of the foreign capital, increase in industrial and other economic activities and their contribution to the long term gains.

The success of the economic reforms depends on how well they are designed and implemented. The term economic reforms indicates necessary structural adjustment to external events.

The Success of the Economic Reforms Requires

(i) The reduction in public expenditure and thereby reducing fiscal deficit

(ii) The flexible nature of the institutions, organisations and system in order to suit to the changing requirements and internal and external resources,

(iii) Positive and quick response of the institutions towards structural adjustments.

(iv) Response from the private sector to promote investments, building institutions and create competitive environment.

(v) The involvement of the government and governmental organisations in designing and implementing economic reforms programme.

(vi) The government to set the minds of the businessmen, industrialists, consumers and people in favour of reforms.

ECONOMIC REFORMS IN INDIA

India had been observing the changes in the nature of markets, institutions, organisations, structure of business firms, social relations between production and markets across the globe.

India responded favourably to these changes in 1985. Rajeev Gandhi, the then Prime Minister, in 1985 declared the **New Economic Policy**. In this policy he emphasised on the high level productivity, introduction of advanced technology, fuller utilisation of capacity and encourage private sector.

The Measures Taken to Encourage Private Sector Include:

(i) Changes in industrial licensing,
(ii) Technology upgradation,
(iii) Elimination of controls and restrictions.
(iv) Allowing foreign equity capital
(v) Allowing changes in fiscal policy
(vi) Rationalising and simplifying the system of fiscal and administrative regulation.
(vii) Encouraging exports
(viii) Liberalising imports.

The liberalised economic policy stressed on removing unnecessary restrictions in issuing licenses, in denying industrial licensing to MRTP companies and in making adjustment of output to administered prices. In this connection, the measures introduced by the government include:

(i) **Cement :** Cement was totally decontrolled. Private Sector units were issued licences for additional capacities.
(ii) **Sugar :** The share of free sale of sugar in open market was enlarged.
(iii) Asset limit : The ceiling of the asset limit of big business houses was enhanced from Rs 20 crores to Rs 100 crores.
(iv) **Broad - banding :** The scheme of broad - banding of licences was introduced to bring variety in the production of two wheelers. Later this was extended to 25 other industries like chemicals, four wheelers, petrochemicals, pharmaceuticals, type writers etc.
(v) **Drugs :** 94 drugs were completely delicenced and 27 industries were placed outside the purview of MRTP Act.
(vi) **Textile :** New textile policy of 1985 was introduced. This policy abolished the distinction between mill, powerloom and handloom sectors. It also abolished the distinction between natural and synthetic fibre for licensing purposes.
(vii) **Electronics :** Electronics industry was liberalised from MRTP Act restrictions. The entry of FERA companies was also liberalised.
(viii) **Foreign Trade :** Export - Import policy 1985 was announced. It provided for quicker access to imports, strengthening export production base and for facilitating technological upgradation.
(ix) **Long Term Fiscal policy :** Long term fiscal policy, 1985 was announced. It provided for the implementation of the seventh plan in a smooth manner.[1]

NEW ECONOMIC POLICY, 1991

The economic liberalisations announced in 1985 were not implemented effectively. Consequently, the deficit in the balance of trade account gradually increased. The deficit in the balance of trade increased from Rs 5,935 crores during the sixth plan to Rs 10,841 crores during

1. P.K. Dhar, *'Indian Economy'*, Kalyani Publishers, New Delhi, 1998, pp. 971-972.

the seventh plan. Receipts on invisible account has also dwindled. These problems plunged the country into a serious balance of payments crisis.

Government of India, in order to overcome this crisis, approached the International Bank for Reconstruction and Development (IBRD) popularly known as world Bank and the International Monetary fund. The Government requested these institutions to extend loan to the extent of about US $ 7billion. International Monetary Fund while granting the loan insisted the Government of India to place the economy on the right track.

The Government of India committed to the condition of the IMF and the then Finance Minister of the Country communicated the acceptance of the Government to the Managing Director of the IMF in his letter of August 27, 1991. The Finance Minister of the Government of India informed IMF the proposal certain macro economic targets and the initiation of certain policy measures in order to bring certain structural readjustment of the Indian economy.

Need for Economic Reforms:

The context of huge fiscal deficits, crisis in the Balance of Payment (BOP) situation, falling foreign exchange reserves, growing trade deficits and mounting foreign debts, declining India's credit worthiness in international business community and conditions imposed by the International Monetary Fund on India regarding radical economic reforms consisting of liberalisation, macro economic adjustments and structural reforms, to become eligible for large loans, necessitated for the announcement of economic liberalisations by the Government of India. The economic liberalisation launched in India since July 1991 have resulted in radical change of the direction and structure of the nation. The direction has tended towards market economy from the then existing socialistic pattern and globalization of Indian economy.

Aims and Aspects of Liberalisation:

Liberalisations aimed at freeing industry, business and trade from the clutches of control, decontrolling macro economy of the country and its economic institutions and changing the structural infirmities.

Liberalisations include liberalising industry, business and trade both domestic and foreign. Economic reforms are broader in scope. They include reforms of fiscal and monetary policies besides liberalisation of industry, business and trade.

Liberalisation of industrial policy, includes delicensing of industries and removal of restrictions of foreign investment, relaxation of Foreign Exchange Regulation Act (FERA) and Monopolies and Restrictive Trade Practices Act (MRTP), curtailment of the role of public sector and application of commercial principles to the public sector industries. Liberalisation of trade policy includes liberalisation of imports, linking of imports to exports and lowering of tariffs, introduction of new exchange rate system, encouragement of exports and foreign investment. Economic reforms include fiscal and monetary reforms, inflation control and financial sector reforms. Structural adjustment includes controlling subsidies and introduction of a market driven environment, restructuring the public sector and exit policy.

Result of the Economic Reforms:

The economic reforms announced by the Government change the direction of the country from socialistic pattern to market economy. The trends of market economy result in intense and vibrant competition, entry of new multinationals and consolidation of existing multinationals, increasing the stake of multinationals in their Indian partnerships, intensification of competition due to import liberalisation, increased competition due to the emergence of buyer's market and changed notions about small scale industry. The vulnerability of Indian Industry and frequent changes in international environment are other basic causes for competition. Thus, the major result of economic reforms is competition and all-round competition. Thus, the major result of economic reforms is competition and all-round competition. This situation necessitated for the Total Quality and Productivity Management (TQPM) and minimisation of cost through attracting positive factors and eliminating hindering factors.

Now, the survival and development of industry in India, mostly depends on its ability to compete with other Indian firms, multinationals and in foreign markets. The ability to maintain high quality and maximise productivity determine the competitive ability of Indian firms, which in turn is largely dependent on the quality and commitment of human resources.

Objectives of Economic Reforms : The main objectives of economic reforms were :

(i) to attain economic growth at the rate of 3 to 3.5 per cent in 1991-92 and at 4 percent in 1992-93

(ii) to reduce the annual rate of inflation by 9 percent in 1991-92 followed by 6 per cent in 1992-93,

(iii) to relieve the critical balance of payments situation and to rebuild foreign exchange reserves to US $ 2.2 billion in 1991-92,

(iv) to reduce current account deficit in the budget from 2.5 percent of G.D.P in 1990-91 to 2.0 percent by 1992-93,

(v) to ráise GDP growth to around six percent by the mid 1990s.

Policy Measures : Government of India has initiated several policy measures in order to achieve the objectives of the New Economic Policy. These measures include :

(i) *Fiscal Policy Reforms :* These reforms include controls over public expenditure, raise the tax and non tax revenue, imposition of fiscal discipline by both central and state governments, reduction of subsidies, developing a more efficient expenditure system, encouraging state governments to streamline the functioning of state public sector undertakings, withdraw the budgetary support to central public sector units with a view to improving their performance and profitability.

(ii) *Monetary Policy Reforms :* Reserve Bank of India has been announcing monetary policy reforms inorder to control inflation and improving the balance of payments position. These reforms include bank rate, cash reserve ratio (CRR) and Statutory Liquidity ratio (SLR).

(iii) *Pricing Policy Reforms :* Government increased the administered prices of various commodities and inputs like petroleum products and fertilisers. Government also sanctioned freedom to the public sector enterprises to fix the prices based on the market forces. These measures help the government to reduce budgetary support, subsidies and to promote more flexible price structure.

(iv) *External Policy Reforms :* Government in order to reduce current account deficit in balance of payments introduced stabilisation and import compression measures.

(v) *Industrial Policy Reforms :* These reforms include

(a) abolition of industrial licensing, except for 8 industries related to security, strategic importance and environmental concerns, (b) Reducing the area of public sector reservation from 17 to 8 industries in order to encourage private sector (c) elimination of the system of pre-entry scrutiny of investment decisions of the MRTP companies and controlling only 'unfair or restrictive business practices', (d) liberalisation of location policy (e) abolition of phased manufacturing programmes earlier enforced to increase the pace of indigenisation, (f) removal of mandatory convertibility clause.

(vi) *Foreign Investment Policy Reforms :* The new policy encourages the inflow of foreign investment in connection with technology transfer, marketing expertise and introduction of modern managerial techniques. The specific reforms include:

(a) Automatic permission is given to 34 industries for foreign direct investment upto 51 per cent of equity. (b) Automatic permission is given with regard to foreign technology agreements in high priority industry for royalty payment upto 5% on domestic sales, 8% on export sales or a maximum payment of Rs 1 crore, (c) Foreign trading companies are allowed to raise their foreign equity holdings upto 51 percent for export activities.

(vii) *Public Sector Policy Reforms :* As mentioned earlier, Government of India, realised the need for reducing the role of public sector in business and announced various public sector policy reforms. These reforms include :

(a) Reduction of reservation list for public sector industrial units from 17 industries to 8 industries. (b) Allowing the review of public investments where social considerations are not important and private sector can function efficiently. (c) Efficiently run public sector undertakings are given freedom and management autonomy through the system of Memorandum of Understanding (MOU), (d) Reduction of budgetary support to public enterprises (e) Encourage the private participation in investment of public enterprises through disinvestment of government holding. This measure is aimed at improving the efficiency of the pubic sector units. (f) Rehabilitation, reconstruction or rationalisation of chronically sick public sector enterprises by referring them to the Board for Industrial and Financial Reconstruction (BFIR), (g) Allowing the formation of joint ventures with foreign companies (h) Creation of National Renewal Fund for training and redeployment of workers.

(viii) *Trade Policy Reforms :* These reforms include:

(a) Progressively eliminating the system of licenses and quantitative restrictions particularly for capital goods and raw materials (b) Reducing the monopoly of the public sector in exports and imports.

(ix) Social Policy Reforms : These reforms include allocation of higher amount of outlays on elementary education, rural drinking water supply, assistance to small and marginal farmers etc.

The successful implementation of the new economic policy brought encouraging results in savings and investment (see tables 6.1 and 6.2) and in various key economic areas (see table 6.3)

TABLE 6.1 DISPOSITION OF GROSS DOMESTIC PRODUCT

	Percentage change over the previous year							
	(At current prices)				*(At 1993-94 prices)*			
	1994-95	*1995-96*	*1996-97P*	*1997-98Q*	*1994-95*	*1995-96*	*1996-97P*	*1997-98Q*
COMPONENT								
Total final consumption expenditure	15.7	15.2	16.5	10.1	7.2	7.8	7.5	6.4
Govt. final consumption expenditure	11.4	18.5	13.4	20.7	7.7	15.1	11.3	19.4
Pvt. final consumption expenditure	16.4	14.7	17.0	8.4	7.1	6.6	6.8	3.9
Gross domestic capital formation	34.1	19.3	15.1	7.1	23.0	8.9	8.5	3.0
Exports of goods and services	17.9	28.7	11.1	10.7	–	–	–	–
Less Import of goods services	21.8	38.4	11.1	12.7	–	–	–	–

TABLE 6.2 SAVING AND INVESTMENT

	1993-94	1994-95	1995-96	1996-97 (P)	1997-98 (Q)
	(As per cent of GDP at current market prices)				
Gross Domestic Savings	**21.8**	**24.2**	**24.1**	**24.4**	**23.1**
Public	0.5	1.5	1.9	1.5	1.0
Private	21.3	22.7	22.2	22.9	22.1
House hold sector	17.9	19.3	17.4	18.8	18.3
Financial savings	10.8	11.6	8.2	9.8	10.3
Physical savings	7.1	7.7	9.3	9.0	8.0
Gross Domestic Investment*	**22.4**	**25.4**	**25.8**	**25.7**	**24.8**
Public	8.1	8.5	7.4	6.7	7.0
Private	12.7	14.4	18.2	16.5	16.4
Gross Domestic Investment*	**22.4**	**25.4**	**25.8**	**25.7**	**24.8**
GFCF	20.9	21.4	23.8	23.2	22.9
Change in stock	-0.2	1.5	1.8	-0.1	.5
Saving Investment Gap@	**-0.6**	**-1.2**	**-1.7**	**-1.3**	**-1.7**
Public	-7.6	-7	-5.5	-5.2	-6.0
Private	8.6	8.3	4.0	6.4	5.7

Note : (i) Gross Domestic Investment denotes Gross Domestic Capital Formation (GDCF)

(ii) Figures may not add up due to rounding off.

* : adjusted for errors and omissions.

@ : refers to the difference between the rates of saving and Investment

GFCF : Gross Fixed Capital Formation

P : Provisional estimates, Q - Quick estimates; *Source*-Central Statistical Organisation.

Source : The Economic Challenger 1(3) April - June 1999, p.14

TABLE 6.3 KEY ECONOMIC INDICATORS

	Absolute Values				*% change over previous period*			
Gross National Products (Rs '000 cr)	*'95-96*	*'96-97*	*'97-98*	*'98-99*	*'95-96*	*'96-97*	*'97-98*	*'98-99*
At current prices	1089.8	1272.2P	1413.2Q	NA	17.1	16.7 P	11.1Q	NA
At 1993-94 prices	913.8	988P	1038.7Q	1099.7A	7.8	8.1P	5.1Q	5.9A
Gross Domestic Product (Rs '000 cr)								
At current price	1103.2	1285.3 P	1426.7Q	NA	16.9	16.5P	11.0Q	NA
At 1993-94 prices	926.4	99.0P	1049.2Q	1110.0A	7.6	7.8P	5.0Q	5.8A
Agricultural production (1)	16.0.7	175.4	164.9	171.3P	-2.7	9.1	-6.0	3.9P
Food grain production (mill tonnes)	180.4	199.4	192.4	195.3P	-5.8	10.5	-3.5	1.5P
Industrial production (2)	122.3	129.1	137.6	139.2#	12.8	5.6	6.6	3.5#
Electricity generated (billion KWH)	379.9	394.5	420.6	329.4#	8.4	3.8	6.6	6.6#

Wholesale price index (3)	299.5	320.1	337.1	353.9*	4.4	6.9	5.3	4.6*
Consumer price index for ind. workers (4)	319.0	351.0	380.0	429.0@	8.9	10.0	8.3	15.3@
Money supply (M3) (Rs '000 cr)	604.0	701.8	825.4	934.7 (5)	13.7	16.2	17.6	13.2 (6)
Imports at current prices								
Rs crore	122678	138920	151553	132447#	36.4	13.2	9.0	23.2#
$ million	36678	39133	40779	31583#	28.0	6.7	4.2	7.1#
Export at current prices								
Rs crore	106353	118817	126286	101850#	28.6	11.7	6.3	11.7#
$ million	31797	33470	33980	24287#	20.7	5.3	1.5	-2.9#
Foreign currency assets (7)								
Rs crore	58446	80368	102507	116515(8)	-11.5	37.5	27.5	37(8)
$ million	17044	22367	25975	27429(8)	-18.1	31.2	16.1	5.6(8)
Exchange rate (Rs/$) (10)	33.45	35.50	37.16	41.99(9)	-6.1	-5.8	-4.5	11.5(9)

Note : Gross national product and Gross domestic product figures are at factor cost (new scale with base 1993-94). **Q** - Quick estimates, **A** - Advance estimates; **P** - Provisional; **NA** - Not available

1. Index of agriculture production (of 46 crops, including plantations) with base triennium ending 1981-82 = 100. **2.** Index of agriculture production 1993-94 = 100. **3.** Index with base 1981-82 = 100 at the end of fiscal year. **4.** Index with base 1982 = 100, at the end of fiscal year. **5.** Outstanding as on January 15, 1999 for 1998-99 and of financial year for previous years. **6.** April, 1998 to January 15, 1999. **7.** Outstanding at the end of fiscal year. **8.** At the end of January, 1999. **9.** April-January 1998-99. **10.** Per cent change indicates the rate of appreciation/depreciation (-) of the Rupee vis-a-vis the US Dollar. As on 30.1.1999 (Provisional) @ December 1998# April-December, 1998.

Source : The Economic Challenger, 1(3) April-June 1999, b.12

COMPONENTS OF THE NEW POLICY

The New economic policy has four components viz., liberalisation. privatisation, globalization and stablisation.

Liberalisation

The new economic policy dispensed with the regulations and controls. It provides freedom to the entrepreneurs/industrialists to enter any business or industry, produce and/or distribute any product, render any service and earn any amount or rate of profit. The liberalisation measures include :

(i) Licensing is abolished except for 8 industries.
Licensing for almost all bulk drugs is abolished.

(ii) Limit for equity participation in Indian companies by the foreign companies is increased upto 51 per cent.

(iii) Fixation of minimum lending rates by the Reserve Bank of India for the loans granted by commercial banks exceeding Rs. 2 lakhs is abolished.

(iv) MODVAT was extended to capital goods and petroleum products.

(v) Five year tax holiday was granted to the industrial units set up in back ward areas.

(vi) Statutory Liquidity Ratio (SLR) was reduced to 31.5%. Exhibit 6.1 presents the main features of new credit policy.

(vii) Import duties on capital goods were reduced to 15 per cent on export related capital goods and 25 per cent for project imports and most capital goods.

(viii) Corporate tax rate was reduced from 45 per cent for widely held companies and 50 per cent for closely held companies to 40 per cent for domestic companies. The same was reduced from 65 per cent to 55 per cent in case of foreign companies.

(ix) Major over haul of the excise tax structure including rationalisation of rates, elimination of most end use exemptions and general shift from specific to advalorem duties.

(x) Full convertibility of rupee on current account is allowed through the introduction of the Liberalised Exchange Rate Management System.

(xi) Controller of capital Issues was abolished.

(xii) Securities and Exchange Board of India (SEBI) was made statutory.

(xiii) Foreign Exchange Regulation Act was relaxed.

(xiv) Setting up of private banks was encouraged.

(xv) Private investment was allowed in power and telecommunications sectors.

(xvi) 100 per cent Export Oriented Units (EOUS) and units in Export Processing Zones (EPZS) are approved automatically.

(xvii) Greater thrust is laid down on exports to manage balance of payments.

(xvii) Establishment of Insurance Regulatory and Development Authority (IRDA) on the lines of SEBI. This act will allow the private insurance companies and foregin insurance companies to operate in India. This act will also allow insurance companies to enter into financial sector and financial companies to enter into insurance sector.

Privatisation

Governments of various countries across the globe experienced with the poor performance of public sector. Due to this factor, the governments favoured privatisation of public sector industrial units and encouragement of private sector to set up business and industrial units. Government of India also realised this and fell in line with the other governments and included the privatisation as a component of the new economic policy.

Before 1991, private sector in the country worked under administrative controls. Government dispensed with these controls and started encouraging the private sector freely and in market friendly environment.

Exhibit 6.1 : Main Features of the New Credit Policy

- CRR cut by 0.5 per cent to 10 per cent with effect from May, 8, 1999
- Freedom to banks for deciding SLR for different maturities.
- Fixed rate loans for project finance term loans.
- Freedom to banks for deciding interest rates on deposits for the period exceeding 15 days.
- Advances to depositors against fixed deposits can be made without reference to SLR celling.
- General refinance facility withdrawn with immediate effect and replaced by collateral lending facility (CLF)
- Starting Interim Liquidity Adjustment Facility ('ILAF') under which loan can be obtained at repo rate by pledging government securities.
- Create a special cell in RBI to raise with NABARD and micro-credit institutions for augmenting flow of credit to self-employed and rural areas.

- Interest rates on loans given by banks to micro-credit organisations and to their members to be left to the discretion of banks.
- National payments council set up under the chairmanship of a deputy governor to streamline payments and settlement system.
- M_3 growth target of 15.5 -16 per cent.
- A 'common fund' of government securities to be created for promoting retail selling market.
- Permitting 'forward cover' to FIIs.
- Scheduled commercial banks have been authorised to make available Export Credit Refinancing Facility at Bank Rate from April 1, 1999.
- UTI, LIC, IDBI and other non-bank participants in the money market to access short term liquidity through repos.
- Cheque facility to exporters for foreign exchange earned by them.

Source : The Economic Challenger, 1 (4) July-sept. 1999, p.13.

Under privatisation more emphasis is given on the market orientation of economic activities in the place of policy driven thrust. Owners and managers in the private sector are guided by core competencies, competitive strengths, competitive edge, customer satisfaction etc. One aspect of privatisation is to encourage the private ownership, investment and control in the business and industrial activities.

Another aspect of privatisation is to reduce the role of public sector to the lowest possible level. Government of India in its New Economic Policy reduced the role of public sector to mere six areas from as many as 17 industries. The rest are open to the private sector. Government also started the process of disinvesting its equity holding in public sector industrial units in favour of private investors. Further, Government also permitted foreign investment upto 51 per cent of equity in Indian industries. This measure of privatisation makes the Indian business and industry more dynamic and responsive to the changes in the global business. This would also help for the faster economic development of the country and increase in the living standards of the people.

Globalization

Indian economy was not closely knitted with the global economy before 1991. There were strict controls regarding imports, exports, entry of foreign capital, entry of multinationals etc. Indian Government minimised these controls to the lowest extent in its New Economic Policy. Further, a number of measures were introduced to knit the Indian economy in the global economy. Devaluation of Rupee in 1991 is a measure to do away with the artificially controlled exchange rates. Further, Rupee is fully convertible on current account. In this direction, the government reduced custom duties on imports at par with world rates. Government also liberalised the norms regarding the entry of foreign private capital. India's membership in World Trade Organisation is another step in this direction.

Stabilisation

Stabilisation refers to maintaining the price level at the lowest possible level from the present 14 per cent level. Price level can be brought down by :

(i) reducing fiscal deficit, to around 4 per cent of GNP

(ii) improving the supply of food stocks though public distribution system

(iii) liberalising imports,

(iv) avoiding wasteful expenditure and
(v) improving productivity.

EVALUATION OF THE NEW ECONOMIC POLICY

The primary agenda of the new economic policy includes :

(a) Elimination of primary deficit in three years to cut interest burden, (b) Broaden tax base, implement VAT and lower average tariffs, (c) Replace quantitative restrictions on imports with custom duties (d) Allow unfettered agricultural trade and free input and output prices and (e) Delicense and dereserve industries further, freeing foreign investment.

It would be appropriate to enquire into the aspect of finished agenda and unfinished agenda of new economic policy. This evaluation helps for understanding the position of implementation of economic reforms, level of implementation, reasons for the unfinished agenda, need for future course of action and the type of future course of action for effective implementation of the liberalisations.

Agriculture :

India is basically an agriculture country. Therefore the roots of reforms must be shown in the country's agriculture. Bringing agriculture upto date is an essential part of the reforms. According to Ashok Gulati, the incomplete market reforms in agriculture, if not complemented with supply-side reforms will lead to rising prices and stagnating output. Liberalisation of agricultural sector improves the terms of trade.

The agenda of the new economic policy regarding agriculture sector include :

(a) remove controls on imports and exports (b) eliminate licensing for wholesale trade (c) phase out public sector procurement (d) wind up the Food Corporation of India (e) phase out public distribution system, replace with food stamps as in USA, (f) allow futures trading in more commodities (g) abolish heavy prices for sugar, rice, molasses (h) allow leasing of cultivate land in all states (i) subsidise investments instead of inputs (v) make agricultural users pay for power (k) index water and power tariff to inflation (l) make cooperatives manage inputs (m) adopt group lending for rural credit (n) decontrol urea prices, decanalise imports.

The accomplishments of new economic policy regarding agriculture sector include :

(a) raise of procurement prices of food grains (b) raise of issue prices though public distribution system to the extent of 60% to 100% (c) export quota for quality rice abolished (d) duty cut on edible oil imports (e) stocking limit for exporters abolished (f) revamped public distribution system in 1,775 blocks (g) minimum export price system abolished (h) quality inspection for exports scrapped (i) scope for crop insurance scheme expanded (j) non-nitrogenous fertilizers prices freed (k) fertiliser subsidy reduced to 0.68 per cent of GDP (l) edible oil imports placed under open general license (OGL) (m) marginal decanalisation of trade and (n) branded agricultural exports promoted. Table 6.4 presents sectorial real growth rates during 1994-99

Industry

Government announced the new industrial policy on July 24, 1991. Since then, industry has been the focus of liberalisation. With the delicensing of all but 9 industries, the entry of private

2. K. Aswathappa, *"Business Environment"*, Himalaya Publishing House, Mumbai, 1997, pp. 525-527.

sector to 11 industries earlier earmarked for the public sector, and the easing of the restrictions on raising capital both at home and abroad, the agenda of industrial reforms had made more progress than any other.

The agenda of new economic policy regarding industry include :

(a) delicense all but security and strategic related industries
(b) decontrol prices of sugar and molasses
(c) phase out product reservation for small scale industries
(d) restrict incentives to only tiny sector
(e) open up coal, mineral and oil sectors
(f) enact laws to tackle anticompetition mergers and amalgamations
(g) allow free foreign direct investment flows into all sectors
(h) expand automatic approval of foreign direct investment
(i) stop case by case approval of foreign direct investment
(j) evolve transparent norms for foreign direct investment approval
(k) thoroughly revise companies bill
(l) introduce exit policy for industry
(m) restructure national renewal fund (NRF), elicit private contributions
(n) amend laws to allow exit from business.

The accomplishments in this regard include :

(a) licensing was abolished for all but 15 sectors (b) licensing for product diversification was slashed (c) MRTP act was amended to allow expansions (d) areas reserved for public sector undertakings was reduced to nine. (e) permission was granted to hire foreign technicians (f) steel prices were decontrolled fully and the prices of coal are decontrolled partially (g) foreign equity upto 51 per cent was allowed in 36 sectors (h) fully owned transactional corporation subsidiaries were permitted (i) curbs on use of brand names were removed (i) convertibility clause on foreign institutional loans were removed. (k) national renewal fund was set up (l) scope of BFIR was widened.

TABLE 6.4 : SECTORIAL REAL GROWTH RATES

Industry	*Percentage change over the previous year*				
	1994-95	*1995-96*	*1996-97* (P)	*1997-98* (Q)	*1998-99* (A)
I. Agriculture and Allied Sectors	5.4	.2	9.4	-1.0	5.3
II. Industry	9.3	12.2	6.0	5.9	4.7
1. Mining and quarrying	9.2	7.4	1.2	2.7	.1
2. Manufacturing	10.6	15.0	7.7	6.8	5.7
3. Electricity, gas & water supply	9.3	6.7	5.7	6.6	6.3
4. Construction	5.3	8.2	2.9	4.1	2.3
III. Services	8.5	9.8	8.0	8.2	6.7
5. Trade, hotels, transport and communications	12.8	11.5	8.6	5.7	6.8
6. Financing services	5.6	8.3	7.9	8.4	7.7
7. Community, social and personal services	3.4	7.8	6.7	13.3	5.8
Total GDP at factor cost	7.8	7.6	7.8	5.0	5.8

A = advance estimate; P = Provisional; Q = Quick estimate

Source : The Economic Challenger 1(3) April-June 1999, p. 13.

Infrastructure

Infrastructure is the backbone for economic development in general and for industrial development in particular. In fact, infrastructure is the bottle neck for India's economic development. Mostly, public sector used to concentrate on providing infrastructure facilities in India as the latter was treated as public utilities. Private investment was not attracted by the infrastructure due to low returns. Infrastructural facilities cannot be developed to the extent necessary unless and until the private investment is attracted. Therefore, the agenda of the new economic policy must centre around commercialisation of public utilities so that the flow of private capital into infrastructure is speeded up.

The agenda of the new economic policy regarding infrastructure include :

(a) restructure state electricity boards as commercial corporations (b) set up a power regulatory authority (c) formulate guidelines for private entry (d) lower the number of clearing agencies (e) involve panchyats in power distribution (f) form a telecom regulatory authority (g) corporatise the department of telecommunications (i) break VSNL monopolies (i) remove limits on foreign equity in telecom (k) corporatise port trusts (l) operationalise hiring from labour boards (m) levy fuel tax to recover highway costs (n) corporatise Indian Railways. (o) stop cross- subsidy in railway fares. (Table 6.5 presents growth rates of core and infrastructure sectors).

Banking & Finance

The only factor of production closest to being freed is capital. The abolition of controls on new issues, the development of secondary markets, and the clearance for foreign institutional investors and private sector mutual funds have strengthened the capital markets. In the banking sector, steps such as interest rate decontrol, a phased reduction in statutory co-option of resources by the government, the introduction of capital adequacy stipulations and prudential norms regarding income recognition, asset classification, and provisioning for bad debts, and the lowering of entry barriers have set the stage for further reforms to capitalise on these initiatives.

The agenda of new economic policy regarding banking and finance include :

(a) eliminate controls on interest rates (b) cut priority sector lending to 10 percent (c) phase out statutory liquidity ratio (SLR) and gradually reduce cash reserve ratio (CRR) (d) strengthen prudential regulations (e) reduce government's holdings in banks (f) scrap branch licensing system (g) implement Goiporia committee proposals (h) open up the insurance sector (i) free foreign institutional investor participation in debt markets (j) allow provident funds to invest in corporate debt (k) strengthen primary dealer network (i) register all sub brokers (m) improve settlements in capital markets.

The accomplishments of the new economic policy with regard to banking and finance include:

(a) lending rates for loans over Rs 2 lakhs are freed (b) Interest rates on term deposits above 2 years are freed (c) direct credit categories are lowered (d) incremental statutory liquidity requirements is reduced to 25 per cent (e) incremental cash reserve ratio is eliminated altogether (f) agreements capping ad-hoc T-bills are signed (g) norms for income recognition are introduced (h) asset - classification norms are changed (i) private banks entry and expansion are allowed, (j) insurance regulatory authority is announced (k) free pricing of equity issues is permitted (l) foreign institutional investors are allowed into capital markets (m) private sector mutual funds are permitted (n) auction of central government securities is introduced.

TABLE 6.5 GROWTH RATES OF CORE AND INFRASTRUCTURE SECTORS

(Per cent p.a)

Sectors	*Weight (IIP)*	*1993-94*	*1994-95*	*1995-96*	*1996-97*	*1997-98P*	*1997-98P@*	*1998-99P@*
Infrastructure Sectors (IIP)								
1. Electricity generation	10.2	7.5	8.1	8.4	3.8	6.6	5.6	6.6
(a) Hydel		0.7	17.5	–12.2	–5.5	8.6	2.6	13.8
(b) Thermal (incl.nuclear)		9.5	5.6	14.8	6.1	6.2	6.3	4.9
2. Coal production	3.2	3.3	3.2	6.4	5.7	3.6	4.9	0
3. Steel	5.1	6.2	8.3	8.9	1.6	.6	–0.1	–2.6
4. Crude Oil	4.2	.3	19.3	9.1	–6.5	3.0	2.7	–3.6
5. Refinery through put	2.0	1.5	4.1	3.9	7.2	3.5	3.5	3.2
6.Cement	2.0	5.7	9.9	6.6	8.6	12.8	9.0	3.7
Overall	26.7	5.0	9.1	7.9	2.6	4.8	4.1	2.0
Other infrastructure sectors								
1. Railway revenue-earning goods traffic		2.5	1.7	7.0	4.7	5	6.1	–2.5
2. Cargo handled at major ports	7.6	10.0	9.1	5.6	10.6	12.4	0	
3. Tele communications:								
New telephone connections provides (DELs)	24.5	44.0	23.3	17.5	27.1	31.9	26.1	

Source : The Economic challenger 1(3), April- june 1999, p–16

P. Provisional @ = April - December

International Trade

International trade has been benefited enormously from liberalisation with the level and dispersion of tariffs being cut sharply, quantitative restrictions on imports eased, and plenty of incentives to exports, the numbers spell out a success story. The trade - to - Gross Domestic Product ratio has increased from 15.5 per cent in 1990-91 to 19.8 per cent in 1994-95. Exports as percentage of imports have increased from 66.2 percent in 1990-91 to 86.6 per cent in 1995-96. The burden of external debt dwindled from 41 per cent to 33 per cent of GDP during 1991-92 and 1995-96. And yet, the export cluster of east Asian countries continues to elude India. A study by the Indian Institute of Foreign Trade has identified computer education, hi-tech. medical services, waste management and printing as the service areas where India holds a competitive advantage over its Asian rivals. Policy initiatives must be taken to improve the quality of Indian products allowing Indian brands to be established. Table 6.6 presents foreign direct investment.

The agenda of the new economic policy with regard to international trade include :

(a) replacing licensing of imports with tariffs (b) lower average imports tariff tc 15 per cent (c) eliminate variations in import duties (d) decanlise oil and agricultural trade (e) remove export subsidies as tariffs fall (f) replace licensing of exports with duties (g) levy low, flat tax on export income (h) counter anti - dumping measures (i) reformulate Export processing zone and export oriented unit policy (j) promote brands to boost unit prices (k) resolve market access issues in services (l) seek membership to trade blocs (m) free the way for investment in foreign joint ventures (n) extend convertibility to capital account.

The accomplishments of new economic policy regarding international trade are :

(a) peak tariffs are reduced from 400 per cent to 50 per cent (b) average tariffs are cut from 87 per cent to 27 percent (c) dispersion decreased from 41 percent to 21 percent (d) capital and import goods imports are freed (e) manufactured goods imports are decanalised (f) export control is halved to 200 items (g) export tax on minerals and farm items is removed (h) most direct export subsides are eliminated (i) current account convertibility is introduced (j) Rupee exchange rate is freed (k) interest rates on Non Resident Indian (NRI) deposits are moderated (l) cap set on external commercial borrowings (m) exports focused through product mix (n) India brand promotion fund is set up. Table 6.7 presents balance of payments during 1990-99.

Fiscal Reforms

The fiscal deficit has been whittled down from 8.3 per cent of gross domestic product (GDP) in 1990-91 to 6.4 per cent in 1995-96. But the gains were concentrated in the initial years of the structural adjustment programme. Most of the government revenue is spent to meet the interest bill of the Government of India. Interest burden consumes nearly half the revenue receipts.

The agenda of the new economic policy with regard to fiscal reforms include :

(a) eliminate primary deficit within three years (b) phase out food and fertiliser subsidies (c) identity and cut wasteful expenditure (d) eliminate all budgetary support to public sector undertakings (e) make zero-based budgeting mandatory (f) dispersal for government schemes on performance (g) phase out all grants - in - aid to states (h) cut tax rates and withdraw exemptions (i) extend presumptive taxation (j) levy minimum tax on profit making firms (k) move towards a comprehensive value added tax (VAT) (l) introduce value added tax (VAT) at the state level. (m) eliminate taxes on inter-state trade (n) simplify forms and procedures.

TABLE 6.6 FOREIGN DIRECT INVESTMENT

	1991	*1992*	*1993*	*1994*	*1995*	*1996*	*1997*	*1998**	*Total ('91-98)*
Approvals									
Rs crore	739	5256	11189	13590	37489	39453	57149	25103	189968
US$ million	325	1781	3559	4332	11245	11142	15752	6132	54268
Actual inflows									
Rs crore	351	675	1786	3009	6720	8431	12085	8433	41490
US $ million	155	233	574	958	2100	2383	3330	2073	11806
Actual inflows as % of Approvals (In US $ terms)	47.7	13.1	16.1	22.1	18.7	21.4	21.1	33.8	21.7

Source : RBI

* Upto September 1998, Figures are provisional. Note : The approval and actual inflows figures include NRI direct investments approved RBI

Source : The Economic challenger, (3) April - June 1997, p. 17.

TABLE 6.7 BALANCE OF PAYMENTS

(In US $ million)

	1990-91 (P)	1991-92 (P)	1992-93 (P)	1993-94 (P)	1994-95 (P)	1995-96 (P)	1996-97 (P)	1997-98 (P)	1998-99 (P) (Apr.Sep)
1. Exports	18477	18266	18869	22683	26855	32311	34133	34849	16634
2. Imports	27915	21064	24316	26739	35904	43670	48948	51126	24712
of which : POL	6028	5364	6100	5753	5928	7526	11036	8217	2910
3. Trade balance	**–9438**	**–2798**	**–5447**	**–4056**	**–9049**	**–11359**	**–14815**	**–16277**	**–8078**
4. Invisibles (net)	–242	1620	1921	2898	5680	5460	10321	9804	4993
Non factor services	980	1207	1129	535	602	–186	851	1143	744
Investment Income	–3752	–3830	–3423	–3270	–3431	–3205	–3307	–3520	–1141
Pvt. transfers	2069	3783	3852	5265	8093	8506	12367	11830	5269
Official grants	461	460	363	368	416	345	410	351	121
5. Current Account Balance	**–9680**	**–1178**	**–3526**	**–1158**	**–3369**	**–5899**	**–4494**	**–5473**	**–3085**
6. External assistance (net)	2210	3037	1859	1901	1526	883	1109	899	–135
7. Commercial borrowing (net) @	2248	1456	–358	607	1030	1275	2848	3999	4605
8. IMF (Net)	1214	786	1288	187	–1143	–1715	–975	–618	–199
9. NR deposit (Net)	1536	290	2001	1205	172	1103	3350	1125	–393
10. Rupee debt service	1193	–1240	–878	–1053	–983	–952	–727	–767	588
11. Foreign Investments (net)	103	133	557	4235	4807	4604	5838	4993	707
of which :									
(i) FDI (net)	97	129	315	586	1228	1943	2526	3165	1239
(ii) FIIs	0	0	0	1665	1503	2009	1926	979	–601
(iii) Euro equities & others	6	4	242	1984	2076	652	1386	849	69
12. Other flows(net)+	2284	101	–245	2800	2604	–2235	–1131	735	–994
13. Capital account total (net)	**8402**	**4563**	**4224**	**9882**	**8013**	**2963**	**10312**	**10366**	**3003**
14. Reserve use (– Increase)	**1278**	**–3385**	**–698**	**–8724**	**–4644**	**2936**	**–5818**	**–3893**	**82**

(P) : Preliminary actuals

@ Figures include receipts on account of India Development Bonds in 1991-92 and related repayments, if any, in the subsequent years. Besides, figure for April-Sept. 1998 includes receipts on account of Resurgent India Book (RIB).

\+ Include, among others, delayed exports receipts and errors and omissions. For the year 1992-93, it also includes errors and omissions arising out of dual exchange rates applicable under the Liberalised Exchange Rate Mangement System (LERMS).

Source : The Economic Challenger, 1(3) April-June 1999, p.15.

The accomplishments in this regard include :

(a) Fiscal deficit is cut from 8.3 per cent of GDP to 6.3 per cent
(b) Primary deficit is reduced to 1.2 per cent of GDP
(c) Resource to monetisation is cut
(d) Real capital expenditure is reduced by 18.8 per cent.
(e) Budgetary support to central public sector units is lowered
(f) Corporate tax is reduced from 57.5 per cent to 46 per cent
(g) Tax on foreign companies is reduced to 55 per cent
(h) Import duties are unified and number of rates are cut.
(i) Specific excise rates are replaced by *ad valorem*
(j) Number of duty rates are brought down to 10.
(k) Number of end-use exemptions are reduced
(l) MODVAT is extended to capital goods
(m) Top personal income tax rate is cut from 56 per cent to 40 per cent.
(n) Presumptive tax is introduced for small traders.

The agenda for unfinished fiscal reforms is : redirect expenditure towards productive uses, cutting across semantic distinctions between categories like revenue and capital, development and non-development, plan and non-plan.

Public Sector

Missed opportunities litter the trail of public sector reforms in the country. Normally sparked off by either an economic crisis – which makes financial support units difficult or by a change in government policy, India's dalliance with public sector units privatisation had the advantage of both the triggers.

The agenda of the new economic policy with regard to public sector include :

(a) Eliminate indirect state budgetary support.
(b) Allow foreign investment in public sector units businesses.
(c) Induct professionals into boards.
(d) Empower boards to clear investments.
(e) Allow joint ventures and alliances with transnationals.
(f) Free Public Sector units (PSUS) to decide on products and prices.
(g) Minimise controls on public sector units.
(h) Offer pay parity with private sector.
(i) Draw-up sector-wise privatisation policy.
(j) Segregate public sector units for disinvestment strategies.
(k) Set up ministry to execute public sector units reforms.
(l) Cut exemptions for public sector units in bankruptcy law.
(m) Improved targeting of funds for National Renewal Fund.
(n) Provide incentives for retraining.

The accomplishments of public sector units reforms include :

(a) Disinvestment of public sector undertakings' shares is initiated.
(b) 24 per cent of public equity is earmarked for sale.
(c) Sick public sector units are brought under BFIR.

(d) Public sector undertakings in 9 sectors are made to compete.
(e) Budgetary support is cut to 0.8 per cent of GDP.
(f) Access to capital markets is increased.
(g) Preferential access to credit is removed.
(h) More performance contracts are signed.
(i) Retraining programmes are introduced.
(j) Law permitting liquidation of public sector units is adopted.
(k) 140 public sector units are referred to BFIR but not a single unit is closed.
(l) Report on privatisation is submitted in 1993.
(m) National Renewal Fund to bank roll worker rehabilitation is set up.
(n) National Renewal Fund is used for 60,000 workers in 40 public sector units.

Administration

Liberalisation cannot be implemented effectively unless bureaucratic bloat and legal labyrinths prosper, thwarting business.

The agenda of New Economic Policy regarding administration include:

(a) Freeze public sector recruitment for 3 years.
(b) Halve the number of ministers.
(c) Implement single - window clearance.
(d) Catalyse centre-state cooperation.
(e) Adopt advocacy system for coordination.
(f) Retrain bureaucrats for development.
(g) Amend Industrial Disputes Act.
(h) Amend P & T Act to legalise couriers.
(i) Amend urban land ceiling regulation Act.
(j) Clear redrafted companies Bill.
(k) Clear new Arbitration Bill.
(l) Simplify legal framework for small scale industries.
(m) Repeal Essential commodities Act.
(n) Prune the concurrent list.

The accomplishments in this direction include :

(a) Controller of capital Issues was abolished.
(b) Securities and Exchange Board of India was made statutory.
(c) External directors are nominated to Reserve Bank of India..
(d) Government staff strength is proved by 3.3 per cent.
(e) MRTP Act and FERA were amended.
(f) Indian Electricity Act was amended.
(g) National Highway Act was amended.
(h) Motor Vehicles Act was amended and enforced.
(i) Air Corporation Act was repealed.
(j) Multimodel Transportation Act was enacted.
(k) Coal Mines (Nationalisation) Act was amended.

(l) Mineral Exploration Act was amended.
(m) Rent Control Act, Delhi, Merchant Shipping Act and Banking Act were amended.[3]

Implementation of the new economic policy helped in increasing exports. Increase in exports resulted in increase in foreign currency reserves. Price level has been brought down. Though the central government has announcement the economic liberalisations, governments at the different levels particularly at the state level should implement the new economic policy effectively, state Governments have to provide basic infrastructure necessary for the industrial development and attract the industries (see Exhibit 6.2) The state of Andhra Pradesh has been striving hard to provide infrastructural facilities necessary for industrial development.

UNITED FRONT GOVERNMENT'S POLICY ON ECONOMIC REFORMS

Status and stance of various parties of united front government and reforms are presented in Exhibit 6.3

The major economic issues highlighted in the common Minimum programme of the political parties in the United Front Government include :

(a) reviewing all anti-poverty programmes and providing them with larger funds.
(b) introducing a special plan for infrastructure development to be taken up in 100 most backward and poorest districts.
(c) incorporating programme for guaranteeing 100 days of employment for every unemployed person to be implemented through panchayat Raj Institutions,
(d) maintaining a 12 per cent growth in industrial sector
(e) devising suitable credit and taxation policies for channelising bulk of investment, both domestic and foreign, into the core and infrastructure sectors.
(f) discouraging entry of multinational companies into low priority areas though suitable fiscal and other measures.
(g) earmarking need and capacity absorb to least $ 10 billion worth of foreign direct investment.
(h) to make the public sector undertakings strong and competitive
(i) establishing a disinvestment commission to advise the government on these steps.
(j) carrying out further reforms of the financial sector
(k) fiscal deficit to be brought down to 4 per cent of GDP.
(l) subsidies will be targeted for the really needy and poor.
(m) continuing the tax reforms, and
(n) strengthening of the public distribution system and barring the affluent sections of the society from its access.

Exhibit 6.4 Presents the economic reforms announced by the united front Government.

EXHIBIT : 6.2

Industrial Policy Reforms : Selected State Government Initiatives

Haryana

* Several steps taken to simplify procedures and ensure time bound clearances,
* Industrial Assistance Group as a single window services further extended to district level to ensure effective coordination among various government organisations.

3. Rohit Saran and Rukmini Parthasarathy, *'The Unfinished Agenda'*, Business Today, May 22– June 6, 1996 pp. 78-99.

* Powers to allot, transfer, lease, and rent industrial plots/sheds; sanction/disbursement of loans by Haryana Financial Corporation, sanction of electric load upto a certain limit-delegated to district level.
* Time bound clearance/sanctions encompassing all aspects – Project Approval (15 days), Registration as small unit (1day), NOC (no objection certificate) by State Pollution Board (15 days), allotment of plots/shed (10 days) from receipt of application.
* All sales tax barriers through the state removed.
* High level coordination committee set up to ensure all clearances within the stipulated time. An Empowered Group (including representatives from various organisations) set up to revamp administration.
* High Powered Committee set up to take spot decisions on foreign investments, NRI projects and 100 per cent export oriented projects.
* A state level grievance committee set up to address problems faced by entrepreneurs.
* Visits of inspectors has been streamlined and rationalised.

Kerala

* Several steps are proposed/have been undertaken for attracting more investments and for procedural/rules simplification.
* State Industrial Development Committee will be formed for ensuring speedy clearance of applications of new SSIs, within prescribed time limit, review and maintenance of good industrial relations and monitoring of industrial development activities.
* District Development Committee to be formed in each district.
* Industrial Relations Committee to be extended to all existing and potential industrial areas.
* A new Green Channel Scheme will be introduced for expediting all clearances and all unnecessary licensing and clearances will be abolished.
* An Industrial Infrastructure Development Authority will be established.
* A special cell will be created to coordinate activities relating to central projects.
* New units will be exempted from all state taxes for the first seven years.
* Investment subsidy will be increased to 15 per cent, with certain ceilings.

Orissa

* A nodal committee constituted at the state government level of clearance of proposals for providing infrastructural facilities and government assistance, and to recommend measures for rehabilitation of sick industrial units.
* The Foreign Investment Division in the Industrial Promotion and Investment Corporation of Orissa will act as a single window for investments by Non-Resident Indians and foreign investors.
* Nodal committees constituted at the district level to resolve local problems faced by entrepreneurs.

Punjab

* A new package of incentive to attract investments, avoid multiplicity of incentives and procedures, create new job opportunities and speedy clearance of new enterprises announced and made applicable from October, 1992. Steps undertaken/contemplated include :
* A committee constituted for providing 'land off the shelf'
* Udyog Sahayaka acting as a single window service for clearing projects.
* State government signed MOUs with selected industrial units to upgrade Industrial Training Institutes.
* Privatisation of Public Sector Units to be undertaken.
* Develop selected industrial corridors as part of infrastructural development. Use private initiative for infrastructure development, specially power.

* Procedures for providing credit by State Financial Institutions to be simplified. For promoting exports, foreign bank branches to be set up in Ludhiana.
* The state is formulating a policy to ensure granting of clearances for setting up industries within 24 hours of receipt of request.

Rajasthan

* Several steps taken for expanding and strengthening infrastructure, simplifying rules and procedures, ensuring speedy availability of inputs/clearances, increasing role of private sector, enhancing employment and investment.
* Power generation, telecom services, tourism and hotelling in the private sector encouraged.
* Enabling legislation put in place to allow private parties to collect tolls from roads/bridges constructed by them.
* Amendments made in rules relating to conversion and allotment of land for industrial purposes.
* 155 SSI industries exempted from obtaining No Objection Certificate from State Pollution Control Boards. Power to grant NOCs decentralised.
* Industries to be inspected under Factories Act reduced from 15 to 3. Common inspection in accordance with a checklist prepared for the purpose. Even simpler procedure for SSIs.

West Bengal

* State, wherever appropriate, welcomes foreign technology and investments.
* State recognises the importance and the key role of the private sector in accelerating growth.
* An Empowered Committee at the State level, under the Chairmanship of the Chief Secretary, to take quick decisions on investment proposals.
* The Single Window Agency of the West Bengal Industrial Development Corporation Ltd., strengthened to provide effective 'Escort Service' to new projects.
* Committees in each district formed under the Chairmanship of District Magistrates to ensure quick decisions on land, employment, and other related matters.
* Private sector investment in power generation encouraged to meet increased demand.

Source : Govt of India, Economic Survey 1994-95, Quoted in Aswathappa K, op.cit.

EXHIBIT 6.3

Status and Stance of various parties of

THE UNITED FRONT & THE REFORMS

PARTY	STATUS	STANCES
Janata Dal	Led by PM H.D. Deve Gowda, the Janata Dal wants to accelerate, But Ram Vilas Paswan and Sharad Yadav prefer the brakes	Strongly Pro
Tamil Manila Congress	In P. Chidambaram, the party has a champion of the reforms. But G.KMoopanar believes in protecting Indian industry	Strongly Pro
Dravida Munnetra Kazhagam	Closely connected with business, Industry Minister M.Maran supports the reforms. But he would prefer to support Indian Industry	Strongly Pro
Telegu Desam Party	Andhra Pradesh CM C.B. Naidu's thrust on the reforms, and Commerce Minister B. Rammaiah's business links provide a pro-reforms stance	Middlingly Pro

Communist Party of India	Agriculture Minister Chaturanan Mishra opposes the reforms, But his objections are not being articulated	Weakly Anti
Samajwadi Party	While Defence Minister Mulayam Singh is busy managing his political future, the party has not defined its stand on the reforms	Middlingly Anti
Communist Party Of India (Marxist)	Although outside the government, it is demanding curbs on the reforms despite the presence of moderates like Jyoti Basu and H.K. Surjeet.	Middlingly Anti
AGP; AIML; Cong-T; FB; MPVP; NC; RSP;	Bereft of any strong stand of their own, these minor constituents are throwing their weight behind Deve Gowda	Middlingly Pro

AGP : Asom Gana Parishad;AIML : All India Muslim League;FB :Forward Block
MPVP : Madhya Pradesh Vikas Party;NC: National Conference;RSP : Revolutionary Socialist Party

Source : Business Today, March 7-21, 1997, p. 77

EXHIBIT 6.4

Economic Reforms Announced by the United Front Government.

JUNE, 1996

- Austerity measures to save Rs 3,000 crore a year announced.
- FIPB restricted and brought under the Union Industry Ministry.
- Restrictions on the number of Euro-issues in a year by a corporate removed
- Administered prices of petrol, LPG, and diesel hiked.

JULY, 1996

- Non-statutory Insurance Regulatory Authority set up
- External Commercial Borrowings guidelines eased for infrastructure projects
- Foreign investment proposals taken out of CCEA's ambit
- Surcharge on corporate tax reduced from 15% to 7.5%
- Further reductions in excise and Customs duties
- Disinvestment Commission and Expenditure Commission proposed
- Draft committees for the revamp of the Companies and Income Tax Acts set up
- Infrastructure Development Finance Corporation constituted
- Foreign Investment Promotion Council set up

AUGUST, 1996

- Power Projects under Rs 1,000 crore exempted from CEA clearance

SEPTEMBER, 1996

- Exemption limit under Section 80–L of the Income Tax Act raised to Rs 15,000
- Capital gains tax on partnerships lowered from 30% to 20%
- Mutual funds dedicated to infrastructure made eligible for tax concessions
- Investment limits for FIIs in debt instruments removed

OCTOBER, 1996

- Private sector investment in port services permitted
- Ceiling on ECBs raised from $6 billion to $7.9 billion

NOVEMBER, 1996

- New Mining Policy announced
- Entertainment electronics industry delicensed

DECEMBER, 1996

- Automatic approval allowed for 74% foreign stake in 9 industries
- Automatic approval of 51% foreign equity allowed in 16 more industries

JANUARY, 1997

- Insurance Regulatory Authority Bill tabled
- New Aviation Policy announced
- Ordinance on decontrol of sugar exports issued
- Divestment of upto 74% in non-strategic and non-core PSUs cleared
- Infrastructure Development Finance Corporation registered
- Department of Telecommunications brought under TRAI's purview
- Telecom projects given infrastruture status
- Norms for selection of independent power producers eased
- Central Electricity Regulatory Commission constituted
- Private sector allowed into transmission of power
- Guidelines for private sector projects in roads and highways presented
- Legal hurdles in land acquisition for construction of highways cleared
- Independent regulatory authorities set up for major ports
- New Takeover Code approved
- Capital Gains Tax waived on shares of priority sector public undertakings
- FIIs allowed to investing government debt instruments
- Proprietary FII funds allowed to invest
- Interest on housing loans of over Rs 50,000 deregulated
- Partial deregulation of oil sector announced
- Petrochemicals units allowed to borrow from DFIs
- Plan for index-based futures cleared by Union Law Ministry
- Guidelines for non–automatic FDI approvals announced
- Gold import ceiling for non-resident Indians doubled to 10 kg
- Automatic FDI approvals announced
- Phase – out of quantitative list of imports by 2002 cleared
- National Environment Appellate Authority set up
- Approach paper to Ninth Five-year Plan approved

FEBRUARY, 1997

- Coal mining opened up to private sector, and coal-prices decontrolled
- Tariff Commission approved by CCEA
- Restructuring of 49 public sector units approved
- Investment ceiling for SSIs raised to Rs 3 crore; for tiny industries to Rs 25 lakh
- Imports of 69 consumer goods freed

- WTO pact of telecommunications signed
- Draft Broadcast Bill approved by CCEA
- Urea prices raised by 10%
- PDS prices of wheat, sugar, and rice hiked

ECONOMIC REFORMS AND THE BJP AND ITS ALLIES

The Bharatiya Janata Party and its allies have signed the "National Agenda of Governance. Closing the Gap between peoples' Aspirations and Government's performance" on 18th March 1998.

The key points of the Agenda are :

(a) Economic reforms will continue but the process will have a strong swadeshi thrust,
(b) Earmarking 60 per cent of plan funds for investment in agricultural and rural development,
(c) Farm subsidies to continue with modifications.
(d) Resuming public expenditure on infrastructure and
(e) Improving public distribution system and ensure price stability.

Action plan for the National Agenda of the BJP and its Allies :

Important measures announced by the Prime Minister in his agenda on 13 – point action plan are :

(a) Appointment of a commission to review within a stipulated time frame all administrative laws, rules and regulations governing industry and trade and outmoded laws are to be scrapped.
(b) National Housing Policy will be announced with in 60 days
(c) Schemes to mobilise investible funds from idle resources will be announced so on.
(d) Companies Act will be drastically over hauled.
(e) Replacement of existing FERA through legislation consistent with current needs.
(f) setting up of National Information Technology Task force.
(g) Government will substantially increase investment in infrastructure development and extend support for private sector investment here.
(h) Prime Minister's office will directly monitor all projects capitalised at more than Rs 100 crores each in power, roads, bridges, dams, irrigation, telecom, oil, railways etc. and also reduction in time and cost over run in projects particularly in the power sector.
(i) Steps to reduce current untenable level of NPAs of banks and financial institutions.
(j) Immediate steps to reforms in PSUs including restructuring, transparent, disinvestment and reducing losses.
(k) Government will formulate transparent, non-discriminatory, non-discretionary policies governing foreign direct investment.
(l) Foreign Investment promotion Board is to be empowered to approve or reject every proposal involving FDI within 60 day deadline.
(m) Introduce carefully calibrated approach towards globalization while depending on internal liberalisation.

CHAPTER 7

MAJOR MACRO POLICIES

Industrial Policy
Small Sector Industrial Policy
Foreign Trade Policy
Infrastructure Policy
Drug Policy

INDUSTRIAL POLICY

Industrial sector plays significant role in any economy. Industrial development / growth, its direction and structure influence the economic development and its direction. Direction, structure and growth of industrial development mostly are directed by the industrial policy issued by the Government from time to time.

The industrial scenario in India was quite discouraging at the time of attaining independence in 1947. The government called an industrial conference in December 1947 to improve the situation, remove the uncertainties in the minds of the investors and industrialists. The conference recommended for a clear-cut division of industries into public sector and private sector.

Industrial Policy Resolution, 1948

Industrial Policy Resolution, 1948 was the first policy resolution announced by the Government of India. The main features of the policy resolution were :

1. Acceptance of the importance of both private and public sectors

The policy resolution accepted the importance and due role of both private sector and public sector. The state expressed the view that, "the mechanism and resources of the state may not permit it to function forthwith in industry as widely as may be desirable." The resolution adopted a strategy of (i) expansion of the state sector in the areas where it was operating and in new lines of production and (ii) allowing the private sector to subsist and expand albeit under proper direction and regulation.

2. Division of Industrial sector

The policy resolution divided the industries into four categories viz., (i) state monopoly industries like arms and ammunition, atomic energy and rail transport.

(ii) Mixed sector where both state and private sectors have the role to play. The existing private sector industries were allowed to continue. The industries in this sector include coal, iron and steel, aircraft manufacture, ship building, manufacture of telephone, telegraph and wireless apparatus.

(iii) The field of Government control : This category contains 18 industries of national importance. These industries are run by the private sector but are regulated and controlled by the government. Some of the industries included in this category are automobiles, heavy chemicals, heavy machinery, machine tools, fertilizers, electrical engineering, sugar, paper, cement, cotton and woollen textiles.

(iv) The field of private enterprise : The industries which are not included in the first three categories are open for private sector.

3. Role of small and cottage industries

The policy emphasises on the small and cottage industries due to the importance and role played by them in providing employment.

4. Foreign capital

The role of foreign capital in industrial development was recognised by the policy. The policy stated that Indians should have a say in the ownership and management of the firms where foreign investment is necessary.

5. Labour-Management Relations

The policy emphasised on the need for sound labour-management relations.

This policy could not provide direction for industrial development for longer time due to the changing scenario in the country. Hence, the Government announced another policy in the year 1956.

Industrial Policy Resolution, 1956

The objectives of the Industrial policy Resolution, 1956 were :

(a) to accelerate the rate of growth and to speed up industrialisation (b) to develop heavy industries and capital goods industries (c) to expand public sector (d) to reduce disparities in income and wealth (e) to build up a large and growing cooperative sector, (f) to prevent monopolies and the concentration of wealth and income in the hands of a small number of individuals.

Features of the Industrial Policy Resolution, 1956

1. Division of Industries : Industries under this policy were divided into (a) monopoly of the state (b) Mixed sector of public and private sectors and (c) Industries left for private sector.
   (a) Monopoly of the state : This category included 17 industries. Only the state was allowed to establish and develop the industries in this category. They were grouped under five categories viz., defence, heavy industries, minerals, transport and communication and power. Industries in this category were referred to as industries listed in schedule A.
   (b) Mixed Sector : This category included 12 industries. State would establish new units in this category. Private sector was also allowed to setup new units and expand the existing units in this category.
   (c) Private Sector : Industries not covered in schedules A and B were included in this category. Private sector had full freedom to establish and expand the industries in this category. However, state was expected to provide necessary facilities to establish the industries of this category.
2. Inter dependence of public sector and private sectors : This policy emphasised that public and private sectors were not completely independent and they were mutually dependent on each other.
3. Assistance and control of private sector : The Government was expected to assist the expansion of private sector by participating in its risk capital and by providing various services. However, the private sector would remain within the regulations of the government.
4. Significance of small and cottage Industries : This policy recognised the importance and role played by the small and cottage industries.
5. Reduction of Regional imbalances : The policy called for the reduction of regional imbalances and achieve the balanced regional development through the industrialisation in less developed areas.
6. Technical and Managerial personnel : The policy recognised and emphasised the need for and importance of technical and managerial personnel to carry out the rapid industrialisation.
7. Industrial peace : The policy emphasised on the significance of industrial peace for rapid industrialization.

Industrial Policy Statement, 1977

Janata Government announced the policy statement in 1977.

The salient features of the policy included :

1. Small scale Industrial Sector : The main thought of the policy was on the development of small scale and cottage industries. The measures included : (a) Expanding the list of items reserved. (b) Establishment of 'District Industries Centres' to provide all kinds of facilities (c) Revamping khadi and village industries commission, (d) appropriate technology for small industries.
2. The statement limited the areas for large scale industries. They were : basic industries, capital goods industries, high technology industries etc.,
3. Big business houses : The policy statement imposed limitations on the big business houses including imposing ceiling on the production capacities.
4. Role of public sector : Public sector was encouraged to develop strategic industries, ancillary industries and transfer of technology.
5. Promotion of technological self reliance.
6. Labour-Management Relations : The policy statement emphasised on the increase in industrial production though maintaining labour-management relations.

Critical Analysis of Industrial Policy Statement, 1977

Since independence, our Government had announced two important industrial policy resolutions. One in 1948 and the other in 1956. The main feature of the 1948 Policy was that it bade good-bye to the policy of laisez-faire by imposing State Control in some areas. The 1956 resolution laid emphasis on public sector and large scale sector, due to which the country at present is in a comfortable position in terms of food-grain, exchange reserves, and technology. However, the economy today faces a bleak prospect in certain spheres, particularly employment situation, balanced regional and sectoral development, and reduction of income in equalities. The small industries (small-scale industries, tiny sector, cottage industry, village and Khadi industries etc.) also were not given a proper role to play.

Mr. George Fernandes, Union Minister for Industries, said that the 1956 Policy, full of "buts, nevertheless and however", had resulted in 30 million unemployed. In another few months, six million more unemployed would be joining the ranks. The policy, he said, was "everything to everybody" and did not give special attention to small scale units. The situation had necessitated the Janata Government to frame a new Industrial Policy putting "man in the centre of things."

Since the large scale industry has achieved a break through in various aspects of development, the emphasis given by the Government to small scale and tiny sector now is justifiable in the present economic environment.

'Tiny sector' is a new coinage of the Government for a policy to suit the rural needs, since a tiny unit requires less capital than a small-scale unit. The total investment in plant and machinery in the former does not exceed Rs. 1 lakh and it is to be located in a place having less than 50,000 population. The proposal for the tiny sector has been made because the bulk of the assistance meant for small-scale sector has been appropriated by the better organised small units.

In the past, there were several agencies and schemes to encourage small industries. But their performance shows that they have tended more to confuse the average small and rural entrepreneur than to encourage and help him. They have functioned more in isolation than in co-ordination with others, even in the same geographical area. The problems of small industries cannot be tackled with a fragmented approach. Hence the idea of constitution of District Industries Centres is rightly mooted by the Government.

Under the single roof of the DIC, all possible support required by small entrepreneurs will be provided, starting from investigation of the project to research and development. The DIC will get the various formalities expedited which will go a long way in fulfilling the objective of establishing industries in small towns and villages.

Besides the reservation to the small-scale sector, the large sector is given a clear role to play in some important areas to which it is best suited viz., basic industries, capital goods industries and high technology industries. However, future expansion of this sector will be guided by some principles so as to restrain them from disproportionate growth.

Another feature of the policy is that the public sector will act as a stabilising force in maintaining essential supplies as it provides a counterveiling power to the growth of large houses and encourages the development of a wide range of ancillary industries.

The Government has laid greater emphasis on the development of small industries which create more employment openings. A labour-rich and capital-scarce country, India should go for labour intensive industry.

The Annual Survey of Industry of the planning commission for 1975 highlighted the small scale and tiny sector's significant contribution to employment generation. The small industries account for one-third of the employment with only a 6.5 percent share in the industrial sector's total fixed capital. Those in the tiny sectors were responsible for 14 percent of the employment with no more than a 2 percent share of the total fixed capital.

Small industries employ indigenous technology; they are labour intensive and require low capital investment. Investment required to create one job in this sector ranges from Rs. 4,000 to 6,000; on the other hand, large scale industry requires Rs. 40,000 to Rs. 60,000. It shows that employment capital ratio is very high in small scale industries compared to large industries.

Another phenomenal point which highlights the significance of small industries is that, with the capital required for a single heavy industrial plant, two million hectares of land could be irrigated or 300 small agro-industries developed.

Besides this, the focal point of the development of small industries is effective decentralisation to achieve the objective of balanced regional development. By establishing small industries in villages, more jobs will be opened with additional source of income to the villagers. Moreover, the fruits of the development can be derived immediately with the setting up of small industries as they have a short gestation period.

For a long time, industrialisation had been inhibited by the small size of the market. The consumer goods sector as a whole is catering to hardly five million people at present. The new strategy is to bring about a diffusion of purchasing power, increasing the buying capacity of the villagers. The growing rural market would be a strong stimulant to industrial development.

Total industrial production in 1976 was Rs. 15,000 crores. The small scale sector alone produced in this goods worth Rs. 6,000 crores. According to the Small Industries Development Organisation, the number of small units during the period 1966-75 increased by 317 percent. One of the notable achievements of the small-scale sector was that, 750 of the 2,400 products produced by the units, were export-oriented. According to the Central Statistical Organisation, 75 percent of the factories are in the small-scale sector.

The new industrial policy will not only accelerate rural development and create millions of jobs but will also help the Government to tackle a number of problems faced by urban centres like immigration, pollution, and shortages of water supply, transport, sanitation and housing etc.,

No doubt, theoretically, the new policy is well suited to the needs of the country. But how far will it serve the purpose practically ? The small sector is still backward even after two decades of encouragement. The development of small industry on desired lines is not easy in a vast country like India. Several complex problems arise with the implementation of the new industrial policy. Doubts and criticisms on its various aspects are therefore voiced among different sections of the society.

Industrial circles allege that it is a hasty exercise in thinking, riddled with several contradictions. The policy talks bravely of the development of the small and tiny sectors without realising the effects of heavy reliance on them.

In fact, the Congress Government had considered a similar scheme four years ago, but it did not implement the idea probably because of lack of financial and administrative resources.

The development programme of the small-scale sector has not worked smoothly because of the apathy of the state Governments. Witness how several thousand bogus units came up only to avail themselves of the incentives offered by the Government. How then will the Government make sure that the tiny sector is used for genuine development ? Also we cannot afford to ignore the basic fact that the development of large industry has put the nation among the first ten industrially developed countries of the world.

In an age of rapid technological advancement it is further argued, labour intensive technology is ipso facto a lower type of technology. Perpetuation of labour intensive technology in a wide spectrum of production will, beyond a point, mean miscalculation of valuable resources. Small units at present are complaining that their products are priced out by the large-scale units and, therefore they should be given exemption in taxes and protection in all other aspects. If the Government abides by it, it ultimately leads to charging higher prices from consumers, and encouraging lower skills and lower levels of efficiency in production.

The Government has asked the large scale sector to depend increasingly on their internal resources for their future needs without leaning on the exchequer and banking system. This will create a lot of problems, particularly at a time when the large scale industries are badly in need of resources for their modernisation, replacement and revival from sickness. Moreover, this affects their profits and imposes limitations on the declaration of bonus and dividends, which hampers the market value of the shares.

The government's intention not to permit expansion in the weaving capacity of the organised and powerloom sector seems self-defeating for the objective of the policy. Cloth being an essential requirement must be produced at the lowest cost possible. Costs can be reduced only with the help of technological breakthroughs, possible only in large scale industries. Hence the reservation of mass consumption goods for small industry has no relevance. Even though the textile industry is labour intensive, the government denies it natural growth by freezing the capacity of the weaving sector, which will undoubtedly lead to sickness and stagnation. The capital-out-put ratio and capital-employment ratio of the footwear industry does not favour the small scale sector. So, there is a need to re-examine these issues.

Small industries cannot produce goods of higher quality at low costs as compared to large-scale industries. The consumers will suffer on both the counts. Workers and society as a whole may be at disadvantage with the development of small industries since the workers will be paid lower wages and society will have to sacrifice a part of the social gains in providing facilities and incentives to the small sector.

The new Industrial Policy did not make any reference to the medium sector which produces a substantial part of the total industrial output. The major problem is to find the entrepreneurship to form the nuclei of industrial development. Aiming at targets without providing infrastructural facilities and socio economic amenities is futile. The real problem is how best the government can mobilise funds in providing these. Reservation of certain areas of production for small industries shall not be viewed as a Government decision based on economic reasoning since 80,000 small units were reportedly sick in 1976 due to finance and marketing difficulties.

Undoubtedly small industries should be given encouragement but this should not imply further limitations on the largescale sector. Mere reservation will not by itself promote their growth. The Central Government should insist upon the State Governments to increasingly work for the success of this policy by giving them appropriate fiscal and monetary incentives. The Governments must ensure that if the small industries fail to come up to the expectations, the other sector must be allowed to make up the shortfall. Every effort should be made to enable small industries as a 'dynamic and go-ahead' sector instead of 'concession-seeking and over-protected' sector.

Experience shows that while capital intensive technology may not directly offer more jobs in the short-run, the very large output, achieved with the help of technology, creates a wide range of jobs in the small-scale, ancillary and services sectors in the long run. The policy of taking immediate and direct employment generated by a particular industry as criteria for framing the preferences, by neglecting the cumulative effects of large industry on employment, is highly deplorable.

Industrial Policy Statement 1980

The Congress (I) Government announced Industrial Policy Statement in 1980. The objectives of the statement included :

(i) Optimum utilisation of installed capacity.
(ii) Maximising production and enhancing productivity.
(iii) Correction of regional imbalances .
(iv) Strengthening of agricultural base.
(v) Development of export-oriented and import-substitution industries.
(vi) Development of infrastructural facilities.

The measures of the policies included :

(i) Effective operational system of management of public sector.
(ii) Integrating industrial development in the private sector by promoting the concept of economic federation.
(iii) Development of nucleus plants which would concentrate on assembling and act as ancillary units.
(iv) promotion of industries in the rural areas.
(v) Removal of regional imbalances.
(vi) Liberalisations of existing capacities.
(vii) Automatic expansion of industries.
(viii) State policy towards industrial sickness.

Industrial Policy, 1990

The Janata Dal Government has announced the new policy in 1990. The objectives of the policy were :

(i) to promote and develop small scale and agro-based industries.

(ii) to re-orient the industrial growth.

(iii) to disperse industries in rural and backward areas.

(iv) to increase the exports of small scale industries.

(v) to change the procedures for industrial approvals.

The policy raised the investment ceiling of small scale industries from Rs. 35 lakhs to Rs. 60 lakhs.

Industrial Policy Resolution, 1991

The Congress (I) Government led by P. V. Narasimha Rao announced its industrial policy on July 24, 1991.

The objectives of the policy include

Objectives : The prime objectives of the policy are to (i) undertake the Indian industrial economy from the cobwebs of unnecessary bureaucratic control (ii) to build on the gains already experienced. (iii) to correct the distortions / weaknesses involved in the system (iv) to introduce liberalisation measures in order to integrate Indian economy with the rest of the globe, and (v) to liberalize the domestic enterprises from the restrictions of MRTP Act.

Abolition of Industrial Licensing : The new industrial policy, 1991 abolished industrial licensing in order to free the industries from the hindrances of bureaucracy. The licensing was abolished for all the industries except for 18 Industries viz., (i) coal and lignite (ii) petroleum (other than crude) and its distillation products (iii) Distillation and brewing of alcoholic drinks (iv) Sugar (v) Animal fat and oils (vi) Cigars and cigarettes of tobacco and manufactured tobacco substitutes (vii) Asbestos and asbestos based products (viii) plywood and decorative veneers and other woodbased products (ix) Raw hides and skins, leather, charmois leather and patent leather (x) Tanned and dressed skins (xi) Motor car (xii) Paper and news print except bagasse based units (xiii) Electronic aerospace and defence equipment-all types (xiv) Industrial explosive (xv) Hazardous chemicals (xvi) Drugs and pharmaceuticals (xvii) Entertainment electronics (xviii) white goods such as domestic refrigerators, washing machines, microware ovens and air conditioners.

Public Sector's Role Diluted : The number of industries reserved for public sector has been reduced from 17 to 6. The industries reserved for public sector include : (i) arms and ammunition and allied items of defence equipment, defence aircraft and warships, (ii) atomic energy (iii) Coal and lignite (iv) mineral oils, (v) minerals specified in the schedule to the atomic energy and (vi) rail transport.

MRTP Limits Goes : Before 1991, the MRTP Commission used to grant approvals for MRTP firms case by case. The new policy states that the condition of MRTP firms is no longer required. These firms are now at par with other firms.

Foreign Investment and Foreign Technology

The new industrial policy prepared a specified list of high technology and high investment priority industries in which automatic permission is available for direct foreign investment upto

51% of foreign equity. Automatic permission is provided in respect of foreign technology agreements in high priority industry up to a sum of Rs. one Crore

Location Policy Liberalised

The new policy states that, no industrial approvals from the centre are required except for industries subject to compulsory licensing.

Abolition of phased manufacturing programmes : Phased manufacturing programmes have been in force in a number of engineering and electronic industries in order to force the space of indigenisation in manufacturing. The new policy abolished such programmes as there is no longer any need for enforcing the local content requirements.

Removal of Mandatory convertibility clause : The new policy provided for the convertibility of loans provided by the banks and financial institutions into equity.

SMALL SECTOR INDUSTRIAL POLICY

The Government announced its policy regarding the small sector on 6th August 1991. The main features of the policy are :

The small scale industrial sector has emerged as a dynamic and vibrant sector of the economy during the eighties. At the end of VII plan period, it accounted for nearly 35 % of the gross value of output in the manufacturing sector and over 40% of the total exports from the country. It also provided employment opportunities to around 12 million people.

The primary objective of the SSI policy during the nineties would be to impart more vitality and growth-impetus to the sector to enable it to contribute its mite fully to the economy, particularly in terms of growth of output, employment and exports.

Tiny Enterprises : Government. has already announced increase in the investment limits in plant and machinery of small scale industries, ancillary units and export oriented units to Rs. 60 lakhs, 75 lakhs and 75 lakhs respectively. Such limits in respect of Tiny enterprises increased from Rs. 2 lakhs to Rs. 5 lakhs, irrespective of locations of the unit.

❖ All industry related service and business enterprises, inrespective of their location, would be recognised as SSIs.

❖ Widen the scope of National Equity Fund scheme to cover projects upto Rs. 10 lakhs for equity support.

❖ Single window loan scheme has been on large for cover projects upto Rs. 20 lakhs with working capital margin upto Rs. 10 lakhs available only through State Financial Corporations and twin function Small Scale Industrial Development Corporations.

Financial Support Measures

1. Emphasis on subsidised/cheap credit (except for specific target groups) and efforts would be made to ensure both adequate flow of credit on a normative basis and the quality of its delivery, for viable operations of this sector.
2. Provide access to the capital market and to encourage modernisation and technological upgradation.

3. Allow equity participation by other industrial undertakings in the SSI. (not exceeding 24% of total shareholding) which will lead to boost of ancillarisation leading to expansion of employment opportunities.
4. Solving the problem of delayed payments by setting up of 'factoring' services through Small Industries Development Bank of India.
5. Network of services throughout the country operating through commercial banks.

Infrastructural Facilities

1. A Technology Development Cell (TDC) has been setup in the small Industries Development Organisation (SIDO) which would provide technology inputs to improve productivity and competitiveness of the products of the small scale sector.
2. TDC would coordinate activities of the Tool Rooms, Process-cum-Product Development Centres (PPDS) and would also interact with other industrial research and development organisations to achieve its objectives.
3. Ensuring adequacy and equitable distribution of indigenous and imported raw materials.

Marketing and Exports

1. National Small Industries Corporation (NSIC) would concentrate on marketing at mass consumption items under common brand name and organic links between NSIC and SSIDC's would be established.
2. SIDO has been recognised as the model agency to support the small scale industries in export promotion.

Modernisation, Technological and Quality Upgradation

1. Industry associations would be encouraged and supported to establish quality counselling and common testing facilities. Technology and markets would be established.
2. A reoriented programme of modernisation and technological up-gradation aimed at improving productivity, efficiency and cost effectiveness in the small scale sector would be pursued.
3. IITs and selected Regional / other Engineering colleges will serve as Technological Information, Design and Development Centres.

Promotion of Entrepreneurship

1. Government's continued support to first generation entrepreneur through training and its support in their efforts.
2. Large number of EDP trainees and motivators will be trained to significantly expand the EDP. they would also be encouraged to participate in this venture effectively.
3. Women entrepreneurs will receive support through special training programmes.

Village Industries : Handloom Sector

1. The policy of Government is to promote handloom to sustain employment in rural areas and to improve the quality of life for handloom wearers.

2. Janata cloth scheme which sustains weavers often on a minimum level of livelihood will be phased out by the terminal year of the VIII plan and replaced by the omnibus project package scheme under which substantial funds will be provided for modernisation, training, better designs, better dyes and marketing assistance.

Handicraft Sector : The key areas in handicrafts that could contribute towards a faster pace of rural industrialisation are production and marketing. Schemes for training and design development and for production and marketing assistance will be given encouragement.

Other Village Industries

1. Government recognises the need to enhance the spread of rural and cottage industries towards the stepping up of non-farm employment opportunities.
2. The activities of Khadi & Village Industries Commission and the state Khadi and Village Industries Boards will be expanded and the organisations strengthened to discharge their responsibilities more effectively.
3. The programmes of intensive development of Khadi and Village Industries through area approach with tie-up with DRDA, TRYSEM and ongoing developmental programmes relating to weaker sections like SC,s, STs and women would be extended throughout the country.

Mr. Yashwant Sinha, while presenting the 1998-99 budget had proposed certain initiatives to tackle the credit problems of SSI Sector.

1. At present, for SSI units having aggregate working capital requirements upto Rs. 2 crores, the working capital limit is determined by the banks on the basis of a simple calculation of 20% of their annual turnover. This facility is being doubled to Rs. 4 crores. This will ease the flow of bank credit to SSI.
2. To moderate the cost of credit to SSI units, Reserve Bank of India will advise the banks to accord SSI units with a good track record, the benefit of lower spreads over the prime lending rate.
3. Enhanced process would be delegated to bank managers of specialised SSI branches to ensure that most credit proposals are decided at the branch level.
4. At present SIDBI is a subsidiary of IDBI and IDBI is the major shareholder of SFCs. To equip SIDBI to play its apex role in SSI credit provision more effectively, SIDBI will be delinked from IDBI and IDBI shareholding in SFCs will be transferred to SIDBI.
5. SSI units are often handicapped by delays in the settlement of their dues from larger companies. To tackle this problem, RBI was asked to strengthen the existing mechanisms available to SSI for discounting of bills.
6. RBI will also modify its guidelines to commercial banks on credit appraisal to give greater weight to the amount of overdue outstandings that large units have in respect of SSI supplier.

New Small-sector Industrial Policy

The new small-sector industrial policy is called 'Policy Measures for promoting and strengthening small, Tiny and Village Enterprises'. The salient features of the policy are :

1. De-regulation, de-bureaucratisation and simplification of rules, regulations and procedures in connection with the establishment and maintenance of small scale industrial units.
2. Increase of investment limit in fixed capital of 'Tiny sector industrial units' Rs. 2 lakhs to Rs. 5 lakhs.

3. Recognition of industry related services and business enterprises within small scale industries with investment upto Rs. 5 lakhs.
4. Arrangement of continuous flow of credit. Improvement of quality and delivery of products of small scale units.
5. Establishment of a special monitoring agency to look after the genuine credit needs of the small scale sector.
6. Arrangement of enactment of a legislation to ensure prompt payment of small industries bills.
7. Introduction of a scheme of integrated infrastructural development for small scale industries.
8. Setting up of a Technology Development cell in Small Industries Development organisation for providing technology inputs.
9. Development of market for the products produced by small scale sector.
10. Establishment of Export Development Centre in small Industries Development Organisation.
11. Introduction of limited partnership Act. The purpose of this act is to limit the financial liability of new and inactive / sleeping partners and to allow foreign capital upto 24 percent.

FOREIGN TRADE POLICY

Importance of Foreign Trade for a Developing Economy

Before independence the pattern of India's foreign trade was typically colonial. India was a supplier of foodstuffs and raw materials to the industrialized nations and an importer of manufactured goods. This did not permit industrialisation at home. With the attainment of independence, the colonial pattern of trade had changed to meet the needs of a developing economy. An economy which decides to embark on a programme of development is required to extend its production at a faster rate. It has to import machinery and equipment which cannot be produced in the initial stages at home are essential These imports of machinery and equipment for increasing the production capacity are called developmental imports. Secondly, a developing country which sets in motion the process of industrialisation at home, requires the imports of raw materials and intermediate goods so as to properly utilise the capacity created in the country. Imports which are made in order to make a full use of the productive capacitiy are called maintenance imports.

India's Trade Policy

Advanced countries like Germany, U.S.A. and others used their trade policy to (a) restrict their imports and provide a sheltered market for their own industries so that they could develop rapidly. (b) Promote their exports so that their expanding industries could secure foreign markets. India did not have a clear cut trade policy before Independence, though some type of import restriction was adopted since 1923 to protect few domestic industries against a foreign competition. It was only after Independence that a trade policy, as part of the general economic policy of development, was formulated by India.

Main Features of India's Trade Policy

On import side : India has been in a disadvantageous position vis-a-vis advanced countries which are capable of producing and selling almost every commodity at low prices. This meant India could not develop any industry without protecting it from foreign comptetion. Since Independence, the Government of India has broadly restricted foreign completion through a judicious use of import licensing, import quotas, import duties and in extreme cases even banning on import of specific goods. The Mahalanobis strategy of economic development through heavy industries called for (a) banning or keeping to the minimum import of non-essential consumer goods (b) comprehensive control of various items of imports (c) liberal import of machinery, equipment and other developmental goods to support heavy industries based economic growth (d) favourable climate for the policy of import-substitution. Mahalanobis strategy was strengthened by the serious foreign exchange crisis which India faced in 1956-57 and government lightened import controls as well as foreign exchange controls.

On the export side : In the Indian contest trade policy does not consist only of import restrictions but of export promotion as well. To pay for its essential imports and to minimise dependence on foreign countries, export expansion becomes very essential. The vigorous export promotion was emphasized after the second plan to earn foreign exchange to overcome the acute foreign exchange crisis. In the 1970's the importance of export promotion was again emphasised because of mounting debt service obligations and the goal of self-reliance.

Phases of India's Trade Policy

Five distinct phases in India's trade policy can be noted.

I Phase (upto 1951-52) : India liberalized imports on account of restrictions imposed by UK on the utilisation of sterling balances. Our balance of payments with the dollar area was heavily adverse. An effort was made to screen imports from hard currency areas and boost exports so as to bridge the gap. This necessiated India to devaluate rupee in the year 1949.

II Phase : (1952-53 to 1956-67) : Liberalisation of foreign trade was adopted as the goal of trade policy. An effort was made to encourage exports by relaxing exports control, reducing export duties etc., Liberalisation led to tremendous increase in imports but exports did not rise. Consequently there was fast deterioration in our foreign exchange reserves. This necessiated a reversal of trade policy.

III Phase : A very restrictive import policy was adopted. On the other hand vigorous export promotion drive was launched. In addition to the export of traditional items export of newer items was also encouraged. Import substitution industries were also encouraged.

IV Phase : The phase started after the devaluation of the rupee in June 1966. During this period trade policy attempted to expand exports and strangely liberalized imports too. During this phase the recommendations of moduliar committee (1962) were implemented.

V Phase : (1975-76 onwards) : Government adopted a policy of import liberalisation with a view to encourage export promotion.

India's Foreign Trade Policy (1991)

The first major liberalisation was done by Rajiv Gandhi Government. As a result, in the four years from 1986-89 to 1989-90 exports surged forward and this period witnessed a record average annual growth of 17 percent in dollar terms. Unfortunately this declined to 9 per cent in 1990-91 and to only 4.4 % in 1991. So government made major reforms which are as bellow :

1. Rep will become the principal instrument for export related imports. It is called Exim-scrip and can be freely traded.
2. All exports will have a uniform Rep rate of 30% of f.o.b. value.
3. The new Rep scheme gives maximum incentives to exports whose import intensity is low.
4. All supplementary licenses shall stand abolished except the case of small scale sector and for producers of life saving or shipment.
5. All additional licences granted to export houses shall stand abolished.
6. The exim policy contains a category known as unlisted OGL. This category stands abolished and all items falling under this category may be imported only through the red scheme.
7. Advance licensing has been an alternative to the rep route for obtaining imports for exporters.
8. In three years time the objective was to remove all import licencing for capital goods and raw materials.
9. The goal of government is to decanalise all items except those that are essential.
10. The financial institutions are allowed to trade in exim scrips.

A new package of incentives was given for export oriented units and export promotion zones. They were

1. The basic rate at which exim scrips were to be issued against exports was 30% of FOB value.
2. An additional exim-scrip entitlement-of 10 percentage points was given in addition to 30% to products such as value added agricultural products.
3. The EOUs and EPZ units, exim scrips at 30% of NFE were given.
4. Exim scrips has to be issued only after export procedure has been realised with in 48 hours of the receipt of application.
5. Procedure for Advance licenses has been simplified.
6. The number of documents accompanying Advance license applications has been reduced from 9 to 3.

New Trade Policy

The main features of the new trade policy are :

(i) Free Imports and Exports : The importers are broadly grouped into (i) actual users for industrial and non-industrial products, (ii) Exporters and (iii) Others. As far as licenses are concerned, they are categorised into (i) Open general licence (ii) Automatic licence (iii) Supplementary Import Licence and (iv) Imports through government-owned canalised agencies. The policy publishes the negative list of items which does not fall under Open General Licence. All the goods and commodities which are not published in the negative list can be imported. The negative list of imports consists of (i) Prohibited items (ii) restricted items and (iii) canalised items.

Exhibit 7.11 presents the objectives and Highlights of Export-Import policy 1992-97 and Exhibit 7.2 presents new economic policy 1997-2002.

Decanalisation : The 1992-97 Policy decanalised imports of a number of items including newsprint, non-ferrous metals, natural rubber, intermediates and raw materials for fertilisers.

However, 8 items viz., petroleum product fertilisers, edible oils, cereals etc., are to be canalised.

Facilities to EOUs and EPZs : The 1992-97 Policy seeks to provide higher benefits to 100 per-cent Export Oriented Units (EOUS) and units in Export processing Zones (EPZs) compared to those exporting among the Domestic Tariff Area (DTA). The EOUS and unit in EPZs dealing with broad agro-based products can sell 50% output in the DTA.

Trading Houses : Export houses and trading houses are allowed by 1991 policy to import a wide range of items. These houses were provided with the benefit of self certification under the advanced licence system under the 1992-97 trade policy.

Export promotion capital goods scheme : The Export promotion capital goods scheme (EPCG) had only one window with a concessional customs duty rate of 15% with export obligation. Under the simplification scheme of 1994-95 third party exports were permitted. Service sector is placed at par with the supply of goods by the 1995-96 policy.

Export scheme for the service sector : Trading in service sector plays a vital role particularly in developing countries like India. In view of this vital role, a new scheme 'Export scheme for the service sector' has been introduced. Under this scheme professionals are allowed to import capital goods at a concessional duty rate of 15 percent.

Duty Exemption Scheme Enlarged : Under the enlarged duty exemption scheme, imports are provided at two concessional rates of 15 % and 25%. A choice to opt for advance import licences under the duty exemption scheme with under quality based or value based norms have been given to the exporters.

Deemed Exports : A number of benefits were offered for deemed exports in the 1992-97 policy. These benefits include duty exemption scheme, duty drawback schemes, exemption from terminal excise duty and special import licences. Suppliers in key infrastructural sectors, and local manufacturers supplying to duty free licence holders are given deemed exporter status.

Rupee Depreciation and Convertibility

Indian Rupee was devalued against US $ several times. The important among them are in 1966, 1975 and 1991.

(i) *Partial Convertibility of Rupee :* Liberalised Exchange Rate Mechanism System was announced by the Government in 1992-93. A dual exchange rate was fixed under this system. Under this system 40% of foreign exchange earnings were to be surrendered at the official exchange rate and the remaining 60 per cent were to be converted at a market determined rate.

(ii) *Full convertibility on Trade Account:* Full convertibility of Rupee on trade account was introduced in 1993 - 94 budget. The full conversion was extended for merchadise trade transactions and for all receipts, but not all payments.

(iii) *Full convertibility on current Account :* Full convertibility on current account refers to the freedom to buy or sell foreign exchange for the international transactions like (i) all payments due in connection with foreign trade, business including services, and normal short term banking and credit facilities (ii) Payments like interest on loans, income on other investments (iii) Payments on moderate amount of amortisation of loans or for depreciation of direct investments and (iv) moderate remittances for family living expenses. The Reserve Bank of India in February 1994 announced liberalisations on invisible transactions like Exchange Earner's Foreign Currency Accounts, basic travel quota, studies abroad, gift remittances, donations, payments of certain services by foreign parties.

Exhibit 7.1 The Objectives and Highlights of Export-Import Policy, 1992-97

The objectives of the policy are :

(a) To establish the framework for globalisation of India's foreign trade;

(b) To promote the productivity, modernisation and competitiveness of Indian industry and thereby enhance its support capabilities;

(c) To encourage the attainment of high and internationally accepted standards of quality and thereby enhance the image of India's products abroad;

(d) To augment India's exports by facilitating access to raw materials, intermediaries components, consumable and capital goods from the international market;

(e) To promote efficient and internationally competitive import substitution and self reliance under a deregulated framework for foreign trade;

(f) To eliminate or minimise quantitative, licensing, and other discretionary controls in the framework of India's foreign trade;

(g) To foster the country's Research and Development (R&D) and technological capabilities; and

(h) To simplify and streamline the procedures governing exports and imports.

Highlights of the Policy

The highlights of the policy are :

(i) Units undertaking the export of their entire production of goods may be set up under the Export Oriented Unit (EOU) scheme or Export Processing Zone (EPZ) scheme.

(ii) Permit the EOU/EPZ units to freely import capital goods, raw materials and allied inputs, photo-types and material handling equipment, provided these are not listed in the Negative List of Imports.

(iii) Permit EOU/EPZ units to export goods through Export House/Trading House/Star Trading House.

(iv) EOU/EPZ units shall be entitled to :

(a) Concessional rent,

(b) Concessional plot,

(c) Tax holidays,

(d) International price reimbursement for supply of iron and steel, and

(e) 100% foreign equity.

(v) All goods to be exported without any restriction except those in the Negative List of Exports.

(vi) Export contracts to be denominated in freely convertible currency.

(vii) Personal baggage of Indian passengers to be exported along with the passengers. If unaccompanied, to be exported within one year before or after the departure of the passengers.

(viii) Goods of the value exceeding Rs. 3,000 not be exported as a gift.

(ix) Merchant and manufacturer exporters and trading companies, Export Oriented Units (EOUs) and units located in Export Processing Zones (EPZs) are recognised Export housed, Trading Houses or Star Trading Houses.

(x) Export Houses/Trading Houses/Star Trading Houses shall have validity for a period of three years.

(xi) Export Houses/Trading Houses/Star Trading Houses shall be entitled to special import licences for the import of items included in the Negative List of Imports.

(xii) Export Promotion Councils to function as professional bodies and would be autonomous. Monetary or fiscal support of the government would depend upon

a) Effective discharge of their functions :

b) Democratisation of their membership; and

c) Timely audit of their accounts.

xiii) Encourage the manufacturers and exporters to attain internationally Accepted standards of quality for their products.

(xiv) To extend support and assistance to trade and industry associations to launch a nationwide programme on quality awareness.

(xv) Recognise and award manufacturers who have acquired the ISO 9000 (series) or to BIS 14000 (series) or any other internationally recognised equivalent certification of quality.

(xvi) Assist in the modernisation and upgradation of test houses and laboratories in order to bring them on part with international standards.

(xvii) Deemed exemption scheme;

(a) Duty exemption scheme;

(b) Duty drawback scheme;

(c) Return of terminal excise duty;

(d) Special import licences.

The new exim policy needs to be appreciated for its thrust on simplification, debureau cratisation, export promotion, quality improvement, globalisation, and above all for its five-year tenure. It is hoped that the new policy will go a long way in boosting our exports.

Source : K. Aswathappa, *op. cit.*, pp. 280-282.

Exhibit 7.2 New Exim Policy for 1997-2002

The new 5-years Export and Import Policy for the period 1997-2002 aims at giving a major thrust to acceleration of India's exports through restructuring and revamping of various export promotion schemes and wide ranging measures for simplification and streamlining of procedures with a view to making them more transparent and easy to administer. The Policy, which will be co-terminus with the 9th Plan (1997-2002), aims at consolidating the achievements made possible during the preceding 5-years Exim Policy for 1992-97, while continuing the process of trade reforms and trade liberalisation with a view to achieving a higher rate of export growth. Unveiling the Policy at a press conference recently, the Commerce Minister, Dr. B. B. Ramaiah, said that the new Exim Policy focused on the need to allow the exporters to concentrate on the manufacture and marketing of their products globally in an environment unhindered by discretionary controls and procedural bottlenecks. The Policy aims at enabling the industry to enhance its competitiveness in the global market and to achieve its full, potential in the areas of its strength. Stating that he had close interaction with the Finance Minister in formulating these policy and procedural changes, Dr. Ramaiah said that his Ministry has been assured by the Revenue Department that Customs notifications to give effect to various provisions of the new Exim Policy were being issued simultaneously, wherever required.

Significant changes have been made to reduce the multiplicity of various export promotion schemes and to improve the attractiveness of such schemes. Instead of the number of schemes contained in the earlier policies to facilitate easy access to inputs required for export production such as the Quantity-Based Advance Licence, Value-Based Advance Licence (VABAL), Special Value-Based Advance Licence for electronics engineering, ready-made garments, pharmaceuticals, etc. and the Pass Book Scheme, the new Exim Policy has only two schemes, *viz.*, Advance Licensing Scheme (corresponding to the quantity-based advance licence) and the new scheme known as Duty Entitlement Pass Book (DEPB) Scheme. This entitlement would enable the exporters to import inputs required for export production duty free. He can also make use of this credit to import any freely importable item and such credit can be transferred but will be valid within the same port. This new scheme incorporates the concept of the old Pass Book but with simplified procedures and greater coverage and transparency in the matter of giving credit entitlements. The scheme respectively covers manufacturers, exporters and merchant-exporters.

Under the Export Promotion Capital Goods (EPCG) Scheme, duty on capital goods has been reduced from 15 percent to 10 percent. Under the zero duty EPCG scheme, the threshold limit for zero duty imports has been reduced from Rs. 20 crores to Rs. 5 crores for agricultural and allied sectors.

In a major boost to the agro-sector, double weightage will be given for agro exports in calculating the eligibility for Export House, Trading House status etc. and 1 percent additional Special Import Licence (SIL) on total value of exports will be given for export of fruits, vegetables, floriculture and horticulture products if such exports constitute 10 per cent of total exports. Export Oriented Units (EOUs)/Export Processing Zones (EPZs) in agriculture and allied sectors can now sell 50 per cent of their output in the domestic tariff area (DTA) on payment of duty without stipulation of any value-addition condition.

Deemed export benefits have been extended to oil and gas sectors in addition to the power sector. In a bid to encourage domestic sourcing of inputs, domestic manufacturers supplying against export promotion capital goods (EPCG) licences will be entitled now for deemed export drawback facility. In case of supply to zero duty EPCG licence holder, the domestic supplier will be entitled to import raw materials duty-free under the Special Imprest Licence.

In order to promote export of gold jewellery, the number of nominated agencies permitted to stock gold has been increased, whereas at present this is being done only by MMTC, STC, SBI and HHEC under the gem & jewellery replenishment (REP) scheme, third party exports have been allowed so that small exporters are able to sell their products in the international market and can claim REP licences based on disclaimer certificate from the third party. Another significant feature is that the facility of bulk licence for import of rough diamonds has been further liberalised to enable the bulk licence holder to import from any source and not necessarily from the Diamond Trading corporation, London, as hitherto. Further, EOU/EPZ units in the gem and jewellery sector will be permitted to sell 10 per cent of their output in the TA on payment duty.

Special Import Licence (SIL) on export of products of small-scale industries (SSIs) has been increased from 1 per cent to 2 per cent. As a special incentive for export of SSI products or products from North Eastern states, additional SIL of 1 per cent on total value of exports will be given to Export Houses, Trading Houses, etc., where such exports from the North Eastern states constitute 10 per cent or more of their total exports. Additional SIL will also be given for exploration of new markets.

In keeping with the objective of promoting quality standards for enhancing global competitiveness of Indian exports, the special import licence entitlement of exporters holding ISO 9000 or IS/ISO 9000 certification has been increased from 2 per cent to 5 per cent.

In the software sector, where India has a distinct competitive advantage, software units are being allowed to undertake exports using data communication links or in the form of physical exports through the courier service also. Further, software units will be permitted on-line communications of DTA sales. Software can use a computer system for commercial training and such units will also be allowed to import goods on loan from clients for specified period.

Existing eligibility criterion for recognition as Export House / Trading House / Star Trading House / Super Star Trading House based on average annual export performance of the preceding 3 years has been revised from Rs. 10 crore, Rs. 50 crore, Rs. 250 crore and Rs. 750 crore respectively to Rs. 20 crore, Rs. 100 crore, Rs. 500 crore and Rs. 1,500 crore respectively keeping in mind the target of exports to be achieved by the turn of the century in order to increase the country's share at the global market and the fact that such status holders contribute nearly 60 to 70 per cent of the country's total exports.

As part of the move towards further liberalisation and globalisation so as to meet the challenge of global competition, the Negative List has been pruned as in the earlier Exim Policies. 542 restricted items have been transferred from Restricted List to the Special Import Licence and the freely importable list.

In order to fully address concerns being expressed about dumping, institutional mechanism and safeguard provisions for anti-dumping are also being strengthened. Out of the total number of 41 petitions received during the period 1992-93 to 1996-97 investigations in 22 cases were initiated of which 11 cases have been finalised so far; and in 11 more cases preliminary findings were completed.

In the area of procedural simplification, the number of documents prescribed has been drastically reduced, repetitive nature of information sought in every application has been dispensed with and application forms have been greatly streamlined so as to elicit only the barest essential information required for giving exporters the benefit of various Exim Policy schemes. Counter Assistance System in the DGFT Headquarters and all Regional Licensing Offices are being further strengthened so that there is no delay in processing applications under different Exim Policy schemes. Delegation of powers to Development Commissioners of the EPZ/EOU/Hardware Technology Parks (HTP)/ software Technology Park (STP) schemes will enable decision-making within 15 days at the Development Commissioners' level. Norms for disposal of scraps and rejects in EOU/EPZ schemes have been simplified. Financial powers of regional licensing authority for issue of licence where input-output norms have already been fixed and for issue of EPCG licences have been enhanced so that parties can get the facilities at the nearest point.

Work in all offices of DGFT will be computerised by September 1997 to facilitate computer-based on-line processing of all applications, receipts and issues under export promotion schemes, the facility of submitting application on floppy in all DGFT offices would be operational by 1 October 1997 which would help in the speedy disposal of applications. From 1 January 1998, licence/applications can be filed through the computer network in DGFT offices on E-mail. The application format has been simplified to eliminate submission of information repeatedly, thereby cutting delays and paperwork. The Minister said that in response to urgings of the trade and industry for a Green Channel facility for clearance of export and import consignments by Customs, the Commerce Ministry had recommended that this facility should be extended to all status holders and manufacturer-exporters with a good track record and indicated that guidelines in this regard would shortly be finalized by the Department of Revenue.

Overall, interface with the DGFT has been reduced considerably. For instance, the export obligation period under advance licence has been increased from 12 months to 18 months and similarly, validity of the advance licence has been enhanced from 12 months to 18 months so that the exporter gets more time for exports and imports with a greater degree of automaticity without coming to DGFT for such purposes.

The Minister said that the Exim Policy had attempted a micro-management approach while ensuring that the Policy environment at the macro level was made liberal and free. He said the process of implementing commodity-specific measures would be strengthened further to give the required thrust to the country's exports.

Source : Foreign Trade- Trends and Tidings, April 1997, pp. 16-17.

INFRASTRUCTURE POLICY

The prosperity of a country depends directly upon the development of agriculture and industry. Agricultural production, however, requires power, credit, transport facilities, etc., Industrial production requires not only machinery and equipments but also skilled labour, man-power, management, energy, banking facilities, marketing facilities, transport services which include railways, roads and shipping, communication facilities, etc., All these facilities and services constitute objectively the infrastructure of all economy and the development and expansion of these facilities are all essential pre-condition for increasing agricultural and industrial production in a country.

In the words of Dr. VKRV Rao, "The link between infrastructure and development is not once for all affair. It is a continuous process; and process in development has to be preceded, accompanied and followed by process in infrastructure, if we are to fulfil our declared objectives of a self-accelerating process of economic development."

Infrastructure is a word which encompasses the entirety of a nation. Infrastructure includes:

1. Energy : Electricity, Coal, Oil and non-conventional sources.
2. Transport : Railways, Roads, Shipping and Civil Aviation.
3. Communication : Post and Telegraphs, Telephones and Telecommunications.

Growth of Infrastructure

The basic infrastructure services in India have until recently been provided by public monopolies and quasi monopolies. Now this sector has been opened to the private companies to develop the infrastructure in India. With the entry of private companies the growth of infrastructure has been at a faster pace.

ENERGY

Energy is the most important determinant of a country,s economic growth. There is a direct correction between the degree of economic growth, the size of per capita income and per capita consumption of energy.

Energy is created through several sources.

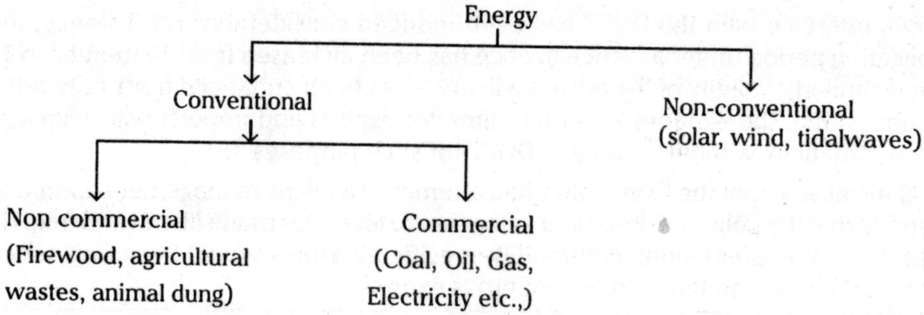

The energy is divided into two:

1. Conventional 2. Non-conventional

Conventional is divided into two – commercial and non-commercial

Commercial energy is so called as it commands a price and the user is expected to pay for its use. Non commercial energy commands no price (theoretically).

Non conventional energy is a recent discovery and its use is confined to limited pockets in our country.

The different types of commercial energy are –

Coal: It is the main source, accounting for 67 percent of the total energy consumed in this country.

Power : There are two modes of generating power – 1. Thermal 2. hydel. The total power generation in 1993-94 stood at 323.5 billion kwh. Power has been bugbear of our economy. Lack of sufficient power supply has checked the growth of industries all over the country.

To meet the future demands Government has given 5 years tax Holiday for new power projects. It has also allowed private companies develop new power plants in India. Exhibit 7.3 presents power sector reforms.

Oil : The wheels run with oil (petrol, diesel etc) without which the whole economy would come to stand-still.

As part of ongoing economic reforms government has allowed imports and distribution of certain petroleum products like domestic LPG and kerosene by private sector. Private and foreign companies are allowed to invest in oil exploration and production in joint ventures with ONGC or OIL.

Exhibit 7.3: Power sector reforms

THE ENERGY SUMMIT held in Chennai last week under the aegis of the confederation of Indian Industry (CII) focused attention on some worrisome features of the so-called 'reform process' in the energy sector. Ambitious power generation targets visualised in the Five Year Plans have not been matched by achievements. During the Eighth Plan period, the capacity addition was far short of the revised target of 30,000 MW. Resource constraints do not adequately explain the disappointing performance. Free supply of power has become a politically competitive and sensitive issue among the states and few have the will to take a realistic stand on pricing electricity for different categories of consumers. Without proper pricing, the State Electricity Boards (SEBs) and other power generating agencies are unlikely to regain their financial health.

The Central law envisaging regulatory outfits to determine the power tariff was indeed a bold step but most states are still dragging their feet on restructuring their generation and distribution systems. Private investors find the situation understandably 'frustrating' despite the ministerial assurances that the reform process is the place. The summit has served to highlight their problems. While the private sector has to play an effective role in the creation of additional power generation and distribution capacities in the country, inordinate delays in clearances will only drive the investors away to more lucrative areas.

Given the incentives, foreign investment in the power sector may increase substantially in the years ahead, During the Eighth Plan period, the private sector's share in power generation showed a marked increase. If the projects in the pipeline are completed soon, the private sector's share will increase further in the Ninth Plan. It is unfortunate that bureaucratic delays have led to cost and time over-runs in several key projects. Unless the thermal and hydel power mix is improved, the power generation utilities will be faced with an acute shortage in meeting the peak demand. For this the hydel resources should be harnessed more effectively to raise their share in power generation. But this is easier said than done.

Inronically, although Chennai and its neighbourhood continue to experience persistent power cuts disrupting normal life, both the Tamil Nadu Cheif Minister, Mr. M. Karunanidhi, and the Union Power Minister, Mr P. R. Kumaramangalam, have held out high hopes for the future. Tamil Nadu plans to double its existing power generating capacity to meet the projected demand of 13,000 MW in less than a decade from now. The Central power agencies are expected to add 6,000 MW. The prospect of surplus power in Tamil Nadu will be a major incentive to private investors. But restructuring of the overmanned SEB to cope with the emerging situation is still way off. Also the process of setting up the electricity regulatory agency is yet to be completed.

As the independent power producers and foreign financial institutions continue to insist on 'guarantees' and 'escrows' to cover their investment risks – they seem to overdo it on some 'hypothetical' considerations – the Centre should expeditiously issue appropriate guidelines to give more teeth to the contracts. There is also the urgency to cut the high transmission and distribution losses to the SEBs, estimated at over Rs . 11,000 crores. Such huge losses have further strained the resources of the SEBS. Firm steps are needed to cut these losses and for the reforms to be effective. For competition to be meaningful, power should be reasonably priced and supplied to the consumer. That is the message of the summit.

Source : The Hindu Dated November 16, 1998.

Transport

If agriculture and industry are regarded as the body and the bones of the economy, transport and communication constitute its nerves. Transport system helps to broaden the market for goods and by doing so, it makes possible large-scale production through division of labour.

Railway : The most important form of transport system in India is the Indian Railways, which is also the country's largest single undertaking. The Indian railways consist for an extensive network spread over 62,462 km.

Road : India is essentially an agrarian economy and roads constitute a critical element in the transportation infrastructure. Road construction and maintenance generate sizable employment opportunities. Indian planners, accordingly, gave considerable significance to rapid expansion of roads.

Shipping : India has a vast coast line and there are 10 major ports and 139 minor ports. Indian shipping accounts for only one percent of total world fleet.

Civil aviation : Air transport has a significant role to play in a vast country like India with major industries and commercial centres located far apart. In recent years important policy decisions have been to speed up the development of civil aviations.

Other transport are inland water transport etc.,

Communications

The communication system comprises posts and telegraphs, telecommunications systems, broadcastings, televisions, Internets, and information services. The communication system helps to bring the buyers and sellers together effectively and help accelerate the growth of economy.

Telecommunications is a vital input for global competition and for India's success in the international market. It is important not only because of its role in bringing the benefits of communication to every corner of India but also in solving the new policy objectives of improving the global competitiveness of the Indian economy and stimulating and attracting foreign direct investment.

Infrastructure is important in present context as it is becoming a tiny world. If India wants to complete with the world, it has to improve the infrastructure.

Road Sector Policy

Road sector policy include :

(i) Abolition of 'pathkar' by all states and octroi by many to reduce overall transit time and to help free flow of traffic.

(ii) to invite private individuals to invest in road construction and development.

(iii) Collection of basic 5% tax on petrol and diesel for road maintenance and development. It is estimated that the income from this source would be Rs. 2,000 crores per year.

(iv) Private parties can construct and develop roads on Build, Operate and Transfer (BOT) basis. The National Highways Act has been amended to enable levy of a fee on a selected sections of national highways. The amendment to the Act allows the private sector to construct and / or develop roads and charge a fee.

(v) The Motor Vehicles Act, 1998 was amended (effective from November 1994) in order to simplify procedures to give more powers to the state Government in respect of granting driving licences and permits for motor vehicles.

(vi) Declaring the road sector as an industry to facilitate borrowing on easy terms and to permit floating of bonds.

(vii) Relaxation of MRTP provisions to enable large firms to enter the Road Sector.

(viii) Reduction of custom duties on construction equipment and streamlining of its procedures.

(ix) Selection of private parties for construction and maintenance of roads on 'competitive bidding' basis.

(x) Develop 'Way side facilities' like motels, shopping malls, petrol and diesel stations, telephone booths, health clinics etc.

(xi) Provide a five year tax holiday and 30% tax relief on income tax for the next five years.

(xii) Private sector can also develop by passes, lane conversions, bridges etc.

(xiii) Government will guarantee a fixed rate of return on the capital employed by the private sector, if the project is financially non viable.

(xiv) Foreign investment upto 74% is allowed for road construction and development. It will be increased upto 100%, if necessary.

(xv) Continuous upgradation of technology for road construction, development and maintenance.

Telecommunications Policy

The major features of the National Telecommunication Policy are :

(i) Target for telephone on demand.

(ii) Phone connection for every village.

(iii) Installation of one public call office for every 500 persons.

(iv) All value-added services internationally to be operational.

(v) Ensuring quality of telecom services in the country to be of world standard.

(vi) Special attention to avoid consumer complaints, dispute resolution and public interface.

(vii) Providing widest permissible range of services to meet consumer demand at a reasonable prices.

(viii) To ensure that the country emerges as a major manufacturing base and a major exporter of telecom equipment.

(ix) Association of private sector on a large scale to bridge the resource gap.

(x) Use the private initiative to complement the efforts of the Department of Telecommunications (DOT)) and increase the internal generation by adopting various means like deferred payments, Build, operate and Transfer (BOT), Build, Lease and Transfer BLT) etc.,

(xi) Establishment of Telecommunications Regulatory Authority of India (TRAI).

(xii) To ensure fair competition and protect and promote consumer interest.

(xiii) Ending the monopoly of DOT by 1999 and Videsh Sanchar Nigam Limited (VSNL) by 2004 for fair competition and to provide full range of services of world standard at lowest possible price.

DRUG POLICY

Prior to the announcement of the New Drug Policy in 1991, almost the entire pharmaceutical sector was totally delicensed through the De-licensed Registration Scheme, 1985, and the Exempted Industries Registration Scheme of 1988.

With the abolition of these two schemes, the drug industry has been temporarily placed under compulsory licensing. The drug industry also has been complaining about the constraints of price control and has asked for the control mechanism to be made more realistic and flexible so as to take care of the rising cost of production and for encouraging new investment.

The drug policy has been inforce since 1995.

The important features of the drug policy include :

- The number of price controlled Products has been decreased from 142 to 74.
- Pharmaceutical companies producing from the initial stage were guaranteed the Lower amount of return on net worth of 18 per cent or profits based on 26 per cent return on capital employed.
- MAPE for essential drugs is lifted from 75 per cent to 100 per cent in line with the allowance for non-essential drugs.
- Formulation with sales in excess of Rs. 40 million and with at least 10 formulators (among which five bulk drug producers) with no single producer having a market share of 40 per cent. The policy favours the large scale companies against the small scale companies by abolishing controls with turnover upto Rs. 40 million.
- Drugs in which there is monopoly situation, which is to be determined on the basis of annual turnover of the bulk drugs of Rs. one crore or more and the existance of a single formulator with 90 per cent or more market share in the retail trade should be included.
- The policy proposed one per cent cess on production of drugs and pharamaceuticals to promote domestic reserch and development.
- There will be automatic approval of bio-technical agreement with foregin companies. Those companies with 51 per cent Indian equity will be at par with Indian companies.
- Manufacturing of medicines, except five bulk drugs used in the National Health Plan and those having DNA, is delicensed.
- Automatic approvel of foreign drug policy and foreign technology agreements.
- Higher rate of returns are to be allowed for price - controlled drugs. This may be reimposed, if prices rise very rapidly.
- National Drug Authority to be setup to monitor drug audit.
- Ceiling prices for standard pack size of price controlled formulations.
- National Pharmaceutical Pricing Authority (NPPA) was set-up to monitor the prices. Time limit for processing of application for bulk drug and formulations has been fixed as two months and four months respectively.
- New indigenously developed bulk drugs which have not been produced else where have been exempted from price control to encourage R&D.

Thus the new drug policy / DPCO covered all aspects of the drug industry.

CHAPTER 8

ORGANISATIONAL STRUCTURAL ISSUES

- **Work Organisations**
- **Principles of Organisation**
- **Authority Relationship**
- **Organisation Structure**

WORK ORGANISATIONS

As one author has rightly said 1 + 1 makes an Organisation, i.e., where there are two or more persons, there is, in effect, an organisation. Some individuals prefer to work independently in isolated circumstances. But the vast majority of all work in today's environment takes place within the context of a structure organisation – a grouping of individuals into a unified, common effort. The structuring may be a loosely knit one in which inter-relationships are scarcely discernible (for they relate to any natural self-grouping of individuals according to their needs), or the organisation pattern may be a highly formalised one in which authority relationships (between the President/or Board of Directors and the operative workers) are clearly defined in detail and the prescribed worker behaviour is expected. The former type of structure is known as 'informal', and the latter as 'formal' organisation. An organisation without some structure could be compared to an airport that has no ground or air control over the aeroplanes using the facilities. It would create chaos and disturb the entire working of the airport.

An organisation may be a manufacturing firm, a business concern, an insurance company, a governmental agency, social organisation, hospital, a university, a public school system, or a religious trust, cause–oriented group, and even a family. It may be small or large, simple or complex. An organisation is a human grouping, in which work is done for the accomplishment of some specific goals or missions. For example, the goal of a public utility, like a power supply station, might be to provide adequate source of energy to the consumers at a reasonable rate. The goal of a manufacturing concern might be to produce and supply the goods and services to satisfy the demands of a market. A hospital may provide preventive and curative health services to the people of the area; or the business's goal might be not only to earn profit but also to do service in the competitive market for long. However, the goals of the organisations will not be the same, but an organisation has its own objectives, which may remain relatively constant, but they are likely to be modified over a period of time, as per the changing needs and circumstances. Organisational objectives are most likely to be multiple, as the organisations try to achieve several goals and to serve a number of different categories of people.

In order to achieve the goals, a well-run organisation works out a set of rules, sometimes called policies, programmes, rules, regulations, procedures or guidelines and sanctions. These are designed not to restrict creativity but to assist its members in the accomplishment of organisational goals.

People who Manage

To look after the various functions set for the organisation, adequate resources in human resources and material have to be arranged by individuals who serve as managers or supervisors within organisations. Such people have to make things happen to aid in the achievement of the organisational objectives, to coordinate the resources of the organisation – four important Ms., *viz., money, material* (raw or semi–manufactured), *machinery* (or fixed assets and plants), and *Men* (or human resources). It is on the effective combination and dovetailing of these factors that the success or failure of the organisation depends. The resources by themselves will not help the organisation to accomplish the objectives, unless there is an effective coordination and utilisation of these human and non-human resources.

While the human resources available to management in an organisation are only one part of the resources which must be coordinated, it is through the combined efforts of the people that monetary and material resources are utilised for organisational objectives; without human efforts, organisations cannot accomplish their objectives. Rensis Likert rightly observed, "All the activities of any enterprise are initiated and determined by the persons who make up that institution. Plants, offices, computers, automated equipment, and all else that make a modern firm use are unproductive except for human effort and directions... of all the tasks of management, managing the human components is the central and most important task, because all else depends on how – well it is done."

Consequently, the managers have a central responsibility not only for the behaviour and performance of other people, but also of their own behaviour. Managers are appointed at various levels to organise and coordinate the activities of the team members or fellow work associates. This constitutes a hierarchy of management, where individuals perform different roles. Some are at the top level management, others are at the intermediate and lower levels of the management group. Those at the lower levels are responsible to persons at a higher organisational level. The greater the commitment of the members of organisational objectives, the greater is the degree of effectiveness with which the organisation works.

People at Work

The principal component of an organisation is its 'human resources' or 'people at work'. Human resources have been defined as: "*from the national point of view*, the knowledge, skills, creative abilities, talents and aptitudes obtained in the population; whereas *from the viewpoint of the individual enterprise*, they represent the total of the inherent abilities, acquired knowledge and skills as exemplified in the talents and aptitudes of its employees."[13] Jucius calls these resources "human factors", which refer to "a whole consisting of interdependent and interacting physiological, sociological and ethical components."[14]

It is this human resource which is of paramount importance in the success of any organisation, because most of the problems in organisational settings are human and social rather than physical, technical or economic. Failure to recognise this fact causes immense loss to the nation, enterprise and the individual. In the words of Oliver Sheldon, "No industry can be rendered efficient so long as the basic fact remains unrecognised that it is principally human. It is not a mass of machines and technical processes, but a body of men. It is not a complex of matter, but a complex of humanity. It fulfils its function not by virtue of some impersonal force, but by human energy. Its body is not an intricate maze of mechanical devices but a magnified nervous system."

'People of work' comprises a large number of individuals of different sex, age, socio-religious groups and different educational or literacy standards. These individuals in the work place exhibit similar behaviour patterns and characteristics to a certain degree, but they also show many dissimilarities. Each individual who works has his own set of needs, drives, goals, and experience. Each has his own physical and psychological traits. Each human being is not only a product of his biological inheritance but also a result of interaction with his environment. Family relationships, religious influences, racial or caste backgrounds, educational accomplishments, the application of technological innovations, and many other environmental-experimental influences affect the individual as he works. Among the environmental factors that influence work behaviour are various organisational elements (authority relationship; organisational goals, procedures, rules

13. Megginson. Leon C., *Personnel and Human Research Administration*, 1977, p.4.
14. Jucius, Michael J., *Personnel Management*, 1976.

and policies; informal group relationship, the type and manner of supervision received by the employee, etc). People come to work with certain specific motives — to earn money, to get employment, to have better prospects for future, to be treated as a human being while at the place of work, etc. They sell their labour for a reasonable wage/salary and other benefits. It is these people who provide the knowledge and much of the energy through which organisational objectives are accomplished.

The manager must, therefore, be aware not only of the organisational but also employee and self-needs. No one of these can be ignored. The achievements for the organisation, the "people at work", "who manage them" (i.e., managers themselves), and other groups of the public such as consumers, shareholders, entrepreneurs, government, suppliers, etc are possible through a concerted effort. He develops a four-dimensional relationship : (i) those between management and workers : (ii) those among the workers themselves; (iii) those among the managerial personnel, and (iv) those among different members of the organisation and the community. In other words, he develops 'human relation', "the purpose of which is *not* to enable him to discover clever techniques for winning friends and influencing people through personality development; *nor* to enable him to manipulate people as though they are puppets, *but* to assist him in working more effectively with other people in the organisation."

Definition of Organisation

"Organisation is a process of dividing work into convenient tasks or duties, of grouping such duties in the form of posts, of delegating authority to each post and of appointing qualified staff to be responsible that work is carried out as planned."[15]

"Organisation is the process of identifying and grouping the work to be performed, defining and delegating responsibility and authority and establishing relationships for the purpose of enabling people to work most effectively together in accomplishing objectives."[16]

According to Sheldon, "organisation is the process of combining the work which individuals and groups have to perform with the faculties necessary for its execution so that the duties so formed provide the best channels for an efficient, systematic, positive, and coordinated application of available effort."[17]

"An organisation is the rational coordination of the activities or roles of a number of people for the achievement of some common explicit purpose or goal, through division of labour and function, and through a hierarchy of authority and responsibility."[18]

"Organising is the process of defining and grouping the activities of the enterprise and establishing authority relationships amongst them. In performing the organising function, the manager defines departmentalisation and assigns activities so that they can be most effectively executed."[19]

Some other definitions of organisation are :

"An organisation *consists of people* who carry out differentiated tasks which are coordinated to contribute to the organisation's goals" (G. Dessler).

15. Deveill, C.S., *Business Administration and Management.*
16. Allen, Louis, A *Management and Organisation*, 1958, p. 57.
17. Sheldon, Oliver, *Philosophy of Management*, 1923, p. 23.
18. Schien, E.H., *Industrial Psychology.*
19. Theo, Haimann, *Professional Management.*

"It is a form of human association for the attainment of a common purpose – *it is a process of relegating specific duties or functions* in a coordinated whole" (Mooney and Reiley).

"It is an identifiable group of people contributing their efforts towards he attainment of goals" (McFarland).

"*It is the adjustment of diverse elements* so that their mutual relationships may exhibit more predetermined quality." (North Whitehead).

"*It is the arrangement or structure of relationships*, power, objectives, roles, activities, communications and other factors that exist when people work together to accomplish certain objectives."

"*It is a structured process* in which individuals interact for achieving stated objectives" (Hicks and Gullet).

From these definitions, certain broad features of an organisation may be drawn. *One*, it means a structure, an association, and entity or network of specified relationships – superior–subordinate relationship among individuals. *Two*, it means a process of on-going activity, i.e, of organising.

Structural Issues in Organisation

The structural issues involved in organisation are :

(i) Identifying and grouping tasks to form individual jobs;

(ii) Grouping jobs into sections, departments and higher administrative units, i.e., divisions;

(iii) Delegating authority, allocating responsibility, exacting accountability, and determining the number of levels in the managerial hierarchy on the basis of 'span of control or supervision';

(iv) Providing organisational climate so that people are activated to give their best in accomplishing organisational objectives; and

(v) Designing communication system for effective decision making, control and co-ordination.

Functions of an Organisation

An organisation tries to establish an effective behavioural relationship among selected employees and in selected work places in order that a group may work together effectively.[20]

There are three kinds of work which must be performed whenever an organisation comes into being, viz., division of labour, combination of labour and co-ordination, i.e., the work, the people and the relationship between them. These are known as fundamentals in every successful organisation.[21] These are now briefly dealt with.

(i) Division of Labour : Since an organisation is a structure of human association for the achievement of common goals, it involves individuals and groups of individuals. When two or more individuals join together to perform certain tasks, it follows that some division of work is done. Properly or improperly, fairly or unfairly, work is divided among those who participate in a productive organisation. With effective planning and organisation in an enterprise, the division of labour leads to a fixing of responsibility, the delegation of authority, specialization, and other conceptual schemes which are frequently called the principles of an organisation.

20. Terry, George, R., *Principles of Mangement*, Richard D. Irwin, Homewood, 1968, p. 289.
21. Newman William, H., Charles E. Summer, and E. Kirky Warren. *The process of Management*, Prentice–Hall, New York, Third Ed., 1972, p.49.

(ii) Combination of Labour : With work divided and assigned to the members of an organisation, their activities are grouped together, forming operations; and operations are arranged to establish systems and procedures. From a structural point of view, this grouping of activities results in units, departments and divisions of an organisation. The basis for this grouping of activities may be the skills of the workers, the tools and machinery used, the nature of the product, the materials employed, or some other elements. Whether it is logical or not, there is always some reason for the arrangement of tasks in a work place.

(iii) Co-ordination : This all-inclusive principle emerges because of the need in every organisation for the integration of activities and the coordination of individuals and groups of individuals performing their tasks. Co-ordination is achieved through leadership; in the structural sense, it involves the fixing of responsibility and the delegation of authority. It establishes controls which provide for an efficient scheduling and performance of activities.

Organisation implies not only a purpose or a set of purposes but a form appropriate to carry on the activities to achieve the objectives. The greater the range of activities of an organisation, the more complicated, and specialised does its structure become. It is the organisation which carries on the activities of life by means of parts or organs more or less separate in function but mutually dependent. As the business enterprise grows, the separation and definition of functions increase, but the oneness of the whole is nonetheless important.

To conclude, we may define organisation as : "*the process of determining the total activities to achieve a given objective/objectives, grouping of the activities, assigning grouped activities to individuals, delegating to them authority necessary to perform the activities assigned and establishing authority relationships among different positions in the organisation*.

In other words, organisation is an entity which provides a structural framework of duties and responsibilities. On the one hand, it establishes authority relationships, and on the other, provides a system of communication. A good organisation must fulfil four main functions:

(i) It must enable management to maximise output or resources through the provision of an efficient man-machine system.

(ii) It must ensure an effective net-work of communication (up-ward, downward, horizontal) and information.

(iii) It must offer interesting and meaningful jobs to all individuals working in the organisation.

(iv) It must create, maintain and develop its own image or individuality.

Significance of Organisation

Organisation forms the backbone of the management because without its proper care at higher, middle and lower levels of administration, it may be practically difficult and/or impossible for any management to run smoothly. Organisation is not an end in itself, but a means to the end of business performance and business results. A sound organisation can, therefore, contribute greatly to the continuity and success of the enterprise. As Lounsbury Fish has observed:

"Organisation is more than a chart – it is the mechanism through which management directs, coordinates and controls the business. It is, indeed, the foundation of management. If the organisation plan is ill-designed, if it is merely a makeshift arrangement, then management is rendered difficult and ineffective. If, on the other hand, it is logical, clear-cut and streamlined to meet present-day requirements, then the first requisite of sound management has been achieved."

Organisations bring about the following benefits to the enterprises[22]

- Disposes off conflicts between individuals over jurisdiction.
- Prevents duplication of work.
- Decreases likelihood of 'run–arounds'.
- Makes communication easier through keeping the channels clear.
- Shows promotional possibilities, which are useful in executive development. Organisation charts and position descriptions show where a man can expect to go, what qualifications are needed to fill a superior job, what additional training is needed to prepare a man in one position for superior post.
- Provides a basis for appraisal and rating of individual performance and capabilities. If one knows what an individual is supposed to be doing, it is then possible to measure how well he is living up to the requirements of the job.
- Aids in wage and salary administration. The analysis of duties for the higher executives performs the service as job descriptions do for those at the lower level.
- Permits expansion with adequate control and without killing off top executives. Activities are administered in manageable units, so that no one person has to bear a heavy load.
- Permits changes to be made in the right direction as opportunities present themselves. In the absence of a plan, changes are likely to be made on the basis of expediency, with the likelihood of perpetuating original mistakes.
- Increases cooperation and feelings of freedom. Each person works best with others when he knows for what he is responsible, to whom he is responsible, and the value of cooperative relationships with others. A feeling of freedom comes when responsibilities are definite and known and when delegation is actually practised.

Importance of sound organisation will be clear from the following :

1. *It facilitates administration and management* : Good organisation facilitates the various managerial functions of planning, staffing, directing and controlling by proper division of labour, consistent delegation or clear job definition and clarity of authority and responsibility relationship.

2. *It facilitates growth and diversification* : Sound organisation helps in keeping the various activities under control and increases the capacity of the enterprise to undertake more activities.

3. *It provides for the optimum use of technological innovations* : High cost of installation, operation and maintenance of new innovative machinery and plants call for proper organisation. Being flexible, a sound organisation makes it possible for the new changes to be introduced.

4. *It encourages optimum use of human resources* : A sound organisation fits the right man to the right task for peak performance.

5. *It stimulates creativity* : A sound organisation stimulates independent, creative thinking, and initiative by providing well-defined areas of work with a broad latitude of the development of new and improved ways of doing things.

6. *It facilitates coordination among various departments* : This is done by creating a clear-cut relationship between them. This is further facilitated by the provision of communication channels in the organisation.

22. Ranbe, S. Avery, *"Principles of Good Organisation"*, in Company Organisation Charts, National Industrial Conference Board, New York, 1954, p.13.

PRINCIPLES OF ORGANISATION

Like the engineer who designs his bridge to meet the special need of joining the two areas, the organisation planner, in designing a company structure, applies the same principles. Through years of experience, it has been found that if certain principles are followed, regardless of the size of the enterprise, the result will be good organisation. Some of these principles are :

1. There must be clear lines of authority running from the top to the bottom of the organisation (the principle of the 'Chain of Command' or 'Scalar principle')
2. No one in the organisation should report to more than one line supervisor. Everyone in the organisation should know to whom he reports and who reports to him (the principle of 'unity of command').
3. The responsibility and authority of each supervisor should be clearly defined in writing.
4. Responsibility should always be complied with corresponding authority.
5. The responsibility of higher authority for the acts of its subordinates is absolute, i.e., although a supervisor delegates authority, he still remains responsible for what is done by those to whom he has delegated it.
6. Authority should be delegated as far down the line as possible, i.e., decision-making power should be placed nearer the scene of action.
7. The number of levels of authority should be kept at minimum.
8. The work of every person in the organisation should be confined, as far as possible, to the performance of a single leading function.
9. Whenever possible, line functions should be separated from staff function, and adequate emphasis should be placed on important staff activities.
10. There is a limit to the number of positions that can be coordinated by a single executive (*viz.*, the principle of 'Span of Control of Supervision').
11. The organisation should be flexible so that it can be adjusted to the changing conditions.
12. The organisation should be kept as simple as possible.

Concepts of Organisation Structure

Several fundamental concepts describing the essentials of a sound organisation structure have been presented by the traditional school of thought. These deal with the following essentials.

(1) Task Accomplishment or Personnel Satisfaction : The emphasis is on organisational accomplishment, i.e., the structuring of work relationships should be so planned that both the objectives of the organisation and the individual are realised simultaneously.

(2) Delegation of Authority : It is the delivery by one individual to another of the right to act, to make decisions, to requisition resources, to direct others to act and to perform other tasks in order to fulfil job responsibilities. *Authority is ineffective without ability to exercise it*. An individual is given the authority to make it possible for him to fulfil his organisational obligations. Authority generally goes hand in hand with responsibility, which may be defined as an *obligation or duty that the employees have been directed to carry out by someone with authority over them*. Once the responsibilities are identified, the appropriate authority can be extended to the individual by his superiors. However, some personal factors within the superior and his subordinate may interfere with this delegation.

Besides delegation of authority the management has also to decide whether to keep most planning, decision-making and controlling activities within their own power or whether to transfer these to their subordinates, i.e., whether to *centralise or decentralise* authority.

(3) Proper Span of Supervision : A formal organisation structure determines the breadth of a supervisor's responsibilities by indicating the number of individuals who are directly accountable to that supervisor. The span of supervision is important because it determines the amount of attention each supervisor can give to each subordinate, and it effects ease in communicating, methods of decision-making that can be used, and other superior-subordinate relationships.

(4) The Degree of Specialisation : Under specialisation, limited duties are performed regularly and repetitively. From the individual's point of view, specialisation makes the learning of job routines easier and makes the worker an expert in his job. From the organisation's point of view, it allows proper utilisation of the abilities of an individual worker and makes coordination of activities easier, facilitates the development and implementation of essential controls, encourages the efficient productiveness of workers, quickens the training process. But too much specialisation often results in making the work monotonous; the worker feeling little pride of accomplishment; and it may also affect a person's opportunity for growth. Therefore, some freedom and flexibility is needed.

(5) Communication Channel Should be Proper : Communication between the subordinates and their bosses should pass through each rung of the ladder without omission as a message is moved upward or downward. No manager in the vertical chain should be bypassed as the communication queue moves its way. When messages are to be conveyed at the horizontal level, they should move upward vertically from the sender to the point where the sender and the receiver have a common superior, then the message can move downward vertically to the receiver.

AUTHORITY RELATIONSHIP

Every manager in an organisation needs authority because without it he cannot secure compliance of orders from his subordinates. Lack of authority creates chaos in an organisation. It is, therefore, considered as an essential tool in the hands of management to discharge managerial responsibilities.

"Authority" has been defined by Henry Fayol as "the right to give orders and the power to exact obedience. It may be derived by position or by personality of the manager." Louis Allen views authority as : "the sum of the powers and rights entrusted to make possible the performance of the work delegated." Accordingly, authority may be of knowledge; of position; or legal authority. According to Theo Haimann, "Authority is the rightful legal power to request a subordinate to do a certain thing or to refrain from doing it, and if he does not follow these instructions, the manager is in a position, if need be, to take disciplinary action, even to discharge the subordinate... Without authority, only anarchy and chaos would result." Barnard states that "The concept of authority as being a right transmitted from basic social institutions to individual managers has been called formal authority."[23]

23. Chester, I. Barnard, *The Business of Executive*, Hardvard University Press, Cambridge, Mass., 1938, p. 162.

In short, authority may be considered as *the right to take decisions, which includes the right to use the resources; and the right to issue orders, and ensure compliance of orders by subordinates.*

Sources of Authority

Regarding sources from which authority emanates, there are three views: *one*, the formal authority theory, *two*, the acceptance theory of authority; and *three*, the competence theory.

The *formal authority theory* states that "Authority flows in a scalar chain from the highest level to rank and file employees." Private property is the source of all managerial authority. The Constitution of India guarantees the right of private property. An individual has a right to own and use his property. In a joint-stock company, the ultimate authority is vested in the shareholders who delegate this authority to a Board of Directors. It, in turn, delegates authority to the Chief Executive Officer or the departmental head. He in turn delegates authority to subordinate managers. The subordinates accept the order of a manager because their time has been hired by the business unit. Managers enjoy the powers to punish subordinates if they do not accept the authority. (fig 8.1)

The *Acceptance Theory of Authority* states that the manager's authority is determined by the acceptance of it by the subordinates. Subordinates may or may not accept this authority. However, they accept it because: (i) they may consider it necessary for achieving organisational objectives; (ii) for getting certain rewards such as increased pay, promotion, prestige, status, etc.; (iii) because of their regard for old age, experience, competence, character, etc,; (iv) to avoid responsibility; (v) because of the fear of losing the job, financial and non-financial rewards; and (vi) for setting an example to others.

The *Competence Theory* states that authority is generated by personal qualities which a manager possesses, *viz.*, knowledge, intelligence, skills, etc.

Limits of Authority

Authority is limited by such restrictions as :

(a) the codes, mores, laws and social values; and legal and political considerations;

(b) the enterprise objectives, policies, procedures and programmes which limit a manager's authority;

(c) biological constraints which limit authority because human beings do not have the capacity to do certain things.

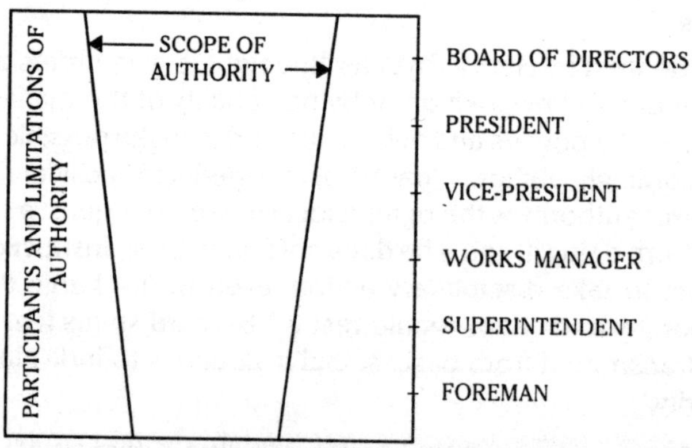

Fig. 8.1 Limits of Authority.

Nature and Types of Authority

Generally, in a business organisation, we come across three types of authority, *viz.*,

- the line authority,
- the staff relationships, and
- the functional authority.

Line Authority

It refers to the common relationship between the superior and subordinate level. It is the administrative authority having the right and power to plan the activities, issue orders, stimulate greater efforts, check up and evaluate the performance of the subordinates, to exact accountability, and to discipline them. The authority links the lowest level operative, through successive levels of supervision, to the chief executive. The line authority constitutes a chain of communication, coordination and delegation. Each management position in this line assumes and retains accountability for each end result.

Authority should always carry with it a corresponding responsibility. Responsibility is the obligation of a subordinate to carry out duties assigned to him. When a subordinate accepts a job, he incurs an obligation to perform it successfully. This is his responsibility.

There are basically three almost inseparable aspects of every relationship between an executive and his subordinates. *First is the assignment of duties*, i.e., what the person is expected to accomplish. *Second*, this assignment must be accompanied by *authority* (permission) because without it, subordinates cannot discharge the duties assigned. This means that they should have the power to acquire the necessary facilities to purchase raw materials, office equipment and machines, and use them; make commitments regarding appointment and training of personnel; give orders to other employees or direct their activities and take such other action, within the framework of company plans, as are necessary to fulfil these duties. *Third*, there is then a *responsibility* (obligation) on the part of the subordinate to the executive for satisfactory performance of his duties.

The important facts to note are that : (i) "authority and responsibility are co-extensive", without one, the other cannot work; (ii) Responsibility cannot be delegated. However, additional obligations can be created between an executive and his subordinates, but this does not permit the executive to duck out of the relationship; (iii) Only one manager should have line authority over an employee; for dual subordination often results in conflict and inefficiency because an individual cannot serve two masters well; (iv) Authority flows downwards, whereas responsibility (accountability) flows upward through the chain of command or through the organisation pyramid. Each manager from the bottom is held responsible to his superior; (v) The downward flow of authority and upward flow of accountability must have parity at each position in the management hierarchy; (vi) Responsibility is derived from functions assigned. Authority is derived from responsibility. Accountability is derived from authority. All the three of these should be balanced if a stable equilibrium is desired.

Staff Relationship

Staff authority indicates the relationship between peers, colleagues, and fellow-workers across the organisation. Individuals located on the same level normally have no authority over each other. They are rather equal in terms of the amount of authority and formal influence they have. They are more or less equal in social status also. Such horizontal structure helps to clarify authority relationship, to understand communication patterns and to discern more about social interactions. Personnel at this structure often work in a team.

As a company grows and engages in more complex activities, the staff or advisory authority relationship has to be recognised. Staff functions have no direct responsibility for accomplishing the objectives of an enterprise. They only help the 'line' to work most effectively in achieving the primary objectives of an enterprise. The 'staff' is generally used by a busy executive to assist him to do his work. He investigates, undertakes research, arranges information on troublesome problems, keep an eye on particular aspects of operations such as expense ratios, governmental regulations, or inventory turnover. Such staff is generally termed as '*Staff Assistants*', who work subject to the approval of their superior and often act in the name of their superior. Such staff may be either 'personal staff', e.g., personal assistant to or 'personal secretary' or a 'general staff', e.g., assistant to, say, Mr. X. A pure staff authority has no right to command; for it is the prerogative of a line authority.

Staff activity is an organisational component existing mainly to provide technical or special advice and service to line personnel. Staff may be appointed by an executive to help/advise him on special matters/problems, e.g., on legal, accounting, public relations, marketing research, production control, quality control, operations research, sales promotion, advertising, engineering or organisation planning, etc. Through this arrangement, the technical/special knowledge of the staff is available to the senior executive and his other subordinates who come in contact with the staff man.

The work of the staff specialist, in course of time, becomes so heavy that he may need other people to work with him. Consequently, a small unit may be developed within the organisation, known as 'Office' or 'Service' division.

The staff relationship, it would be clear, implies that the man is working on behalf of an executive; he is doing things the executive himself would do, if time permitted; he has no authority to issue orders, and if he does pass along instructions or interpretations, this is done in the name of the senior executive.[24] Staff relationship may be used in any department of a business enterprise. For example, the sales promotion director in the sales department, an industrial engineer in the production department, the cost analyst in the accounting department, an economist in the purchasing department, and safety director in the personnel department are examples of staff relationship

Under staff relationship, three types of staff authority are in vogue, viz.,

(i) *Service authority* where a staff specialist offers a specific service to the line organisation, e.g., purchasing supervisor, production planning and control supervisor provide special services to the plant manager.

(ii) *Advisory authority*, where a staff specialist may offer only expert advice to the line organisation, e.g., and industrial engineer, a quality control supervisor and an accountant provide specialised advice to the plant manager.

(iii) *Functional speciality*, where a staff specialist may exercise effective direction and control of a functional speciality. For example, a staff member may be allowed to take decisions and assume power to command in a given functional area.

Functional Authority

Functional authority is permission to issue directions to people not under line supervision. Such directions deal with specified activities or certain aspects of those activities, for instance, an

24. Newman, William H. and James P. Logan, *op. cit.*, p. 465.

industrial engineer may select equipment and prescribe the tools and the methods to be used in production operations. The *sales production* manager may stipulate the methods of presenting new products and the time the products are to be introduced. A *production planning manager* may pass orders in matters of personnel problems, production planning, use of safety devices, and quality control; or a *finance executive* may be authorised to acquire from other departments the budgetary reports and other records.

In all these examples, the executives with functional authority does part of the planning activity. He may prescribe policy, set up methods, or determine the time when activities are to be undertaken. In doing so, he is saying how the activities are to be performed. The line executive, on the other hand, is responsible for seeing that the instructions given by the functional authority as well as from the executive are carried out.

However, it should be noted that extensive grant of functional authority may seriously damage the basis of line authority, i.e., the unity of command. The dangers are.[25]

1. If several different people exercise functional authority over a given operative executive, he may be swamped by specialised instructions. A branch manager, for instance, may find it almost impossible to carry out all the directions received from the chief accountant, maintenance manager, warehouse manager, sales promotion manager, credit manager, personnel manager, and public relations manager, if each of these home office experts has a wide degree of functional authority. Moreover, under such circumstances, it is quite possible that some of the instructions may be inconsistent with others in actual operation.

2. The effectiveness of line supervisors may be weakened by a heavy use of functional authority. As more and more instructions come from the functional authority, the status of the line boss may be undermined. In the eyes of his subordinates, the boss has become merely a go – between, and they will turn directly to the specialists for guidance.

"Functional authority sometimes leads to autocratic and inflexible administration. The functional specialist may become narrow in his viewpoint and insist that his plans be followed even though they are not well suited to a specific local situation. In a large concern, he is likely to be distant from the scene of operations and reluctant to make modifications in his generalised plan".

Functional authority should, therefore, be granted only when it is essential. The good practice is to minimise this to a line or staff position; and provision should be made to see that it is not arbitrary. *Further*, it should be established by prior agreement among the departments affected, preferably in written procedures that are approved by the executive officer.

Functional authority works well in certain situations such as : (a) when only a minor aspect of the total operating job is covered; (b) when technical knowledge of a type not possessed by the operating executives is needed; and (c) when consistency of action in several departments is important.

Many times, cases of composite relationships are available, when a single executive has a wide variety of relationship, depending upon the subject and who the other person is, for example, a personnel manager; (a) have line authority over the employment office, cafeteria, and other employee service operations; (b) exercises functional authority in respect of compensation ranges, length of vacation, dismissal procedures; and (c) provides much constructive advice regarding training, promotions, motivation, etc in a staff capacity.

25. Newman, William H., and James P. Logan, *op. cit.*, p. 468.

This example of composite relationship brings to the forefront the futility of having a man as 'line' or 'staff'

Delegation of Authority

Delegation of authority is an important managerial practice of getting things done through others by sharing authority with them. It is the delegation by one individual to another of the right to act, to make decisions, to requisition resources, to direct others to act and to perform other tasks in order to fulfil the job responsibilities. According to Allen, "It is the entrustment of a part of the work of responsibility and authority to another and the creation of accountability for performance; and responsibility is the work assigned to a position."[26] O.S. Hinger observes that "Delegation takes place when one person gives another the right to perform work on his behalf and in his name, and the second person accepts a corresponding duty or obligation to do what is required of him."

It should be noted that *delegation is the granting of authority to subordinates and exacting responsibility from them when the volume of work to be done is in excess of an individual's capacity*. Through delegation, the manager shares the burden of his work with others by: (i) entrusting to others the performance of the part of the work he would otherwise have to do himself; and (ii) providing a means of checking up on the work what is done for him to ensure that it is done as he wishes.

All authority of the manager cannot be delegated. For the purpose of delegation, such an authority has been divided into three categories :

(a) *authority which must be delegated*, such as authority to take decisions for the accomplishments of tasks;
(b) *authority which can be delegated*, such as administration of policies; and
(c) *authority which cannot be delegated*, such as authority to take policy decision.

One man's business requires no delegation because the owner-manager performs every task himself. But with the growth of size and complexity of business, delegation becomes essential. Through it substantial assistance can be obtained by a manager, who is over burdened with work and, therefore, short of time for doing everything by himself, by sharing know-how, responsibility, authority, budgetary information, materials and equipment to the degree necessary to get the work done and achieved.

Delegation helps in maintaining healthy relationship between the executive and his subordinates by clearly defining the 'authority' and 'responsibility' of the subordinates. According to Douglas C. Basil, "Delegation can be one of management's best technique for satisfying needs and for motivating subordinates to better performance. *In terms of technical aspect of business*, delegation, through task assignment, can achieve decisions more quickly and eliminate a cumbersome information system. *In terms of behavioural aspect*, delegation can satisfy man's demands for responsibility, recognition, and opportunity to exercise authority.

Components of Delegation

The process of delegation covers the following three elements :

1. *Entrustment of responsibility* to the subordinate for performance;
2. *Granting of authority to make* use of resources, and take necessary decisions for carrying out the responsibility; and

26. Allen, Louis, A., *Management and Organisation*, p. 116.

3. *Creation of an-accountability or obligation* on the part of the person accepting the authority to perform in terms of standards established. These three attributes of delegation (Responsibility – Authority – Accountability or RAA) are like three legs of a stool, which are all interdependent.

1. *Entrustment of Responsibility* : Responsibility is the 'obligation' of an individual to perform assigned tasks/duties. Responsibility arises from a superior-subordinate relationship, i.e., the superior (manager) has the authority to require specified services from a subordinate. Authority flows from the superior to the subordinate, when duties are assigned; and, at the same time, responsibility is the obligation of the subordinate to accomplish those duties. By holding a subordinate responsible, the superior does not relieve himself of any part of the original responsibility. Delegation only authorises some one else to undertake the work. In actuality, *responsibility is a series of obligations contracted between any two organisation levels*. (Fig 8.2)

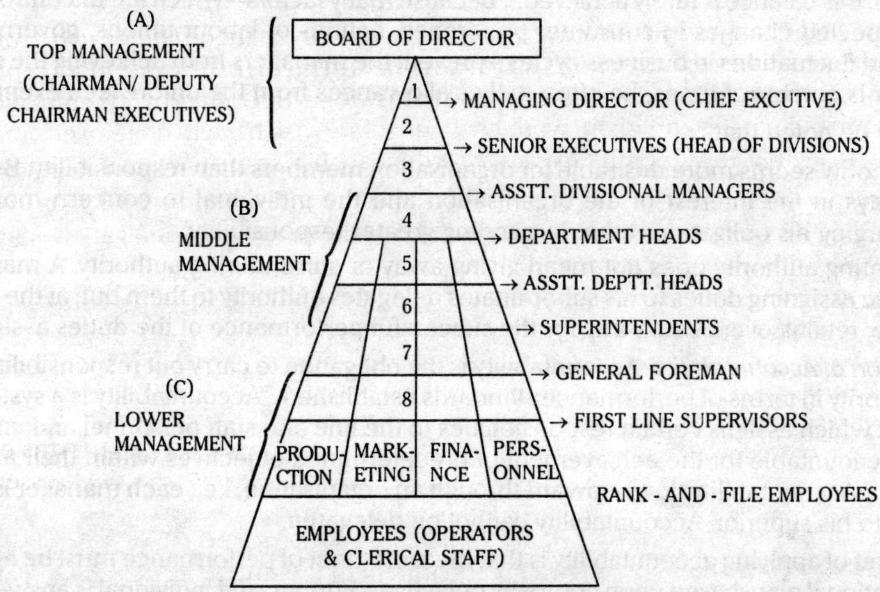

Fig. 8.2 Organisational Pyramid.

Responsibility flows through the entire organisation. The process of delegation takes the form of a pyramid. At the head are the shareholders, who entrust the task of managing a company to the Board of Directors. The Board of Directors hold the President or the Chief Executive or the General Manager responsible for total operational performance. He in turn, holds various vice-presidents, Deputy Managers responsible for marketing, production and finance functions. They repeat the process, resulting in a series of obligations to be performed at various organisation levels. At the lowest, supervisors hold operational personnel – machine operators, office workers – responsible for their activities. If the assigned task is not fulfilled at the lowest level, the supervisor is responsible for the action of his subordinates to the next higher level and so on upto the ladder.

One thing is to be noted that *although the work is shared, the person assigning the task is always accountable for the results achieved*.

Before responsibility can be assigned, certain conditions must be fulfilled:

(a) *Work–load must be divided among the personnel.* Individual jobs – based on units of responsibility – are specified by grouping similar functions into individual work programmes, i.e., the principle of 'functional similarity' should be followed.

(b) *Overlapping of responsibility should be avoided.* Gaps in responsibility develops when all requirements for performing work have not been properly foreseen.

(c) *Delegation of responsibility should be avoided for* functions that do not contribute to organisation objectives.

2. *Granting of Authority* : Authority is the right to perform certain assigned tasks. It is the power to order or command and is delegated from the superior to the subordinate to discharge his responsibility for the assigned work. *The amount of authority should be commensurate with the responsibilities undertaken;* there must be a balance between responsibility and àuthority. But in practice, this balance is rarely achieved.[27] Because many factors – which are uncontrollable such as unexpected changes in consumer preference, actions of labour unions, government legislation, and fluctuations in business cycles – prevent the managers from achieving the goals. If the superior is abreast of times, he often makes allowances from the unforeseen events.

It should be noted that :

(i) Authority seems more desirable for organisation members than responsibility. But it is always in the interest of the organisation and the individual to concern more for enlarging his obligations than demanding greater responsibility.

(ii) Granting authority does not mean giving away or surrendering authority. A manager while assigning duties to his subordinates delegates authority to them but, at the same time, retains overall authority for the successful performance of the duties assigned.

3. *Creation of Accountability* :Accountability is the obligation to carry out responsibility and exercise authority in terms of performance standards established. "Accountability is a system of management which assigns certain responsibilities to the line and staff personnel and, in turn, holds them accountable for the achievement of predetermined objectives within their area of responsibility." Accountability flows upward through an organisation, i.e., each manager is held accountable to his superior. Accountability cannot be delegated.

The secret of applying accountability is that measurement of performance must be against specific operational plan, based upon company objectives. Further, and individual is answerable to only one immediate superior, and no more. The reason is that single accountability promotes not only discipline, resulting from a good understanding of what is expected of the individual but also promotes coordination and minimises clash of interests.

Why Delegation?

Delegation of authority is felt necessary because :

(i) An individual's energy and time is limited and hence, he cannot do more than his capacity to do. His work, therefore, is distributed among others to get the work accomplished effectively;

(ii) Certain activities are rather complex and need expertise for doing these. The services of staff specialists are, therefore, utilised by delegating some of the responsibility.

(iii) When business is not diversified but also scattered over a large area, new branches need be opened and these require delegation of authority to persons working there under the head office.

27. McGregor, Douglas, *The Human Side of Management*, McGraw -Hill Book Co., New York, 1960, p. 158.

(iv) Delegation is a crucial step in management development, for it offers ample scope to the manager for self-expression and self-advancement through and taking decisions on many vital issues on his own account.

In short, *delegation is a must when the work costs too much in money and time for a manager*. Generally, routine duties needing programmed decisions are delegated to subordinates.

When Delegation Not Possible

Delegation cannot be made when the following situations occur :

1. When qualified subordinates are not available to carry out the assigned task;
2. When subordinates are available but they shirk responsibilities due to lack of self-confidence; fear of committing mistakes; lack of incentives; desire to play safe, depending on the boss for all decisions;
3. When a superior has no confidence in his subordinate, he may consider them incapable of doing and taking decisions.
4. When the manager is compelled to maintain direct and absolute control over a certain job;
5. When the manager feels his importance, or when he wants his presence felt everywhere, i.e., his desire to dominate others puts a check on delegation;
6. When the work-load is small or when the organisation is a one-man show;
7. When an executive himself is incapable of directing the work;
8. Absence of selective and sensitive controls that give a warning of possible difficulties may also be a reason for non-delegation;
9. When the manager himself suffers from a inferiority or fear complex that his subordinates will outshine him, get more recognition and attention;
10. When the subordinates are already overburdened with work and are unwilling to accept new assignments which call for thinking, initiative and involve more time;
11. When the organisation structure is itself defective and the authority - responsibility relationships are not clearly defined; and
12. When there is inadequate planning, and infringement of the principle of "Unity of Command".

However, these reasons do not constitute legitimate grounds for non-delegation of authority. An effective manager should always be willing to delegate authority as needed to accomplish the desired organisation objectives but a manager himself cannot evade his own responsibility. He is directly responsible for: (a) *planning* (formulation of objectives, policies, programmes, procedures and budgets); (b) *organising* (developing an organisation structure, defining responsibility, authority and establishing relationship for his unit – the line, the staff and line staff and functional relationship); (c) *motivating* (counselling, coaching, guiding and leading); (d) *co-ordinating* (assessing and reconciling all personnel involved to secure the best integration of group efforts); and (e) *controlling* effectively the work of the subordinates. In other words, the *manager cannot relieve himself of the ultimate responsibility to perform the overall managerial functions*.

Guidelines for Better Delegation

Delegation is an art which requires that proper planning and organisation should be developed beforehand. For this, the executive should know what his subordinates do at a particular time, what they need next and what it will require to be done. Accordingly, a manager should clearly instruct his subordinates what they are required to do, how it is to be done, when and where it is to done. To get the work done efficiently, the tasks or duties must be assigned to individuals concerned.

The following guidelines should prove useful in making delegation successful :

1. The assignments should be clearly defined in terms of goals or results expected. Sufficient authority should be granted for doing the work.
2. There should be a two-way communication between the manager and the subordinates so that proper understanding could be established. Clear, unambiguous instructions, guidance should be given to the subordinates, when needed.
3. Outline of the job set must be clear and proper control limits and standards of performance should be prescribed. Performance should be appraised periodically and feedback of information encouraged to keep the subordinate in self-improvement,.
4. Observance of principles of delegation like "parity of authority and responsibility", "unit of command" and "creation of accountability" should be strictly adhered to.
5. The subordinates must be trusted and, as far as possible, there should be little interference in their work.
6. Managers must develop proper attitudes favourable for delegation, viz., (i) willingness to welcome ideas from subordinates; (ii) willingness to delegate authority whenever required; (iii) willingness to let others learn by mistakes/trial and error method; and (iv) willingness to establish and use broad controls.

Centralisation and Decentralisation of Authority

One of the fundamental problems of organisation is to decide how much authority should be centralised in the hands of the Chief Executive and how much should be distributed among the lower level management, i.e., what should be the right degree of centralisation or decentralisation. Complete centralisation is possible only in a one-man enterprise. But the moment its scope is enlarged, decentralisation becomes inevitable.

'Centralisation' means concentration of power of decision-making at one point or in a few hands. According to Allen, "Concentration is the systematic and consistent reservation of authority in the central hands in the organisation."[28] Its implications, are that: (i) decision-making power in regard to planning, organisation, coordination and control is reserved in the hands of the top executive; (ii) operating authority is reserved with the middle level managers; and (iii) operations at lower levels are subservient to command, consent and control by the higher level authority in time.

'Decentralisation.' On the other hand, means delegation of business decisions by the owners to their subordinates, and then the others further down in the management hierarchy. Allen defines decentralisation as "The systematic effort to depute the lowest levels all authority except that which can only be exercised at central points."[29] This implies the (i) reservation of some authority at the top level; and (ii) delegation of authority to make decisions at points as near as possible to where actions take place.

If decision-making power is centralised in the hands of a single individual, the organisation is fully centralised; but when the power of decision-making is widely scattered throughout the organisation, it is a decentralised set-up. As George Terry puts it: "Decision-making and

28. Allen, Louis, A., *Management and Organisation*, p. 158.
29. Allen Louis, A., *op. cit.*, p. 162.

responsibility are centralised in that authority and formal activities are centralised in fewer and fewer managers as the organisation structure is relieved from the lower to the higher organisation levels. At the very top, all decision-making and responsibility theoretically emanate from the apex of the chief manager. In contrast, proceeding from the top to the bottom levels, decision-making and responsibility are decentralised, in that they are dispersed among an increasing number of management members, the greatest number being at the lower organisational level."[30]

An organisation may be highly centralised although its physical facilities and employees are widely dispersed. Similarly, an organisation may be highly decentralised even though all employees and physical facilities are located at one place. The point to note is that *neither the actual performance of work by the employees nor the physical dispersal of activities is the factor determining a centralised or a decentralised organisation*. The determining factor is: who is authorised to make decisions, i.e., who enjoys the decision-making power, whether this power is centralised in a few hands (centralised) or it is widely dispersed throughout the organisation (decentralised). *Everything that goes to increase the importance of the subordinate's role in decision-making is decentralisation; and everything which goes to reduce the subordinate's role (as decision-maker) is centralisation*.

Centralisation and decentralisation are the opposite ends of an organisation continuum. Basically, "centralisation procedures, uniformity of policy and action utilise the skills of centralised and specialised staff and enable closer control over operating units. Decentralisation, on the other hand, tends to effect faster decision-making and action 'on the spot' without consulting the higher level; and creates a tendency towards greater interest and enthusiasm on the part of subordinates."[31]

Carwell has succinctly described the strengths and weaknesses of centralised and decentralised organisation structure thus : [32]

Strengths	*Weaknesses*
Centralised Organisation	
1. Assumes uniformity of standards and policies among organisational units	1. Flood communication lines to a few. individuals at the top of the organisation.
2. Allows use of outstanding talent in managers by the whole organisation rather than a single unit.	2. Makes great demands on a few managers rather than spreading responsibility.
3. Decisions are uniform	3. Personalises decisions to the judgements of a few key decision-makers.
4. Helps eliminate duplication of effort and activity.	4. Forces top managers to possess a broad view that may be beyond their capacity.
	5. Gives vast amounts of power to a few individuals
	6. Reduces sense of participation for all but a few people.

30. Terry, George R., *Principles of Management*, Richard D. Irwin., Homewood, 1972. p. 375.
31. Thierauf, Robert, J. Robert C. Klekamp and Daniel W. Geeding, *Management Principles and Practices*, John Wiley & Sons, New York, 1977, p. 339.
32. Carwell Fred G., *Human Relations in Business*, Macmillan Company, New York, Second, Ed., 1975, p. 356.

Decentralised Organisation	
1. Reduces total responsibility to more managerial units.	1. Lack of uniformity of standards and policies among organisational units.
2. Helps develop more personnel in decision-making process.	2. Capable managers are not always available or willing to participate in decision-making.
3. Shortens line of communication.	3. Creates problems or coordination among separate organisational units.
4. Places decision-making close to situation affected by decisions.	4. Inter-unit rivalry can interfere with the total organisation's operation.
5. Allows more people to use skills and talents in decision-making.	5. Requires training programmes that may be time-consuming and costly.
6. Disperses power among many persons.	

Absolute centralisation is impossible in a large business unit because that would mean considerable cost and delay. Absolute decentralisation is also not possible, because in that case entire authority will be delegated to lower level managers, and the top manager will be left with no authority.

When Centralisation Desirable?

However, a higher degree of centralisation is needed:

(i) to facilitate personal leadership when the company is small;

(ii) to provide for integration and unification of the total operations of the enterprise; and

(iii) to promote uniformity of action, credit, price, etc. by the operating levels in a better way; authority for overall planning, organisation, coordination, control, etc. must be reserved for the top executive.

When Decentralisation Desirable?

Decentralisation, on the other hand, is considered desirable:

(i) When more decisions are to be made at the lower levels;

(ii) When more important decisions (such as purchasing of plant and machinery or construction of building) are made at lower levels in the organisation structure;

(iii) When more decisions relating to all or almost all functional areas are made at lower levels; and

(iv) when no checkings are required.

Some degree of decentralisation is usually found in every big enterprise. Allen has given three criteria for guiding the degree of decentralisation, *viz.*, (a) what kind of authority is delegated? (b) to what extent the authority is to be delegated? and (c) how consistently it is to be delegated?

These criteria may be applied to know the degree of decentralisation in different areas such as hiring of employees, promotion of employees, acquisition of capital equipment, approval of travel expenses and increases in pay/wages, procurement of raw materials, acceptance of sales order.

The *locus* or *place* of decision-making is another criterion. The lower the rank of executives who make given decisions, the greater the degree of decentralisation.

In determining the degree of decentralisation, it has to be remembered that an enterprise has both *formal* and *informal decision making rules*. Official policy statements may be one type of decision making, but actual may be quite different.

Another criterion is the degree of decision-making power at the lower levels. This can be determined by studying the authority which can be exercised: (1) without any check with higher authority at all (routinised decisions such as the billing procedure, safety enforcement, purchase of stock orders); (2) with a check or regular report after the decision is made and carried out (engagement of clerical personnel, purchases of equipment covered by budget); or (3) with a check before the decision is made or put into effect (decisions with precedent, special appropriation request). Or these may be the simple requirement to check with a superior on all matters of policy changes, of financial appropriations, or potential and actual disagreements.

Considerations Regarding Centralisation/Decentralisation

1. *Size and Complexity of the Organisation* : The larger the organisation, the more authority and responsibility must be delegated to subordinates by the top executive. If an organisation is a conglomeration involving several industries, the limitation of expertise dictates the need for decentralisation of authority to head the individual units. The rationale behind this is that each product group is likely to have different types of marketing, manufacturing, distribution, and financial problems. Even where a large firm having many units produces the same basic type of product, decentralisation is desirable. On the other hand, if the firm is relatively small, centralisation of authority is advisable.

2. *Competency of Organisational Personnel* : If there are adequate number of capable personnel in an organisation, who can take decisions quickly, decentralisation works effectively. On the other hand, if management personnel are followers and lack initiative, centralisation of authority is preferred.

3. *Dispersion of Organisation Units* : If the organisation has many units scattered over a large area, decentralisation for better results is generally the practice. Although operational control is employed at the lowest level of its divisions, the same is not true for finance. It is generally centrally controlled to maximise the firm's control over its total assets.

4. *Effectiveness of Communication System* : The degree of centralisation or decentralisation is highly determined by the adequacy or otherwiseness of the communication system. If the communication system is quick (such as telegraph, telephone, radio, teletype), centralisation can be an effective means of issuing direct orders to distant subordinates. With the development of electronic devices, computerized management information system, operations research, the issue of directions on matters like sales and production orders, inventories, etc., facilitates the centralisation of certain information for managerial purposes. On the other hand, if the communication system is ineffective, there is a tendency towards decentralisation.

5. *Degree of Standardisation in the Organisation* : The greater the degree of standardisation in the organisation, the greater is the degree of centralisation. If repetition and standardisation of operations can be introduced to a large degree in the work place, events can be controlled more easily; and they can also be predicted more accurately. Therefore, authority tends to be centralised.

6. *The Span of Control*: When there is a narrow span of control and numerous levels in management hierarchy, organisations are 'tall' and authority is centralised. Contrarily, if the span of control is wide and there are only a few levels of management, organisations are 'flat' and authority is decentralised.

7. When quick, responsible, adaptive, creative action is necessary to be taken on the spot a level at which it is required with a view to cashing on the opportunity present, decentralisation is desirable. On the other hand, where delay does not matter, centralisation is adopted.

Hartman and others have observed thus: "Centralisaton or dencentralisation may be, in part, merely the result of circumstances. Many of the problems are handled centrally because the laws of the country require it or the union insists on it. Many operating or sales decisions are decentralised because it would be physically impossible to operate successfully if they were centralised. Frequently, the centralisation or decentralisation of a decision is merely an accident. Finally, there is an increase in the variety of possible human behaviour, a vast multiplicity of minute, undiscoverable causes and effects that cannot be encompassed in any principle or standard or evaluation. Thus, there is a large area in which necessity, intrusion, and luck decide the issue between centralisation and decentralisation."[33]

Balanced View Needed

However, where neither absolute centralisation or absolute decentralisation is preferable, there should be a balance between the two. General motion under the leadership of Sloan adopted the balance between managerial centralisation and decentralisation by following this management philosophy: "Centralised policy and control and decentralised operations and administration"[34] That is, *major policy and decision-making powers were duly centralised; and decisions involving execution of major plans, policies and programmes were duly decentralised in the operating units.*

Delegation vs. Decentralisation

1. Delegation is a process while decentralisation is the end-result of planned delegation.
2. Delegation is always between the superior and his subordinate; while decentralisation is company-wide delegation as between top management and divisions and/or departments.
3. Delegation is a must for management and it creates an organisation, while decentralisation is optional and appears on the scene when the organisation grows and is large and complex.
4. The superior exercises supervision and control over the subordinate, while in decentralisation, the top management exercises broad and minimum control.

Merits of Decentralisation

Decentralisation of authority has certain advantages, such as:

1. *Diversification of activities* : It reduces the burden of the chief executives with making routine decisions. They can easily devote the time available for important activities such as diversification of products, raising necessary finance, obtaining licenses and starting new lines of production and solving crucial problems of the business concern, while less important and routine may be left to the middle and supervisory levels.
2. *Development of the Managerial Personnel* : As the business grows in size, it requires the services of a large number of managers and here decentralisation provides a training ground for the would-be managers. The managers learn by experience within the organisation concerned.

33. Quoted by Sherlekar, S.A., and V.S., Sherlekar, *Principles of Business Management* (with *Case Problems*), Himalaya Publishing House, Mumbai, 1983, p. 258.

34. Hartman, Richard, I., Terreuce P. Hogan, and John T. Wholihan, *Modern Business Administration: Introductory Readings*, D.B. Taraporevala Sons, Mumbai, 1975, p. 106.

3. *Effective Control and Supervision*: Decentralisation leads to effective control and supervision. Since concerned managers enjoy full authority to make changes in work assignment, to take disciplinary actions, to change production schedules or to recommend promotions, they are in a position to supervise the subordinates' activities.
4. *Improvement of morale* : Improvement in managerial ability leads to an increase in their morale and this results in a higher productivity.
5. *Satisfaction of human needs* : Decentralisation is an important tool for satisfying human needs of power, independence, status and prestige. This satisfaction helps in building a cadre of satisfied managers, who feel their responsibility towards company's work.
6. *Quick and wise decision possible* : Since decision-making authority is as near as possible to the place where action takes place, those having this authority can make reasonably accurate, wiser and timely decisions because they are well aware of the realities of the situation. Decentralisation also minimises the delay in communicating information.
7. Other economies may be achieved through the better utilisation of lower and middle management, greater incentive, more and improved training opportunities, insurance that some products will not be pushed at the expense of others.
8. Closer and better employee management and community relations are possible in small administrative units for business as a whole, where decentralisation may mean a more widespread distribution of roles and purchases, which may reduce proportionately the unfavourable impact of sales decline.
9. Decentralisation may result in an increase in the managerial social net product, i.e., benefits to the community as distinct from benefits to the company. These general benefits may include more freedom of action for individuals, more widespread opportunity for constructive individual participation, less social stratification within the business.

Demerits of Decentralisation

1. Decentralisation makes the utilisation of the services of exceptionally talented people difficult. Because of weak financial resources, appointment of such persons may not be possible.
2. It increases the problems of coordination among the various units.
3. In some cases, decentralisation may not be possible at all. External factors make this difficult, such as company wide strikes.
4. It increases the administrative expenses because highly-paid managers have to be appointed.

ORGANISATION STRUCTURE

Peter Drucker has observed that : "Organisation is not an end in itself, but a means to the end of business performance and business results. Organisation structure is an indispensable means and a wrong structure will seriously impair business performance and may even destroy it. The organisation structure must be designed so as to make possible the attainment of the objective of the business for five, ten, fifteen years hence." According to him, there are three *specific* ways to find out what type of structure is required to attain the objectives of an enterprise, *viz.*, (i) Activities analysis, (ii) Decision analysis; and (c) Relation analysis.

(i) *Activity Analysis* : Since policies of a company affect its form of organisation greatly, it is necessary at the outset to identify its policies and then to analyse the activities necessary for achieving these policies. Newman and Logan have identified four major policy issues in business enterprises, *viz.*, in sales, production and purchases; personnel; and finance areas.[35] These have been given in the appendix to this chapter as *Exhibit 1*.

It may be stated that each business has a set of specific functions to perform, such as manufacturing, marketing, engineering, purchasing, personnel, financing etc. With prior analysis, these functions can be applied everywhere and to every thing. If the activities of various business houses are analysed, it will be noted that each has some specific functions which may be the most important function of the typical functions mentioned above. When an overall structure of organisation is being considered, a listing of major activities would be adequate; but when individual jobs are there, they need a listing of minute details. The analysis is a continuing process.

(ii) *Decision Analysis* : Through decision analysis activity, the management tries to find out what is needed. In regard to decision analysis, Peter Drucker has emphasised four basic characteristics, viz. :

(a) the degree of futurity in the decision;
(b) the impact that decision has on other functions;
(c) the character of the decision determined by a number of qualitative factors such as basic principles of conduct, ethical values, social and political beliefs; and
(d) whether the decisions are periodically recurrent or rated as recurrent decisions may require a general rule whereas a rated decision is to be treated as a distinctive element.

He has further emphasised that "Decision should always be made at the lowest possible level and as close to the scene as possible."

The analysis will show what structure of the top management the enterprise needs, and what authority and responsibility different levels of operating management should have.

(iii) *Relation Analysis* : Under this, the job of manager in terms of the activity he leads is defined. Peter Drucker has emphasised that, "The first thing to consider in defining a job is the contribution his activity has to make to the larger unit of which it is a part," i.e., the 'upward relationship' (*vertical*) should be analysed and established first and then the sideways (*horizontal*) relations must be analysed.

The grouping of activities into major departments and units within these departments may be regarded as a vertical division of activities and, hence, the *vertical authority*. When horizontal strata are created within each of the vertical divisions, i.e., in a plant, machine operations are put on one level, foremen on another, then shop superintendents, and then the plant managers, this creates a *horizontal relationship* among them.

The chief elements that make up the design of relationship in an organisation, thus, take these forms :

- Line authority
- Staff relationship
- Functional authority

35. New, William, H and James P. Logan, *Business Policies and Central Management*, Mumbai, 1970, pp. 410-411.

- Decentralisation of authority.

These will be discussed at a later stage in this chapter.

Departmentation or Grouping of Activities

Once an organisation's activities have been defined and listed in the order of their importance, the next step is to decide how these can be grouped together into manageable sections, departments or divisions or units. This activity is known as *departmentation*. For example, the General Manager of a big company cannot look after the activities of different departments. He may, therefore, transfer (i.e, delegate) some of his functions to the Departmental Managers, who, in turn, may delegate some of their responsibilities to Deputy Managers, and so on (Fig 8.3)

The purpose of departmentation is to specialise activities, simplify the tasks of managers, and maintain control. There is no single formula which may apply to all situations for departmentation. However, the following criteria may help the organisation planner.[36]

1. Similar activities may be grouped together, based upon likeness of personal qualifications or common purpose, for example, medical and dental personnel;
2. An activity may be grouped with other activities, with which it is used, for example, safety and production.
3. Activities may be grouped to encourage competition among departments or to avoid friction among them.
4. Functions may be assigned to the executive who is most interested in performing them well.
5. If it is difficult to make definite distinctions between two activities, they may be grouped together.
6. Certain functions require close coordination and if separated, would increase the problems of higher level managers; in this case, such functions should be grouped together.

Departmentation in manageable units provides an optimum contribution of (i) specialisation of expertise (with respect to function, product, customer or any other factor that is important in a specific situation, (ii) aid to control; (iii) aid in coordination; (iv) adequate attention; (v) adaptation to local conditions, and (vi) low expenses.[37].

Activities are grouped on the basis of products, processes, customers or markets, territories and functions.

(a) *The grouping of activities on the basis of product* becomes feasible when organisations grow into multi-product enterprises having extensive markets. All functions related to particular products are brought under the control of a Product Manager who is deputed with operating authority by the top executive. For example, in an electricity company, one department may be for manufacturing and selling of household appliances; another large generators, and so on.

(b) *The grouping of activities on the basis of process* may be feasible when similar machines are grouped into separate sections that are used for a distinct operation of each. For example, lathe machines, drill machines, grinding machines, etc are put each in a distinct unit.

(c) *The grouping of activities on the basis of customers or markets* is resorted to by enterprises engaged in specialised services. This is done with a view to giving individual attention to the different groups of buyers. Sales activities are usually divided into several parts.

36. Massie, Joseph, L., *Essentials of Management*, Prentice Hall of India, New Delhi, 1973, pp. 69.70
37. Newman and Logan, *Ibid.*, p. 441.

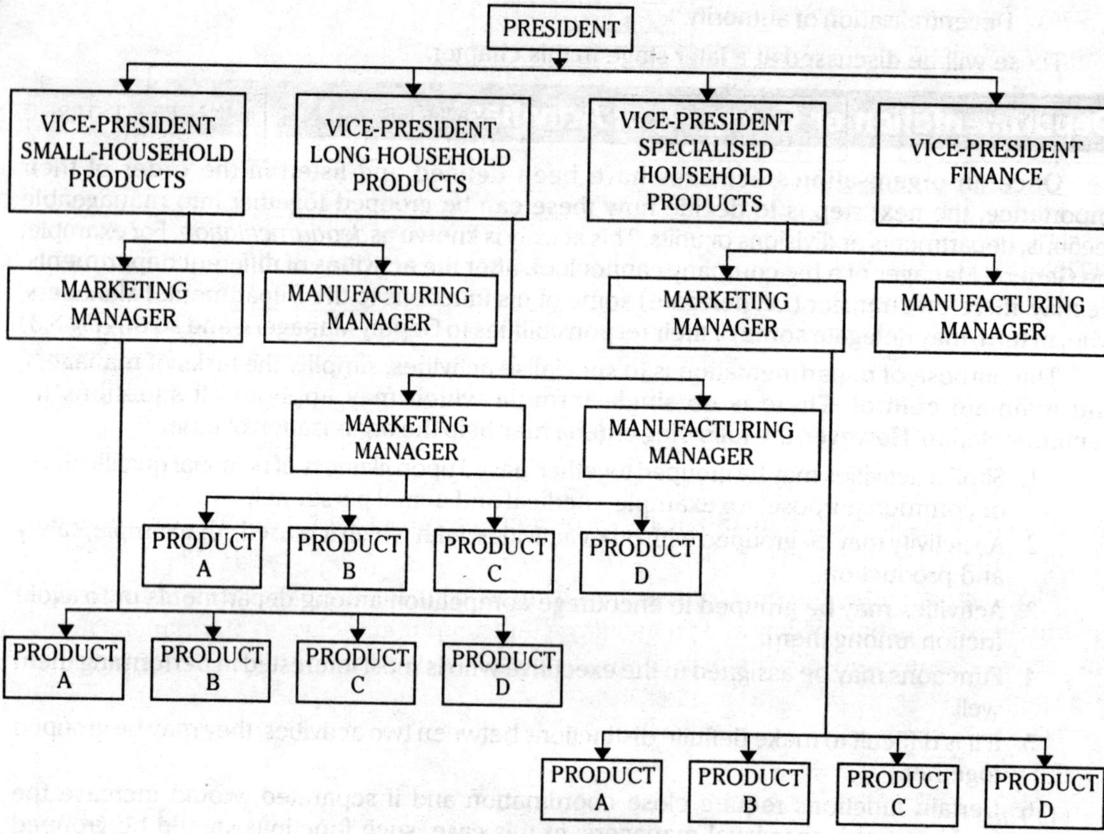

Fig. 8.3 Product-type of Organisation Structure.

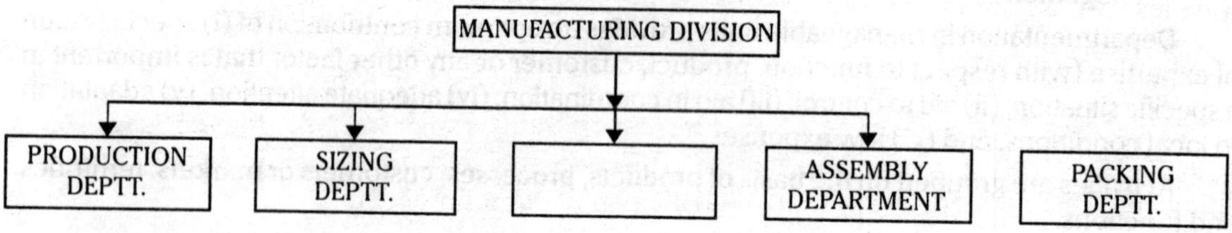

Fig. 8.4 Process-wise Organisation Structure.

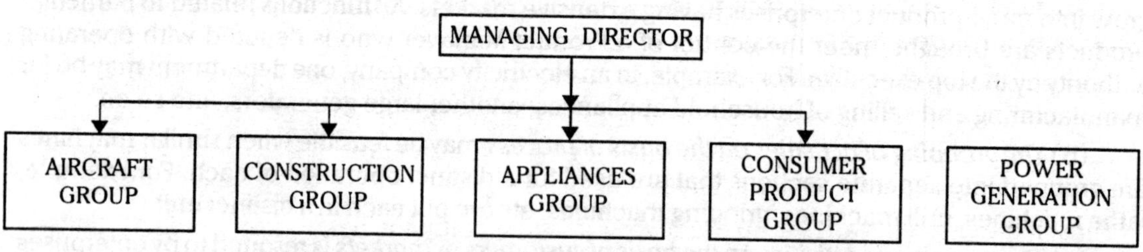

Fig. 8.5 Customer-wise Organisation Structure.

(d) ***The grouping on the basis of territories*** **is done when the market is to be broken into sales territories such as Northern, Southern, Central or Western India. Each territory is in charge of a Sales Executive under whom there are field salesmen.**

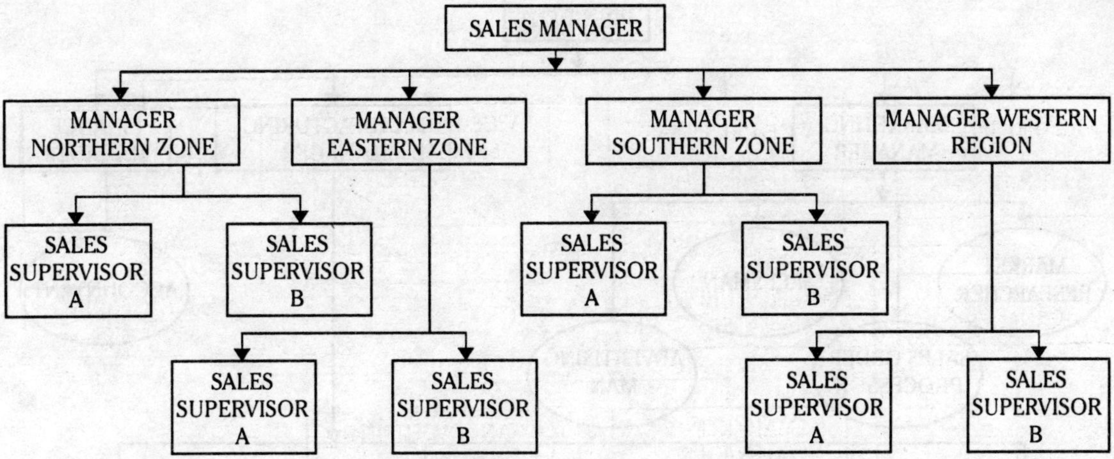

Fig. 8.6 Territorial Organisational Structure.

This basis is suitable for the physically dispersed enterprises. Activities are grouped area-wise and assigned to the heads of the respective areas.

(e) *The grouping on the basis of functions* is done in small enterprises for creating major departments. Production, selling and financing are three important activities of a manufacturing concern. For example, the production department may be divided into engineering, quality control and inspection department. The marketing or sales department may deal with marketing research, advertising, sales promotion and personal selling.

But there are certain drawbacks in the process of departmentation, viz.,

(1) *The problem of coordination gets complicated*. The greater the number of department/levels, the more difficult becomes the task of coordination and with poor coordination, there is always less of managerial efficiency which may ultimately lower the overall output.

(2) *The work of communication, control, supervision and planning becomes more difficult* and increases the cost of managing a concern

(3) Because of the layering of executives, operatives may be far removed from top management, creating a large gap between the two and this lessens the chance of direct relationship. This causes a loss of morale on the part of the subordinate.

In sum, departmentation results in expensive working in terms of money and effort and in undermining of operating efficiency of the business concerned. In spite of these drawback, departmentation is deemed necessary in a modern business.

In practice, an organisation may use one or more bases of departmentation. For instance, a national multi-product diversified corporation may adopt geographical, product-wise departmentation and within the division, it may have a functional base having functional departments like production, finance, and marketing.

Thus, if departments are set up product-wise and a company handles six products, there will be 6 major units. When territorial or functional grouping of activities is used, many sub-divisions of work can be possible. But then, it has to be decided how many persons an executive or other head can supervise effectively, i.e., to decide the 'span of management' or 'supervision'. This refers to the number of subordinates an executive can supervise efficiently.

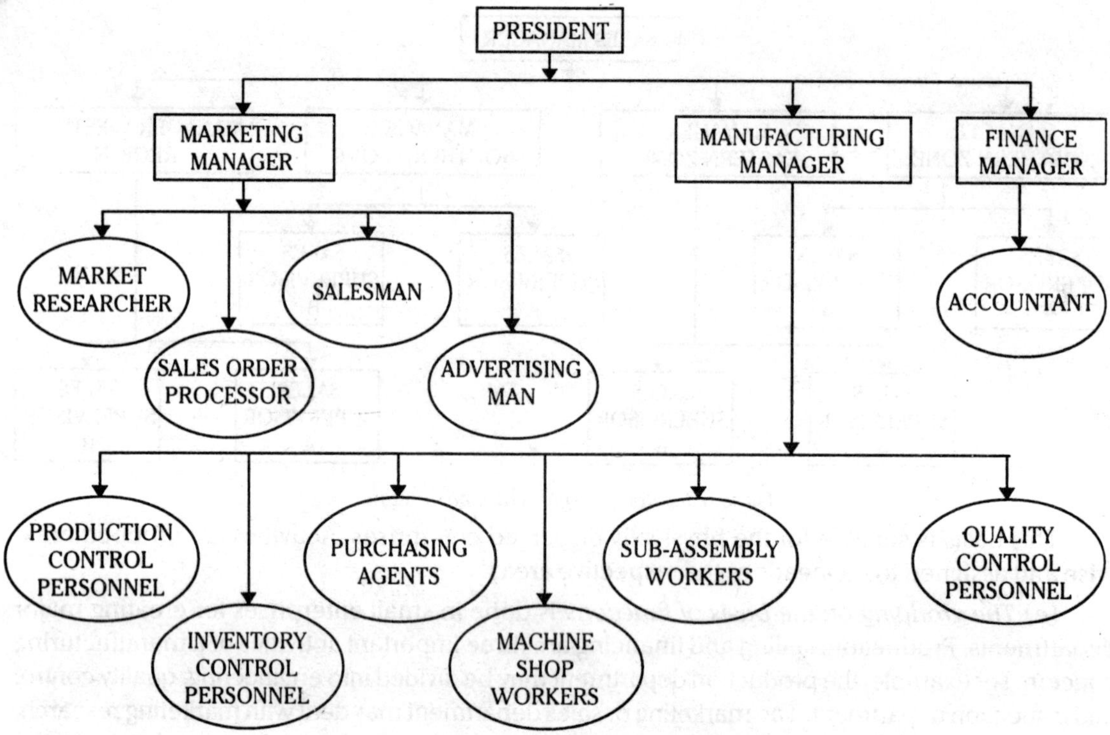

Fig. 8.7 Functional Organisation Structure.

Span of Control or Supervision

The number of people manager can control and still accomplish organisation objectives effectively is referred to as the *span of control*. Various management authors have suggested limiting the span of control from 3 to 9; 6 to 15; and 10 to 13 persons[38]. In general practice, many business firms tend in the direction of a narrow span contributing to the creation of a 'tall organisation'

Lyndall Urwick suggested a specific span limit of 3 to 6 persons for a manager.[39] Graicunas states, "No executive should attempt to supervise directly the work of more than 5 or at the most 6, direct subordinates whose work interlocks."[40] He termed this as a principle of 'Control' or 'Supervision'. Other management experts have suggested differing numbers of personnel to be supervised. Davis recommended that the span be limited to approximately 3 to 9 when supervising subordinate managers, if the work is difficult. [41] When one is supervising operative employees, acceptable spans are 10 to 30.[42] Keith Davis suggests a span of control of from 6 to

38. Davis, Ralph, C., *The Fundamentals of Top Management*, Harper and Brothers, New York, 1951, p. 276; and Keith Davis, *Human Relations at Work*, McGraw-Hill Book Co., 1962, p. 226.
39. Urwick, Lyndall, F., "The Managers' Span of Control", *Harvard Business Review*, May-June, 1956, pp. 39-47.
40. Graicunas, V.A. "Relationship in Organisation," Papers *On Science of Administration*, ed, L. Gulick and L. Urwick, New York, 1937, pp. 183-187.
41. Davis, Ralph; *op. cit.*
42. *Ibid.*, p. 271.

15 managers when little supervision is required of the managers and only access to the supervising manager is necessary.[43] Still others recommend 15 to 20 persons for an effective span of control. These varying spans are caused by the types of persons being supervised, the job itself, and the abilities of the supervisor.

If the span of control is 'narrow' or limited, there is a greater need for close supervision, which means, more *layers* of executives between the operatives and the general manger. However, additional layers of executives have also been regarded objectionable on various grounds such as: [44]

(i) it contributes to inflexibility; for it takes time to communicate, especially if the executives are busy or are off station; and this slows down the speed of adjustments to changing conditions;
(ii) when a company is divided into many segments, vested interests are likely to arise which may resist changes;
(iii) morale tends to be lower in companies with many layers of executives. Operators do not know the 'big boss' personally; and they may lack a sense of participation and feel just like a cog in the wheel. Too many levels of span create problems of coordination and control; they breed conflicts and add to inordinate delay.

According to one authority, "a tall structure often results in over specialisation and over-funtionalisation of activities and job assignments. Individuals work under close, constant supervision, therefore they may be exposed to undue pressure from the formal hierarchy, superior-subordinate relations are strained as a result of intense supervision and control."[45]

On the other hand, the larger the span, more the organisation structure is '*flat*', i.e, longer or wider which means greater individual freedom, resulting in fewer levels of executives. This enables the executive to delegate more authority to his subordinates, thereby allowing more freedom on the job. A wide span means fewer managers and therefore, reduced managerial costs and also a reduced number of problems of communication.

Donnelly and others observe that, "Organisations with fewer levels and wider spans of control yield a less complex organisational system. The wide span of supervision forces management to delegate authority. In addition to delegation, the flattening technique requires a better trained management team, shortens communication networks, and also reduces the administrative distance between levels of management."[46]

To determine what should be the optimum span, many factors need to be considered. Since the managers are accountable for the performance of their subordinates, the span of supervision is made a workable proposition. It is a function of a number of variables, such as :

(i) the similarity or dissimilarity of functions performed by the individuals being supervised;
(ii) the physical nearness of the workers to each other;
(iii) the level of complexity or simplicity of functions needed to be performed;
(iv) the amount and degree of continuing attention, needed on the part of the supervisor, towards each subordinate;

43. Davis, Keith, *op, cit.*
44. Flippo, Edwin, B and Garg, M, Munsinger, *Management*, Allyn & Bacon, Boston, 1975, 3rd Ed., p. 169.
45. Worthy, James, C. "Organisational Structure : Employee Morale:" *American Sociological Review*, 15. No. 2. April 20, pp. 169-179.
46. Donnelly, James, H. Jr., James L. Gibson and John, M. Ivancevich, *Fundamentals of Management*, Business Publication, Texas, 1971, p. 224.

(v) the effort required to coordinate and correlate the actions of subordinates;

(vi) the importance and complexity of future programmes and objectives and the time required to review and establish them;

(vii) the amount of support and help the supervisor receives from line and staff assitances[47].

A few more factors have been added, such as: (a) the level of cohesiveness of the workers; (b) the degree of member consensus and identification with common goals; (c) the amount of job satisfaction derived by subordinates from their jobs; and (d) existing levels of performance and productivity [48].

Besides these, some other factors also affect the span, such as:

(i) the communication system within and between the levels of organisation structure;

(ii) the time the executive has to devote to supervision;

(iii) the variety and importance of the work supervised;

(iv) the effect on morale, and the flexibility of additional layers of executives; and

(v) the authority delegated to subordinates.[49]

Based on these factors, the span of control should be :	
Short	for complex work.
Longer	for work similar jobs.
Large	if both supervisors and subordinates are capable
Lower	if the location of the supervisor is higher in the mangement hierarchy.
Wide	if more authority is delegated.
Lower	if there is a fear of possible rival
Limited span	if the activities are highly dynamic and volatile.
Limited span	if the communication is frequent and involved.

A manager's philosophy (Theory X or Theory Y) towards his subordinates also affects the number that he feels can be supervised effectively. However, a *correct span will vary from manager to manager*. The usual number is from 4 to 8 at the higher level of management. *The people involved, the jobs involved and the environment are the major deciding factors of the span of control.*

Committee Organisation

Committees are usually relatively formal bodies, with a definite structure/organisation, which are delegated definite responsibility and authority for doing a specific job, such as reviewing budgets, formulating plans for new products, making policy decisions on wages and salary and compensation plans. Others may only have the power to make recommendations and suggestions to a designated official. Whatever be the task, committees generally enjoy authority/power for carrying out the assigned tasks.

A Committee has been defined as "a group of individuals who meet for the purpose of effecting an integration of ideas concerning a solution of some problem."[50] Allen has defined a

47. Stieglitz, Harold, *Organisation Planning*, National Industrial Conference Board, New York, 1966, p. 15.
48. House, Robert, J, and John, B. Miner, "Merging Management Theory: The Interaction Between Span of Control and Group Size," *Administrative Science Quarterly*, Vol. 14, No. 3, Sept., 1969, p. 461.
49. Newman, W.H., and James, P. Logan, *op. cit.*, p. 451.
50. Davis, Ralph, C., *The Fundamentals of Top Management*, Harper & Brothers, New York, 1951, p. 469.

committee as a "body of persons appointed or elected to meet on an organised basis for the consideration of matters before it."[51]

The principal features of a committee are :

1. A committee is a gathering of people representing different functions or spheres of knowledge, who come together to promote a common purpose or fulfil a common task or solve a problem, by interchanging of views.

2. The character and composition of a committee is often spelled out in the bylaws or administrative procedures of the company.

3. A committee usually has a fixed membership. In most cases, members are appointed, although sometimes, as with the board of directors, they may be elected.

4. In its deliberations, a committee usually follows certain definite written rules and procedures. Some committees can function if a quorum is complete; others only if all the members are present.

5. A committee may be granted authority to make or recommend decisions, or it may serve merely in an advisory capacity.

6. Committees may be set up for different functions to be performed, such as for acting only rather than for advice (i.e., Control Committee); to help line executives in laying down plans, policies and objectives (such as *Legislative Committee*); to gather facts relating to a problem (such as *Fact Finding Committee*): to settle grievances or disputes and to determine the validity of the past and present courses of action (such as the *Grievance or Judicial Committee*); to bring coordination among the activities of the organisation members through interchange of views, opinions, and information (such as *Co-ordination Committee*); to decide other personnel matters like wages, promotions, merit pay, compensation, leave etc. (such as *Wage Committee*). In fact, there is a myriad of committees in government, educational, religious and business organisations. Although they are more frequent at the top of the pyramid, there is usually some type of formal committee at every level of organisation.

A commitee may also be set up on a standing basis (Standing Committee) which is of a permanent nature; or on an *ad hoc* basis, which may be for a specific purpose only. It may be formal or informal.

Advantages of Committees

A committee is usually used for bringing about organisational effectiveness as a device for helping the line executive in the performance of his managerial functions. According to Allen, a committee is created and used for the following purposes.[52]

1. *To carry out responsibilities that may otherwise be delegated to a simple individual.* Committees are used properly when individuals in regular established positions cannot adequately carry out a specific responsibility.

2. *To make use of the collective knowledge and judgement of a number of people on complex problems*, which may result in a solution better than the one that is generally available from an individual. Committees perform several functions. These may act in a service, advisory, coordinating information or final decision-making capacity.

51. Allen, Louis A., "Making Better Use of Committee", *Management Record*, New York, Dec. p. 467.
52. Allen, Louis, A., *Ibid.*

As the old adage goes, 'two heads are better than one', a group of people offer a wider range of experience, knowledge, ability and personality characteristics, a more through survey of facts, and a more diverse and specialised background than one person can possibly bring to bear on a problem. The situation resulting from oral exchange of views can clarify problems and help develop new ideas and solutions. When problems are diverse and complex, the combined judgement of the group is superior to that obtained from individual judgement.

3. The committee deliberations tend to ensure participation of all to suggest, criticize and make recommendations – on policies and projects, which are binding on all the parts of the organisation, and hence, it can work more smoothly. In other words, a *committee* increases motivation and commitment derived from participation. By being involved in the analysis and solution of the problem, individual members more readily accept and try to implement what has been decided.

4. A committee is extremely useful in coordinating plans and in integrating and unifying varying points of view as well as in facilitating their execution.

5. A committee not only permits organisation personnel to obtain an overall picture of plans and their place in the plans, but also allows its members to contribute valuable suggestions 'on the spot' for improving the plans and other related managerial problems.

6. A committee may exercise a staff role by providing advice to a specific individual of the organisation at large. They may be used to advise and counsel a top executive in policy formulation.

7. A committee sometimes serves as a decision-making body in the field of finance, personnel, etc.

Disadvantages of Committees

Committees suffer from many disadvantages too. Attacks have been on the usefulness of the committee, as the following statements show :

- "A camel is a horse designed by a committee."
- "The best committee is a five-person committee, with four members absent."
- "In a committee, minutes are taken but hours are wasted."
- "A committee is a collection of the unfit appointed by the unwilling to perform the unnecessary."
- "Nothing is even accomplished by a committee unless it consists of three members, one of whom happens to be sick, and another absent" (Hendrick Van Loon, a Dutch-American historian).
- "Committees are too dilatory, irresponsible and time-consuming for normal administration."
- "It is like a corporation with neither a soul to be damned nor a body to be kicked."
- "There is a group or corporation, but no individual responsibility or accountability. It is used as a 'shield to avoid personal responsibility for bad decisions or mistakes' using justification as 'why would I bother with this problem'."
- "Madness is the exception in individuals but the rule in groups" (Nietzche, the German Philosopher)

Committees also suffer from other disadvantages as given below :

1. *Committees encourage managers to shirk or evade decision making responsibilities* : If a manager/chairman is an accountable person, he may fall back upon the committee as a scapegoat, or escape the consequences of an unpopular decision. If the committee as a whole is held

accountable, accountability is so diffused as to be impossible of assignment. Some managers utilise the committee as a means of avoiding the difficult process of logical thinking that leads to a sound decision.

2. *Slow decision-making* :Committee action is always invariably slow and unwieldy compared to individual decision-making as much of the time is wasted through irrelevant discussion on trivial topics that do little to further the organisation's good. This seriously handicaps management of the enterprise, because the very technique of calling people together and providing for discussion is time-consuming. Absenteeism, lack of preparation before meetings and substitutions in membership slow down decision-making.

3. *May serve to mesh inefficient management* : Committees are mostly popular with managers who are inadequate in their own right. The committee serves as a crutch for concealing the weaknesses of the managers.

4. *Committees are dominated by a few individuals who force their opinion on other members:* Committee decisions, therefore, often represent the views of these influential personalities. In most cases, these decisions are not in conformity with the wishes of the members as a whole. The committee decisions, therefore, do not find favour at the implementation stage.

5. *The committee develops, what is known as Group think* : Group think is a process of deriving negative results from group decision making efforts – a result of pressures. People do tend to be influenced by their peers. Since no one wants to break up the cohesiveness of the group, the members become the victims of 'group think'. Group-think type of atmosphere is encouraged before the meeting even begins. The other members are there merely to rubber-stamp pre-determined decisions. Group leaders may also assume that silence on the part of the participants means consent or agreement to decisions actually made unilaterally by the leader.

6. *Group decision-making often results in costly delays* : Other tasks are neglected while committee members are in session, and there tends to be more indecisiveness rather than any candid and creative thought among members as they try to arrive at reasonable decisions and conclusions.

Guidelines for Effectiveness of Committee Operations

The effectiveness of a committee can be improved if attention is given to the following factors:

1. *The committee should have a clearly-stated purpose in unambiguous terms*. It should comprise function and scope, responsibilities, authority, and organisational relationships. The purpose should be made clear to all the members beforehand. The duties and the authority of the committee should be defined clearly. Unless all members have a clear idea of the purpose of the committee and the subjects it is to cover, considerable time is likely to be lost in irrelevant discussion. The committee should know whether it is advisory or whether the decisions are to be final. When decisions are final, there should be an understanding of who will carry them out because it is obviously impractical for an entire group to be responsible for executing any plans.

2. *Members of the committee should be carefully selected*, preferably from among persons of equal status, and possessing ability to help fulfil the purposes of the committee. For example, a Salary Committee should be composed of a few highly respected and objective individuals, whereas a Coordinating Committee should include operating executives from different departments to be coordinated. When representation is important, committees may have to be large. In other situations, there should be a few members and then to invite other people to sit in

when subjects of interest to them are being discussed. Allen observes, "Some individuals are constitutionally incapable of effective membership with subordinates they are domineering; with superiors, they are obsequious; and with peers, they are quarrelsome." Selection of members must, therefore, be made on the basis of personality differences, ability in expression and status.

3. *The chairman of the committee should understand his role properly*, which is that of expediting and facilitating the progress of the meeting. For this, he should possess expert knowledge, experience, and ability to cope with different situations. With his expertise, the chairman can see that discussion is kept on the subject, effective staff work has been done in advance of the meeting, and standard procedures are observed.

4. *The committee should be of a proper size*. If it is too large, many members might not get an opportunity to express their viewpoints, and the situation, at times, may become chaotic. If it is too small, it becomes difficult to secure well-thought-out views. Those committees are ideal where the members range between 5 and 9.

5. *There should be adequate preparation for the committee meeting*, properly prepared agenda, provision of adequate staff and all necessary facts/data needed, proper setting of beginning and ending time of the meeting, arguments on types of information needed to make a decision, and summary of this information on a standard form, etc. So that the work of the committee is greatly expedited.

6. *Committee members should have open communication, and conflicts* should be confronted and resolved with a problem-solving approach.

7. *Logical procedure should be followed in conducting the meeting* so that discussion may be carried on in an orderly fashion and lead to a logical conclusion.

This procedure consists of:

(i) reviewing of the pertinent facts by the chairman;
(ii) analysis of the problem in terms of what caused it, if this has not already been brought about, and determining how committee members feel about it;
(iii) suggested solutions;
(iv) group decision or recommendation; and
(v) securing of consensus of meeting, either by majority vote, or concurrence by all members, or acceptance of the recommendation of the majority, and recording of the viewpoint of the dissenters.

8. *Adequate follow-up is necessary* : Minutes of committee should be prepared and distributed to each member and the top executive, in all cases, as early as possible.

9. *The work of the committee should be constantly evaluated*. This is done to find if the committee is operating effectively in terms of the purpose for which it was set up and whether that purpose is still valid. If this is not done, committees often become self-perpetuating.

10. If the committees are appointed only when they have a significant role to perform, and if the preceding guides for effective operation are allowed, committees can become an important part of the organisation structure of a company.

In sum, before establishing a committee, due consideration should be given to the benefits and demerits of the committees besides the social setting in which they are required to work. This will include such things as availability of competent members; their training, background and personality; previous experience with committees and the prevailing attitude towards them; the technique of supervision normally used; and the general operating climate.

Project Organisation

This is an approach for bringing together all the necessary talent and organisational resources to accomplish a specific project goal.[53]

This type of organisation structure is found in industries with highly complex product systems, such as the aerospace or weapon industry. In this structure, project members are chosen for their special capabilities in the light of the goals to be accomplished from different functional departments, *viz.*, production, engineering, quality control, marketing research, and marketing. When the project has been completed, this task force is dissolved and personnel are returned to their regular organisation units.

Although the regular functional departments do not work, the project manager is responsible for the completion of the project. He specifies *what* is to be done, *when* it is to be done, and *how much* of the available resources are needed. The functional managers decide *who* in their units will do the work and *how* it will be done. The project organisation, thus, is a complex structure that facilitates the coordination and integration of many project activities.

Such an organisation is known as a *grid* or *matrix* organisation because here, vertical flow of functional authority and responsibility is combined with the horizontal flow of project authority and responsibility. The project manager acts as a coordinator of all project activities and the work of different specialists lent by the functional departments. The project manager has authority over the functional managers regarding *what*, *when* and *how much* of the activities; the functional manager determines *how* support will be given and who will give the support.

According to Middleton, there are four types of organisations[54].

(i) an *individual project* manager to whom no one is required to report;

(ii) a *unit project organisation* where the manager is provided unit help in scheduling and coordinating as well as supervising the funds of the project;

(iii) *an intermix project* in which some of the operative functions or existing departments are assigned full time to the project and others remain intact; and

(iv) *the aggregate organisation* in which all activities and personnel are assigned to the project manager.

Merits of Project Organisation

1. It is an effective way of producing highly complex product systems.
2. Project organisation, based on team concept, is the best means of getting the right things done right.
3. In a turbulent environment, such organisation is preferable for planning, implementing and control of costs projects.
4. Diverse interests are consolidated to the above problems.
5. Creativity is developed through interaction with various specialists.
6. It leads to the development of strong team-work and teams with identity fully with project goals.

53. Thieramp, Robert J., Robert C. Klekamp, and David W. Geeding, *op. cit.*, p. 365.
54. Middleton, C.J., "How to Set Up a Project Organisation," *Harvard Business Review*, March-April, 1967, p. 75.

Demerits of Projects Organisation

1. A deliberate conflict is established between the project officer and the existing department heads because of the overlapping of authority delegation.
2. At the close of the project, there is every likelihood of insecurity of employment.
3. There always lurks and danger of over-specialisation in the course of project involvement.
4. Rotation from project to project reduces employees' loyalty to the parent functional department.

Exhibit 1: Major Policy Issues in Business Enterprises

Sales	*Production and Purchasing.*
A. PRODUCTS AND SERVICES	A. EXTENT OF VERTICAL INTEGRATION
1. Diversification vs specialisation	B. PRODUCTION PROCESSES
2. Product differentiation	1. Choice of technology
3. Frequency of design change	2. Division of labour and automation
	3. Size and Dispersion of plants
	4. Involvement in process research.
B. CUSTOMERS	C. CAPACITY AND FACILITY BALANCE
1. Types of consumers	1. Peak vs. normal load
2. Location of consumers	2. Backward taper of capacity
3. Channels of distribution	3. Provision for growth
4. Size of customers	
C. PRICES	D. MAINTENANCE AND REPLACEMENT
1. Relation to competing products	E. MAKE-OR-BUY SUPPLIES AND SERVICES
2. Relation to costs	
3. Prices of individual items	F. SELECTION OF VENDORS
4. Quantity and trade discounts	1. Number of vendors
5. Price changes	2. Type of vendors
D. SALES PROMOTION	G. TIMING, PRODUCTION AND PURCHASING
1. Sales appeal	1. Stock vs to order
2. Advertising	2. Size of inventory and orders
3. Personal solicitation	3. Stabilising production
	4. Anticipating price changes
Personal	*Finance*
A. SELECTION	A. USES OF CAPITAL
1. New Employees	1. Fixed asset investment
2. Promotion	2. Uses of Circulating capital
3. Discharge	3. Mergers and acquisitions
B. TRAINING	B. SOURCES OF CAPITAL
1. Place in Management	1. Owners
2. Specific purposes	2. Long-term creditors
3. Types of training	3. Short-term creditors
	4. Financial structure

C. COMPENSATION
1. Amount of pay
2. Methods of payment.

D. ARRANGEMENTS OF WORK
1. Hours of work
2. Vacation
3. Working conditions

E. EMPLOYEES SERVICES
1. Social and recreational
2. Protection from risks

F. INDUSTRIAL RELATIONS
1. Character of relations
2. Support of union
3. Scope of bargaining
4. Use of outside agencies

C. PROTECTION OF CAPITAL
1. Reduction of hazards
2. Insurance
3. Hedging
4. Calculation of profits.

D. DISTRIBUTION OF EARNINGS
1. Ploughing back of earnings
2. Stable dividend rate
3. Adequacy of surplus

Source: Newman, William H. and James P. Logan, *Business Policies and Central Management*, 1970, pp. 410-411.

CHAPTER 9

BEHAVIOURAL POLICIES

MOTIVATION AND MOTIVATION THEORIES

What is Motivation?

Every human action is the result of a need or desire. One experiences a sort of mental discomfort as long as that need remains unsatisfied in him. The moment the action is ignited he makes an attempt to get over the discomfort. So what causes an action is the need or desire. What causes a need is called the stimulus. Therefore, the manager's duty is to create the stimulus that causes a need which ignites action that leads to satisfaction.

There should be a repetitive process for the action to continue. All this is called 'motivation' in management.[1]

Motivation is derived from the word motive. "A motive is an inner state that energizes, activates or moves and directs or channels behaviour toward goals".[2]

"Motivation represents an unsatisfied need which creates a state of tension or disequilibrium, causing the individual to move in a goal directed pattern towards restoring a state of equilibrium by satisfying the need".[3] According to the Encyclopaedia of Management, "motivation refers to the degree of readiness of an organisation to pursue some designated goal and implies the determination of the nature and locus of the forces, including the degree of readiness."[4]

Motivation is a process that starts with a physiological or psychological deficiency or need that activitates behaviour or a drive that is aimed at a goal or 'incentive'. Thus, the process of motivation lies in the meaning of and relationship among needs, drives and incentives (Fig.9.1)

Needs →	Drives →	Goals/Incentives
(Deficiency)	(Deficiency with Direction)	(Reduction of drives and fulfils deficiencies)

Fig. 9.1: The Basic Motivation Process.

Need: Need is deficiency. Needs are created whenever there is a physiological or psychological imbalance.

Drive: is a deficiency with direction. They are action-oriented and provide an emerging thrust toward goal accomplishment.

Incentives: Incentive is anything that will alleviate a need to reduce a drive.

Types of Motives

Motives are divided into three categories viz., Primary Motives, General Motives and Secondary Motives.

Primary Motives: These motives are unlearned and physiologically based. They include hunger, sleep, avoidance of pain, sex and maternal concern.

1. C.B. Mamoria, *op. cit*., p. 652.,
2. Berelson et. al., *"Human Behaviour"* Harcourt Brace & World Inc., New York, 1964, p. 240.
3. Carris S. Viteless, *"Motivation and Morale in Industry"*, W. W. Nonb & Co., New York, 1953, p. 73.
4. C.B. Mamoria, *op. cit*., p. 652.

General Motives: These motives are unlearned but not physiologically based. These motives include curiosity, manipulation and activity motives and the affection motive.

Secondary Motives: Secondary motives are closely tied to the learning concept. A motive must be learnt in order to be included in the secondary classification. Important among them are: achievement the affiliation, power, security, status and immediate feedback.[5]

"The task of management is to arrange organisational conditions and methods of operation so that people can achieve their own goals best by directing their own efforts toward organisational objectives". Successful supervisors will be those who integrate the goal-oriented actions of individual workers with the pursuit of organisational goals. The goals of the individuals and the organisation can be achieved through stimulating workers toward productive performance — called *activating or motivational process*. It is a process of arousing action, sustaining the activity in progress, and regulating the pattern of activity.[6] It attracts and initiates action and also serves as a factor in the continuation of activity until objectives have been attained.

Motivation may be defined as "a willingness to expend energy to achieve a goal or reward. It is a force that activates dormant energies and sets in motion the actions of the people. It is the function that kindles a burning passion for action among the human beings of an organisation."

Objective of Motivation

The purpose of motivation is to create conditions in which people are willing to work with zeal, initiative, interest and enthusiasm, with a high personal and group moral satisfaction, with a sense of responsibility, loyalty and discipline and with pride and confidence in a most cohesive manner, so that the goals of an organisation are achieved effectively.

Motivational techniques are utilised to stimulate employee growth. This was indicated by Clarance Francis when he was Chairman of General Foods. He said: "You can buy a man's time, you can buy a man's physical presence at a given place; you can even buy a measured number of skilled muscular motions per hour or day; but you cannot buy enthusiasm. You cannot buy initiative; you cannot loyalty; you cannot buy devotion of hearts, minds and souls. You have to earn these things."

Types of Motivation

If a manager wants to get work done by his employees, he may either hold out a promise of reward for them for doing work in a better or improved way, or he may constrain them, by instilling fear in them or by using force, to do the desired work. In other words, he may utilise a positive or negative motivation. Both these types are widely used by the managers.

A *positive motivation* involves the possibility of increased motive satisfaction, while a *negative motivation* involves the possibility of decreased motive satisfaction.[7]

Positive Motivation

Positive or incentive motivation is generally based on reward. Accordings to Flippo, "positive motivation is a process of attempting to influence others to do your will through the possibility of gain or reward." People work for incentives in the form of the four P's of motivation: Praise, Prestige, Promotion and Pay cheque.

5. Fred Luthams, *op, cit*., pp. 231-235.
6. Young Paul, T., Motivation and Emotion, John Wiley & Sons, New York, 1961, p. 17.
7. Kazmier, Leonard, *Principles of Management*, 1977. p. 458.

Positive motivation, in fact, includes: (i) praise and credit for work done, (ii) a sincere interest in subordinates as individuals; (iii) competition; (iv) participation; (v) status and pride; (vi) job security; (vii) job enlargement, (viii) job rotation; (ix) job load; and (x) pay or financial security.

According to Peter Drucker, the "real and positive motivators are responsible for placement, high standard of performance, information adequate for self-control and the participation of the worker as a responsible citizen in the plant community."

Incentive motivation is the 'pull' mechanism. It has its own benefits. The receipt of awards, due recognition, and praise for work well done definitely lead to good team spirit, co-operation and a feeling of happiness.

1. *Appraisal, Praise or Recognition:* When he does his work well, the employee naturally wants it to be praised and recognised by his boss and fellow-workers. "Praise seems to have its greatest value when given and received as recognition, and is not perceived by either party as an attempt to control the behaviour of the recipient."[8] Recognition satisfies human need for esteem by others and for self-esteem. This recognition may be shown in the form of praise, of a pat on the back of the employee or a recommendation for a pay rise, promotion, or assignment of more interesting tasks. Awards may be given in the form of articles, banquets honouring certain individuals, certificates and plaques, too, may be given, or the employee's name may be entered on the Honours Board.[9]

Such recognition may generally be given for good workable suggestions leading to a reduction in time or cost or in improving the quality of a product; for valuable services in an emergency, as when a fire breaks out, or there is a breakdown, or there are riots or accidents; exceeding sales beyond the set quota, and regularity in attendance on the job.

2. *Status and Pride:* Status refers to 'the social rank of a person,' and satisfies social and egoistic needs. A management often tries to satisfy these needs by establishing status symbols and distinctions in its organisation providing costly furniture, carpets on the floor, picture on the wall, artistic curtains, a separate stenographer, a few peons, and a personal assistant. Individuals try hard to gain these status symbols; and once these have been achieved, there is a craving for higher status symbols.

Persons working in similar positions and enjoying the same status in an organisation should be treated on equal footing and provided with identical facilities, such as those of a private locker, a separate chamber or cabin, easy-chairs, suitable desks with drawers, peons, etc.

Pride is a nebulous concept and it is somewhat difficult to define. However, "good products, dynamic leadership, fair treatment, service to the community, ethical conduct and such other things serve to stimulate an employee's pride in his work and organisation." This pride is regarded as a powerful and valuable motivator towards higher productivity.

3. *Competition:* As a form of motivation, competition is widely used in an organisation. Individuals do compete with one another if they feel they have chances of winning and satisfying their 'ego'. This competition may be in regard to sales, production, or safety measures. The person who is adjudged the best is awarded the coveted prize. But sometimes, competition generates jealousy and hostility among the competing members, may give rise to a sense of frustration among the losers, and may even destroy team-spirit.

8. Maier, Norman, R.F., *Industrial Psychology*, p. 460.
9. Beach, D.S., *Managing the Personnel At Work*, p. 395.

4. *Delegation of Authority*: An authority is the right to act, to direct, and to requisition resources needed to properly perform the job. The delegation of a substantial amount of responsibility to execute a given task often proves to be a strong motivating force. The subordinate is more or less on his own. The supervisor trusts him. He feels that he must show results. But for persons who lack confidence, this technique of motivation often proves disastrous.

5. *Participation*: It implies the physical and mental involvement of the people in an activity, especially in that of decision-making. This satisfies one's ego and self-esteem, and the needs of creativeness and initiative. A management may encourage employees to help in such areas of decision-making as production methods, materials handling, safety measures, cost reduction, employee-management problems, and improvement in working conditions.

Participation may be in regard to: (a) institutional arrangements for worker's participation in decisions within undertakings (Work Councils and Joint Council bodies); (b) participation of workers in management organs (particularly in managing welfare facilities); (c) participation at the shop-floor level and at the board level.

6. *Job Security:* For some employees, this is an equally important motivator. Job security implies that an employee would continue on the job in the same plant or elsewhere, and that he shall enjoy economic and social security through health and welfare programmes providing security against sickness, unemployment, disability, old age, and death.

Job security may be provided either by properly regularising the amount of work that must be done by fixing of the hours of work and by finding out work for those who have been rendered surplus because of changes in techniques of production or lines of production or recessionary conditions in the market, or by adoption of schemes of rationalisation, modernisation and automation.

Job security may be provided by: (i) ensuring that catastrophes will be avoided as far as possible; (ii) implementing elaborate programmes of fringe benefits; and (iii) adjusting surplus labour in an organisation.

7. *Job Enlargement or Whole Job Concept:* It is the process of increasing the complexity of the job in order to appeal to the higher-order needs of workers. It implies that the employee performs more varied tasks, which are all on the same level, the idea being to make the jobs less monotonous. According to Strauss and Sayles, "it implies that, instead of assigning one man to each job, a group of men can be assigned to a group of jobs and then allowed to decide for themselves how to organise the work." Such changes permit more social contacts and greater control over the work process.

The technique suggests that attempts are made to give workers more complete, or whole jobs to perform. Efforts are made to develop an environment in which employees are able not only to be actively involved in their jobs, but also to participate in both planning and evaluating the results of their efforts. An example of job enlargement would be to allow a person on an assembly line to perform more than one specialised function.

Jobs can be enlarged both in the horizontal dimension and in the vertical dimension. The former refers to the number and variety of operations that an individual performs on a job; while the latter refers to the extent to which the job-holder controls the planning and execution of his job and participation in the setting of organisational policies.[10]

8. *Job Rotation:* It implies the shifting of an employee from one job to another so that monotony and boredom are reduced. The basic objective of job rotation is to increase the skill

10. Lawler, Edward E., "Job Design and Motivation." *Personnel Psychology*, Vol. 22, 1969, pp. 26 - 35.

and knowledge of the employee about related jobs. In job rotation, workers learn to do all the different activities necessary for an operation or unit of work.

Sometimes, an unpleasant job is made an entry-level *position*. Employees can be told that the job is monotonous, but temporary. Another possibility may be to put all 'dull jobs' up for grabs each day. *Sleepy or hung-over workers* may even prefer a day on a job not requiring much use of their minds. Another possibility is that *physically* or *mentally handicapped workers might be* given simple jobs.

9. *Job Loading*: It implies making the job more interesting. A *horizontal job loading* assumes that if employees are given more work at the same level at which they are currently performing, they will be motivated to work harder and also be more satisfied with their work. In a *vertical Job loading,* changes in jobs include larger areas of responsibility. Jobs are restructured so that they will become intrinsically more interesting. The worker is motivated because his job is more challenging and more meaningful. He is given as much responsibility as possible, and is encouraged to be accountable for his work with little supervision.

10. *Job Enrichment*: It is a form of changing or improving a job so that a work is likely to be more motivated. It provides the employee with the opportunity for greater recognition, advancement, growth and responsibility. Through job enrichment, the job is made more interesting and challenging. It is designed to be less specialised and more enriched. Usually this is accomplished by giving the worker more autonomy and by allowing him to do much of the planning and inspection formerly done by his supervisor. Job enrichment implies a deliberate upgrading of responsibility, scope and challenge.[11] The goal of job enrichment is not merely to make the work more varied but to make "every employee a manager." An employee whose job is enriched will perform the management functions of planning and control so far as his own work is concerned. According to Herzberg, "job enrichment would provide an opportunity for the employee's psychological growth."

In an enriched job, an employee knows the overall deadlines and the quality standards he must meet and within that framework he plans the order in which he will tackle the various tasks and the time that should be devoted to each. He holds himself responsible both for meeting the deadlines and for producing work of the necessary quality, and he does not pass his work or let others to judge it till he is satisfied that it meets the required standards.

11. *Pay or Financial Security*: Such motivation is connected directly or indirectly with money. Wages and salary, bonuses, profit-sharing, leave with pay, medical reimbursement, etc. are included under this type of motivation. At a first glance, money would seem to be one of the 'lower level' needs, a need that is quickly satisfied. But in reality this is not true. The reason is that money is more than just a medium of exchange. It is more than a vehicle through which one can satisfy other higher-order needs. When a person goes out to buy a car he is doing more than just spending his money; he is buying at least in his own eyes — prestige, recognition, and a visible symbol of his achievements. He uses money to satisfy some of higher-order needs — self actualization, ego and social needs besides the safety and physiological needs. For this reason, money is sometimes regarded as the most esteemed needs and hence, a most important motivator.

12. *Others: (a) Quality of Work Life*: This covers all aspects of worker's life with particular reference to his interaction with his 'work' and 'working environment'. Besides adequate compensation, this includes: (i) *safety and healthy working conditions,* including reasonable

11. Hersey, Paul, and K.H. Blanchard, *Management of Organisational Behaviour*, Prentice Hall of India, 1980, p. 58.

hours of work and rest pauses, physical working conditions that ensure safety, minimise risk of illness and occupational diseases and special measures for protection of women and children; (ii) *security and growth opportunity*, including factors like security of employment and opportunity for advancement and self-improvement; (iii) *opportunity to use and develop creativity*, such as work autonomy, nature of supervision, use of multiple skills, worker's role in total work process and his appreciation of the outcome of his own effort and self-regulation; (iv) *respect for the individual's personal rights*, such as the application of the principles of natural justice and equity, acceptance of the right of free speech and the right to personal privacy in respect of the worker's off the - job behaviour; and (v) *work and family life*, including transfers, schedule of hours of work, travel requirements, overtime requirements, etc.

(b) *Good Treatment*: This includes: (i) prompt and considerate handling of grievances: (ii) looking after the interests of the subordinates; (iii) opportunities for promotion; (iv) improvement in working conditions; (v) recognition as an individual; and not as a mere wheel in the machine; and (vi) giving due consideration to his self-respect; (vii) assignment of work according to his skill, intelligence, ability and craftsmanship. These recognitions cultivates a sense of accomplishment in the subordinates.

The skilful executive will analyse the attitude and aspirations of his subordinates and then try to arrange operations so that each individual will be challenged to put forth his best effort.

Guidelines for Motivating Employees and Managers

We suggest below the lines of guidance for motivating people:

1. The management should let his subordinates know that he considers them valuable, capable individuals, i.e. should treat them with respect and honesty.
2. He should make sure that subordinates have the tools to get the job done for achieving the goals.
3. The person should be fitted on the job where he can set his own standard, get concrete feedback and deal with moderate risks.
4. He should avoid building 'dissatisfiers' into the job, i.e. he should make sure that salary and working conditions are adequate.
5. He should set fair, achievable goals and communicate them to the employees, for understanding what they are shooting for helps adequate accomplishment of the goals.
6. The people should be made known, through feedback, how they are doing.
7. All such techniques as reinforcement incentives, MBO, job enrichment and maintenance of high morale should be utilised.
8. Job analysis, selection and training should be used to ensure that people are hired who could do the jobs if they wanted to — people with the required skills and abilities.

Steps in Motivation

According to Judious, the following steps should be adopted in motivation.

1. Sizing up situations requiring motivation.
2. Preparing a set of motivating tools.
3. Selecting and applying an appropriate motivator.
4. Following up the results of the application.

Sizing up: This step mainly involves understanding of different needs of people. Having assessed the needs, one can determine what motivates them.

Preparing a set of Motivating Tools: this list of motivators should be prepared based on the revealed needs of the people.

Selecting and applying Motivators: Out of the list of motivators, few should be selected and applied wherever and whenever they are needed.

Feedback: Having applied the motivators, it is important to find out how effective has a particular motivator been.

Theories of Motivation

There are several theories on motivation. The significant among them are: Maslow's hierarchy of needs, Herzberg's Two-factor theory, Vroom's Expectancy Theory, Alderfer's ERG Theory and the Porter and Lawrel Model Expectancy Theory.

1. Maslow's Theory of Hierarchy of Needs

According to Maslow, human needs form a hierarchy, starting at the bottom with the physiological needs and ascending to the highest need of self-actualisation as shown in Fig. 9.2. He says when one set of needs are satisfied they no longer work as motivators as a man seeks to satisfy the next higher level needs.

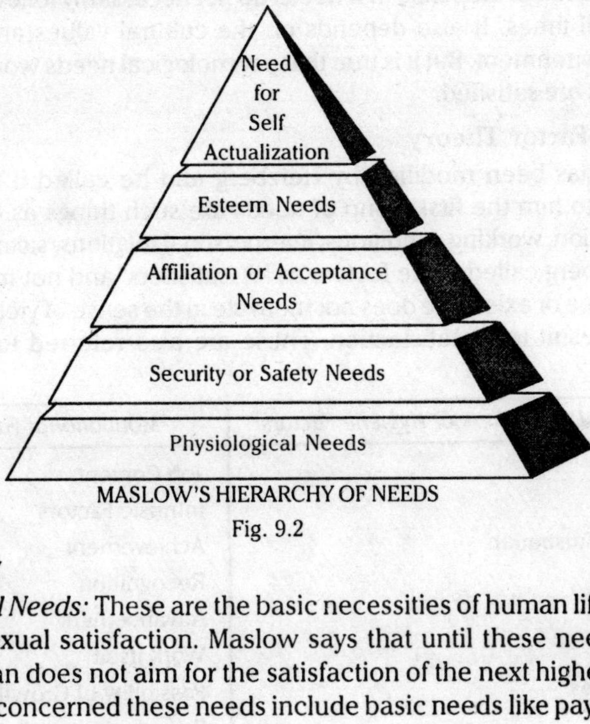

MASLOW'S HIERARCHY OF NEEDS

Fig. 9.2

The Need Hierarchy

(i) *Physiological Needs:* These are the basic necessities of human life-food, water, warmth, shelter, sleep and sexual satisfaction. Maslow says that until these needs are satisfied to the required level the man does not aim for the satisfaction of the next higher level needs. As far as work organisation is concerned these needs include basic needs like pay, allowance, incentives and benefits.

(ii) *Security/safety Needs:* These refer to the need to be free of physical danger or the feeling of food, job or shelter. When the physiological needs are satisfied man starts thinking of the way by which he can continue to satisfy these physiological needs. Security needs spring up the moment he makes an effort in the direction of providing himself the source of continuity of physiological needs. This is exactly the reason why attitude towards security is an important consideration in choosing the job. These needs as far as work organisation is concerned include: conformity, security plans, membership in unions, severance pay etc.

(iii) *Social Needs (Affiliation or Acceptance Needs)*: When the Physiological and security needs are satisfied these social needs begin occupying the mind of a man. This is exactly why he looks for the association of other human beings and strives hard to be accepted by its group. Social needs at work place include: human relations, formal and informal work groups.

(iv) *Esteem Needs*: These needs are power, prestige, status and self-confidence. Every man has a feeling of importance and he wants others to regard him highly. These needs make people aim high and make them achieve something great. These needs for employees include status symbols, awards, promotions, titles etc.

(v) *Self-actualisation Needs*: This is the highest need in the hierarchy. This refers to the desire to become what one is capable of becoming. Man tries to maximise his potential and accomplish something, when this need is activated in him.

Critical Analysis of Maslow's Theory

The first question that arises is "do needs follow hierarchy?" Studies and surveys conducted by experts reveal that needs do follow hierarchy to some extent. But it should be remembered that it cannot be generalised in the sense that needs do not necessarily follow the same hierarchy among all people at all times. It also depends on the cultural values and personality of the individuals and their environment. But it is true that psychological needs would emerge only after the physiological needs are satisfied.

2. Herzberg's Two-Factor Theory

Maslow's theory has been modified by Herzberg and he called it two-factor theory of motivation. According to him the first group of needs are such things as company policy and administration, supervision, working conditions, interpersonal relations, salary, status, job security and personal life. Herzberg called these factors as 'dissatisfiers' and not motivators. By this he means that their presence or existence does not motivate in the sense of yielding satisfaction, but their absence would result in dissatisfaction. These are also referred to as 'hygiene' factor (See. Fig. 9.3).

Maintenance Factor or Dissatisfiers or Hygiene Factors	*Motivational Factors or Satisfiers*
Job Context	Job Content
Extrinsic Factors	Intrinsic Factors
Company Policy and Administration	Achievement
Quality of Supervision	Recognition
Relations with Supervisors	Advancement
Peer Relations	Work Itself
Relations with Subordinates	Possibility of Growth
Pay	Responsibility
Job Security	
Work conditions	
Status	

Fig. 9.3: Herzberg's Classification of Maintenance and Motivational Factors.

In the second group are the 'satisfiers', in the sense that they are motivators, which are related to 'Job content'. He included the factors of achievement, recognition, challenging work, advancement and growth in the job. He says that their presence will yield feelings of satisfaction, but not dissatisfaction.

Comparison of Maslow's and Herzberg's Models

If we compare Herzberg and Maslow's models we can see that Herzberg's theory is not much different from that of Maslow. Most of the maintenance factors of Herzberg come under lower level needs of Maslow (see Fig. 9.4). Maslow says when the lower level needs are satisfied they stop being motivators and what Herzberg says is the same in the sense that they are maintenance factors (not motivators). But one particular difference that can be talked off here is that Maslow emphasises that any unsatisfied need, whether of lower or higher level, will motivate people and Herzberg clearly identifies certain needs and calls them as maintenance factors which can never be motivators.

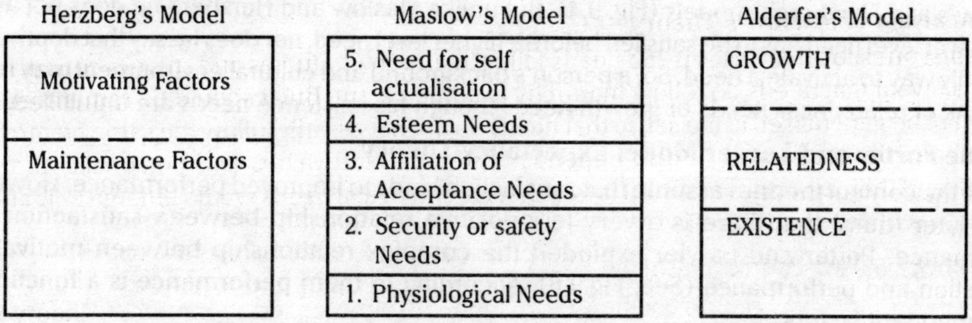

Fig. 9.4: Comparison of Maslow's, Herzberg's and Alderfer's ERG Models.

3. Vroom's Expectancy Theory of Motivation

Victor Vroom felt that content models were inadequate explanations of the complex process of work motivation and he developed relatively new theory of motivation. According to his theory, motivation of any individual depends on the desired goal and the strength of his expectation of achieving the goal. Vroom's model is built mainly on three concepts — valance, instrumentality and expectancy (See. Fig. 9.5).

Valance: Vroom says that valance is the strength of an individual's preference for a particular outcome. It can be taken as equivalent of value, incentive, attitude and expected utility. The valance to be positive the person must prefer attaining the outcome to not attaining it. A valance of zero occurs, when the individual is in different towards the outcome. The valance is negative when the individual prefers not attaining the outcome to attaining it.

Instrumentality: Another major input into the valance is the instrumentality of the first level outcome in obtaining desired second level outcome. For example, assume that an individual desires promotion and feels that superior performance is a very strong factor in achieving that goal. His first outcomes are then superior, average or of poor performance. His second level outcome is promotion. The first level outcome of high performance thus acquires a positive valance by virtue of its expected relationship to the preferred outcome of second level promotion.[12] In this case the person is motivated to achieve superior performance because he has the desire to be promoted. The superior performance (first level outcome) is seen as being instrumental in obtaining promotion (second level outcome).

Expectancy: The third major variable in the Vroom's theory is expectancy. Though the expectancy and the instrumentality appear to be the same at the first glance, they are quite

12. J.J. Rent and J.W. Hill, "*The New Look in Motivation Theory in Organisation Research*", Summer 1969, p.104.

different. Expectancy is a probability (ranging from 0 to 1) or strength of a belief that a particular action or effort will lead to a particular first level outcome. Instrumentality refers to the degree to which a first level outcome will lead to the second level outcome. Vroom says the sum of these variables is the motivation.

4. Alderfer's ERG Theory

Alderfer theory also states that needs should be categorised and that there is basic distinction between lower order needs and higher order needs. Alderfer identifies three groups of needs viz., Existence, Relatedness and Growth and that is why his theory is called the ERG theory. The existence needs are concerned with survival or physiological well-being. The relatedness needs talk of the importance of interpersonal and social relationships. The growth needs are concerned with the individual's intrinsic desire for personal development. This theory is somewhat similar to that of Mashow's and Herzberg's models (Fig. 9.4). But unlike Maslow and Herzberg he does not assert that a lower level need has to be satisfied before a higher level need, nor does he say that deprivation is the only way to activate a need. So, a person's background and cultural environment may make him think of relatedness needs or growth needs though his existence needs are unfulfilled.

5. The Porter and Lawler Model Expectancy Theory

All the content theories assume that satisfaction leads to improved performance. However, it was later found that there is a very low positive relationship between satisfaction and performance. Porter and Lawler exploded the complex relationship between motivation, satisfaction and performance (See. Fig.9.6). According to them performance is a function of three important factors viz:

(i) If an employee wants to perform, he must be motivated.

(ii) Motivation alone does not ensure performance and hence a person must have the necessary abilities and skills as well.

(iii) An employee must have an accurate knowledge of the requirements of the job.

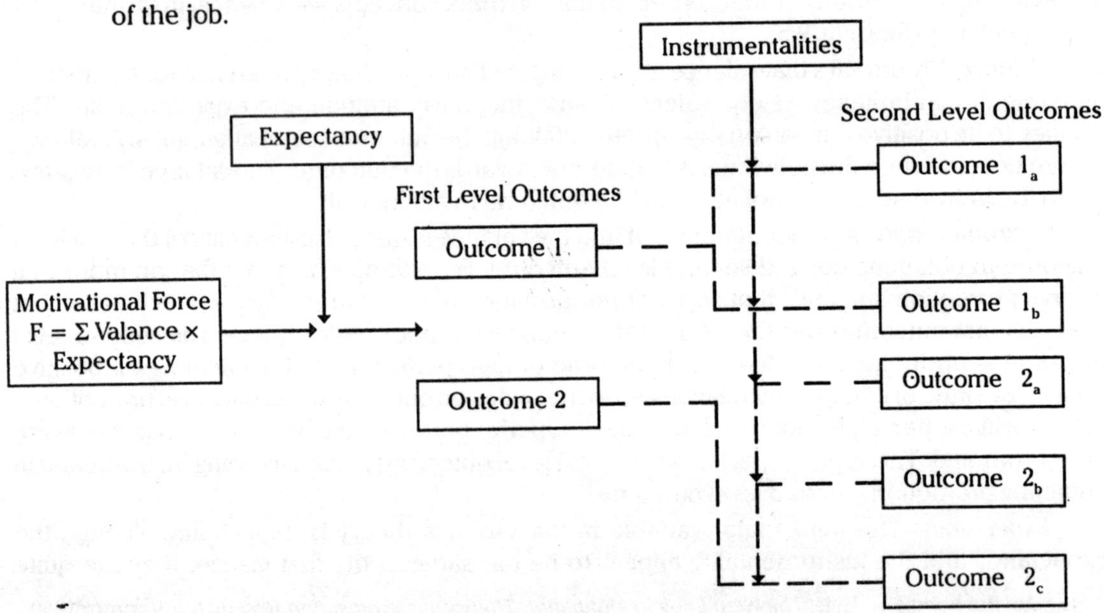

Fig. 9.5: The Vroom's Expectancy Theory of Work Motivation.

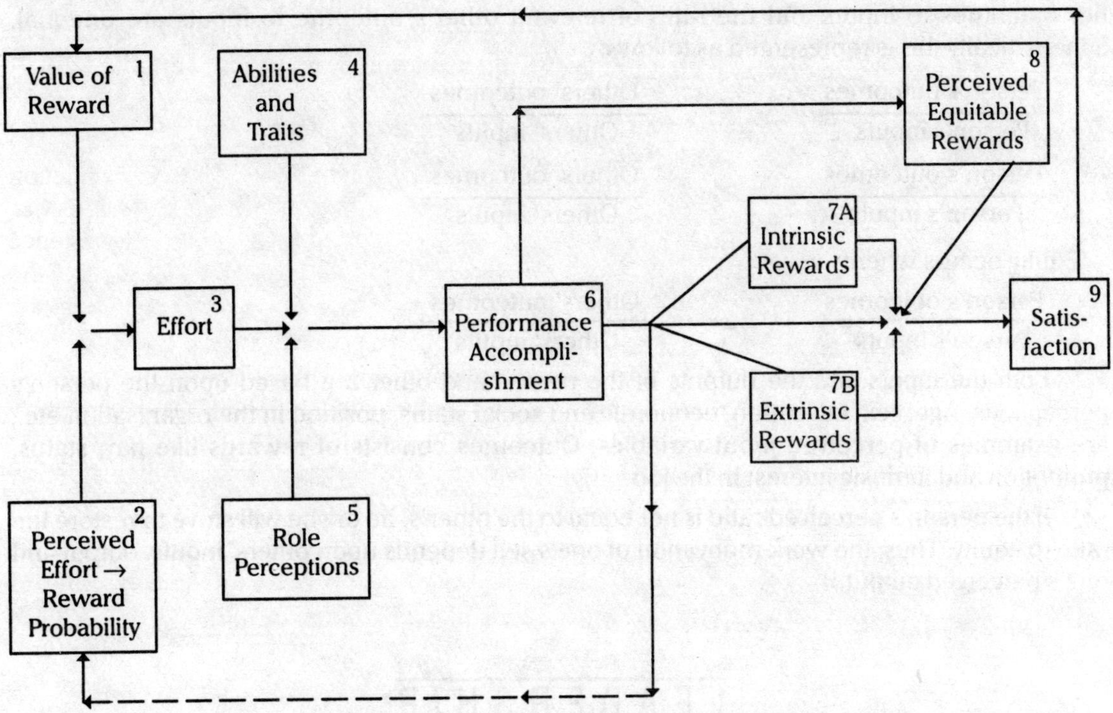

Fig. 9.6: The Porter — Lawler Motivation Model.

Source: Fred Luthans, *op. cit.*, p. 249.

The following are the key-variables in this model.

Motivation: Satisfaction and Performance.

Effort: Effort does not directly lead to specific levels of performance. Effort is only the amount of energy exerted by an individual to achieve a specific task. It is only the result of the attractiveness of the reward and how he perceives a relation between effort and pay off. The individual will exert greater effort if he perceives that there is a greater probability that his effort will lead to the reward. So motivation is seen as a force on the employee to expect effort.

Performance: Effort alone is not enough, as performance results only when the effort is continued with the ability. Effort and performance cannot be taken as the same.

Reward: A person gets intrinsic reward himself by performing a task well. Intrinsic reward will be a feeling of accomplishment. Extrinsic rewards like pay, promotion and status are offered by the organisation.

Satisfaction: The satisfaction depends on the perceived rewards and the actual rewards. If an individual feels that he should have received more for what he had done, it results in dissatisfaction and *vice-versa*.

Thus, motivation and achievement result in satisfaction or dissatisfaction of an employee about the job, organisation and the like.

6. Equity Theory of Work Motivation

Credit of developing this theory goes to J. Stacy Adams. This theory argues that a major input into job performance and satisfaction is the degree of equity (or inequity) that people perceive in their work situation. Inequity occurs when a person perceives that the ratio of his or her outcomes to inputs and the ratio of relevant other's outcome to inputs are unequal. Schematically this is represented as follows:

$$\frac{\text{Person's outcomes}}{\text{Person's inputs}} < \frac{\text{Others' outcomes}}{\text{Others' inputs}}$$

$$\frac{\text{Person's outcomes}}{\text{Person's inputs}} > \frac{\text{Others' outcomes}}{\text{Others' inputs}}$$

Equity occurs when:

$$\frac{\text{Person's outcomes}}{\text{Person's inputs}} = \frac{\text{Others' outcomes}}{\text{Others' inputs}}$$

Both the inputs and the outputs of the person and other are based upon the person's perceptions. Age, sex, education, economic and social status, position in the organisation etc., are examples of perceived input variables. Outcomes consists of rewards like pay, status, promotion and intrinsic interest in the job.

If the person's perceived ratio is not equal to the other's, he or she will strive to restore the ratio to equity. Thus, the work motivation of one's self depends upon others' inputs, output and one's perceived output.[13]

LEADERSHIP

Leadership is defined as the relationship in which one person (the leader) influences others to work together willingly on a related task to attain goals devised by the leader and /or group. Thus, the leadership is a key element in human resource in any organisation. Leadership is a part of management, but not all. Leaders require and use three different skills in influencing and interacting with people to attain goals, viz., technical skills, human skills, and conceptual skills.

Leading (or as it is also known as directing, executing, supervising, ordering and guiding) concerns the total manner in which a manager influences the actions of the subordinates. It includes: issuing of orders that are clear, complete, and within the capabilities of subordinates to accomplish. It implies a continual training activity in which subordinates are instructed to carry out the practical assignment in the existing situation. It necessarily involves the motivation of workers to try to meet the expectations of the manager. Finally, it consists of maintaining discipline and rewarding those who perform functions and duties properly. In short, leading or directing is the final action of a manager in making others act after all preparations have been completed.

People working in business organisations need leaders – individuals who could be instrumental in guiding the efforts of groups of workers to the achievement of goals and objectives. both of the individuals and the organisation. The objectives may not be very far-reaching and the actions of the leaders may not be so dramatic, but the successful performance of the leadership role is essential for the survival of the business enterprise. Goods and services are to be provided. products and customers need to be united and the workers' efforts require integration and coordination. The leader guides the actions of others accomplishing these tasks.

13. Fred Luthans, *op. cit.*, p. 251.

Leadership has been defined as "The relationship in which one person, or leader, influences others to work together willingly on related tasks to attain that which the leader desires."[14]

Leadership is that outstanding aspect of management which manifests ability, creativeness, initiative and inventiveness, and which gains the confidence, co-operation and willingness of the people to work, by organising and building employee morale.[15]

" It is the name for that combination of qualities by the possession of which a person is able to get something done by others, chiefly because through his influence they become willing to do it".[16]

Cartwright and Zander have observed that the definitions of leadership are so many and so varied that there is very little consensus about what leadership is or what it should be. They give a number of statements based on various definitions, viz., [17]

(i) Most leaders are too bossy or are not bossy enough.
(ii) A leader's job is to develop responsibility and initiative among his subordinates.
(iii) A leader's job is to take decisions and exercise authority.
(iv) A group is as strong as its leader.
(v) The trouble in most groups and organisations is that a few persons run everything.
(vi) Once the leader shows weakness, he is dead.
(vii) To be a leader, you must be aggressive and ambitious, and tell people what they should do.
(viii) If you want to be a leader, you have to be sensitive to the needs of others and tell them what they want to hear anyway.

The common thread running through these definitions is that leadership is a process whereby one individual exerts influence over others, through five different types of power — as pointed out by French and Raven — viz., coercive power, reward power, legitimate power, expert power, and referent power.[18]

It needs be noted that : (1) Leadership involves persons, (2) Leadership operates from some organisational position, (3) The act of leadership occurs within a specific situation. The leadership act takes place when these three factors interacts with each other.

Research studies done on leaders and non-leaders suggest that leaders "tend to be brighter, tend to be better adjusted psychologically, tend to display better judgement, tend to interact more than non-leaders, tend to give more information, tend to ask for more than non-leaders and tend to take the lead in interpreting a situation."[19] Paul Hare says, "there are indications that certain traits such as intelligence, enthusiasm, dominance, self-confidence, social participation and equalitarianism are frequently found to characterize leaders."[20]

14. Terry, Geroge R., *Principles of Management*, Richard D. Irwin, Homewood, 1972, p. 458.
15. Glover, John G., *Fundamentals of Professional Management*, Simmons Broadman Publishing Corporation, New Delhi, 1958, p. 148.
16. Ordway, Tead, *Human Nature and Management*, p. 149.
17. Cartwright, D. and A.F. Zander, *Group Dynamics,* pp. 535-536.
18. French, John, R.P. and Bertrim, Raven. '*The Basics of Social Power*'.
19. Hollander, E.P. 'Emergent Leadership and Social Influence.' in *Current Perspectives in Social Psychology: Readings with Commentary*, ED. E.P. Hollander and Raymond G. Hunt, Oxford University Press, New York, 1963, pp. 468-475.
20. Hare, A Paul, *Handbook of small Group Research*, The Free Press of Glencoe. 1962, p. 292.

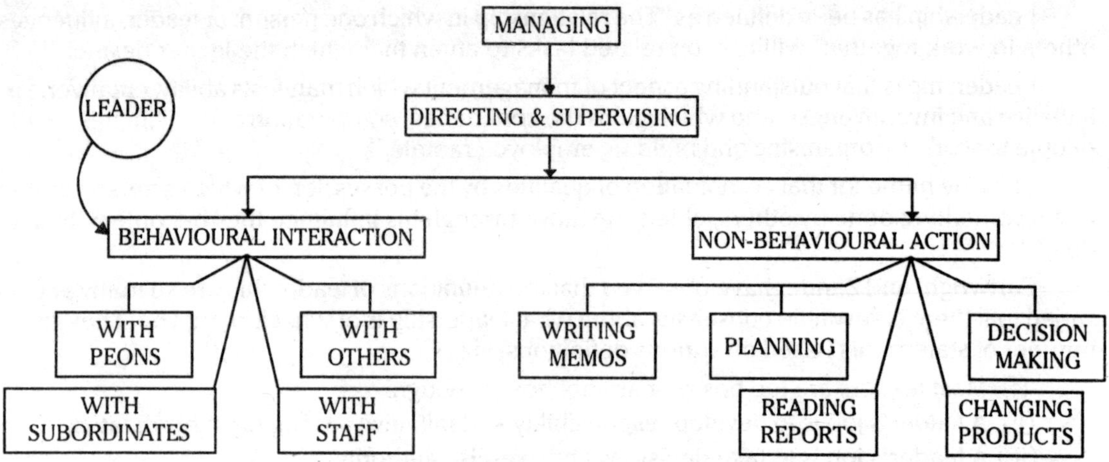

Fig. 9.7: Determinants of Leadership

He plays more than one role, viz., *group task* — definition and solution of problems; *group building and maintenance*; and *individual roles* — satisfaction of individual needs. These roles have been classified by Benne and Sheats as below:[21]

A. *Group Task Roles.*

(1) Initiator — contributor, (2) information seeker, (3) opinion seeker, (4) information giver, (5) opinion giver, (6) elaborator, (7) co-ordinator, (8) orienter, (9) evaluator-critic, (10) energizer, (11) procedural technician, and (12) recorder.

B. *Group Building and Maintenance Role*

(1) Encourager, (2) harmonizer, (3) compromiser, (4) gatekeeper and expediter, (5) standard setter or ego ideal (6) group observer and commentator, and (7) follower.

C. Individuals Roles

(1) Aggressor, (2) blocker, (3) recognition seeker, (4) self – confessor, (5) playboy, (6) dominator, (7) help seeker, and (8) special help pleader.

Functions and Responsibilities of a Leader

Different authors have differently given the functions of a leader. Most listings of leadership duties and responsibilities stress the leader's obligation to attain organisational goals and give attention to the needs of the individuals who are his subordinates.

Kahn, for example, is both organisation and work-oriented in his list of leadership functions. He states the leader serves best when he:[22]

1. Provides direct satisfaction to his followers.
2. Structures the path to goal attainment (in doing this, the leader provides the subordinate with cues towards fulfilling personal needs while attaining organisational goals).
3. Removes barriers to goal attainment;
4. Modifies employees' goals so that their personal goals can also be organisationally useful.

21. Benne, K. and Sheats, 'Function Role of Group Members', *Journal of Social Issues*. Vol. 4 No.2, 1948, pp. 42-48.

22. Kahn, R.I., 'Human Relations in Shop Floor' Hugh Jones Edward, *Human Relations and Modern Management*. North Holland Publishing Co., Amesterdam, 1958.

Killian, in a study published by the American Management Association, states that a leader's functions are:[23]

(i) To render a service (by multiplying the contribution of every individual who is its beneficiary);

(ii) To take decisions (leading others to sufficient understanding, not a reckless shooting from the hip but a calculated searching for, and weighing of, facts);

(iii) To elicit response (leading others to sufficient understanding, of the need for accomplishing the job in hand);

(iv) To achieve results (by guiding the energy of others in a definite direction for a specific purpose); and

(v) To be willing to be different; to have discipline and a standard of performance which is higher than that of the non–leader.

In sum, a leader undertakes the following functions:

(i) He represents the undertaking and its purposes, ideals, philosophy and problems to those working for it and to the outside world;

(ii) He initiates all the measures that are necessary for the purpose of ensuring the health and progress of the undertaking in a competitive economy;

(iii) He administers the undertaking by arranging for the forecast, planning, organisation, direction, co-ordination and control of its activities;

(iv) He interprets the objectives of the organisation and the means to be followed to achieve them; he appraises his followers, convinces them, and creates confidence among them;

(v) He integrates the activities of his group, develops its team spirit and cohesiveness, and brings about unity of action and approach among its members.

(vi) He identifies himself with group goals. Whether or not a leader has helped to formulate goals, he must always help the group attain them;

(vii) He satisfies the group's ego. The group ego develops by (a) integrating the group's needs and goals with the reality outside the group; (b) satisfying interpersonal needs within the group; and (c) creating an atmosphere free of conflict for group members.

(viii) When a decision cannot be reached easily, the leader makes a decision, for better or worse, with group compliance. Leaders can help clarify possible alternatives of action and they can prevent a group from stalemating or turning into a debating society.[24]

(ix) When groups experience internal differences, whether based on emotional or intellectual clashes, a leader can often resolve the differences. He acts as an arbitrator to prevent serious group splintering.

To be effective, the manager must do the following:[25]

1. *Create Support*: This behaviour on his part will let others feel that they are of worth and importance.

23. Killian Ray, A., *Manager Must Lead: A supervisory Road-map to Advancement*, A.M.A. New York, 1966. p. 20.
24. Applewhite, *Organisational Business*, p. 358.
25. Bowers, David, G. and Stanley E. Seashore, "Predicting Organisational Effectiveness with a Four - factor Theory of Leadership", in *Organisational Behaviour and Human Performance*, Ed, Cummings L.L. and Scoff, W.E. Irwin-Dorsey, 1969, pp. 599-615.

2. *Facilitate Interaction:* This behaviour will encourage members of the group to develop close, positive, warm, satisfying relationships.

3. *Emphasize Goals*: This will stimulate an enthusiasm among people to meet the performance goals of the group.

4. *Facilitate Work*: This is related to goal attainment and includes scheduling, coordinating, planning, and providing technical knowledge, tools and materials.

5. *Meet the Needs:* The manager should see that the needs of the formal and informal organisations are met.

Qualities of Leader

The leader is expected to play many roles and, therefore, must be qualified to guide others to organisational achievement and must also be a capable handler of interpersonal relations. Robert Dubin says. "All people are potential leaders. And, given the desire and opportunity, people can develop into effective ones.........A group abhors confusion, including the confusion resulting from being leaderless. Every organisation has many people in it who can exercise leadership, at least temporarily, than there are positions of leadership to be filled. It is often in situations of crisis, where an individual, not previously known to possess such qualities, become a leader, that officials of an organisation learn where the potential leadership skills are to be found."[26]

As group goals and tasks change, new leaders and shifts in power occur. Leadership in a group depends on the group standards and what leadership rules are acceptable.

Although no set of absolute traits may be identified, the individuals who possess abilities to lead others must have certain attributes to help them in performing their leadership roles.

According to Ordway Tead a leader must possess:

1. Physical and nervous energy;
2. Enthusiasm,
3. Sense of purpose and direction,
4. Technical mastery,
5. Friendliness and affection,
6. Integrity,
7. Decisiveness,
8. Intelligence, and
9. Faith.[27]

Chester Barnard thinks that a leader should have (1) vitality and endurance, (2) decisiveness, (3) persuasiveness, (4) stability in behaviour, (5) intellectual ability, and (6) knowledge.[28]

In our opinion, a good leader should possess the following qualities:

(i) *Energy*: A leader should have both mental and physical energy to work for sufficiently long hours without feeling tired.

(ii) *Emotional Maturity and Stability:* A leader should act with self confidence, avoid anger, take decisions on a rational basis and think clearly and maturely. He should not be whimsical but

26. Dubrin Robert, *The World of Work: Industrial Society and Human Relations*, Prentice-Hall, Englewood Cliffs, 1958, p. 393.
27. Tead, Ordway, *Art of Leadership*, McGraw - Hill Book Co., New York, 1935, p. 83.
28. Barnard, Chester, *The functions of Executives*, Harvard University Press, Cambridge, 1938, p. 260.

consistent in his actions because of his emotional stability and his cool mind. According to Koontz and O' Donnell: "Leaders cannot afford to become panicky, unsure of themselves in the face of conflicting forces, doubtful of their principles when challenged, or amenable to influence."[29]

(iii) *Knowledge of Human Relations*: A leader should have an understanding of human behaviours, that is, he should know people, know their needs, sentiments, emotions, as also their actions and reactions to particular decisions, their motivations, etc.

(iv) *Objectivity*: A leader's approach to any issue or problem should be objective and not based on any pressure, fear, bias, prejudice or preconceived notions. His decision should be based upon reasoning, facts, and a careful analysis of a problem. Objectivity is a vital aspect of analytical decision making. Objectivity also helps to ensure a fair, consistent course of action from the leader.

(v) *Empathy*: A leader should be able to look at things objectively and from the point of view of others. He should respect the rights of others, their beliefs and sentiments. In other words, he should equip himself to meet the challenges emanating from the actions and reactions himself to meet the challenges emanating from the actions and reactions of other people. The leader should be perceptive or empathetic towards his subordinate-followers so that he can discern their strengths, weaknesses, and ambitions and can give them the attention they deserve. He should also be perceptive introspectively (toward himself) so that he can know his own strengths, weakness and goals and can give proper consideration to them.

(vi) *Personal Motivation*: This involves the creation of enthusiasm within the leader himself to get a job done. It is only through enthusiasm that one can achieve what one wants.

(vii) *Communication Skill*: A leader should be able to talk and write clearly and forcefully. He should have the ability to persuade, to inform, stimulate, direct and convince his subordinates that it is in their own interest to offer him their willing co-operation in the performance of his task. Good communications seem to find all responsibilities easier to perform (those of planning, organising, controlling and especially those involving leading) because they relate to others more easily and can better utilise available data.

(viii) *Teaching Ability*: A leader should have the ability to demonstrate how to accomplish a particular task, to correct errors, prepare followers for achievement, and ask questions and offer suggestions.

(ix) *Technical Competence:* He should have a thorough knowledge of, and competence in, the principles, procedures and operations of a job. Technical skill involves specialised knowledge, analytical skill, and a facility in the use of the tools and techniques of a specific discipline.

(x) *Integrity*: A leader should be morally sound. In the words of Fredrick Taylor, "integrity is that straight forward honesty of purpose which makes a man truthful, not only to others but to himself; which makes a man high-minded, and gives him high aspirations and high ideals."

(xi) *Conceptual Skill*: He should have the ability to look at the enterprise as a whole, to recognise that the various functions of an organisation depend upon one another and are inter-related, that changes in one affect all the others. In the words of Chester Barnard, "the essential aspect of the executive process is the sensing of the organisation as a whole and the total situation relevant to it."

(xii) A leader should have the moral courage to do things which, he believes, are right, and stand by the decision he has taken. According to Field Marshal Slim, "without courage, there are

29. Koontz, Harold and Cyril O' Donnel, *Principles of Management,* McGraw - Hill Book Co., New York, 1972, p. 440.

no virtues; for faith, hope, charity and all the rest do not become virtues until there is courage to exercise them."

(xiii) *Flexibility of Mind:* A leader should have a flexible mind so that he may change in obedience to the change in circumstances. Carlyle has said: "A foolish consistency is the hobgoblin of a little man."

(xiv) *Ability to Establish Proper Priorities*: The leader must be capable of sorting out 'the chaff to get the real kernel of grain' — in other words, he must have the ability to see what is important and what is not. When decisions are necessary, the gifted leader knows which alternatives are worthy of consideration and which are not. When supervisory action is stable, the priority-oriented leader gives attention to the critical and most meaningful areas. He is not distracted by surface issues but pierces the heart of the matter.

In sum, a leader must have a dynamic personality — not necessarily a strong body, a good height, a beautiful complexion, a fine nose, a sharp and lustrous eye, a broad chest and a muscular body, but something much more important — character, intellectual attainments, striking features, and such special traits as a powerful voice, a sweet and amiable disposition, a modest and unassuming temperament, and knowledge of how to deal with his followers.

He must have a keen sense of social justice and be fully appreciative of the rights and interest of the men and women at work, as well as of the economic necessities of management. His philosophy of social justice should include two fundamental concepts:

(i) industry is a partnership between management, men and owners whose objective is to earn profits through service;

(ii) industry can profit greatly by developing and coordinating the capacities, the interests, and the opportunities of each worker and of each member of management. He must be able to couple this sense of social justice with a warm personal interest in people. This, in turn, must be controlled by a wealth of common sense, which will protect him from sentimentality, on the one hand, and from coldness, on the other.

The manner in which a manager directs activities depends upon his own personal *traits* and *situation* in which he finds himself. In leading, the manager must determine his own approach after surveying the possibilities open to him. Each manager will do well to be himself and must try to act as he observes others acting. Moreover, a manager will find himself in various situations — calling for different approaches in leading. If his subordinates are unskilled and need detailed instructions, the manager may find the direct, simple order advisable. If the subordinates are highly educated persons, he may find that a permissive and consultative approach is advisable. In cases of emergency, the manager may assume a 'take charge' role and give short clear authoritative commands, whereas if the action is not pressing, he may assume a deliberate and analytical attitude.

Type of Leadership Styles

According to the philosophies of leaders towards their followers, the techniques of leadership and its patterns and styles may be classified as below:

(i) Autocratic leadership, or authoritarian or leader-centered leadership;
(ii) Consultative, participative, democratic or group–centered leadership;
(iii) *Laissez-faire*, free-rein, or individual-centered leadership;
(iv) Bureaucratic or rules-centered leadership;

(v) Manipulative leadership; and

(vi) Expert leadership

(i) *Autocratic or Authoritarian Leadership:* An autocratic leader is work-centered or leader-centered. He concentrates all the authority and all the decision-making powers in himself. He structures the complete work situation for his employees. There is no participation by his subordinates in the decision-making process; they simply do what they are told to do. He tolerates no deviation from his orders, His subordinates fully depend upon him and are unaware of the goals of the organisation. The leader takes and assumes full responsibility for decision-making, for initiating action, and for directing, motivating and controlling his subordinates. This is because the autocratic leader many think that he is the only competent and capable individual, and that his subordinates are incapable or unwilling to guide themselves, or he may have other reasons for assuming a strong position of guidance and control. The response expected from the subordinates is obedience and adherence to his decisions. The style can be "soft sell", but it is usually perceived as "hard sell" — in either case, subordinates are permitted little freedom.

Autocratic style is efficient; needs little or no time to consult others during the decision-making process; and it works well in developed situations when decision must be made and acted on quickly and without question. But employees often present and resist leadership that excludes them from may involvement. Since autocratic communication is essentially one way, the resulting lack of feedback can lead to a misunderstanding and subsequent mistakes. Making decisions without first listening to the advice of others can result in poor decisions. Finally, this type of leadership is usually negative because the followers are generally ill-informed, unsecure and afraid of the leader's authority. Individual growth is far more difficult to attain within an autocratic framework; and it may fail to develop the workers' commitment to the objectives of the organisation. However, autocratic style might be used during an emergency occasioned by the breakdown of machinery with which the manager is familiar or when fire breaks out and there is a danger of the property and building being completely engulfed in it.

(ii) *Consultative, Participative, Democratic, or Group-Centered Leadership*: This type of leadership centralises managerial authority. The leader's decision are taken after consultation with his followers and after their participation in the decision-making process. He involves the members of his group in the decisions on the feasibility and workability of an idea, or a job and its content, and on the extent and the content of the problems that affect them. He believes that their co-operation in the attainment of organisation goals can be enlisted only if they are committed to the organisation, and that commitment can be ensured only by an honest and open communication of ideas with them and by the development of a team spirit. He encourages his subordinates to function as a social unit, and makes full use of their talents and abilities. "He is the conductor or an orchestra rather than a one-man band; and he realises that his job is to co-ordinate the willing work of his employees."

Participative leaders call for subordinates to exercise a high degree of both responsibility and freedom. They use as little authoritarian control as possible, and are concerned with group relationships as well as getting the job done. They do not delegate their right to make final decisions and to give specific directives to their subordinates, but do seek their thoughts and opinions on many decisions that affect them. Such leaders cultivate the decision-making abilities of their subordinates and encourage to increase their abilities, to exercise self-control and urge them to assume greater responsibility for guiding their own efforts.

Participative style is very useful in many ways. When workers feel their ideas are important and being made use of, they feel considerably committed to changes in which they have participated. Workers also develop a greater feeling of self-esteem. They maximise their potential in creative and productive ways and experience personal satisfaction and accomplishment of their tasks. Further, when most people are given a little freedom, they develop and grow personally and in job competence. Often they will take on more responsibility than their job descriptions call for because of the pleasure they take in their work.

On the other hand, participative leadership can be very time consuming and requires a great deal of energy. Sometimes participation can mean that little or no planning gets done at all, which can result in situations getting out of control. Participation can be used by people with authority as a guise for shirking their own responsibilities and as a way to pass on the buck to others. Another potential problem with participation is that group members whose ideas have been rejected may feel alienated.

Participative style of leadership is more appropriate under conditions in which:

(i) the company has communicated its goals and objectives to the subordinates and subordinates have accepted them;

(ii) where the company practices use of rewards and involvement as the primary means of motivation and control;

(iii) where the leader-supervisor truly desires to hear the ideas of others before making decisions;

(iv) where the leader wishes to develop analytical and self-control abilities in the subordinates;

(v) where the workers are reasonably knowledgeable and experienced;

(vi) where subordinates desire involvement in matters that affect them;

(vii) where the group has a proven record of cooperation and performance; and

(viii) workers are able to work independently with little or no direct contact with the supervisor.

(iii) *Free-rein or Laissez Faire or Group-Centered Leadership*: This is often described "*as no leadership at all*," for there is absence of direct leadership. Under this style, the leader delegates the authority for decision-making into the hands of the subordinates rather completely. A task is ordinarily presented to the group, which establishes its own goals and works out its own techniques for accomplishing those goals within the framework of organisational policy.

The leader expects his subordinates to assume responsibility for their own motivation, guidance, and control. Except for the stating of a minimum number of ground rules, the leader provides very little guidance and support for the followers. He acts principally as a liaison between outside sources and the group and ascertains that necessary resources are available to the group.

Discipline and control are not enforced in the hope that the employees will themselves enforce them, whenever necessary. The free-rein leader believes that one who leads the least leads best.

The behaviour of the leader in the *laissez-faire* style of leadership involves little direction; there is complete group or individual freedom in decision-making, and no appraisal or regulation of the performance of the subordinates is made.

This pattern of leadership suffers from some drawbacks. For example: (a) The work group generally has some members who refuse to co-operate; (b) It is unable or unwilling to reach a decision; (c) It is either too large to work effectively, or it lacks the necessary cohesion which may enable it to arrive at a decision and (d) in some instances, it could degenerate into chaos.

The free-rein style of leadership would be most effective:

(i) Under companies where its goals and the subordinates' goals are highly compatible; and they have been thoroughly communicated and are acceptable to the subordinates; (ii) when the leader desires to delegate decision-making fully; (iii) when the leader has a high degree of confidence in the abilities of his subordinates; (iv) when the subordinates themselves are well trained and highly knowledgeable concerning their jobs, are willing to assume responsibility for decision-making and self control; (v) when the subordinates have a high need for independence; (vi) when the subordinates derive large personal satisfaction from their work; and (vii) where performance demands allow some room for error if mistakes occur in a rather decentralised arrangement.

To some degree free-rein leadership is found among certain professional workers such as university professors, route salesmen, engineers, scientists, as there is a limited amount of supervision on people in these areas.

Besides these three main styles, there are others too.

(iv) *Bureaucratic or Rules-Centred Leadership*: The leader's behaviour is characterised by a high degree of reliance on rules, regulations and procedures, to which both he and his subordinates subscribe.[30] As a result, the process of administration is reduced to a series of routine actions. The rules specify the obligations of the subordinates, and enjoin upon them to do particular things in specific ways. There is no participation or initiative on their part. This style of leadership fosters workers' apathy. The rules serve as a specification of the minimum level of acceptable performance. It is possible for workers to remain apathetic, for they know just how little they should do to remain secure in their jobs. This leads to what is called bureaucratic sabotage — a deliberate apathy fused with resentment so that every act of conforming to the letter of the rule is accompanied by a conscious intention to violate it. Rules make it possible for workers to indulge in activity without participation; they enable them to work without being emotionally committed to work. Rules also lead to red tape and the habit of passing the buck, too much paper work and too great a desire to play safe.

(v) *Manipulative Leadership:* This style of leadership is based on the belief that employees are persons who should be manipulated by the leader so that his goal may be attained. It exploits the aspirations of the employees. Under this style of leadership, employees know that they are being manipulated, and therefore, become resentful and bitter. A manipulative leader, however, is very sensitive about the needs and desires of his employees as individuals. But the information gathered as a result of this sensitivity is not used for the benefit of the employees; instead, it is utilised by him for his own personal profit.

But this style of leadership is effective only in specific situations; for example, when co-operation and co-ordination have to be achieved on a project and previous leaders were unable to motivate the group properly; or when highly motivated employees are needed for short-duration projects. They are often given the illusion of reward, and are thus motivated for short periods.

However, manipulative leadership is not effective when: (i) A relationship of long-standing is involved; and (b) the structure of an open organisation is so controlled that the ability of the manipulator to wheel and deal is severely restricted.

(vi) *Expert Leadership:* This is an emerging style of leadership, resulting in part from the complexity of modern organisation. The basis for expert leadership is the individual leader's knowledge and ability; and he assumes the role of the leader regardless of his age, sex, physical or other attributes. It depends largely on the approximate mix of skills and the needs of others in a situation. With any change in a particular situation, another person may become the leader,

30. Jennings, Engene Emerson, *The Executive Autocrat-Bureaucrat*, Harper & Row, New York, 1962, pp. 164-165.

who would meet the needs arising out of the change. In these circumstances, a person is looked upon by group members as an expert who must continuously demonstrate his expertise in order to maintain his position as a leader.

Such expertise can be successful in these situations: (i) When the group members are convinced that they can reach their goals by following the advice and guidance of the expert; and (ii) When a situation develops in which specific expertise is necessary for the survival or performance of the group.

However, the situations in which this style of leadership usually fails are: (i) When an individual is no longer recognised as an expert; and (ii) When the situation changes to routine or to one calling for a different kind of expertise.

Theories of Leadership

There are several approaches to the study of leadership, but important among them are classified as: (a) Trait theory; (b) Behavioural theory; (c) Situational theory.

(a) Trait Theory

This theory assumes that leader are born, not made. This study focuses on personal traits or characteristics that distinguish the leaders from the followers and a successful leader from an unsuccessful leader. Stogdil[31] classified these traits into five categories, viz: (1) Intelligence and scholarship; (2) Physical trails like age, weight, strength; (3) Personality characterised by self-confidence, honesty, integrity, creativity and imitation; (4) Social status and experience: and (5) Task-orientation.

Contingency Theories of Leadership: Contingency approaches to leadership take the position that there is no 'one best way" to lead in all situations. Effective leadership styles vary from situation to situation depending on several factors like responsibility predispositions of the leaders, the characteristics of the followers, the nature of task being done, and other situational factors.

Tannenbaum and Schmidt's's Leadership Pattern: Tannenbaum and Schmidt used a contingency framework to discuss effective leadership patterns taking a situational approach. They suggested that the use of authority by the manager or the area of freedom given to the subordinates is a function of the: (i) Forces of the managers: (ii) Forces in the subordinates; and (iii) Forces in the situation (Fig. 9.8). They concluded that a successful leader is one who can accurately assess the forces that determine what behaviours would be most appropriate in any given situation and they are able to be flexible enough to adopt the most functional leadership style.[31]

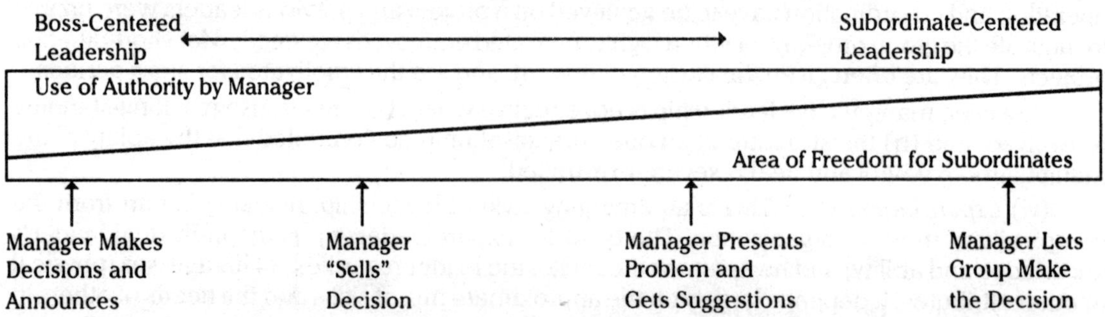

Fig. 9.8: The Tannenbaum and Schmidt Contingency Model.

31. Umasekharan, *"Organisational Behaviour"*, Tata McGraw-Hill Publishing Co. Ltd., New Delhi, 1989, p. 156.

Fielder's Contingency Theory: Fidler developed a model to predict work group effectiveness by taking into consideration the 'fit' or match among — (i) The leader's style (task/relationship-oriented); (ii) The leader-member relations; (iii) Task-structure; and (iv) The position power of the leader (Fig. 9.9). Certain combinations of the last three factors are considered to be situations where the leader finds himself/herself to be in either a high degree of control or low control over the situation one finds oneself in.[32]

Situational Characteristics

Leader-member Relations Task-Structure Position-Power	Good High Strong	Good High Weak	Good Low Strong	Good Low Weak	Poor High Weak	Poor High Strong	Poor Low Strong	Poor Low Weak
Situational Control of Leader	High			Moderate				Low
Effective Leadership Style	TASK-ORIENTED			RELATIONSHIP-ORIENTED				TASK-ORIENTED

Fig. 9.9: Fielder's Situational Variables and Effective Leadership Styles.

Path Goal Theory of Leadership: This theory of leadership is developed by Martin Evans and Robert House using contingency approach based on the expectancy theory of motivation.

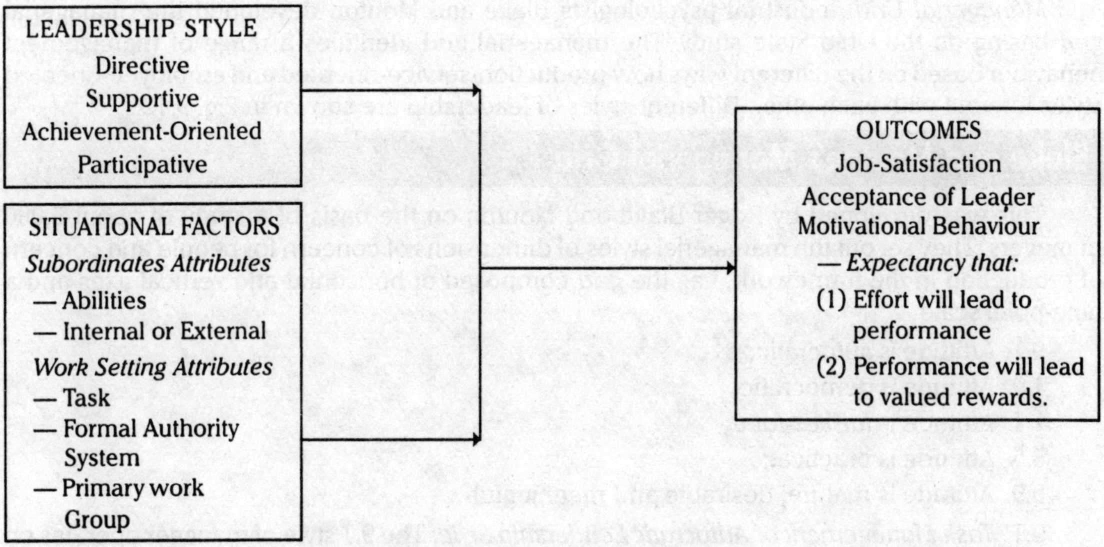

Fig. 9.10: Path Goal Theory of Leadership

This theory states that leaders can exercise four different kinds of styles viz., directive (giving directions), supportive (friendly and approachable), participative and achievement oriented (setting challenging goals) leadership. It also states that the leader can use any of these styles

32. *Ibid*, p. 157.

depending on situational factors like subordinate characteristics (ability, internal locus of control) and attributes in the work-setting (task characteristics, formal authority system and primary work groups). A good fit between leadership style, situational factors will result in job satisfaction of subordinates accept and value the leader as a dispenser and will engage in motivated behaviour (Fig. 9.10).

(b) Behavioural Theories

These theories opine that a leader's style is oriented either an employee centered or a job-centered emphasis. In the employee-centered orientation, the leader develops friendly relations and open relationships with employees. A Job-centered leader emphasis in getting things done by the people.

Lewin, Lippit and White suggested a continuous theory of leadership which identified three basic styles of leadership, i.e., autocrat, democrat and *laissez-faire*. Robert McMurre suggested the benevolent autocrat between autocrat and democrat leadership. Bank managers used to adopt autocratic style before 1969. But, this style proved to be ineffective after 1969 in view of new values, expectations, desires, culture etc., inducted in banks with the massive entrance of new employees with massive branch expansion. However, the bank manager feel that even the democratic style has not proved effective, leading to indiscipline in most situations. In view of this it is suggested that the bank managers may adopt a benevolent autocratic style.

Likert's Four Systems: Rensis Likert suggests that managers operate under four different system. In system-1, the leader behaves like a exploitative authoritatives and exploits the subordinates. In system-2, leader takes a paternalistic approach and in system-3, he uses democratic approach, where he consults subordinates in decision-making. In system-4, the leader allows his subordinates to participate in decision-making process and the decisions are taken by the leader and subordinates (Fig. 9.11)

Managerial Grid: Industrial psychologists Blake and Mouton developed the managerial grid basing on the Ohio State study. The managerial grid identifies a range of management behaviour based on the different ways how production/service-oriented and employee-oriented styles interact with each other. Different styles of leadership are shown in Fig. 9.12.

Blake and Mouton's Managerial Grid

This was developed by Roger Blake and Mouton on the basis of a study of about 5,000 managers. They set out the managerial styles of dimensions of concern for people and concern of production in the framework, i.e., the *grid* composed of horizontal and vertical axes and a nine-point scale.

9.1 Attitude is autocratic;
1.9 Attitude is democratic;
1.1 Attitude is *laissez-faire*;
5.5 Attitude is practical;
9.9 Attitude is mature, desirable and meaningful.

9.1 *Task Management or Autocratic Leadership Style:* The 9.1 style of manager operates on the assumption that there is an inherent contradiction between the organisational needs and the individual's personal need. Therefore, if one is to be achieved, the other has to be scarified. The 9.1 orientation seeks to resolve the problem by arranging the conditions of work in such a manner that it would minimise the interference of human feelings with the efficiency of output.The 9.1 manager is a hard taskmaster. He drives himself and his subordinates to execute what he has planned. By and large, he operates on the assumption of Theory X, that "an average human being has an inherent dislike of work and will avoid it if he can," Hence, he must be constantly watched, coerced, controlled and threatened if a job is to be properly done. His second assumption is that if His subordinate was intelligent enough, he would not be in that subordinate position. Third, he assumes that the unintelligent sub-ordinates are immature, unreliable and irresponsible persons. Therefore, they should be constantly watched during the course of their work.

Here, the manager's goal is likely to be very high; but the goal of the subordinate is more or less ignored. The manager believes that his ideas should not be questioned. He, therefore, practises only one-way communication, which is not communication in the true sense of the term. Office circular, bulletins, notice boards, etc. convey the orders from the top, and upward communication is limited to reporting production figures and the attainment of targets.

1.9 *Country Clubs or Democratic Leadership Style*: The 1.9 manager largely avoids the use of power to get a job done. He believes that a desired organisational behaviour can be obtained if employee needs and wants are satisfied. Therefore, he not only issues orders but interprets them and sees to it that the employees have the necessary skill and tools to carry out their assignments. He assigns a fair work load to his personnel, and recognises the job that is well done. There is a team approach to the attainment of organisational goals.

By and large, the 1.9 manager acts on the assumption of Theory Y, that "people are capable of doing work and assuming responsibility if they are given opportunities and incentives." The 1.9 style focusses attention on the comfort and safety of the employees. The subordinates are supervised, guided and aided rather than threatened and commanded to work. In return, the manager expects loyalty and devotion, rather than accountability, from his subordinates. Mistakes are not received seriously. The assumption is that disciplinary action breads discontent and frustration among employees and creates an unhealthy work environment.

There is room for information communication in the 1.9 managerial style. It provides an outlet for the social and emotional aspects of the relationship. Conflict is not suppressed but is resolved by discussion. The acceptance of decisions by subordinates is very important. The democratic attitude of the manager enables him to maintain a high level of morale; and the involvement of his employees in the decision-making process gives them a sense of belonging.

1.1 *Improverished or Laissez-Faire Leadership Style*: The 1.1 style manager does not exercise power or authority to get work done or to maintain unity of command. He follows the rule of minimum exposure to accountability. He relieves himself of responsibility and is ready to blame his subordinates if something goes wrong. He has no clear idea of the goals to be attained. He is more security conscious than status conscious.

The communication system in this style of management very much resembles that of a government department, that is, the messages are delivered; nothing else is done. The 1.1 manager is not willing to communicate with his superiors and subordinates unless it is absolutely necessary to do so. There is no place for creativity under this style of management.

This style of management is followed by those who are constantly bypassed at the time of promotion, or who function mostly in unchallenging work situations. They try not to rock the boat, and accomplish just enough to avoid pressure from their superiors.

5.5 *Middle-of-the-Road or Practical Leadership Style*: Under the 5.5 managerial style, employees are not driven, pushed, or forced, but are requested and motivated to do a job. A fair and firm approach is adopted to get work done. The most fundamental function of a 5.5 manager is to achieve organisational goals with a minimum effort within the shortest time possible and ensure the utmost employee satisfaction.

9.9 *Team Management or Matured, Desirable Leadership Style:* Under the 9.9 style of management, both the people and production are closely involved. The manager's prime responsibility is to see to it that each and every activity leads to the attainment of organisational goals. For this purpose, the manager delegates authority to subordinates and makes them accountable for the work allocated to them. The 9.9 manager says: "My job is not only to take sound decisions but also to ensure that they are effectively carried out." Under this style the assumption is that if people have a clear understanding of organisational goals, a strict control of their activity would not be necessary.

Mistakes provide an opportunity for learning. Employees are committed to attain the targets of production because individual and organisational goals are complementary.

Based on the findings, Blake and Mouton, concluded that administrators work best under a 9.9 style, as contrasted with the 9.1 (task oriented) or 1.9 (country-club) type leader.

Characteristic	*SYSTEM 1 (Exploitative Authoritative)*	*SYSTEM 2 (Benevolent Authoritative)*	*SYSTEM 3 (Consultative)*	*SYSTEM 4 (Participative Group)*
Trust in Subordinates	None	Condescending	Substantial	Complete
Motivation Accomplished by	Fear and threats	Rewards and Punishment	Rewards, Punishment, Involvement	Group Participation, Involvement
Communication	Very Limited	Limited	Fairly Widespread	Widespread
Interpersonal Interaction	Very Limited	Limited	Moderate Amount	Extensive
Decision-making	Centralised	Mostly Centralised	Broad Participation Allowed	Dispersed
Goal Setting	Centralised	Mostly Centralised	Some participation Allowed	Participation Allowed
Control	Centralised	Mostly Centralised	Moderate Delegation	Extensive Delegation
Informal Organisation	Always Developed and in Opposition to the organisation	Usually Developed and partially in Opposition to the Organisation	May be Developed and May Support or Oppose the Organisation	Informal Organisation is the same as the Formal Organisation

Fig: 9.11 Likert's Four system Construct.

1.9 (COUNTRY CLUB) Thoughtful attention to needs of people leads to a friendly and comfortable organisation atmosphere and work tempo.	(TEAM 9.9) Work accomplished is from committed people with interde-pendence through a common stake in organisation purpose and with trust and respect.
Adequate performance through balance of work 5.5 (Middle Road) Requirements and Maintaining satisfactory morale.	
Exertion of minimum effort is required to get work done and sustain organisation morale 1.1 (Impoverished)	Efficiency results from arran-ging work in such a way that human elements have little effect (Task) 9.1

(CONCERN FOR PRODUCTION/SERVICE THE MANAGERIAL GRID)

Fig. 9.12

Main Source: Adapted from R.R. Blake and J.S. Mouton, *The Managerial Grid*, Gulf Publishing Company, Houston, Texas, 1964, p.10.

The style 1-1 is impoverished management – low concern for both people and production. This style is also called laissez-faire management. Style 1-9 management is country-club management – high concern for employees, but low concern for production. Style 9-1 management is task or authoritarian oriented high concern for production and low concern for employees. Style 5-5 is middle-of-the-road management – and intermediate amount of concern for both production and employees. Style 9-9 management is team or democratic management – a high concern for both production and employees. Blake and Mouton Strongly argue that the 9-9 management style is the most effective type of leadership style.[33] Hence, it is felt that the management may adopt 9.9 style for effective goal attainment.

Hersey and Blanchard's Life Cycle (or) Situational Approach

It is an extension of the managerial grid approach, Hersey and Blanchard's approach identifies two major styles viz., task style and relationship style. Hersey and Blanchard incorporated the maturity of the followers into their model taking the lead from some of Fiedler's work on situational variables. The level of maturity is defined by these criteria viz., degree of achievement motivation. Willingness to take on responsibility and amount of education and/or experience. The key for leadership effectiveness is this model (Fig. 9.13) is to match up the situation with the appropriate style. The four styles are:

(i) Telling Style: This is a high task, low relationship style. It is effective when followers are at a very low level of maturity.

(ii) Selling Style: This is a high task, high relationship style. It is effective when followers are on the low side of maturity.

(iii) Participating Style: This is a low task, high relationship style. It is effective when followers are on the high side of maturity.

(iv) Delegating Style: This is a low task, low relationship style. It is effective when followers are at a very high level of maturity.[34]

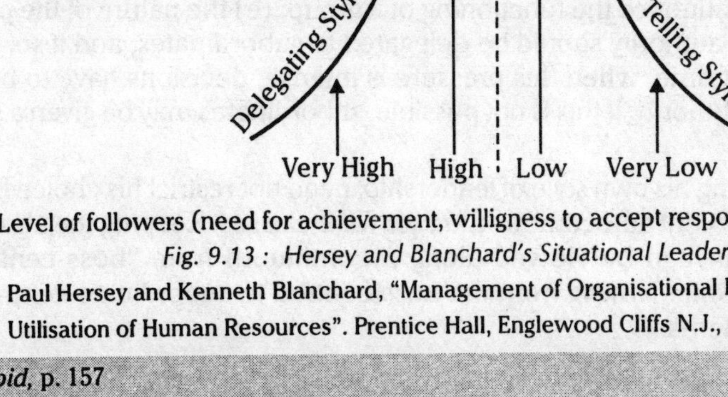

Maturity Level of followers (need for achievement, willigness to accept responsibility, and education/experience

Fig. 9.13 : Hersey and Blanchard's Situational Leadership Model

Source : Paul Hersey and Kenneth Blanchard, "Management of Organisational Behaviour: Utilisation of Human Resources". Prentice Hall, Englewood Cliffs N.J., 1977, p. 170.

33. *Ibid*, p. 157
34. Fred Luthans, *op. cit.*, p. 475.

Factors Affecting Choice of Leadership

As a manager works with his organisation, his choice of a leader is governed by certain forces. These are:[35]

(i) Forces acting on the manager;
(ii) Forces acting on the subordinates; and
(iii) Forces acting on the situation.

(i) *Forces Acting on the Manager*: In any given situation, the behaviour of the manager is influenced by his own personality; that is, leadership is perceived on the basis of his background, knowledge and experience. The important forces affecting him are: (a) his value system; that is, the relative important he attaches to organisational efficiency, the personal growth of his subordinates, and company profits; (b) his confidence in his subordinates, which is influenced by the knowledge and competence they have; (c) his own leadership inclination; that is, whether he can function comfortably and naturally or whether he is uncomfortable when operating in team, and (d) his feeling of security is in an uncertain situation. In other words, his tolerance of ambiguity is taken as an important variable in his dealing with problems.

(ii) *Forces Acting on the Subordinates*: The leader needs a knowledge of the factors which influence his employee's personality. The manager may grant greater freedom to his subordinate if he is assured that: (a) the subordinate has a relatively high need for independence: (b) he is ready to assume responsibility for decisions; (c) he is interested in the problem which is important; (d) he has a relatively high tolerance of ambiguity; (e) he understands, and identifies himself with, the goals of the organisation; (f) he has the necessary knowledge and experience to deal with problems; and (g) he has learnt to expect that he would share in the decision-making process.

(iii) *Forces Acting on the Situation*: Some aspects of a general situation affect the manager's behaviour. These are (a) the type of organisation for which he works, its values and traditions which are communicated through job descriptions, policy announcements and public statements by the top executives; (b) the qualities of the leader. Some organisations require that their executives should be dynamic, imaginative, decisive, persuasive, while others place emphasis on their ability to work effectively with people; and (c) the size of a working unit, its geographical location, and the extent of inter and intra-organisational security which is needed to attain company goals — these also affect the quality and extent of employee participation. (d) group effectiveness, i.e., the leader should know that a group which has a long standing is in the habit of working in co-operation. Moreover, the confidence which members of a group have in their ability to solve a problem as a group is also to be borne in mind. Cohesiveness, permissiveness, mutual acceptance and a common purpose also influence the functioning of a group; (e) the nature of the problem itself may determine whether authority should be delegated to subordinates, and if so, to what extent; and (f) the pressure of time; when this pressure is intense, decisions have to be taken quickly with a high degree of authority. If this is not possible, subordinates may be given a share in the decision-making process.

The manager, in developing his own style of leadership, need not restrict his choice from the autocratic, democratic, benevolent autocratic and *laissez faire* classes. Keeping the above facts in view, leadership behaviour can be viewed along a continuum from "boss-centred" to "subordinate-centred" leadership. Moving from the boss-centred to subordinate-centred, one can observe the following systems:

35. Tanneubaum, Robert and Warrier H. Schniedt, "How to Choose a Leadership Pattern", *Harvard Business Review*, March-April, 1950, pp. 95-101.

1. The manager makes the decision and announces it.
2. The manager "sells" his decision.
3. The manager presents his ideas, invites questions.
4. The manager presents a tentative decision subject to change.
5. The manager defines the limits and requests the group to make a decision.
6. The manager permits the group to make decisions within prescribed limits.

Followership Styles — A New Approach

There is a misconception that an effective leader is enough to mould and direct the group behaviour towards the attainment or organisational goals. But attainment of organisational goals more or less equally depends on the committed and effective followers. In fact no leader can be effective without effective followers. Here the term effective follower is used in the sense that the follower should be potential and he should be in a position to willingly contribute most of his potentialities towards the organisational goal.

Most of the academicians, practitioners and writers have emphasised on the leader for effective functioning of the organisation totally ignoring the follower. Almost all the theories of leadership like Trait Approach, Behaviours Approach, Situational Approach, Electric Approach, Path Goal. Theory, Reddin's Three Dimensional Model, Managerial Grid of Blake and Mouton, Likert's Four Systems Model and Vrooms' Yetton Normative Model concentrate only on leadership styles and leader behaviour not on the follower for effective management. But there is a little mention about the follower under the concept of environment in the Social Learning Approach and the maturity level of the follower is dealt with by the Paul Hersey and Ken Blanchard. In the Hersey and Blanchard approach, various styles of leadership are suggested depending upon the follower's level of maturity. Four types of styles of followers are identified. They are: (1) Telling style; (2) Selling style; (3) Participative style; and (4) Delegating style.

The followership styles are not given due recognition except mentioning them at the maturity level of followers. Various authors have failed to recognise the significance, of the follower in the leader-follower interaction.

In fact, the follower is as important as the leader in any situation. In view of this background an attempt is made in this paper to develop the followership styles suitable to situational requirements.

Adoption to Situational Requirements: Who has to Initiate?

There is no single style which is appropriate for all situations. Hence, the styles of both the leader and follower are to be changed in accordance with then situational effectiveness. Generally, the follower is reluctant to change his style. Hence, the leader these to take initiative and try to change his style as well as the style of the follower. If a situation requires the combination of 'Exploitative-Autocratic Yes-Boss' style the leader has to enter into exploitative autocratic style and make the follower to be in 'Yes-Boss' style by exercising his authority and/or by convincing the follower.

If the situation warrants the combination of 'Participative Critical Style' the leader, whatever his original style based on his traits may be has to enter the participative style and convince the follower to be in critical style with a view to maximising human resource contribution to the organisation.

When the followers in the styles like 'No Boss', 'Grumbling', Escaping and Intellectual Arrogancy', the leader has to change their styles either to the 'Yes-Boss' style of Critical style depending upon the situation by offering incentives and benefits and by providing challenging work, delegating authority responsibility and conferring new designation on the follower.

Sometimes, the followers may change their styles on their own depending upon the style of the leader and the situational requirements. If the follower does not meet the requirements or if the change in the followership styles is not in tune with the situational requirements, the leader has to take the initiative and change the followership styles to suit the situational needs.

Development Phase of the Followers

Most of the employees are not able to utilise their existing level of skill and knowledge of the fullest extent possible due to various reasons. The important among them is failure to exchange their options, knowledge and experiences with their superiors due to mismatch of their styles with their leader and these two with the situation. Moreover, training on the job and off the job takes car of the development of the employees relating to the job knowledge. Hence, it is felt that training in psychological aspects is also essential to develop the followers.

The employee development programme in the arena should cover developing of the follower from the negative of critical through Yes-Boss and Grumbling stages. Content of the training programme regarding the development of the follower should include the making of the follower to become aware of this self, including his strengths, potentialities, his weaknesses, his attitudes, way of pursuing the things, traits, motivational factors etc. It should also include the identification of the potentialities of the leader, his weaknesses, perception, attitudes, emotions, styles, traits etc. Further the training programme should aim at enhancing the follower's abilities to know himself and about the leader to change his style to match with that of the leader and situational requirements. Similarly, the follower should also be developed in the abilities of convincing the leader to change the later's styles based on followers styles and situational requirements. Thus, This programme helps him in attaining an effective interpersonal interaction with the leader.

Training of Leaders too

The leader should understand his self, followers' self, situational requirements and change his styles, follower's style to the situational requirements. It will be his task, in future, to convince the followers in order to change their style to match the same with situational requirements. Moreover, if the followers want change this style to match the same with situational requirements. The leader will have to change his own style in future, in tune with the followership style. Hence, the leaders should also be trained in intransactional analysis, assertiveness, stroking and other areas of interpersonal relations.

Techniques

Various training techniques like role play, transactional analysis may be employed to develop the follower to reach the stage of critical and change his style depending upon the situational requirements. Quality circle can be used as a better technique to develop the employee as they encourage them to express their views and exchange their experiences freely. Further the leader in the quality circles mostly resort to the democratic style. Hence, this technique enables the follower to develop through different stages and reach the stage of critical style. But this technique may not be effective in developing the employee to become adoptable to different situational requirements. This lacuna can be bridged by other new techniques i.e., Dynamics of Organisational Climate. Organisational Climate is not static and it goes on changing without any voluntary action from any side. It can also be changed through voluntary influence of the management, Management creates different natures and degrees of Organisational Climates with a view to influencing the people to act differently compared to that of the present. Moreover, employees are automatically trained in new interactions designed by the management. Thus, dynamics of Organisational Climate can also be used as a training technique in the development of the followership styles and in developing the follower to adapt his style based on change the later's style in accordance with situational requirements. Similarly, the leader also learns to change the follower's style towards the situations. The leader and the follower through their close interaction in varying organisational climatic conditions learn now to move with each other, how to interact with each other, how to influence or to be influenced and the art of convincing each other, based on the strengths and weaknesses of the other party (ultimately) based on situational requirements. The emphasis on the followership styles clearly states that there is a greater deed for convincing the leader by the follower as the follower sometimes may have better ideas, rich experiences worthwhile attitudes controllable emotions, right aptitude than what the leader should have. As such listening to the follower and considering the follower's views greatly enriches the opportunities for situational success. Under such environment the techniques of organisational climate effectively trains the leader to realise this truism and adopt himself based on followers style and situational requirements. This technique further trains the follower to reach the level of the leader in various respects which in turn improves Organisational Climate and places the organisation at a higher ladder.

GROUP DYNAMICS

Group dynamics describe how a group should be organised and conducted. It encompasses the dynamics of interaction patterns within the group, the subtle and not-so-subtle pressures exerted by group members, the manners in which decisions are made in the group, how work gets done and members' needs are met. Understanding these group dynamics will enable managers to completely harness the synergy of the group members. Individuals join groups for security, social relations, affiliation, leadership etc.

These are numerous types of groups. The important among them are primary groups, secondary groups, formal groups and informal groups. Primary groups are small groups enough for face-to-face interaction, having a feeling of commandership, loyalty and a common sense of values among its members. Coalitions are very relevant to organisations. Coalition is group of groups.

Formal groups are collections of employees who are made to work together by the organisation to get the job done. On the other hand, informal groups emerge on their own due to the affinities that develop among the group members.

Norms can be described as shared beliefs among groups members as to what behaviours are appropriate, if one desires to be a part of and belong to the group. Status refers to the importance and deference that people give to others. Cohesion refers to the extent of unity in the group and is reflected in the member's conformity to the norms of the group, feeling of attraction for each other and wanting to be members of the group.

Interactive Behaviour and Conflict

Conflict is the difference between the perceived/expectation and reality. Conflicts are of different types.. They are intrapersonal, interpersonal, intragroup, intergroup and organisational conflict.

Intra-personal (or) Intra-individual Conflict

Within every person there are generally — (a) A number of competing needs and roles; (b) A variety of different that drives and roles can be expressed; (c) Many types of barriers which can occur between the drive and the goal; and (d) Both positive and negative aspects attached to desired goals. These complicate the human adaptation process and result in conflict. Intra-personal conflicts can be analysed in terms of frustration model, goals and roles.

Conflict Due to Frustration: Frustration occurs when a motivated drive is blacked before a person reaches a desired goal.[36] The barriers which block may be outward or inward. Frustration normally triggers defence mechanism in a person. The defence mechanisms include: aggression, withdrawals, fixation and compromise. For example, the need of a clerk in a bank is to enhance his economic and social status His drive is to complete CAIIB course and appear for interview. His goal is to get promotion for officer post. If he could not get through the CAIIB examination due to (barriers like) lack of time for preparation or his psychological weakness he may be frustrated. Then the defence mechanisms available to the clerk are: behaving aggressively with colleagues or family members (aggression), discontinuing the course (withdrawal) taking the examinations again and again until the course is completed (fixation) and trying for another job in other organisation (compromise).

Goal Conflict: Another common source of conflict for a person is a goal which has both positive and negative features or two or more competing goals. But, in frustration model single motive is blocked, before the goal is reached.[37] Three separate types of goal conflict are normally identified.

(a) Approach-approach Conflict: A person is motivated to approach two or more positive but mutually exclusive goals. For example trying for promotion from clerk to officer's position in the same bank and trying for appointment officer's position in other bank.

(b) Approach-avoidance Conflict: A person is motivated to approach a goal and at the same time is motivated to avoid it. The single goal is contains both positive and negative features.[38] For example trying for promotion and at the same time avoid it if the promotion is accompanied by transfer to a disturbed place.

(c) Avoidance-avoidance Conflict: A person is motivated to avoid two or more negative but mutually exclusive goals. The person may not choose either of them and simply leave the situation. For example: preferring a transfer to a branch in either Punjab or Kashmir at present.

Role Conflict

In any bank a variety of functions which are divided into jobs, positions and tasks should be performed by human beings of that bank. They perform these functions with a view to attain objectives of the bank as well as the individual employees. This function results in specific behaviour of the individual.

36. *Ibid*, p. 398.
37. *Ibid*, p. 401.
38. *Ibid*.

Role is defined as the action performed by the person to indicate the occupation on this position.[39] Keith Davis viewed the role as the pattern of actions expected of a person in activities involving others. Similar opinion is also expressed by Newcomb that roles are ways of behaving towards others, which are defined for different positions. A role is dynamic. It refers to the behaviour of the occupants of a position, not all their behaviour as person's but to what they do as occupant of the position.[40] Role reflects a person's position in the social system with its accompanying rights and obligations, power; and responsibility. People need some method to anticipate others' behaviour in order to be able to interact with each other. Role performs this function in the social system.[41] Thus, the role theory views the person as a member of the social system. Thus, a person has several roles in the society like occupational role as a worker, family role as a parent, social role as a club member, religious role as a disciple, role in marketing as a consumer, etc. The role behaviour of an employee is influenced by the various sub-systems of the organisation system, the economic system, the social system, the religious system, policies, objectives, goals and programmes of the company etc.

Role Perceptions

Activities of bank employees are guided by their views about their behaviour, i.e., how they think about their behaviour at work. In other words, they are guided by their imagination about their own roles in reaction to the roles of the others at work. This is called the perception of employees about their own roles. Bank employees must be highly adaptable to different situations in order to change from one role to the other without any delay as they perform difficult roles in dynamic situations. Bank managers have to essentially change the roles quickly as they work with different levels and types of people like their superiors, subordinates, colleagues, field supervisors, technical and non-technical employees. Thus, for each bank manager there are three different roles like superior, subordinate and colleague. Obviously, one cannot meet the other employees, unless one can perceive what they expect.[42]

Conflicts

Each bank manager experiences conflict of different roles as bank employees, managers, customers and government officials perceive and expect differently from his role and he cannot meet all his expectations without limiting/resisting others. This is mainly because a human being has limited resources and time. Thus, every bank employee has a role conflict.

Role Ambiguity

It exists in the banks when roles are either defined inadequately or substantially unknown. In this situation bank employees are not quite sure of playing their roles. The role ambiguity and role conflict reduce job satisfaction and need fulfilment.[43]

Bank managers should set themselves as models in acting their role as their followers tend to follow what and how the superiors play. Further, they have to adopt different styles of leadership in different situations and while playing different roles.

39. Theodore R. Sarbin, *"Role Theory"* in G. Lindzey (Ed.) *"Hand Book of Social Psychology"*, Adison-Wisley, Cambridge, 1954, pp. 223-258.
40. Theodore M. Newcomb, *"Social Psychology"*, Dryden Press, New York, 1980.
41. Keith Davis, *op. cit.*, p. 32.
42. *Ibid*, p. 33.
43. Corag E. Schmier, *"Behavioural Modification — Training the Hardcore Unemployed"*, *Personnel*, May-June 1973, pp. 65 - 69.

Interpersonal Conflict

Interpersonal conflict arises when two or more individuals interact with one another. Interpersonal conflict can be explained through — (i) Transactional analysis; and (ii) Johari window Transactional Analysis (TA).

Transactional analysis is developed and popularised by Eric Berne through his book on 'Games People Play' and Thomas Harris through his book on I'm OK — You're OK respectively. Transactional analysis is the analysis of transaction between two or more persons. The major areas of Transactional analysis can be explained through ego states, transactions and stroking.

The ego is a hypothetical construct and is used to help explain the complex dynamics of the human personality. Transactional Analysis uses three ego states viz., Child (C) ego; Adult (A) ego and Parent (P) ego.

Child ego is the state in which the individual acts like an impulsive child. The characteristics of child ego include submissive or insubordinate, emotional, joyful or rebellious. The child state is characterised by immature behaviour. For example the officer of a bank branch says to the branch manager you know better, when he is asked to offer a suggestion.

In the Adult ego an individual acts like a matured person. The characteristics of adult ego state include 'cool-headed', rational behaviour, calculative, objectivity, fairness, gathering and analysing information, logical choice etc.

In the present ego state, individual acts like a dominating parent. The characteristics of parent ego state include: protective, loving, controlling, nuturing, critical etc.

Transactions between Ego States: A number of transactions take place between two or more individuals. They are classified as complementary, crossed and ulterior transactions. The transactions are complementary, if the message sent or the behaviour exhibited by one person receives the appropriate and expected response from the another person's ego state (See Fig. 9.14) conflict does not arise between the transacting persons in complementary transactions.

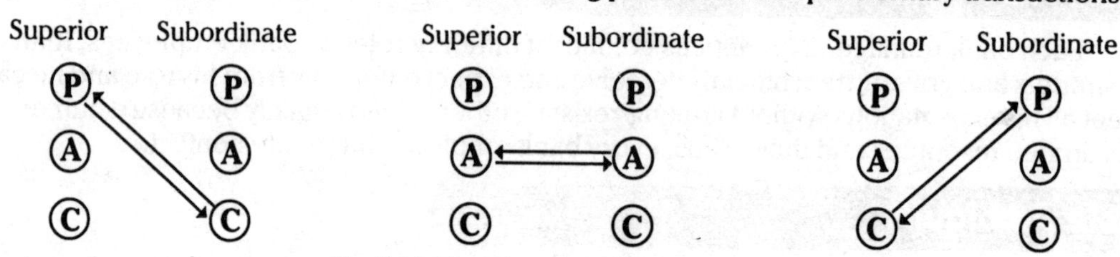

Fig. 9.14: Complementary Transactions

Crossed transaction occurs when the message sent or the behaviour exhibited by one person's ego state is reacted to by an incompatible, unexpected ego state on the part of the other person[44] (See Fig. 9.15). For example: A bearer came to the branch after business hours to withdraw from his account to encash a cheque and the branch manager ordered the officer concerned to pay the money (transaction is parent ego to child ego), but the officer replied as: withdrawals are not allowed after business hours (transaction is adult ego to adult ago). Crossed transactions are the source of much interpersonal conflict. The consequences of this type of transaction are hurting the feelings and frustration on the part of the parties and dysfunctional consequences of the bank.

44. Fred Luthans, *op. cit*, p. 408.

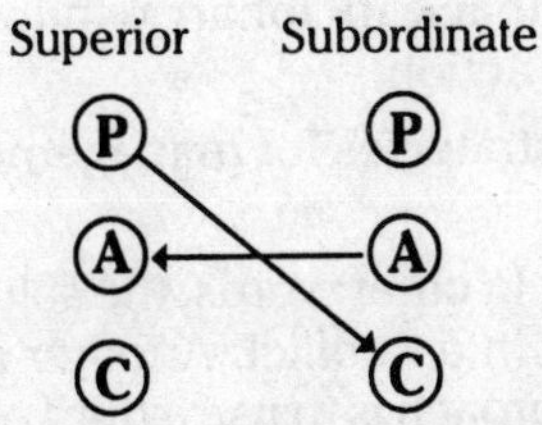

Fig. 9.15: Crossed Transactions.

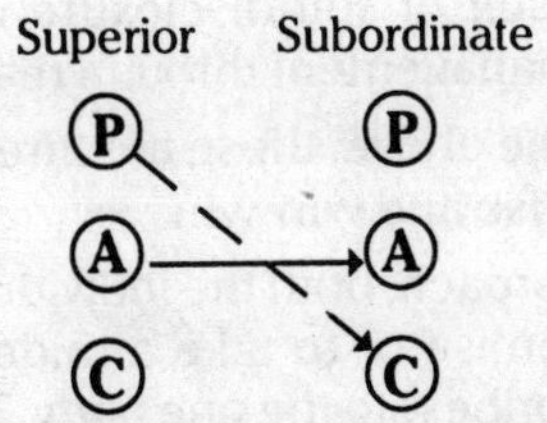

Fig. 9.16: Ulterior Transactions.

The ulterior transactions involve at least two ego states on the part of a person. The individual may say onething but mean quite another (See Fig. 9.16). For example: branch manager says to an officer: Come to me if you can't balance the day book. But the branch manager really means is don't come to me with your troubles. Find answer within yourself. These transactions are very complicated and result in interpersonal conflict. These transactions damage psychic of the two parties and interpersonal relations.

Stroking: Stroking is recognising the presence of the others. Stroking may be positive, negative, circastic or mixed. Positive stroking develops interpersonal relations, whereas negative and mixed stroking damage interpersonal relations. But circastic stroking is highly dangerous to interpersonal relations.

The Johari Window: The other framework to explain interpersonal conflict is Johari Window developed by Joseph Loft and Harry Ingham (Johari). These are certain things that a person knows about himself and there are certain things that are unknown. This valids good for other persons also. This idea is the basis for Johari window. Four cells are identified based on the above assumption (See Fig. 9.17). They are: Open self, hidden self, build self and undiscovered self.

	The person knows about the other	The persons does not know about the other
The person knows about himself/herself	1 OPEN SELF	2 HIDDEN SELF
The person does not know about himself/herself	3 BLIND SELF	4 UNDISCOVERED SELF

Fig. 9.17 : The Johari Window.

In the open self form of interaction, the person knows about himself/herself and about the other. This situation results in openness and compatibility and a little interpersonal conflict. In the hidden self situation, the individual knows about himself/herself, but does not know about the other. The person remains hidden from the other since he does not know how the other might react. Thus, the person close his true feelings or attitudes. This situation results in potential interpersonal conflict.

In the blind situation, the individual knows about the other but blind about himself. The individual may be unintentionally irritating to the other and hurting the other's feelings. The situation is also prove to high interpersonal conflict. In undiscovered self-situation the person does not know about himself/herself and about the other. This situation results in much misunderstanding, and interpersonal conflict. Thus this is potentially the most explosive situation.[45]

Strategies for Interpersonal Conflict Resolution

The simple strategies for interpersonal conflict resolution include: complementary transactions (particularly Adult ego estate to Adult ego state) in transaction analysis, moving

44. *Ibid*, p. 412.

towards the open self of self-disclosure and feedback in Johari window model, emotion management and management through reason and action.

In addition to the above, these are three basic strategies for management of conflict. They are: lose-lose, win-lose and win-win.

In lose-lose approach, both the individuals lose. In other words, the solution to the problem would be a compromise or to take a middle point in a conflict. Another approach is pay off (mostly in the form bribes) to the one party. Third approach is to use a third party as an arbitrator. The fourth approach is to resort to the bureaucratic rules and regulations to resolve the conflict. Both the parties in this strategy.

Win-lose approach is not in India. In this approach one party wins and the other party loses. This strategy is common in competitive type of culture. In a win-win strategy, energies and creativity are aimed at solving the problem rather than beating the other party. This strategy takes the advantages of win-lose strategy and eliminates many of the dysfunctional aspects. The need of both the parties are met and both the parties receive rewards.[46]

Intergroup Conflict

Conflict between two groups or departments in an organisation refers to intergroup conflict. Conflict between production department and marketing department is an example for intergroup conflict. Intergroup conflict arises due to overlapping roles, absence of cooperation and collaboration between groups and lack of a comprehensive, understanding about the total understanding.

Strategies to Reduce Intergroup Conflict

(a) Avoidance: Keep the conflict from surfacing at all.

(b) Defusion: Deactivate the conflict and cool off the emotions, and hostilities of the groups.

(c) Containment: Allow some conflict to surface and contain it carefully by pointing out which issues are to be discussed and how they are to be resolved.

(d) Confrontation: Bring all issues to the open and allow the conflict groups confront directly in an attempt to reach the mutually satisfactory solution.

(e) Team building: Build the interdepartmental teams and encourage the people to work beyond their departmental boundaries.

(f) Collaboration: Teach the groups about the total organisational productivity, profitability and effectiveness and encourage collaboration, among all groups and avoid organisational politicking.

BUILDING WORK TEAMS

Team building is a method improving organisational effectiveness at the team level by diagnosing barriers to team performance and improving interteam relationships and task accomplishment. Team building analyses the activities, resource allocations and relationships of a group or team to improve its effectiveness. This technique can be used to develop a sense of unity among members.[47] Team building is for two types of teams viz., an existing or permanent

46. *Ibid*, p. 414
47. James A.F. Stoner and R. Edward Freeman, *op. cit.*, p. 421.

team comprising of manager and his/her subordinates often called a family group and a new group made through a merger or other structural changes in the organisation or formed to solve a specific problem called the special group.

Team work needs collaboration among its members. It is said that one plus one may be three in team work. Moreover, the synergitic effect is evident in team work. Each team is a linking pin to another team and to the total organisation. Teams do wonder. They make the impossible things possible.

Team building activities, for both kinds of groups, aim at diagnosing barriers to effective team performance, improving task accomplishment, improving relationship between team members. Understanding and managing group process and culture, role analysis technique for role clarification and definition and role negotiation techniques (See. Fig. 9.18).

Diagnostic meeting may involve the total group and several sub-groups and require only a brief time in order to identify strengths and problem areas and to conduct a general critique of the performance of the group. Actual team building requires a subsequent longer meeting ideally held away from the work place. The purpose of this meeting is to improve the team's effectiveness through better management of task demands, relationship demands and group processes. The role analysis technique is designed to clarify role expectations and obligations of team members to improve team effectiveness. Role negotiation intervenes directly in the relationships of power, authority and influence within the group.[48] A follow-up meeting evaluates the success of the action steps.

The purpose of team building are: (i) To set goals or priorities; (ii) To analysis/allocate the way the work is performed; (iii) To examine the way a group is working and its process; (iv) To examine the relationships among people. The primary goal of team building activity is task accomplishment and maintenance of interpersonal relationships is secondary.

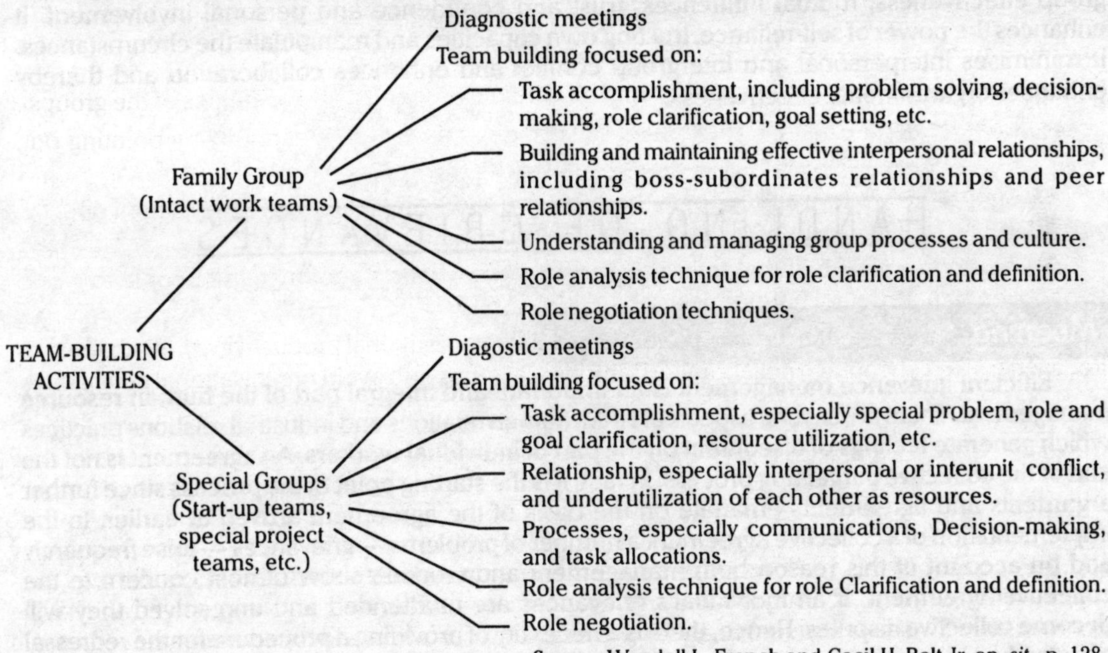

Source: Wendell L. French and Cecil H. Belt Jr. *op. cit.*, p. 128.

Fig. 9.18 : Varieties of Team Building Interventions.

48. Wendell L. French and Cecil H. Bell Jr., "*Organisational Development*", Prentice-Hall of India (P) Ltd., New Delhi, 1989, pp. 142-148.

The essential conditions for team building include: (a) Every member must have a clearly assigned role; (b) The team must take collective responsibility for the action of each of its members; (c) Team must speak with one voice; (d) No appeal from one member to another; (e) Good team is small in number; (f) No inordinate difference in salary or members; and (g) Each member should be able to handle responsibility of other members.

The major ingredients of team building are: (a) Get the right people together; (b) Have a large block of uninterrupted time; (c) Deal with high priority problems/opportunities; (d) work on all the identified problems; (e) Structure in all ways to enhance the likelihood of success; (f) Develop realistic solutions and action plans; (g) Implement the solutions enthusiastically; and (h) Follow up to assess actual is expected results.

The essential hints to the manager to build the team successfully are: (a) Hold small and informal meetings for minor problems and large and long meetings for strategic issues; (b) Create a climate of cooperation; (c) The rule of order is to pick easy problems first; (d) Keep the atmosphere casual and light; (e) Compliment the participants and strengthen the spirit of cooperation and collaboration; (f) Keep an open mind; (g) Don't harp on a pet idea and do not let any one else hog the floor either; (h) Encourage the subordinates to formulate the goals through you are the boss; (i) Workers expect something, so fulfil their goals; (j) Help the members when they need it; (k) Protect the workers when they do something wrong; (l) Provide the members all necessary material, finance etc; (m) Follow feed forward and feedback and keep the members informed always; and (n) Aware that the democracy is almost always the best policy.

The main factor the success of Japan is team work. It does wonders. It can do the things what the hi-tech. cannot do. It creates an open and participatory climate. It improves communication problem solving and interpersonal skills of the members. It results in high level group effectiveness, mutual influences, trust and confidence and personal involvement. It enhances the power of self-reliance, trusting own capacities and manipulate the circumstances. It minimises interpersonal and intergroup conflict and enhances collaboration and thereby enhances organisational effectiveness.

HANDLING OF GRIEVANCES

Meaning

Efficient grievance management is an important and integral part of the human resource management. There are several aspects of HRM, human relations and industrial relations practices which generate feelings of discontent on the part of individual workers. An agreement is not the end of the collective bargaining process. In fact, it is the starting point of the process since further arguments and agreements emanate on the basis of the agreement arrived at earlier. In the implementation of a collective agreement a number of problems — grievances — arise frequently and on account of this reason both management and workers show utmost concern to the collective agreement. If an individual's grievances are unattended and unresolved they will become collective disputes. Hence, there is a necessity of providing a procedure for the redressal of individual grievances.

A grievance is a sign of the employee's discontent with job and its nature. The employee has got certain aspirations of expectations which he thinks must be fulfilled by the organisation where he is working. When the organisation fails to satisfy the employee needs, he develops a feeling of discontent of dissatisfaction. For instance, the employee expects proper implementation of the Central and State Government's laws, collective agreements, company policies and management responsibilities. A violation of any one among these cause dissatisfaction on his part. Thus, grievance is caused due to the difference between employee expectation and management practice.

The concept 'grievance' has been defined in several ways by different authorities. Some of the definitions are as follows:

Beach defines as grievance as "any dissatisfaction or feeling of justice in connection with one's employment situation that is brought to the notice of the management",[49] whereas Flippo indicates the grievance as "a type of discontent which must always be expressed. A grievance is usually more formal in character than a complaint. It can be valid or ridiculous, and must grow out of something connected with company operations or policy. It must involve an interpretation or application of the provisions of the labour contract".[50]

Jucious defines a grievance as " . . . .any discontent or dissatisfaction, whether exposed or not, whether valid or not, arising out of anything connected with the company which an employee thinks, believes or even feels to be unfair, unjust or inequitable".[51]

The above definitions indicate that a grievance may be factual or imaginary or disguised and it is problem whether expressed or not, valid or not. When an employee presents a problem, the grievance redressing authority, has to analyse the problem, find out the root cause of the problem rather than viewing it from legal aspects and solve it based on humanitarian approach. This approach of grievance redressal is known as clinical approach to grievance handling. Hence, a grievance may be viewed as complex psychological phenomenon calling for human rather than any procedural or legal action in its analysis and solution.

Characteristics of Grievances

A grievance may have the following characteristics:

(a) Factual: The employer-employee relationship depends upon the job contract in any organisation. This contract indicates the norms defining the limits within which the employee expects the organisation to fulfill his aspirations, needs or expectations. When these legitimate needs of expectations or aspirations are not fulfilled, the employee will be dissatisfied with the job. Such dissatisfaction is called factual grievance. For instance, when an employee is not given promotion which is due to him or when work conditions are unsafe, grievances of employee relating to these issues are based on facts. In other words, these grievances reflects the drawbacks in the implementation of the organisational policies.

(b) Imaginary: When the job contract is not clear-cut and does not indicate the norms defining the limits within which the employee expects the organisation to fulfill his needs or aspirations, the employee develops such needs which the organisation is not obliged to meet. Here, grievances are not based on facts. Even then the employee feels aggrieved. Normally, the organisation does not feel any kind of responsibility for such grievances and their redressal, because they are based not only on wrong perceptions of the employee but also on wrong information. However, such grievances can have far-reaching consequences on the organisation because the employees are likely to develop an altogether negative attitude towards the organisation which decreases their effectiveness and involvement in work.

49. Dale S. Beach, *op. cit.*, p. 583.
50. Edwin B. Flippo, *op, cit.*, p. 430.
51. Michael J. Jucious, *op. cit.*, p. 4.

(c) Disguised: In general organisations consider the basic requirements of their employees. Psychological needs of the employees such as need for recognition, affection, power, achievement etc., are normally unattended and ignored for instance, an employee complaining very strongly about the working conditions in the office may in turn be seeking some recognition and appreciation from his or her colleagues. Hence, disguised grievances should also be considered since they do have far reaching consequences in case they are unattended and ignored.

Nature of and Causes of Grievances

A grievance is a problem and submitted by an employee or several employees of different types. If may be concerning a situation or likely to affect the terms and conditions of employment of one worker or several workers. If a problem is related to and endorsed by all or majority of employees or if trade union submits a problem as a general claim it falls outside the scope of grievance procedure and generally comes under the purview of collective bargaining. Thus, if an issue is wider in scope of general in nature it will be outside the grievance machinery. For example if majority of employees or the trade union in an organisation demand wage revision, such issue does not come under the scope of grievance machinery and falls within the scope of collection bargaining. In contrast if the workers of different departments submit to the management that their wage is not in accordance with the award given by Wage Boards and if they ask the management to correct the wage inequity such issue falls within the scope of grievance machinery. Thus, a grievance — (a) Has a narrower perspective; (b) Is concerned with the interpretation of a contract or award as concerned to an individual or a few employees of different types.[52] As such policy issues do not fall within the scope of grievance machinery.

Causes of grievances related to interpretation of all personnel policies: National Commission on Labour states that "complaints affecting one or more individual workers in respect of their wage payments, overtime, leave, transfer, promotion, seniority, work assignment and discharge would constitute grievances."[53] The causes of grievances include the interpretation of areas like placement, transfer, promotion, working conditions, payment of wages, allowances overtime pay, victimisation, medical benefits, housing facilities, increments, granting loans, conditions of work, leave, seniority, safety measures, fines, conditions of work, suspension, break in service and the like.

Pre-requisites of a Grievance Procedure

The efficiency of a grievance procedure depends upon the fulfilment of certain pre-requisites. These are as follows:

(a) Conformity with Prevailing Legislation: While designing the grievance procedure due consideration must be given to the existing statutory provisions. In other words, the existing grievance machinery as provided by law may be made use of.

(b) Clarity: There should be clarity regarding each and every aspect of the grievance procedure. An aggrieved employee must be informed about the person to whom a representation can be made, the form of submission (written or oral), the time limit for the redressal of grievance etc. Similarly, the redressing authority should be very clear about what is expected from him, what measure he can take, the limits within which he should resort to an action etc.

(c) Simplicity: The grievance procedure should be simple. Every employee must understand different stages of the procedure, the forms to be filled up, the witnesses required etc. If there

52. Arun Monappa and Mirza S. Saiyadain, *op. cit.* p. 237.
53. Report of the National Commission on Labour, *op. cit.*, p. 458.

are too many stages in the procedure, too many forms to be filled up, too much going around etc., the very purpose of the procedure is defeated. Instead of resorting to the formal procedure an employee may ignore it.

(d) Promptness: The promptness with which a grievance is processed adds further to the success of the grievance procedure. Since justice delayed is justice denied the procedure should aim at rapid disposal of the grievances.

(e) Training: The success of the procedure also depends upon imparting training to the supervisors and union representative in handling grievances.

(f) Follow-up: The successful working of a grievances procedure depends upon a proper follow-up by the personnel department. The department should periodically review the procedure and introduce the essential structural changes making it more effective.

Grievance Interview

Despite the fulfilment of the above pre-requisites, there is some inherent empersonality in the procedure which makes it insensitive to imaginary and disguised grievances. Hence, they should be supplemented or sometimes replaced by a good personal approach i.e., the grievance interview. This also facilitates the identification of the basis — whether factual or not. Even when the basis is factual the grievance interview reduces the magnitude of the problem and develops an understanding between the aggrieved and the organisation.

The effectiveness of the interview depends upon the skills on the part of the interviewer. He must give a patient listening to the employee and the employee should feel free to ventilate his grievances. If the interviewer is competent in professional handling of the situation and well conversant with the techniques of interview he can draw the aggrieved to him and in the process of interview he can bring about an integration of the employee's objectives with the organisational objectives.

The Open-door Policy

How to minimise/eliminate the source of an employee's grievances?

This question is normally ignored and prevention of grievances is a neglected part of grievance management in a number of organisations. What is required is the development of 'sensitive feelers' within an organisation for tapping the sources of dissatisfaction. In other words, the upward channels of communication should be free from bloacks of hindrances. Unfortunately, in many organisations there is a notion among superiors that a negative content generates dissatisfaction on the part of the higher-ups, and gives a negative feeling about the concerned department. Hence, an endeavour is made for suppressing the grievances and individuals are prevented from 'speaking out'. To overcome the barriers of upward communication some experts have suggested an 'Open-door Policy' which requires effort and willingness from the individual's superior. In other words, there should be a general invitation to all employees to walk-in at any time and speak over their grievances. However, this policy is workable only in small organisations. Since the principle of management by exception is practised in large organisations, the top level management have neither time to look after the in numberable grievances of their employees nor familiarity with their work situation.

Grievance Procedure

The Model Grievance Procedure suggested by the National Commission on Labour has provided for the successive time bound steps each leading to the next in case of lack of satisfaction (Fig. 9.19).

At the outset an aggrieved worker shall approach the foreman and informs its grievance orally and seeks the redressal of his grievance. If it is not redressed to his satisfaction he approaches the supervisor who has to give an answer to the complaint of the worker within 48 hours. If the decision (answer) is not acceptable to the worker or if the superior does not give an answer, the worker can go to the next step. At the third stage the worker can, either in person or accompanied by his departmental representative, approach the head of the department who has to give an answer before the expiry of three days. If the department head fails to do so or if the decision given by him is not acceptable to the worker then the worker can resort to the Grievance Committee which comprises of the representatives of employers and employees. This Committee shall communicate its recommendations to the manager within seven days of the grievance reaching it. If there are unanimous decisions, these shall be implemented by the management. In case, unanimous decisions have not been arrived at, the views of the members of the Committee shall be recorded and all the relevant records shall be placed before the manager for decision. The manager shall communicate his decision within three days. The worker has got a right to appeal against the manager's decision. These appeals shall be decided within a week. If the aggrieved desires, he can take along with him a union official for discussion with the authority. In case a decision has not been arrived at, at this stage, the union and management may refer the grievance to voluntary arbitration within a week of receipt of the management's decision by the worker.

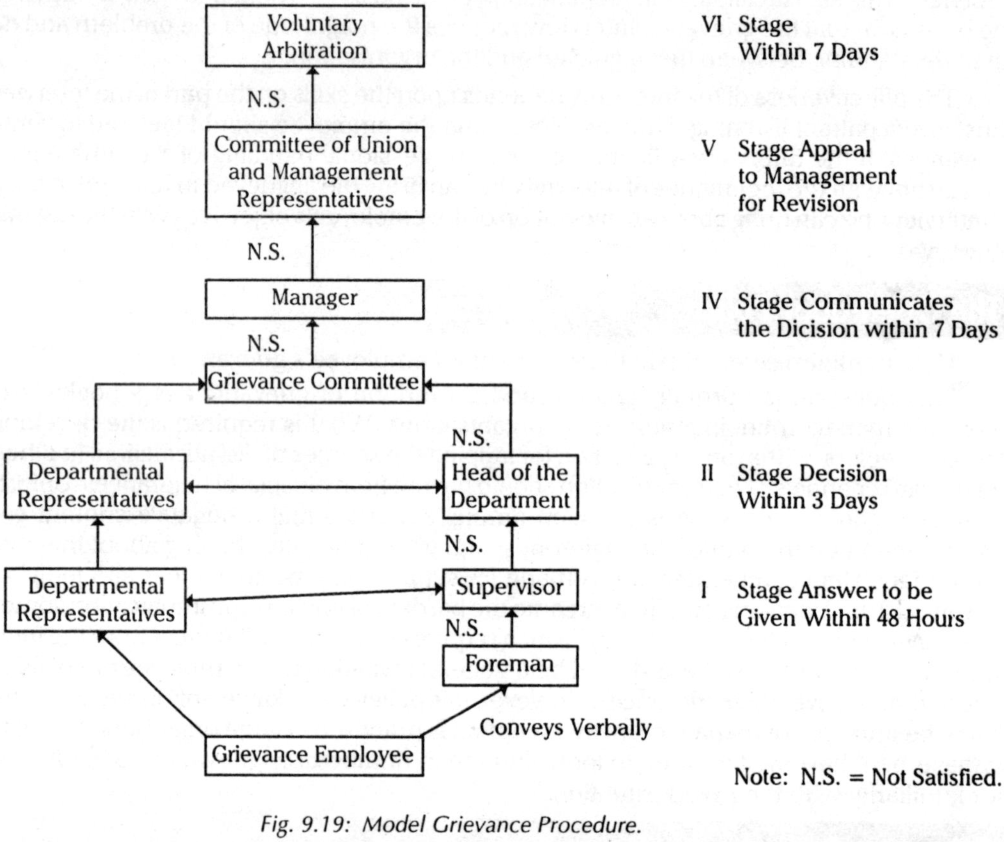

Fig. 9.19: Model Grievance Procedure.

All the above mentioned steps may not be resorted to by a worker. In case the grievance arises on account of dismissal or discharge of the worker, he can resort to the second step. In the latter stage he can make an appeal to the dismissing authority designated by the management within a week from the date of dismissal or discharge.

Thus, there is voluntariness in so far as the implementation of the Model Grievance Procedure is concerned. But, there is a great need for providing a statutory backing to the grievance machinery since voluntariness failed to get the desired result in a number of cases. Further, there is a need to introduce suggestion schemes which are helpful in overcoming the barriers in upward channels of communication. In the Western countries suggestion schemes have helped a lot in harmonising the relations between labour and management. In India also, suggestion schemes have been a success in some organisations due to monetary rewards, establishment of suggestion committees and dissemination of full information about the suggestions received. Hence, the importance of suggestion schemes should be recognised and measures should be initiated for the introduction of such schemes.

EFFECTIVE SUPERVISION

Supervision is most important activity in motivating and utilising human resource. Further, it is a moderately important source of job satisfaction of employees. Leadership style of the supervisor is an important dimension. One of the leadership style of the supervisors is an important dimension. One of the leadership style of the supervisors is employee-centeredness supervisor takes a personal interest in the employee's welfare. It is normally manifested in ways such as checking to see how well the subordinate is doing, providing advice and assistance to the individual and communicating with the employee on a personal as well as an official level.

The other dimension is participation or influence supervisor allows the employees to participate in the decision-making. In most cases this approach leads to higher job satisfaction. A participative climate created by the supervisor has a more substantial effect on workers' satisfaction than does participation in a specific decision.[54]

The supervisor should create strong orgnisational culture by providing effective supervision. The effective supervision should include providing initiative to the individual workers, degree of risk tolerance, providing support for the acts of workers, maximum freedom in doing the work, minimum controls, free-flow of communication, reward system based on performance, allowing free criticism and identify the employees with the organisation. Supervisor should take care of employees personal and family problems.

COMMUNICATION

Communication is one of the most basic functions of management. The manager can make a good decision, think out well-conceived plans, establish a sound organisation structure, and even be well linked with his associates. But he cannot get the work done through the employees unless he is sure of some basic facts, viz., that the workers are to be communicated of what he wants to be done. He has to decide how it is to be communicated, and what results can be expected from the communication. In the following table is given the relationship between these issues and the managerial communication.

54. Fred Luthans, *op. cit.*, p. 185.

TABLE 9.1 MANAGERIAL COMMUNICATION AND ITS CONSEQUENCES

Communication Questions	*Possible Outcomes*
1. What to communicate?	Factual Information Information about Opinions and Attitudes
2. How to communicate?	Verbally (oral or written) Non-verbally
3. What to expect?	Compliance Behaviour, Changed Behaviour

Communication forms a basis for management by objectives, long-range strategic goal setting and policy formulation, strategic planning, organisation development and organisation effectiveness, control, decision-making and allied managerial activities aimed at effective achievement of organisational goals.

What is Communication?

Communication refers to the sharing of ideas, facts, opinions, information and understanding.[55] It has been defined as "The process of passing information and understanding. From one person to another. It is essentially a bridge of meaning between people. By using this bridge of meaning, a person can safely cross the river of misunderstanding that separates all people."[56] Prof. Das Gupta is of the view that "To communicate is to inform, to tell, to show or to spread information. Whatever its etymological meaning, from the managerial point of view, communication is the means by which a management gets its job done. It can affect both the morale and efficiency of employees. Communication is a skill of management."[57] According to Allen, "Communication is the sum of all things that one person does when he wants to clear a misunderstanding in the mind of another. It is a bridge of meaning. It involves a systematic and continuous process of telling, listening and understanding."[58] Dr. McFarland views communication as "a process of meaningful interaction among human beings. More specially, it is the process by which meanings are perceived and understandings are reached among human being."[59] Vardaman and Helterman have given a very comprehensive definition of communication thus: "By communication we mean the flow of material, information, perception, and understanding between various parts and members of an organisation....all the methods, means, and media of communication *(Communication technology)*, all the channels, network and systems of communication *(Organisation Structure)*, all the person-to-person interchange (interpersonal communication)....It includes all aspects of communication: up, down, lateral, speaking, writing, listening, reading, methods, media, models, channels, networks, flow, interpersonal, interorganisational."[60]

55. Kazmier, Leonard J., *Principles of Management: A Programmed Instructional Approach*, Tata McGraw Hill Book Co., 1977, p. 266.
56. Davis, Keith, *Human Behaviour At Work*, Tata McGraw - Hill Publishing Company Ltd., New Delhi, 1977, p. 372.
57. Das Gupta, A., *Some Management Skills*, University of Delhi, Delhi, pp. 48-49.
58. Allen, Louis A., *Management and Organisation*, p. 144.
59. McFarland, D.E., *Management: Principles and Practice*, p. 552.
60. Vardaman, George, T., and Carroll C. Helterman, *Managerial Control Through Communication*, John Wiley & Sons, New York, 1968, pp. 3-4.

Basic Elements of Communication

The key elements of communication are:

1. *It is a process*, which exists as a flow through a sequence or series of steps. These steps include the generation of an idea: putting it into some logical sequence, transmitting it through some media; and its reception by someone at the other end; his understanding of the message sent and his acting upon the message received.

2. Communication involves that information not only be transmitted but also understood. If information has been transmitted and not received or received but not accurately interpreted, then miscommunication occurs.

3. The third element is that *information senders (encoders)* and *receivers (decoders) are either human* (animate) or non-human (inanimate) objects. It should, however, be remembered that communication is a broad field of human interchange of facts and opinions and not the technologies of the telephone, the radio and the like.[61]

4. *There must be some channel or medium through which information or understanding could be transmitted*: Transmission may be done by word of mouth, by written material, pictures, body language, etc. "Communication is generally understood as spoken or written words. But, in reality, it is more than that. It is the sum total of directly or indirectly, consciously or unconsciously, transmitted words, attitudes, feelings, actions, gestures and tones."[62]

5. *Communication may consist of three interlocking circuits transmitting information*: It may be upward in regard to knowing the effectiveness of orders, ideas, comments, actions, reactions, attitudes, reports, complaints, and grievances from the lowest level; downward may flow instructions, directions, clarifications, interpretations, of rules, regulations, orders, policies and procedures; and intra-scalar or cross contact, where information may be exchanged between two departmental heads or two or more persons who are of equal status.

The rating-scale method is easy to understand and easy to use, and permits a statistical tabulation of scores. A ready comparison of scores among the employees is possible. These scores indicate the worth of every individual. It is the most common evaluation tool in use today.

Importance of Communication for Management

The importance of communication in any managerial process can hardly be overemphasised. If an organisation is to operate as an integrated unit, it is necessary that the top management should keep the lower level supervisors and employees well-informed of its ultimate objectives and how it wants each person to endeavour for their realisation. By freely sharing information, the management takes employees into its confidence, prepares them for changes, avoids misunderstanding, and removes it if at all it develops, and makes them more knowledgeable about the problems and policies of the enterprise.

Communication is essential for management for the following reasons:[63]

1. It is a prerequisite to work communication. Management cannot communicate to workers unless management itself is informed. Not only must management *know* but it must also

61. Kelly, Joe, *Organisational Behaviour,* Richard D. Irwin, and the Dorsey Press, Homewood, 1974, p. 587.
62. Scott, and sprigel, *Personnel Management*, 1977.
63. Richard, Max D., and R. Williams, A Nielander, *Readings in Management*, D.B. Taraporevala Sons Ltd., Bombay, 1971, pp. 156-157.

understand the information well enough to interpret it to others. "Just as a photograph can be no clearer than the negative from which it is printed, the manager cannot transmit more clearly than he understands."

2. *It is essential if a manager* is to make proper judgements and decisions. The manager is often completely isolated from the point of performance, and he can serve as a "decision centre" only to the extent that reports and other informations reach him. This requires two-way communication.

3. The scope of manager's influence is typically greater than a worker's. Therefore, inadequate communication to any one manager can have a direct effect on profit, productivity, or morale because his wide span of control and coordination affects many people and different activities.

4. Management communication is necessary because most of the links in the chain of communication from top to bottom and bottom to top, are in the management group. Each link attends a new opportunity for distorting, fading and delay.

5. It is important because, even though members of management are not defined as "employees", they are in fact employees, which means that they have need for communication and understanding just like any other employee.

In discussing the importance of communication, Drucker says; "The manager has a specific tool: information. He does not 'handle' people; he motivates, guides, organises people to do their own work. His tool to do all this is the spoken or written word or the language of numbers. No matter whether the manager's job is engineering, accounting or selling, his effectiveness depends on his ability to listen and to read, on his ability to speak and to write. He needs skills in getting his thinking across to other people as well as skills in finding out what other people are after."[64]

It would be obvious that communication is the 'life-blood' and 'foundation-stone' of the successful working of an organisation, for it puts a check on many rumours, misunderstandings and gossip when plans, ideas, information, etc., are circulated among employees. At the same time, it makes their reaction known so that any difficulty in the proper implementation of policies and the observance of rules may be removed.

Peter has said: "Good communication is the foundation for sound management,"[65] It is through a well-laid system of communication that the management succeeds in establishing links between different management functions. viz., those of planning, organisation, co-ordination direction and control. Peterson and Plowman regard communication as an essential function of management, because it is through it that subordinates come to know of the relevant instructions and orders of the boss, and their own duties and responsibilities.[66] It is through communication that they submit their grievances, work reports, suggestions, etc. In fact, an effective and speedy communication ensures that there are no delays, bottlenecks, confusion, misunderstandings and distortion of facts, and establishes unity among all the concerned persons and departments. For proper co-ordination and control, communication is a must, for in its absence there cannot be any synchronisation of activities, unity in thinking and working, and co-operation among the employees. Mary Cushing Nyles writes: "Good communications are essential to co-ordination. They are necessary upward, downward and sideways through all the levels of authority and advice for transmission, interpretation and adoption of policies, for the sharing of knowledge and information and for the more subtle needs of good morale and mutual understanding."[67]

64. Drucker, Peter F., *The Practice of Management.* Harber & Row Publishers, New York, 1954, p. 346.
65. Peters, Raymond W., *Communication Within Industry.*
66. Peterson and Plowman, *Business Organisation and Management,* p. 444.
67. Niles, Mary Cushing, *The Essence of Management,* pp. 390-391.

Purposes of Communication

A management depends on communication to achieve organisational objectives. Since managers work through others, all their acts, policies, rules, orders and procedures must pass through some sort of communication channel. The purposes of communication are:

(i) To develop information and understanding which are necessary for group effort;
(ii) To foster an attitude which is necessary for motivation, co-operation and job satisfaction;
(iii) To discourage the spread of misinformation, rumours, gossip, and to release the emotional tensions of workers;
(iv) To prepare workers for a change by giving them the necessary information in advance;
(v) To encourage ideas, suggestions from subordinates for in improvement in the product and work conditions, for a reduction in the time or cost involved and for the avoidance of the waste of raw material;
(vi) To improve labour-management relations by keeping both in contact with each other;
(vii) To ensure such free exchange of information and ideas as will assist all the employees in understanding and accepting the reasonableness of the status and authority of everyone in the organisation;
(viii) To satisfy such basic human needs as the needs of recognition, self-importance and a sense of belonging;
(ix) To serve auxiliary functions such as entertainment and the maintenance of social relations among human beings.

In brief, a good communication system not only ensures the transmission of information and understanding among individuals and groups, but unifies group behaviour, which provides the basis for continuing group co-operation. The efficient functioning of any organisation depends on how well its communication channels operate.

According to Miner and Miner, there are four basic types of objectives of communication activities which combine to form a communication network.[68]

(a) A regulative network ensures security, conformity to plans and the achievement of productivity through the communication of policy statements, procedures and rules.
(b) The innovative network is concerned with problem-solving and change through such techniques as suggestion systems and meetings.
(c) The integrative network is directly related to considerations of employee morale and organisational maintenance and uses methods ranging from the informal group-wise presentations to formal presentations by the management.
(d) The informative network relates to employees' effectiveness and productivity through a direct dissemination of information and training programmes.

Functions of Communication

Thayer has divided the functions of communication into four specific categories: the information function, the command and instructive function, the influence and persuasion function, and the integrative function.[69]

68. Miner J.B. and Miner M.G., *Personnel and Industrial Relations,* 1973, p. 545.
69. Thayer, Lee, *Communication and Communication System,* Richard D. Irwin, Homewood, 1968, pp. 187-239.

1. *The information function* serves to provide knowledge to the individual's need for guidance in his actions. It also fulfils worker's desires for awareness of things that affect him.

2. *The command and instructive functions* serve to make the employee aware of his obligations to the formal organisation and to provide him with additional guidance on how to perform his duties adquately.[70]

3. *The influence and persuasion function* (also known as motivational function) encourages the appropriate individual to perform or to exhibit a certain behaviour. Messages communicated are used to convince individuals that their actions can be personally or organisationally beneficial.[71]

4. *The integrative function* refers to the fact that the communication of message, ideas, if properly handled, should help to relate the activities of the workers to their efforts, complement rather than detract from each other. Work efforts are unified rather than frangmented as a result of properly integrative communication.[72]

If the functions of communication are to be accomplished, communication within the organisation must be three-dimensional—downward, upward and horizontal. Downward communication serves all the four functions; upward communication particularly provides operational information needed by those high in the organisational hierarchy and also facilitates the achievement of integrated activities; and *horizontal communication* is important for all purpose, but it specially helps in the performance of information and integrative functions.

Responsibility for Effective Communication

Though communication is the responsibility of every person in an organisation, yet a successful communication programme depends upon the top management which initiates and sparks it. In other words, it should be established by the top management, though the subordinates may also be asked to do the same. Employees must communicate with others, and they must also be able to judge when, where and how to communicate.

In any operation, the supervisor or the first-line manager is the key communicator. He should learn and interpret clearly the company's ideals and policies to the workers; and he should be able to understand his worker's problems and put across management's viewpoint in their own interests. A successful and good supervisor is one who "shows understanding" and "to whom one may talk".

The supervisor must understand clearly the following facts so that he may be able to communicate effectively:

(i) He must understand clearly the needs and policies of the company, and keep himself abreast of its new policies or changes in its structure. He should be acquainted with the broad outline of the company's policy in general.
(ii) He must understand the interest of the workers.
(iii) He must set clearly his own goals and ideals.
(iv) He must know his work group and know its feelings and emotions.

Types of Communication

Basically, the two most important types of organisation are formal and informa communications.

70. *Ibid.*, p. 205.
71. *Ibid.*, p. 226.
72. *Ibid.*, p. 239.

(a) *Formal Communications* are those that are "official", that are a part of the recognised communication system which is involved in the operation of the organisation. These communications may be oral or written. A formal communication can be from a superior to a subordinate, from a subordinate to a superior, intra-administrative, or external.

Communication between superiors and their subordinates represents *downward communications flow*. These are administrative communications, which provide instruction, information, and clarification. When subordinates initiate communication to their superiors, the *flow is upward*, and the messages may include participation in decision making, expression of dissatisfaction, or opinion. *Intra-administrative communications* pass across the organisational levels. They are frequent between line and staff units.

Formal Communications take place externally from the organisation i.e., with outside groups, such as suppliers, clients, unions, government agencies, and community groups.

(b) *Informal communications* grow out of the social interactions among people who work together. These are not bound by any chart on the wall but are bound by conventions, customs and culture. Such communications provide useful informations for events to come, in the form of grapevine.

Communication may also be *oral* (silent) and *written*.

An *oral communication* generally takes place when the audience is largely illiterate and there are problems of languages difficulty. Such communication is direct between the supervisor and the worker, and is often known as face-to-face (or one-to-one) communication. It takes the form of talks, a public address, verbal discussions, telephonic talk, telecommunication (or on the intercom system) and other artificial media, such as audio- visual aids (slides, movies, tape records, films, broadcasts, whistles, bells or call bells), speeches and orders, holding of meetings and conferences, lectures, social get-together, training sessions, public address systems, museums, exhibitions, counselling.

A written communication is always put into writing and generally used when the audience is at a distance or when a permanency of record is required or where its preservation is essential in case it is needed as evidence in cases of dispute. It is generally in the form of instructions, orders, rules and regulations, policies, procedures, posters, memos, reports, information bulletins; in the form of items in magazines, newspapers, circulars, house journals; or in the form of pictorial messages, hand-outs; or it is written down in employee's hand books, training and job manuals; or when a grievance procedure is laid down, or when a performance appraisal is effected; or it may be put upon notice boards, display stands; or it may be in the form of suggestion schemes and personal letters written to employees.

Habbe gives comparative advantages of written versus oral communications. These are:[73]

Advantages of a Written Communication

— Authority
— Accuracy
— Permanence
— Coverage (can be of adequate length and can be duplicated and distributed to all individuals who should receive it)
— Miscellaneous (retention rate from reading is high; written communications are economical)

73. Habbe, S., "Communicating with Employees", *Studies in Personnel Policies*, No.29, National Industrial Conference Board, 1952.

Advantages of Oral Communication

— Personal
— Two-way (ideas can be exchanged, questions asked)
— Flexible (can be adapted to receive, can be presented in the right tone of voice, with a smile, with gestures)
— Effective
— Miscellaneous (easy, simple, fast, places responsibility for communication where it belongs– on the immediate supervisor).

In a good organisation, the management uses both the media — the verbal and the written– of communication. To be effective, these media have to be clear, purposeful, concise, complete, and should express mutual confidence at appropriate levels. A proper communication has to play an important role in a large organisation, and there has to be a proper balance between the oral and written forms of communication.

It need hardly be said that the choice of any one method depends upon the purpose to be accomplished and the likelihood of its success. Quite often, it is better to use more than one methods to convey the same information so that one can reinforce the other.

Direction of Communication

Communication flows in various directions. Generally, however, it is transmitted down or flows across an organisation.

Vertical communication (also known as *upward and downward or inter-scalar communication*), is one in which communication flows from top to bottom as well as from the rank-and-file workers towards the management. Thus, it consists of downward and upward communication.

Messages moving along vertical channels travel along the same paths (downward and upward communication), the content, nature and problems of the two vary considerably. "Downward communication is like water streaming down from a waterfall or streamhead. It pours down easily with great force and wets a large area, while upward communication is like a small spurt of water shooting up from a fountain against the pull of gravity. The higher it travels, the more it loses its force. Official top-to-bottom communication channels flow down with great force and reach a great many people, but official bottom-to-top channels flow up with difficulty and reach relatively few people."[74]

Downward Communication

It is the transmission of ideas or information from executives to the subordinates. It is generally a directive in the sense that it causes action to be initiated by subordinates. It is the best form of communication in the vertical chain of communication, is accepted more at the face value, and is reacted to more vigorously. Instructions, directions, clarification, interpretations, orders, policies, rules and regulations, procedures, a specific conduct of jobs, changes in work rules, time schedules, safety and welfare measures, orders for transfers, promotions, information on working conditions, leave, etc., have to flow downwards from those at the top of the pyramid to the rank-and-file workers at lower levels who form the base; and this flow may be in the form of an oral or written communication.

74. Halloran, Jack, *Applied Human Relations*, Prentice-Hall, New Delhi, 1978, p. 63.

Upward communication in companies is just as vital and yet inadequate as downward communication. It is, therefore, necessary that both the upward and downward flow of communication should receive equal attention. This flow becomes a complete circuit. If this circuit is broken by a poor upward flow, the following benefits would be lost to management:[75]

(a) Stimulation of employee interest and participation;
(b) Receipt and use of valuable employee ideas;
(c) Evaluation of effectiveness or otherwise of downward communication;
(d) A proper and objective understanding of employees' problems; and
(e) More and better information for better evaluation and decision-making;

Horizontal, Intra-Scalar or Lateral Communication

This is communication from persons at one level in an organisation to others at the same level. It is particularly frequent, between the line and staff units. It provides a means by which managers at the same level of an organisation co-ordinate their activities without referring all the matters to their superior. A writer has called this a gang plank. His idea is that many matters can be handled at the same level of an organisation. In this way, one acts speedily and, at the same time, relieves superiors of unnecessary problems. For example, multiple copies of memoranda that flow to all the positions needing the information increase the co-ordination of effort.

Communication at the horizontal level is also important at the executive level. Dimock remarks: "The influence an executive has with other executives is partly a matter of his position in the hierarchy, partly a question of his competence and party dependent upon a complete and sensitised communication system.."[76]

Extra-Organisational Communication

This type of communication takes place between agencies outside an organisation and the people within it. Communication is generally effected through letters and passing of annual reports to the creditors, bankers, the Government and trade organisations.

Media of Communication

In its relations with the outside world, an organisation might use these forms of written communication: advertising materials; training and instruction materials; employee recruiting programmes, brochures and news releases. Under oral communication may be used sales contracts, verbal presentations to individuals and group participation in conferences and speeches.

The media most commonly used are: employee handbook, house magazines and newspapers, employee papers, financial reports to employees, published statements concerning personnel and other policies, information racks or display stands, bulletin boards, audiovisual aids, posters, exhibitions, notice boards, and suggestion system. Meetings and grievance handling procedures are also utilised for the purpose. Each of these media has its merits and demerits, which a manager keeps in view while deciding which one to adopt.[77]

75. Gulati T.S. 'Communication Vital for Organisational Integration', *Industrial Times*, Vol. 9, No.. 17, 1967, p. 13.
76. Dimock, *Executive Action*.
77. Mamoria C.B., *Personnel Management*, Himalaya Publishing House, Mumbai, 1982, pp. 553-558.

Communication with Management

Management communication is a pre-requisite to employee communication and should, therefore, receive due attention. Management or intra-management communication helps managers to arrive at sound decisions. Inadequate information to manages often affects the broad area of performance, because their spans of supervision affect many persons and activities. Moreover, management communication is needed for its own sake, rather than as a means of informing workers. Therefore, most companies use such practices as newsletters, bulletins, special booklets, management journals, management lunch or coffee rooms to keep managers informed of policies, services and production.

For an effective management communication, the following universally accepted ways should be tried:

(i) The management must think clearly before communicating. It must give proper attention to the attitudes of the receiving audience; for "it is no good opening the tap if there is nothing in the tank."

(ii) The purpose of communication must be clearly known as to what is to be achieved. Too many objectives should not be achieved with one single communication.

(iii) The audience must be thoroughly known, as also the timing and the media of communication.

(iv) Before communicating, it is always better to consult someone who knows about communication. This will lend objectivity to the approach.

(v) The language used, the tone of voice, expression and emotion should receive proper attention (for all these affect the success of communication).

(vi) The management should be prepared to help the receiving audience and make the information clear to it.

(vii) It should encourage comments, ask questions, have follow up and encourage feedbacks. Without these, communication will go haywire.

(viii) Communication should be based not only on present requirements but also on future needs.

(ix) Communication should always be supported with appropriate action, for "action speaks louder than words."

(x) The management should cultivate the habit of listening.

Communication with the Public

Communication with the public—the shareholders, customers, suppliers, Government, community, and the general public are communicated through such media as mass communication, comprising public meetings, advertisement in newspapers, periodicals, radio and television broadcasting etc.

The purpose of communication with the public is (i) to make the company known as a producer of quality goods and services and to improve its image in the public mind; (ii) to build a reputation of the company as a good and reliable firm with which to do business; (iii) to get recognition from the public that the company is socially responsible to the society; and (iv) to secure and maintain public understanding of the company, its organisation, policies, problems and operations.

Channels or Network of Communication

A communication channel is a pathway, route or medium through which information and understanding are passed a sender to a receiver; for example, a chain of commands, or a grapevine is a channel. Communications between departments or between two companies constitute channels.

The communication channel may comprise of the centralised or decentralised network. The centralised network means that all communication is forced through a central position; one member has more channels and more information than the other members of the group. A centralised network generally facilitates efficient performance of routine problem-solving activities (especially in the assembling of information), strengthens the leadership position, and results in quickly stabilised sets of interactions among the members of a group.

As against this, there are decentralised networks, in which there is no central member; all the members have an equal number of channels and the opportunity to share an equal amount of information. Such networks systematically produce higher levels of satisfaction (probably because they are more democratic in nature), facilitate the handling of ambiguous and unpredictable situations and are more likely to be responsive to innovation.

Communication networks are usually identified according to their component configurations. Patterns such as a circle, a chain, a wheel, all-channel, star, 'Y' and pyramid have been utilised. Each of these patterns has certain merits and demerits. The most effective manner of communicating messages will depend on such situational factors as speed, accuracy, cost and time limitation. The best organisational results are, therefore, obtained by using various networks and media of communication instead of just one.

It is interesting to note that, "for a group of five people," writes Leavitt, "ten channels of communication are possible; but when the number increases to 10,45 channels open up; and when the number is 100, 4, 950 communication channels are possible."[78]

Barriers to Communication

Communication, when it is impeded and does not reach the receiver, is often somewhat ineffective, and the impediments are known as barriers. These barriers have been classified into three categories by Sterglitz.[79]

A. Barriers arising from the act that individuals are involved in communication and they differ from one another because of their different background—geographic, economic, social, educational and occupational. These barriers may be called "pre-existing barriers to communication" which a company inherits because they are not common to society. They involve the unwillingness of the top management to communicate; or it may have no means to communicate; or it may have only a one-way communication; or it may not even understand the need for communication. For it, "communication may denote idle chit-chat; meetings, a waste of time."

B. Barriers arising from the company's climate which tends to stultify communication. Under this are included;

(a) *Fears:* (i) Fear of being misinterpreted when an employee talks about a rise in pay because of good profits in a particular year; (ii) Fear of disortion by the grapevine, when a message reaches the members of a group in a filtered manner; (iii) Fear of exposing oneself to criticism for having too little to offer; or knowing very little; this prevent an individual from withholding some information for which he cannot given an explanation. Information is held

78. Leavitt, Harold, *Managerial Psychology*, University of Chicago Press, Chicago, 1964, p. 373.
79. Sterglitz, Harold, "Barriers to Communication", *Management Record*, Vol. 20, No.1 January 1958, pp. 2-5.

back deliberately by an employee or supervisor lest the suggestion should be scrapped or provoke a derisive look;

(iv) Fear of reprisal, where an employee holds back information, for a frank criticism, a verbal grievance, a non-conforming opinion may get him pleasant duties, may get him transferred or even may cost him a rise or a promotion, or may result in the loss of his job.

(b) Poor supervision is another barrier to communication. The supervisor may act as a self-appointed censor and block information from going up or down. His unwillingness to communicate and his failure to understand the need for communication makes for dead spots in communication.

(c) Insincerity and lack of confidence are inter-related. "Insincerity" means that communication is superficial, while "lack of confidence" implies that what is being communicated or the one who is communicating is distrusted.

(d) Mechanical barriers are connected with the technical impediments in the way of communication within a company. They comprise barriers arising out of organisational structure, where responsibility and authority are not properly assigned. "If channels are not clear, if there are dead ends, blocked passages or bottlenecks, communication is chaotic and non-existent."

C. *Others*: These comprise barriers arising out of geographical distances, lack of time for communication, and lack of training.

To these may also be added:

(i) *Personal barriers* which arise from the judgements, emotions and social values, and give rise to a psychological distance. It has been rightly said that "our emotions act as filters in nearly all our communication. We see and hear what we are emotionally 'tuned' to see and hear. Thus, communication cannot be separated from our personality."

(ii) *Semantic barriers* arise due to the difference in meaning which different people attach to different things. "The meanings of words are not in words; they are with us". Semantic problems impede the communication that is essential for effective organisational performance. A poor choice of symbols, confused meaning of symbols, or the ignoring of non-verbal ones could disort communiques.

(iii) *Psychological barriers* are connected with the status symbol of an executive—his private dining room, higher position, status, prestige, etc., make subordinates feel a sense of inferiority or embarrassed in his presence; and this creates hierachical levels.

(iv) *Physical barriers*, which are due to environmental factors, such as weather disturbance, physical distance, distracting noises, etc.

Physical distance between people is also created because of excessive hierarchy in organisation. The reliance upon the "unity of command" concept requires that formal communications follow prescribed channels through the organisation. As a result they must frequently pass through many layers of the organisation, each offering a potential for distortion.

Human limitations also a hindrance to effective communication. Instead of listening in a rational, objective manner, to what is being said, one occasionally becomes emotionally involved. Judgements are imposed in place of rational fact appraisal. People inject their value systems into what they hear or read and, often instead of deciding objectively, lose rationality—either because they do not agree with what is being said or, if they have mentally stereotyped the sender, by perceiving the message to be other than the way it was intended. Consequently, the receiver hears only what he expects to hear.

Thus, *filtering of messages* occurs both in what the receiver is willing to acknowledge receiving and in the interpretation given to the message. Messages are consistent with the receivers' self-image and useful knowledge may be received and interpreted carefully. Messages that theaten his self-image or negatively affect his desires and expectations may either be ignored or interpreted in a less threatening way.

Again, if the receiver's mind is free from bias, optimism, and is forward looking, the communication and interpretation of messages is more likely to be objective and accurate. If, on the other hand, the minds of the receivers are anxious, emotional and predispositioned, communications and interpretations will probably be biased, subjective and sometimes unrealistic.

Another form of distortion of messages in *exaggeration*. With exaggeration, the message is received and then overstated or over reacted to. The message is interpreted to mean more than it really does. This often results from the perception of a large amount of authority carried by the sender to the message, particularly a high-level official.

Faulty expression or bad translation, as a result of which communication is vague, and is badly expressed in inadequate words; it shows a poor organisation of ideas which leads to lack of clarity and precision.

Finally, the stumbling block of the proper interpretation of messages is the fact that the message reaches the receiver at a time when he is not ready to utilise the message (it is premature), or the message is too late to be helpful, or the message is received at a time when the receiver is preoccupied with other matters and, therefore, misinterprets the meaning.

Guidelines for Improving Communication Barriers

The following guidelines may prove useful in removing communication barriers:

(i) *Identify and Analyse the Barriers:* Find out the possible barriers in the way of effective communication and then try to remove them. To make the communication clear, make use of the listener's language and avoid faulty translation.

(ii) *Top Management Must be Convinced of the Need of Communication*: A good communication is good human relations, and good communication is good business. It is not enough that communication should be convincing, it should also be practised, for "Practices are contagious".

(iii) *Emphasis on Written Statement of Policies:* This is the best means of letting everyone know how a company feels about communication. It sets the tone for the type of communication that everyone throughout the organisation should have. It sets the basis for the procedures and practices which will be used to implement policy. The formulation must take into consideration such questions as:

(a) What and how much should employees be told? How about good news, bad news, sensitive information?

(b) On what matters should employees have a chance to be heard: grievances, grapevine, methods, products, profits?

(c) How can a company ensure day-to-day acceptance and conformity with its communication policy? How can it protect the employees against reprisals?

(d) To remove mechanical barriers, it is necessary that an organisation should see to it that the job specifications of each supervisor include the responsibility for communication; the organisation structure should clearly designate the channels of communication; the staff responsibility for co-ordinating and controlling communication process should be clearly fixed.

(iv) *Recognise that Communication is a Two-way Process*: It is, therefore, necessary to know whether it has been properly received and perceived. This can be done by encouraging action, responses, asking questions, removing confusion and explaining clearly the meaning of the message sent.

(v) *Consistency and Coherence are Essential for Successful Communication*: Orders should be consistent with the objectives of the organisation and in keeping with its other activities.

(vi) *Overcome Disadvantage of the Distance Barriers*: For this purpose, utilise, whenever possible, physical devices like the telephone and the intercom, and see to it that people understand, i.e., the sender should see to it that information is not distorted, misinterpreted or stopped by those who are responsible for passing it on to others.

(vii) *Communication is a Continuing Process*: It cannot be compartmentalised or reduced to one or more communication programmes, because the goal of communication is complete understanding. Therefore, there should be a never-ending process of listening and reading. Communication should be constant, habitual and automatic.

(viii) *Empathetic speaking and hearing are essential* for effective communication. Therefore, the speaker should know his audience, and be sensitive to their needs and feelings when he speaks and listens; otherwise he may short-circuit important communication network.

(viii) *Optimum Timing is Important in Communication*: The best time for communicating important messages is when they are competing the least with other situations affecting the listeners. Messages are most likely to be considered and attended to when they provide a solution to a problem affecting the receiver.

(x) *The use of feedback improves the communication process* and reduces the chance of major disparities between the information or idea receive and the one intended.

(xi) *Repetition of Messages may be Helpful in Conveying the Intended Thoughts*: Often a single transmission of an idea may not be received or decoded properly. A second or third message may assist the receiver in his understanding and use of the concept. Repetition should be done by using various media and different formats. For example, an organisation which seeks to promote safety may place "Think Safety" messages on bulletin boards, on operating equipment and in the house journal, and also remind employees of the slogan at weekly departmental meetings. Advertisers use repetition in their communication to increase their effectiveness on television, the radio, on billboards, in magazines. etc.,

(xii) Messages should be timed so that they are received when they are needed and are not misconstrued as a result of other thoughts on the receiver's mind.

(xiii) If the communication process is to function effectively, reciprocal confidence and trust on the part of the members of the organisation is absolutely essential.

Conditions for Effective Communication

It is important to recognise that the environment within the formal organisation structure will have an effect upon the successful transmission of concepts and ideas from the appropriate sender to the receiver. For example, a clearly defined channel of formal communication will influence the ease and accuracy for formal communication. If the employees are clearly aware of superior-subordinate relationships and horizontal networks, the employees will know whom they should communicate directly and what communication needs and expectations the receiver will have. If lines of authority and channels of communication are not known, an abundance of miscommunication, excessive communication or lack of communication will occur.

Further, the span of control for supervisors and the number of intervening levels in the organisational authority hierarchy, from top to bottom, also influence the success of failure of organisational communication. Communication tends to become more impersonal if the span is too wide.

Scholz describes some of the factors which influence the effectiveness of communication thus.[80]

(i) The credibility of the communicator and the motive attributed to him have a profound influence on the reception of his message.

(ii) The most successful communications are those which reinforce at least some of the audience's beliefs, those which state conclusions as well as premises and those which call for action.

(iii) People are interested first in people, then in things, last in ideas. Their attitudes and opinions are strongly influenced by the groups to which they belong or want to belong.

(iv) It is better to communicate information little by little over a period of time than all at once. Repeating a communication obviously prolongs its influence.

(v) Short sentences, familiar words and active verbs helps to make communication both interesting and persuasive.

(vi) In changing opinions, an oral presentation tends to be more effective than the written word.

(vii) Only rarely is it possible for communication, particularly over a short range, to change deep-seated attitudes or beliefs.

(viii) Mass communication alone is hardly ever an effective agent of change.

In an organisation, the manager-supervisor, as a result of his position and responsibilities, is primarily responsible for the successful communication of messages and the proper activity of communication networks.

Ways of Improving Communication

Some ways of improving communication may be summarised thus. An awareness of these points is of basic importance of good communication; the symbolic nature of languages and messages (i.e. words and symbols represent idea); the faltering process; and the distortions that can be expected; the effects of the receiver's attitude and his background of experience.

80. Scholaz W., *Communication in Business Organisation*, Prentice-Hall, New York, 1962.

CHAPTER 10

PERSONNEL POLICIES

Introduction
Manpower and Job Analysis
Selection and Allied Policies
Employee Training
Management Development
Performance Appraisal
Compensation

INTRODUCTION

Personnel Policies are the tools for the personnel department to achieve the objectives of the organisation. Yoder says:

"Personnel or labour or industrial relations policy provides guidelines for a wide variety of employee relationships in the organisation. These guidelines identify the organisation's intentions in recruitment, selection, promotion, development, compensation, organisation, motivation and otherwise leading and directing people in the working organisation. Personnel policies serve as a road map for managers."[1]

Aims and Objectives of Personnel Policies

A management's personnel policy should have two types of objectives, general and specific. The statement of *general objectives* should express the top management's basic philosophy of human resources and reflect its deep underlying convictions as to the importance of people in an organisation and of the management activity which deals with people, i.e., personnel administration. The management must formulate and develop a basic creed, which should contain a clear-cut statement of the company's general objectives of the personnel management's major responsibility. The statement of *specific objectives* should refer to the various activities of personnel administration connected with staffing, training, developing, wage and salary administration, motivation, employee services and benefits, employee records, labour relations and personnel research.

The aims of personnel policies should be/are:

(i) To enable an organisation to fulfil or carry out the main objectives which have been laid down as the desirable minima of general employment policy;

(ii) To ensure that its employees are informed of these items of policy and to secure their co-operation of their attainment;

(iii) To provide such conditions of employment and procedures as will enable all the employees to develop a sincere sense of unity with the enterprise and to carry out their duties in the most willing and effective manner;

(iv) To provide an adequate, competent and trained personnel for all levels and types of management;

(v) To protect the common interests of all the parties and recognise the role of trade unions in the organisation;

(vi) To provide for a consultative participation by employees in the management of an organisation and the framing of conditions for this participation, which, however, shall not take place in technical, financial or trading policy;

(vii) To provide an efficient consultative service which aims at creating mutual faith among those who work in the enterprise : (a) by developing management leadership which is bold and

1. Yoder Dale, *Personnel Management and Industrial Relations*, Prentice-Hall of India, New Delhi, 1976, pp. 27-28.

imaginative and guided by moral values; (b) by effectively delegating the human relations aspects of personnel functions to line managers; (c) by enforcing discipline on the basis of co-operative understanding and a humane application of the rules and regulations; and (d) by providing for a happy relationship at all levels :

(viii) To establish the conditions for mutual confidence and avoid confusion and misunderstanding between the management and the workers, by developing suggestion plans, joint management councils, work committees, etc., and by performance appraisal discussions;

(ix) To provide security of employment to workers so that they may not be distracted by the uncertainties of their future:

(x) To provide an opportunity for growth within the organisation to persons who are willing to learn and undergo training to improve their future prospects;

(xi) To provide for the payment of fair and adequate wages and salary to workers so that their healthy co-operation may be ensured for an efficient working of the undertaking;

(xii) To recognise the work and accomplishments of the employees by offering non-monetary incentives; and

(xiii) To create a sense of responsibility on the part of those in authority, for the claims of employees as human beings, who should be guaranteed protection of their fundamental rights and offered enough scope for developing their potential.

In brief, personnel policies should respect human dignity and personal integrity, ensure fair treatment to all, irrespective of caste, creed, or colour, and offer reasonable social and economic security to employees. They should be so designed as to ensure that work and accomplishment are properly recognised, that safe and healthy conditions of work are created, that common interests are promoted and employee participation encouraged, that the role of trade unions is recognised and their functions and responsibilities are respected, and that the employees' satisfaction and motivation and their development as individuals are properly looked after.

Need for Personnel Policy

The *raison d'etre* for formulating personnel policy is basically two fold : *One,* to have a formal statement on corporate thinking which will serve as a guideline for action. *Two,* to establish consistency in the application of the policies over a period of time so that each one in the organisation gets a fair and just treatment.

Personal policies need be specifically created because of the following reasons : [2]

(i) The basic needs and requirements of both an organisation and its employees require deep thought. The management is required to examine its basic convictions as well as give full consideration to practices in other organisations.

(ii) Established policies ensure consistent treatment of all personnel throughout an organisation. Favouritism and discrimination are thereby minimised.

(iii) Certainty of action is assured even though the top management personnel may change. The tenure of office of any manager is finite and limited; but the organisation continues, and along with it continue the policies; and this continuity of policies promotes stability in the organisation.

(iv) Because they specify routes towards selected goals, policies serve as standards or measuring yards for evaluating performance. The actual results can be compared with the policies to determine how well the members of an organisation have lived up to their professed intentions.

2. Beach, Dale, S., *Personnel Management of People,* MacMillans Collier, New York, 1977, pp. 48-49.

(v) Sound policies help to build employee enthusiasm and loyalty. This is specially true when they reflect established principles of fair play and justice, and when they help people to grow within an organisation.

(vi) They set patterns of behaviour and permit participants of plan with a greater degree of confidence.

Principles of Personnel Policies

In designing personnel policies, the management must balance the needs, goals; objectives and values of both the employers and the employees. Since these policies are rules of conduct, they are based on the following principles :

(i) *Put the right man in the right place* by a careful selection and placement to make sure that he is physically, mentally and temperamentally fit for the job he is expected to do and that the new employee may be reasonably expected to develop into a desirable employee, so that "there will be the minimum number of square pegs in round holes."

(ii) *Train everyone for the job to be done,* so that they qualify for better jobs, so that their accomplishments are limited to their ambitions and abilities, so that they do their present work very efficiently.

(iii) *Make the organisation a co-ordinated team* through proper co-ordination and administration of different departments and divisions, so that there is a minimum amount of friction and unproductive or unnecessary work. This calls for proper planning and organisation, control and direction of the entire organisation without destroying the initiative of the individual employee.

(iv) *Supply the right tools and the right conditions of work,* for the better the tools, facilities and working conditions, the larger the output produced with the same human effort at lower costs so that, ultimately, higher wages may be paid and more good jobs provided.

(v) *Give security with opportunity, incentive, recognition.* In order that he may stick to his job, each employee should have sound incentives for work, such as fair compensation, recognition for results achieved, reasonable security, and opportunity and hope for advancement in the organisation.

(vi) *Look ahead, plan ahead for more and better things.* Superior products should be produced and distributed, and these should be attractive and meet the demands of consumers. This calls for research and a policy of continuing product planning and development.

In brief, the principles should ensure that equity and justice are accorded to all the employees; that wages and salaries are adequate and fair; that every employee has scope for development to the limit of his capabilities; that fairness is guaranteed in maintaining discipline and that these principles are followed without discrimination against any grade of employees.

Essential Characteristics of a Sound Personnel Policy

The main features of a good personnel policy are :

(i) The statement of any policy should be definite, positive, clear and easily understood by everyone in the organisation.

(ii) It should be written in order to preserve it against loss, to stimulate careful consideration before its implementation and to prevent the promulgation of numerous differing and temporary oral policies.

(iii) It must not be rigid.

(iv) The policies of an enterprise have to be balanced with the kind of reputation an enterprise wants to build up with special reference to the social and human needs, objectives and values.

(v) It should indicate that the management knows that workers prefer to deal with the management on an individual basis.

(vi) It should recognise the desire of many workers for recognition as groups in many of their relationships.

(vii) It should be formulated with due regard for the interests of all the concerned parties– the employers, the employees and the community.

(viii) It must provide a two-way communication between the management and the employees so that the latter are kept informed of the latest developments in the organisation and employers are aware of the actions and reactions of the employees on particular issues.

(ix) It must not only have the support of the management but the co-operation of employees at the shop floor level and in the office.

(x) Before evolving such a policy, trade unions should be consulted in matters of industrial relations; and the role of the trade union should be restricted only to this area.

(xi) It should be progressive and enlightened, and must be consistent with professional practice and philosophy.

(xii) It must make a measurable impact, which can be evaluated and qualified for the guidance of all concerned, especially in the field of the three Rs of personal management, viz., recruitment, retainment, and retirement.

(xiii) It should be uniform throughout the organisation, though, in the light of local conditions, slight variations may be permitted in specific policies relating to staffing, compensation, benefits and services.

Original and Sources of Personnel Policies

Policies stem from a wide variety of places and people. They are not created in a vacuum but are based on a few principal sources, which determine the content and meaning of policies. These are :

(i) The past practice of an organisation;
(ii) The prevailing practices among sister concerns in the neighbourhood and throughout the country in the same industry;
(iii) The attitudes, ideals, and philosophy of the Board of Directors, top management and middle and lower management;
(iv) The knowledge and experience gained from handling day-to-day personnel problems;
(v) Employee's suggestion and complaints;
(vi) Collective bargaining programmes;
(vii) State and national legislation;
(viii) Changes in the country's economy;
(ix) International forces, such as may operate in times of war;
(x) The culture of the plant and its technology, its business environment, its social and political environment;

(xi) The extent of unionism;

(xii) The attitudes and social values of labour;

(xiii) The ethical points of view or the social responsibility of the organisation toward the public; and

(xiv) The goals of the organisation.

Types of Personnel Policies

There are various types of policies. Jucius identifies two types, viz., functional or organisation groupings of policies; and the centralised policies. The *functional grouping of policies* are those policies which are grouped for different categories of personnel, e.g., for the management dealing with personnel planning, organising and controlling or for management concerned with functions of procuring, developing and utilising manpower. The *centralised policies* are framed for companies with several locations. They are formulated at the head office and apply throughout the organisation.

Policies may also be classified as major and minor. *Major policies* pertain to the overall objectives, procedures and control which affect the organisation as a whole. They cover in general way nearly every phase of the enterprise and its product and methods of financing, its organisational structure, plant location, its marketing and personnel. Such policies are formulated by the Board of Directors, and a framework is established within which major executives fit the remaining policies necessary to carry out the major objectives of organisation. *Minor policies*, on the other hand, cover relationships in a segment of organisation, with considerable emphasis on details and procedures. Such policies are the outgrowth of major policies and preserve their unity of purpose.

Coverage of the Policies

The subject matter of personnel policies is as varied as the practices of the Personnel Department; and any itemization would serve merely as a laundry list. The norms of personnel policy vary from industry to industry; and with its management structure, the economic and social conditions prevailing in it at a particular time, the attitudes and ideals of the top management. They also vary with changes in public opinion, area and regional traditions, customs and practices, the country's industrial system, the labour and industrial policies of the State and the Central Governments, the influence of trade unions, national agreements between representatives of employers, managers, employees and the government. The policies and influences of business associations, employers federations, technological development, competition and social approval, the prevailing attitude of the organised labour, government regulations, the extent of unionisation in a particular industry, the decisions of triparte conference, Industrial or National Tribunals or Labour Courts–these, too, determine the norms of personnel policies. In other words, they cover such a wide variety of items and are so broadbased that every possible item which affects the interests of anyone in an organisation is included in them.

The National Industrial Conference Board of USA is of the view that the following matters should be included in a personnel policy:[3]

(i) History of the company's growth.

3. N.I.C. Board, "Personnel Policies in Factories and Offices", in *Studies in Personnel Policies*, Nos. 145 and 146.

(ii) Employment practices and conditions of employment–minimum qualifications preferred services for recruiting personnel, physical examination, psychological and occupational interest and aptitude test; methods of wage payment and pay period, hours or work overtime work, shift work and shift relations; the basis of promotion and promotion channels, lay-offs, and re-hiring, discharge, voluntary separations; seniority rights, guaranteed employment after attaining a certain length of service and when an employee is considered as a regular employee.

(iii) Grievance redressal procedure.

(iv) Safety rules and regulations, and responsibilities of employees while at work.

(v) General practices–employee identification, punching time cards and reporting in and out of the plant or department; checking of tools, purchases from the company usually at a discount; procedure for getting pay; absence, leave of absence, change of address and solicitation on company premises.

(vi) Sickness, death and maternity benefits or allowances.

(vii) Freedom for the employees to discuss any item of interest with the management.

(viii) Company Stores.

(ix) Social security and other kinds of compensation and unemployment and accident compensation, provident fund, pension, gratuity, compensation for employees injured while on duty, invalidity.

(x) Collective bargaining and recognising the employee's rights to join any union of his choice, recognition of a particular bargaining agency, procedure to be followed in settling grievances or the interpretation of a bargaining contract, and the right of an individual to be heard.

(xi) Procedures for disseminating information on company policies.

(xii) Maintenance of discipline and adherence to rules; penalties available.

(xiii) Garnishments.

(xiv) Public relations.

(xv) Labour-management relations and union-management co-operation.

(xvi) Prohibited activities–smoking, gambling, imbibing liquor and soliciting on company premises and during working hours.

It may be noted that this list is by no means exhaustive; it is only indicative of the scope of personnel policies.

In India, ordinarily personnel policies cover the following :

(a) *Policy on Recruitment or Hiring of Employees* : In finding and selecting the right calibre and number of people required to perform the operations of the organisation, these subjects are taken into account; (i) whether recruitment is needed: (i) how much manpower is required and at what levels, (iii) selection procedures, (iv) age limits for employment, (v) marital status, minority groups, SC/ST, women, (vi) pre-employment medical check-up and (vii) establishing order of preferences between relations of employees, employment exchange candidates, and outsiders in the matter of selection; and (viii) induction and placement, etc.,

(b) *Policy of Manpower Planning and Development* : This covers : (i) work study, job evaluation, (ii) selection and recruitment techniques, (iii) identifying training needs and preparing training programmes; (iv) promotional avenues; and (v) opportunities for self-development and advancement in organisation, etc.

(c) *Policy on Terms and Conditions of Employment* : This covers terms such as hours of work, overtime, shift working, lay-off, termination of services, and welfare, wage policy, payment methods, pay-period, job evaluation, etc.,

(d) *Policy on Industrial Relations,* in broad terms considers (i) whether to recognise trade unions, and conditions of recognition, (ii) collective bargaining, (iii) grievances handling procedure, (iv) workers participation in management, etc.

(e) *Policy on Communication with Employees*, at all levels, covers (i) suggestion system; (ii) formal/informal meetings between top management and junior management.

Responsibility for Policy-Making

The actual formulation of personnel policies is the responsibility of the personnel manager; but its ultimate approval, or any change or modification in it, comes from the top executives, and his decision depends upon the financial ability of a company, the obligations imposed upon it by legislation, the agreement between employers and employees, the repercussions of such decisions on the various levels of employees as well as on neighbouring industries and on the community. The executive role is one of mediating, reconciling, persuading, convicing, expressing and communicating the policy, developing tools and machinery, guiding, directing and evaluating the effectiveness with which these tools are used in the application of policy. The responsibility for personnel administration rests squarely upon the shoulders of the line management. The Personnel Department assists in communicating policies to those for whom they are meant and exercises control over it in order to ensure fairness and uniformity. If it is not communicated and interpreted correctly, even a sound policy may lose much of its usefulness.

Policy Administration

Essentially, in the administration of personnel policy–

(i) A large sum of money is involved;

(ii) An unsound decision may endanger the company's bargaining power and position.

Therefore, a thorough consideration must be given to the following issues :

(i) What purpose and objectives will it serve ?

(ii) What principles, concepts, practices and philosophies of the organisation will it project?

(iii) How much would be its implementation cost ?

(iv) What benefits will it offer and to whom ?

(v) Is it administratively feasible and fair to the employees ?

(vi) What areas will it cover ?

(vii) What authority will it give to personnel at different levels ?

(viii) Will it be acceptable and consistent ?

Mechanism of Policy Formulation

Policy generation is a complex process, calling for the help of experts. Personnel policies are so designed as to reflect the current good practices in society. The *first step* in the mechanism of formulating a policy is the identification of a problem area or situation in which decisions of a similar and repetitive nature are involved. To some extent, policy-making involves all levels in the working organisation. It is the personnel staff who study the existing documents, survey industry and community practices, review the prevailing conditions in the company, interview other executives in the organisation to collect appropriate information, and get their suggestions and co-operation on personnel activities. *The formulation of a policy is not a job for any ivory-tower specialist.* The person preparing a draft of it must be thoroughly familiar with the subject from personal experience and involvement.

After the policy draft has been prepared, the *second step* is to circulate its copies among all those who may be expected to operate under it. Their constructive criticism and suggestions would be very valuable. A second draft is then prepared and finalised, and the policy statements are given shape and promulgated throughout the organisation. Policies are developed after a thorough discussion so that all the managers involved in related areas of responsibility are personally committed to them. Developed in this manner, these policies will stand the test of time, and will hold even "under conditions of stress". A set of policies may be compared to the rope holding the mountain-climbers together; since they are thus together, no climber can be lost, but they must co-ordinate their activities, "or the rope will get in their way."

The *third step* is to undertake a periodic review, evaluation and revision of policies. This is essential if organisational complacency and managerial stagnation are to be avoided. It is a part and parcel of the means of keeping an organisation "vibrant" and "on it does". If a policy is cancelled or withdrawn, it should be substituted by a new one, failing which mismanagement is likely to result. "The authority for implementing personnel policy must come from the top management. The responsibility for implementation rests with the line management at the level of the department head and that of administration of day-to-day matters with the lower level of management. The responsibility for assessment review, and follow-up action should lie with the personnel department".

Personnel Policies Should be in Writing

Someone has said that an idea does not exist unless it can be put in writing. A policy, conceived as a management tool, also does not exist unless it is in writing.

There are distinct advantages of written formal policies. *In the first place,* the writing of policies makes a commitment on the part of an organisation. When they are written, it should be apparent to management representatives, employees and union officials that the "top management does what it says." *Secondly,* writing ensures iniformity of application, minimises favouritism and discrimination among the personnel and assures continuity of action even when the top management is changed, for a policy is not just a fad of one particular boss, to be jettisoned when he leaves the organisation. *Third,* it earns the loyalty of, and builds enthusiasm among, the members of an organisation in so far as they are assured of fair play and justice. *Fourthly,* it limits the freedom of action on the part of the management, for a supervisor cannot go off han-cocked and come up with his personal interpretation of the organisation's intent. *Fifthly,* writing helps to ensure that the professed policies are right, for an organisation tries to put its best foot forward. *Finally*, written policies provide something concrete on which to base an appeal if there is any disagreement about what the organisation's policy is.

All well-established concerns should have published Policy Manuals for all its managers, supervisors, and employees. Handbooks, house bulletins and booklets may also be used for the purpose. The moment a policy is written down or published, it encourages the staff to be constantly alert so that it may be properly implemented. Francis Clarence says; "If you write it (policy) down, you have got to live up to do it or die trying. If you set a high standard, you will fall far short of perfection. But your performance, simply because you have pledged yourself to the standard, will be better than it would be if you lacked a special goal."[4]

BOX 10.1

THOMSON PRODUCTS' HUMAN POLICY

Thomson products', an American concern's, Human Relations Policy gives the following pledge :

Our Pledge

"We pledge, so long as the affairs of this company are in our hands, that the following principles will govern our relations with members of the organisation.

1. We will pay wages which will always compare favourably with prevailing rates in the area of occupation. Any employee or group of employees at any time may request a wage survey to verify the fairness of the rate.

2. With friendliness, we will meet with employees from any group or department, or their proper representatives, to discuss any requested improvements in conditions, hours, policies or practices.

3. Any grievance will be fairly and promptly settled through steps provided in our Grievance Procedure.

4. Practices with respect to paid vacations, paid holidays, overtime premiums, recognition of length of service, retirement benefits, and general conditions such as safety, cleanliness and employee accommodation will always compare favourably with good community practices.

5. We will devote our best efforts and thinking to building a growing business within which will prevail an atmosphere of friendship and harmony with steady jobs and opportunity for all."

BOX 10.2

TATA STEEL'S PERSONNEL POLICY

The Statement of Objectives of the Tata Steel gives a clear-cut policy toward employees:

i. "by a realistic and generous understanding and acceptance of their needs and rights and an enlightened awareness of the social problems of industry :

ii. "by providing adequate wages, good working conditions, job security, an effective machinery for redressal of grievances and suitable opportunities for promotion and self-development through in-company and external programmes;

iii. "by treating them as individual, giving them a sense of self-respect and better understanding of their role in the organisation and satisfying their urge for self-expression through closer association with management:

iv. "by creating a sense of belonging through human and purposeful activities as an integral part of human relations ensuring their willing cooperation and loyalty."

MANPOWER PLANNING AND JOB ANALYSIS

Importance of Human Resources

"Manpower" or "human resource" may be thought of as " the total knowledge, skills, creative abilities, talents and aptitudes of an organisation's workforce, as well as the values, attitudes and benefits of an individual involved...It is the sum total of inherent abilities, acquired knowledge and skills represented by the talents and aptitudes of the employed persons."[5] Of all the "Ms" in

4. Clarence, Francis, "The Causes of Industrial Peace", 1948, Quoted by D. Yoder in *Personnel Management and Industrial Relations*, 1972, p. 43.

Management (i.e., the management of materials, machines, methods, money, motive power), the most important is "M" for men or human resources. It is the most valuable asset of an organisation, and not the money or physical equipment. It is in fact an important economic resource, covering all human resources–organised or unorganised, employed or capable of employment, working at all levels–supervisors, executives, Government employees, "blue" and "white" collar workers, managerial, scientific, engineering, technical, skilled or unskilled persons, who are employed in creating, designing, developing, managing and operating productive and service enterprises, and other economic activities. Human resources are utilised to the maximum possible extent in order to achieve individual and organisational goals. An organisation's performance and resulting productivity are directly proportional to the quantity and quality of its human resources. Hence, the importance of human resources.

Process of Human Resource Planning

The process of human resource planning is one of the most crucial, complex, and continuing managerial functions which, according to the Tata Engineering & Locomotive Company, "embraces organisation development, management development, career planning and succession planning." The process has gained importance in India with the increase in the size of business enterprises, complex production technology, and the adoption of professional management techniques. It may be rightly regarded as a multi-step process, including various issues, such as :

(A) Deciding goals or objectives ;
(B) Estimating future organisational structure and manpower requirements,
(C) Auditing human resources.
(D) Planning job requirements an job descriptions ; and
(E) Developing a human resource plan.

(A) *Objectives of Human Resource Planning :* Human resource planning fulfils individual, organisational and national goals; but, according to Sikula, "the ultimate mission or purpose is to relate future human resources to future enterprise needs so as to maximise the future return on investment in human resources."[6] In effect, the main purpose is one of matching or fitting employee abilities to enterprise requirements, with an emphasis on future instead of present arrangement.[7] The objectives may be laid down for a short–term (i.e. for one year). For example, the short-term objective may be to hire 25 persons from Scheduled Tribes or Backward Classes for purposes of training. The long-term objective may be to start a new industry, to expand the market, to produce a new product, to develop its own sales force rather than depend on distributors, or to have minority group members eventually in the position of middle and upper management cadres.

(B) *Estimating the Future Organisational Structure and Forecasting Manpower Requirements:* The management must estimate the structure of the organisation at a given point of time. For this estimate, the number and type of employees needed have to be

5. Megginson, Leon C., *Personnel and Human Resource Administration,* 1977, p. 4.
6. Sikula, A.F., *Personnel Administration and Human Resource Development,* 1978, P. 148.
7. Cox, Arne, "Personnel Planning : Objectives and Methods-Presentation of Integrated System," *Management International Review,* Vol. 8, No. 4-5. 1968, pp. 104-114.

determined. Many environmental factors affect this determination. They include business forecasts, expansion and growth, design and structural changes, management philosophy, government policy, product and human skills mix, and competition.

Forecasting provides the basic premises on which the manpower planning is built. Forecasting is necessary for various reasons, such as :

(a) The eventualities and contingencies of general economic business cycles (such as inflation, wages, prices, costs and raw material supplies) have an influence on the short-range and long-run plans of all organisations. (b) An expansion following enlargement and growth in business involves the use of additional machinery and personnel, and a re-allocation of facilities, all of which call for advance planning of human resources. (c) Changes in management philosophies and leadership styles. (d) The use of mechanical technology (such as the introduction of automatic controls, or the mechanisation of materials handling functions) necessitate changes in the skills of workers, as well as changes in the number of employees needed. (e) Very often, changes in the quantity or quality of products or services require a change in the organisation structure. Plans have to be made for this purpose as well.

After estimating what the future organisation structure should be, the next step is to draw up the requirements of human resources, both for the existing departments and for new vacancies. For this purpose, a forecast of labour force is needed, and requisitions should be obtained from different departments, i.e., forecast has to be made in terms of functional category : the number needed; and the levels at which they are required. Vacancies, occurring in any department, should be notified in writing by different department heads to the personnel department, stating clearly the number of vacancies to be filled, job or category-wise types of personnel needed, their technical qualifications and experience, and the reasons for acquisition (i.e., whether for replacement or addition); a statement of duties, types of jobs, pay scales, age, and previous experience should also be made. Requisitions should be based on accurate job specifications by first line supervisors. They should, as far as possible, be clear-cut about the exact demands of a job.

In determining the requirements of human resources, the expected losses which are likely to occur through labour turnover–quits, retirement, death, transfers, promotions, demotions, dismissals, disability, resignations, lay-offs, and other separations–should be taken into account. Changes in the human quality resulting from the experience gained in the jobs during the period and the training achieved also need to be considered. The addition of new lines of production and new projects also influence the demand estimates of human resources. The basic fact to remember is that the human resource in an organisation constantly changes in terms of its present and future size. Additional human resources are gained through new employment of personnel, promotions, through transfers and demotions; but personnel is lost through voluntary quits, death, dismissals, terminations and retirements.

After making adjustments for wastage, anticipated and expected losses and separations, the real shortage or surplus may be found out. If there is a shortage, efforts are made to meet it either by new recruitment or promotion from within, or by developing the existing staff. If there is a surplus, it is to be decided how it will be dealt with, i.e., whether there should be transfers, lay-offs, retrenchment or reduction in the hours of work of all.

Underestimation of the quality and number of employees required would lead to shortfalls in performance, while overestimation would result in avoidable costs to the organisation.

It may be noted that for purposes of manpower planning, the main dimensions to be taken into consideration are :

(i) *The total number of personnel available could be obtained* from the pay-rolls and other personnel records, such as applications for employment. The total number has to be classified on some basis, such as manual workers (i.e., daily-rated, weekly-rated or monthly-rated); clerical employees, ministerial staff, managers and other executives; specialists and skilled and unskilled workers; sex-wise distribution, etc.

(ii) *The job-family*, i.e., a detailed job-description for each position such as stenographers who may belong to various departments, e.g., finance, marketing, personnel, public relations, general administration, etc.

(iii) *Age distribution of the employees*, available in the present departments, say in the age-groups 20-29 years; 30-45 years; 46 years and above.

(iv) *Qualification and experience desired*, such as a person with 5 years/10 years experience in a particular branch/job; and whether under-graduate, post-graduate, or MBAs or graduates in Science, Commerce, Arts, engineering, or professional diploma holders, etc.; or with specialised knowledge in the field of marketing, finance, computer programming or engineering work.

(v) *The salary range*, etc.

(C) *Auditing Human Resources* : Once the future human resource needs are estimated, the next step is to determine the present supply of manpower resources. This is done through what is called "Skills Inventory." A skills inventory contains data about each employee's skills, abilities, work preferences and other items of information which indicate his overall value to the company.

The above facts are usually recorded by an employee in some form from which the information is fed into a computer. Other data pertaining to his performance ratings and his superior's evaluation of his potential for promotion may also be fed into the computer.. The result may either be kept in a file (on tape or otherwise stored) containing information as to the number of employees in the organisation, and other data about each employee, and an indication of his fitness for promotion.

BOX 10.3

SKILLS INVENTORY PROFORMA

Personal Factors

Name	Birth Place
Age	Occupation of parents
Sex	Present address
Dependants	Permanent address
Martial status	Telephone Number (if any)

Education and Training

School attended with years
Degrees/Diplomas obtained
Training achieved

Experience and Skills

Job areas	Special skills (such as ability to speak/write foreign languages)
Job titles	Reasons for leaving supervisory responsibilities
Job dates	

Additional Information	
Salary	Test results
Grade	Performance ratings
Absenteeism record	Location of relatives
Disciplinary record	Appraisal data
Career plans	Any other information

Some organisations do not compile a Skills Inventory but prepare *Organisation Charts* (as they do in Hindustan Lever) to determine "how many people, at what level, in what position and what kind of experience and training would be required to meet the objectives." These charts show a person's age, the number of years he has been in a particular position, and his fitness for promotion. These Charts or Skills Inventories help in determining and evaluating the quantity and quality of the present human resources of an organisation. They tell us "what exists in stock" and "what is needed to be added to that stock", taking into account the capability, qualifications, experience, skill, knowledge and promotional potential of employees. Some companies maintain a *Manning Table*, which lists all the jobs in the unit and the number of workers holding each job. Other companies also use *Manpower Replacement Charts,* which show the present performance of each position holder and the promotion potential of possible replacements.

Once the present manpower resources are determined, the personnel department can estimate what changes will occur in the present labour force in the next few years, say, 5 years.

(D) *Job Analysis* : After having decided how many persons would be needed, it is necessary to prepare a job analysis, which records details of training, skills, qualification, abilities, experience and responsibilities, etc. which are needed for a job. Job analysis includes the preparation of job descriptions and job specifications. This is been discussed in a later section of this chapter.

(E) *Developing a Human Resource Plan:* This step refers to the development and implementation of the human resource plan, which consists in finding out the sources of labour supply with a view to making an effective use of these sources. The first thing, therefore, is to decide on the policy : should the personnel be hired from within through promotional channels or should it be obtained from an outside source. *The best policy* which is followed by most organisations *is to fill up higher vacancies by promotion and lower level positions by recruitment from the labour market.*

The labour market is a geographical area from which employers recruit their workforce and labour seeks employment. Here, the forces of demand and supply interact.

The personnel manager should have a thorough knowledge of the labour market. Which particular source in the labour market will be tapped will depend upon the policy of a firm, the position of labour supply, the arrangements with labour unions, and Government regulations. However, it is always safe for the personnel manager to be in close liaison with these different sources and use them as and when the need arises.

Responsibility for Human Resource Planning

Human resource planning is the responsibility of the personnel department. In this task, it is aided by the industrial engineering department, the top management and the team of directors of different departments. It is mostly a staffing or personnel function. The overall responsibility lies with the Board of Directors because, as the manpower planning scheme of Hindustan Lever indicates, "these members are in a position to direct the future course of business, set appropriate goals for the management concerned in the formulation of personnel policies." The personnel department's responsibility is "to recommend relevant personnel policies in respect of manpower planning, devise methods of procedure, and determine the quantitative aspects of manpower planning."

Points to Consider [8]

The Personnel Department/Director must first decide on a plan period, i.e., the time span for which the plan is to be made. A plan period of less than three years or more than five years would be unrealistic. The process of recruitment, training and placement often takes three or more years.

Having decided on the time span (say five years), it should be seen that it runs a span of five years and in blocks. Only then can the plan be kept realistic and functioning.

The plan should be worked out in sufficient detail. It implementation should be evaluated and controlled properly. *This requires a great deal of tenacity, persistence and vigilance on the part of personnel managers.*

Every component of the plan has to be compatible with policies regarding recruitment, promotion, termination, inter-departmental transfers, retirement and training. *Policy formulation is an essential pre-requisite for manpower planning.*

Whatever plan is made, it has to be realistic. A plan has to be put into operation and, therefore, *whatever is not feasible should be excluded.*

For every part of the plan, allowances should be made for lead time, otherwise the result will be adversely affected. A balance between çonflicting requirements of standards and time available has to be achieved. In other words, *practicability has to be given precedence over perfection.*

Finally, the paramount consideration should be to make the plan an integral part of the corporate plan. *It has to mesh with plans in other functional areas.*

Manpower Plan Component

The manpower plan can be broken down into three components : (i) *Forecasting*–estimating future needs and stock–taking of available resources in the organisation; (ii) *Recruitment plan,* to meet the gap between the internal resource and estimated need by external recruitment; (iii) *Training and Development plan* to utilise fully the human resources of the organisation and to develop the potential resources.

In practice, it has been found that short-term (under 2 years) and medium-range plans (2 to 5 years) are easier to formulate with greater degree of uncertainty.

Short-range forecasts usually grow out of normal budgetary processes. The parameters of short-range forecasting usually are fairly well defined. They are handled in the normal course of budget preparation and require simple arithmetical calculations. Long-range planning is more complex and is dependent upon mathematical and statistical models, knowledge of demand variables and appropriate measurement techniques.

Two general kinds of forecasting techniques are used : indirect and direct methods. *Indirect methods* involve the forecasting of the general rules-production figures, for example – that must be translated into specific requirements or measures. *Direct techniques* involve the use of methods of estimate (directly) labour hours, number of supervisors or particular occupational needs.

8. Basu, K.S., *New Dimensions in Personnel Management,* the Macmillan of India Ltd., New Delhi, 1979, pp.40-42.

Job Analysis

Developing an organisation structure results in jobs which have to be staffed. "Work" is an organisation's primary function. The 'Basic work activities' may relate to three categories–Data, People and Things. Under *Data* are included synthesizing, co-ordinating, analysing, compiling, computing, copying and comparing activities. *People* relate to monitoring, negotiating, instructing, supervising, diverting, persuading, speaking, signalling, serving and taking instructions. *Things* are concerned with setting up precision working, operating-controlling, driving-operating, manipulating, feeding-off bearing and handling.

Purpose and Uses of Job Analysis

A comprehensive J A programme is an essential ingredient of sound personnel management. It is the major input to forecasting future human resource requirements, job modifications, job evaluation, determination of proper compensation, and the writing of job descriptions. It is of fundamental importance to manpower management programmes because of the wider applicability of its results. The information provided by J A is useful if not essential in almost every phase of employee relations.

(i) *Organisation and Manpower planning :* It is helpful in organisational planning, for it defines labour needs in concrete terms and co-ordinates the activities of the workforce, and clearly divides duties and responsibilities.

(ii) *Recruitment and Selection :* By indicating the specific requirements of each job (i.e., the skills and knowledge), it provides a realistic basis for the hiring, training, placement, transfer and promotion of personnel. "Basically, the goal is to match the job requirements with a workers's aptitude, abilities, and interests. It also helps in charting the channels of promotion and in showing lateral lines of transfer."

(iii) *Wage and Salary Administration* : By indicating the qualifications required for doing a specified job and the risks and hazards involved in its performance, it helps in salary and wage administration. Job analysis is used as a foundation for job evaluation.

(iv) *Job Re-engineering* : Job analysis provides information which enables us to change jobs in order to permit their being manned by personnel with specific characteristics and qualifications. This takes two forms : (a) *Industrial engineering activitity,* which is concerned with operational analysis, motion study, work simplification methods and improvements in the place of work and its measurement, and aims at improving efficiency, reducing unit labour costs, and establishing the production standard which the employee is expected to meet; and (b) *Human engineering activity,* which takes into consideration human capabilities, both physical and psychological, and prepares the ground for complex operations of industrial administration, increased efficiency and better productivity.

(v) *Employee Training and Management Development* : Job analysis provides the necessary information to the management of training and development programmes. It helps it to determine the content and subject matter of in-training courses. It also helps in checking application information, interviewing, weighing test results, and in checking references.

(vi) *Performance Appraisal :* It helps in establishing clear-cut standards which may be compared with the actual contribution of each individual.

(vii) *Health and Safety* : It provides an opportunity for identifying hazardous conditions and unhealthy environmental factors so that corrective measures may be taken to minimize and avoid the possibility of accidents.

In sum, it may be noted that job analysis is a systematic procedure for securing and reporting the information which defines a specific job. It has many uses in the management of personnel. It determines the qualifications required for a job; provides guidance in recruitment and selection; evaluates current employees for transfer or promotion; and establishes the requirements for training programmes. It is used as a foundation for job evaluation and helps in employee development by means of appraisal and counselling; for establishing improved methods of analysing problems of health, safety and fatigue; it functions as a guide in connection with disciplines and grievances and as a basis for transfers, lay-offs and as a basis of comparison of the pay rates obtaining in other organisations; and it establishes workloads and job assignments. It also helps in redesigning the jobs to improve operational performance or to enrich job content and employee improvement. Managers may develop ways of giving their employees an increased sense of personal accomplishment and control over themselves and their work.

J A produces four kinds of documentation and procedures that are crucial to personnel activities : (i) Job descriptions; (ii) Job specifications; (iii) Job evaluation, and (iv) Personnel assessment. In turn, the procedures and documentation are basic inputs for diverse personnel functions.

Contents of Job Analysis

A job analysis provides the following information :[9]

(i) *Job identification* : Its title, including its code number;

(ii) *Significant characteristics of a job* : Its location, physical setting, supervision, union jurisdiction, hazards and discomforts :

(iii) *What the typical worker does* : Specific operation and tasks that make up an assignment, their relative timing and importance, their simplicity, routine or complexity, the responsibility or safety of others for property, funds, confidence and trust :

(iv) *Which materials and equipment a worker uses* : Metals, plastics, grains, yarns, milling machines, punch presses and micrometers;

(v) *How a job is performed* : Nature of operation–lifting, handling, cleaning, washing, feeding, removing, drilling, driving, setting up and many others :

(vi) *Required personnel attributes* : Experience, training, apprenticeship, physical strength, co-ordination or dexterity, physical demands, mental capabilities, aptitudes and social skills;

(vii) *Job relationship* : Experience required, opportunities for advancement, patterns of promotions, essential co-operation, direction, or leadership from and for a job.

It is obvious from the foregoing that a job analysis is usually a clear indication of a *job description* and *job specification*.

The Steps in Job Analysis

There are five basic steps required for doing a job analysis, viz.,

Step 1: Collection of Background Information: According to Terry, "the make-up of a job, its relation to other jobs, and its requirements for competent performance are essential information needed for a job evaluation. This information can be had by reviewing available background information such as *organisation charts* (which shows how the job in question relates to other jobs and where they fit into the overall organisation); *class specifications* (which describes the general requirements of the class of job to which the job under analysis belongs); and the existing *job descriptions* (which provide a starting point from which to build the revised job description).

9. Yoder, D., *Personnel Management and Industrial Relations*. 1972, p. 210.

CHART 10.1

JOB ANALYSIS

(A Process for Obtaining All Pertinent Job Facts)

Job Description Statement containing items such as :	**Job Specification** A statement of the human requirements for doing a job :
(a) Job Identification (job title, location, occupational code, alternative name in use, name of division, department and unit where it exists).	(a) Physical make-up or characteristics.
(b) Job Summary (gives a quick capsule explanation of the contents of a job, its hazards and discomforts).	(b) Psychological characteristics.
(c) Duties performed (says the what, how and why of a job; also describes a worker's responsibilities in regard to custody of money, supervision of other workers, training of subordinates, etc.)	(c) Personal characteristics.
(d) Relation to other jobs (gives how many persons may be supervised).	(d) Responsibilities.
(e) Supervision given/taken (helps in locating a job in the job hierarchy).	(e) Other factors of a demographic nature (sex, age, education, language, ability to read, write and speak).
(f) Machines, tools, equipment (what type of tools/equipment material is used).	
(g) Materials and forms used.	
(h) Conditions of work (*Location*– factory/office/inside/outside/overhead/underground/solitary gang: *Time*–day, night, overtime, peak loads, uniformity of work; *Posture*–standing, sitting, stopping, clinging, walking, reaching, lifting; *Speed*–quick, moderate, slow; *Accuracy*–coarse, fine, exacting; *Health hazards*–ventilation, illumination, nerve strain, eye-strain, physical strain, moisture, heat, dust, humidity, fumes, acids, exposure to such disagreeable features as dirt, noise etc.	
(i) Hazards (accident hazards).	

Step 2: Selection of Representative Position to be Analysed: Since the analysis of all jobs would be time-consuming, flow representative positions should be analysed.

Step 3: Collection of Job Analysis Data: Job data on features of the job, required employee qualifications and requirement should be collected either from the employees who actually perform a job; or from other employees (such as foremen or supervisors) who watch the workers doing a job and thereby acquire knowledge about it; or from the outside persons known as the *trade job analysts* who are appointed to watch employees performing a job.

Step 4: Developing A Job Description: The information collected is to be developed in the form of a job description. This is a written statement that describes the main features of the job, as well as the qualifications/activities which the job incumbents must process.

Step 5: Developing Job Specification: The last step is to convert the Job Description statements into Job Specifications, i.e., to specifically mention what personal qualities, traits, skills and background are necessary for getting the job done.

Techniques of Job Analysis Data

The determination of job tasks, the concomitant skills and abilities necessary for successful performance, and the responsibility inherent in the job can be through such *methods* or *approaches* as the following:

(i) Personal Observation;
(ii) Sending out questionnaires;
(iii) Maintenance of log records; and
(iv) Conducting personal interviews.

(i) *Personal Observation:* The materials and equipment used, the working conditions and probable hazards, and an understanding of what the work involves are the facts which should be known by an analyst. Direct observation is especially useful in jobs that consist primarily of observable physical ability, like the jobs of draftsman, mechanic, spinner or weaver.

(ii) *Sending out Questionnaires*: This method is usually employed by engineering consultants. Properly drafted questionnaires are sent out to job-holders for completion and are returned to supervisors. However, the information received is often unorganised and incoherent. The idea in issuing a questionnaire is to elicit the necessary information from job holders so that any error may first be discussed with the employee and, after due corrections, may be submitted to the job analyst.

(iii) *Maintenance of Log Records*: The employee maintains a daily diary record of the duties he performs, marking the time at which each task is started and finished. But this system is incomplete, for it does not give us any desirable data or supervisor relationship, the equipment used, and working conditions. Moreover, it is time-consuming.

(iv) *Personal Interviews* may be held by the analyst with the employees, and answers to relevant questions may be recorded. But the method is time-consuming and costly.

However, it may be noted that the personal observation and interview approach are more or less complete and accurate. If a particular job is simple and repetitive, observation may be the only technique required. Otherwise, in most cases, interviews coupled with observation constitute the desirable approach.

Caroll L. Shartle, Ottis Lenhert have provided the following suggestions for making the job analyst's task simple [10].

(i) Introduce yourself so that the worker knows who you are and why you are there;
(ii) Show a sincere interest in the worker and the job that is analysed.
(iii) Do not try to tell the employee how to do his job;
(iv) Try to talk to the employees and supervisors in their own language;
(v) Do not confuse the work with the workers;
(vi) Do a complete job study within the objectives of the programmes; and
(vii) Verify the job information obtained.

10. Shartle, Carol.L, *Occupational Information*, 1952, Chapter 2, and Ottis, Jay L, and Lenhert, Richard H., *Job Evaluation*, 1954, Quoted by Flippo E.B., *op. cit.*, 1971, pp. 120-122.

Position or Job Description (JD)

"Job description" is an important document which is basically descriptive in nature and contains a statement of job analysis. It provides both *organisational information* (location in structure, authority, etc.) and *functional information* (what the work is). It defines the scope of job activities, major responsibilities, and positioning of the job in the organisation. It provides the worker, analyst, and supervisor with a clear idea of what the worker must do to meet the demands of the job.

Uses of Job Description

Job description has several uses, such as:

(i) Preliminary drafts can be used as a basis for productive group discussion, particularly if the process starts at the executive level.

(ii) It aids in the development of job specifications, which are useful in planning recruitment, in training and in hiring people with required skills.

(iii) It can be used to orient new employees towards basic responsibilities and duties.

(iv) It is a basic document used in developing performance standards.

(v) It can be used for job evaluation, a wage and salary administration technique.

Job description helps top executives, especially when they jointly discuss one another's responsibilities. Overlapping or confusion can then be pointed out; questions can be raised about the major thrust of each position, and problems of structure can be identified. *A job description becomes a vehicle for organisational change and improvement*.

Some companies have more than one job description for each job. A detailed version may be used in training and in evaluating a job, while a shorter version may be used in planning and hiring of management.

Components or Contents of Job Description: A job description contains the following data;

(i) *Job identification, or Organisational Position* which includes the job title, alternative title, department, division, plant and code number of the job.

(ii) *Job summary* serves two important purposes. *First*, it provides a short definition which is useful as an additional identification information when a job title is not adequate. *Second*, it serves as a summary to orient the reader towards an understanding of detailed information which constitutes the job.

(iii) *Job duties and responsibilities* give a comprehensive listing of the duties together with some indication of the frequency of occurrence or percentage of time devoted to each major duty. *It is regarded as the heart of a job*. It tells us what needs to be done, how it should be done, and why it should be done. It also describes the responsibilities related to the custody of money, the supervision of workers and the training of subordinates.

(iv) *Relation to other jobs*: This helps to locate the job in the organisation by indicating the job immediately below or above it in the job hierachy. It also gives an idea of vertical relationships of work flow and procedures.

(v) *Supervision*: Under it is given the number of persons to be supervised along with their job titles, and the extent of supervision involved—general, intermediate or close supervision.

(vi) *Machine, tools and equipment* define each major type or trade name of the machines and tools and the raw materials used.

(vii) *Working conditions* usually give us information about the environment in which a job holder must work. These include cold, heat, dust, wetness, moisture, fumes, odour, oily conditions, etc. obtaining inside the organisation.

(viii) *Hazards* give us the nature of risks to life and limb, their possibilities of occurrence, etc.

Limitations of Job Description

In any use of job description, it should be remembered that these descriptions are not perfect reflections of the job. "The object of a job description is to differentiate it from other jobs and set its outer limits." Further, executives tend to carry work patterns with them into new jobs, thus modifying the job drastically.

To avoid such problems, care must be exercised in writing a job description to make it as accurate as possible, and at the managerial or professional level, it should be reviewed and discussed after the job. *Jobs tend to be dynamic, not static, and a job description can quickly go out of date. Therefore, jobs should be constantly revised and kept up-to-date*, and the personnel and the other departmental heads should be appraised of changes.

Both supervisors and subordinates should understand the uses to which a job description would be put so that appropriate information is recorded by them. The relevant parties should agree that a job description fairly reflects that job; otherwise job evaluation and job performance review would seem to be unfair.

Job Specifications

The job specification takes the job description and answers the question: "What human traits and experience are needed to do the job well?" *It tells what kind of person to recruit and for what qualities that person should be tested.*

Job specifications translate job description in terms of the human qualifications which are required for a successful performance of a job. They are intended to serve as a guide in hiring and job evaluation. As a guide in hiring, they deal with such characteristics as are available in an application blank, with testing, interviews, and checking of references.

Job specifications are developed with the co-operation of the personnel department and various supervisors in the whole organisation. The personnel department co-ordinates the writing of job descriptions and job specifications and secures agreement on the qualifications required.

These specifications relate to physical characteristics, psychological characteristics, personal traits of temperament, responsibilities and other features of a demographic nature.

SELECTION AND ALLIED POLICIES

In this chapter, we shall discuss the selection, promotion, demotion, discharge policies, etc.

Selection

Selection embraces all policies by which a company regulates the choice of employees. In other words, it includes not only the hiring of new employees but also selecting those who are to be promoted or discharged.

While formulating a selection policy, due consideration should be given to organisational requirements as well as technical and professional dimensions of cost factors, extent of formality, etc. Hiring responsibility is generally assigned to the Personnel or Employment Department to whom the demands of various departments for various types of employees is made. This department bases the actual requirement for employees on the analysis of the workforce. It also prepares a standard with which a prospective employee may be compared, i.e., a comprehensive Job Description and Job Specification as developed by Job Analysis is prepared.

Selection Policy may embrace several issues such as extent to promotion from within, attitudes of enterprise in recruiting its old employees, handicaps, minor groups, women employees, part-time employees, etc. Therefore, a well-considered and well-planned policy must take into consideration the needs of the personnel area-wise, job-family-wise; the qualifications needed and the responsibilities expected; and preferred sources of recruitment. Such a policy should be in conformity with its general personnel policies; it should be flexible; and it should be so designed as to ensure employment opportunities for its employees on a long-term basis.

For selection, the top executive has to decide whether persons will be taken-up from within or outside the company, i.e., whether to tap the *internal* or *external* sources available..

Internal Sources

Internal sources are the most obvious sources. These include personnel already on the pay-roll of an organisation, i.e., its present working force. Whenever any vacancy occurs, somebody from within the organisation is upgraded, transferred, promoted or sometimes demoted.

This source is used by many organisations, but a surprisingly large number ignore this source, especially for middle management jobs. In other words, this source is the code that is rarely mind.

External Sources

These sources lie outside the organisation. They usually include: (i) New entrants to the labour force, i.e., young, mostly inexperienced potential employees—the college students; (ii) The unemployed—with a wide range of skills and abilities; (iii) Retired experienced persons such as mechanics, machinists, welders, accountants; (iv) Others not in the labour force, such as married women and persons from minority groups.

For tapping external sources, three methods may be employed;

1. *Direct Methods*: These include sending travelling recruiters to educational and professional institutions, employees' contacts with public, and manned exhibits. One of the widely-used direct methods is that of sending of recruiters to colleges and technical schools. Most college recruiting is done in co-operation with the placement office of a college. The placement office usually provides help in attracting students, arranging interviews, furnishing space, and providing student resumes. For managerial, professional and sales personnel, campus recruiting is an extensive operation. Persons reading for MBA or other technical diplomas are picked up in this manner.

2. *Indirect Methods:* Indirect methods involve mostly advertising in newspapers, on the radio, in trade and professional journals, technical magazines and brochures.

Advertising in newspapers and/or trade journals and magazines is the most frequently used method, when qualified or experienced personnel are not available from other sources. Senior posts are largely filled up by such methods when they cannot be filled up by promotion from within. Advertising is very useful for recruiting blue-collar and hourly paid workers, as well as scientific, professional, and technical employees.

3. *Third Party Methods*: These include the use of commercial or private employment agencies, state agencies, placement offices of schools, colleges and professional associations, management consulting firms, indoctrination seminars of college professors; and friends and relatives.

Promotion

A promotion is a vertical or horizontal move in rank and responsibility of an employee. The purpose of promotion is to provide incentive to initiative, enterprise, and ambition; to minimise discontent and unrest; to attract individuals, and to reward the employee for his co-operation, long service and loyalty. It brings satisfaction of esteem, belonging and security needs.

A sound promotion policy must satisfy the following criteria:

(a) It should enjoy consistency, i.e. it will be applied irrespective of the persons concerned. Consistency demands that the policy should be so correlated to career planning that there should not be a sudden spurt of promotion in the organisation conferring premature benefits on a number of persons, followed by a long period of absence of promotion.

(b) It should be fair and impartial, i.e., the management should be able to remove all suspicion of arbitrariness, *ad hocism*, improvisation to suit particular individuals, nepotism, etc.

(c) Promotion should be a planned activity, i.e., the management should make a correct assessment of the requirements or opportunities of promotion within the organisation so that there are no phenomena of "bunching" or no period of "promotion drought", i.e., no overestimation or underestimation.

The promotion policy should involve six elements as follows;

1. Promotion Policy Statement, which should consider whether vacancies are primarily to be filled up from within an organisation or by recruitment from outisde. Is any preferential treatment to be given to direct recruits? Would it be sound to deny promotion to otherwise qualified personnel? Whether an increase in pay is to be given, if so, when and how much? Usually, internal promotions are preferred over external recruitment and increase is given at the time of promotion, otherwise promotion is meaningless.

2. Establish a Plan of Jobs, i.e., decide on what basis promotions are to be given. Whether on performance appraisal, or on the basis of confidential records, or job and post-bid system. Which positions are to be filled up? Usually promotions are decided on the basis of performance appraisals. "Job-post and bid system", i.e., posting of job vacancies indicating job titles, duties, pay and qualifications on company notice boards, is also utilised.

3. Trace Transfer Routes, i.e., having some type of formal and systematic promotion channels, ladders giving paths of advancement, promotional charts, opportunity charts or fortune sheets clearly distinguish each job and by lines and arrows, connect various jobs; and show the lines/routes of advancement upto and away from them. Stepping jobs should be clearly identified and recorded on paper. Dead-end jobs should be labelled and the path upward well marked.

4. Prepare employees for advancement, through the provision of some training either on the job in professional/technical institutions, or through job rotations, multiple management, under-study and conferences.

5. Communicate the Policy. The organisation should communicate its promotion policy either in the form of a manual or in the agreement signed with union or in the form of a set of Standing Orders.

6. Detailed Personnel and Service Records are kept ready, on the basis of which promotions may be made.

Promotion Policy

The usual policy is to take merit into consideration. Sometimes, length of services, education, training, courses completed, previous work history, etc. are factors which are given weight to while deciding on a promotion. Although promotions are made on the basis of ability, hard work, co-operation, merit, honesty, many informal influences are powerful determinants of a promotional policy.

For higher posts, persons are picked by the top executive: (i) who think and feel just as he does; (ii) who value loyalty to him and to the organisation; and (iii) who have social, political, economic and religious interests similar to his own.

Seniority versus Merit: "Seniority" refers to length of service in the company or in its various plants, or in its departments, or in a particular position. Under straight plant-wise seniority in all jobs, promotions go to the oldest employees, provided that he is fit for the job. Occupational seniority may be within a department, within a division or in the entire plant.

There is a great controversy on the question of whether promotions should be given on the basis of seniority or ability. Trade unions are of the view that promotions should be given on the basis of seniority, while managements favour promotions on the basis of merit and ability.

If a promotion is given to a qualified man in recognition of his performance or with a view to creating incentive for him, then it should be based on his ability.

If, on the other hand, promotion is given to recognise and reward senior employees, then it should be on the basis of seniority.

The most widely used basis for promotion combines both ability and seniority. The best policy would be to ensure that whenever there are two employees of equal seniority, ability or merit should be the deciding factor in a promotion. Where, however, there are two employees of almost equal competence, seniority should be the decisive factor. Such a policy would satisfy the management with prefers ability, and trade unions which prefer seniority.

Demotion

It is the assignment of an individual to a job of lower rank and pay usually involving lower level of duties and responsibility.

The demotion policy should satisfy these conditions:

(i) A clear and reasonable list of rules should be framed, violations of which would subject an employee to demotion;
(ii) This information should be clearly communicated to the employees;
(iii) There should be a competent investigation of any alleged violation;
(iv) If violations are discovered, there should be a consistent and equitable application of the penalty, preferably by the immediate supervisor;
(v) There should be a provision for review. (In a unionised case, this will be automatic via the grievance procedure; in a non-unionised case, the employer will need to make other provisions for review.

Demotions serve a useful purpose in the sense that they keep the employees alert and alive to their responsibilities and duties.

For persons with a long and meritorious service, there should be no demotion. However, some of their duties and responsibilities may be taken from them and assigned to others. The other alternative is to create a job for the person at the same pay and status but with lower job demands.

A demotion should never be made as a penalty for a violation of the rules of conduct, poor attendance record, or insubordination because such action will not improve the performance of the individual. Only discipline and training can set things right.

Transfer Policy

A transfer is a lateral shift causing movement of individuals from one position to another, usually without involving any marked changes in duties, responsibilities, skills needed or compensation.

A good transfer policy should:

(i) Specifically clarify the types of transfers and the conditions under which these will be made;
(ii) Locate the authority in some officer who may initiate and implement transfers;
(iii) Indicate whether transfers can be made only within a sub-unit or also between departments, divisions/plants;
(iv) Indicate the basis for transfer, i.e., whether it will be based on seniority or on skill and competence or any other factor;
(v) Decide the rate of pay to be given to the transferee;
(vi) Intimate the fact of transfer to the person concerned well in advance;
(vii) Be in writing and duly communicated to all concerned;
(viii) Not be made frequent and not for the sake of transfer only.

In making transfer, the usual policy that is followed is to pay the employee the actual cost of moving the household to the place of transfer.

Discharge

A discharge involves permanent separation of an employee from the pay-roll for certain specific reasons, such as:

1. Changes in policies that may result in discontinuing the activities in which the employee has been engaged.
2. Seasonal and cyclical trends that make necessary a reduction in the number of employees.
3. Unadaptability or inefficiency of the employee.
4. Disability of the employee through old age, illness or other causes.

The following elements should be present in a discharge programme policy:

(i) The reasons for discharge should be clearly stated. (ii) The individual concerned should be adequately informed about the reasons for his discharge. (iii) The supervisor in charge of initiating discharge action should be fully conversant with the rules and regulations of the organisation. (iv) The facts regarding violations of the rules and regulations should be carefully analysed. (v) Line officials should handle the discharge affairs. (vi) There should be a well-thought-out procedure for settling the discharge cause. (vii) Adequate provision should exist for the review of the discharge employee's case. (viii) A discharged employee needs a reasonable notice or an equivalent of pay in lieu of notice, because it carries with it certain penalties, such as difficulty of re-employment, loss of benefits and, in certain cases, the loss of a part of the provident fund, etc.

It is fair and just that an employee should be discharged with as little humiliation and ill-feeling as possible, both because this is humane and because it is advantageous from the point of view of the company.

In sum, the workforce is an asset of the company and, therefore, if it is to be run efficiently, the selection of employees must be done with all necessary precautions; and if a later stage, the employee is found unsuitable or not properly doing this job, he may be discharged or training is provided to him to mend his ways.

EMPLOYEE TRAINING

Every organisation needs to have well-trained and experienced people to perform the activities that have to be done. If the current or potential job occupant can meet this requirement, training is not important. But when this is not the case, it is necessary to raise the skill levels and increase the versatility and adaptability of employees. Inadequate job performance or a decline in productivity or changes resulting out of job redesigning or a technological break-through require some type of training and development efforts. As the jobs become more complex, the importance of employee development also increases. In a rapidly changing society, *employee training and development is not only an activity that is desirable but also an activity that an organisation must commit resources to it if is to maintain a viable and knowledgeable workforce.*

Basic Training Issues

In the field of training, the manager has to consider the following basic issues:

1. The need why training should be impaired to the employees.
2. Whose responsibility is the training to be?
3. What steps of training should be adopted?
4. What should be the training policy and in which areas it should be given?
5. What should be the duration of the training period?
6. Who should be given the training?
7. What types of training will best meet the purpose?

Training Policy

Every company or organisation should have a well-established training policy. Such policy represents the top management's commitment to the training of its employees, and comprises rules and procedures governing the standard and scope of training. A training policy is considered necessary for the following reasons:

(a) To indicate a company's intention to develop its personnel; to provide guidance in the framing and implementation of programmes and to provide information concerning them to all concerned.

(b) To discover critical areas where training is to be given on a propriety basis; and

(c) To provide suitable opportunities to the employee for his own betterment.

Training Courses

Training may range from highly specialised instruction in the procedures to be adopted while performing a particular job to very general instruction concerning the economy and society.

Training courses in general areas usually aim at making an employee a rounded individual, a happier worker and a good citizen, and at training him for "larger responsibilities" and future advancement. Such training exerts a remarkable influence on production and labour. From the producers' point of view, output would increase with decreases in scrap, spoilage, waste and the cost of production. From the point of view of labour, the employees' morale would improve; so would the rate of turnover, excessive absenteeism and accidents. Training programmes are no doubt expensive; but their worth to a growing concern cannot be over-emphasised.

Training in general areas is given in such subjects as general and home economics, basic English, instruction in letter writing and report drafting, reading and using gauges, the operation of machines, fire-fighting and safety devices on the job, shop practices and secretarial practices, elementary mathematics, sociology, industrial psychology, time study, personal hygiene, public speaking and public relations, selling and communication with people.

So far as women employees are concerned, they are given training in telephone etiquette, personal hygiene, good grooming, sales talk and handling of sales and courtesy.

Duration of Training Period

The duration of a training period varies with the skill to be acquired, the complexity of the subject, a trainee's attitude and ability to understand and the training media used.

Generally, a training period should not be unduly long; if it is, trainees may feel bored, and uninterested. The ideal session should not go beyond 2 to 3 hours at a stretch, with a break in between two sessions. If convenient, employees may be trained for a week or a fortnight for an hour or two every day after work hours.

The training period may extend from 3 weeks to 6 months of even more, depending upon job requirements.

The physical location of the programme should be in pleasure surroundings away from the noise and tension of the work place.

Training for Different Employees

Employees at different levels require training. *Unskilled workers* require training in improved methods of handling machines and materials to reduce the cost of production and waste and to do the job the most economical way. *Such employees are given training on the job itself; and training is imparted by their immediate superior officers*. The training period ranges from 3 weeks to 6 weeks.

Semi-skilled workers require training to cope with the requirements of an industry arising out of the adoption of mechanisation, rationalisation and technical processes. *These employees are given training either in their own sections of departments, or in segregated training shops where machines and other facilities are usually available.* The training is usually imparted by the more proficient workers, bosses or inspectors, and lasts for a few hours or a week, depending upon the number of operations, and the speed and accuracy required on a job.

Skilled workers are given training through the system of apprenticeship, which varies in duration from a year to three or five years. Such workers are usually trained in training centres and industry itself in industrial jobs and operations.

Salesmen are given training so that they may know the nature and quality of the products and the routine involved in putting through a deal. They are trained in the art of salesmanship and in handling customers and meeting their challenges.

Supervisory Staff need training the most, for they form very important link in the chain of administration. The training programmes are mostly tailored to fit the needs of the increasing demands of the enterprise in practically wide areas.

Why Training Fails?

The following factors have been regarded as the main reasons for the failure of training programmes

1. The benefits of training are not clear to the top management.
2. The top management hardly rewards supervisors for carrying out effective training.
3. The top management rarely plans and budgets systematically for training.
4. The middle management, without proper incentives from top management, does not account for training in production scheduling.
5. Without proper scheduling from above, first line supervisors have difficulty in maintaining production norms if employees are attending training programmes.
6. Behavioural objectives are often imprecise.
7. Training external to the employing unit sometimes teaches techniques and methods contrary to the practices of the participants' organisation.
8. Timely information about external programmes may be difficult to obtain.
9. Trainers provide limited counselling and consulting services to the rest of the organisation.

Improving Effectiveness of Training

The training programmes can be effective and successful if the following hints are considered:

1. Specific training objectives should be outlined on the basis of the type of performance required to achieve organisational goals and objectives. An audit of personal needs compared with operational requirements will help to determine the specific training needs of individual employees. This evaluation should form a well-defined set of performance standards toward which each trainee should be directed.

2. Attempts should be made to determine if the trainee has the intelligence, maturity, and motivation to successfully complete the training programmes. If deficiencies are noted in these respects, training may be postponed or cancelled till improvements are visible.

3. The trainee should be helped to see the need for training by making him aware of the personal benefits he can achieve through better performance. He should be helped to discover the rewards and satisfactions that might be available to him through changes in behaviour.

4. The training programme should be planned so that it is related to the trainee's previous experiences and background. This background should be used as a foundation for new development and new behaviour.

5. Attempts should be made to create organisational conditions that are conducive to a good learning environment. It should be made clear why changes are needed. Any distractions in the way of training environment should be removed. The support of the upper levels of management should be obtained before applying training at lower levels.

6. If nécessary, a combination of training methods should be selected so that variety is permitted and pedagogy becomes broad-based.

7. It should be recognised that all the trainees do not progress at the same rate. Therefore, flexibility should be allowed in judging the rates of progress in the training programme.

8. If possible, the personal involvement or active participation of the trainee should be got in the training programme. He should be provided with opportunity to practice the newly-needed behaviour norms.

9. As the trainee acquires knowledge, skills or attitudes and applies them in job situations, he should be significantly rewarded for his efforts.

10. The trainee should be provided with regular constructive feed-back concerning his progress in training and implementation of newly acquired abilities.

11. The training should be provided with personal assistance when he encounters learning obstacles.

MANAGEMENT DEVELOPMENT

The manager is the dynamic life-giving element in a business. The calibre and performance of managers will largely determine the success of a business. If the business wants to improve the quality of its managers, it must expend money and effort and introduce imaginative and systematic development schemes for them in which managers themselves play a crucial role. All enterprises need to devote great attention to the continuous supply of their future managers, both functional and general.

A manager's tasks include certain skills which can be improved, even perfected or nearly so. The major and more elusive task of management development is to mould and fashion the behaviour component into a virile and unmixed weapon of enterprise achievement. The secret of effective management lies in vitality, a conceptual attitude of mind concerned with profitable results matched by determination and integrity in management and managers.[11]

Why Management development?

The causes of, or factors which bring about, management development programmes may be stated thus:

(i) The rapid rate of technological and social change in society has necessitated the training of managers so that they may cope with these developments.

11. *Ibid.*, pp. 113-114.

(ii) The introduction of automation, intense market competition from foreign countries, the growth of new markets in the underdeveloped countries, enlarged participation of labour in management, and greater interest by the public and the government in the actions of businessmen have all led to the need for the development of managerial personnel.

(iii) Increased recognition by business and industrial leaders of the social and public responsibilities of management has necessitated the development of managerial personnel.

(iv) The increased size and complexity of most organisation—governmental, industrial, commercial, non-profit public services—require trained managers.

(v) The frequent labour-management strifes have necessitated the services of trained personnel.

(vi) The changes in socio–economic forces, including changes in public policy and the concepts of social justice, industrial democracy, problems of *ecology* (smog or pollution), *ekistics* (the problem of human settlements), *ergonomics* (the problem of working environment), and *cultural anthropology* (the problem of fitting machines to men) — all these demand increasing attention of the management for decisions in these diverse fields. If management development programmes are not evolved, the managerial personnel would become "obsolete". Managerial obsolescence may be due to redundancy, mergers and take-overs, reorganisations, changes in technology, products and trade and individual causes. Such obsolescence may lead to lay-off, which may cause a great emotional trauma and disturbance, David Ewing has rightly said: "The managerial personnel must realise that they will not survive unless they keep pace with modern management education, research theory, principles and practices."[12]

The stages involved in a management development programme are:

Organisational Planning, to determine the company's present and future needs;

Programme targeting, to focus the company's efforts on the most pertinent areas;

Ascertaining key positions requirements to stress the basic requirements of particular managerial positions;

Managerial appraisal, to evaluate periodically the abilities and performance of individuals with a view to identifying managers showing a promise of future development and meeting their training needs;

Replacement of skills inventories, to indicate persons qualified for managerial replacements;

Planning individual development programmes, to provide specific development programmes for promising managers; and

Appraising existing programmes, to ascertain areas of improvement to be incorporated in future programmes.

Organisational Climate for Management Development

Management development cannot take place unless a favourable climate for it is created at the top which extends down through each level of the organisation. It may come to a stand still if encouragement is not available to the persons concerned. If the growth stops at the middle management, it is impeded at the level; and then the first line management and non-supervisory employees too, suffer. Therefore, the creation of a proper organisational climate is a "must" for the success of any development programme.

12. Erving David, W., "The Knowledge of an Executive", *The Educational Development Series – I*, p. 181.

By "organisational climate" is meant the circumstances or conditions in which the management guides the development and growth of the people at all levels by training, counselling, delegation and communication. The growth process is largely influenced in the home environment of a company by the manner in which superiors and peers manage the affairs, the manner in which they treat people, how they delegate authority, how they encourage ideas initiative and enterprises, how they provide opportunities to experiment and test new concepts, tools and techniques and how they project company goals, policies and philosophy.

In order that a proper development climate is created, it must be borne in mind that;

First, development is a learning rather than a teaching process; the burden for final growth rests on the individual.

Second, growth takes place through a striving process in which sights (objectives) are set high and tasks involve "stretching."

Third, development takes place largely by building on the strength of the people rather than by a concentration of the elimination of weaknesses.

Fourth, a feeling of confidence in, and approval of the process of development must be generated among those who are to be a affected by it. They is seldom possible when the superior has a negatively critical point of view.

Fifth, at all levels, a genuine faith in development is necessary, a belief that people *can* and *will*, with proper goals and encouragement, do better.

Finally, all concerned must, with an open heart and mind, be willing to welcome and accept any change in a point of view.

To develop a proper management climate, it is vital to pay a vigorous and constant attention to the administration of a development programme. There must be a comprehensive and co-ordinated planning, and the plan should be communicated to all those who have to administer and function under the programme. Further, a plan should apply first to the top to so that management at that level may, by its own efforts, set an example for personnel development.

Administering a Management Development Programme

While administering the programme, due consideration should be given to the following points:

1. *An M.D.P. should support a systematic career planning for managerial personnel*, otherwise the frustrated trainees, might seek opportunities elsewhere and the whole investment made in training programmes would go waste.
2. *Management development does not comprise involvement in a series of structured courses*, but there should also be an active interaction between the trainee and the management.
3. *Training programme should cover, as far as possible, every manager, capable of showing potential for growth,* i.e., "the crown prince or heir apparent" approach should not be adopted in the selection of the trainees. As Peter Drucker puts, it, "The eight men out of every ten who were not included in the programme will understandably feel slighted. They may end up by welcoming less effective, less productive, less willing to do new things."
4. *The entire programme should be properly planned*. The trainees should take part in it. An individual may stay out, but it should be made clear that he does so at some risk to his future promotion. The company should not normally allow any manager to opt out of a training programme.

Courses for Management Development

Although foremen, department heads, plant managers, and vice-presidents are all members of management, the nature of their duties and responsibilities differ greatly. There are certain areas in which development courses may be regarded as essential for all levels of management (such courses as on the company, on management principles and techniques, on economic, social and political environment, on personal skills and human relations). However, certain areas are more appropriate for one level than another. For example, foremen are not directly involved in the economic, social and political environment of a corporation; but the executives are. Further, in some areas, not only the content but also the depth of knowledge and skill varies with the personnel involved.

Courses for members of the middle management contain elements of both top and lower level management programmes. Middle level managers, however, devote a considerable time to human relations and personnel management principle because these are essential at all levels of management. They should have a solid grounding in such management techniques as cost analysis and control, data processing, production planning and control, wage and salary administration, work study, **PERT/CPM**, value engineering, etc.

Courses for first level supervisors concentrate upon the technical process of the business, human relations and personal skills, for they are immediately practicable and are closely related to a supervisor's day-to-day job. According to Prof. Beach, the subject matter of a course for management development may comprise:

Basic Requisites for the Success of Management Development Programmes

(i) The top management should accept responsibility for getting the policy of development executed. For this purpose, a senior office may be placed in charge to initiate and implement the MDP (Management Development Programme).

(ii) Management development is essentially a "line job". It takes place on the job and involves both the man and his boss.

(iii) Every manager must accept direct responsibility for developing managers under his control on the job, and high priority should be given to this task.

(iv) Management development must be geared to the needs of the company and the individual.

(v) A policy of *promotion from within* is a necessary incentive for managers to develop in an organisation.

(vi) Management development starts with the selection of the right material for managerial ranks. It is essential to ensure that really good material is fed into the programme at the entry levels.

(vii) There should be a realistic time table in accordance with the needs of a company. This time table should take into account the needs for managerial personnel over a sufficiently long period and the resources which are available and which will be required.

Management development programme should be based on a definite strategy, which should spell out the type, coverage and objectives of the programme. The multi-tier supervisory and management development programme should start from the first line supervisor and go all the way up to the top management.

Techniques of Management Development

A large number of management development methods and techniques are used. These include lectures, conferences, seminars or group discussions, case studies, films and slides, outisde reading and private study panels, forums, role playing, and workshop. Other techniques are: under-study, job-rotation, coaching and counselling, position rotation, professional classes, membership in professional and technical classes, membership in professional and technical associations, committee assignments, management courses in colleges and professional institutions, multiple-management syndicate, incident method, project management or in-basket management game and sensitivity training.

With respect to particular management development methods, it may be said that there is no one technique which may be considered as most effective. Flippo observes that the techniques such as in-basket methods, business games, and case studies purport to develop *decision making skills,* while role-playing, sensitivity training and structural insight are likely to develop *interpersonal skills* of the managers. Further, on the job-experience, coaching and understudy provide *job knowledge* and position rotation and multiple management enhance *organisational knowledge,* while special projects, counselling, etc. meet the *specific needs of the managers.*[13]

The methods of management development have been classified in two broad categories, viz., the *leader-centre method* and the *student–centre method.*

Under the *leader–centre method*:

(a) Suggestions are evaluated by the instructor who advises or leads the class to correct their conclusions;

(b) Techniques and steps for activities are given by the instructor;

(c) The instructor, rather than the student, considers and handles questions and individual problems; and

(d) The instructor is the focus of attention. Student to student attention happens rarely or very occasionally.

Lecture and lecture-cum-discussion methods are typical examples of the leader-centre method.

Under the *student-centre method*:

(a) The instructor encourage suggestions from students and uses this procedure to stimulate the class to carry out class activities.

(b) Techniques and steps for activities emerge from group discussions;

(c) Group consideration of individual problems is encouraged by the instructor; and

(d) Students direct their attention to one another. The instructor becomes the focus of their attention only when discussion or activity requires guidance.

Group discussion, decision-making, group activities (including case method, role–playing, T-Group training etc.) are examples of this method.

13. Flippo, Edward, B., *Personnel Management,* 1976, p. 228.

PERFORMANCE APPRAISAL

Performance appraisal, which aims at measuring employees job performance, is critical area of human resource management. Inspite of a number of researches carried out by psychologists, behaviouralists and practising managers, on employee behaviour, they have failed to understand human the black box. The human being, however, is capable of attaining a high level of performance in a proper environment and with proper motivation. The system of appraisal is not only concerned with reporting an individual's performance once a year or so with a view to deciding about pay increases or promotions. But a system which provides a complete and comprehensive feedback to the employees about their performance has a strong motivating effect on their work behaviour. That is why this has been regarded as an important aspect of human resource management. The performance appraisal is an important sub-system of personnel management, around which a host of personnel issues revolve; therefore, while deciding upon an appraisal programme, the management should try to seek answers to the following questions:

(a) Why is performance appraisal necessary?
(b) How can it be brought about?
(c) What traits are required to be measured?
(d) Who will carry out the appraisal?
(e) When should employee be rated?
(f) What are the common problems associated with appraisal and how can they be minimized?

CHART 10.2

Appraisal Questions

Who?

Appraised: All

Appraisers:
1. Immediate supervisor
2. Peers or Colleagues
3. Subordinates
4. Personnel Manager
5. Rating Committee
6. Assessment
7. Self-Appraisal

What ?

Object: Human beings Time frame
1. Current performance
2. Future Potential

Specifics
1. Personal traits
2. Achieved results

Why ?
1. Maintain workforce
2. Improve performance
3. Determine organization training needs

4. Determine personnel development opportunities
5. Basis for promotions, transfers, lay-offs, discharges, etc.
6. Basis for pay increase, aid in recruitment, selection, placement and indoctrination processes.
7. Feedback and communication mechanism

When?

Formal	Informal
1. Annually	1. Weekly
2. Semi-annually	2. Daily
3. Quarterly	3. Continuously

Where?

On the Job	Off the job
1. Boss's office	1. Consultant's office
2. Subordinate place of work	2. Social or recreational setting
3. Everywhere	3. Everywhere

How

Methods		Problems
Traditional	Rating scale, employee comparison, check lists, free form essay, interviews, critical incidents	1. Halo effect 2. Leniency or strictness 3. Central tendency 4. Similarly error 5. Miscellaneous biases
Modern	Assessment Centres, M.B.O., human asset accounting, self appraisal	

Why Appraisal is Necessary

The basic objective of management is to epitomize efficiency by an adequate utilization of non-human and human resources. The non-human resources are well within the control of the management. There is, therefore, no problem in harnassing them to their maximum. But human resources differ in their skill, capacity and motivation; they therefore affect productivity in a great many ways. In the circumstances, it is necessary to know the relative worth of individuals, so that their job proficiency, skill and interpersonal competence may be enhanced by proper feedback mission in a much more effective way. This calls for a systematic appraisal of their performance against the targets of role description and specification.

Most organization conduct an annual review of their employees, performance in a more or less ritualistic way. The superior just fills up the appraisal report in a quite casual manner, because he feels that it is only required for the purpose of deciding about certain time-honoured personnel functions (like promotion, pay increase or demotion). Such an appraisal report gives an apparent rather than a true idea of reality.

Therefore, before embarking upon any appraisal programme, the management should determine its rationale and objective. A different programme should then be designed for different categories of employees keeping in view the kind of information to be gathered for the purpose of taking appropriate personnel action.

In view of the fact that performance appraisal is an important aspect of human resource management, it is considered to be a significant and indispensable tool which furnishes the management highly useful information on the various personnel issues which have a direct bearing on the effective working of an organization. If valid, timely, accurate, objective and standardized performance data are available, sound and progressive human resource development policies can be practised to achieve optimal organization effectiveness.

An ideal appraisal programme should help the management in following ways:

(i) Performance Improvement: Performance feedback makes it possible for individuals and management to intervene with an appropriate plan of action to improve upon the shortcomings that have been identified.

(ii) Placement Decisions: Performance evaluation decisions assist the management in assessing the cases for promotion, transfer and demotion.

(iii) Training and Development Needs: Training and development enables decision-makers to determine as to who deserves a pay rise and low performance may indicate a need for training or retraining. A good performance may show that there is room for further training to release the hidden untapped potential of the employees.

(iv) Compensation Adjustments: As the appraisal assists the management in assessing the relative worth of an individual, it enables decision-makers to determine as to who deserves a pay raise and additional incentives.

(v) Informational Inaccuracies: A poor performance may indicate serious flaws in role analysis, human resource planning and development, and other personnel functions. This knowledge would guide the management in introducing improvements in various personnel practices to achieve a higher level of effectiveness.

(vi) Job Design Error: A poor performance, besides other functional factors, may result in an ill-conceived job design. The appraisal helps the managers to diagnose the error.

(vii) External Challenges: Traditionally, it was believed that performance was largely influenced by skill and job-related factors. But now it has been recognized that factors associated with one's family, financial status, health and other personal matters affected the quality of job performance. These factors, if brought to light during an appraisal, may enable the personnel department to embark upon various assistance programmes.

The How of Appraisal

The how of appraisal is concerned with deciding the methods to be utilized to carrying out a task, for a appraisal is concerned with assessing the total performance of an individual on the basis of some objective criteria. Subjectivity cannot be altogether eliminated even by the use of very modern and sophisticated method. However, continuing efforts should be made to ensure that rating is objective, and not dependent on the indiocyncracies of rates.

A variety of techniques of appraisal are available for evaluating the performance of an employee. The methods and scales available differ for a variety of reasons. *First*, they differ in respect of traits or qualities to be appraised. The qualities may differ because of differences in job requirements, statistical requirements and the opinions of the management. *Second*, they differ because of the different categories of personnel who are to be evaluated, viz., workers, executives or salesman. *Third*, the variations may be caused by the degree of precision attempted in an evaluation. *Finally*, they may differ because of the methods used to obtain weightings for various traits.

There is little agreement on the best method of evaluating managerial, professional or salaried employees. A great many personnel management experts have suggested different methods. For instance:

Robbins gives three categories of appraisal, viz.,

(i) Single-trait, single subject, in which the subjects are not compared with any other person, and each trait is measured by itself. The check list, the numerical and graphic scales methods are popular for this rating.

(ii) Single trait, multiple subject, in which the subjects are compared with other subjects. Group order ranking, individual ranking and pair comparison methods are best used for this purpose.

(iii) Multiple trait, single subject, in which forced choice rating is done by either the subject himself or the traits offered for evaluation.

The widely used category is that given by Strauss and Sayles. They have classified performance appraisal methods into traditional and modern methods. The traditional methods lay emphasis on the rating of the individual's personality traits, such as initiative, dependability, drive, responsibility, creativity, integrity, leadership potential, intelligence, judgement, organising ability, etc. On the other hand, modern methods place emphasis on the evaluation of work results–job achievements — rather than on personality traits. Result–oriented appraisals tend to be more objective and worthwhile, especially for counselling and development purposes.

CHART 10.3

Methods of Performance Appraisal

Traditional Methods	Modern Methods
1. Straight Ranking Method	1. Appraisal by Results or Management by Objectives
2. Man-to-Man Comparison Method	2. Assessment Centre Method
3. Grading	3. Human Asset Accounting Method
4. Graphic Rating Scales	4. Behaviourally Achored Rating Scale.
5. Forced Choice Description Method	
6. Forced Distribution Method	
7. Check Lists	
8. Free Form Essay Method	
9. Critical Incidents	
10. Group Appraisal	
11. Field Review Method.	

What of Apprisal

The *What* of appraisal is concerned with the identification of the traits that are required for evaluating an individual's performance. As the gravity and intensity of appraisal varies with one's position in the organization, responsibility, nature of the job, etc., the management should prepare different appraisal formats for appraising the performance of different categories of personnel. Though it is quite difficult to make a precise list of the traits which measures one's performance best, if we include too many factors in the programme, it will make appraisal difficult. The inclusion of fewer traits, on the other hand, will hinder effective evaluation. Therefore, at any point of time, it is desirable to have a "tailor-made programme" which should be in conformity with the targets of the job description and the job specifications of a particular job.

Who is to do Appraisal!

Before implementing a performance appraisal programme, the management should take a policy decision as to who would evaluate the performance of the personnel working different levels of the organization. The success of the appraisal programme depends on the rater. If he is free, frank, firm and fair, the evaluation may really be effective. But if he is biased or prejudiced, the whole purpose of evaluation will be defeated. Therefore, great caution should be exercised in the selection of the rater. The appraisal may be brought about by the following:

(i) Immediate supervisor
(ii) Peers or colleagues
(iii) Subordinates
(iv) Personnel Manager
(v) Rating Committee
(vi) Assessment Centre
(vii) Self-appraisal

We shall now briefly discuss the relative importance of different rating sources.

COMPENSATION

Compensation is a reward to an employee for the work done. It is usually financial remuneration in the form of wages, salaries, bonuses, and other forms of direct financial reward. The manager has to consider three basic issues, such as: how much compensation is to be paid? What method of payment should be used? and What steps should be taken to establish a wage structure for the organisation. These issues are the foundation stone of wage and salary administration, which refers to the establishment and implementation of sound policies and pratices of employee compensation. Its scope is rather wide, and it includes such areas as job evaluation, survey of wages and salaries, analysis of relevant organisational problems, development and maintenance of wages structure, establishing rules for administering wages, wage payments, incentives, profit-sharing, wage changes and adjustments, supplementary payments, control of compensation costs and other related items.

The *basic purpose* of wage and salary administration is to establish and maintain an equitable wage and salary structure. Its *secondary objective* is the establishment and maintenance of an equitable labour – cost structure, i.e., an optimal balancing of conflicting personnel interests so that the satisfaction of employees and employers is maximised and conflicts minimised. The wage and salary administration is concerned with the financial aspects of needs, motivation and rewards. Managers, therefore, analyse and interpret the needs of their employees so that reward can be individually designed to satisfy their needs. For, it has been rightly said that "people do what they do to satisfy some need; before they do anything, they look for a reward or pay-off."

Amount of Compensation

The wage policies of different organisations vary somewhat, Marginal units pay the maximum necessary to attract the required number and kind of labour. Often, these units pay only the minimum wage rates required by labour legislation, and recruit marginal labour. At the other extreme, some units pay well above the going rates in the labour market. They do so to attract and retain the highest calibre of the labour force. Some managers believe in the economy of higher wages. They feel that, by paying high wages, they would attract better workers who will produce more than the average worker in the industry. This greater production per employee means greater output per man-hour. Hence, labour costs may turn out to be the lowest than those existing in firms using marginal labour. Some units pay high wages because of a combination of favourable product market demand, higher ability to pay and the bargaining power of a trade union. But a large number of them seek to be competitive in their wage programme, i.e. they aim at paying somewhere near the going rate in the labour market for the various classes of labour they employ. Most units give greater weight to two wage criteria, viz., job requirements and the prevailing rates of wages in the labour market. Other factors, such as changes in the cost of living, the supply and demand of labour, and the ability to pay are accorded a secondary importance.

A sound wage policy is to adopt a job evaluation programme in order to establish fair differentials in wages based upon differences in job contents. Besides the basic factors provided by a job description and job evaluation, those that are usually taken into consideration for wages and salary are:

(i) *Organisation's Ability to Pay:* Wage increases should be given by those organisations which can afford them. Companies that have good sales and, therefore, high profits tend to pay higher wages than those which are running at a loss or earning low profits because of the high cost of production or low sales. In the short run, the economic influence on the ability to pay is practically nil. All employees, irrespective of their profits or losses, must pay no less than their competitors and need pay no more if they wish to attract and keep workers. In the long run, the ability to pay is very important. During times of prosperity, employers pay high wages to carry on profitable operations and because of their increased ability to pay. But during a period of depression, wages are cut because funds are not available. Marginal firms and non-profit organisations (like hospitals and educational institutions) pay relatively low wages because of low or no profits.

(ii) *Supply and Demand of Labour*: The labour market conditions or supply and demand forces operate at the national, regional and local levels, and determine organisational wage structure and level. If the demand for certain skills is high and the supply is low, the result is a rise in the price to be paid for these skills. When prolonged and acute, these labour-market pressures probably force most organisations to "reclassify hard-to-fill jobs at a higher level" than suggested by the job evaluation. The other alternative is to pay higher wages if the labour supply is scarce; and lower wages when it is excessive. Similarly, if there is a great demand for labour expertise, wages rise; but if the demand for manpower skill is minimal, the wages will be relatively low.

(iii) *The Prevailing Market Rate:* This is also known as the comparable wage or going wage rate, and is the most widely used criterion. An organisation's compensation policies generally tend to conform to the wage-rates payable by the industry and the community. This is done for keeping wages at the competitor's level; for attracting and maintaining a sufficient number and quality of personnel; for meeting the provisions of law and demands of trade unions.

Belcher and Atchison observe: "Some companies pay on the high side of the market in order to obtain goodwill or to insure an adequate supply of labour, while other organisations pay lower wages because economically they have to, or because by lowering hiring requirements, they can keep jobs adequately manned."[14]

14. Belcher, David, "Fringe Benefits: Do we know enough about them" in Langsner and Zollitsch (ed), *Wage and Salary Administration*, South-Western Publishing Co., Cincinnati, 1961, p. 488.

(iv) *The Cost of Living*: The cost-of-living pay criterion is usually regarded as an automatic minimum equity pay criterion. This criterion calls for pay adjustments based on increases or decreases in an acceptable cost of living index. In recognition of the influence of the cost of living, "escalator clauses" are written into labour contracts. When the cost of living increases, workers and trade unions demand adjusted wages to offset the erosion of real wages. However, when living costs are stable or declining, the management does not resort to this argument as a reason for wage reduction.

(v) *The Living Wage:* Criterion means that wages paid should be adequate to enable an employee to maintain himself and his family at a reasonable level of existence. However, employees do not generally favour using the concept of a living wage as a guide to wage determination because they prefer to base the wages of an employee on his contribution rather than on his need.

(vi) *Trade Union's Bargaining Power:* Trade unions do affect the rate of wages. Generally, the stronger and more powerful the trade union, higher the wages.

(vii) *Job Requirements:* Generally, the more difficult a job, the higher are the wages. Measures of job difficulty are frequently used when the relative value of one job to another in an organisation is to be ascertained. Jobs are graded according to the relative skill, effort, responsibilities, the degree of supervision received, and job conditions required.

Each job is rated on these bases for classifying all jobs upto the "Executive" level, say, into about 15 grades. Jobs in any one grade are about equal in difficulty and importance, and hence, are entitled to the same day. If, however, the experience required is greater for one job than another, it is classified in a higher grade.

(viii) *The Quality and Quantity of Work Turned Out by Individuals on the Same Job*: These are not equal. Rarely is a man these days assigned a job as valuable to the company as his fellow-worker who has been doing that kind of work for several years. Therefore, it is desirable to adjust pay in recognition of these differences in individual performance.

(ix) *Psychological and Social Factors*: These determine in a significant measure how hard a person will work for the compensation received or what pressures will he exert to get his compensation increased. Psychologically, persons perceive the level of wages as a measure of success in life; people may feel secure, have an inferiority complex, seem inadequate or feel the reverse of all these. They may or may not take pride in their work, or in the wages they get. Therefore, these things should not be overlooked by the management in establishing wage rates. Sociologically and ethically people feel that "equal work should carry equal wages" that "wages should be commensurated with their effort," that "workers are not exploited", and that no distinction is made on the basis of caste, colour, sex or religion. To satisfy the conditions of equity, fairness and justice, a management should take these factors into consideration.

(x) *Managerial Attitudes*: These have a decisive influence on the wage structure and wage level, since judgement is exercised in many areas of wages and salary administration, including whether the firm should pay below average, average, or above average rates, what job factors should be used to reflect job worth, the weight to be given for performance or length of service, and so forth, both the structure and level of wages are bound to be affected accordingly. These matters require the approval of the top executives. Lester observes. "Top management's desire to maintain or enhance the company's prestige has been a major factor in the wage policy of a number of firms. Desires to improve or maintain morale, to attract high calibre employees, to reduce turnover, and to provide a high living standard for employees as possible also appear to be factors in management's wage-policy decisions."[15]

15. Lester, *Labour Economics.*

Wage Administration Rules

The development of rules of wage administration has to be done after the rate ranges have been determined. Rules have to be developed to determine to what degree advancement will be based on length of service rather than on merit; with what frequency pay increases will be awarded; how controls over wage and salary costs can be maintained; what rules will govern promotion from one pay grade to another, etc.

At the next stage, the employees are to be informed of the details of wage and salary programme. Although most hourly-paid workers are informed through the wages contract about the details of wage programme, a substantially smaller number of salaried employees have such information about their jobs. It is considered advisable, in the interest of the concern and the employees, that the information about average salaries and ranges in the salaries of group are made known to the employees concerned; for secrecy in this matter may create dissatisfaction; and it may also vitiate the potential motivating effects of disclosure.

Finally, the employee is appraised and the wage fixed for the grade he is found fit.

Employees Benefits

Introduction

Management is concerned with attracting and keeping employees, whose performance meets at least minimum levels of acceptability; and at keeping "absenteeism" and "turnover" to tolerable levels. The provision of "benefits" and "services" can be and are important in maintaining the employees and reducing or keeping turnover and absenteeism low.

It is important to note that "financial" incentives are paid to *specific employees* whose work is above standard. "Employees' benefits and services," on the other hand, are available to *all employees* based on their membership in the organisation. The purpose of such benefits and services is to retain people in the organisation and not to stimulate them to greater effort and higher performance. They foster loyalty and act as a security base for the worker.

On the basis of their identification, however, benefits may be classified as under;

(a) *Employee Security Payments:* (i) Employer's contributions stipulated in legal enactments; old age, survivor, disability, health and unemployment insurance; (ii) payments under the Workmen's Compensation Act; (iii) Supplemental unemployment benefits; (iv) Accident Insurance; (v) Pensions; and (vi) Contributions to savings plans and health and welfare funds.

(b) *Payment for Time not Worked*: Under these are included call-back and call-in pay; clean-up time; health-in-the-family leave; family allowance; holiday pay; lay-off pay; medical time; paid lunch periods; portal-to-portal time; pay for religious holidays; reporting pay; pay for rest periods; severance pay; paid sick leave; payment for time spent on collective bargaining and on the redressal of grievances; vacation pay; pay for the time spent in offering evidence in a court of law or other statutory bodies; and payment for the time spent on casting one's vote at election time.

(c) *Rest Period:* Among office jobs and those jobs requiring heavy exertion, high repetition, or diligent concentration, certain "breaks" popularly known as a *Rest Period* or a *Coffee break* are allowed during the day to allow the worker to rest. The idea is to allow the worker some mental and physical diversion from his job.

(d) *Holidays*: Certain days in the year are stipulated as paid holidays, in Western countries like the USA, the USSR and the U.K. Christmas, New Year, Thanks-giving, Labour days are particularly included, for which the employees are paid and do not have to work. In India, Independence Day, Republic Day, Gandhi Jayanti, Deepavali, Dasshera, Holi, Id. Christmas, Gurunanak Jayanti, Mahaveer Jayanti are gazetted holidays.

(e) *Vacations:* Paid vacations vary from 15 days to 1 month in a year. These are given to the employees after he has put in a specified period of time. The rationale behind paid vacation is to provide a break in which the employee can refresh himself.

(f) *Sick Leave* provides an employee pay when he is out of work due to illness. Full pay for a specified number of "permissible sick days are granted to the employee.

(g) *Severance Pay*: This provides a non-time payment when employees's service is terminated. This is done on humanitarian grounds.

(h) *Leave of Absence*: This covers leave of absence for which pay is provided. *Educational Leave* is given to managers or management-trainees during the training period.

(i) *Pension Programmes*: A Pension represents a fixed payment, made regularly to a former employee or his surviving dependants, provided an employee has fulfilled specific conditions of employment for a specific length of time.

(j) *Insurance*, which may be life, health and accident. It may be individual or group.

(k) *Bonus and Awards*: These consist of such financial amenities and advantages as holiday, overtime and shift premiums; attendance bonus; Diwali bonus; bonus for good quality workmanship; safety awards; profit-sharing bonus and service bonus; suggestion awards; waste elimination bonus; and year-end bonus.

CHAPTER 11

MARKETING POLICIES

- **Introduction**
- **Product Policies**
- **Service Policies**
- **Distribution Policies**
- **Pricing Policies**
- **Promotional Policies**

INTRODUCTION

In the 20th century, the role of marketing in the success of a business cannot be underestimated. In this context, Peter Drucker remarks: "If we want to know what a business is, we have to start with its purpose. And its purpose must lie outside the business itself, it must lie in society since a business enterprise is an organ of society. There is one valid definition of business purpose: To create a customer'.[1]

Essentially, the "creation" of customers involves the identification of their needs, and the finding of ways and means to satisfy them through the optimisation of corporate goals. This can be effectively brought about if the organisation designs, implements and adheres to sound sales policies. A sales policy is a systematic process of developing, co-ordinating, monitoring the various decisions that have a direct bearing on the company's sales. The objective of such policies is to furnish effective guidelines for corporate efforts to optimise customer satisfaction, besides stimulating the company's profitability and competitive strength.

A manufacturing firm needs to design sales policies relating to:

(i) The products to be offered for sales, i.e., Product Policies;
(ii) The categories of customers to whom the products will be sold, i.e., Distribution Policies.
(iii) The prices at which the products will be sold, i.e., Pricing Policies; and
(iv) The promotional methods utilised for the sale of products, i.e., Promotional Policies.

The various sales policies are closely related. For example, if a producer of men's ready-to-wear clothes intends to add women's ready-to-wear clothes to his product line, he will have to design those garments which are definitely superior to the competitor's brands (Product Policy); to go in for competitive prices (Pricing Policy); and, finally, to popularise the products (Promotional Policy).

The interdependence of a sales policy constrains a management to make a systematic and logical analysis of the various issues involved in it.

Formulation of Sales Policy

Among the various organisations, there is considerable variation in the formulation of sales policies. In some enterprises, policies are laid down by the top management, while in others they are referred to the chief marketing executive. However, they require the final approval of the top management. In most enterprises, sales policies are formulated by a group of marketing executives.

A predetermined sales policy avoids differences and ill-will and prevents annoyance and indecision on the part of the executives who have to control these activities. The complications which may arise out of a haphazard, indeterminate or fortuitous manner of doing business do not develop, and the road to progress is kept clear of these unnecessary pitfalls and hindrances. Once a policy is determined, and as long as it is in existence, it should always be given the force of a law. In practice, the value of sound business is comparable to the value of good laws in guiding the administration of a government. In the formulation of marketing policies, the opinion of one man should not be considered as final. The consequences of policies are far too important to any arbitrary or careless formulation.

1. Drucker, Peter F., *The Practice of Management*, Harper and Row, New York, 1954, p. 37.

Like good laws, sound policies are developed as a result of the application of experience and thought. It is not always possible to lay down the right policy immediately after the commencement of a business. But the best thought and experience available should no doubt be given on the formulation of the policies to be followed; thereafter, as further experience calls for modifications, these should be given proper consideration, and the desired changes made in the existing policies.

Product Policy Decisions

Over $ 20 billion are spent annually by the United States' industry on technological research and the development of new product.[2] The expenditure of this huge magnitude underscores the importance of product policy decisions to a business. Product policy decisions in today's business world have become the focal point round which a firm's marketing philosophy revolves, because they govern marketing decisions relating to prices, promotion and distribution which, to a considerable extent, project the corporate image.

The impact of product decisions affects not only the company's marketing activities but also such major corporate levels and functions as R & D, resource allocation and long-range planning. From the point of view of marketing the firm's competitive strength in the market place largely flows from its effective product policy decisions coupled with other elements of the marketing programme and its overall corporate strategy.

The quality of the prevention of the risk of product failure, the history of marketing reveals glaring examples of the failure of a majority of new products because of lack of marketing insight. It has been noted that a large number of products abort in the process of development – even before they are put on the market.

The pace of S & T changes does not permit any effective alternative to product planning and development. In fact, it tends to intensify the uncertainty. Its effects have well been summarised by Weston: "The manifestation of increased technological changes are: higher rates at which older products have been obsoleted; the shorter life of individual product cycle; the increased rise of product substitution; and of attractive growth potentials in the new and diverse sections of the economy."[3]

In an era of cut-throat competition, companies are making strenuous efforts to innovate, modify or even to abandon existing products with a view to capturing a larger market share; those which fail to do so find a burial site near yester-year's barrel-markers. Products bring social and economic wealth to the nation; but there is the negative side of its social importance—for instance, a product that pollutes the environment, or is not safe to use, or is of a spurious quality, poor design, impairs the reputation of the manufacturer.

As this chapter is devoted to the study of product planning, it would be desirable to know what a product is. In the words of Stanton, "a product is a complex of tangible and intangible attributes, including packaging, colour, price, manufacturer's prestige, retailer's prestige, and manufacturer's and retailer's services which a buyer may accept as offering satisfaction of wants or needs."[4]

2. "R & D: Still a Growth Industry", National Conference Board Record, May 1970, pp. 38-40.
3. Weston, J.F., *New Technologies: Competition and Anti-Trust*, National Conference Board, New York, 1970, p. 9.
4. Stanton, J.W., *Fundamentals of Marketing*, 1983, p. 161.

PRODUCT POLICIES

"Product is a bundle of utilities consisting of various product features and accompanying services."[5] The bundle of utilities consists of those physical and psychological satisfaction which the buyer receives when he buys the product which the seller provides by selling a particular combination of product features and associated services. For example, when the manufacturer produces a toothpaste, the consumer expects from it whiter and cleaner teeth, pleasant taste, fewer cavities, stronger gums, sweet-smelling breath and sex appeal. It is in the hope of receiving a real or an imaginary benefit that the consumer really buys a product, and not because it is something in itself.

Product Policies — Nature and Types

Product policies tend to focus on two objectives :

(i) Whether product planning decisions tend to facilitate goal attainment;

(ii) What types of decisions should be avoided, which are not in harmony with organisational goals.

A product policy tends to achieve one or more objectives. However, here we shall discuss only those policies which are concerned with product management. There are many parameters concerning the achievement of product objectives. Moreover, there is a set of decisions in selecting a consistent policy relative to each of these parameters. Here, we shall discuss six parameter types of policies that are quite often considered by an organisation.

(i) Growth Elements: Product policies are largely designed to cater an environment which facilitates the desired growth. Therefore, while deciding upon product policies, the direction of growth must be clearly spelled out. This may be brought about by properly selecting policies relating to:

(a) Marketing development; and

(b) Product development.

Ansoff[6] has nicely depicted a four-called growth matrix. The four general policy choices shown in Table 11.1 which are open to a firm to guide its growth in a particular direction.

TABLE 11.1
GROWTH VICTOR COMPONENTS RELATIVE TO DEGREE OF INNOVATION

	(1) *Present*	*(2)* *New*
(A) Present	Penetrate current market for high rate of usage	Develop approved or new products to serve present markets
(B) New	Develop market and usage for present product	Diversify into new products to service new markets

Product policy A-1 seems to be conservative in contrast to Product policy B-2, which seems to be quite radical. Wider gradation than the present and a new dichotomy would be required in

5. Alderson, W., *Marketing Behaviour and Executive Action*, 1957, p. 214.
6. Ansoff, H.I., "A Model for Diversification", in *Management Science*, July 1958, p. 394.

a growth-oriented product policy.[7] While formulating a product policy, due consideration must be given to environmental factors, for these have a profound influence on product growth or failure.

(ii) Risk and Return on Investment: While designing product policies, organisations must have a clear perception of the risk that is likely to occur when a product is launched. Moreover, it should provide for a fair rate of return on investment. Generally speaking, there is an inverse relationship between these two objectives. For instance, if a company goes in for a low risk, the return is bound to be low. However, it can manage to earn a high rate of return through minimising risk, and this can be effectively brought about by carefully designing the product line which can best suit the different market segments.

(iii) Revenue and Profit: Specific policies pertaining to sales and other financial aspects are required, besides the often talked-about polices of the rate of return. The policies which fall in this category are:

(a) The desired level of profit as a percentage of the sales volume tends to maintain the desired company-wise average;
(b) The minimum sales level policy to be adopted for assessing the fate of the product line;
(c) The minimum market share policy to be adopted to keep the business on its toes.

(iv) Differential Benefits: An effective product policy provides a firm with some unique advantages over its competitors. Some of these advantages are:

(a) Technological superiority;
(b) Product/brand image;
(c) Location of monopoly;
(d) Market franchise;
(e) Market places in the distribution network; and
(f) Aggressive sales force.

If a firm lacks the ability to compete with its rivals, restrictive policies should be adopted to avoid them.

(v) Width and Depth of Product Line: A variety of products can be produced in a variety of shapes, sizes, designs, colours and a variety of materials. These factors determine the possible demand for a product or products. If a company produces a few varieties, their prices can be maintained at a low level. But if the number of varieties is large and no effective sales forecast is made, the products may be sold at higher prices.

(iv) Service: A firm's policy relating to the type of services it extends to its buyers is a determinant in the selection of the channel of distribution. It also depends upon the type of product sold–e.g., a consumer durable of hihh value needs more after-sales service. A wide variety of services can be considered in such contexts as (1) Warranty or guarantees; (2) Maintenance and repairs; (3) Application assistance (4) Returned goods; (5) Adherence to sound service, to boost the company's image.

Product Mix Strategy

Most companies–whether large or small, whether in manufacturing or retailing—generally handle a variety of products. In the course of time, they may expand new lines or contract old lines, alter an existing product or develop new uses for the existing products. These activities involve managerial strategies and policy-making with respect to the company's line of products and services.

7. Kotler, P., *Marketing Management*, 1972, p. 439.

The proliferation of products within a company indicates that product policy decisions are made at three different levels of product aggregation, viz., product item, product line and product mix.

(a) Product item is a specific version of a product that has a separate designation in the seller's list.[8] For example, Hindustan Motor's Ambassador Mark II is a product item.

(b) Product lines — A group of products that are closely related either because they satisfy a particular need or are used together, are sold to the same customer group, are marketed through the same types of outlets, or fall within the given price ranges, or are considered a unit because of marketing, technical, or end-use considerations.[9] In other words, a broad group of products which are meant essentially for similar uses and possess reasonably similar physical characteristics constitute a product line. For example, Kodak cameras or wearing apparel is a product line; non-food product lines for babies including baby clothes, nursery equipment, vaporizers and toiletries.

(c) Product mix: The product offered for sale by a firm or a business unit are known as a product mix. In other words, a product mix is a full list of all the products offered for sale by a company. For example, Kodak's cameras, photographic supplies, chemicals, plastics and fibres are its product mix; Tata's hair oil, cosmetics, locomotives, textiles, iron and steel goods, Mercedes, Benz trucks, etc., are its product mix.

Structure of Product Mix

The structure of a product mix has dimensions of both "width" and "depth".

By the "width of the product mix" is meant the number of different product lines dealt in by the company. In other words, *breadth* is measured by the number of product lines carried by it. For example, Bajaj Electricals produce bulbs, fluorescent lamps, mixers and grinders, toasters, pressure cookers and a host of other electrical appliances.

The phrase "depth of the product mix" refers to the average number of items offered by a company within each product line. In other words, depth is measured by the assortment of sizes, colours, models, prices and quality offered within each product line.

The phrase "consistency of product mix" refers to how closely related the various product lines are in terms of consumer behaviour, production requirements, distribution channels, or in some other way. For example, the product produced by the General Electricity Company have an overall consistency in that most products involve the use of electricity in one way or the other.

TABLE 11.2
PRODUCT MIX

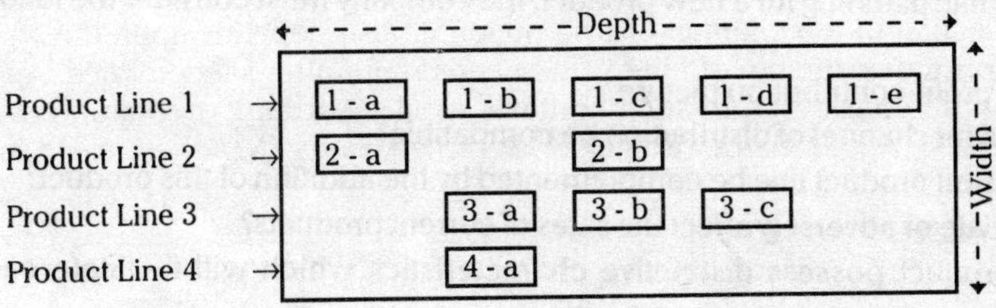

Product Mix Items = 12
Number of Lines = 4
Average Depth = 3

8. *Ibid*, 1976, p. 185.
9. Holmes, P.M. and Bartel, R. (ed)., *Readings in Marketing*, Charles E. Merill Book Inc., Colombus, Ohio, 1963, pp. 316-319.

In this connection, Kotler observes: "All the three dimensions of a product mix have a market rationale. Through increasing the width of the product mix, the company hopes to capitalise on its good reputation and skills in present markets. Through increasing the depth of its product mix, the company hopes to entice the patronage of buyers of widely differing tastes and needs. Through increasing the consistency of its product mix, the company hopes to acquire an unparalleled reputation in a particular area of endeavour."

The dimensions of the product mix and the ways in which they relate to each other are important for marketing management. Changing the product items involves such discussion as whether to modify or add or drop product items. Changing the width of the product mix involves altering the policy at the product-line level-whether to deepen or shorten an existing product line. Changing the product mix involves such issues as what markets the marketer should enter or leave, and how to handle competition to the various product lines or items.

Major Product-Line Strategies

In order to survive, organisations develop and grow in a hostile marketing environment, and deploy several strategies bearing on the width, depth and consistency of the product mix. Most of these strategies involve a change in the structure of the product mix. The major product line strategies may be identified as under:

(i) New product development strategy.
(ii) Product-line modification strategy.
(iii) Product-line contraction strategy.
(iv) Product-line diversification strategy.
(v) Product segmentation and market differentiation strategy.
(vi) Product design strategy.
(vii) Branding and allied strategies.

New Product Development Strategy

Any product that a customer considers in addition to the existing product may be considered a new product. It includes a modified product, duplication of the competitor's product, product acquisition or discovery of an original product. Of all product policy decisions, those bearing on new product policy are quite crucial for any manufacturer, for they involve a variety of sub-decisions affecting the various departments of the organisation, and involving heavy investment and risk. Therefore, while planning for a new product, the company must consider the following questions:

(a) What is the profit-contribution picture?
(b) Will the present channel of distribution be compatible?
(c) Will the present product line be complemented by the addition of this product?
(d) Will it stimulate or adversely affect the sales of current products?
(e) Does the product possess distinctive characteristics which will facilitate ease of promotion?
(f) What is the expected life cycle of the product?
(g) What is the size of the potential market for this product?
(h) Will it be affected by cyclical or seasonal variations?
(i) Can it be produced by using existing plant facilities?[10]

10. Pessemier, E.A., "New Product Ventures", *in Business Horizons*, August, 1968, pp. 7-8.

New Products Planning Process

New Product Objectives: Before developing a new product, product objectives should be determined. Since it is the market which accepts or rejects the product, product objectives serve as guidelines for product innovation. A firm's product objectives are usually oriented toward the satisfaction of the customer's needs; and as the market or its needs change, the company adjusts its products accordingly. The other product objective is to state the firm's philosophy with regard to the desired degree of product leadership. Other product objectives are derived from each major company objective, whose attainment depends upon the product line in some way. All product objectives must be consistent with the other components of marketing strategy, such as company objectives of marketing channels and distribution, promotion and price. When either the company objective or marketing strategy changes, product objectives should be reappraised for their continued suitability and, if necessary, revised.

The Planning Process: New product planning process consists of the creation of new ideas, their evaluation in terms of sales potential and profitability, production facilities, resources available, designing and production testing, and the marketing of the product. The main task of product planners is to identify specific customer needs and expectations, and align the growth possibilities of the company with the changing market demands. In each of these stages, the management decides whether:

(a) To move on to the next stage;
(b) To abandon the product; or
(c) To seek additional information.[11]

Product planning is the function of the top management personnel and specialists drawn from various functional areas. This group considers and plans for new and improved products in different phases such as:

(a) Idea Formulation.
(b) Evaluation or Screening of Ideas
(c) Business Analysis
(d) Test Marketing
(e) Commercialisation or Market Introduction.

(a) Idea Formulation: In the beginning of a successful product is a creative idea. For the generation of new ideas, knowledge of the unfulfilled needs of the consumers, their attitudes, the attributes that may be required in a product to be of use to the customer, and some useful information relating to it have to be gathered. This step starts with a sound need-oriented analysis and assessment of market opportunities and company resources. For this purpose, a careful inventory of the company's resources along the lines given below has to be made. Every company is unique as a result of its history, experience and personnel; it has certain strengths and weaknesses which distinguish it from other organisations.

The ideas for new product generation may come from the company's own research and development studies, from its technicians, scientists, from the management's judgement, from the company's salesmen, employees, consumers and industrial users and middlemen, from its suppliers of raw materials, its competitors and their products from governmental agencies, trade associations, etc. Consumer's complaints or dissatisfactions can also be a source of new

11. The term "characteristics" refers to such attributes as design, style, colour, size, weight, method of operation, guarantees and servicing. The management determines product characteristics in the light of three product objectives: (i) providing target consumers with particular benefits; (ii) emphasising areas of strength; and (iii) fulfilling social responsibilities. Peterson, Robin: *Marketing: A Contemporary Introduction*, 1977, p. 252.

ideas. As a matter of fact, consumers are said to be one of the best sources of new ideas. In this connection, Cannon and Wicher observe: : "A meat-packer began producing onion soup at the suggestion of a company executive's wife. A pottery manufacturer produced a new vase after viewing a museum exhibit. Whatever may be the source of an idea, it must be in conformity with corporate goals and customer's needs."

(b) Evaluation or Screening of Ideas: This involves the evaluation of the company's capabilities and its technical know-how in terms of possible new product development and product improvements. The basic idea is to find out whether and which ideas warrant further study. The screening should be rigorous enough to eliminate poor stuff, but not so rigorous as to eliminate potentially good possibilities. A list of information required in evaluating new product possibilities should be drawn up in such a way as to throw some light on profit possibilities, and on the risk and cost of capital involved in it.

The various departments of the firm must screen ideas by making a thorough investigation into various questions, such as whether the new product is to be produced or not; and if it is to be produced in what quantities; what facilities are available within the plant to produce this quantity; what new plant/machinery would be needed; whether packaging materials is available and, if so, of what size and shape the packages should be; through which marketing channels it should be promoted. After these questions have been considered, the profitability of the product should be evaluated.

(c) Business Analysis: At this stage, new product ideas are carefully evaluated for their economic worth. Estimates of sales, costs and profits are important components of any business analysis, and forecasts of market penetration and market potential are essential. More precise estimates of the environmental and competitive changes that may influence the product's life cycle or its replacement or repeat sales are also required to develop and launch a product. A complete cost appraisal (both manufacturing and marketing costs) is necessary besides the evaluation of the profitability of the project.

While making a business analysis, the following questions may be posed:

- Is the company capable of developing and producing a product idea?
- How quickly can new facilities for producing a new product be built up?
- Does the product fit in with the company's existing "product mix" and "product lines"?
- Is the necessary finance available on terms consistent with a favourable return on investment?

At this stage, the "idea on paper" should be converted into a "working model", i.e., a physical product. It should be converted into an exact prototype that should reveal the tangible and intangible attributes associated with the product in the consumer's mind. "Pilot models" or small quantities of the product are manufactured in accordance with specifications and characteristics. Laboratory tests and other technical evaluations necessary to determine the engineering and production feasibility of the article are made. Steps are taken to review copyrights, preliminary advertising copy, packaging and labelling to determine legal ramifications, and to plan personal selling and distribution to ensure an effective integration of all elements of the marketing mix. Marketing research is also conducted to ascertain the potential sales level for the prospective product. Market research makes and facilitates the establishment of the production volume, cost, quality, goals, and hence the scheduling of men, materials and machines.

(d) Test Marketing: Often, intertwined with the process of product development is the process of "product testing". In a broad, sense, this involves not only an internal laboratory testing of the proposal, production in terms of characteristics and pilot testing of production

processes but also consumer (or mini-market) testing in which the product is tested under conditions existing in the field.[12]

Test Marketing is generally done by consumer goods companies rather than by industrial goods firms which usually try out new products with selected customers or obtain general reactions by having their sales people demonstrate products when they make their rounds.

Test marketing helps marketers in the following ways:

(i) It provides an opportunity for examination of a product in a natural marketing environment to obtain a measure of its sales performance.

(ii) While the product is being marketed in a limited area, it is possible to identify the weaknesses of the product in the overall marketing plan.

(iii) It helps the management to develop a profile of potential customers and their purchasing habits.

(iv) It enables marketers to evaluate alternative marketing strategies, if need be.

(v) It offers an opportunity for measurement of consumer reactions to the test product and competing products.

(e) Commercialisation or Market Introduction: This stage involves the launching of the product with a full-scale marketing programme. This introduction should be guided by a complete marketing plan which establishes sales, share-of-market, and profit goals for the introductory campaign; map out the strategic and tactical approaches which are to be made to reach these goals; and provide for the yardsticks by which the results of the introductory programme may be measured and corrective action taken, if necessary. The channels of distribution must be filled with the product, and all the selling agencies should be fully informed about the new product, the planned marketing programme and their role in it.

While launching a product in the market, the market has to make a choice of two alternatives:

(i) Whether to launch the product in a selected market or to approach the entire market;

(ii) Whether to place the product market-by-market (known as roll-out) or to get an immediate entry in the State or national market.

Though every new product through all the stages, a majority of them are discarded or abandoned in the early evolutionary process.

A Study by Boor, Allen and Hamilton has revealed that two out of forty originating ideas survive to the point of commercialisation. The delay in the survival of new product ideas at different stages has been depicted in Fig. 11.1.

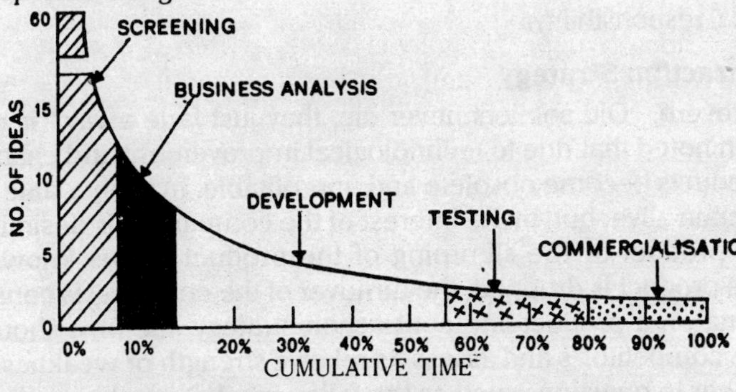

Fig. 11.1: Morality of New Product Ideas

Source: Boor, Allen and Hamilton Inc., *Management of New Product*, p. 9.

12. Leighton, D.S.R., *International Marketing: Text and Cases*, McGraw-Hill, New York, 1966, p. 190.

Alder noted that the time which elapsed between the date of conception and the date of commercialisation was one year per product like, for example, Coldene cold tablets and as long as thirty years in the case of a product like Talon Zippers.[13]

Product-Line Modification Strategy

Product-line modifications generally involve changes in products or their respositioning by the enhancement of the promotional focus. The changes in product often furnish superior product satisfaction, thereby generating high initial buying and greater switching from existing brands. Product-line modifications largely aim at customers retention, customer satisfaction and improving the company's competitive strength, which invariably increases sales by stimulating demand through an increased purchase rate. It may be brought about by:

(a) Functional changes
(b) Quality changes
(c) Style changes
(d) Environmental impact changes.

(a) Functional Changes: These include redesigning of products functionally or by the addition of new features to products. If functional features are distinct and demonstrable, they enhance product image and gratify the unmet and at times unidentified needs of customers. They also facilitate the functioning of the sales force and of the dealers in the market place. The redesigning of sanitary napkins to tampons is an instance of how a functional change may be more beneficial or convenient to buyers.

(b) Quality Changes: The buyers get more durable products through changes in design and material. These changes aim at enticing various categories of customers. At times, it is found desirable to upgrade the quality of products to cater to those segments of the market which crave for goods of superior quality. Contrary to these, in some cases, product quality is required to be downgraded with a view to capturing more profitable market segments which demand goods at lower prices.

(c) Style Changes: The style improvement aims to enhance the aesthetic appearance of a product. It may include changes in label and packaging. These changes indicate at times a unique brand identification.

(d) Environmental Impact Changes: In some cases, manufacturers have to modify their products or product lines in obedience to pressure from the government, competitors or its commitment to social responsibility.

Product-Line Contraction Strategy

The ancient proverb, "Old soldiers never die, they just fade away," is equally true of old products. It has been noted that due to technological improvement and changes in customer's tastes over time, products become obsolete and unprofitable. In such a state of affairs, it is true that products do remain alive: but, in the interest of the company, it is desirable to drop them.[14] This dropping of a product or the slimming of the product line is known as product-line contraction. When a product is dropped, the turnover of the company is considerably affected. So, before embarking on a product-line contraction strategy, the firm should compare each item with that of the competitor's and assess its relative strength or weaknesses. Specifically, it should seek an answer to questions such as the following: Why is the product used? Where is

13. Alder, Lee, "Time Lag in New Product Development" in *Journal of Marketing*, January 1966, pp. 18-21.
14. Alexander, *Journal of Marketing*, April 1964, p. 2.

it used? When is it used? The answers to these questions will help the firm in not only designing an effective product-line contraction strategy, but in helping it to assess its overall market position.

If a product is not profitable, it should be dropped. However, before dropping it, due consideration must be given to such factors as low prices and efficient promotional programme to increase its profit performance. There are certain products such as spare parts, which, by nature, are profitable but cannot be dropped because they cater to the needs of the buyers who have already purchased the firm's goods. Moreover, markets are heterogenous, and each segment has its own features. Many firms find it desirable even to continue unprofitable products to promote the sale of established profitable products. As a rule, however, though subject to certain desirable expectations, unprofitable products should be dropped. A product should be dropped it if causes the sales force to divert its attention from profitable products. The products with a slow turnover should be dropped if middlemen lay stress on fast-moving products. Last but not the least, any product which does not fit logically into the basic line should be eliminated. According to Stanley Richard and Thomas,[15] product be dropped under the following conditions:

(a) Declining absolute sales volume.
(b) Sales volume decreasing as a percentage of the firm's total sales.
(c) Decreasing market share.
(d) Past sales volume not upto expectations.
(e) Expected future sales disappointing.
(f) Future market potential for products or services not favourable.
(g) Return on investment below the minimally accepted level.
(h) Variable costs exceed revenues.
(i) Variable costs as a percentage of sales consistently increasing.
(j) Increasingly greater percentage of executive time required.
(k) Consistent need to lower prices to maintain sales.
(l) Consistent need to increase promotional budget to maintain sales.

While deciding on product-line contraction, adequate attention must be given to the following facts:

- The product should not be dropped abruptly because certain products require service and replacement. So if a firm stops producing spare parts, the intermediaries may shift to competing brands which will not only grab the firm's market, but will tarnish its image in the eyes of its customers.
- When a firm drops a product, it does not abandon the market. Therefore, a successor product must be made available well in time to maintain its market share.
- Timely information on product abandonment must be given to distributors, so that they may modify or design their marketing strategy for the sale of the new products.
- When the successor product is marketed, dealers must be given additional price concession to meet any loss incurred on the sale of old products.
- Adequate appraisal of the product line should be made so that the opportune time of product abandonment may be identified.

Product-Line Diversification Strategy

The growth objectives of a firm are quite restricted when the established product lines crosses its growth limit. These objectives are further depressed when the company faces

15. Kratchman, S.H., Richard, T.H. and Thomas U., "Management Decision to Discontinue a Product." in *Journal of Accountancy*, 1975, p. 53.

problems in maintaining its market share or is on the verge of dying. In such circumstances, its future can be safeguarded, if adequate and timely decisions are taken on the diversification of the product line. The product-line diversification takes place when the company seeks to enter new market segments with a completely different product or products. Generally speaking, product-line diversification policies aim at exploring new avenues of growth opportunities, sales stability and higher profitability. However, the firm's object in this context varies considerably. Some firms diversify to survive; others to grow and prosper; and yet others to reduce their costs. In the present case, when competition is very intense, "diversify or die" becomes the need of the hour for the marketers. Marketers have identified five ways of diversification. These are:

Synergestic Diversification

In synergestic diversification, new products are marketed. When the resources for manufacturing and marketing are highly compatible with the existing resources of the firm, the synergies sport from commonalities in the production process R & D facilities, sales-force competence, and distribution network. The Bush Company, by resorting to synergestic diversification, has profitably expanded its market for a wide variety of its products, such as radios, transistors, two-in-one, three-in-one recorders, TV (coloured and black and white) and videos.

Conglomerate Diversification

Such diversification is designed to take advantage of growth opportunities without bothering about any synergestic effect. Under such a diversification programme, although financial considerations are dominant, product consideration does play a vital role.

Product-Line Extension

Product-line extension policies aim at reaching those market segments which the firm has not yet penetrated. Product-line extension may be valid if it is an area in which the consumers enjoy a wide variety of brands to choose from and are accustomed to switch over from one to another, or if the competitors lack a comparable product or if they have themselves expanded into these areas. The Bakeman, the well-known biscuit producers, have extended their product line by adding bread, cake and confectionery to their existing line. Similarly, VIP, a leading producer of banians and briefs, has added socks and panties to its product line. Extension in the present product mix may be done by increasing the number of lines and/or the depth within a line. Such new lines may be related or unrelated to the present products. For example, a large provision stores may add drugs, cosmetics and housewares (width), while at the same time, increasing its assortments of dry fruits, baby foods, detergents (depth), etc.

Product Proliferation

Proliferation is a limited form of diversification. It involves the development of new varieties of an initial product or of take-offs that are similar to that product (not being a new product). When the manufacturer of biscuits adds a new flavour, such as orange or pineapple, there is a product proliferation, for there is nothing new to be mastered or risked.

New-Field Entry

It involves the entry of a firm in those categories of products which are new to it. In this type of diversification, the firm starts producing those goods which are quite unrelated to its product line. For instance, a confectionary firm may diversify its product line by producing frozen foods or soaps, etc. The Bakemans, well-known biscuit manufacturers, have profitably expanded their export market by diversifying into soap and detergents. Similarly, the Reliance Group, besides producing textiles, caters to the needs of the chemicals market.

A firm may resort to more than one type of diversification at a time. For instance, a paint manufacturer may, for a long-range product, think of entering the market for Sunmica; for an intermediate range, it can go in for paints that are pollution-resistant. On a short-term basis, it may diversify into the production of bright and sophisticated looking paints which bear more a bright and pleasing look.

Occasionally, there are some specific reasons for resorting to diversification. For instance, textile industries producing sarees may find it desirable to bring out sarees of different types to cater to the needs of different classes of buyers. Lakme, by diversifying, has profitably extended its export cosmetic market.

Factors Governing Diversification

The company's diversification programme is related to a variety of factors which, collectively and individually, determine its extent and nature. One of the important factors is the customer himself. In some lines, a customer prefers to buy a variety of products from one source. For instance, a dealer in sanitaryware must supply a variety of sanitaryware to cater to the specific needs of customers. But if the manufacturer provides only a few products, the dealer may refuse to stock them and will definitely shift to those producers who supply a wide product range. Likewise, dealers and retailers in most cases buy the entire product line from one manufacturer. This is understandable because they want to deal with one manufacturer to enjoy the benefit of the company's promotional performance in terms of trade.

In same cases, product line diversification becomes essential in order to ensure that customers do not establish relations with other vendors. Thus, a tube manufacturer may find it desirable to make tyres as well. Otherwise, customers will prefer to deal with those manufacturers producing both tubes and tyres. In many cases, it is always profitable to market more than one product in order to counter the effects of seasonal or cyclical fluctuations. For instance, a woollen clothing manufacturer may find it desirable to enter the market of ready-to-wear clothing.

Some firms diversify to spread their risks. A highly successful textile manufacturing firm, to avoid excessive competition, may enter the business of chemicals and dyes. In any diversification programme, however, the pressing problem is to determine the variety of items that are to be added to the product line. Salesmen quite often feel that their sales volume will increase substantially with the addition of a number of products in a line. Also, a marketing executive considers diversification as an important tool for increasing the company's market share and competitive strength. Quite often, it has been noted that companies yield to the pressure of their marketing men and start selling new products. In the initial stages, sales show a profitable growth, but later on they begin to decline. This is mainly because in the early stages, due to the enthusiasm of salesmen to sell the product, the retailers' tendency to try out new products and also consumer curiosity about them increase the sale; but subsequent sales may decrease if the product fails to satisfy the needs of consumers. So before embarking on any diversification programme, the company should make an intensive market research and then design its sales forecast.

Impact of Diversification on a Firm

All the M's of Management (i.e., Men, machine, material, money and methods) are affected by a diversification programme. The company should therefore designs its various policies and procedures after carefully weighting the advantages and disadvantages of diversification. The ways in which diversification may influence the sales of a company's products have been discussed in the following paragraphs.

(a) More often than not, a salesman cannot effectively handle the entire product line. If he is asked to sell a variety of items, he tends to focus on those items which are fast-moving and relatively costly rather than on those that enjoy the customer's patronage. This will result in the neglect of uneconomical products. For instance, if a biscuit manufacturing firm adds new varieties of spicy biscuits at a low price, there is every likelihood that salesmen would neglect this line because of its newness to the market.

(b) Usually, firms cannot efficiently produce a wide range of products at the same time. For instance, manufacturers of high-quality machinery find it difficult to take up the production of spare parts. Similarly, mills producing superfine cloth may find it difficult to venture into the production of cheaper varieties, because the manufacture of these varieties would necessitate the setting up of an altogether different production system and quality-check procedure. Obviously, a roadside hotel cannot be converted into a five-star.

(c) Another danger of diversification is that the ability of the management to direct and control the activities related to the sale of a large number of products is quite restricted. For instance, if a textile manufacturer enters the field of chemicals and drugs, the marketing executive will find it difficult to manage the sale of products which are entirely new to him; and this fact may force him to divert his attention from the existing product to newer products, which may, at times, prove quite harmful to the company.

(d) A critical factor governing diversification is the availability of company resources (both human and non-human) for the production of new products. If new products are to be produced, the company will have to incur additional expenditure on adequate technology, raw materials and expertise, etc. Moreover, it will require salesmen to focus their attention on newer products which at times may result in the diversion of their interest from profitable to non-profitable lines. And if, inspite of concentrating on the new product, the salesmen fail, the company's financial health will be in jeopardy.

(e) The production of a wide variety of products has a marked effect upon the cost structure of the company. It calls for the installation of plant, machinery, procurement of tools, spare parts, etc. Unless the new product achieves a higher sales volume, it will unduly inflate the per unit cost of production, as a result of which the objective of diversification will be defeated.

Many factors have to be considered while deciding upon diversification or specialisation. While venturing into a new product line, the existing situation in the company and the market environment at any given time may exhibit so many variations that it may not be possible for it to reach the best decision. It has been noted that a large number of companies have suffered as a result of diversification, whereas others have reaped benefits.

Product Differentiation and Market Segmentation

In order to survive in a competitive and hostile market environment, the firm must make its products distinctive from those of its competitors. The design, package, promotional appeal and service can be profitably utilised to achieve product differentiation. The differentiation strategy is suitable if the brand is quite popular and can be continued in the market through effective promotion. While deciding on product differentiation, emphasis must be placed on the following two factors:

(a) Quality of Product: The quality of a product is an important consideration for the customer when making a purchasing decision. There is no precise definition of quality, for it varies with the product and the customer who buys the product. Even with the same individual it often carries different meanings at different times. While purchasing a kitchen appliance, an

individual's concept of quality may be based on its "durability". For luxury goods, their outward appearance is important, whereas for eatables purity, taste and nutritive value count more than anything else. For industrial goods, the term quality may count uniformity and high operating efficiency. A product differentiation strategy may therefore be designed to optimise customer satisfaction.

(b) Style of Product: The change in product style is another way of achieving product differentiation. Most firms restyle their products when there is a shift in fashion or when the existing product becomes outdated. The policy of a company in regard to style must be in conformity with the needs and desires of customers. For instance, when a furniture manufacturer goes in for product differentiation, he must decide whether he will manufacture furniture of modern style or will just follow a conservative style.

When embarking upon product differentiation, a firm must bear in mind the fact that customers have a variety of tastes which are subject to change with changes in fashion and that, therefore, style change should be adopted only after proper market research; otherwise the company will have to incur heavy losses. To a considerable extent, a product differentiation policy is closely related to market segmentation and product design.

Market Segmentation Strategy

The total market for most of the products is not homogeneous but heterogeneous because people have different needs and values. The marketer cannot, therefore, derive the maximum benefit from an analysis of marketing as a whole. For example, there may be a total market for textiles, electrical appliances, refrigerators, etc., but within the total of each of these products, there may actually exist many sub-markets which differ vitally from each other. In the textile market, in one section of the population, there may be a huge demand for cotton cloth; in another for synthetic fibre; in a third for pure silk garments. This diversity may be due to differences in the income of the people, their tastes, buying habits or motives. Further, no two customers are alike in their demand. Therefore, to take advantage of this situation, the marketers may divide the total market into smaller groups of consumers on the basis of the significant differences in buyer characteristics or in buyer responses to marketing programmes. By tailoring product designs, pricing policies, promotion and distribution channels to meet the needs of these small groups, marketers often gain a competitive advantage. This kind of marketing strategy is also consistent with the marketing concept, which requires the identification of consumer wants and needs and the development of marketing programmes to satisfy them.

Degrees of Segmentation

A segmentation of market is generally consistent with the changing needs of the population. Consequently, any one of the following kinds of segmentation may be practised by marketers:

(a) Partial market segmentation where the entire market is divided along broad categorical lines. For example, in the automobile market, one consumer may be looking for a station wagon, or a jeep; another may want to buy a car run on diesel, or a light vehicle, such as a scooter or a Luna cycle. In such situations, some manufacturers market separately to suit each group.

(b) Extreme market segmentation occurs when marketers cater to the specialised needs of selected customers. This type of segmentation occurs specially in luxury goods industries, for example, the tailor makes a dress according to the measurements of the lady concerned, or the hosiery dealer may sell "bras" or "panties," or only ladies' toilet preparations.

(c) Market aggregation is often practised by a company that is production-oriented. Here, the entire market is treated as a single homogenous unit, all parts of which are uniform. In such

segmentation, marketers develop one product and one marketing design to reach as many customers as possible. The company is thus able to maximise its production on a large scale at a low cost, and to make it production economical. Examples of such markets are those for blankets, suiting, refrigerators, radios, cycles, etc.

Market Targeting Strategies or Segmentation Decisions

Marketing segmentation identifies the following strategic option of marketing viz., concentrated marketing, differentiated marketing and undifferentiated marketing. Under the first two strategies, "rifle shots replace shotgun blasts at the market." Very rarely is it possible today for a firm to successfully follow an undifferentiated strategy of one product offered with one marketing mix to the total market.

Concentrated Marketing

It is concerned with "focussing all available resources on one segment within the total market." It is an attempt to match what the firm can do best with a market niche devoid of strong competitors—a strategy of differential advantage. It means one marketing mix, or rather a narrow product line and some unique competence, which is the basis for the firm's competitive advantage in a chosen segment.[16]

Concentrated marketing takes a variety of forms, for example, high fashion boutiques and design-oriented houseware shops. Such marketing has been followed by Ford, Rolls Royce, Ambassador Cars, HMT, Quartz and Rolex Watches and glass manufacturing units. Johnson & Johnson's strategy for infant market (for baby food, baby talcum powder etc.) is a good example of concentrated marketing.

The chief advantage of concentration is that an organisation can become a specialist in the needs of its chosen market segment. This enables it to save costs through large scale production of a few products; and it also tends to have a positive impact on advertising and distribution.

This type of marketing results in a quasi-monopoly position. Highly satisfied customers develop strong loyalties. New products can ensure continued favour in the chosen market niche.

But its main problem is that "it is an all-the-eggs-in-one basket" strategy. Due to changes in preferences, there is a risk of decreasing effectiveness. Further, for one product, a company may concentrate so much on one market segment that it may neglect another that might also prove profitable. Again, if demand slackens suddenly, or if competition seriously begins to adversely affect market share, such a company is likely to suffer more.

Differentiated Marketing

This means to capture the entire market by designing different products and marketing programmes for different segments of the market. In doing so, the marketers hope to achieve additional sales and increased customer identification with the brand or company name. This type of marketing is followed by most medium and large-sized firms doing business in many markets with a broad product line. For example, Golden Tobacco Company in India markets cigarettes under the brand names of Panama, New Deal, Gold Flake, Taj, Sainik, Gaylord, Tajmahal, Square, Target and Diamond, Hindustan Lever Ltd. manufactures and sells toilet soap under different names, such as Lux, Lux Supreme, Lifebuoy, Rexona, Pears, Lyril, etc. Usha Fan Company markets fans under three different names – Usha Prima, Usha Delux and Usha Continental. Lipton and Brooke Bond reach all segments of the market through a large number of brands of tea in various price ranges, and promoted through a variety of appeals. Tatas market their hair oil under Swastik, Jasmine and Coconut.

16. Webster, F.E., *op. cit.*, p. 46.

Such marketing strategy usually involves some differentiation among products and brands as well as in pricing, promotion and distribution. This is often a characteristic of affluent markets, and consumer needs and wants are so precisely defined that a new type of marketing (fragmented marketing) has developed. Under this situation, markets become more and more segmented and sub-divided to such an extent that segments are no longer economically viable.

Undifferentiated Marketing

It treats the entire market as its target by competing successfully with the use of the same marketing mix. Such marketing is resorted to when it is found that there are some products which have a broad-based appeal and that there is, therefore, no need for their segmentation.

Such marketing proves weak in every segment because there is specialised competition in each segment. Coca Cola, Pepsi-Cola, Thums Up, are instances of this type.

Selecting a Strategy

Which of the foregoing three strategies should be selected would depend upon such factors as the competitor's strategies, company strengths and weaknesses, the size of the market and of individual segments, and the availability of distribution channels and promotional media for the implementation of the chosen strategy. While selecting a market segmentation strategy, the following criteria must be given adequate attention:

Identity: The Marketing Manager must have some means of identifying the members of the segment, i.e., some basis for classifying an individual as being or not being a member of the segment. There must be clear differences between segments. Members of such segments can be readily identified by common characteristics which result in similar behaviour.

Accessibility: It must be possible to reach different segments for purposes of both promotion and distribution. In other words, the organisation must be able to focus its marketing efforts on the chosen segment. Segments must be accessible in two senses: *First*, firms must be able to make them aware of their products or services. *Second*, they must get these products to them through the distribution system at a reasonable cost.

Responsiveness: A clearly-defined segment reacts to changes in any of the elements of the marketing mix. For example, if a particular segment is defined as being cost-conscious, it should react negatively to price rises. If it does not, this is an indication that the segment needs to be redefined.

Size: The segment must be reasonably large enough to be a profitable target; and this depends upon the number of people in it and their purchasing power. For example, makers of luxury goods may appeal to small but wealthy target markets, whereas makers to cheap consumption goods may sell to a large number of persons who are relatively poor. The idea is that enough potential buyers must exist to cover the costs of production and marketing in that segment.

Product Design Strategy

Product distinction may be achieved and maintained through frequent changes in product design. In this regard, marketing executives have to take two important policy decisions, viz.,

(i) The frequency with which the product is required to be changed; and

(ii) The extent to which product design should be protected from being imitated by the competitors.

The decision pertaining to change in product design is quite costly, for it involves huge expenditure on the part of production, R & D., market research, testing and tooling sections for the redesigned product. Even for a simple product like a gas stove or cosmetics, the preparation expenses run into lakhs of rupees. For such sophisticated complicated products as computers, automobiles, etc. the preparation expenses are quite substantial; and they rise if the product is changed frequently. Also the cost of inventories goes up, for enough stock of the old product is required to be maintained to feed the existing demand, and a higher inventory level of the new products is required to cope with the uncertain demand for them. There are also many problems of distribution at various levels with wholesalers, retailers and, at times with customers. The production of a new model often leads to wide fluctuations in the inventory levels of manufacturers. If they want to keep the channels well stocked, they have to accept old stocks or provide price concessions to wholesalers and retailers. The service problem, too, is accentuated by a change in design, for the service staff of both producers and middlemen are forced to refurbish their technical expertise. Finally, more competent and trained staff is required to deal with production problems. But how-so-ever risky or costly a product redesign decision may be, a manager cannot ignore the pressure of changes. In fact, S&T changes force companies to change their design so that they may best satisfy customer needs. The electronic revolution of the present century has sounded the death-knell of radios, transistors, etc., by flooding the market with such products as videos, cassette players, TVs, etc. In industries like textiles, electronics, ready-to-wear garments, and domestic appliances, changes in product design have become a focal point of marketing strategy.

It goes without saying that a change in the product design helps in breaking down sales resistance, reducing emphasis on price, and assisting the sales personnel in achieving a high sales target.

A company's policy in respect of product decision protection is closely linked with its policy of frequent design changes. In certain industries such as textiles, women's apparel and electronics, the pace of change is quite rapid. It is not, therefore, feasible to protect a new design. However, in industries where design changes are less frequent or rare, a legal protection of product design is both practical and desirable.

Branding and Allied Strategies

Branding involves the use of distinctive names, symbols, signs or names on a product to differentiate it from other similar competitive offerings.

A *brand* is name, term, symbol, or design, or a combination of all these which is intended to identify the goods or services of one seller or group of sellers and to differentiate them from those of the competitors.[17]

A *brand name* consists of words, marks, symbols or some combination of these that can be communicated orally.

A trade mark is a band that has legal protection, because it is capable of exclusive appropriation (i.e., only the owner can use it). *A brand* mark is part of the brand which appears in the form of a symbol or design or distinctive colouring or lettering. It is recognised by sight but is not expressed when a person pronounces the brand name.

Brand names should not be confused with trade names, for a brand refers to a product while a trade name refers to a company. The name of the firm is its trade name. A brand name can come from its trade name.

The relative significance of branding as a means of boosting a company's image varies with the product and the company's objectives of branding.

An enterprise brands its products for three reasons: physical identification, legal protection, and as a basis for promotional efforts.

17. Committee on Definitions, American Marketing Association, *A Glossary of Marketing Terms*, Chicago, 1960, pp. 9-10.

A *physical identification* of individual products and product lines is important in shipping, sorting, grading, labelling and managing the inventory of various products.

There are three recognised degrees of brand identification:

(a) *Brand insistence*. Consumers insist on a particular brand when they perceive it as having few close substitutes. Brand insistence is the ultimate goal of product differentiation and market segmentation.

(b) *Brand preferences* may stem from habit or experience. Preferences exist among groups of consumers for almost all well-known brands.

(c) *Brand recognition* results when consumers remember having seen or heard of a particular brand but make no special attempt to purchase it because they are satisfied with their present brand.

Legal protection is vested in the trade mark or brand over which the organisation has an exclusive right. Trade mark details have been given elsewhere.

The most important reason for branding is marketing effort. The purpose of the marketing programme is to convince the consumer that the organisation's product will satisfy his wants and needs. To achieve this purpose, the consumer is first acquainted with the brand, so that he may recognise it when he wants it. It is through the brand that this recognition is sought.

Branding Policy

One of the prime objectives of branding is to generate or increase recognition of a product or of information pertaining to its various aspects. Branding has, therefore, become an important element in the overall marketing strategy of a firm. It goes without saying that the brands that are most widely recognised have a large market share than the less important ones. A definite brand policy is called for if the market potency of a firm is not to be blunted. While deciding on a brand policy, the manufacturer should give due consideration to the following:

(a) Will there be a family brand for all types of products or a special brand for each type of product?
(b) Will the company concentrate on a single brand, or will multiple brands be utilised for increasing its market share?
(c) Will the manufacturer make products for a private brand similar to those bearing its own brand name.
(d) Will a national brand policy be followed?

Family Brand

A family brand is used by firms that offer all their merchandise under one name. A product line containing closely-related products are quite often sold under one brand name. The IBM in the USA, Tatas, Modis and Mafatlal in India follow the family brand name policy. Family brand name such as Lakme or Ponds for cosmetics, Dipys for fruit squashes and syrups, Bakeman's for confectionery, Dabar for Ayurvedic medicines are quite popular. When a family brand is successfully advertised, a favourable reaction to one item often leads to an increase in the sale of the product line. Contrary to this, an unfavourable experience may set the consumer against the entire product line. Due care must, therefore, be taken to ensure that all items of a family brand must meet the consumer's expectations.

Products lacking common marketing attributes are usually sold under individual brands, for nothing can be gained from their joint association with one single brand. At times, there may be an adverse reaction to sales resulting from the family branding. For example, there is no point in putting vegetable ghee, detergent or soap under a family brand. This is obvious from the branding policy of Hindustan Lever, where every item is sold under an individual brand name. Here, vegetable ghee is sold under the brand name of Dalda, washing powder under the brand name of Surf, detergent soap under the brand-name of Rin.

Single Brand and Multiple Brand

In order to strike a greater market penetration some manufacturers employ a multiple brand strategy. Under this strategy, they market two or more products that are labelled under different brands but are designed to appeal basically to the same category of customers. For example, Hindustan Lever is selling various toilet soaps under different brand names. Malhotras market shaving blades under different brand names. In such cases, each of these brands competes with the other brand. The decision to have separate brands or to stick to one single brand depends on whether different brands have developed dissimilar images that appeal to different market segments.

Mixed Branding

Manufacturers may adopt a strategy of marketing a part of their output under the brands of one or more middlemen. By following this policy, the manufacturer can grab a larger market share, besides stregthening his financial status. Where the policy of private branding is adopted, both the manufacturer and the middlemen are expected to take a policy decision. The middlemen must give due consideration to the fact that they would be able to sell and compete with the manufacturers' brand. Manufacturers, too, must be able to evaluate whether they would be able to compete with the middlemen's brands which sell at a lower price. Such a policy is usually adopted for the sale of hosiery, woollen and sports goods, etc.

National or Manufacturer's Brand

The policy of having a national brand is followed by producers who enjoy wide geographical distribution.

The national or manufacturer's brand is a brand used by the producer who enjoy a wide geographical distribution. "This they are able to achieve because they have a high annual sales value, extensive warehousing and physical distribution facilities; the capacity and experience in conducting marketing operations, which include maintaining a large sales force and conducting comparative and national advertising programmes; continued consumer and marketing research programmes and maintaining extensive warranty and service programmes.[18] Because of these facilities, companies using national brands can easily compete with others. National brands, once acceptable to the consumer, bring large profits to the distributors and the product. Secondly, such brands help merchandise a product, because promotional campaigns can be developed around the brand.[19]

Choosing the Brand Name

The selection of a proper brand name is one of the vital tricky elements in developing a new product. "A good product with a lacklustre name may not sell as well as a mediocre product with an intriguing name. And once it is chosen and the product is out on the market, changing

18. Cook, V.J. and Schutte, T.F., *Brand Policy Discrimination*, Allyn and Bacon, Boston, 1967, p. 68.
19. Gensmer, Blair, E., "Brand Name, the Most Vital Element in Developing New Products", in *Marketing News*, 13 February, 1976, p. 4.

or modifying the name is not only harmful, but also rather difficult. Getting it right the first time is essential."[20] A good brand name should be such as would help sell the product. Some of these names are:

(i) Names that sound interesting, but have no meaning ("Kodak", "Sony");
(ii) Names whose meanings have to connection to the producer ("Araville Scooter", "Arrow Shirts", "Metex Underwears');
(iii) Names that suggest a function or quality of the product ('Cool Foam", "Agfa Films");
(iv) Names that are borrowed from words in other languages ('Lux");
(v) Names that belong to the company founders ("Ford", "Tata") or to famous people ("Gandhi", "Pratap");
(vi) Names that are taken from myths and legends ("Atlas", "Hercules") or
(vii) Names that are company initials (HMV, GEC, etc.)

In each of these categories, various innumerable possibilities may be explored, but the main criterion is that the selected name should help to sell the product.

A good brand name should possess as many of the characteristics as possible. It would, however, be difficult to find a brand name which would posses all of them. A brand name should have the following features:

(i) It should be easy to pronounce, spell and remember. Simple, crisp, one-syllable names are best: "Charminar" (cirgarettes), "HMT" (watches), "Anchor" (thread), "Topaz" (blades), "Sony" (cassettes), "Promise" (toothpaste).
(ii) The brand should suggest product benefits or qualities. Examples are: Allywn Refrigerator, HMT Tools, Surf/Sway detergent, Lijjat pappad, Tiger locks, Vicco Vajradanti tooth powder or toothpaste, Snowcem paints, Gold Spot (cold drink), Dessert Cooler, etc.
(iii) The brand should be distinctive, because brand names are attention-compelling, and have interest, appeal and memory value. Dull and unimaginative names will have no influence on customers. Examples are: Kodak, Philips, Murphy, Godrej, Quink, Showwhite, Every-ready, Tinopol.
(iv) The name should be capable of being registered and protected legally under a statutory law, i.e., it should not be too closely associated with an existing brand.
(v) It should be easy to advertise and promote. Some names lend themselves to brand marks and eye-catching graphics. Others require great effort to promote.
(vi) Brand names and trade marks must be suited to markets, buyers and products. Women consumers are attracted to feminine names and trade marks and men to masculine ones, e.g., "Evening in Paris" (Perfume) and "Prince" (blades).
(vii) The brand should have a suggestive quality so that interest may be aroused and the performance of the seller's advertising may be enhanced. A name may suggest the product itself, or the product's quality, or some benefit, features or characteristics, of the product; e.g. "Binaca" (toothpaste), "Betterfix" (brassiers), "Kissans" (tractors), "Dippy's" (squashes) "Ceat" (Tyres).
(viii) The brand name should be short, of seven or eight letters or even less: e.g., "Coke" (not Coca cola), "Fiat" (car) "Pears" (soap), "Carefree" (sanitary towels) "Xerox".

20. Littlefield, J.F. and Kirkpatrick, *Advertising: Mass Communication in Marketing*, 1971, pp. 75-78.

Trade Mark

A trade mark is any sign, mark, symbol, word or words, which indicate the origin or ownership of a product as distinguished from its quality and which others have not the equal right to employ for the same purpose.[21] A trade mark or brand may be registrable or non-registrable. A trade mark, to be registered, must observe some legal formalities; such as:

(i) It must not be identical with or confusingly similar to marks already in the same field;

(ii) It should be one by which the public can recognise the goods;

(iii) It must not possess a flag or coat-of-arms of a foreign nation;

(iv) The brand or mark must be associated by the public with a definite source of supply and it should not be possible to confuse it with anything else;

(v) The public gives its own meaning to the words and terms it uses in trade, even as it does to any other word, and this use of a word or term cannot be controlled or restricted by the proprietors of a brand or trade mark;

(vi) The word, term or slogan selected as a brand or trade mark must be one which can be monopolised and used exclusively for the identification of the owner's goods without interference with the rights of others.

A registrable trade mark must not be deceptive or descriptive of the goods, their use, character or quality. To be influential, it should be:

(i) Distinctive and attractive to the eye and ear;

(ii) Easy to remeber, simple and short;

(iii) Similar to that already in use;

(iv) Easy to pronounce;

(v) Easy to illustrate strikingly; and

(vi) Easy and economical to reproduce.

Selection of Brand or Trade Mark

It is difficult and important to choose a brand or trade mark carefully, for it is tedious and expensive to make any change after it has been put into use. It is also necessary to consider the legal provisions governing the use of a brand or trade mark in order to avoid unnecessary and costly harassment later on. Courts protect trade mark rights only when they actually exist at the time an action is brought before them. While selecting a particular brand, due caution should be exercised to eliminate certain words which are either not required by law or which, from the point of view of a monopoly, are unsatisfactory. Some important points to be borne in mind in this connection are:

(i) Any word that is an imitation or duplication of any brand or trade mark already in use in connection with goods of the same kind should not be used.

(ii) Descriptive terms include all words that show the kind or quality or use of the product, or which praise the quality of the goods or recommend or advertise their quality. For example, the words "Cork Tipped" should not be used as a trade mark or brand for cigarettes. First, because they are not registrable, and secondly because they do not constitute a monopoly. Anyone who has the right to use the English language may also apply them to his cigarettes.

21. Adapted from "Package Needs Again Stressed by Management", in *The Nelson Research*, May, 1969, p. 12.

(iii) Geographical names are also objectionable. They are not registrable except in exceptional circumstances.

(iv) Family names are sometimes unsatisfactory, though there are a great many well-known trade marks that are family names: Colgate, Waterman, Tata, Birla, Vimal, Mafatlal, Bajaj, Patanwala, etc. The main objection against them is that family names may become troublesome, for others entitled to the same name have the right to use it is connection with a product of the same class.

Generic Brand Names

A brand name becomes generic or descriptive when the public refers to that type of class of product by the manufacturer's brand name. These generic terms which were brand names once upon a time; linoleum, aspirin, celluloid, cellophane, kerosene, nylon, milk of magnesia. Brand names in danger of becoming generic are: Coke, Formica, Kodak, Frigidaire.

The use of generic names leads to loss to the owner, for it involves loss of time and loss of money and effort spent on establishing them.

The following steps may be taken to prevent a brand name from becoming generic:

(i) Use two names, the brand name in conjunction with the company name or the brand name together with the generic name, such as Eastman Kodak;

(ii) To give actual notice to the public that the brand has been copyrighted.

(iii) Protect any and all misuse of the brand name. The market must be policed vigorously.

(iv) Take legal action.

Packaging

Packaging is a key element in merchandising. It is concerned with formulating a design of package, and producing a safe and attractive container for the product. There are a variety of reasons for packaging a product—to protect it, to differentiate and identify it, to make it more eye-catching, to provide for ease in handling, and to furnish information to the consumer about it.

In keeping with the "total product" philosophy, the management must give due weightage to the packaging of its products. To increase sales, it is not necessary for the company to market a new product or change its design. Anything that makes a product new in the eyes of customers is new in terms of product planning. In some cases, packaging is so unique that the product is known by its package rather than its features. The best example of it is the coco-cola bottle which itself speaks of the peculiar feature of the product throughout the world. Other distinctive packages or designs which act as shelf salesman are Amul Butter package, Modern Bread package, Wrapping of Carefree sanitary napkins, etc.

Every product requires packing—whether it is a consumer product or an industrial one. Because packaging is an important element in boosting the company's sales. For example, if the package is used for brand differentiation and identification, it should bear some peculiar features that make it identifiable among a variety of similar products lying on the shelf, and it should remain intact until purchased by the consumer.

In the case of consumer goods, where it is meant to identify the product at the point of purchase or to stimulate impulse buying, packaging should be attractive, as goods like Cadbury's Chocolate and Britannia Biscuits. In the case of products like spices, ghee, other eatables and medicines, it is meant for the prevention of adulteration. In the case of milk, curd, cheese and butter, packaging largely aims at the prevention of adulteration and maintenance of the freshness of products.

Packing Policy

The package is the producer's last chance to communicate product message to the consumer. After all the advertising and public relations work has been done, the package must frequently stand on its own in a face-to-face confrontation with customers in the market place. Hence, the need for a sound packaging policy, which should give attention to the following points:

(i) Package design.

(ii) Package size.

(iii) Package cost.

(iv) Package material.

(i) *Package Design:* One of the important ingredients of a package policy relates to its design. Package design is largely related to the function it wants to serve when it is primarily used as a promotional device and should attract and hold customer's attention and stimulate them to buy. And packaging depends on the size and shape of the product. All are equally important and, therefore, a decision on these elements should reflect the preferences of the target customer group. When it is primarily protective, design decisions are, by and large, protective and should give due weightage to the cost of material, the product's shape, etc. It must give consideration to product handling, both by middlemen and consumers, and should facilitate easy display in retail outlets.

(ii) *Package Size*: Package size decisions arise from a number of interrelated factors, but the most pressing and important ones are the rate of consumption and consuming units. For instance, bread, butter and cakes are consumed by households; so they are required for group consumption. In contrast, cigarettes, chocolates and cosmetics are packaged in units for individual consumption. Similarly, eatables like wheat, sugar, salt, etc., are required to be packed in large packages, for they are meant for family consumption. Sometimes, packages are required to be modified when a customer has a strong liking for a particular package size; for example, in the case of washing soap, people prefer to buy a package of 4 or 6 cakes. Therefore, the manufacturer must decide on the form of packaging. The different types of available packages are:

A consumer package is one which holds the product for ultimate consumption and is within the means of a buying household. In other words, the consumer has the option to purchase the pack size which he considers adequate for the consumption of his family over a length of time and which does not involve extra investment during that period.

A *bulk package* is its opposite. It is either for the industrial consumer's use, e.g., steel drums for paint or 4-gallon or 18-litre kerosene oil can, a sack of rice, etc. The consumer package itself very often requires an outside package in which it is transported which is sometimes referred to as a transit package or an outer container.

An *industrial package* may either be described as a bulk package or a package for durable consumer goods. It is a basic package type, although many sub-divisions can be listed, e.g. a strip package or a multiple package.

A *dual use package* is one which has a secondary usefulness after its contents have been consumed. Drinking glasses, boxes of jewellery or cigarettes, wastepaper baskets, refrigerator dishes, cloth from flour and feed sacks are examples of this type of package.

(iii) *Package Cost*: While framing their packaging policy, manufacturers should bear in mind the cost of packaging. The protection required to deliver the item to the user in good condition determines the cost of packaging; but quite often, consumer preferences and likings increase the packaging cost. A cardboard container or a tin may be less expensive, but because of customer choice, the marketer at times uses them as containers for certain products. Similarly, a reclosable package, although more expensive than the throwaway, allows customers to retain their products for a long time. Again an empty container, such as that of vegetable ghee or powdered milk, can fetch a good price when sold. When a package is used as a promotional tool, its cost is higher than that of a package solely meant for protection.

As packaging performs different functions and meets different requirements, manufacturers must consider the question of the importance they attach to packaging in their overall marketing strategy.

(iv) *Package Form*: A variety of material containers are available, such as tin cans or cardboard containers, polythene bags, paper or cloth or gunny bags, wooden boxes, teak chests, square bottles, collapsible tubes, aluminium foils, clear film wrappings, plastic containers, etc. Colour can be used to identify sizes, models, flavours and qualities.

Packages are often selected on *prima facie* grounds of cost, international practice, type of product to be packaged, the quality of the product, the conditions of display, likely consumer appeal; and this often done without regard to the true economy of packaging, operation, filling, selling, storing, handling and distribution.

Essentials of a Good Packaging Policy

The expenditure incurred on product development and marketing is meaningless if the package of a product fails to achieve the desired results. While deciding on package, the marketing manager must seek to answer the following questions:[22]

— Does the package tell consumers what they want and need to know?
— Does it instantly identify the type of product the package contains, i.e., does it reflect quality?
— Is the package distinctive?
— Is it compatible with the firm's advertising image?
— Does its size make it compatible with similar products?
— Is it adaptable to other products? Does it suit the product?
— Is it acceptable to the trade? Will it stack properly?
— Will it last? Is it tamper-proof?
— Does it look distinctive from other packages?
— Is it easy to open?
— Does it protect the product?
— Is there a prominent place on it for the display of price?
— Are the brand, symbol and name easy to see?
— Does the package have promotable features?

Labelling

A label gives verbal information on the product. It identifies the name and place of manufacture of the product. It mentions its ingredients. And it indicates how it should be used. It carries date of its manufacture and the date of its expiry, the price to be charged, the brand

22. Udell, J.G. and Anderson, E.F., "The Product Warranty as an Element: Competitive Strategy," in *Journal of Marketing*, October 1969, p. 7.

name, and the net quantity of the contents (weight, measure, numerical count, etc.) Some labels consist of tags attached to the product or package, as in the case of most clothing or hosiery articles. Others are imprinted on the product itself. Labels are part of the printed material on the package. It is a strong sales tool and is an integral part of the point-of-purchase advertising.

Although some products may be adequately identified by the name of the product and the producer, most require a somewhat more extensive description of their nature and use. For example, processed foods, patent drugs, some cosmetics, textiles and other goods are required by law to carry a fairly complete idea about their ingredients. Many products must also furnish instructions for their use, as in the case of commercial plant food. Safety warnings are also necessary on labels of all potentially hazardous products or packages. If a substance is poisonous, the label must tell the user what steps to take if any is ingested and must list the antidotes. For example, there is often a warning on medicines; "To be used under the direction of a medical practitioner."

Labels are classed as brand, grade, descriptive and informative.

A *brand label* is simply the brand name applied to the product or to the package: e.g. some clothing carries the brand label "Sanforised."

A *grade label* identifies the quality by a letter, number or word, such as canned mangoes may be graded as, A, B, C or Fancy Grade 1, 2, 3 etc.

The terms "descriptive labels" and "informative labels" are used synonymously. These give written or illustrative objective information about the characteristics, use, construction, care, performance or other features of the product.

Labels are designed to help the promotion of a product. The arrangement of type, illustrations, and colour is designed to attract the consumer's eye, make a package distinctive, and encourage recognition by the consumer who often views it in the midst of many other products.

Guarantees and Warranties

A guarantee is generally offered by producers/manufacturers with regard to defective products. Guarantees expressed or implied are the obligations assumed by the seller, promising buyers that they will receive certain services or satisfactions. Thus, a guarantee is a bundle of satisfactions a buyer receives when he buys a product.

Warranty is an assurance of quality, service and performance given by the producer to the consumer. It is a written guarantee of the instrinsic value of a product. It accepts the responsibility of the maker for repairs, service and maintenance of consumer durables. The warranty is the outcome of the rule of law, viz., let the buyer beware. Producers develop warranties to create confidence in the buyers' mind and to provide compensation in case the product is not upto reasonable expectations.

The warranty usually gives clearly the name of the warrantor, which products and parts are covered and which are not, exactly how they are covered, who pays and the period for which the warranty applies.

A guarantee may serve any one of the two purposes:

(i) To protect producers against the abuses of the "service" policy and to limit their liability; or

(ii) To provide an additional promotional factor in their programme of selling against the competitors.

Promotional guarantees are used in a number of different situations in the market introduction of a new product. They help in overcoming buyer resistance, gaining initial distribution, adding new dealers and opening new market areas. In introducing new products or remerchandising established products, promotional guarantees are most effective when:

(i) The product has a high retail price — the higher the price, the greater assurance the buyers want that the product will perform as represented.

(ii) The product is purchased infrequently.

(iii) Buyers visualise the product as complex. Complex products frequently are costly to repair, and complexity is likely to increase buyer's uncertainty.

To satisfy the consumer and to provide the services guaranteed by the warranty, the manufacturer may adopt the following guidelines:

(i) Ensure the integrity and credibility of the warranty.

(ii) Institute a meaningful education programme about the use of the product.

(iii) Strengthen the company programme for quality control in manufacture.

(iv) Provide high quality maintenance and repair service.

If these guidelines are followed properly by the manufacturers, repeat sales are bound to be stimulated.

Sampling

Sampling is an old trade custom. Everyone is familiar with the artifice of the sweetmeat-seller who generally gives the children a sample of the sweets to induce their parents to make purchases. Some business houses, through advertising, make an offer to send a sample if the coupon attached therewith is filled in and posted. They also send their wares on a trial basis for a period of time. The idea which works behind this strategy is the same i.e., create interest in the customers to make purchases of the product offered.

The main function of sampling is to make prospective or would-be customers more intimately acquainted with the qualities of the merchandise offered for sale, and induce them to buy it. All types of goods can be sampled in one way or the other. Customers may be given an opportunity to use, try, handle, taste, hear or see the articles offered for sale. In modern marketing, sampling should be understood as giving the prospective customer an opportunity of discovering the qualities of the product for himself.

(a) Sampling with Small Packages: Some goods by nature lend themselves to sampling in packages that are smaller than those placed on the market for sale. Sampling of such products is very simple and does not cost much; but they yield very good results. The goods under sampling should also fulfil the following conditions:

In no case should the customer be put to any trouble or inconvenience in testing the sample.

In making the test, the purchaser should get a good idea of the nature and different qualities of the product.

(b) Making Sampling Advantageous: A definite decision should be taken to use samples on a large scale, without testing the result of several alternative schemes in a restricted area. A typical town or a part of a large city should be chosen for each scheme of sampling the manufacturer desires to test. The results of the investigation should be kept on the record of the different activities of sampling in that area. A proper comparison of the cost and achievements in the area will indicate which scheme is the most satisfactory one. Some traders doubt or question the wisdom or the utility of such experiments, but it should not be forgotten that the

general mass of people do not always react in the manner we think, and it is essential for the success of any scheme of sampling that we know precisely how the public responds and what can be expected before large sums of money are spent.

Sometimes goods are sold in a large container whose price is high enough to warrant giving it away as a sample; a small sample of it may be inadequate and may not give a true idea of its qualities. Such products can effectively be sampled by offering the large container or a sufficiently large sample at a greatly reduced price i.e., just sufficient to cover the manufacturing cost. This procedure would discourage sample collectors and ensure that samples are received by those who are genuinely interested.

Sampling largely depends on the nature of the goods and of the market where they are put on sale. For example, publishers who sell costly editions of books send many sample pages, together with a copy of the index or contents and descriptive matter bound in the same style as the books to interested persons or parties. Such methods of sampling, together with follow-up letters and other sales literature and extensive publicity, generate sufficient business. The margin of gross profit has, of course, to be large enough to cover their costs. Where sampling is incovenient to the recipient, it is often possible to do the sampling by showing the advantages which flow from the use of the product. A product like varnish or colour wash for the walls of houses or oil paint can be sampled by sending pieces of cardboard or slips or wood or other fabrics covered with the distemper or paint. Such samples will not only show the different shades of colour but also give some indication of the appearance of the finished work. If such samples are accompanied by suitable sales literature, illustrated in colours and showing the products as used by those who have already purchased them, the recipient gets a fairly accurate idea of its look, quality and value. At times, the value of many samples is lost when proper care is not taken to prevent each person or family from getting more than one sample; When distributed through the dealer, his help may be necessary; but when samples are sent by mail in response to enquiries solicited in newspaper and magazine advertising, one or the other system of check has to be followed. The most common is to have a card index with a card for each recipient. Over and above the name of the recipient, his address is also included. In this way, it is possible to avoid-sending more than one sample to an individual family in a very large number of cases.

(c) Sampling Channels: Samples may be distributed through two different channels:

(i) From the manufacturer or sales agent directly to the homes of consumers by post or through a sampling crew.

(ii) From the manufacturer to dealers who distribute the samples to their customers.

Persons to whom the samples are to be given may be selected as follows:

(i) From a compiled list of persons who would probably be interested in the product. The names and addresses of such persons are obtained from dealer or from some director, or selected by members of sampling crew during their itineraries on some predetermined basis; for example, persons who live in houses with a rent of more than Rs. 100.00 per month or persons who own motor cars or radios, or who have telephones in their homes.

(ii) Through advertising in newspapers and magazines and using a coupon to be filled in and posted by the enquirer asking for a sample.

When sample is introduced, some of the following principles must be considered:

(i) Through getting people to test the product by using, handling, tasting, hearing or seeing. This is often the quickest way to make them customers, for it must be remembered that human nature attaches very great value to anything that can be had for nothing.

(ii) People like to receive samples free of cost. But when they are able to obtain several samples easily without having to pay for them, they resent it later when the samples are not procurable and find that they have to pay for what they want.

(iii) Before samples are distributed, people should be made to desire the product by advertising that directs their attention to its benefits and advantages. Value should be attached to the sample itself both by advertising and by making a small charge for it or by otherwise insuring that the recipient does something to deserve it.

(iv) Before a new product is sampled, the suspicion and distrust of people for all innovation must be overcome either by educational advertising or by demonstrating the product use or consumption, or the results of using it, or by combining both advertising and demonstration, i.e. the product must be made acceptable to the public before samples are offered to it.

(v) Sampling has other uses than the introduction of a new product or the placing of an old one in a new market. Competition can often be satisfactory fought by frequent distribution of samples, say, once a year, to selected customers. This keeps the product and its advantages in the minds of customers and prevents their being enticed by competitors, or wins them back if they had been disloyal.

(vi) When advertising precedes or accompanies the distribution of samples, its claims must be modest and true; otherwise; the test made by the recipients of samples will only prove their exaggeration and falsity and all confidence lost in the manufacturer.

(vii) Samples should be put attractively packaged and their presentation should be similar to the standard packages offered for sale.

(viii) Sampling should be neither condemned nor rushed into without due consideration of its value and purpose, and tests on a small scale should be made to obtain some idea of the results which may be expected.

(ix) The relative value of small-sized and standardised packages for use as samples should be considered.

(x) The need for keeping the value and benefits of the product before the recipients of samples during the time they are testing the product should not be forgotten.

(xi) The relative value of the two channels of distribution for samples should be carefully studied before making a choice.

(xii) When results are disappointing, look for the cause, not forgetting the other factors in successful marketing, distribution, advertising and dealer co-operation.

SERVICE POLICIES

Service strategies aim at increasing the utility of a product without effecting a change in product by the intangible additions. A firm's policy pertaining to the type of service to its buyers is an important factor in the decisions on the products which the supplier intends to market. Service may also facilitate the extension and promotion of the market for existing products. The several kinds of services should be considered while designing strategies to this effect. These include:

(a) Application assistance;

(b) Returned goods;

(c) Shipping;
(d) Parts;
(e) Distribution network;
(f) Maintenance and repairs (after-sales service).

In the era of consumerism, service in all forms, especially after-sales service, is of paramount importance. This is mainly because today's customers are definitely better educated than his predecessors. Moreover, in the wake of the price spiral, quality and advertising competition, customer service provides an excellent basis of competition.

After-sales service is an important aspect of a marketing transaction. Such service covers repairs, smooth maintenance, availability of spare parts at lower prices after the product has been sold and is used. These services are important because they ensure that there is no dissatisfaction, frustration and ill-will among consumers against the manufacturer's product they are using — so far as the quality of its working is concerned. Free services for repairs and replacement of defective parts are given during the guarantee periods and thereafter at lower charges to retain customers for future sales.

As a matter of fact, after-sales service for costly and durable goods, such as electrical appliances and equipment, complex machinery, refrigerators, coolers, air and water duplicators, TV sets, radios, tape recorders, stereos, washing and sewing machines and automobiles, cars and scooters, etc. is essential.

The marketers often provide after-sales service in a number of ways:

(i) By upgrading the efficiency and reliability of dealer-provided service through training programme;
(ii) By developing company-owned service centres which repair consumer goods;
(iii) By placing greater emphasis on product design through vigorous testing, research and quality control than before.

IBM service has become an integral part of its marketing programme. Its emphasis on the marketing of a total package of computer service, including maintenance of hardware and software, by providing systems expertise or programming consultants and even computer operators.

Product Life Cycle (PLC)

Products, like people, have a certain length of life during which they pass through different stages. From the time the product idea is born, during its development and up to the time it is launched in the market, a product goes through various phases of development. Its life begins with its market introduction; then it goes through a period during which its market grows rapidly. Ultimately, it reaches marketing maturity, after which its market declines; and finally the product dies. It is worth noting that the duration of each stage is different for different products. Some take years to pass through the introductory stage, while others may be accepted in a few weeks. Further, not all products go through all the stages; some fail in the initial stages, others may reach the maturity stage after a long time. In the case of most products, decline and possible abandonment are almost inevitable because:

(i) Competitive products establish their superiority over existing products;
(ii) The product goes out of date;
(iii) The company lacks an aggressive sales strategy.

The product life cycle passes through five stages:

(i) Introductory, pioneering or development stage.

(ii) Growth or the market acceptance stage.

(iii) Maturity stage.

(iv) Saturation stage.

(v) Decline stage and death stage.

Introductory, Pioneering or Development Stage

With the end of the gestation period (i.e., when activities like idea screening, pilot modelling and test marketing are completed), the product is born or, say, the product is placed on the market. This is known as introductory stage of the PLC. The product placed on the market may be entirely new or it may be well known with a new feature added to it. In the early stage, the demand for a product can be boosted up by aggressive promotion, elaborate feedback and adjustment in the marketing strategy. At this stage, if customer satisfaction is reinforced by adequate promotion, the product may enter the "take-off stage."

In many respects, the introductory stage is a very risky and expensive one, for there is a high degree of product failure, Quite often, operations at this stage are characterised by low sales volume, high cost, limited distribution and high promotional cost.

Growth or Market Acceptance Stage

The growth phase sets in following rapid acceptance and repeat purchases of the products which survived during the introductory phase. At this stage, competition becomes keen if the profit performance of the product has been promising. With the acceleration of product growth, the firm increases its distribution network, and its promotional and pricing policies aim at generating a larger volume of sales. The manufacturer shifts to "buy-my-brand" rather than to "buy-my-product strategy". At this stage, it is desirable for the firm to think about new uses and new markets for product.

Market Maturity Stage

During this stage, sales continue to increase but at a decreasing rate. While the sales curve is levelling off, the profits of both the manufacturer and the retailers start to decline because of rising expenditure and lower prices. Marginal producers, therefore, drop out of the market. Price competition becomes increasingly fierce, and the producer assumes a greater share of the total promotional efforts in order to retain his dealers. New models are also introduced to broaden their lines. Supply exceeds demand for the first time, making demand stimulation essential through advertising and salesmen's efforts.

The Saturation Stage

At this stage, each of the characteristics mentioned under the different stages is intensified. The replacement sales dominate the market. The sales curve reacts to changes in economic conditions. Owners of durables (like automobiles and appliances) are bombarded with pleas to trade in their present possessions "for new and improved models", while users of non-durable goods (such as cosmetics, and toiletry) are reminded constantly to keep on buying their favourite brands.

The Decline Stage

This stage is characterised either by the product's gradual replacement by some new items or by an evolving change in consumer buying behaviour. For example, paper napkins replace linen napkins because of their being more convenient. Buyers do not buy as extensively as they did before. New and superior products are introduced in the market, many of which meet the customer's demand and needs more fully. The sales drop off and many of the competitors withdraw from the market. Cost control becomes increasingly important when the demand drops. Advertising and other promotional activities are drastically curtailed, and the price factor is used more and more frequently to obtain business. The emphasis now is on efficient distribution at the lowest cost. The sales become concentrated among a relatively few large and efficient mass distributors. Most management shift their attention to other products, gradually phasing out the declining product as its future grows increasingly dark. Some stay with the dying product a little longer and try to revive the market, usually with disappointing results.

Fig.11.2 Depicts the successive stage of the PLC, by a curve of the sales volume.

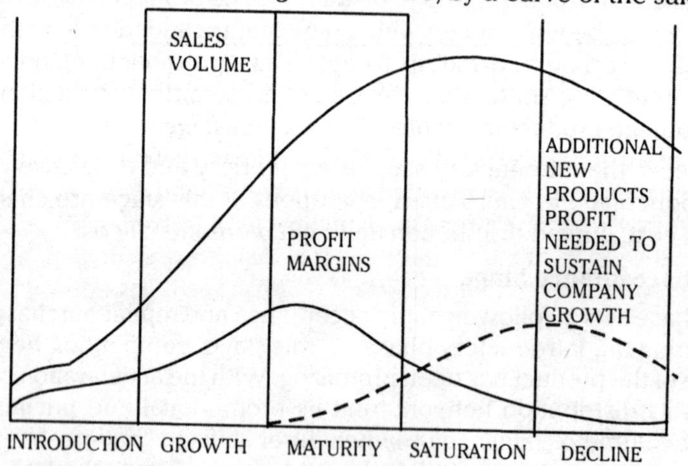

Source: Booz, Allen and Hamilton, Inc., *Management of New Products.*

Fig. 11.2

Fig. 11.2 depicts the total sales volume of a variety of products. If there are three products appearing in the market over the product life, their individual life cycle can be depicted by Fig.11.3 which shows the sale of the individual product as compared to total sales, which may follow different life patterns.

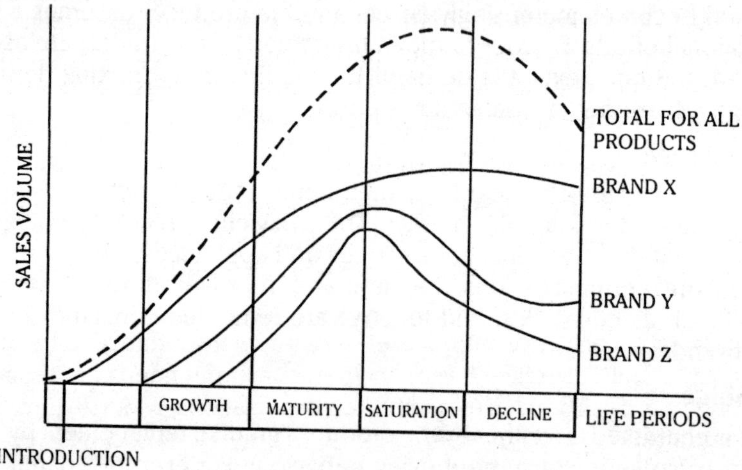

Fig. 11.3: Product Life Cycle.

The above sales curves are hypothetical and represent the tendencies that some products show during their life cycle. There are certain products which, due to their popularity, show sky-rocketing sales but have a shorter life span. Also, there are products which show a gradual increase in sales but have a longer life cycle.

Inspite of greater variation in the life span of a product, the concept of PLC provides a useful insight into the designing of an appropriate marketing strategy. It is a common place observation that in today's rapidly changing business environment, sales pick up in the growth stage and reach the peak during the late-growth or early-maturity stage, and begin to decline at the end of the maturity stage. The introduction of new products at regular and frequent intervals is the only means of maintaining high profitability.

DISTRIBUTION POLICIES

Over the years, managerial philosophy with regard to marketing has undergone a radical change. The increased pressure of competition, consumerism and government regulations has forced businessmen to cast away their traditional philosophy of "Caveat Emptor" and to embrace the newer one, "Caveat Vendor". Today, it has been increasingly realised that the prime task of a business is to create a customer; and if this aim is achieved, a business can attain its goal or mission.

Therefore, customer policies of every company should strive to provide every possible benefit which customers expect from the manufacturer's products.

Though India is still in a developing stage, the progress achieved by the country in the various spheres of the economy cannot be underestimated. If we look at industries, it would not take long to realise that we have already crossed the "take-off stage", and are progressing rapidly toward industrialisation. The goods once treated as luxuries have now almost become a part of our daily life. The increased employment opportunities, rising standard of living of the people, increased *per capit*a income, higher level of literacy have all accelerated the demand for a variety of goods. Today, in the changed socio-economic conditions, the demand for electrical and electronic appliances, labour-saving kitchen devices, fashionable clothing, furniture, automobiles, etc., has sky-rocketed in urban areas. In rural areas, the green revolution has already revolutionised the pattern of consumption. The people's needs are not only confined to goods such as farm machinery, insecticides and consumer durables but extend to goods like fine clothing, automobiles and electrical appliances.

Distinction Between Consumer and Customer

The words consumer and customer are widely used in marketing, though many fail to distinguish between them properly. A consumer is a person whom uses a product or service for his own personal satisfaction or benefit, whereas a customer is anybody who buys a commodity. A customer may or may not be a consumer.

The needs and desires of a consumer are of paramount importance to the manufacturers who intend to sell any product/service. It is only when consumer needs are properly identified that the desired goods can be produced to satisfy their expectations, which in turn, determine the prosperity of the organisation.

Various Dimensions of Customer Policies

Keeping in view the corporate goals and the target customers it wants to serve, a company has to design its plans to optimise results. Consequently, a company is expected to concentrate on the following issues:

(i) The location of customers.
(ii) The number of customers.
(iii) The channels of distribution.

Location of Customers

The demand for many products varies significantly, depending on the geographical location of the customers, i.e., where potential consumers live; the area which is profitable enough to be covered; and the issues which are required to be considered while choosing customers.

(a) Rural and Urban Customers: The pattern of rural and urban distribution of customers affects the demand for goods in a variety of ways. This is largely due to the differences in their background, educational and social levels, habits and life styles, etc. In India, rural and urban consumers are poles apart. India is still a country of villages, for only one out of every 5 persons resides in an urban area. In 1921, 88.8% lived in villages; in 1951, the percentage was 82.7 and in 1971, it was 80.1. In 1981, the proportion was 76.8%. This indicates that gradually people are shifting to urban areas. Even so, the rural market is a very large one. The movement of modernisation to rural areas, through contact with urban people, the progress in literacy and press propaganda induce the rural population to go in for the satisfaction of their needs for synthetic textile, consumer electronics, fashion-wear, electrical appliances, tractors, fans, agricultural machinery, and fertilizers. The Green Revolution has increased purchasing power of the farmers who are using the new products in a big way. The marketer, by studying the needs of the rural population, can plan his marketing strategy in a very satisfactory way.

India was 575, 936 villages spread over 32,89,483 sq. kms of land. The villages are of different sizes. The Census has classified these into six categories, as shown in the table on the next page.

It will be seen that about 62% of the villages have a population of less than 500, and about 21% have less than 1,000 persons. This means that a shrewd marketer would try to build up his market in these villages, may be for clothing, utensils, daily necessities, cheap toiletries, etc. Hindustan Lever, Brooke Bond and Bata have taken advantage of the rural market by undertaking surveys and satisfying the needs of the villagers by opening retail stores or appointing travelling salesman in these areas. Apart from the expenditure on food and farm inputs, farmers now want to posses and do actually possess consumer durables like transistors, bicycles, steel furniture and wrist watches.

Distribution of Villages by Population (1971)

Population Range	*No. of Villages*
(i) Less than 500	318,633
(ii) 500 to 999	132,990
(iii) 1000 to 1999	81,973
(iv) 2000 to 4999	36,005
(v) 5000 to 9999	4,974
(vi) 10000 and over	1,358
Total:	575,936

But the penetration of rural markets is a difficult task. About two thirds of our villages are of a very small size, accounting for nearly 20% of the rural population. About 5,000 villages with over 5,000 population account for less than 10% of the rural population. Even these villages are situated far away from the pucca roads; most of them are cut off from the surrounding areas during the rainy season; Hence, without adequate transport and communication facilities, these cannot be covered.

Further, the nature and character of the rural market differ from those of urban markets. People in the villages are creatures of traditions, habits, preferences, and are subject to social pressures. The task of educating them in the advantages of new products is not easy. It calls for the exercise of imagination, skill and drive. A suitable marketing strategy based on study and an understanding of the specific needs of villagers is essential.

About 23.7% of the population lives in urban areas, towns and cities, which number 3,245.

Of these 60.37% lives in Class I towns, 11.65% in Class II, 14.35% in Class III, 9.52% in Class IV, 3.61% in Class V, and 0.50% in Class VI towns. Of the total urban population, 94.29 million or 26.90% lives in 12 metropolitan areas/cities. These cities are Calcutta, Mumbai, Delhi, Chennai, Bangalore, Hyderabad, Ahmedabad, Kanpur, Pune, Nagpur, Lucknow and Jaipur.

The urban population may need such products as cosmetics, tailored garments, decorative pieces and scooters, electrical kitchen appliances, modern furniture and furnishing, reading material (comics/magazines), radio and television, etc. For many products, urban households represent not only a rich but also a larger market segment than the rural households; for example, for articles of luxury and comfort such as cars, scooters and electrical appliances.

(b) Regional Distribution of Customers: The regional distribution of population also affects the manufacturer's strategy on the marketing of a variety of goods because of sectional differences flowing from climate, religion, social norms and customs. In our country, U.P. (with a population of 110.8 million) is the most populous state. Bihar, with 69.8 million, and Maharashtra, with 62.7 million, occupy the second and third places respectively. These three states retained their respective ranks in 1961, 1971 and 1981, West Bengal (54.5 million) which occupied the fifth place in 1961, moved up to the fourth place in 1981, at the expense of Andhra Pradesh (53.5 million), which slipped to the fifth rank. Similarly, Madhya Pradesh (53.1 million), which ranked seventh in 1961, moved up to the sixth place in 1981. The remaining States and Union Territories more or less maintained their ranks, with the exception of Assam (19.6 million), which ranked fourteenth in 1961 but moved to the thirteenth place at the expense of Punjab (16.6 million). It may be noted that about 90% of the total population lives in U.P., Bihar, Maharashtra, West Bengal, Andhra Pradesh, M.P., Tamil Nadu, Karnataka, Gujarat, Rajasthan, Orissa and Kerala – in that order. Therefore, it would not be incorrect to say that the biggest markets of the country lie in these states. The largest rates of increase are Delhi (52%), Nagaland (49.7%), Assam (36.9%), Rajasthan (32.3%) and Haryana (28.0%).

A knowledge of the regional distribution of population is essential for marketers because sectional differences exist in the demand of many products. For example, warm clothes are required in winter in Northern India, and none in the South Indian States, where the demand is for cotton fabrics. In winter, more tea may be used in North India and coffee in Southern India; in summer, cold drinks, ice creams may be in large demand throughout the country. In the extreme North, woollens are necessary almost all through the year.

Shifts and trends in the regional distribution of population may also influence policies relating to channels of distribution. As the distant markets grow, firms may open a large number of branches of retail stores, as has been done by Corona Sahu and Bata Shoe Co., Hindustan Lever, Indian Tea Marketing Company, Bombay Dyeing, Mafatlal, D.C.M., Oswal, Tata Textiles, Vimals, Raymonds, Calico Mills, Century Rayons, Gwalior Suitings, Atlas Cycle, etc. They may also increase their sales force to cover markets which had previously been assigned to wholesalers or manufacturer's agents.

(c) Foreign Markets: A business has no geographical limits; it can prosper in any part of the world, provided that the environment is conducive to its growth. Today, international trade has become a part and parcel to every economy, for no economy is self-sufficient; it has to depend on others for some goods or raw materials. Literally all countries of the world import raw materials, semi-finished goods and technological expertise to keep their industries on their toes. To earn hard currency and to achieve a favourable balance of trade, most of the countries provide a variety of concessions to their manufacturers to capture foreign markets.

However, marketing in foreign countries raises many thorny problems, for every country has its own bearing on exchange control, currency regulations, import restrictions, tax structure, regulations of foreign companies, terms of trade, etc., which make trading quite difficult. Moreover, the social, political and ethical environment of a country imposes a variety of obstacles in the way of trade. Admittedly, there are a host of difficulties in trading with other countries; but one cannot deny the fact that foreign trade is quite attractive, both in terms of money and prestige.

A profitable exploration of foreign markets calls for a scientific analysis for such markets, which is undertaken so that a firm may really market goods which are required by foreign customers. The pressing questions which require a firm's attention are:

(1) Is tapping of a foreign market really profitable?
(2) Is the firm capable of catering to the needs of foreign markets?
(3) Can it supply goods of the desired quality at a competitive price?
(4) Will it be able to tailor its marketing policies to various regulations imposed by foreign countries?

If these questions are thoroughly studied, a company can wisely design an effective strategy for tapping foreign markets.

Foreign markets may be tapped by various means other than by way of exports. A company may enter into agreements with local firms in a foreign country or erect its plant in the host country.

Size of Customers

(i) Small Customer: Often a manufacturer needs a definite guideline to the size of customer with whom he wants to deal. A company should know what it costs to serve each type of customer, and whether these customers are really profitable for it. For example, a company dealing in consumer goods was catering to about 10,000 outlets in North India. But it was noted that 65% of the outlets accounted for 8% of the total purchases which was only Rs.8 lakhs per year. On the basis of the profitability of outlets, dealer-wise sales figures were analysed. It was then decided to drop about 6,000 outlets. This resulted in the reduction of the sales force from 186 to 72. Consequently the selling cost went down substantially.

However, this is an extreme case. It has been noted that in order to expand their sales, companies often sell all those customers who desire its products. Salesmen, too, are tempted to increase their sales by covering all those areas which may serve as outlets for the sale of goods. In deciding whether to eliminate small customers, adequate weight should be given to their total purchases vis-a-vis the actual purchases of a particular product or product line in which the company deals. If small manufacturers have the capacity to increase their actual purchases, they should not be ignored or bypassed. Moreover, conditions in a market for its product will indicate to the company whether it is desirable to keep small customers or drop them altogether.

(ii) Large Customers: On the other hand, some companies, instead of focussing on many small customers, find it profitable to deal with a few large customers. For example, a big automobile company has eight big distributors; but if four of these cancel their contracts with the company, its position will be vulnerable, because the loss of about 50% of its customers will create a big financial problem for the company.

A small auto spare parts manufacturer was selling its products to a big automobile company. During the course of an investigation it was noted that its sales increased tremendously from year to year.

In the first five years, the figure was 30 percent and at the end of ten years, it was 55 percent. The company earned a handsome profit from this customer and undertook many ambitious projects to enter new fields.

Although sales to other customers of the company were quite promising, they were not significant enough in comparison with those of the auto company. Even so, the company enjoyed a fair market. But, suddenly, the auto company cancelled its contract, as a result of which the auto parts manufacturer was confronted by the spectre of financial disaster. The preceding illustration does not suggest that a company should not have only one or a few customers. It should, however, be in a position to withstand the loss caused by the cancellation of contracts by such customers. This can be accomplished by entering into contract with a large number of customers of different sizes.

Channels of Distribution

When a product is finally ready for the market, it has to be determined what methods and routes will be used to bring it into the market, i.e., to ultimate consumers and users. This process involves the establishment of distribution strategies, including channels of distribution, and providing for the physical handling and distribution of the product. Distribution is concerned with various activities, such as the movement and storage of goods or the transfer of ownership from the producer to the consumer or user. A channel of distribution for a product is the route taken by the goods as they move from the producer to the ultimate consumer or user.

According to the American Marketing Association, "a channel of distribution is the structure of intracompany organisation units and extraordinary company agents and dealers, wholesale and retail, through whom a commodity, product or service is marketed."[23] In other words, it is the sequential linkage of institutions and relationships through which a product flows from the producer to the consumer.

23. American Management Association, *A Marketing Definitions: A Glossary of Marketing Terms*. New York, 1960. p. 10.

The intermediaries (wholesalers and retailers) direct the products and services to consumers. The consumers are the ultimate end in the channel of distribution, for it is for them that goods are purchased; and it is they who purchase them. Each of these three participants has a stake in the distribution channel and contributes to its operation.

Every marketing channel contains one or more of the transfer points at each of which there is either an institution or a final buyer of the product. Moreover, the transfer of title may be direct, as when the producer sells the product outright to a wholesaler or retailer, or it may be indirect, as when an agent-middleman simply negotiates its transfer to the consumer. From the viewpoint of the producer, such a network of institutions for reaching a market is known as the marketing channel. A channel always includes both the producer and the final customer for the product, as well as all the agents and merchant-middlemen involved in the transfer of the title. However, a channel does not include such firms as the railroads, which render a marketing service but play no role in negotiating purchases and sales. If a consumer buys wheat from the cultivator, or if the publisher sells a book by mail direct to a professor, the channel is from producer to consumer. On the other hand, if the publisher sells books to booksellers who, in turn, sell them to students and teachers, the channel is from producer to retailer to consumer.

Generally speaking, when business expands, it is expedient to take the assistance of professionals in the distribution of the product — specially if the market to be covered is dense and large. Here comes the role of intermediaries, who bridge the gap between producers and consumers most efficiently. The channel of distribution is a structure which is organised and represents a choice among alternative channels of distribution; or it may involve a description of the different marketing situations faced by retailers, wholesalers and producers within the structure. It may be considered as a series of functions which must be performed to market products effectively. This structure is highly complex and is made up of a variety of institutions, such as middlemen, merchants and agents, retailers and wholesalers, and producers (i.e., the enterprises engaged in manufacturing in mines, the extractive industries, and farming). The channel starts from the producer and extends to the last person who buys it without any significant change in the form of the product. When its form is changed, another product emerges, and a new channel is started.

To bring maximum profits to all institutions concerned, a channel of distribution should be treated as a unit — a total system of action. The activities of manufacturers need to be co-ordinated with those of the middlemen used in the distribution of a given product. However, a marketing channel is often treated as a fragmented assortment of a competing, independently operating organisation. For example, a manufacturer may look upon his own retailers as his competitors; or a middleman may be in conflict with his supplier.

Types of Channels of Distribution

(i) Through Jobbers: This is perhaps the oldest and widely used channel of distribution. Under this system, a jobber assembles products from a variety of producers, stores them and sells them to retailers. In doing so, he assumes the risk of a price rise or price fall and of product obsolescence. He provides credit facilities to retailers and sells the product to retailers on the basis of their requirements.

All these functions are essential in the distribution system, regardless of the channel of distribution used. When a large number of purchases come from retailers distributed over a wide territory, it is more desirable for the manufacturer to enlist the services of a wholesaler than to undertake such activities himself. Lower-order shopping and convenience goods are generally sold in this manner.

(ii) Direct to Consumer: In this system of distribution, there is no intermediary. Sales are directly made to consumer either by producers, or house to house visits of salesmen. This channel is largely utilised when the product is of such nature that technical expertise is required in connection with its sale and after its sale. For example, this channel is utilised by producers of computers, ripographers and industrial machinery.

Secondly, producers of a variety of consumer goods employ this channel to a certain extent. For example, producers of medicines, cosmetics, ready-to-wear clothes, furniture and, at times, publishers use this method. The producers of consumer goods utilising this method often advertise that a variety of expenses made by various intermediaries are totally eliminated and that the selling company bears all the costs of distribution. But for consumer goods this channel is not very desirable or economical.

(iii) Direct to Retailers: The distribution by the producer direct to the retailers has some distinct advantages. By utilising this method, he can put in a more aggressive sale effort to boost the sales of its products. This method also enables the producer to have first-hand information about the market and consumer's interests.

By utilising this method, the producer an exercise direct control over the final sale and establish a better relationship with retailers — a fact which plays a vital role in gearing up the sales for he is not dependent on an intermediary. He is also in a better position to influence price, promotional aids and other factors which have a direct bearing on the sales and goodwill of the organisation.

Some companies that manufacture a variety of products set up their own sales branches which, in many ways, perform the functions of jobbers, i.e., they sell goods directly to retailers. The distributor may also have a place in the retail shops of the manufacturer as in case of Bata Shoe Company or Bombay Dyeing Mills. Under this system, the manufacture is always in touch with trends in demands and consumer attitudes towards his products. But this system can only be profitably used by large manufacturers.

(iv) Through Brokers or Agents: In contrast to the jobber, a broker usually sells one type of product or a few closely-related products. Agents are largely employed for the distribution of producer's goods, though they may also be utilised for the distribution of consumer goods. For example, he can be extensively used for the sale of electronic goods, agricultural goods, farm machinery, fruits and vegetables, etc. This channel is largely utilised by small manufacturers with a limited product line who sell in a widely dispersed market.

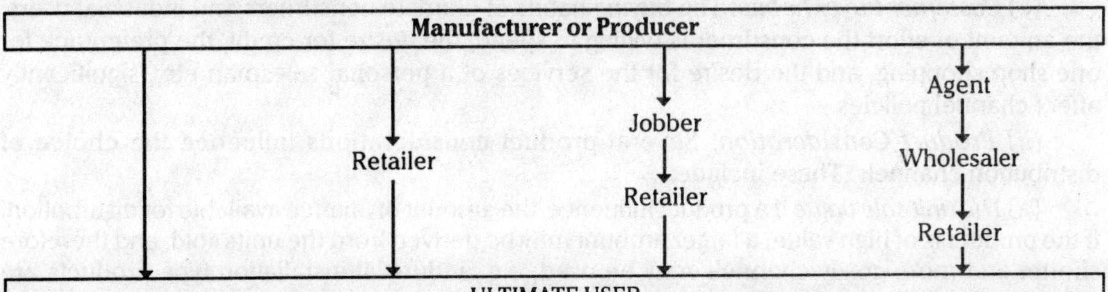

Choice of Distribution Channels

A large number of channels of distribution are available to the manufacturer to carry his product to the ultimate consumer. From this vast number of potential distribution arrangements, the marketing executives must screen those that may be appropriate for the distribution of the product at the least cost per unit of merchandise and the maximum volume of sales. Efficient distribution at the least cost and the attainment of the desired volume of sales are ends that can be secured only after a proper analysis of the market has been done. The nature of the product, its unit value, its technical characteristics, the extent of its differentiation from competitive products, and other product characteristics, financial resources, available expertise with the company, the availability of a suitable middleman, etc. are the factors which may limit the number of "potential channels alternatives". Individually or in combination, they may restrict the alternatives available in a given line of trade to those containing a certain number of distribution levels, or to those for which middlemen are equipped to provide technical services and repair facilities, or to those where middlemen have specialised storage facilities or are specialists in some aspects of marketing.

The Factors affecting the choice of channels may be discussed under five heads:

(i) Market consideration;
(ii) Product consideration;
(iii) Company consideration;
(iv) Middlemen consideration;
(v) Consumer consideration;

(i) Market Consideration: (a) The nature of the market is regarded as one of the important factors. For example, is the product meant for consumers or for industrial buyers? If it is for the consumer market, retailers will have to be employed. If it is for both the markets, more than one channel will have to be employed.

(b) The *number* of potential customers. If it is large, the services of a number of middlemen will be required; and if it is small, only the company's sales force may be used.

(c) *Geographic concentration* of the market. If the potential customers are concentrated in a few areas, direct selling may be done effectively. But a large number of middlemen will have to be employed if the customers are widely spread over the entire country. In densely populated areas, selling may be done through company's sales offices or branches.

(d) *Order size*: If the sales volume is large, direct selling may be economically feasible; for example, sales of food products to chains of grocery stores. Industrial supplies are sold through industrial distributors.

(e) *Customer buyer habits*: The buying habits of ultimate consumers and industrial users, the amount of effort the consumer is willing to spend, the desire for credit, the preference for one-shop shopping, and the desire for the services of a personal salesman etc., significantly affect channel policies.

(ii) Product Consideration: Several product considerations influence the choice of distribution channels. These include:

(a) *The unit sale value* if a product influence the amount of finance available for distribution. If the product is of high value, a larger amount may be derived from the units sold, and therefore shorter and more costly channels may be used; e.g., industrial installation type products are sold directly, while small accessory equipments are sold through agents.

(b) *Bulk and Weight*: Heavier and more bulky items, when freight forms a significant part of the total value, are transported in truck load or wagon load quantities to minimise freight cost.

(c) If the product is perishable, a shorter channel will be preferred, while for non-perishable products a wider choice of channels is available.

(d) The technical nature of the product requiring services will necessitate its sale through sales-and-service men, who may explain the utility of the product to the customer and even provide pre-sale and post sale services.

(e) The *broader the product line, the shorter the channel*. The producer of only one item will use wholesaling middlemen, while that with a number of product lines may directly deal with the customer.

(f) *The nature of the product.* If the product is custom-made, it may be distributed directly by the producer to the ultimate customer or industrial user. But if it is tailor-made, the selection by the customer of the product may be made from samples, catalogues, etc.

The nature of the product to be marketed must be taken into consideration. If the sale of the product calls for special skill on the part of the seller (a product like a charcoal gas generator for motor cars), it may be necessary to use trained salesmen to sell it directly to prospective consumers. But as the volume of sales necessary for an adequate profit would necessitate the employment of a large sales force, it would probably be less costly and more efficient to appoint district sales agents. This would also provide the means for the necessary maintenance services.

If the product is hard to sell or its price is too low to permit the use of salesmen calling directly on consumers, retailers should be approached. They should be given an attractive margin of profit and should be induced to sell the product. When the demand for it grows, wholesalers often go to the manufacturer for supplies, and the manufacturers may decide to let them handle the line, for they will be able to sell in large lots, which will lower their packing, handling and delivery expenses; these savings may then be passed on to the wholesalers are their remuneration. In actual practice, it is often necessary to sell some goods directly to the retailers. Such retailers have the capital to purchase large quantities prefer to buy directly, while those who lack capital are more or less financed by wholesalers and prefer to buy through them.

(iii) Company Consideration: Company considerations are of paramount importance in deciding the channels of distribution. Financially strong companies are able to avail themselves of the services of middlemen, and are in a position to exercise a definite control over various channels of distribution. In this context, two points may be kept in mind:

(a) Financially sound companies may utilise the services of their sales force and branches in a much better may. They can grant credit for a long period or warehouse their products, whereas weak concerns are obliged to get these services from middlemen.

(b) The desire for the control of channel may influence the producer in establishing a short and direct channel, even though it may be more costly. A more aggressive sales promotion may also be undertaken.

(iv) Middlemen Consideration: This should take into account the following:

(a) Middlemen's services influence channels. If the product needs aggressive promotion or special storage facilities, which can conveniently be provided by the wholesaler and which ordinarily cannot be provided by the manufacturer, the services of the middlemen are to be utilised.

(b) *The channel* which offers the maximum sales volume is preferred to the channel offering little business.

(c) In making a choice of sales channels, the cost of each proposed channel should be estimated on the basis of the unit of sale. That method of distribution should be chosen which will give the desired volume at the least cost. For example, a particular method of distribution may require a small layout of money; but the number of units sold may be so small that the cost of selling is much higher than it would be if some other method were used.

(v) Consumer Consideration: From consumer's point of view, the justification of the marketing processes is that they make it easy for them to buy goods. While some marginal buyers of a product may weigh the question of its price, logical consumers do not mind paying for the marketing processes which enable them to obtain products in the quantities they desire, at the time they want them and/or the terms on which they prefer to buy. For example, a very large number of people prefer to buy from retailers who sell to them on account. They know that they pay a little more for their products, but they believe that the convenience of paying once a month is well worth the extra cost. There are some commodities, such as radios or refrigerators, whose price is higher than the majority of logical consumers can afford to pay at one time. The convenience of buying this class of goods on easy instalment basis justifies the higher price.

But perhaps the advantage which the consumer most desires is that the goods he wants to buy are available at a convenient location. The significance of "convenient location" differs from commodity to commodity. For example, when milk, butter, bread, and other articles of daily consumption are purchased, consumers like to have them delivered to their homes. But when they buy groceries, they go to their grocer and select the things they want once a month, or once a week, according to their habit and convenience.

Often, a manufacturer may use multiple channels to reach different markets when:

(i) the same product (sporting goods, typewriters, fans or sewing machines, shoes, etc.) is sold to both the consumer and the industrial markets;

(ii) unrelated products (paint and margarine or rubber products and plastics) are to be sold;

(iii) the manufacturer wants to reach the same market, but one in which there are differences in the size of the buyers or the densities within parts of the market. For example, a producer of industrial machinery may use his own salesmen to sell directly to the users in concentrated markets; but he may also employ manufacturers' agents to reach customers in dispersed markets.

Selection of Channels for New Product

When a new product is added to the existing product line, or an unrelated product is marketed, or a new company starts functioning with a new product, three important factors need to be taken into consideration.

First, the newness of the product and the extent to which consumers realise that they want it.

Second, aggressive promotion, either through the manufacturer's own sales force to call directly on retailers or by the employment of agents.

Third, all possible efforts will have to be made to use any appropriate channel available.

Intensity and Extent of Distribution or Market Coverage

After deciding upon the channel of distribution, the manufacturer has to determine how many middlemen should be in the channel, i.e., the intensity of distribution to be used at the wholesaling and retailing levels in the channel has to be considered. Manufacturers recognise three degrees of intensity: two are extremes, the third is a middle course. These are intensive distribution, exclusive distribution or selective distribution.

Intensive Distribution: This strategy is used by producers of convenience goods and common raw materials. The purpose is to saturate the market as much as possible with their products. Such strategy is generally employed when the product is inexpensive and frequently purchased. Consumers want it near their areas; and where the market is competitive, the unit of purchase is usually small, the price per unit is small, and retailers enjoy a high stock-turnover on a small inventory. The responsibility for advertising is that of the manufacturers themselves.

Exclusive Distribution: Under this strategy, the manufacturer sells his products to a particular middleman or retailer in a particular area, i.e., here, exclusive distribution rights are granted to a particular distributor (wholesaler or retailer, as the case may be); and he is prohibited from handling a directly competitive product line. This strategy is adopted in a relatively large area and for goods which are frequently purchased, consumed over a long period of time, and call for service or information for their use. Product features and consumer buying habits are quite different from those in intensive distribution. Extremely expensive glassware, farm machinery, large construction equipment, watches, radios and commercial heating and air-conditioning equipment are often retailed in this manner. At the wholesale level, the manufacturer's agents, brokers and occasional wholesalers enjoy sole selling privileges in their respective areas.

Selective Distribution: Under this strategy, intermediaries are selected form among those who will most probably contribute to the attainment of specific sales volumes and profit goals. This strategy is used for speciality and shopping goods and also for convenience goods — such as industrial accessory equipment, pens, silverware, shoes, watches, etc. The manufacturer's product is available to all department stores, jewellery stores, and clothing stores.

It should be noted that the consumer's preferences determine the intensity of distribution. If consumers, for example, are not willing to spend much time and effort on shopping and buying, manufacturers must provide for intensive distribution. If consumers are willing to spend time and effort on buying an electrical appliance, the distribution can be much more selective.

Channel Decisions

Channel decisions are among the most critical of marketing decisions because channels of distribution affect product, price and promotion decisions. Channel decisions are not always made prior to other marketing decisions; but they exercise a powerful influence on the rest of the marketing mix. Another significant aspect of marketing channels is that the relationship among the channel members (producers, wholesalers and retailers) usually involve relatively long-term commitments. While prices can usually be changed and producers may have considerable control over products and promotion, marketing channels are less flexible. There are legal commitments to intermediaries, and replacing or bypassing them means extra botheration, effort and responsibility. Therefore, the decision has to be taken with caution.

Stanton provides some guidelines for the use of marketing management while developing channels of distribution.[24] These are:

The channel analysis should begin with the final customer and work backward to the producer because essential channels of distribution are determined by consumer buying habits, i.e. appropriate outlets should be available to the customers.

Channels finally established must be totally appropriate to the basic objectives of the firm's marketing programme.

The channels should provide a firm with access to a predetermined share of the market, including a definite level of intensity of market penetration.

24. Stanton, W.G., *Fundamentals of Marketing*, 1983, p. 239.

The channel must be sufficiently flexible to ensure that the use of one channel will not permanently close off another.

There is high degree of interdependence among all the firms in the channels for any given product, i.e., there should be no weak link in the chain if it is to be successful.

Constant evolutionary and sometimes almost revolutionary changes occur, which necessitate that economic forces should be taken into account while marking decisions for constant changes.

Middlemen survive only when their existence is based on sound economic considerations and is socially desirable. Moreover, new middlemen and channels arise to do new jobs or to do those that are not being done properly.

PRICING POLICIES

Prices and pricing policies are probably the most tricky aspects of marketing management. It is largely assumed that consumers will buy a thing if the price is reasonable. But to determine a reasonable price is an uphill task, for it is affected by a variety of interacting and interdependent factors. The price at which a product is sold has a definite impact on its production, distribution and promotion and also on the purchasing power of customers.

The competitor's pricing strategy and legal restrictions on pricing also determine the overall pricing policy of an industry. The final market price is the net result of a variety of interacting forces.

The complexity in the determination of prices in most cases puts the management in a difficult situation. While some firms feel that experience is the best guide for price determination, others embark on elaborate economic studies for its determination. This calls for new methods of determining specific prices to guide marketing personnel in their daily activities.

The pricing policies of a firm must be co-ordinated with its policies relating to product, channels to distribution, and sales promotion. For example, if a company wants to sell its high-quality product to select market segments, its pricing policy obviously will differ from that of the company which aims at selling a low-quality product to a broader market segment.

In determining prices, the company must concentrate on the following questions:

(i) What are the objectives of pricing?
(ii) What will be the relationship of prices with those of competing products?
(iii) What will be the relation of prices to the cost of production and distribution?
(iv) How will different items of the product line be priced?
(v) What will be the price differential policy?
(vi) How frequently and under what circumstances will the prices be changed?
(vii) What will be the pricing policy over the product life cycle?

Objectives of Pricing

Prices and price policies are of great importance to the manufacturer, wholesaler, retailer and the consumer in general. That is why considerable attention is given to their determination. The market price is the price at which a particular good changes hands. It is the price at which a good is offered for sale by one person to another. A low or a high price may make for the success or failure of a product, depending somewhat upon the scale of production. It is, therefore, the duty of the marketing manager to spell out the objectives of pricing before he determines the price itself. Pricing objectives are overall goals that describe the role of price in an organisation's long-range plans.[25] These objectives provide guidance to decision-makers in formulating pricing policies, planning pricing strategies and establishing actual prices. The most important objective of the companies is to earn maximum profits.

Other goals in pricing may be;

(a) To achieve a target return on investment;

(b) To stabilise prices;

(c) To maintain or improve a target share of the market;

(d) To meet or prevent competition;

(e) To maximise profits;

(f) To ensure survival; and

(g) To maintain an image.

(a) To Achieve a Target Return on Investment: An adequate return on investment or net sales is one of the main objectives of pricing. The target return may be a fixed percentage of sales; or a return on investment (ROI); or a fixed amount. The idea is to secure a sufficient return on the capital employed in the manufacture of specific products so that the sales revenue may ultimately yield a pre-determined average return to the whole company. This is generally a long-range goal. This objective is commonly used by companies that are "industry leaders" and those that sell in established markets (where there are no substitutes, i.e., "protected markets"). The achievement of a target rate of return requires an annual cash inflow large enough to cover production costs and provide a specific profit. For example, a company produces a single product, such as sewing machines, and expects to sell, say, 20,000 machines a year. The total investment amounts to Rs.20 lakhs. At 20,000-unit sales, the total unit cost is Rs.150. If the target return on investment is set at 30% before taxes, a return of Rs.600,000 is required in an average year. The company's pricing calculation would be something like this:

Total cost for 20,000 units @ Rs. 150 per unit	Rs. 3,000,000
30% before tax on investment of Rs. 20 lakhs	Rs. 600,000
$\frac{\text{Rs.}3{,}600{,}000}{20{,}000}$ = Rs. 180/-	Total Sales Rs. 3,600,000

The target rate is a helpful yardstick for a product's performance, especially if it is new. For large companies, target-return pricing is little more than a useful reference point, which has to be adjusted periodically to account for inflation and other fluctuating market factors.

(b) To Stabilise Prices: The objective of stabilising prices is to even out, or, if possible, eliminate, cyclical price fluctuations. During periods of depressed business or scarcity, marketers lower their output and keep prices from falling too low; and during periods of good business or prosperity, they increases their output and sell large quantities of goods at reasonable prices, and try to prevent prices from rising. Companies seeking stability in their prices are anxious to avert price wars when the demand is declining. Price leaders tend to take a long-run view of achieving stability. Their goal is "to live and let live."

(c) To Maintain or Improve Target Share of Market: The market position or sales in relation to competition are a very meaningful benchmark of success. Therefore, a company may set a target market share as its major pricing objective so that by focussing attention on it, it may not

25. Price, W.H. and Farrel, O.C., *Marketing: Basic Concepts and Decisions*, 1977, p. 210.

lose its former market position, It tries to maintain at least the *status-quo*, or to improve its position through continuous low pricing and through price penetration.

For example, the leading manufacturing concerns reduce the prices of their electrical and electronic appliances with a view to capturing and keeping a larger share of the market than they had when the product was very expensive. In many other areas, too, a number of companies cut prices in order to edge out competitors. Others offer unusually low prices in the hope that their market share and sales will benefit. This is what airlines often do.

When a favourable situation exists, any change might represent a threat, whether it is caused by customers, competitors or the government. Many companies may seek to maintain the *status-quo* within an industry to avoid price wars that reduce overall profits.

(d) To Meet or Prevent Competition: A pricing policy generally enables a firm to meet or even to prevent competition. If a company is the industry's price leader, it may set prices designed to discourage new competitors from entering the market. Similarly, companies that are price followers set their prices in order to meet the competitors' prices. When introducing a new product, low prices are often set in order to discourage competition.

One way in which this objective may be achieved is by pre-emptive pricing. This entails matching the competitor's prices to maintain the *status-quo* within an industry. Sometimes a firm may cut its prices drastically to prevent competitors from entering the market. Pre-emptive pricing policy tends to reduce the incidence of price wars.

(e) To Maximise Profits: This objective aims at making as much profit as possible. The goal is to maximise profits on the total output rather than on each single item. A manufacturer may maximise profits by pricing some products so inexpensively that he attracts the buyers' attention and stimulates the sales of other products. A retailer may sell goods at a very small profit; but if he attracts a large number of customers as a result, his overall profit is enhanced considerably.

A price maximisation policy is usually pursued by smaller firms or firms that are little known. A policy of "charging what the traffic will bear" tends to make a firm unpopular with consumers. An excessively high rate of return in an industry may lead to the rapid entry of competitors and to lower prices in the long run.[26]

(f) To Ensure Survival: The fundamental pricing objective is to survive. Most organisations can tolerate short-run losses, internal upheaval, and many other difficulties if these are necessary to their continued existence. Price is used to increase the sales volume to a level that matches the organisation's expenses.

(g) To Maintain an Image: A company's image is important for its success. This is largely influenced by its pricing policy. A firm with an established reputation based on existing price curves may introduce a new line at either higher or lower prices to appeal to a different market segment. If this segment has not earlier bought any of the company's products but is aware of its prestige, it might desire to purchase its products because price is no longer a deterrent factor.

Factors Which Determine Pricing

There are no cook-book rules or formulae for the management to arrive at effective pricing decisions. These are influenced by many interacting forces. Such decisions must be consistent with the company's desired public image, i.e., they should derive directly from the company's objectives. Secondly, price policies should be consistent with pricing objectives, and pricing

26. Bell, Martin, L., *Marketing Concepts and Strategy*, Hongton Co., Boston, 1972, p. 860.

strategies should be in conformity with both price policies and pricing objectives. Thirdly, pricing decisions can be made only on the basis of the company's knowledge of its overall marketing environment, viz., the internal factor (such as company objectives, company brand image, the nature and objectives of the promotional effort, marketing channels, and the physical distribution system) and the environmental factors (such as competition, economic climate and government controls/regulations). (Fig. 11.4)

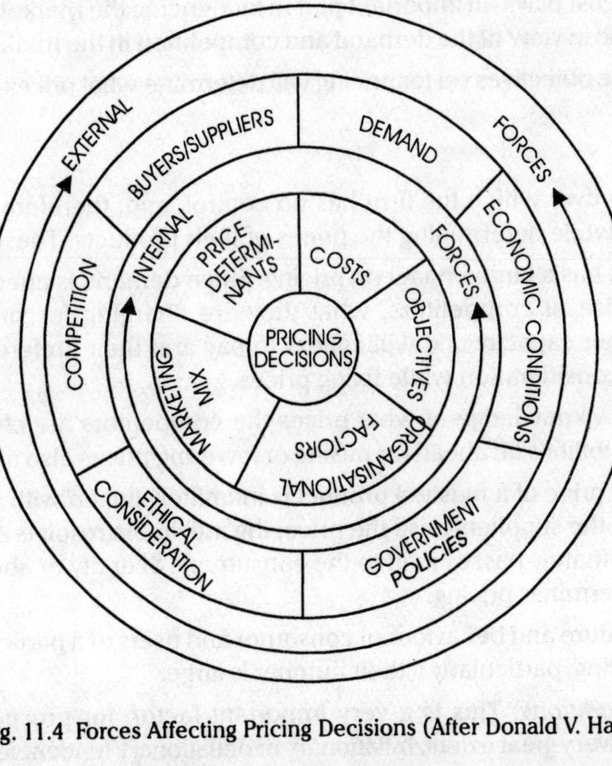

Fig. 11.4 Forces Affecting Pricing Decisions (After Donald V. Harper).

Internal Factors

These are the factors which can be controlled by a firm to a certain extent. These are: organisational considerations, marketing-mix product differentiation, costs and objectives.

(a) Organisational Factors: It is the top management which generally has full authority over pricing. The marketing manager's role is to administer the pricing programme within the guidelines laid down by the top management. Pricing activities have such a direct effect on the sales volume and profit that the marketing manager cannot keep himself aloof from pricing, policy making and strategy formulation. However, in many companies, some authority is granted to subordinate executives for setting prices, especially where the pricing policy varies in different markets; or where there are numerous products and frequent pricing decisions are required. But it is the top management which should retain the primary responsibility for determining pricing objectives, policies and strategies.

(b) Marketing Mix: Price is one of the important elements of the marketing mix, and therefore must be co-ordinated with the other three elements: production, promotion and distribution. In some industries, a firm may use price reduction as a marketing technique; others may raise

prices as a deliberate strategy to build a high-prestige product line. In either case, the effort will fail if the price change is not commensurate with the total marketing strategy that it supports.

(c) Product Differentiation: Generally speaking, the more differentiated a product is from competitive products, the greater the leeway the firm has in setting prices. When its product is basically of the same quality as that of its competitors, it may differentiate its own image by building a solid reputation among customers by charging different prices.

(d) Costs: Often, cost plays an important part in influencing the marketer in his decision on what prices are realistic in view of the demand and competition in the markets.

(e) Objectives: The objectives set for pricing will determine what prices should be fixed for a particular product.

External Factors

These are factors over which the firm has no control, and, therefore, marketers have to face many difficulties while determining the prices of their products. These factors are:

(a) Demand: This has a large impact on pricing. Since demand is affected by such factors as the number and size of competitors, what they are charging for similar products, the prospective buyers, their capacity and willingness to pay and their preferences, these factors have to be taken into consideration while fixing prices.

(b) Competition: A knowledge of what prices the competitors are charging for a similar product and what possibilities lie ahead for raising or lowering prices also affects pricing.

(c) Suppliers: The price of a finished product is intimately linked with the price of the raw material; etc. Hence, if the suppliers raise the price, the inevitable result is a rise in price by the manufacturer, who ultimately passes it on to the consumers. Scarcity or abundance of the raw material, therefore, determines pricing.

(d) Buyers: The nature and behaviour of consumer and users of a particular product, brand or service do affect pricing, particularly if their number is large.

(e) Economic Conditions: This is a very important factor, for prosperity or depression influences demand to a very great extent. Inflationary or deflationary tendencies also affect pricing. To meet shortages or rising prices and decreased demand, several pricing decisions are available. Some of these are:

(i) Prices may be boosted to protect profit against rising costs;

(ii) Price protection systems may be linked with the price on delivery to current costs;

(iii) The emphasis may be shifted from sales volume to profit margin and cost reduction.[27]

(f) Government Regulations: The regulatory pressures and antiprice rise and control measures effectively discourage companies from cornering too large a share of the market or controlling prices.

(g) Among the other important factors that affect the general price level are: pressure for higher wages, competition, business productivity, buyer resistance, seller resistance, speculation, and government policy.

Below are given the factors that "push up" and "push down" prices in the market.

27. Mandell, M.I., and Larry, J.R., *Marketing*, 1983, p. 239.

Factors that Tend to Push Prices Up and Down.[28]

Forces that Tend to Push Up prices	*Forces that Tend to Push Down prices*
1. Short supply relative to demand.	1. A large supply relative to demand.
2. An increase in wages not matched by an increase in productivity.	2. Stable wages as productivity rises.
3. Weak competition and non-price competition.	3. Strong competition and competition on the basis of prices.
4. Lack of efficiency in the use of land, labour and capital.	4. The efficient use of land, labour and capital by business.
5. Buyers eager to acquire owernship (a bullish attitude).	5. Buyer resistance to purchasing for any reason (bearish attitude).
6. Sellers holding out for higher prices (a bullish attitude).	6. Sellers eager to sell (bearish (attitude).
7. Widespread speculation based on belief that prices will rise.	7. Belief that prices will go down.
8. Government action to increase the supply of money and reduce interest rates.	8. Government action to decrease the supply of money and raise interest rate.
9. Deficit spending by government, especially duirng periods of inflation.	9. A balanced government budget or a budget surplus.

Relations or Price to Competing Products

A firm, in making a pricing decision, must anticipate the reaction of competitors. The competitors' pricing activities or the possibility of such activities set a lower limit to prices. In deciding prices, firms must give due weight to the quality of their product and services in comparison with the competitors' standing in this regard.

Comparative Quality and Price

The quality of a variety of products can be accurately measured, and well-defined grades or standards can be established. For example, in agricultural produce, chemicals and some minerals, where quality can be precisely measured with a high degree of accuracy, the variation from the going market price is almost impossible with the variation in the quality of product; but different categories can be established bearing different prices. In the case of fruits, it has been noted that before they are marketed, they are graded and sold at different prices. In the case of standardised goods, the quality distinction is clearer still. When a significant quality-and-service differentiation exists, the manufacturer must decide whether:

(i) A higher price than that of the competiting product will be charged;
(ii) The price will be kept at par with that of competing products;
(iii) High prices will be charged initially to "skim the cream off the market", and later the prices will be slashed.

The choice of any of these alternatives will be contingent on such factors as: To what extent the company will be able to maintain its quality distinctiveness; the capacity of the consumer to pay of superior quality on the basis of which prices can be easily altered to face competition.

28. Schwartz, D.J., *Marketing Today: A Basic Approach*, 1977, p. 528.

Reaction of Competitors

In determining a pricing policy, a company should not only consider the immediate effect of prices, but also give due weight to the reaction of competitors. It should call for an effective market intelligence of the competitors' pricing policy. For example, if a company keeps prices below the market price with the intention of earning a huge profit in the short run, it must bear in mind the fact that the competitors, too, may resort to price cutting. In that case, they will be able to keep pace with the company's action.

Differences in Quality and Services

Quite often, for the vast majority of products, there are no commonly accepted standards of quality. They are largely determined by the producers' policy with respect to a particular market or market segments and by the tastes of individuals. For example, the different dishes served at a luncheon in a five-star hotel will carry a higher price than those served in an ordinary hotel or a road-side restaurant. In this particular case, the price depends on the class of hotel and the type of customer. Therefore, for pricing such products, the manufacturer must consider the quality of his product *vis-a-vis* the quality of his competitors products.

Differences in services rendered also influence the pricing policy of an enterprise. If a department store delivers an order free of charge or allows its customers one or two months' credit, its price will naturally be higher than that of the supermarket or ordinary retailer who sells goods on cash basis. The manufacturer catering to the needs of industrial buyers provides services in the form of credit, free delivery and advertisement. He has a different price policy from that of the local supplier providing goods in small quantities.

Size of the Company

The size of the company influences its pricing decision or price changes to a considerable extent. For example, the price charged by a large reputed manufacturer in a particular industry will have an impact on the pricing policies of that particular industry. Among small manufacturers, it is a common practice to quote lower prices than those of major producers, because their total sales volume in no way poses a threat to big producers. In the case of textiles, small manufacturers are able to increase their sales by quoting prices which are much lower than those of the leading manufacturers.

Market Conditions

The condition of the market profoundly affects the prices of products. For example, the textile industry in our country is suffering from a demand recession due to unfavourable government policies and reduction in the purchasing power of consumers. But no immediate or huge cut in price has been resorted to because the manufacturers know that their competitors may match any reduction in price. Nevertheless, the overall wholesale prices have decreased.

Relation of Prices to Cost

An effective pricing policy must bear some relation to cost. Attempts must be made to ensure that the prices of products generate a desirable level of profits.

In connection with price determination, industries do enjoy some discretion in setting the prices of their products above or below the market level. They, therefore, set prices in relation to cost. They may consider it desirable to sell products at prices which bring them a normal profit.

Selling at Normal Profit

Many industries price their products in such a manner that they cover the cost of production, distribution and normal profit. For instance, the textile industry, which is suffering from demand recession, has followed the policy of keeping the prices relatively stable. Large textile industries operating at a reasonable sales volume at these prices earn normal profits. In this condition, the maintenance prices by large producers have provided an "umbrella" under which small manufacturers flourish. For the last two years, the electronics industry has been facing an altogether different situation, for though advances in technology have facilitated reductions in the cost of production; yet no significant change in the prices of finished goods has been witnessed. Due to the high profit margin, a variety of competitors market goods at lower prices than those of reputed manufacturers.

Selling below Cost

There is a variety of forces which at times tempt companies to sell their products below the cost of production. Every producer has to incur certain expenses — rent, interest, wages, etc. —which have to be recovered whatever the level of sales. Besides this, the expenditure on material and labour varies with the volume of the product.

But it is not desirable for a company to sell goods below its total cost. With a view to increasing sales, some manufacturers resort to the policy of selling below cost of production. But if the turnover is low, this may lead to heavy losses and distort the market. Moreover, once the price is reduced, it is difficult to return to the previous level. Therefore, the pricing policy followed at one time may substantially affect the company's future pricing, beside affecting its sales.

Liquidation of Inventory

When there is overstocking of finished goods and the demand is at a low ebb, it is desirable to sell the goods below cost. In fact, it is desirable to do so in certain circumstances; for example, if a company does not enjoy good financial health and there is extreme paucity of funds, and bankruptcy is apprehended, it is desirable to sell goods below cost. Even financially sound companies at times find it desirable to sell goods below cost. For example, if market prices show a declining trend, it is desirable to sell the goods at any price they bring rather than stock them for a period, where they may fetch even lower prices. A similar condition may arise in a firm dealing in fashion goods or perishable goods, when circumstances compel middlemen to sell goods at a low price.

Loss Leader

Some retailers sell one or more standard goods below cost and the loss so sustained is made good by selling some other product at a relatively higher price or in some other way. At times, companies sell some goods below cost to provide service to its customers or to compete in a specific product line.

Effect of Volume on Cost and Profit

The cost of a product varies with the volume of production. The fixed expenses always remain the same, whether the volume is doubled or reduced to half; but with a variation in the volume of production, the per unit cost is substantially influenced. For example, an electric generator producer company estimated that it would cover its cost by selling 1500 units. The actual sales volume, however, was of the order of 1,100 units with the result that the company sustained a heavy loss because the total cost could not be reduced in correspondence with the decrease in sales. As a result, the average per unit cost increased. But the company could not increase the selling price of the generator, for it had to face competition. Besides, its overhead expenses did not vary with the decrease in the units of production. The cost of production also varies with changes in the prices of raw material. An increase in wages and salaries of employees increases or decrease selling and promotion costs. All the factors should, therefore, be considered by executives in determining the actual selling price of a product.

Estimation of Profit for Different Price Levels

As the cost of production varies with the volume of sales, the executives should estimate the quantum of products that can be sold at different prices, because changes in per unit cost affect the selling price which, in turn, determines the profitability of a concern.

This may be explained by an illustration that indicates the variations in profit with changes in prices. A company is able to sell 500 pieces of gloves each at the rate of Rs.15, and makes a profit of Rs. 2,000. By reducing price to Rs.12, it was able to sell 800 pieces; but when the price was reduced to Rs. 6, the company sold 1,400 pieces. Table below shows the possible effect of reduction in prices on the volume of sales, per unit cost, and total profitability. As is obvious from the table, with a decrease in price, there is a substantial increase in sales.

Effect of Prices of Volume, Cost and Profit

Price Rs.	*Number of Units sold*	*Cost per Unit (Rs.)*	*Profit per unit Rs.*	*Total Profit (2) x (4)(Rs.)*
15	500	10.00	4.00	2,000
12	800	9.90	4.25	3,400
10	1,000	9.60	3.90	3,900
8	1,200	9.50	3.40	4,080
6	1,400	9.40	2.50	3,500

In most cases, the unit cost does not decline rapidly when prices are reduced; consequently the profit margin decreases, as shown in column 4. The profit per unit is not the final yardstick of the desirability of a particular price, because emphasis must be placed on the number of units on which profit is earned. At times, an increase in price may lead to a higher profit per unit.

As is obvious from the table, the total profit earned depends on the volume of sales as well as the unit cost. But the relationship of profit to unit cost is not so simple, for it depends on a variety of factors. Some of these have been discussed below.

Competitor's Strategy in Relation to Price Changes

While establishing the desired sales volume for earning a definite profit, managers must bear in mind the strength of the competitive forces. If competition is excessive, and various competitors, to maintain their share, adjust to every price change, there is little chance that an industry would be able to earn a profit by reducing prices.

Elasticity of Demand

Another important factor that determines profitability is the elasticity of demand; for example, a grocer can increase its sales by reducing the price of certain standardised products. However, an electricity company cannot increase its profitability by reducing electricity charges.

Buyer's Attitude to Future Market Situation

Industrial buyers as well as various intermediaries adjust the volume of their purchases in anticipation of price changes. If a company reduces the prices of its various products, the buyers may curtail their purchase in the hope that prices may be further slashed. If an increase in prices is taken as an index of future scarcity of goods, the buyer may go in for heavy buying.

Besides these, there are a variety of factors which influence prices. The complexity of the problem is not due to varied problems but the inability to get correct information.

Composite Policies

Often, companies consider both their cost prices and the competitors' prices in determining the general price level. For example, a newly-established shoe company may use a low price as a sales appeal; it may follow a policy of selling at 5% below the price of a reputed competitor; and sales below cost may be made temporarily to compete with price leaders. However, in contrast to this, a company dealing in high quality electronic goods may fix prices that are at par with those of the competitors. In this case, at times prices are adjusted in the light of intensity of competition that is faced.

Policies Regulating Price of Individual Items

Price Lining

If a company sells several varieties of the same product, the price of one product is required to be established in relation to that of the others. For example, a ready-to-wear garment company may sell stockings at different prices, say at Rs.9.50, Rs.15.50 and Rs.20.50. This procedure is quite common with big department stores and retailers, who sell a wide variety of the same product. Some stores may carry one or two varieties of different products at each price level, whereas others may handle a variety of products at different prices. Moreover, they attempt to have a price spread throughout the range — from the lowest to the highest — instead of concentrating on a few points, thereby creating a wide price gap. Most consumer goods producers have a regular product line and a deluxe line; and if competition is acute, the super deluxe brand may be added to face it.

The price lining has attractions both for the consumer and the retailer. The consumer's buying decisions are simplified, since the number of prices from which he must make a selection is limited. The retailer finds the policy attractive because it helps him plan his buying. However, during periods of rising wholesale prices, it is often difficult to replenish stocks at costs low enough to permit retailing at established price lines; in such cases, the price retailer must either "trade down" his stock, i.e. have lower quality items or adjust his price line upward.

Different Price for Different Customers

One Price Versus Variable Price: Every industry, whether its products are sold at the same price to different customers or at different prices to different customers, can follow a one-price policy or a variable price policy

Under the one-price policy, the product is offered at exactly the same price to all similar types of customers who purchase more or less the same quantities on essentially the same terms of sale. Such a policy builds customer confidence in the seller at all levels. Weak bargainers with not then feel that they are at a competitive disadvantage. Since prices are not negotiated with individual customers, the selling time and the selling costs are reduced. This makes for a more orderly transaction process. It provides a uniform return on each sale and raises fewer problems in forecasting sales volumes and profits. Finally, this policy can be adopted whether personal salesmen are used or not, for it tends itself to service retailing and mail order selling.

Under the variable price policy, more or less the same quantities are sold to similar buyers at different prices. It is in common use where individual sales transactions involve large sums. Such prices are offered when sellers want a business of certain customers. The policy enables the seller to have flexibility in his dealings with different customers. The seller may offer concessions to woo a buyer way from a competitor, or he may want to give a buyer a better deal because the customer shows promise of becoming a large-scale buyer in future. But such a policy generates considerable ill-will when people learn that some buyers acquired the product at lower prices. Variable pricing can trigger a price war and call forth strong retaliation in some industries. The customer who feels that Rs.5.00 is too much to pay for a cloth handbag may buy the same if the price is, say, Rs.4.95.

Discounts and Allowances

Discounts and allowances are granted in the hope that the customer will in return perform some marketing whose value to the seller will be equal to the amount of the discount or allowance granted to him. These include quantity trade, cash and seasonal discounts, and promotional brokerage and freight allowances.

Quantity discounts are deductions offered from list prices by a seller in order to encourage a customer to buy larger quantities or to concentrate his purchases with a particular seller. This discount may be a non-cumulative discount or a cumulative discount. The former is offered on an individual order of one or more products. Wilson pens may be sold at Rs.1.50 each or 3 for Rs.4.00. The latter is based on the total volume purchased over a period of time. These are patronage discounts because the greater the volume of the business a buyer gives to a seller, the larger is the discount. Either type of these discounts may be used for selling related or unrelated products which are purchased by a single buyer. The slow-moving item may be sold with a more popular item if some attractive discount is offered. Such a discount also brings the advantage of large-scale economies of the seller.

Cash Discount

This is a deduction from the price granted to the buyer by wholesalers of manufacturers so that he may be prompt in payment, whether the payment is of a bill which is not yet due or a cash payment. The discount is calculated on the net amount due after first deducting trade and quantity discounts from the initial price. The functions of cash discounts have been clearly described by Prendergast. He observes:

"For the seller, the cash discount affords a ready means of judging the credit standing of his customers and also for eliminating the credit risk on a considerable part of his account. It enables him to concentrate his attention on the poorer credit risks which do not take the discount and, hence, tends to ensure the efficiency of his credit work at the same time curtailing the total amount of such credit work and reducing the cost of the credit department. In consequence, it should tend to decrease the total amount of loss due to bad debts. More rapid turnover of capital and more accurate planning of financial needs are also accomplished.

"From the point of view of the banking and credit system, the use of the cash discount results in having the buyer, as far as possible, obtain his funds directly from the bank instead of having recourse directly to the seller through buying on time and taking the net terms. The bank then measures the credit of the buyer directly, and not the seller. The latter only measures the credit of the buyer directly, and not the seller. The latter only measures the credit of the poorer accounts which do not take the discount, and himself borrows from the bank in turn in order to obtain funds with which to carry these accounts. He thus in fact guarantees such accounts to the banking system. He then has either a contingent liability on the receivables he has discounted, or a direct liability for his own borrowings, whereas with a buyer who takes a cash discount he assumes no responsibility whatsoever."[29]

The privilege of cash discount is sometimes abused. First, taking unearned discounts or, in other words, taking the discount after the expiry of the discount period. Second, the abuse of cash discount arises when buyers, who know themselves to be excellent customers and who buy comparatively large quantities, insist upon special discounts for cash. "This state of affairs is due partly to the method employed by some stores of penalizing departments whose buyers fail to secure a specified minimum discount. If the buyer fails to receive the required discounts, his department is charged with the difference between the discount obtained and the discount required. Similarly, the department is credited with the discounts which are secured in excess of the required figures. This practice is known as 'loading' and is regarded by enterprises which use it as a means of making sure that all buyers secure the largest possible discount. Another argument in its favour is that it enables executives to judge the abilities of various buyers on a uniform basis. Because of this practice, hard and unusual terms are demanded of sellers, with the result that the cash discount system is greatly harmed and sentiments are thereby generated for its abolition."[30]

Trade Discount or Functional Discount

This is granted by manufacturers or producers to wholesalers and retailers, and is in the nature of a deduction from the list price or quotation appearing in the catalogue of the firm. The rate of discount to be allowed is not fixed. For example, a manufacturer may quote a retail price of Rs.300 with a trade discount of 30% and 10%. The retailer pays Rs.210 (Rs.300 less 30%), and the wholesaler pays the manufacturer Rs.189 (210 less 10%). He is expected to keep 10% to cover the cost of his wholesaling functions and pass on 30% to retailers. Sometimes very high discounts are offered. Well-established firms, however, offer lower discounts on large single purchases or on large purchases over a period of time. However, a single customer may receive both kinds of discounts. As Clerk says: "It is impossible to determine where one ends and the other begins."[31]

Trade discounts are useful because they indicate to the retailer the prices at which the manufacturers think the merchandise should be resold to the customer. Such discounts, however, are sometimes used to deceive the buyer. This happens when the retailer agrees to order something for the customer which is temporarily out of stock but which is listed in the catalogue. The dealer shows the catalogue and the price list to the purchaser, and agrees to allow a certain percentage if an order is placed and if the customer agrees to take and pay cash for the product, whenever available.

Seasonal Discount

It is the deduction allowed on products which have only a seasonal demand. Manufacturers of electric fans, coolers or refrigerators may allow a discount of say, 5%, 10%, or 20% if an order is placed during the slack season. This type of order enables the manufacturer to level out his production schedule and make a better use of his facilities.

Promotional allowances are deductions allowed to buyers for undertaking promotional services. Promotional aids and materials for display may also be supplied to the buyer free of charge.

29. Prendergast, W.A. and Stainer, W.H., *Credit and its Uses*, p. 29.
30. Beckman, T.N., *Credit Collection in Theory and Practice*, pp. 100-101.
31. Clark and Clark, *Principles of Marketing*, 1947, p. 510.

Geographical Price Differentials

When products are despatched by ship, train or truck, the management has to decide who is to pay the freight. This may be paid by the seller, or by the buyer; or both may share the cost of freight.

F.O.B. Prices

The marketer using on F.O.B. pricing quotes his selling prices ex-factory, and the buyer pays all the freight charges. Buyers in different places have different "landed costs" — each pays the price at the selling point plus the freight from there to its location, thus determining its total costs for the delivered goods. The main attraction of F.O.B. pricing for the manufacturer is that it simplifies price quotations for those with whom he deals directly. However, such a policy may limit a firm's trading area, because customers nearer his place of operations pay less for transportation than those who are located far away. ·

Uniform Delivered Pricing or "Postage Stamp Pricing"

Under this pricing practice, the same delivered price is charged to all buyers regardless of their location. Such pricing system is used where transportation costs are a minor charge on the seller's total cost structure.

Zonal Delivered Pricing

Under it, a seller's market is divided into a number of geographic zones, and a uniform delivered price is quoted within each zone.

The Marketing Approach to pricing

This approach is demand-oriented. It takes into account:

(i) Product life cycles;
(ii) Promotional pricing.

This approach is closely linked with the pricing objectives, which are: achieving a target rate of return on investment; maintaining or improving the market. In this way, prices are competitive and profits are stabilised.

Price policies fall into two general categories:

(i) Those that use Strategies based on the product life cycle; and
(ii) Those that use strategies related to product lines.

Pricing Over the Product Life Cycle

At the introductory stage of a new product, relatively high price per unit is fixed with correspondingly high per unit margins. This is done because the product is generally meant for those customers who have a strong need and ability to pay a relatively high price.

At the growth stage, prices are fixed fairly high; but these begin to decline as the market reaches the maturity stage, and becomes highly competitive.

In the decline stage, the remaining buyers are usually highly conscious and therefore price-cutting is generally resorted to.

A firm pricing a product at the introductory stage of its life cycle has two alternatives. One, skimming, and two, penetration pricing. Which of these two policies should be employed will depend on the nature of the product, the number of substitutes available in the market, consumer shopping habits, the elasticity of demand, and the reaction of the competitors, if any.

Skim the Cream Pricing or Skimming Pricing

This strategy involves the establishment of a very high price so that, in the initial stages, the cream of demand may be skimmed, and enormous profits made for an indefinite period; or the price may be lowered later in order to tap other segments of the market. By this method, the investment made in the product may be quickly realised. Cream skimming is probably most effectively with a highly distinctive article which is aggressively promoted in the early stages of its life cycle.

There are four main reasons why this kind of skimming price policy is worthwhile for new and distinctive products:

First, the quality of the product that can be sold is likely to be less affected by price in the early stages than it will be when the product is full grown and imitations have had time to take effect. This is the period when pure salesmanship can have greatest effect on sales.

Second, a skimming price policy takes the cream off the market at a high price before attempting to penetrate the more price-sensitive sections of the market. This means that more money can be got from those who don't care how much they pay, while building up experience to hit the big mass market with tempting prices.

Third, demand can be felt out in this way. It is frequently easier to start out with a high refusal price and reduce it later.

Fourth, high prices frequently produce a greater volume of sales in the early stage of market development than a policy of low initial-stage prices. If this is the case, skimming pricing will provide the firm with funds for financing expansion into the big-volume sectors of the market.

Penetrating Pricing (Low Pricing)

This strategy involves the setting of a low price of the product as an "entering wedge" to get easily into "mass" markets.

The approach is likely to be desirable under the following conditions:

First, when the quantity of the product sold is highly sensitive to price, even in the early stages of introduction;

Second, when substantial economies can be achieved in unit cost by manufacturing and distributing the product in large volumes;

Third, when the product is faced by threats of strong potential competition soon after introduction;

Fourth, when there is no "elite" market, i.e., a body of buyers who are willing to pay a much higher price in order to obtain the latest and the best.

Finally, when there is a strong possibility that the public will accept the new product as a part of its daily life.

The decision to price so as to penetrate a broad market can be made at any stage in the product's life cycle; but then firm should carefully examine this pricing strategy before the new product is marketed. This possibility should be explored as soon as the product has established an "elite" market. Sometimes a product can be rescued from a premature death by the adoption of a penetrative price policy after the cream of the market has been skimmed. The ease and speed with which competitors can bring out substitute products is probably the most important single consideration in the choice between *skimming* and *penetration* pricing at the time of the introduction of new product. For a product whose market potential is very promising, a policy of low initial prices ("stay-out pricing") makes sense, because the big multiple product manufacturers are attracted by mass markets. If the price is set low enough to begin with, the large competitor may not feel it worthwhile to make a big production and distribution investment for slim profit margins. In any event, the firm should appraise the competitive situation very carefully for each new product before it decides on its pricing strategy.

Reserve Pricing Strategy

This type of strategy is sometimes used by firms when they fix up the retail price of a product before the design and production costs are estimated. The price of the product determines how much should be budgeted for manufacturing and marketing it rather than *vice versa*. A reverse price policy may be adopted either because the product will be competitive, price-wise, with existing products or because the product should have a certain position in its product line.

Promotional Pricing Policies

The term *promotional pricing* is generally applied when low prices are offered as a major advantage of a particular product or service. The other advantages may be special low-price sales, offers of premiums or trading stamps, provision of special low-price sales, offers premiums or trading stamps, provision of special displays or advertising or promotional allowances (known as Push Money (PM) paid directly to the salesman for pushing the product. Such allowances may also be granted for trade-ins, providing installation and repair services, handling, financing, repayment or storage.

Promotional pricing policies include:

(a) Leader pricing; and

(b) Bait pricing.

(a) Leader Pricing: This type of pricing is used mainly by retailers, for example, by supermarkets. Its purpose is not to get customers to buy bargains but rather to buy other items once they have been drawn into the store.

(b) Bait Pricing: This is designed to get consumers into the store to buy other products. It is an unethical practice, through which a salesman tries to convince the customer that the product is really worth buying and then to switch him to another, higher-margin product.

Psychological Pricing Policies

Psychological pricing is an attempt to select prices that have some kind of emotional appeal for the customer. This sometimes means choosing a price that appears to be lower than it actually is. For example, a customer who feels that Rs. 5.00 is too much to pay for a cloth handbag may buy the same if the price is, say, Rs.4.95.

Such pricing policies are practised at the retail level in the form of odd or even pricing, customary pricing, prestige pricing.

Odd or Even Pricing

This pricing refers to the setting of retail prices that end in odd amounts — say, Rs. 10.95 or Rs. 11.87 rather than 11.00 or Rs. 12.00. The rationale for this policy is that customers perceive the odd prices as a better buy. Even expensive products appear less expensive when priced in this way. On the other hand, even number pricing appears to be more effective in selling prestigious products about which consumers have little knowledge.

Customary Pricing

This type of pricing is usually done for products which reach the maturity stage of their life cycle. These are the prices which consumers are expected to pay.

Prestige Pricing

Such pricing is done to enhance the image of other products in the same product line. Such a policy is based on the assumption that a high priced product will be sold better and taken to be of good quality than a low-priced product.

PROMOTIONAL POLICIES

The promotional policy is the key element in the overall marketing strategy of an undertaking. The first element is the product policy, which focusses upon fitting the product and its features to the target market's needs and wants. The second element, the customer policies, is concerned with deciding about the location of the final consumers and the ways of reaching them. The third element, the pricing policy, relates to the conditions on which the product will be sold. The fourth and most essential ingredient of the marketing strategy is promotion, which refers to the activities and processes designed to change or reinforce the behaviour and/or the ideas of the consumers through communication, so that they are persuaded to buy what they might not otherwise buy, or what they don't really want to buy. Promotion is *telling* and *selling*. It is an exercise in information, persuasion and influence. These three are inter-related in the sense that to "inform is to persuade;" and if "a person is persuaded, he is informed."

The main object of a promotion programme is to induce customers to buy the company's product at its established price. To achieve this objective, the manufacturer is expected to undertake all such programmes as would develop the consumer's interest in his product, and lead him to the point of purchase. The important decisions pertaining to promotion focuses on:

(A) Advertising;

(B) Sales Promotion;

(C) Personal Selling;

Advertising

"Wherever we turn, advertising will be forcibly thrust on us in an intensive orgy of abrasive sound and sight, all to induce us to do something we might not ordinarily do or do it differently. This massive and persistent effort crams increasingly more commercial noise into the same, few, stained 24 hours of the day."[32]

The reason for the heavy bombardment of advertisement which people experience is quite simple to communicate, inform and persuade them to buy some good or commodity which has been advertised. It is a basic fact about marketing life that even when a product is designed as per the customer's specifications and sold at a reasonable price, it would not be successfully marketed unless customers are informed about its availability and usage.

32. Theodore Levitt, "The Morality of Advertising," in *Harvard Business Review*, No.4, July-August 1970, p. 84.

Advertising is the art of influencing human action; the awakening of the desire to possess; and posses the product. It is a mass persuasion; and it is any form of publicity given to products or services at the expense of the person who wants such publicity to bring his products and services to the notice of the general public.

Advertisement is an important medium through which producers communicate to the customers about their product or services. But mere communication is not enough, for it often fails to yield the desired results. Therefore, to reap the benefits of advertising, the management should give due consideration to the following questions:

(i) For what purposes will the advertisement be used?
(ii) Which media will be utilised to attain the objective?
(iii) What will be the organisation for advertising?
(iv) How will advertising be budgeted?
(v) How will the effectiveness of advertisement be measured?

The Purpose of Advertisement

For a given market target, there are six purposes which an advertisement seeks to attain. It is possible to achieve more than one type of objective with one single campaign; but that is both difficult and costly. Whenever a company seeks to achieve more than one purpose through an advertisement, it must make sure that the various purposes are in conformity with its overall marketing strategy.

The basic purposes of advertisement are:

(a) Awareness;
(b) Reminder to use;
(c) Changing belief about the brand;
(d) To assist salesmen in marketing products;
(e) Generating direct sales;
(f) Building the company's image.

(a) Awareness: One of the most common objectives of advertisement is to increase the recognition of a brand name or product, or to communicate information about the availability of the product. This is an important objective from many point of view. First, when a new product enters the market, it does not easily gain the favour of the buyers unless they are well informed about it. That is, an awareness about the product must exist before a favourable attitude toward the brand can be developed. An awareness about the brand is all the more important when several brands compete with each other.

(b) Reminder to Use: For discretionary items having an irregular or unusual pattern, an appropriate advertising policy must aim at stimulating the primary demand. To attain this objective, the buyers must be reminded not only to use the product but also to restock it.

(c) Changing Belief About Brand: If an attribute is already considered important, buyer will examine the relative strength of different brands with respect to that attribute. Accordingly, the objective of advertisement is to improve the buyer's rating with regard to the product advertised *vis-a-vis* the other competing brands. When the attribute of a product is not peculiar, advertisements are floated to establish the superiority of product over other competing brands.

(d) Marketing Product: The manufacturer extensively use advertisement for this purpose. Through advertisement, they try to familiarise the customers with their products and tend to promote a favourable attitude toward them before buyers are approached by salesman. That is

why, when a salesman approaches a customer, it is relatively easy for him to sell the product. For example, companies producing machine tools advertise their goods in those trade magazines which are read by their customers. Such advertisements may induce potential customers to purchase the product. At any rate, they create a favourable attitude toward the product so that the salesman may find it easy to canvass support for it.

Some companies assist retailers in arranging window displays and store decorations. This serves a dual purpose: it creates consumer interest and facilitates a favourable reception of the product by the retailer.

(e) Generating Direct Sales: In some cases, advertising is used for the purpose of persuading the customer to place an order for the product. Mail order houses through leaflets and catalogues, advertise their products in such a manner that customers are convinced of their value and are tempted to write to the institution to get the product without going to a shopping centre or without going into further details about the product.

Products like books, ready-to-wear garments, slimming machines, toys and sports goods can be profitably sold by direct mail advertisements. Through such advertisements, the company lays strees on price appeal, and uses such slogans as "direct from factory to you."

(f) Building Company's Image: Practically all companies try to build their image through advertisements. Some consider it as the primary objective of advertisement. For example, Godrej, Lakme, Vimal, VIP have built up an image through advertisement. It is largely assumed that if the company has some image or reputation in the market, it will be easy to sell its product. For example, Vimal's clothing is very costly; yet it has good sales because of its image.

(g) Selection of Advertising Media: Advertising is a vehicle through which advertisers communicate their messages to customers to induce them to buy the products or services advertised by them. The principal advertising media are:

(i) Press Media;
(ii) Direct mail media;
(iii) Outdoor media;
(iv) Other media;

Though a wide variety of advertising media are available, yet selection and use of an appropriate medium pose a variety of problems, which cannot be altogether solved by the management media specialist or even by an advertising agency. As is obvious from Table 11.1, each medium has its own merits and demerits. It is, therefore, quite difficult to determine which type of medium would be the most desirable one and which one would best influence target audiences.

There are three major policy decisions with regard to the selection of advertising media. First, the management must decide whether *general media like* T.V., Radio, Newspapers or magazines will be used. If magazines are used, will the management make use of such general magazines as *The Illustrated Weekly of India, Dharamyug, Probe*; or will women's magazines and professional magazines be used? If TV or Radio is used, will they concentrate on national advertising or local advertising?

To answer these questions, managers should give due consideration to the factors detailed below.

TABLE 11.3
CHARACTERISTICS, MERITS AND DEMERITS OF MAJOR ADVERTISING MEDIA

Medium	*Type*	*Units of Sale*	*Factors Affecting Rates*	*Merits*	*Demerits*
(1)	*(2)*	*(3)*	*(4)*	*(5)*	*(6)*
Newspapers	Morning Evening Sunday Weekly	Agate lines Column inches Counted words Printed lines	Volume and frequency counts Number of colours Position charges for preferred and guaranteed positions Circulation lelvel	Almost everyone reads a daily newspaper; total circulation is increasing; purchased to be read; national geographical fexibility; short lead time; frequent publication; favourable for co-operative advertising; merchandising services.	Not selective regarding socio-economic groups; short life; limited reproductive capabilities; Large volume prevents extensive exposure for any one advertisement.
Magazines	Consumer Industrial Farm Business	Press Partial pages Columns	Circulation level; cost of publishing; type of audience; volume discounts; frequency discounts; size of advertisement; position of advetisement; number of colours; regional issues.	Socio-economic selectivity; good production; long life; prestige; geographic selectivity when regional issues are available; read in leisurely manner.	High absolute cost; long lead time.
Direct mail	Letters Catalogues Price lists Calendars Brochures Circulars Newsletters Postcards Broadsides Samples Coupons	Not applicable	Cost of mailing lists; postage; production cost.	Little wasted circulation; highly selective; controlled by advertiser; few distractions; personal; stimulates actions, use of novelty. Relatively easy to measure performance; hidden from competitors.	Expensive, no editorial matter to attract readers; considered junk mail by many; criticised as invasion of privacy.
Radio		Programmes; Sole Sponsor; Co-sponsor Sports 5, 10, 15, 30, 60 seconds.	Time of day; audience size; length of spot programme; volume discounts.	Highly mobile; low-cost broadcast medium; message can be quickly changed; can reach a large audience; geographic selectivity; socio-economically selective.	Provides only audio-message, has lost prestige; short life of message; listeners' attention limited because of other activities while listening.

Table 11.3 (Contd.)

(1)	(2)	(3)	(4)	(5)	(6)
Television	Network Local	Programme; Sole sponsor; Co-sponsor; Sports; 5, 10 20, 30, 60 seconds.	Time of day; length of programme; length of spot; volume and frequency discounts; audience size.	Reaches extremely large audience; low cost per exposure; utilises sight and sound; highly visible; high prestige; geographic and demographic selectivity	High cost; highly perishable message; audience may enjoy commercial but ignore message; size of audience not guaranteed; amount of prime time limited.
Inside Transit	Buses and Trains	Full, half and quarter showings are sold on a monthly basis.	Number of readers; multiple month discounts; production costs; position	Low-cost, "captive" audience; geographic selectivity.	Does not reach business nad professional persons; does not secure quick or direct results; limited growth.
Outside	Bus Taxi cabs	Full, half and quarter showing; space also rented on per-unti basis.	Number	Low cost; geographic selectivity; reaches a broad, driverse audience.	Lacks demographic selectivity; does not have high impact on readers.
Outdoor	Prepared posters; painted displays; spectaculars	Prepared posters; sold on monthly basis in multiples called "showing" Painted displays and spectaculars; sold on per-unit basis.	Length of time purchased; land rental; cost of production; intensity of traffic; frequency and continuity discounts; location.	Allows per repetition; low cost; message can be placed close to the point of sale; geographic selectivity; can operate 24 hours a day.	Message must be short and simple; no demographic selectvity; seldom attracts reader's full attention; critised for being a traffic hazard and a blight on nature.

(a) Ranking of Media

While selecting the medium or media, the management has to consider the relative strength of different media that are available. There are many variables which have a direct bearing on the effectiveness of a particular medium to communicate the desired message. It is impossible, therefore, to assess the relative worth of different media which can make an advertising programme effective and advantageous.

In evaluating the relative worth of different media, the management must consider the following issues;

(i) The peculiar feature of the message to be communicated;

(ii) The technical requirement imposed by the medium on the advertisement; for example, many magazines require several weeks' lead time for the submission of advertisements. As a result, the company cannot base its advancements on current events;

(iii) The availability of preferred space and time;

(iv) The manner in which it is received and perceived by audiences;

(v) The extent to which it is used by the competitors.

Which of these variables should be considered and what relative weight should be given to each are questions which have to be considered by the management before selecting a medium or media.

(b) Class of People to be Influenced

The class of people to be influenced by an advertisement is an important determinant of media selection. Customers can be segmented on the basis of different indices—social class, educational level, income level; or on the basis of profession, age group, sex, state of the life cycle, rural and urban background, etc. This segmentation helps advertisers to determine the most effective medium for advertising a particular product. For example, if a company is selling medical kits, it will have to advertise its products in a medical journal; one selling cosmetics and women's wear will have to advertise them in women's magazines; for general consumer goods largely used by urbanities, general magazines, (such as *Dharamyug*, *The Illustrated Weekly* and *Sarita*), would be a very good medium. TV and radio can be tapped for advertisements. Farm machinery, auto parts can be effectively advertised by putting up boards, hoardings, etc.

(c) Objective of Advertisement

Media selection is contingent upon the objectives for which an advertisement aims at. For example, for an advertisement for matrimonial alliance, magazines and newspapers are the most suitable medium. For an advertisement for managerial personnel, magazines *(like Indian Management)* and newspapers (like *The Economic Times)* are a more effective medium than the radio or outdoor advertising. Where advertisement intends to educate the public, for example, an advertisement for family planning or encouragement of the savings habit—TV and the cinema are better than any other medium.

(d) Reputation of the Media

The reputation of a medium is an important determinant of advertising effectiveness. For example, advertisements appearing in reputed magazines (like the *Reader's Digest* and *India Today*) are considered to be more honest than those appearing in local magazines of less repute. The medium recognized for its prestige or expertise on a given subject may be an excellent choice for the advertisement of a certain product or service (for example, *Sports Week* is a good medium for advertising of athletic equipment). Coaching institutes advertise in magazines which are exclusively meant for competitions.

(e) Cost of Media

The companies spend a fairly good amount of their marketing budget on advertisement. Therefore, adequate care must be taken for the selection of media; otherwise the money so spent will fail to generate the desired results. For example, TV sports and film slides are quite effective but very costly in comparison with magazine and newspaper advertising. However, except in the case of media that are usually costly relative to the size of the advertising budget, the manager should not generally eliminate a specific medium from further consideration at this point. Moreover, the actual cost per insertion varies with its size, length and position in any medium.

(f) Requirements of Message

The message to be communicated has a direct bearing on the selection of medium; example, for such products as textiles, ready-to-wear clothing, cosmetics, energy food, etc., which require pictorial presentation, can be most effectively advertised in magazines, on TV, film slides and the radio. But insurance services cannot be properly advertised on TV or radio; for them handbills and magazines are the effective media.

(g) Time and Location of Buying Decision

A medium which reaches the prospective customer, as near as possible to him and at a particular time, can be best chosen for products like groceries, dairy and bakery products, or gasoline, etc.

Before choosing a particular medium, the advertising manager should analyse and study each available medium in the light of the above criteria. Each fact must be given due consideration and compared with others before a final decision is made.

Organisation for Advertising

The effectiveness of an advertisement depends upon the extent to which it is able to elicit the desired responses from desired audiences. This objective can be achieved only if the right type of advertisement is prepared at the right time, and communicated by the right media to the right type of customers. This can be brought about by an efficient advertising organisation when the company has decided to embark upon an advertisement programme. But who will formulate the advertising strategy? Who will plan the advertising programme and design the advertising campaign? Who will write the advertising copy, develop appeals? Who will determine the type of advertisement and arrange for the proper media, and who will sponsor the advertising programme?

To carry out its advertising activities, the management has three available options:

It can have its own advertising department;

It can utilise the service of an advertising agency;

It can synchronise the efforts of the company's advertising department and of the advertising agency.

Advertising Department

In companies where advertising forms a substantial part of the promotional mix, advertising activities are usually entrusted to the advertising department. This department is concerned with the planning, execution and monitoring of the advertising campaign. Though most big business hire the help of an advertising agency, the entire work of advertisement cannot be delegated to it. The advertising executive has to decide about the overall advertising, strategy and has no ensure that it does not negate the company's total marketing strategy. As the advertising manager is solely responsible for the success or failure of the company's advertising campaign whether the job is done by himself or by the agency, it is his responsibility to see to it that advertising not only increases the company's sales but boosts its corporate image as well.

Advertising Agency

An advertising agency is a business organisation specialising in providing counsel on advertising and allied operations of its clients, and actually prepares and buys space and time for advertisements for their products and/or services. It may also offer a broad range of such marketing services as market research, preparation of the sales promotional material, and counselling on varied marketing problems. It is advantageous to entrust the advertising task to an advertising agency. First, a company does not have as many types of specialists as an agency has. Moreover, it is more resourceful and creative than the advertising executive of a company. Second, the cost of advertising is low when advertisements are prepared by an agency, for the latter spreads the cost of staff and other resources to many accounts. In selecting an advertising agency, the management has to take a number of policy decisions. It must determine what services are desired from an agency, and it has to decide which agency among those available would be the most satisfactory one for it. The considerations that may have to be weighed are many; and hence there are no hard and fast rules with regard to the selection of an advertising agency.

The problem of agency selection involves an evaluation of the efficiency of competing agencies and necessitates comparison of their pool talents. The management should, therefore, investigate the background and professional competence of the key personnel of the advertising agency. This evaluation is largely subjective, for it is based on an appraisal of past experience and of other business associates, and an observation of their behaviour in the course of negotiations.

Co-ordination of Company with Agency Personnel

Even when a company has its own advertising department, it often makes use of an advertising agency to optimise its advertising effectiveness. In this case, the advertising manager works with the agency personnel in co-ordinating their activities with those of the company. Quite often he is involved in the agency's planning and preparation of the advertising campaign to ensure that it is in perfect harmony with its overall marketing strategy. Besides this, he is concerned with checking the agency's proposed campaign and providing the cost of agency's co-ordinating research studies with those of the company. When both the advertising manager and the agency work in close co-ordination, it is obvious that the advertising manager does not interfere with the work of the agency and that the agency is not influenced or swayed by the whims and fancies of the top management.

Budgeting Advertisements

One of the important ingredients of advertising policy is the determination of the advertising budget. The company's ability to finance an advertising programme depends partly on the potency of the advertisement to generate the desired level of sales and partly on the availability of funds in the desired quantum. If a company does not have adequate funds to support its advertising campaign, it should concentrate on other promotional ideas.

But when a company intends to embark on an advertising programme, it finds that it is not easy to establish the advertising budget. One of the widely used methods of determination of the advertising budget is to earmark a certain percentage of sales for it, though there is no direct relationship between sales and advertisement because the use of other promotional tools, the competitor's actions and strategy and environmental factors—all these influence sales.

There is another problem, too; and that is that the buyers who have developed a favourable attitude to the product following advertising during a year may buy it in the ensuring year as well. Also, there is no guarantee that increased advertising expenditure will result in higher sales; it is not infrequent that the money spent on advertising fails to yield the desired results because of the poor message design or ineffective media scheduling. But in spite of all these difficulties, it is desirable for the management to determine the advertising budget. Although the specifics of the budgeting process vary with the company, the manager, while doing so, should concentrate on the following points:

(a) To establish a base-line budget;
(b) To estimate the message, design and media cost;
(c) To assess the impact of the programme through experiments;
(d) To revise the budget, if required.

Establishing Base-Line Budget

Those companies which desire to launch a large-scale advertising programme should establish a base-line budget. The various methods of establishing this budget are:

(i) Percentage-of-sale Method: Under this method, a certain percentage of sales is earmarked for the budget. This percentage may be determined either on the basis of gross sales, or on the net sales volume for the preceding year, or on the adverage sales volume for a period of years. In addition to it, an estimate of future sales may be combined with the average. Some are of the opinion that this makes for greater accuracy in determining the amount to be spent on advertising.

(ii) Unit-of-sale Method: This method requires that a fixed sum per unit of product sold will be set aside as an appropriation for advertising. This method is very satisfactory, particularly when it is used in advertising a commodity which is produced in uncertain quantities. The manufacturers of such products as washing machines, automobiles, and domestic oil-burners are in a position to use the unit-of-sale method to good advantage. But it is the least satisfactory method for fashion products, or when market conditions are uncertain.

(iii) Objective-and-task Method: This method involves the consideration of such problems as goodwill, market development, aids to dealers, or the accomplishment of any other purpose desired by the proper officials. The objectives-and-task method allows a great deal of initiative to the advertiser, makes it possible for him to do some thinking for himself, to be free from the domination of his competitor, and to make use of any facts and figures which may have been gathered and furnished to him at considerable expense.

Advertisers sometimes sell direct to the consumers whose orders and inquiries they receive as a result of direct-mail solicitations or of advertising copy inserted in widely-read periodicals. With a given advertisement or series of advertisements, consumers are induced to make direct purchases. There is, then, a direct relationship between the cost of this sales stimulus and the results obtained. While this cost is not constant, the advertiser can, over a period of time, find upper and lower limits between which he may expect to find his selling cost. He can then appropriate for advertising a sum of money set by the cost per sales by usually taking the upper figure. And since this cost per sale is not constant, he must continually test it and keep careful and minute records of advertising response.

Estimation of Message, Design and Media Cost

For a given advertisement, the manager can easily assess the message development cost (i.e., product cost, agency fee, etc.) and media cost (*i.e.,* print space of TV or radio time). Generally speaking, the message development cost contributes less to the total cost of advertising in comparison to the media cost. Particular attention should, therefore, be paid to media cost in preparing the advertising budget.

Assessment of Impact of Programme

Wherever feasible, the advertising manager should test the advertising programme in a limited market area to assess its effectiveness. If different media and different advertisements are used in different markets, the effectiveness of the different media and advertisement can be evaluated. These measures will help the manager to adjust the budget to obtain the most effective media scheduling. The revision of the budget is necessary because of the impact of other promotional measures. Changes in the budget for other programmes compels the manager to redesign his budget so that he may stay within the available resources.

Measurement of Advertising Effectiveness: A well-conceived advertising programme is an integral part of the firm's overal marketing strategy. Therefore, it is obligatory on the part of the management to know whether the campaign has really attained its advertising objectives, and whether its advertisements are as good as those of its competitors.

A number of alternative procedures are available for the evaluation of the effectiveness of advertisements, of which the three important ones are:

(i) Evaluating individual advertising messages in order to assess their relative importance;
(ii) Evaluating the achievement of awareness-and-attitude objectives;
(iii) Evaluating the impact of advertisement as reflected in the sales reports.

These can be measured by a variety of tests. "In fact, the tests of effectiveness are needed to determine whether the proposed advertisements should be used, or they need some improvement; or should be stopped, continued or significantly changed. The advertising measurements usually take two forms; one involves the sales effect of advertising—that is, the sales volume generated by advertising. The other involves the communications effect on advertising, or the degree to which the audience perceives the content of the message. Both of these forms of measurement are important. Sales measurements help determine the optimum advertising budget, and communications measurements help to tell us if the message is working."[33]

To measure sales results, an analysis is made of consumer purchases before and after advertising has been introduced to stimulate sales. Such analysis can be used to estimate whether and to what extent the brand's position has been improved as a result of advertising, and among which consumer segments it has been most effective. Sometimes, store inventory is done before and after the effects of advertising to measure the sales results.

Many advertisements give some idea of the product so that consumer may be persuaded to purchase it. For this purpose, advertisements are pre-tested before target consumers are exposed to them, and post tests are conducted after these consumers have been exposed to the advertisements.

Pre-tests are conducted to find out whether the information communicated to consumers has been successfully communicated. If the tests indicate that advertisements are not potentially

33. Ramond, Charles, *Advertisement Research: The State of the Art,* Association of National Advertisers, New York, 1977, p. 3.

effective, they may be modified, or dropped. Post-tests indicate whether they have been effective or not. If a significant difference is found in sales, the management may decide that the effort is successful and should be continued as planned. Other measures of effectiveness are: readership, awareness of advertising themes, and attitude changes.

Various kinds of effective tests are used. These are: exposure, attention, comprehension, attitude change, and behaviour or action.

Exposure: In order to be effective, an advertisement must gain exposure, i.e., how many consumers have seen or heard about the message. Without exposure, advertising is doomed to failure. Whether the media used has *exposed* the idea can be found out by:

(i) Examining its circulation or audience data (i.e., number of print copies sold, persons passing billboards or riding in city buses, persons living in radio-listening area, etc.); or

(ii) Conducting readership or "listernership" surveys.

Attention: Advertisement cannot be effective unless they get the attention of target consumers. This attention-getting response can be obtained by asking consumers to indicate the degree to which they recognise or recall each advertisement. Various mechanical devices provide indices of attention.

Comprehension: Consumers utilise advertisements as a means of obtaining information. They cannot be informed unless they comprehend the message. Marketers use various tests of comprehension, such as recall tests, i.e., consumers will recall what they comprehend. They may also ask consumers how much they comprehend of a message they recently heard or viewed.

Attitude Change: Attitudes towards the product or organisation, both before and after the appearance of an advertisement, are measured by measuring instruments which normally contains 15 to 20 sales.

Action: Advertising aims at stimulating action or behaviour. The intention can be measured by instruments, and the answers to certain questions may be analysed to find out the future trends in purchasing.

Which of the tests may be used will depend upon the advertising objective and the research budget of the organisation. The test used should assess the degree to which advertising helps achieve the management's objectives. Thus, if the objective is to increase brand awareness, readership or listenership surveys may be quite suitable. But if the objective is to generate immediate action, sales or coupon measurements may be adopted. Sales and readership studies are very expensive for small-scale organisations; these should, therefore, use less expensive tests, such as inquiry tests.

In the evaluation process, the role of advertising managers and product managers is quite critical with regard to monitoring the achievement of advertising objectives. Advertising agencies and specialists play a vital role in determining the relative worth of different messages. The evaluation procedures, to be effective, should be diagnostic; that is, it should not merely indicate which of the alternative messages in superior or how well advertising objectives are being attained; it should also provide for remedial action, wherever necessary.

Sales Promotion

The advertising programme aims to nurture awareness and attitude among customers regarding the product or service. The extent to which such attitude or awareness generates the desired action is reflected in the sales report. In contrast, sales promotion programmes are designed to generate immediate action. They include "those marketing activities, other than personal selling, advertising and publicity, that stimulate consumer purchasing and dealer effectiveness—such as displays, shows and demonstrations, exposition and various non-current selling, not in ordinary routine."[34]

Sales promotion is neither personal selling nor advertising; yet it has the peculiarities of both. Being in the middle-of-the-road position, it makes each activity more effective. The advertising message that appear in the media area, in most cases, are controlled by the advertising agency, whereas sales promotion is internally created and distributed by the company to arouse the enthusiasm of salesmen, middlemen and consumers. It largely aims at achieving short-term sales results, whereas advertising, besides inducing customers to buy, quite often aims at developing brand image and brand loyalty.

With regard to the sales promotion programme, the management has to take policy decisions pertaining to the following issues:

(i) What type of sales promotion programme will be selected?

(ii) How will such programme be financed?

Sales Promotion Programme

The type of sales promotion programme to be followed depends upon the objectives of the programme itself. It is, therefore, the prime job of managers to establish definite promotional objectives. Further, such objectives should support the marketing strategy for the product. The two most widely used sales promotional programmes are:

(i) Consumers promotional programme;

(ii) Dealers promotional programme.

Consumers Promotional Programme

Consumer-directed promotional programmes are sometimes called "quick action stimuli"/ or the "forcing methods" for they are concerned with generating immediate action. These largely aim at achieving two objectives:

(i) To stimulate the purchase of the new product;

(ii) To increase the sales of established products.

In the marketing of such goods as cosmetics, confectionery, soap, etc., manufacturers incur a heavy expenditure on popularising the product. The most commonly used method of consumer promotion takes the form of samples, contests, demonstrations and coupons.

Sampling: Free samples may be distributed among the prospective customers to arouse their interest in the product. Sampling is an effective sales promotion device when the product is frequently purchased. These products are: convenience goods, such as detergents, soap, tea or coffee, deodorants and sausages, etc.

Samples of drugs and medicines are generally given by medical representatives to doctors; or small cakes of soap or free specimen copies of books by publishers to professors concerned. The idea is that the recipient should, if he finds the product suitable for the purpose, recommend it for use to the patient or student, or will himself continue to consume it. Samples may be sent on request in response to some advertisement or given to the prospects of the salesmen.

Contests: These may be conducted to attract new customers or to introduce a new product by asking the prospects to state in a few words why they prefer it. To enter the contest, the

34. *Marketing Definitions*, p. 20.

prospect is first required to purchase the product and submit the evidence (e.g., a label or package or card attached to the product) with the entry form for the contest. Through such contests, even those who are not inclined to purchase the product get interested in using it.

Demonstration: This device is generally used when products are complex and of a technical nature, such as rotary duplicators, computers, field machinery, electrical pumping sets, chemical fertilizers, cosmetics, or apparel. Cosmeticians may provide free lessons on the proper use of make up. Fashion shows may often be arranged at department stores, restaurants, and other locations, where a reasonably affluent market can be reached.

Couponing: Coupons are generally supplied along with the product, which entitle the holder to either a specified saving on a product or a cash refund. Most coupons are designed to:

(a) Introduce a new product;
(b) Increase the sale of an established product;
(c) Sell a new and larger size of a product;
(d) Induce customers to switch brands; or
(e) Encourage repeat sales.

These promotional methods can increase the sale of a product to a considerable extent. But a too frequent use of promotion may tend to diminish the product image in the eyes of customers; and this may result in lower than normal repeat sales. The management should, therefore, determine the right time when a particular method may be adopted or may be dropped, if the situation warrants it.

In order to determine how to deliver an incentive effectively to a target segment, the manager should try to understand the shopping pattern of consumers and the characteristics of the product. Some organisations dealing in consumer goods use the method of sampling and demonstration to reach target market segments, while others reach them with coupons. If the product is introduced for the first time in the market, sampling and demonstration would be the most effective methods—these have often been employed by the Hindustan Lever Ltd. for the marketing of Surf. To boost the sale of an established product, the coupon system seems to be the most effective, which is now largely used for the promotion of Pond's Soap.

The efficiency of a promotion programme can be increased by knowing the buyer's purchasing rate. This requires that incentives should be made available long enough so that all the buyers may have the opportunity to avail themselves of the benefits of the promotional programme during their normal purchase cycle.

Dealer's Sales Promotion Programme

These sales promotion programmes aim at benefiting distributors by encouraged large volume of sales. They are designed to achieve three objectives:

(i) To make distributors carry the product line;
(ii) To stimulate them to promote aggressively the manufacturer's product:
(iii) To encourage to build inventories to meet the customer's demand following the implementation of the various promotional measures.

These objectives can be achieved by offering extra cash or trade discount on the basis of the orders placed, display and advertising allowances, premium for achieving sales above a particular limit, providing POP material, etc.

In formulating a promotional programme, the management must bear in mind the needs of the distributors with respect to a particular product or product line. Some idea of this may be gained from the pricing programme of a distributor. For the retailer, who buys goods in bulk, a price-oriented promotion would be very effective. But the promotions that help to build retailer image in respect of the quality of the product may be more important for margin — oriented *retailers*. Managers should also give consideration to the profit impact of sales promotion of dealers, the assortment of product inventory and space constraints. For example, many manufacturers of similar products attempt to promote their own products. As a result, distributor attention, inventory investment and space will be divided. In this case, the offer of a trade discount and an off-seasonal promotional programme would be much more effective.

Sales Promotion Budget

The sales promotion budget is an important part of the promotional budget. As in the case of the advertising budget, it is difficult to determine how much a company should spend on sales promotion. As a rule, advertising and sales promotion decisions are closely co-ordinated to make the promotional programme effective. Moreover, both programmes are managed by the same individual in the organisation. It is desirable, therefore, to strike a fair balance between advertising and promotion expenditure.

To a considerable extent, this balance is influenced by the competitors' activities, the pressure of distributors and the company's overall marketing strategy. If competitors place premium on sales promotion, the company will be forced to meet his requirements.

In framing the budget, emphasis should be placed on the "cash" factors because all the promotion programmes attract direct fixed and variable costs. Among the direct fixed costs are the cost of the distribution of samples, the premium offered, the cost of mailing coupons, etc. The contribution margin may be reduced because the value of coupons affects the price of the product. Therefore, attention must be paid to the various cost factors. An estimate of market response, too, must be made. But to make such an estimate is an uphill task because of two reasons; first, the cost cannot be properly measured without evaluating the sales response. Second, the sales objective has a direct relationship with the sales volume. When a precise relationship between sales and the cost of promotional expenses can be assessed, it would be possible to arrive at the optimal amount to be earmarked in the budget. The manager should, therefore, undertake elaborate economic studies before determining the size of the budget.

Personal Selling

A dynamic sales force is essential for the successful operation of a marketing strategy. First, the sales force is an important source of marketing information—market position, sales potential, buyer's attitudes of existing and new brands, and competitors' strategies. Second, the sales force gives momentum to advertising and sales and promotional programmes by disseminating information to distributors on product benefits, and motivating them to stock products by providing assistance to them in promotion, displays, inventory policies, and by co-ordinating their various marketing efforts. Finally, customer service policies, designed to inculcate better buyer-seller relationship, are executed by the sales personnel.

The common denominator in these activities is the personal interaction between seller and buyer. When individual buyers or distributors have complex and varied needs, the personal interaction between them can play a critical role by sorting out and solving the problems faced by them. This is true whether a business deals in consumer or industrial goods or even in service.

Scope of Personal Selling Programme

Personal selling includes a vast array of activities that are concerned with selling goods to customers and providing assistance and information to distributors or final buyers. A salesman is more of the company's spokesman than a mere order-taker. He is responsible for finding ways and means that can be profitably adopted to satisfy customer needs in terms of product features, quality, price, service, delivery and inventory requirements.

To effectively manage the sales force and to optimise sales effectiveness, a company is expected to take decisions on:

(i) Determination of the objective of personal selling;
(ii) Management of the sales force;
(iii) Allocation of territory to sales personnel;
(iv) Determination of sales quota.
(v) Determination of personal selling appropriation.

Objectives of Personal Selling

The objectives of personal selling take their deep roots in the marketing strategy of a firm. Quite often managements try to achieve more than one objective through such programmes. Therefore, while designing objectives, managements must see to it that they are specific, that they themselves are competent enough to direct the sales personnel and provide a sound basis for monitoring the programmes.

The sales volume is one of the most specific kinds of objectives that can be established and easily assessed in terms of its monetary value. There is no doubt that it is a quite important objective is the sense that it provides an objective yardstick for evaluating the performance of the sales personnel, territory potential and the effectiveness of the sales programme. But it has been noted that in most cases, it fails to generate the desired results for a variety of reasons.

First, the quantum of sales volume obtained at any time is determined by the competitor's actions, product performance, buyer behaviour, and the environmental and marketing factors that are beyond the control of the management. Moreover, such objectives do not provide any guidelines to sales personnel for increasing or maintaining their sales volume. It is true that there is an increase in the sales volume and that this is an important objective, and if the management wants to achieve this objective alone or in combination with objectives, it should bear in mind the fact that objectives will be effective only if they bear the following features:

(a) They are specific and quantifiable;
(b) They can be evaluated in terms of the efforts of the sales force as well as in terms of total results;
(c) They are in harmony with the company's marketing strategy;
(d) They focus on the activities of the field force.

The most common objectives of the sales force have been discussed in the following paragraphs.

Account Development

This objective is primarily designed to acquire new distributions or new outlets. Although that is not the sole objective of personal selling, it often helps the entire selling programme and serves as an important means of assessing the performance of the sales force. For example, if the sales force is asked to increase its territorial coverage by opening new outlets, the latter will have to divert its attention to the achievement of those objectives on the basis of which their performance will be measured.

Account Maintenance

This is perhaps the most important objective of the salesman's job. It involves the maintenance of an effective selling position with distributors or retailers through regular calls, and aims at furnishing product information, taking orders, eliciting information about the buyers' changing needs, to redressing distributors' grievances, etc.

Distributor's Support

This objective aims at inducing retailers to carry a new product or a full range of products and stock more products, and arrange for more space of products display and co-operative advertising.

Sales Force Management

Human resource management is the prime task of a manager in literally every functional area. But within the marketing area, this is the most critical and important task assigned to him. This is largely so because of the following reasons:

(a) large number of personnel are employed in sales;

(b) The cost of personal selling is fairly high because of salaries and other associated expenses.

(c) The selling operations are highly decentralised.

The effectiveness of a sales programme depends on the operations of a dynamic and efficient sales force. For its management, the sales manager has to perform the following functions:

(a) Establish sales force objectives;

(b) Plan for human resource;

(c) Recruit and select personnel;

(d) Train and develop personnel;

(e) Compensate and motivate personnel;

(f) Evaluate the performance of the sales force.

Establish Sales Force Objectives

A sales manager must develop sales objectives in precise, measurable terms, and they should be specific in so far as the time period and geographic areas are concerned. Sales objectives have to be established, both for the total sales force and for each salesman. These should be stated in terms of volume, market share or profit for the total sales force. For the individual salesman, they should be stated in terms of rupees of unit sales volume, order size, average number of calls per time period, and the number of orders relative to the number of calls.

Human Resource Planning

Human resource planning involves the determination of the number of characteristics of the sales personnel which are required to achieve the sales objectives. The number of sales personnel required during a particular time period depends on the company's marketing strategy and the prevailing marketing environment.

Human resource planning requires that the marketing manager should first establish a marketing plan and then determine the areas to be covered to achieve the sales targets. On the basis of territories to be covered, he should determine the size of the sales force.

Sales managers should determine the desired characteristics of recruits for this, they should prepare job descriptions, which outline the duties and responsibilities of the salesman. The effectiveness of sales force management depends on the completeness and accuracy of the sale- job description. Through an analysis of duties and responsibilities, the management derives a set of qualifications in the form of job specifications which salesmen should possess. The preparation of this job specification derives from the hierarchy of objectives — corporate marketing, promotion, and selling.

Recruitment and Selection

Since the salesman comes directly in contact with customers and reflects the character of the employer, the utmost care should be taken in his selection. An unwise selection will result in slow turnover, inefficient blocking of capital in stocks, loss of goodwill and increased selling expenditure. The process of recruitment involves the identification of the sources of recruits and the selection of an appropriate method of recruitment. The manager should decide whether the company should use internal or external sources. Although internal sources, such as other departments, people working in non-selling activities in sales, etc., are quite profitable, external sources, such as educational institutions, dealers, competitor's salesman persons registered with employment exchanges can also be tapped for recruitment.

The determination of a satisfactory method of selection is essential for the selection of the right type of sales personnel. This may range from a simple one-step procedure consisting of an informal interview to a complicated one involving various methods for eliciting information from prospective sales. The selection process should be based on the successive "handle" technique, where unfit applicants, who fail to cross the barrier at a particular stage, may be dropped from further consideration. The commonly used application method includes an application blank, written examination, psychological tests, personal interview and reference checks.

Training and Development

Trained sales personnel strongly contribute to sales effectiveness. The management, therefore, should give due attention to this aspect of sales promotion. A number of companies conduct training programmes for their newly-hired sales personnel as well as for the development of existing ones.

For newly-hired sales personnel, a formal sales training programme should provide information pertaining to the company, its products and various sales policies, the competitor's strategies, selling techniques, report writing, etc. The orientation programme for existing sales personnel should be tailor-made to meet the specific needs of these employees. In making the training and development programmes effective, the management should take decisions pertaining to the method of training (on-the-job training, or class-room training, or a combination of both), the techniques of training (lecture-group discussions, case studies, role playing, simulation, etc.) the duration and site of training, trainer-training aids, and the methods of assessing training effectiveness.

Compensation and Motivation

The amount of compensation paid to a salesman has a direct bearing on his efficiency and work motivation. Management policy should, therefore, aim at attracting and retaining sales personnel of the desired calibre because sales personnel enjoy a high degree of job mobility. The compensation policy should be approximately at par with the competitors' policy and, if feasible, salesmen should be paid higher salaries and the going rate. The management can use any of the following plans for compensating its sale force:

(i) Straight Competition Plan, which suggests the payment of a certain percentage to the salesman;

(ii) Sliding Commission Plan, which suggests the payment of a given commission on sales effected to a point, automatically increasing the commission rate as definite sales totals are reached;

(iii) Group Commission Plan, which suggests the payment of different commissions at different rates to the salesman of different groups of articles sold;

(iv) A drawing account against commission, under which a salesman is enabled to pay recurring bills without taking recourse to borrowed money; and to help him in developing a new territory.

(v) The Straight Salary Plan under which a fixed monthly salary is given to the salesman. But this scheme does not provide for a proper incentive to the salesman to increase his sales, for he knows that, in spite of his large sales, his salary would remain the same;

(vi) Salary Plus Commission Plan, under which a salesman is given some compensation besides his fixed income. This provides him with an incentive for better work;

(vii) Other Plans include: salary plus bonus; salary plus incentive; profit-sharing; the sales-and-service quota basis; and rating basis.

Motivation

Compensation plans, howsoever beneficial, may not impel the sales personnel to better performance unless some additional benefits are made available to them. The management should, therefore, formulate a proper motivational strategy to stimulate sales personnel to achieve the desired level of performance. A great many companies use a variety of motivational devices, such as bonus, awards, promotions and sales contests for the benefit of their sales force. But it should be borne in mind that performance does not depend on these factors, but also on such factors as the quality of supervision, participation in the determination of selling objectives, quota-setting and the type of selling job to be performed (such as missionary versus trade selling). While designing a motivational strategy, the management should, therefore, give due weightage to all those factors which have a bearing on employee performance and the evaluation of sales force performance.

Evaluation of Sales Force Performance

In order to manage personal selling effectively, the company should design and execute a satisfactory procedure for monitoring the working of the sales force. Unless the sales manager has a complete record of the activities of his field force, he cannot lead and motivate them to achieve a predetermined sales target, nor can he accomplish his own departmental objective. He should:

(i) Identify sales personnel who require additional training;

(ii) Award incentives and bonuses;

(iii) Identify the "problem" geographical areas covered by individual salesmen;

A comprehensive result-oriented sales performance programmes should include the following steps;

(i) Determination of Performance standards;

(ii) Comparison of performance with standards;

(iii) Taking corrective action.

Determination of Performance Standards

The establishment of performance standard requires a thorough knowledge of the selling job, the condition of market and the strategies of competitors. Once the sales manager has obtained vital information on these, he should determine performance standards. The standard of sales performance should facilitate the measurement of the efforts of sales personnel and their contribution to departmental objectives, both general and specific. The evaluation should be scientific and meaningful. Both quantitative and qualitative standard should be set up.

Quantitative Standards

Quantitative standards are generally specific and objective and evaluate the performance on the input-and-output basis. A salesman's effectiveness concept involves the relationship between two variables — the output, which is measured in terms of sales volume and gross margin, and the input as indicated by call frequency, non-selling activities, etc.

The commonly used output variables utilised for the evaluation of sales personnel performance include;

(i) Sales volume by model, product or customer group;
(ii) Sales volume by percentage of quota.
(iii) Sales profitability by rupee gross margin or contribution.

Accounts

These include:

(i) The number of new accounts made;
(ii) Percentage volume increase in key accounts;
(iii) The number of lost accounts.

Order

This should cover:

(i) The size of the order;
(ii) The number of orders.

A new notable input variables utilised for evaluation are:

(i) Calls per day and frequency of calls made during a definite period;
(ii) Non-selling activities;
  (a) The number of demonstrations completed;
  (b) The number of customer's complaints handled;
  (c) The number of enquires followed up.

Qualitative variables

In contrast to quantitative variables the qualitative variables are difficult to measure, but should not be under-estimated for that reason. They perform a vital role in the overall performance of a salesman. These variables include:

(i) Knowledge of product and company policies;
(ii) Knowledge of competitors' strategies;
(iii) Customer relations;
(iv) Ingenuity and creativeness.

To evaluate the performance of the sales personnel, the management must blend both quantitative and quanlitative variables in such a way that they yield the best possible results.

Comparison of Performance with Standards

the evaluation of sales personnel performance against a pre-set standard is a quite difficult and ticklish task. Even when performance standards are well defined or quantified, a host of difficulties are encountered in judging the actual performance against the projected standard. It is obvious that the same performance standard cannot be used to evaluate all the salesmen, for each operates in a different territory which differs from others in terms of its sales potential and the extent of competition. Moreover, quantitative variables cannot be effectively measured. Therefore, while assessing the salesman's performance, the achievement of each should be examined in the light of the market situation and territory personality. Purely quantitative, mechanical and arbitrary methods should not be allowed to colour the evaluation.

Corrective Action

If performance evaluation reveals that sales personnel are not up to the mark, the manager should find out their shortcomings by examining their performance in different territories and then resort to corrective action. The plausible steps which can be undertaken in this context include:

(i) The revision of policies and strategies so that goals may be optimised;
(ii) Raising or lowering the standard used in performance evaluation; and
(iii) Arranging an orientation programme for exceptionally weak personnel.

Allocation of Territory to Sales Personnel

Territory allocation to sales personnel enables the management to match selling effort with sales opportunities. Sales personnel are entrusted with the responsibility of serving a particular group of customers or prospects. This not only helps the management to execute sales policies but furnishes a strong base for planning and monitoring the selling process. In fact, the various objectives of the strategy can be attained by a scientific allocation of territories. A few of these objectives are:

(i) To improve and maximise market coverage;
(ii) To control selling expenditure;
(iii) To improve customer service;
(iv) To facilitate market research;
(v) To co-ordinate personal selling and advertising effort;
(vi) To offset competition effectively so that salesmen may concentrate their efforts on the areas assigned to them; and
(vii) To improve sales force performance evaluation.

These objectives can be effectively attained if sales territories are properly assigned to salesmen. And this can be done only if planning is made not only on a territory-to-territory basis but also on the total market basis. As the nature of the territory varies considerably not only in different parts of the country but also in one particular part, a sizable variation in the nature of the market would often be noticed. While designing the sales territory, the company should, therefore, make a thorough review of its competitive strengths and weaknesses; it should assess its strength in comparison with that of other competitors to optimize sales effectiveness in different territories.

Procedure for Setting up Sales Territories

The success of a selling programme largely depends on a proper selection of territories because if territory potential is properly assessed in terms of the company's marketing plan and the customer's expectations, the organisation can effectively deploy its various marketing programme to gain the optimum benefit from a territory.

One of the quite widely utilised ways of setting up a territory is to base it on some geographical basis. Accordingly, one can have a territory confined to a village, town, city, region, or state. The rationale for designing a territory on a geographical basis is that by clubbing together customers located in one or more particular places, the company will be able to serve them most economically and conveniently. Many companies ignore this geographical consideration, and allocates sales responsibilities to sales personnel on the basis of the class of customers, regardless of their location. In certain cases, companies have highly specialised sales people who are assigned the job of serving customers who are in need of their skills. This is particularly true of companies selling complicated machinery, which may require five to six salesmen, each specialising in a part of the product line or a particular product, and each serving the company's customers regardless of their geographical location. It is, however, not always necessary or desirable for a company to assign geographical clusters of customers or prospects to salesmen. In fact, the determination of such assignment depends on the type of product, customer service requirements, the cost involved in meeting it, etc. While allocating territory, the following facts should be borne in mind:

(i) Territories should be so defined that the expected commission for each salesman may be roughly the same.
(ii) Territories should not be too big, otherwise they will not be properly served;
(iii) They must not be too small, because the size of the territory affects the salesman's earnings;
(iv) A new salesman should not be given an independent territory. He should rather be asked to help a senior salesman in that territory and pick up the technique of work;
(v) Territories should be so planned that the expenditure incurred on covering them is maintained at the lowest possible level;
(vi) Territories should be flexible. A larger territory should be given to a senior salesman as a sort of promotion;
(vii) As far possible, the transfer of salesman from one territory to another should be avoided on account of the limited scope for work. However, for temperamental reasons, a transfer may become desirable.
(viii) With certain classes of product, such as highly technical equipment or materials or speciality goods, the principle is often adopted of creating territories by class of business.

Several important factors have to be taken into account before deciding about the allocation of sales territories, such as:

(a) The number and location of customers a salesman can efficiently deal with:
(b) The frequency of the salesman's visit, i.e. the number of calls he should make on customers;
(c) The place of production;
(d) The nature and type of the product;
(e) The nature of demand—whether seasonal or otherwise;
(f) Transportation facilities available and the facilities that can be given to the salesman;
(g) Sales resistance and competition; because if these are high, each sale will take a longer time to negotiate;

(h) The expenditure incurred;
(i) The ease or difficulty of sale;
(j) The method of distribution;
(k) The frequency of contact with customers; and
(l) Government policy in so far as customers duties, sales tax, etc. are concerned.

The foregoing factors and the supervisory ability of the senior sales staff determine the size of the territory. The main objective is to devise and develop the sales personnel in such a way that they may be able to perform their task in a most effective and economical way.

Determination of Sales Quota

The determination of the quota is the goal or task or part of a share assigned to a marketing unit in the management of sales efforts. A quota may be for a territory, a branch house or for the company as a whole. It may be expressed in terms of sales volume for budgeted items, or in terms of expenses, gross margin, net profit, and return on investment, or a combination of these and other items.

But here we are concerned with the sales quota pertaining to a salesman, i.e., the target that a salesman is expected to achieve during a stipulated period. It is a normal practice that the sales manager lays down the target for his entire department, which is then broken down into small targets, each of which is then assigned to different sales personnel working in different territories. The management establishes quota to attain the following objectives:

(i) To establish a scientific method of planning and controlling sales;
(ii) To set up performance and efficiency standards for salesmen;
(iii) To provide a basis for the remuneration of salesmen;
(iv) To obtain effective budgetary control.

While setting the quota, the sales manager must bear the following in mind:

(i) It must be set scientifically;
(ii) It must be flexible;
(iii) It must relate to the sales potential determined by market research;
(iv) It must be as simple in form as is consistent with its purpose;
(v) It must be set in consultation and co-operation with the salesmen;
(vi) It must provide definite incentives to the salesmen;
(vii) It must be planned in such a manner that it facilitates the performance of company activities.

The attainment of these objectives is contingent upon the kind, amount and accuracy of marketing information available and used in determining and administering the quota system.

CHAPTER 12

PRODUCTION/OPERATIONS POLICES

INTRODUCTION

Though most firms have separate production and purchase departments, the basic problems that require managerial attention are so closely linked that it is desirable to consider production and purchasing policies together.

Historical Perspective

Since the beginning of business activities, the procurement of merchandise was the main problem of businessmen. The discovery of various continents on earth may largely be attributed to traders' hunt for new trade routes. Since then, and centuries thereafter, merchants have gone to different parts of the world with a view to carrying a variety of goods to their own place, and sell them in their domestic markets.

With the advent of the industrial revolution, large-scale production received an impetus. Consequently, both purchase and production problems increased manifold. On one side, there was heavy demand for raw materials for the requirements of the production schedule; on the other, the qualitative aspect of purchase gained increased importance. Also, with the increased sophistication in the production process, excessive competition, consumerism, etc., forced businessmen to adopt more effective purchase and production policies.

Issues Calling for Management Attention

Purchase and production policies, like other business policies, generate a number of intricate problems. A satisfactory handling of these problems is essential if the business is to keep on its toes. Major production and purchase policies involve the following issues :

(i) Selection of the production process;

(ii) Determining the total production capacity;

(iii) Deciding about the extent of vertical interpretation;

(iv) Establishing plans for maintenance and replacement;

(v) Solving manufacturing or buying problems of supplies and services; and

(vi) Considering how the purchasing function should be organised and performed.

The first four problems are considered in this chapter and the last three in the next one.

PRODUCTION PROCESS

All profit-making organisations survive on the basis of the production of goods and services. High profitability can be achieved only if the right type of goods and services are produced, and they are of the right quality in right quantity and produced at the right time. This calls for adoption of a satisfactory production process so that it may yield the desired results. As for the adoption of an effective and efficient method of production, the management has to take a decision on the following:

(a) Selection of appropriate technology;
(b) Degree of specialisation required or necessary;
(c) Extent of mechanisation and automation required or necessary;
(d) Size and decentralisation of plants;
(e) R & D Programmes.

(a) Selection of Appropriate Technology : The effectiveness not only of the production process but of business itself is contingent on the type of technology that is used, for it provides, less expensive, more efficient ways of producing goods and services, besides minimising physical labour and excessive supervision which, in turn, leads to low cost of production; and this enables producers to provide goods and services to customers at low prices. Thinkers like Drucker[1] and Toffler[2,3] have remarked that technology is a force of "creative destruction" in the sense that it compels industries to shed older techniques and embrace newer ones. For example, the advancement of electronic industries has hurt the radio and transistor industries by prȏducing better entertainment goods. Xerox copies are being replaced by riphographers, cotton textiles by synthetic blends, and so on.

The technology environment of the present century is highly dynamic. The success of a business is therefore definitely linked with its ability to keep pace with changing technological trends.

With regard to the choice of technology, industries do not enjoy much freedom. As a rule, they are forced to adopt one which is of maximum advantage to them. It is widely held that the use of advanced technology leads to higher productivity and the production of better quality of goods.

But the use of modern technology calls for a heavy outlay on its development and cash for financing such activities as the procurement of plant and equipments, raw materials, expertise, and training and development of personnel. Moreover, the technology so adopted is not free from environmental threats. Businessmen, therefore, live in a state of utter uncertainty. They are often forced to adjust and readjust themselves to the changing technological environment and this involves a huge investment and high degree of uncertainty.

In deciding about the choice of technology, the management should therefore see to it that the technology to be adopted is effective and efficient and pays off its cost well in time.

(b) Degree of Specialisation : The use of advanced technology has shifted the emphasis on specialisation. In this process, the whole job is divided into many small ones, and each individual, on the basis of his expertise, performs a narrowly defined task. In industries, there may be a fairly great variation in the extent of specialisation, ranging from little specialisation to an intensive one. In the first instance, and individual performs most of the functions involved in a complete task. For example, in a small industry, one may be faced initially with drawings furnished by the supplier and then progress towards completion of the task. Contrary to this is the case of high degree of specialisation; each individual section or unit or department is assigned a narrowly defined

1. Drucker, P.F., *The Age is Continuity: Guidelines to Changing Society,* Harper and Row Publishers, New York, 1980.
2. Toffler, Alvin, *The Future Shock,* Bantam Books, New York, 1970.
3. Toffler, Alvin, *The Third Wave,* Bantam Books, New York, 1980

specialised task. For example, in the manufacture of textiles, the various operations involved in the production of cloth are performed by different experts working in various departments – spinning, weaving, dyeing and printing, etc.

Specialisation creates inter-dependency among individuals and groups. Each specialist carries a definite responsibility for contributing to goal attainment. There are definite advantages of specialisation, for it increases on individual's efficiency, reduces the cost of production, facilitates training, reduces lost time, etc. In deciding about specialisation, the management should pay adequate attention to the problems associated with it.

(i) Expressiveness :Specialisation calls for higher investment in plant and machinery, in the training and development of personnel and in the designing and maintenance of an adequate organisation. In fact, specialists, machines and organisation are quite costly to obtain, train and maintain. Sophisticated technology should, therefore, be employed only when the firm has the necessary resources to bear the increasing financial burden.

(ii) Inflexibility : Specialists, machines and organisations become rigid because they are exclusively suitable only for a particular job. If there is any change in technology or consumer tastes, it becomes difficult for the specialist to easily mend his ways of working and adapt to new and changed situations.

(iii) Alienation and Frustration : In specialisation, a worker is busy all the time performing a small part of the entire task. His own contribution to its completion appears to him to be almost insignificant. Again, the performance of the same task over and over again induces depersonalisation and alienation among workers. In this context, Drucker has remarked that "the use of the worker as a single-purpose tool is a wasteful use of man in the production process." He asserts that the principle of specialisation is productive and efficient when applied to machinery, but is dubious whether we know how to apply the principle to people.

Behaviouralists like Walker,[4] Behling,[5] Argyris,[6] and Herzberg[7] have remarked that excessive specialisation is certainly not beneficial for an organisation.

To overcome the defects of specialisation, management experts have suggested the adoption of the job enlargement philosophy wherein the duties of workers are deliberately diversified to make the job more challenging and rewarding, thereby eliminating their feeling of alienation.

So, in deciding upon specialisation, managers should evaluate the effect of their policies on mechanisation, standardisation of products, and the type of personnel to be employed against the prevailing practices in other industries.

(c) Extent of Mechanisation and Automation : The extent of mechanisation and automation to be undertaken by an organisation has far-reaching implications for the management and the people working in it. In organisations where a high degree of automation is deployed, a large part of the production process is performed by machines, and computers monitor the integrated machine activities.

4. Walker, C.R., and Guest, R.H., *The Man on the Assembly Line*, Harvard University Press, Cambridge, 1952, pp. 38-65.
5. Behling, O.C., "The Meaning of Dissatisfaction with Factory Work," *Management Personal Quarterly* 3, 1964., pp. 11-16.
6. Argyris, C, "The Individual and Organisation : An Empirical Test," in *Administrative Science Quarterly*, 3, 1964, pp. 145-167.
7. Herzberg, F., "One More Time : How You Motivate Employees," in *Harvard Business Review*, January February, 1968, pp. 53-67.

Some organisations have definite policies pertaining to the extent to which their plants can be automated. For example, biscuit manufacturers may establish a policy that all the operations, from start to finish, should be mechanised. In such cases, the product often bears a label "untouched by human hands." Similarly, the telephone department may follow the policy of introducing an electronic exchange in place of the traditional one.

Automation has a variety of limitations which warn the management to decide carefully as to when and where to automate. In this context, managers should remember the following points:

(i) Limited Scope : Automation can be only applied to those processes which are continuous and call for the use of integrated machines and the production of standardised units. It is desirable to automate only the mass production programmes and not the batch production one.

(ii) Inflexibility : In the process of automation, specially designed machines are used to produce special types of products. When there is a technological change, product obsolescence or change in product designs, existing machines become more or less useless, for they cannot be modified to suit the new requirements. Automation, therefore, should not be adopted in cases where rapid change in technology and production design are likely.

(iii) High Cost : Automation is a quite expensive affair, for it calls for heavy investment in fixed assets, and the payback is low. Only a financially sound organisation can therefore venture to take the risk of adopting new technology.

(iv) Dehumanisation of Job : The regard for availing of the benefits of advanced technology tempts businessmen to resort to automation at a rapid pace. The production process is then largely carried out by the machine, and the role of worker is confined to maintaining, adjusting and repairing the equipment involved in the manufacture of products. As a result, their opportunities for social interaction decrease considerably, resulting in the dehumanisation of the job.

Therefore, when to automate or when not to automate is a question which deserves serious attention and calls for imaginative response to challenges. In fact, automation is a tiger on which a blind ride lands one into a dreadful ditch; but a restrained and cautious ride can take one speedily along the desired path.

(d) Size and Decentralisation of Operating Units : An important factor which governs the efficiency of an operating unit is the question of its size and the need for decentralisation. Large manufacturing companies have a wide choice in the selection of size and location of their plants. For a pretty long time, it has been held that bigger industries are more economical than smaller ones. But present thinking has gone beyond these assumptions. It cannot be taken for granted now that it is advantageous to have a large plant. For example, a concern that produces eleven different related items had a policy that each product would be manufactured in a separate plant and that each plant should be located in the vicinity of the registered office, so that easy and frequent liaison might be maintained between them.

Some textile manufacturers in our country have adopted the policy of getting the product manufactured by small producers and marketing the finished product in their own name.

In some industries, such as the pharmaceutical and processing industries, where technology calls for continuous operations, large-scale production is essential to achieve economies of scale. Once a plant is large enough to reap the benefits of economies of production and support specialised services, the question arises whether the existing plant should be expanded or another one set up in a new location. In such cases, it is always desirable to increase the capacity of the existing plant. But is cases where the existing plant is outdated or uneconomical, the erection of a new plant is desirable. A smaller plant in comparison to a bigger one enjoys such advantages as better co-ordination among different departments, direct control and supervision, harmonious relations among various personnel, etc.

(e) R & D Programmes :Effective R & D programmes are the backbone of the industry, for they enable it to discover better methods of work which aim at providing goods and services at a comparatively low prices.

How much an industry should invest in R & D programmes is a difficult question to answer. In industries where the rate of technological advancement is so high that products do not enjoy a long life – as in the case of the pharmaceuticals and electronics – extensive R & D programmes are necessary for survival. In contrast to this, firms dealing in textiles, paper, or printing do not face a high degree of technological threat and they do not, and are not expected to, incur heavy expenditure on R & D programmes.

Whenever an industry embarks on an R & D programme, it should bear in mind the fact that the programme is derived from, and works into, the corporate objectives. It is essential, therefore, that "the technical staff should play a part in the establishment of an overall company strategy, which is not likely to be a good one unless it takes full account of the scientific advances that will affect the future of industry. The relevant information must come mainly from research and development men, and it must be presented at the board level by someone who is fully qualified to appraise it critically. Without effective and continuous communication between the directors of a company and its scientists, good planning is impossible; but until an overall plan has been prepared, it is not possible to produce a programme for the part that research and development are to play in it."[8]

The ever-increasing pressure for R & D has tempted an increasing number of companies to reappraise their corporate goals. We have now witnessed the emergence of top research scientists dubs who are referred to as *The MBA Syndrome* – a super, no–risk management, which not willing to gamble on anything short of a sure thing.

While designing a broad research policy, managers should distinguish between basic and applied research. From the managerial point of view, basic research is the search for knowledge in a sphere related to its business, and not any specific knowledge. This type of research can be only undertaken by financially well off companies, for it involves a heavy expenditure. Moreover there is no certainty that research will pay off. However, research often leads to paying off in the manufacture of new products, new processes or activities which are related or un-related to the present operations. If a firm, therefore, undertakes basic research, it should be willing to exploit the new discoveries.

The objective of applies research, however, is the invention of substitute of raw materials and cheaper processes. But this research is risky, for the company is not sure whether it would enjoy the advantages of this research, nor how long it will take to have them, and what its cost will be. Research activity is basically a defensive activity. It has been observed that firms are always afraid of the technological superiority of their rivals. By resorting to an elaborate research programme, they can, so they believe, keep pace with their competitors.

In deciding about R & D programme, the management should give due attention to the following points :

8. McLeod, R.S., *Management of Research, Development and Design in Industry*, Cower Press Ltd., U.K., 1969, p. 11.

(i) Economic Characteristics of Technology : The economic characteristics of technology have a lot to do with the choice of an appropriate R & D programme. One of the major characteristics of technology is that risks it carries which are both technical and commercial in nature. The technical risks it carries refers to the fact that although firms spend huge sums of money on research, they are never sure that it would really result in the manufacture of a saleable product. Commercial risk refers to the fact that although research leads to the fabrication of a technically feasible product, it may not be commercially successful. In fact, "both types of risks have a bearing on the market function. If the product is genuinely new, markets will have to be created. The parameters of demand potential cannot be easily inferred because previous experience is not there as a guide."[9]

(ii) Expenditure on R & D : In deciding about an R & D programme, one of the important considerations is how much the company should spend. Quite often, a company maintains a fairly constant ratio between R & D expenditure and sales. But the actual amount to be spent on R & D should depend on the management's expectations from R & D programmes.

(iii) Value of Research : The value of research can be assessed only in retrospect. The occasional breakthrough should be accepted as a bonus. R & D people should not be criticised for not making startling discoveries. In fact, they are there to see to it that the company is benefited from their research.

(iv) Abandoning the Project : As it is important to know when to start a project, it is equally important to abandon one which is unprofitable. There is not point in hoping that success would soon crown one's efforts. Nor should one be dazzled by scientific challenges. One should drop a research programme project if it is worthwhile to do so after a careful scrutiny and evaluation.

As R & D programmes are both expensive and risky, industries may follow a policy of sharing the risk. They may enlist the help of national laboratories or furnish, financial support to them or provide finance to universities for a particular research programme. However, such policies are largely beneficial to smaller companies that cannot afford a large expenditure on R & D programmes.

THE QUANTUM OF PRODUCTION

One of the important ingredients of a production policy is the quantum of production, i.e. how much the company should produce. This not only affects the production process but other functional areas of management as well. To arrive at a profitable level of production, therefore, data from a variety of sources should be collected on the sales forecast of the physical volume, policy decision on what will be purchased, and estimates or productivity. In addition, and overriding such data, are several central management policies regarding the desired capacity. In this context, the following policy dimensions must be properly studied :

Peak Versus Normal Load : For any industry, a completely stable level of operations is virtually impossible, for all types of industrial activities are substantially affected by cyclical fluctuations. Moreover, a large number of industries face seasonal, daily or even hourly variations in the volume

9. Parker J.E.S., *The Economics of Innovation*, Longman's Group, London, 1974, p. 46.

of their business. In addition to these, demand is largely affected by S & T changes, the legal and political environment, the whims and fancies of buyers, and many other unforeseen factors. The manager should therefore decide whether he will produce enough to satisfy the demands of customers during the peak periods, knowing that the production capacity will be idle during the slack season, or whether he will plan to produce less and hope that the failure to satisfy customers during the peak period will not have any unfavourable impact on the goodwill which the business enjoys.

Most leading companies try to meet demand during the peak period in any of the following ways :

(i) By increasing the capacity of the plants;
(ii) By producing more during the slack season so that the requirements of the peak period may be easily met;
(iii) By allowing overtime work for the operations not carried out during the preceding 24 hours and
(iv) By sub-contracting some of the work.

The suggested methods involve extra cost and may be more or less satisfactory to customers. A clear policy and guidelines should therefore be laid down is so far as production requirements during the peak season are concerned.

Backward Type of Capacity

Vertically integrated companies may deliberately follow a policy of backward type of capacity. Such companies generally perform final operations on all their products, but only produce a part of their material requirements. For example, a textile manufacturer may have his own separate spinning unit which works at its optimum level. If more yarn is required, it can be purchased from other firms. Such a policy has the advantage of keeping the industry going well in the early stages of production. The success of this policy depends on the willingness of suppliers to meet the fluctuating demands of the industry.

Provision for Growth : While deciding about the size of product, the management should not only concern itself with its present production requirements, but also with the size of future market demand. Business does not always remain static. Over a period of time, it is presented with a number of opportunities. Adequate provision must, therefore, be made for future expansion and growth. To take care of the expansion of business, the management builds production facilities of 40% to 50% more than is actually required; and if its plans materialise because of demand, it can be immensely benefited. But if it has failed because of an improper assessment of the situation, it will have to suffer a great deal. If the management takes decisions as and when the need arises for them, the addition of facilities at frequent intervals on a piecemeal basis will be both expensive and inconvenient to employees and customers.

Therefore, it is always desirable to take the middle ground, if resources permit. A provision for expansion may be made in the initial plan for the land to be purchased, the design of building, the purchase of machinery etc. Whatever may be the basic plan, specific decisions must be taken by the management regarding the investment required to be made in the anticipated plan, if the need for it arises.

Balancing Capacity : In business, each phase of operations – material handling, processing, finishing, warehousing, selling and the like – has its own capacity. It is the prime task of the management to see to it that the functions of all the operations are so synchronized as to ensure a satisfactory balance among the various activities. How a lack of balance can seriously hamper the production process may be illustrated by the following example. A gas stove producing company is involved in such activities as stamping, welding, painting, and enamelling the parts, assembling and testing. The plant has ample capacity to carry out all operations, except enamelling. For this job, the services of another firm were utilised. However, it was noted that the firm was neither sticking to the schedule nor supplying goods at economic prices. The company therefore installed a small plant for enamelling jobs. But unfortunately the desired results were not forthcoming, for its working capacity was limited. Moreover, it was unable to enamel large pieces. The capacity of the entire factory was seriously affected because of the ineffective working of one small plant.

However, even when a balance is achieved through careful planning, it is difficult to maintain it between various operations, because over a time, the character of the technology and the nature may call for a change. Such shifts often cause bottlenecks in production. Even when one bottleneck is removed, another may crop up. Consequently, there seems to be a never-ending cycle of overcoming one bottleneck after another.

Extent of Vertical Integration

Most managements are confronted with such questions as : Should we manufacture what we sell, or should we buy it? If we manufacture, should we assemble the purchased parts or should we make them? The answers to these questions are the key to the long-run success of the company. In fact, a vertical combination may be regarded as a more or less ingenious device on the part of the manufacturer to reduce the cost of production by eliminating intermediate profit. Industries having the following characteristics usually tend to be vertically integrated:

(i) Where the quality of the product is important :
(ii) Where the finished product of one industry can be consumed by another as raw material;
(iii) Where one process is complementary to another; and
(iv) Where balanced production is significant.

Vertical Integration in Automobile Industry : The problem of deciding whether to make or buy products can best to be considered in relation to the automobile industry. About 20 years ago, companies used to procure most of their parts from other manufacturers which were assembled into cars. In fact, a substantial number of automobile manufacturers did nothing more than assembling parts. However, they exercised a great influence on the design of the body of the car. Since then, the picture has changed considerably; but even today large manufacturers do not make certain automobile parts. For example, the production of speedometers and milometers is a specialised job, and most automobile manufacturers consider it economical to purchase them from other manufacturers who have specialised in it. Similarly, tyres and tubes, pistons and rings, etc., are purchased from other companies.

Vertical Integration in Electronic Industry

Vertical integration can best be considered in relation to the electronic industry in this country. In the last four years, the manufacture of electronic goods has registered a steep rise. The manufacturers of these goods, which include TV, Video, Watches, Computers, etc., import most of the key parts from foreign markets and assemble the products before they are sold in the market. For TV picture tubes, the entire circuit and chips are assembled by the indigenous manufacturer.

Determinants of Vertical Integration

It goes without saying that integration policies, if properly designed and adopted, can yield high profitability. But whether the company should opt for integration or not depends on a variety of factors. Some of these important factors have been discussed here.

(i) Possible Savings Resulting from Co-ordination : If a firm produces goods or materials for its own use, it is easier to ensure promptness of delivery to customers and make adjustments in emergencies. If the firm is aware of its needs and the production process, and production schedule, optimum benefits can be achieved.

(ii) Flexibility : Vertical integration tends to limit flexibility in the production design to a considerable extent. The huge investment in plant or raw materials hampers the shift to a new design. But the firm that buys from outside can easily shift to a new product design.

In the short run, integrated firms cut down their purchases or shift to different suppliers. While doing so, they must recognise the effect of such action on unabsorbed overheads.

(iii) Elimination of Marketing Expenditure : If the firm manufactures parts or the raw material required for the production of goods, the expenditure incurred on procuring goods from outside is altogether eliminated.

(iv) Effects of Patents : The control of patents by other companies inflates the cost of production. But if the company obtains control over patents, a policy for large-scale production is desirable. If the company feels that raw materials cannot be procured easily, then, in order to keep up production, it will have to stock the raw materials.

(v) Volume Required for Economic Production : Most of small companies cannot undertake backward integration because the volume of their requirements for any part or material is too small to facilitate the utilisation of the entire plant capacity. To optimise profit, the company therefore sells the balance of the production in the market.

(vi) Financial Status of the Company : One of the important factors governing vertical integration is the financial status of the company. It has been noted that financially weak firms are not in a position to procure capital from the market. On the other hand, financially strong companies can effectively undertake vertical expansion. Their financial strength facilitates improvements in the manufacturing operations.

Vertical integration decisions are of paramount importance in the success of business. These decisions, therefore, should be carefully examined in terms of the various key factors, such as probable sales, the ratio of savings to investments, and the rate of return. A detailed analysis of these will enable the company to design a broad policy.

MAINTENANCE AND REPLACEMENT

Maintenance and replacement of plant and machinery are the very foundation of a production programme because a great many production functions are performed by automated plants, whose maintenance and timely replacement are essential for the success of a business. If no attention is paid to this aspect of the production programme, it will be difficult for the management to stick to its production schedule.

Maintenance

Like human beings machines suffer from fatigue and exhaustion. Machines, buildings and other plant facilities deteriorate because of wear and tear, because of use, overuse, misuse, vibrations, cold and hot fumes, etc. If "diseased" machines are not cured in time or before time, they will become inefficient, which will lower the quality and quantity of production. In fact, the maintenance of machines is essential for the overall efficiency of business. Increased mechanisation has made a proper maintenance of machines, one of the imperatives for the success of an enterprise. It is for this reason that all big industries have a well designed programme for timely and adequate maintenance of various plant facilities. Medium-size and large-scale industries have a full-fledged maintenance department, known as the plant engineering department, whose main job is to ensure that the entire plant is in perfect working order.

Types of Maintenance

Maintenance can be of two types :

(a) Preventive maintenance;

(b) Corrective or repair maintenance.

(a) Preventive Maintenance : In preventive maintenance, precautionary action is taken before the problem arises. If it is apprehended that a certain part of the machine will be shortly worn out, the immediate replacement of that part before it is actually worn out is called preventive maintenance. Preventive maintenance involves a definite programme of routine inspection, cleaning, and servicing of parts and machines.

The best example of preventive maintenance is provided by the automobile. Here, regular servicing after 1,000 kilometres, regular greasing, tuning and oil change after a definite period ensure the smooth functioning of the vehicle.

In industries, the problem of maintenance is very acute. It is always desirable, therefore, to identify the potential source of the trouble well in advance so that timely corrective action may be taken.

But the degree of attention to be paid to the need for maintenance and replacement varies from company to company. For example, the protection required in plants manufacturing poisonous gases is different from the one required in plants manufacturing software. The attention given to a blast furnace is different from that given to the fabrication of wheelbarrows. If interruptions in production are not of a serious nature and if a breakdown can be quickly dealt with, the intensity of preventive maintenance can be relaxed. But in industries like pesticides, chemicals and fertilisers, a high degree of excellence in maintenance is required.

(b) Corrective or Repair Maintenance : As a rule, depreciation in plants, machinery and other equipment takes place because of the passage of time, weather effects and accidents. Worn-out machinery needs repairs and replacement from time to time. Corrective maintenance is concerned with eliminating production bottlenecks by timely repairs or replacement of worn-out parts. Repair maintenance may call for the disassembly of equipment and the detection of malfunctioning, the repair or replacement of broken parts and then a check to make sure that the machinery or equipment functions efficiently.

Replacement : This refers to the substitution of old equipment by new. It is generally needed because of the following reasons :

(i) Natural decay;

(ii) Technological change;

(iii) New demand;

(iv) Improved working.

However, much emphasis is now placed on scheduled replacement because most of the machines/plants require certain parts to be replaced after the expiry of a definite time period.

The top management is not concerned with the petty matters of maintenance and replacement. However, to maintain the optimum efficiency of the plant, senior executives furnish guidelines to their subordinates for maintenance and replacement, i.e., when to slow down replacement or push it, what level of maintenance is required and to what extent.

MAKE OR BUY - SUPPLIERS AND SERVICES

Every firm engaged in the production of one or more type of goods aims at profit-maximisation. To accomplish this objective, it tries to procure the desired material for the operation of its plant at a low cost. It has usually the alternative of satisfying its requirements by producing the goods or material from within the firm itself. In some cases, a firm can manufacture goods in the desired quantity at a relatively low cost; but in certain other cases, the procurement of these goods from outsiders is more advantageous. In determining whether goods or material should be purchased or produced within the firm arises the "make or buy" problem.

In this connection – that is, whether it should make or buy goods – the policies of firms vary considerably. There are certain industries which follow the policy of self-support to the extent of manufacturing all the items required by them. On the other hand, there are concerns which believe in procuring material from other companies that specialise in the manufacture of those items/products. Every company uses a variety of suppliers and services, they need stationery, cartons, polyethylene bags, detergents, chemicals, power, heat, and many others. But it is not possible for them to procure all of them or produce all of them. They, therefore, take decisions on which items they should make and which goods and services they should buy.

Factors Influencing "Make or Buy" Decisions

The "make or buy" decisions are taken on the basis of their financial implications for a growing concern. For small companies, with an annual expenditure of a few lakhs of rupees, it is always desirable to buy materials from outside. In big concerns, where a substantial amount is involved, a full-scale analysis is required covering company matters relating to overall corporate policy, direct cost, personnel relations, plant layout, and other details which are incidental to any manufacturing programme. In the following paragraphs, we shall discuss a few factors affecting the "make or buy" decision.

(i) Manufacturing may be undertaken to ensure a regular supply. This is specially necessary where a close co-ordination between demand and supply is required. The decision to make goods appears to be quite attractive from the point of view of self-sufficiency, the high cost of procurement, and the interruptions in deliveries by vendors confronted with labour difficulties or natural calamities. It has been said that the difficulties which manufacturers are trying to avoid to arise even when they buy material for their own production.

But the danger is less, for there is a greater assurance of regular supply, when the item is manufactured by the user himself.

(ii) In some cases, the decision to make flows from the company's expectations to have goods of a desired quality. It has been observed that, in a seller's market, vendors do not bother about quality and specifications. Sometimes they sell only high quality goods and enjoy a profitable sales volume; they do not, therefore, have any interest in lower quality goods which at times may be needed by some manufacturers. In such a situation, the producer has no option but to manufacture the goods himself.

(iii) There are conditions under which it is profitable for a company to produce certain items more economically than they can be bought from outside. If it discovers a new process which enables it to produce some items at a definitely low cost or if it acquires equipment at a relatively low price that can manufacture goods cheaply, the decision to make goods instead of buying them will be quite profitable.

(iv) During the period of depression or recession, the manufacturer with idle plant capacity may find it desirable to undertake the production of those goods which they were formerly buying. Even during normal times, the decision to make is taken with a view to increasing the total volume of production. In this way, the overhead costs can be distributed.

(v) Sometimes, protection of quality design also tempts companies to make decisions.

Guidelines to "Make or Buy" Policy

The following are often an answer to most "make or buy" decisions relating to supplies and services :

(i) When a dependable source does not exist outside, it is desirable for the company to produce the goods of the desired quality, unless some unforeseen circumstances develop. For instance, most big companies prefer to have their own thermal supply because public power plants are not reliable.

(ii) When a dependable source exists outside which provides goods at an economical price, it should be used, unless there is a strong case for not doing so. For instance, under the following conditions, it is always desirable to depend on their own resources :

(a) When an item is required in large quantities which can be produced at a low cost by the company itself;

(b) When suppliers are not willing to provide goods of the desired quality or cater to the special needs of their buyers; and

(c) When co-ordination with suppliers seems to be quite difficult.

PURCHASING

Irrespective of how a company resolves the issue of "make or buy" or achieves vertical integration, some services and goods have to be purchased. The efficiency of a company's operation, therefore, is contingent upon its making supplies and goods available of a proper quality, in a proper quantity, at the proper place and time and at a proper price. A failure on any one of these counts inflates the cost, and this has a dampering effect on profits because of production bottlenecks, inferior products, disgruntled customers, excessive and unnecessary wastage.

To make purchasing effective, the management has to take policy decisions on the following issues :

(i) What type of purchasing will be there?

(ii) How will vendors be selected?

Types of Purchasing

If the company has a number of plants, purchasing may be centralised or localised under a *centralised purchasing authority* – a single person should be placed in charge of the purchasing department. This is generally so when the company operates only one plant. But this department is created in those companies as well which have more than one plant. In this case, however, a number of factors have to be taken into consideration before deciding whether purchasing should be centralised, such as the extent of the geographical separation of plants, the homogeneity of the product manufactured, the type of material forming bulk of purchase, the location of suppliers, etc.

On the other hand, under *localised purchasing*, each of the units of the plant has its own purchasing department which makes purchases on the basis of its requirements. This usually applies where the company runs a large number of plants in widely separated locations and turns out a variety of products.

Before the discussing an ideal situation, it is worthwhile to consider the relative merits of centralised and localised purchasing.

Merits of Centralised Purchasing

(i) Economy of Large-Scale Purchasing : Centralised purchasing offers the advantages of large-scale purchasing. These are: the availability of raw materials at cheaper prices, better transportation facilities at lower rates and more concessions. It is possible to place orders directly with suppliers so that thereby middlemen may be altogether eliminated.

(ii) Utilisation of Expertise : Manufacturers with a number of working units can afford better paid and better qualified staff which results in more efficient and economical buying.

(iii) More Flexibility : Through centralised purchasing, greater flexibility can be achieved in a variety of ways. First, the surplus material in one plant can be effectively used by other plants or units without any additional expenditure. Second, the emergency requirements of one plant can be met by utilising materials from other plants in the quickest and most economical way.

Merits of Localised Purchasing

Here, purchasing is done by an individual department, which enjoys the following advantages:

(i) Delays and High Reserve Inventories Avoided : Delays in the procurement of materials is usually caused when purchasing is done by the central office. Different units are required to build heavy inventories to compensate for the time lag between the requisition and procurement of material. This is more true when different units are situated at different places, and the central office is not in a position to meet their emergency requirements.

(ii) Efficient Dealing with Social Problems : Every plant or unit usually has its own peculiar problems and differences in the production process which largely affect its procurement needs. Besides these, climatic conditions, transportation facilities, warehousing facilities, laws, supplier's

distribution policies do have a direct bearing on purchasing. The central office is in a better position to understand and manage this complex situation. Purchasing becomes more effective.

(iii) Avoidance of Conflict with Central Purchasing Department: Quite often, there may be a misunderstanding and conflict between different unit heads and the central purchasing department specially when the goods purchased are not of the right quality or are not supplied in time. From the point of view of the supplier, it is not desirable on his part to ask his sales personnel to contact plant managers who have no authority to purchase and for which they are required to contact the purchase manager.

The best solution of the purchasing problem is centralised control. The central purchasing office should concentrate on framing uniform policies and control procedures for the purchasing activities of all the departments. The different units should be allowed to make purchases in accordance with the policies laid down by the head office.

In other words, we may say that the major purchasing activity should be performed by the head office and petty purchases may be made by the respective units on the basis of their requirements. To avoid duplication, friction and confusion, the authority at the head office and unit office should be properly defined and both the head office and the offices should function within the purview of their assigned duties.

Selection of Vendors

The basic ingredient of an efficient purchasing process is the rational selection of the source of supply, i.e., to find capable and willing vendors and to conclude an agreement with them on the pertinent factors of quality, service and prices. In most businesses, it is quite possible to purchase products from several vendors. This raises two important questions :

(i) Whether purchasing from several vendors is profitable;

(ii) What type of vendor is the most satisfactory source of supply.

Number of Vendors

The question of whether the company should have a number of vendors from whom it should procure most of the materials it requires should be given careful consideration, failing which the entire production process may run into difficulties. In regard to the number of vendors, the policies of companies vary considerably. For instance, a medium-size chemical manufacturing company for a number of years followed the policy of procuring materials from a number of vendors. Later, it went through financial difficulties, and regretted the policy of utilising the services of a large number of vendors. Since it used to make small purchases from a variety of vendors, it did not get any credit facility. Instead, each vendor pressed for urgent and immediate payment. Had this firm concentrated on one or two vendors, it might have induced the latter to liberalise their credit policies for it.

The companies that buy large quantities of merchandise quite often deal with one supplier. By doing so, they are able to secure favourable prices, better quality of goods, regular supplies etc. The danger of reliance of this practice is that if, due to any unavoidable circumstances, such as labour trouble, power cut, mechanical failure, transport bottlenecks, the vendor fails to maintain a constant supply, the production process of the company would be adversely affected.

Most firms follow the policy of dealing with a number of vendors and, at the same time, concentrate the bulk of their purchases with one vendor. They find it desirable to procure about 75% to 80% of their total requirements from one vendor who happens to be a desirable source in terms of price, quality and delivery. The remaining part is procured from several other suppliers. Though the placing of small orders with a large number of vendors is certainly not economical, the fact remains that it serves two distinct purposes :

(a) The main supplier is always on his toes, for the manufacturer is in close touch with the market and can shift to another supplier if the terms of trade, the quality of merchandise, and service are more profitable elsewhere;

(b) If the main supplier is unable to supply goods due to any reason, the manufacturer can readily procure his requirements from the other vendors.

Factors Affecting Selection of Vendors

We have already discussed the fact that a variety of advantages and disadvantages limit the number of vendors when purchases are made. It is very desirable to weigh the advantages of better quality and low price against the disadvantages of shifting to a small vendor, if the original one is unable to cater to the requirements of the firm. The various problems arising out of this resolve themselves into the following questions :

(i) Can a limited number of vendors supply the variety of products required?

(ii) What are the advantages of utilising the services of many vendors?

(iii) Which trade concessions and special services will result from concentration?

After seeking answers to these questions, the management should design policies about vendors.

CHAPTER 13

FINANCE POLICIES

- **Introduction**
- **Issue of Securities**
- **Borrowing from Financial Institutions**
- **Public Deposits**
- **Retained Earnings**
- **Use of Capital**
- **Protection of Capital and Distribution of Earnings**

INTRODUCTION

Importance of Finance

Among all the M's (Man, Machine, Material and Money) of management, **MONEY** plays a vital role in the success of an organisation in the sense that the growth and development of a business is contingent upon the availability of finances in the desired quantum. In fact, finance is the life blood of business in today's money economy; and its role has rapidly gained importance. In the modern hostile business environment with its increasing complexity, excessive competition and an unprecedented pace of S & T changes, a business with a sound financial standing is able to survive environmental onslaughts. The management, therefore, ensures that the company always has sufficient financial resources at its disposal, not only for the successful operation of its daily affairs but for meeting contingencies too. A shortfall in finances, besides hampering routine activities, can put obstacles in the production process, prevent the adoption of new technology, endanger human relations and generate an acute financial crisis which may even lead to bankruptcy. Contrary to this an excess of, or an easy availability of capital may to at times tempt the management to make unwise investment decisions which may lead to a negative effect on profitability.

It is, therefore, the prime responsibility of the management to ensure that the financial resources of the company are so utilized that they yield optimum benefit to the company and to society at large.

The requirements of capital of an undertaking depends upon the size and type of its business– the cost of installing plant and machinery and other expenses. Generally speaking, business undertakings require capital for :

(i) Promotion and formation expenses;

(ii) The cost of fixed assets;

(iii) Regular working capital

(iv) The cost of financing; and

(v) The cost of establishing the business.

Classification of Financial Policies

Once the financial requirements of a company have been crystallized, the management must determine the financial policies necessary for achieving the corporate goals. These policies are guides to all the actions that are concerned with procuring, administering and disbursing funds. While designing financial policies, the management must seek an answer to the following questions :

(i) How will capital be procured?

(ii) How will it be utilised?

(iii) How will it be protected?

(iv) How will earnings be distributed?

As all these questions are intimately related, their impact on other issues must be borne in mind, for that will help the management to design comprehensive financial policies.

Procurement of Capital

The management is often confronted with the question of how and from where to obtain capital. There is a closer relationship between the sources and methods of raising capital, and both influence the character of each other. This is largely due to the fact that different sources of capital can be successfully tapped only when the company knows the way in which supplier can finance its activities. For example, if a financial institution is authorised to invest only in debentures and if the firm wants to avail itself of this, it will have to float debentures.

As there are a number of methods of raising finance and a number of sources from which it can be raised, the management must decide which method should be employed and which source (or a combination thereof) should be tapped. In fact, selection of a particular source depends on the purpose and period for which capital is required. Capital for basic necessities like machinery, land and buildings should normally be raised through equity sources; but if borrowed capital is to be raised, it should be in the form of short-term loans. The various sources from which capital can be raised include :

ISSUES OF SECURITIES

(a) Ownership Securities

(i) Common stock;
(ii) Preference stock,

(b) Creditorship Securities

(i) Bonds;
(ii) Debentures;
(iii) Borrowings from financial institutions;
(iv) Public deposits;
(v) Retained earnings.

Ownership Securities

The ownership of a company is generally represented by two types of securities – one, the common stock (equity shares or ordinary shares), the other, preferred stock (preference shares).

(a) Common Stock : Common stock is regarded as the cornerstone of the financial structure of a company. Both for legal and economic reasons, no corporation can exist without it, for it does not carry with it any fixed commitment charges. In this case, if the company earns a huge profit, the stockholders can expect a substantial return; but if it suffers losses or directors do not decide to distribute profits, the shareholders have no recourse.

The common stock provides venture capital even though the company has not started earning profits. Moreover, it does not create any financial obligation on its part, as the declaration of dividend is the exclusive prerogative of the management. So the entire profit earned on the share capital can be employed to strengthen the financial position of company. Besides this, if the funds raised by the company are not required to be refunded during the life-time of the company, it is assured of permanent capital. As the shares issued do not create any charge on the company's assets, it can raise emergency funds against the security of these assets. While raising funds through equity shares, the management should bear the following points in mind:

(i) The exclusive use of equity shares as a fund-raising device deprives the management of the opportunity of trading on equity. This results in loss of opportunity for using cheap borrowed capital.

(ii) The financing of business through common stock is not desirable as this affects the efficiency of the business, particularly when cliques of shareholders are formed.

(iii) Excessive use of equity shares results in over-capitalisation.

(b) Preference Stock :It is a hybrid form of financing in the sense that it has the features of both the debt and common stock. Preference stockholders carry a preferential right to dividends in the normal course of business, and the repayment of capital in the event of the winding up of the business. The preference claim may be cumulative or non-cumulative; in certain cases, preference stockholders participate in the profits of company along with equity shareholders. At times, the company gives an option to its shareholders to convert their shares into equity after the expiry of a certain period if they desire to have the benefit of higher returns. To attract more investors, redeemable preference shares, giving an assurance of redemption after the expiry of a stipulated period, are issued.

This is considered to be a satisfactory method of raising semi-permanent finance. It is beneficial for the company, for it can redeem preference shares carrying a high dividend rate when the money market is favourable. It enables the company to capitalise its reserve and surplus funds. A company issuing redeemable preference shares will not be over-capitalised, for whenever it is in danger of over–capitalisation, it can overcome the problem by redeeming shares as and when desired.

Though it is one of the most widely used sources of funds, what its exact role in meeting the financial requirements of a company is not quite clear. The attitude of most managements in this context varies considerably. This is largely so because of the "in between" nature of this type of security. In creating some sort of normal, but not a legal, obligation to fix dividends, the corporation assumes the risk of its credit rating, the extent of which is unknown. The decision whether or not to use preference stock in a financial plan depends on the management's ability to evaluate its merits and demerits in advance.

The company raises capital through both preference and equity stock; but the right granted to any particular type of stock depends on:

(i) The financial health of the company;
(ii) The condition of the securities market at the time of issue;
(iii) The quantum of outstanding securities the company has at the time of the issue of new securities.

The policy of companies relating to the procurement of additional capital should be designed on the basis of the availability and cost of capital from other sources. The managements must assess the probable impact of new issue on the equity and rights of the existing shareholders.

Creditorship Securities

Creditorship securities are a means by which companies meet their medium and long-term financial requirements. The principal creditorship securities include bonds and debentures. Both of these represent the debts given to a company.

(a) Bonds: Bonds are issued by corporations to meet their long-term financial requirements. The issue is an economic way of raising funds, because the rate of interest that a company offers on its bonds is definitely lower than the expected dividend that it is required to offer to its shareholders. The interest on bonds is an expense deducted from the income before the tax is computed, whereas the profit available for stockholders is the net income after the tax has been paid. The issue of bonds permits trading on equity, which is another important means of raising capital.

Bonds can be secured as well as unsecured. Secured bonds are those bonds which are supported by some property as collateral. The kind of property attached to such bonds may be either real property, personal property or both. Real property includes immovable property — land and buildings — whereas personal property includes such moveable property as stocks and bonds, etc. When the mortgage is given as the first security, it is termed as the first mortgage bond. Bonds carrying the prior claim are known as senior mortgage, while others are referred to as junior mortgage.

A specific mortgage gives the bond-holder the right of lien on some specific part of the business, whereas a blanket mortgage covers the whole range of the company's existing assets as well as those that might be acquired at subsequent dates. In the case of unsecured bonds, the company pays interest to the bond-holder at a fixed rate. After the expiry of the stipulated time period, he is paid a certain sum of money.

While issuing bonds, the company must see to it that its assets are substantially in excess of the amount of the bonds to be issued, and that its annual operating profits are three or four times higher than the interest charges on its entire debt. Since any shrinkage in earnings or asset value must first be borne by stockholders, a fair cushion of protection should be made available to bond-holders.

The rate of interest on bonds should be fixed in terms of the risk of loss associated with them and the interest rates prevailing in money market.

(b) Debentures : Debentures are issued by a company whenever additional or extra funds are required for diversification or improvement. A debenture may be regarded as an acknowledgement of debt by a company, which binds itself to repay it on the basis of the terms and conditions of issue.

A debenture may be secured or unsecured. Secured debentures generally carry a fixed or floating charge on the assets of the company. Under the floating charge on assets, the company is free to deal with the property forming the charge.

Apart from the fact the debentures may be secured or unsecured, there are certain other classes of debentures, such as bearer and registered debentures, redeemable or irredeemable debentures. The interest on registered debentures is payable only to the registered holder, whereas the interest on bearer debentures is cashed by the holder. Redeemable debentures are redeemed at the expiry of the stipulated period. In contrast to this, irredeemable debentures are perpetual in nature and are not to be paid as long as the company is a going concern.

It is obvious from the foregoing discussion that debentures enable the company to meet its intermediate and long-term financial requirements. As long as term finance is available, the company gets an opportunity for adjusting its financial plan to its requirements. This source of finance carries with itself a packet of advantages. These are :

(i) It permits trading on equity;
(ii) It provides tax benefit to companies;

(iii) It does not dilute the control of the enterprise; and
(iv) It appeals to institutional investors.

However, it is not desirable on the part of companies to raise debenture funds which are more than 20 per cent of its gross earnings because the issue of debentures imposes a financial burden on the business. To safeguard the interest of shareholders, therefore, it would be wise on the part of the management not to depend excessively on debentures for borrowed capital.

BORROWING FROM FINANCIAL INSTITUTIONS

Companies can meet their financial requirements by borrowing funds in the desired quantum from financial institutions. A careful study of the Indian money market reveals that institutional financial machinery is composed of :

(i) Ordinary financial institutions, such as commercial banks, investment trusts and the life insurance corporation; and
(ii) Specialised financial institutions, (i.e., development banks).

These financial institutions provide industrial finance in the following forms:

(i) Medium and long-term loans;
(ii) Short-term bank credit;
(iii) Underwriting and subscription of new issues; and
(iv) Purchase of securities.

The financial institutions, by providing financial assistance in different forms, cater to a variety of needs of business enterprises.

From a purely quantitative point of view, commercial banks usually provide short-term loans, whereas other financial institutions meet the mid-term and long-term financial requirements of both large as well as small and innovating undertakings.

PUBLIC DEPOSITS

Besides the use of corporate securities, industries can raise finance by way of public deposits to meet their long and medium-term financial requirements. This method of financing involves an invitation to the public to deposit their money with the company. The company gives a receipt to the depositor, specifying the amount of the loan advanced, the rate of interest payable, the time of the repayment of the loan, etc.

This is a beneficial method of procuring finance at a lower rate of interest. Usually, the rate of interest payable on short-term loan is lower than on long-term borrowings. Moreover, the method involves minimum administration charges because the company is required to issue only a deposit receipt to the depositor. The use of public deposits as a source of funds is justified because this method does not place a burden on the company's assets. Most deposits are unsecured debts.

However, this method cannot be profitably employed during a period of depression, when the depositors become panicky and want to withdraw their funds due to the shaky position of the company. Moreover, public deposits are in the form of unsecured loans. The depositor is therefore afraid of non-payment in the event of the winding up of the company. In spite of stringent measures suggested by RBI to safeguard the interest of shareholders, this method is not much popular in India as a means of procuring finance by industries.

RETAINED EARNINGS

At the very outset, it must be noted that, for financing purposes, only existing companies can take recourse to this method. New business undertakings cannot avail of the advantages of this method. Established concerns do not employ it, when there is a problem of immediate financing of a major programme. However, some companies make it a practice to utilise retained earnings to finance their various projects, besides managing financial requirements pertaining to fixed and working capital.

The peculiar feature of retained earnings is that, contrary to their methods, they are an internal source of finance. They arise from the profit which is not distributed among shareholders. As a result, no long-term debt is incurred, and ownership, by way of the sale of voting stock, is not diluted.

A proper utilisation of retained earnings has the advantage of avoiding the cost of investment that would have been incurred if bonds or stocks were sold to public. There is conclusive proof of the fact that firms which build up its surplus accounts by withholding dividends if stockholders are in a better position to face adverse business conditions than other firms.

Apart from successfully established big businesses, a small business, too, can tap this source of finance for its expansion and development programme.

However, ploughing back of profit should be resorted to with great caution, for excessive ploughing back is detrimental not only to the interests of the shareholders but also to corporate management at large.

From the financial point of view, the profit earned during a financial year is channelized in three directions:

(i) The government shares in profit through income tax;
(ii) The amount payable to stockholders as cash dividends;
(iii) The amount to be retained,

The disposition of the profit through income tax is determined by tax laws. However, with regard to dividends and retention of profit, the management has to take a decision, for there is a close relationship between the dividend paid and the profits retained. If the dividend rate is higher, the amount of retained earnings is bound to be small.

Financial Structure

The amount of capital utilised and its relative importance determines the financial structure of a company. In designing its policies relating to sources of capital, this general structure must be given adequate attention, for the use of one source of capital affects the worth and value of other sources.

The size of the undertaking, its nature, the nature and type of its assets, the amount and stability of its earnings, the position of the financial market, etc., determine the source of capital to be utilised by the company for financing its business. From time to time, the source of capital is changed, either because it can be profitably procured from some other source or because some lender decides to withdraw his capital from the company. The expansion and contraction in the total capital that is employed affect the relative importance of different sources. Therefore, the financial structure of the company should be based on a proper correlation and the adoption of financial policies in relation to existing conditions.

Selecting Source of Capital

The financial structure of a company provides a base for managers to decide about the source to be deployed for procuring finance. It has been noted that, among different companies, there is great variation in capital structure – in assets, in earnings, in the style of management; but in industries dealing is similar types of goods, the capital structure tends to be the same. An effective financial management would ensure that the capital structure of the company is tailor-made. Therefore, while deciding about the capital structure of the company, the management should bear the following factors in mind:

(i) The use to be made of the capital;
(ii) The cost of capital;
(iii) The rights granted to various contributors.

Use of Capital

The funds required to finance temporary or seasonal needs can be effectively obtained from short-term creditors, such as commercial banks. This is a relatively easy and inexpensive method of raising capital and facilitates immediate reduction in the capital so owned after its requirements have been fully met. On the other hand, the finances required for fixed assets or working capital that will be permanently retained in business should be raised by issuing securities or from financial institutions.

The use of capital also affects the company's ability to offer the lender some special security for his loan. As effective guarantee that the loan will be paid well in time, the company may pledge as security one or more assets (such as inventories, machinery, plant and buildings). In this way, it will be able to procure the loan of the desired amount.

Cost of Capital

In business undertakings, capital in the form of shares and debentures has to be attracted and retained. Therefore, the management in assessing the cost of capital, must give due consideration to the original cost in obtaining it as well as to the compensation paid for its use.

The total cost of maintaining loan and share capital should be kept to the minimum, alternative capital structures should be compared, for different proportions of share capital and loan capital yield different results. Different alternative sources of capital at different time periods should therefore be taken into consideration. If other things remain equal, the one which attracts the minimum cost should be chosen. However, care should be taken to ensure that the terms of cheapest loan do not impose any restrictions on the company which are likely to impair its ability to earn maximum profit. In assessing cost of capital, the following elements should be given adequate consideration.

Underwriting and Registration

The companies procuring capital by the issue of bonds or selling stock to public incur considerable amount of expenditure. Securities and stocks are sold through brokers and underwriters, who are resourceful enough to reach prospective buyers. Companies therefore pay a substantial amount of compensation to them for their services. Capital or finance raised by way of sale of property involves legal formalities and publicity cost. Therefore, while procuring capital, the management must see to it that it is able to raise money at minimum cost.

Issue of Rights Shares

The companies issuing new securities generally sell them directly to this existing shareholders. This is particularly true when a company sells additional stock of a similar nature. Some companies have a clear policy to the effect that, on a fresh issue, the existing shareholders will be given priority. When that is the case, if the stock is sold at below market price, the present stockholders will take full advantage of the privilege. When this situation exists, the cost of securing additional capital is made very easy. But, even then it is always desirable to enlist the services of underwriters and brokers, failing which many items of expenditure relating to the sale of securities will have to be incurred.

Adjusting Sources to Prevailing Rate of Interest

The compensation that is paid for the use of capital varies not only with the way in which it is used but is materially affected by the state of the business cycle.

Many companies find it desirable to sell bonds and other long-term securities when low interest rates prevail in order to safeguard themselves against the high cost that they anticipate in future when interest rates would be high. A company may raise funds through short-term loans on the presumption that these can be paid off from the proceeds of long-term bonds which will be sold in future when interest rates are lower. The success of such a plan depends on the efficiency with which the management forecasts the movement of interest rates. But there is always an apprehension that interest rates on long-term obligations will be higher when short debts mature. Moreover, the corporate taxation structure plays such an important role in the profitability of companies that the timing to changes in the capital structure may be based on an attempt to get the most desirable tax structure

Return Paid on New Stock

Whenever new stock is sold, the company is not obliged to pay a specific amount of interest for the use of capital so procured. Moreover, when new stockholders are paid any dividend, there is a reduction in the dividend of existing shareholders. This sharing of dividend is the cost of capital so far as the existing shareholders are concerned.

Many companies find it desirable to raise capital by issuing stock even though it is anticipated that the dividends paid would be definitely higher than the interest that would have been paid on bonds, if the latter had been issued. The willingness of companies to pay higher cost is linked with the fact that dividends do not have to be paid if there are no adequate earnings or cash to justify the declaration of a dividend. Contrary to this, the interest on bonds is required to be paid regardless of the amount of earnings or cash in hand.

It is largely assumed that capital can be procured from any source at any time, provided that a fair compensation is made available to the public. But, as a matter of fact, the sale of bonds or stock during certain phases of the business cycle may be so difficult that capital cannot be procured from these sources.

Right Granted with New Securities

Rights Granted to Creditors

In selecting the source of capital, adequate attention should be given to the authority attached to the different types of capital. If capital is procured from short-term creditors, the latter will have no control over the affairs of the company. But if they are not compensated in time, they may resort to legal action for the enforcement of their claims.

Long-term creditors, too, do not ordinarily have a voice in the current affairs of the company; but a bond-holder may impose certain restrictions on the management. For example, by indenture he may restrict the future debts that the company can incur, or he may insist that the amount be invested in fixed assets, etc. The loan agreement may also restrict the freedom to declare and pay a dividend. Some agreements provide that a dividend cannot be paid if the ratio between the various type of assets is below the prescribed limit, or if there is any default in the payment of interest to long-term creditors. If these requirements are not met and a dividend is declared, legal action can be taken by the bond-holders against the company. These restrictions at times become so cumbersome that the managements prefer to procure capital from other sources.

Rights Granted to Stockholders

If capital is procured by the sale of stock, new stockholders will have certain rights against the company. Quite often, they have full voting rights and they become participants in the future management of the company. In most cases, present stockholders want to retain control of the management and do not want new stockholders to participate in the affairs of the company. The possibility that the sale of stock will change the balance of power among the members of the Board of Directors largely depends upon the size of the new issue as compared to the existing stock, the amount of stock held by existing shareholders and the extent to which existing stockholders purchase the new stock.

The preference shareholders do not exercise any control over the affairs of the company. Normally, they have no right of vote in the election of directors, as equity shareholders have. However, common stockholders usually run the risk of losing control to preference stockholders, if the preference stock remains unpaid for a long time and the charter provides that, under such circumstances, preference stockholders can be given the voting power.

USE OF CAPITAL

Use of Capital

Profit is the prime motto of a business. Therefore, the way in which capital is utilised has a lot to do with its success or failure. The policies relating to the use of capital concern almost every activity of a business. For example, plans for sales, i.e., for the products to be sold, the pricing and promotional strategy to be followed, and plans for production, i.e., decisions relating to manufacture or purchase, the adoption of new technology and plans for the recruitment of expertise, motivational programmes, investment in human resource development – all these dictate the way in which capital may be utilised. The policies relating to the use of capital do not, however, stipulate the specific use of capital; in fact, these are largely monitored by other management decisions.

Circulating and Fixed Capitals

Circulating Capital

Assets like plants, machinery, land and buildings purchased with permanent capital are kept in business for the purpose of earning a profit over a longer period of time. However, in addition to these, there are assets which are normally not retained for a longer period, for they usually change their forms over and again during the course of a year. These are known as current assets, and the capital used to purchase them is termed as circulating capital. In a business cash, inventory and accounts receivable constitute the circulating capital because this capital changes frequently its form. The original capital is typically in the form of cash. This is invested in inventories, general administration, and sales promotional expenses. After making investment inputs, the management sells the output in the market with an intention of recovering the money so spent. When the product is sold on cash, the capital is again made available to the business. And so the cycle goes on.

The circulating capital requirements of a business vary considerably over a period of time; for instance, fluctuations in the sales volume often bring about fluctuations in the size of the capital invest in accounts receivable. These fluctuations in sales may be reflected in purchasing and production programmes. Quite often, managers build up heavy inventories to meet market demands during peak periods. The unfavourable period of business cycles may result in the slow movements of goods and may call for higher credit to intermediaries, which may result in the blocking of circulating capital. As both external constraints and management decisions pertaining to the internal operations of the business affect the size of the circulating capital, sound policies and rigorous control standards must be followed to ensure that the total amount is profitably employed.

Fixed Capital

Every type of business requires a certain amount of fixed capital to carry on its activities. For example, a machine tool producing concern may require a huge amount of capital for the installation of plant, machinery, etc. A retail store may need it for investment in fixtures and furniture. Even a consulting firm has to invest in office decoration, computers and typewriters. The investment made in such form is referred to as fixed capital because these terms of expenditure typically render services over a period of time.

In the words of Betty: "All fixed assets, intangible assets (such as goodwill, patents and trade marks investment) and other assets which are retained permanently in the business are purchased from funds which may be regarded as the fixed or permanent capital[1]." The fixed capital employed in business turns back into cash more slowly than circulating capital.

At any instance, it should not be taken for granted that fixed capital represents the only long-term investment required in a business. Actually, a growing business needs a minimum amount of capital to be invested in account receivables, inventory and other circulating items. The cash from accounts receivable should again be invested in inventories. The requirements of circulating capital are as regular as those of fixed capital. The financial programme of an enterprise should therefore provide for long-term capital to cover both fixed and circulating capital requirements.

The major policy issues concerned with the use of capital may be discussed in terms of:

(i) Use of circulating capital;
(ii) Regulating investment in fixed assets;
(iii) Merger and acquisition.

1. Betty, J., *Management Accountancy*, McDonald Evans, 1982, p. 113.

Use of Circulating Capital

The policies relating to circulating capital should include general restrictions on the amount of capital invested in inventories. The size of an inventory must be consistent with other possible uses of this capital. If a company experiences difficulty in maintaining an adequate cash flow, it should try to minimise investment in inventories in such a fashion that no undue strain is put on its financial resources, and at the same time, an economic order quantity is maintained to maintain the production schedule. As the creditworthiness of a company is assessed by its current ratio, most companies place financial restrictions on inventory building.

Though inventory management is certainly not the main problem of the finance people, it is necessary for them to see to it that the purchase of inventory does not lead to a dilution of the current ratio.

Credit Policies

The term credit policies refers to those decision variables which influence the amount of trade credit, i.e., the investment in receivables. A firm's investment in receivables is largely affected by general economic conditions, the pace of technological change, the extent of the competition, industry norms, and the financial structure of the company itself. Though a firm has no control on these external factors, it can influence trade credit through its credit policies within externally imposed constraints.

Ingredients of Credit Policy

A fundamental prerequisite for designing an optimal credit policy involves the estimation of its diverse aspects. The various decision variables which are required to be considered in this regard include:

(a) Credit standards;
(b) Credit terms; and
(c) Collection period.

Credit Standards

The credit standards adopted by a firm have a significant bearing on sales and receivables. A firm with a loose or relaxed credit standard enjoys higher sales and receivables, whereas one with a tight credit standard finds that there is a dampering effect on its sales and receivables. The credit standards of a firm are largely monitored by:

(i) Willingness of customers to pay;
(ii) Capacity of customers to pay; and
(iii) General economic milieu.

Credit is among a host of factors that affect the firm's sales. The extent to which credit can stimulate demand is contingent upon the severity of other factors. It is desirable for a firm to lower its credit standards to the point where increased sales exceed the associated costs. However, a relaxation in credit standards would result in a lengthening of the collection period, and that may tempt new customers not to pay their bills in time.

In deciding upon a relaxation of credit restrictions, the management should know to what extent it will be able to increase the sales and how much expenditure it will have to incur to achieve this increase.

Credit Terms

The conditions or specifications under which firms sell goods to customers are referred to as credit terms. The important components of credit terms include :

(a) Credit period;

(b) The cash discount terms.

Credit Period

The credit period refers to the time duration for which credit is extended to customers. It is expressed in terms of time. For example, if a firm's credit period is net 30 days, it is expected that the customer will make the payment within 30 days of sale.

Cash Discount

Cash discount is another important aspect of credit terms. Most business undertakings offer this discount to speed up collections. The cash discount policy indicates the rate of discount payable and the period for which it has been offered. The management, in deciding about the quantum and period of cash discount, should assess whether the discount offered will be really helpful in procuring business for it. If not, a cash discount policy would be burdensome for the business.

The cash discount and the credit period are two ingredients of credit terms. These relate to the amount of discount payable, the discount period and the credit tenure. For example, if the credit terms are expressed as "3/15 net 45," it means that 3% discount is allowed if payment is made after 15 days and that if this offer is not availed of, then payment has to be made within 45 days.

Favourable credit terms are largely offered to increase a firm's sale. Though the management is at liberty to design its own credit policies, adequate consideration should be given to the strategy of the competitors, failing which it may sustain undue losses.

Collection Policy

To make the credit policy function effectively, a sound collection policy is indispensable. Most businessmen know that all the customers do not pay in time. Some are slow payers, while others are non-payers. A collection policy helps to accelerate collections from slow payers and tends to reduce bad debts. In order to collect payment from slow payers, a firm should follow a definite policy. For example, if a customer has been granted 30 days credit, and if no payment is received after the expiry of this period, he should be asked to make payment. If the letter asking for payment remains unattended, another letter may be sent; and this may be followed by a registered letter, a telegram, and even a visit by the company's sales personnel. If there is no response, legal proceedings may be initiated. However, before resorting to legal action, the firm's financial position must be studied. If it happens to be financially weak, it is better to compromise for a reduced payment. If the firm does not do so, but adopts a strict collection policy, its permanent customers, who happen to be slow payers for one reason or other, shift their business to those firms which offer liberal credit terms. But if a lenient collection policy, is followed, the profitability of the company will suffer. Firms, therefore, have to be very cautious in implementing their collection policy.

Factors Influencing Credit Policy

It has already been pointed out that the credit policy of a firm is largely determined by general economic conditions, the rate is technological change, the extent of competition, and industry norms. But within the limits of the external environment, it is free to design its credit policy. A sound credit policy should be based on two factors: one, the cost of extending credit which includes interest on money, probable losses due to uncontrollable accounts, the expenditure incurred on handling the account, and, two, the net profit that may be earned on sales generated by the credit policy.

Regulating Investment in Fixed Assets

In all business organisations, a number of proposals are made for the addition of facilities to increase profitability. The managers concerned with product planning or production place emphasis on the deployment of a better technology with a view to achieving higher production at lower cost. One important way to regulate such proposal is to lay down a policy pertaining to investment in fixed assets. Here, we give some samples relating to such proposals.

Long-Term Outlook

A plywood-making industry became worried about the increasing cost of production of one of its plants located in Tamil Nadu. A cost analysis revealed that the plants located in North India were getting raw material at a lower cost than that in Tamil Nadu.

It was, therefore, decided that no further investment in fixed assets should be made at the plants in Tamil Nadu; that only the purchase of miscellaneous equipment and spare parts will be allowed; that attempts will be made to ensure that the existing capacities of the plants located in North India are gradually increased; and that the plant located in Tamil Nadu will be discounted.

The policy relating to the investment in fixed assets should be administered with great caution. A change in government policies and uncertainty of technology often tempt the management to give serious thoughts to the varied problems of investment in fixed assets. If a company deals in wide variety of production lines with a view to increase its profitability, heavy investment in fixed capital may be justified.

Minimum Rate of Return

The policies illustrated so far indicate the type of fixed assets to be avoided or encouraged in a business. Parallel to this, most firms concentrate on the minimum rate of return that must be anticipated, if capital is employed in a specific proposal. For example, a company may decide that the investment in new assets must earn at least 5% on the initial investment after making the necessary provision for depreciation and taxes. All those proposals which yield less than the desired return will then have to be dropped in the very first instance. This sort of policy is quite useful, for the method of estimating the return is quite well defined. The depreciation interest, taxes, net investment and other items can be treated in quite a different manner.

It is largely believed that the permissible rate of return should be the average cost of capital to the company. The minimum rate of return can be properly estimated if due consideration is given to such factors as the desire for expansion, the size of existing funds, plans about future procurement of funds, and assessment of risk. As most executives, who make proposals for investment in fixed assets tend to be quite optimistic in assessing the benefits that are likely to flow from the products, it is desirable that the management should get a high rate of return.

Capital Budgeting

In regulating investment in fixed assets, a company quite often has a variety of plans that can be effectively financed. The technique which is widely utilised to screen various investment proposals is commonly known as capital budgeting. The screening of a proposal calls for the identification of alternatives, feasibility studies, cash flow forecasts, assessments of economic worth vis-a-vis the degree of risk involved, and expected rate of return. Because of its crucial importance, an analysis of various proposals must be done with great caution, for the effective functioning of subsequent plans will depend on the thoroughness with which proposals have been screened. The whole task will be simplified by screening those proposals which are not in conformity with purchase, production, personnel and finance policies.

Effective investment criteria should have the following features :

(i) It should clearly screen the projects which are to be accepted or dropped;
(ii) It should provide a logical base for the ranking of projects in the order of their priority;
(iii) It should furnish a scientific basis for choice from among alternatives.

The important technique of screening investment proposals includes the following :

(i) Payback method;
(ii) Accounting rate of return;
(iii) Net present value method;
(iv) Internal rate of return;
(v) Profitability index.

A firm may use any one of those methods. However, the method to be employed by a particular firm depends on circumstances. A big firm may use more than one method for project appraisal, while a smaller one may stick to one method. Though these appraisal techniques can help the management to make an effective investment decision, managers should utilise their discretion in arriving at a particular decision by giving due consideration to intangible factors as well.

Merger and Acquisition

Growth is an essential ingredient in the success and vitality of an enterprise; and it can be effectively brought about by channelising the firm's capital into various assets in a step-by-step manner, both internally and externally. The internal growth of a firm takes place by following the acquisition of assets and after financing them from external sources or by the retention of earnings. External growth can be brought about by the acquisition of another company.

A merger is a combination of two corporations, as a result of which one loses its corporate entity. The surviving corporation acquires the liabilities, assets, personnel and much of the reputation of the fusing company[2]. A merger is fundamentally different from a statutory consolidation in the sense that it involves a combination of two companies, whereby an entirely new corporation is formed. Both the old companies cease to exist, and the share of their common stock are exchanged for shares in the new company. When two companies of about the same size combine, they usually consolidate; when two companies differ significantly in size, they usually merge. Though mergers are not common, they have a market effect, whenever they do occur. Therefore, in deciding about a merger, the management should pay adequate attention to the following points:

(a) Reasons for entering into a merger;
(b) Alternative ways to finance acquisition;
(c) Problems of compatibility.

(a) Reasons for Entering into a Merger

The reasons for entering into a merger are varied and complex. They are not mutually exclusive. Quite often, more than one reason is involved in a merger. A few important reasons for merger have been discussed in the following paragraphs.

2. Vanhorne, J.C., *Fundamentals of Financial Management,* Prentice Hall of India, 1984, pp. 523-524.

Economic Benefits

Substantial economic benefits can be achieved through a merger. Quite often, one company has some assets which are required by the second company; but the second company cannot obtain them or obtains them at a higher cost. A merger generally does away with these problems. It also checks duplication of efforts and facilities and promotes consolidation of a variety of operations. "When industrial companies merge, a firm with a product that complements an existing product line may fill out the line and increase the total demand for the product of the company. The realisation of such economies is known as 'synergism', the fused company is of greater value than the sum of the parts; that is, 2 + 2 = 5."[3] A typical example is that of the merger of an oil company with uptodate technology in refining and a dynamic marketing organisation with the producer of crude oil. Such an acquisition provides an excellent opportunity for gaining control over raw materials.

Tax-Loss Carry-Forward

An important factor in some mergers is the existence of tax-loss carry-forward. A company with cumulative tax losses may have little chance in future to utilise fully its tax-loss carry-forward. By merging with a profitable firm, it may be possible for the existing company to utilise the carry forward at the expense of the government. This would not be possible for either of the companies independently.

Diversification

Some companies go in for mergers to reap benefits of diversification. By acquiring firms dealing in different products or product lines, a company can reduce the uncertainty of its earnings. For example, an electric equipment company, facing a static demand for its established products, by merging with an electronic goods industry, can eliminate the uncertainty of its earnings to a large extent.

Growth

Normally, a company may not grow at a fast or balanced pace but can attain its objective by acquiring another company. It has been noted quite often that growth by acquisition may be cheaper than internal growth, because the numerous costs and risks involved in undertaking new ventures are avoided by the acquisition of a going and profitable concern.

Personal Factors

In a tightly held company, the individuals, who are at helm of affairs, want their company to be acquired by any other company which has an established market for its stock. They may intend to do so by reason of their ill health or old age. The merger helps them in converting their stock into marketable securities or cash.

(b) Alternate Ways to Finance Acquisition

Once a merger possibility with clear benefits has been identified, the parties to the merger should start financial negotiations. This as a rule depends on the management of the two companies – their liabilities, their need for capital, their tax position, their desire to withdraw and remain active. Broadly speaking, in a merger, the final agreement will probably bear some of the variations in elements indicated below.

3. *Ibid.*, p. 524.

Company A Gives		Company B Gives
Cash Stock – Preferred or Common Bonds, notes or long-term lease Assumption of liabilities Employment Contracts	In Exchange Of	Stock holders of the company give controlling stock or Assets, including good will

The financial and legal details of most mergers quite often become so complicated that final negotiations often drag on for a long time. Major economic benefits should therefore be taken into consideration in concluding merger agreements.

(c) Problems of Compatibility

A merger is more than discovering economic advantages and negotiating a deal. If the amalgamation of two enterprises into a new one is not carried out efficiently and effectively, the expected benefits may not materialise at all. Below we have considered some of the possible sources of friction.

The nature and type of policies adopted by fusing organisation differ so much that, for want of a proper synchronization, their living together may be virtually impossible. As a result, new policies and norms have to be established which have the good features of the fusing undertakings; and the people employed in them should be encouraged to accept new norms and methods of working and discarding the older ones. For example, the manager of an electric switch gear company took over an electronic research firm and started working on developing a new electronic product line. Unfortunately, however, the attitudes and policies of the production were so alien to his team that most of the key personnel left the organisation.

The status, role and personality of the executive should be given due weightage. If, as a result of the new pattern of management, some senior personnel are reverted or placed in difficult situations, they may develop negative feelings towards the new regime. Also, the breaking down of the old "role set" at times makes people uncomfortable in working in a newly formed group, which may breed interpersonal problems.

It has been noted that companies face a host of difficulties in actually reassigning the work because of technological and union complications. It goes without saying that a merger occasionally provides a fast and economical way of moving towards the company's objective. But the management has to take a number of decisions to make it practicable. Before embarking on any merger programme, the company should, therefore, carefully weigh the consequences and benefits that it expects would flow from it.

PROTECTION OF CAPITAL AND DISTRIBUTION OF EARNINGS

Protection of Capital

Twentieth century business is confronted with a very dynamic, unpredictable and hostile environment. There is a continuous influx of new opportunities and threats. To keep pace with changing environment demands from an organisation a high degree of adaptation and innovation which, as a rule, involve a high degree of risk. If a business fails to capitalise on it or sustains heavy losses, financial disaster is inevitable. For example, if the government of a particular country changes its economic policy which suits its political ideology businessmen will be forced to toe the line; but if any technological change occurs and the government is tempted to accept the change in favour of the people, it will force businessmen to fall in line. In other words, their earlier investments in plant, machinery, and training will be unproductive.

Besides the environmental threat, business always faces the risk of product obsolescence, declining sales, industrial strife, fire, burglary, etc.

So if a business fails to minimize its risk a time may come when it will be compelled by circumstances to pull down the shutters.

Therefore, while dealing with risk, the management should establish policies pertaining to

(i) Reduction of Uncertainty;
(ii) Insurance;
(iii) Hedging; and
(iv) Estimation of Profit.

(i) Reduction of Uncertainty

One of the most effective ways of reducing uncertainty is to determine planning premises. These planning premises anticipate the environment in which plans are expected to operate, i.e., the environment which the business will face in the near future, If managers have a clear idea of planning premises, they can effectively design their plans to overcome uncertainties. In this connection, Koontz *et al* have remarked that a "successful manager is not one who just responds to changes as they occur but one who will rather forecast change and take appropriate action"[4].

In this context, two types of premises, namely, *external* and *internal*, are required to be properly studied. The *external premises* fall in three important groups: the *general environment*, which includes economic, technological, political, social and ethical conditions; the *product market*, which includes conditions influencing demand for product and service; and the *factor market*, which has to do with land, location, labour, material parts and capital. The *internal premises* include such things as capital investment in plant and equipment, strategic policies, and approval of sales forecasts.[5]

Though internal premises are contingent on external, yet they form a significant part of the planning scene. Planning premises help companies to reduce uncertainties. For instance, technological forecasting enables an organisation to minimise technological obsolescence; social forecasting unveils the dimensions of the social scene of tomorrow; political forecasting helps businessmen to assess the various political indices which are likely to affect their operations.

(ii) Insurance

Another effective way of dealing with risks that cannot be altogether eliminated is to go in for insurance. Though insurance is not available for all types of risks, yet it offers protection against the loss of capital flowing from some common risks which are usually confronted with.

Insurance helps in eliminating or minimising risk because the insurer undertakes to make good the loss if it occurs. But to be eligible for this the insured company has to pay a premium for the risks against which insurance has been sought. For instance, if there are a hundred factories in a town, there is likely to be a serious fire at least in one or two each year. The management of

4. Koontz, H., O'Donnell, C. and Weihrich, *Management*, Mcgraw-Hill, Koga Kusha Ltd., 1980, p. 217.
5. *Ibid*., p. 218.

these factories does not know when and where the fire will break out, but is quite sure of the fact that, in the event of a fire, it will incur heavy losses. So if each factory contributes a certain amount of money to deal with the risk, an insurance company can create a reservoir of funds that can be utilised to compensate the owner of the factory in which a fire has broken out.

Insurance against a wide variety of risks is available to business undertakings. Here is a partial list of possible types of protection.

Fire
Theft and burglary
Employee compensation
Lift insurance of employees
Public liability
Automobile
Marine
Aviation
Riot
Flood
Tornado
Cash or goods in transit insurance
Engineering insurance
Plate glass breakage
Steam boiler

Although it has become almost a universal practice to have insurance, the fact remains that there are substantial differences in the various policies that are available.

The Type and Amount of Insurance

With regard to the type and amount of insurance, there is a considerable variation in the policies of different companies. Some companies carry a minimum amount of insurance. They cover themselves against the loss arising out of fire, explosion, employee compensation, for which there is not great probability of occurrence. They contend that smaller risks will not break the company. Therefore it is desirable to insure against major contingencies instead of going in for insurance to cover every type of mishap.

At the other extreme, there are some companies which carry insurance against every possible type of risk, for they contend that business is exposed to a host of risks, and that all of them cannot be effectively covered by insurance; hence, whatever risks can be covered will minimise the loss they might suffer.

In between these two extremes, there are some companies which follow the policy of insuring only those risks that exceed a definite amount. They feel that loss upto a certain amount can be easily borne by the company without putting any undue strain on its financial resources and that the premium paid for insurance for a smaller amount is definitely lower than the premium that would otherwise be paid.

In making a rational appraisal of his insurance programme, the manager should give adequate consideration to the following factors:

(a) The nature and extent of the insurable risks of the company must be properly assessed. If grave risks are overlooked, the company may sustain heavy losses; if minor risks are covered, the company may be forced to pay a premium which may well exceed the cost of the possible loss.

(b) The adequacy and cost of the available insurance coverage must be studied in relation to the type and gravity of the risks faced by the company. In covering the risks, it must see to it that the policy purchased protects it against grave risks.

(c) The ability of the company to withstand the quantum of loss. Some companies are financially so strong that they can sustain a loss of Rs. 2 crores to 3 crores, whereas others go bankrupt even if they incur a loss of one to two lakhs of rupees.

(iii) Hedging

Another important protective device that has more or less the same effect as insurance but fundamentally differs in operation from the latter is hedging. Some products like wheat, oil seeds and textiles, which suffer a high degree of price fluctuations, can be sold through forward contracts, which substantially eliminate the risk of these fluctuations.

Hedging refers to "the coincidence of purchase and sale in two differerent markets." The prices in these two markets are expected to move in such a way that any loss suffered in one will be offset by an equivalent gain in the other. The most common instance of a hedging transaction is the purchase and sale of the same amount of the same commodity in the spot and future markets respectively.[6] It is made in the future markets to counteract or neutralise speculative loss (and profit) on the trade contract.

Purpose of Hedging

Risks arising out of price changes in obedience to constant changes in supply and demand conditions affect those businessmen who own commodities in storage (while they are being processed), or when these commodities are in the form of inventories of finished goods until they are sold. Market price risk also affects those businessmen who expect to buy a given commodity at a later date in order to make delivery on a previous sale of such commodity. The market position of such businessmen is known as long in the previous case and short in the latter case. Whether the position is long or short in the market at any given time, all commodity handlers such as flour millers, food processors, distillers, food manufacturers, cotton merchants and many others are deeply concerned with the problem of price changes. Hedging is thus the device which protects dealers in spot and forward markets. The organised Commodity Exchange is the mechanism through which the device is made effective.

Hedging aims at:

(a) Protecting purchases or inventories of a commodity not covered by actual sales of that commodity;

(b) Protecting uncovered forward sales of a commodity;

(c) Protecting or earning an expected carrying charge on the commodities that have been stored;

(d) Protecting a given price for the prospective or estimated production of commodities.

Hedging is widely used for staple commodities. But it is impossible to make a close estimate of the actual number of hedging transactions. Outside the commodity markets, the most important application of the hedging principle is in connection with the risk of fluctuations in foreign exchange. When a merchant buys or sells goods for future payment in a foreign currency, he runs the risk that change in the foreign exchange rate before the settlement date may expose him to heavy losses. To avoid this risk, he may make use of the market in "forward" exchange.

Kinds of Hedging

Hedging may be for the purchase or for the sale of goods. Under hedging purchases, a merchant or wholesaler may go to the spot market and make purchases to resell goods at profit.

6. Converse, Huegx and Mitchell, *Elements of Marketing*, pp. 421-422.

He sells the same commodity in the cash market so that he may protect himself against any loss in price. So long as the spot and futures prices move in unison, the loss incurred by the merchant on the sales in the spot market is offset or counter-balanced by the profit on his dealings in the futures market.

In a hedge sale, a merchant sells the same commodity for cash, but he also sells it in the futures market so that he is protected against a fall in price. Any loss on a forward sale, consequent on a rise in the price of the actual commodity in the spot market, is offset by the gain on the hedge purchases in the futures market.

Limitation of Hedging

The protection furnished by hedging is never perfect. To eliminate completely the risk of price changes, it would be necessary that the relationship between the future price and the cash price at the time the hedging contract is closed should be definitely predictable on the basis of the relationship at the time when it begins. In fact, there is nearly always some fluctuations from month to month in the cash price and the various futures prices. For example, a temporary shortage caused by a delayed harvest, bad roads and transportation difficulties will cause the cash price and the futures to rise, and there is no way in which one can hedge against the decline in prices which will later wipe out these differentials.

A few important limitations of hedging are :

(i) Cash and future prices do not always move together, i.e., in the same direction. Hence hedging cannot prevent losses.

(ii) Prices of contract or basic grade on a futures market and other grades in the cash market do not move together in the up or down direction. Hence, hedging may often fail.

(iii) The unit of trade on the futures market is fixed, i.e., it is 100 tons, or 100 bales or 1,000 kgs. If a hedger's needs fall short of the unit or its multiple, hedging is of limited use to offset losses against profits or *vice versa* as between the two markets.

(iv) Hedging protects a manufacturer against a rise in the cost of production due to a rise in the price of raw materials. But if the rise in the cost of production is due to a rise in wages and other costs, hedging cannot provide protection.

(v) Hedging involves some expenditure–commission to brokers and the expenses involved in the time and effort required to study and analyse price changes in different markets.

(iv) Estimation of Profits

As the survival, growth and development of an undertaking is contingent upon its profits, it is the prime task of the manager to ensure that profits are not estimated in an unwarranted manner. If the profits are overstated, dividends will be paid to stockholders out of the capital. Though the management has significant discretion in the estimation of profits, it should, while doing so, bear in mind that there must be:

(a) Accounting reserves;

(b) Capitalisation of disbursements; and

(c) Inventory valuation.

(a) Accounting Reserves : The accounting reserves set up by the company considerably affect its profitability. The basic issues in this context are concerned with the estimation of expenses on accounting reserves as well as an assessment of the decline in the asset value of such reserves. The expenses, which involve an immediate outlay of cash – outstanding payments or bills payable – can be easily recognised. Contrary to this, for expenses that do not require an

immediate outlay of cash but must be met well in time, their estimation is quite an uphill task; they are subjected to a higher degree of error. The depreciation on equipment and buildings, unassessed taxes, provision of uncontrollable expenses and contingent losses are examples of such expenses.

One of the effective ways of handling such expenses is to make a reasonable estimate of the amount to be charged against operations each year and then to add up this figure along with other expenses as a deduction from the gross income in the estimation of net profit. It should be borne in mind that reserves should not be treated as a separate fund to be put aside to meet an anticipated cash payment. However, they help companies to prevent over-statements of profits.

(b) Capitalisation of Disbursements : One of the important questions – the estimation of profit – is related to the capitalisation of disbursements. For example, in case of product development or improvements in fixed assets, the question arises whether to treat disbursements as expenditure in the current year and thus reduce profits, or to capitalise them. The example of patents states this problem specifically. If a company buys a patent, it has an asset the cost of which should be charged as an expense throughout the life of the patent. But when the patent is the company's own creation, the situation is not very clear. Here, the management has to decide as to how much of the cost should be attached to the asset – should it be treated like an asset or partially written off every year? If a larger part of the cost is capitalised as an asset, the profit will be higher in the current year.

(c) Inventory Valuation : One major problematic area in the computation of profit is inventory valuation. For this purpose, the management has to decide about the inventories which are in demand and those which are to be treated as scrap. The value of inventory depends upon its physical conditions – the future need of companies of spare parts, the ability to procure new inventories. While valuing inventories, the management has to decide whether a specific item is still a good asset or should be written off. If a higher value is attached to the inventory as an asset, the profit will be higher. Therefore, while valuing inventories, the management must ensure that this is done in such a manner that it yields the best possible results.

Policy Issues in Profit Estimation

While computing profits, adequate attention must be paid to a number of issues – the size of the surplus, the valuation of inventories, and the capitalisation of costs. Though it is not necessary for the management to concentrate on the numerous entries involved in profit estimation, it is desirable that it should frame policies indicating the degree of general conservation to be followed in this context.

One of the important considerations of profit assessment relates to policy changes in estimation. If a given method is followed over a period of time, it will tend to balance out the profit postponed from the previous year and show it in the current year; and this largely affects the profit in the present year which is shown as delayed profit next year.

However, if a conservative policy is followed in one year and a liberal one in another one, the effects on the results that are reported during a particular year will be more satisfactory. Some companies stress consistency in the policy of profit estimation, whereas others follow one which minimises the payment of income tax.

Like many other policy issues, profit estimation, too, is inter-related with various aspects of management functioning. The protection of capital calls for a conservative estimation of profit. At the same time, attention must be paid to such factors as income tax, interest, ease in raising new capital, etc.

In designing policies of protection of capital, adequate attention must be paid to the various financial aspects of the company.

Distribution of Earnings

The net profit earned by a company after taxes belongs to shareholders. This dos not mean that the whole profit will be distributed among the shareholders. It is the prime responsibility of the management to determine what part of earnings should be retained and what should be distributed. In deciding about the distribution of profit, the management has to concentrate on the following issues:

(i) Ploughing back of profits.
(ii) Dividends.
(iii) Retained earnings.

(i) Ploughing Back of Profits

Ploughing back of profit is an important means of conservation of profits, for it means reinvestment of retained earning in the business, and becomes an important source of internal financing. In fact, profitable enterprise not only in India but abroad as well, use profit to finance their expansion and development programme.

They find it desirable to plough back profits to finance their various activities rather than to distribute them in the form of dividend and then raise capital from other sources. This method of financing can be effectively employed for the expansion of business. In other words, it is an ideal arrangement from the point of view of corporate management because there is no immediate pressure to pay a return on this portion of the stockholders' equity. In deciding upon ploughing back profits, the management has to decide how much is to be retained in the business and how much is to be paid out to the stockholders in the form of dividends. As a rule, there is an inverse relationship between the dividend paid and profit retained with the company for the purpose of ploughing it back. Therefore, if a higher dividend is paid, the quantum of profit retained for reinvestment will be small. The management must strike a fair balance between these two decisions to ensure that the shareholders' requirements for a steady dividend remain satisfied and that the continuous flow of business is not interrupted for lack of funds. The process of ploughing back of earnings into business instead of distributing them in the form of dividend has proved to be so advantageous that some authorities on finance consider it desirable to distribute only half of the profit to stockholders. Such a policy certainly contributes to the financial strength of an enterprise. But it may lead to unnecessary accumulation of capital if the company does not expand the area of its operations.

(ii) Dividends

One of the crucial decisions pertaining to the distribution of earnings relates to the various aspects of dividends. The policies relating to dividends affect the overall financial structure of a firm, for various issues, such as the retention of earnings, reserves and surplus, ploughing back of profits, profit planning, etc., are monitored by such policies.

Dividend earnings are a reward which shareholders get for providing venture capital. This reward may include, besides the normal interest rate, something more to absorb the risk assumed by stockholders.

In the case of a proprietary organisation, such as a sole trading company or a partnership, proprietors can get their dues from the organisation by securing payments out of the capital or from available profits. Here, the rationale of profit distribution largely arises out of their personal interest. In sharp contrast to this, the impersonal nature of corporations, arising from the divorce of ownership from the management, calls for a fresh look at the problem of profit distribution.

The problem is twofold. *First*, it is the prime responsibility of the management to satisfy the shareholders by offering them a fair return on their investment; *second*, it has to ensure that the financial health of the company is safeguarded even by withholding the dividend, if necessary.

Dividend Policy

The term dividend policy refers to the consistent approach to the retention-versus-distribution decision rather than a decision made on a purely *ad hoc* basis from time to time. A dividend policy embodies in itself decisions pertaining to when and how much dividend is required to be paid.

The formulation of a dividend policy is a crucial and an extremely difficult decision because of the conflicting nature of objectives, and the absence of adequate measures for the computation of an optimal policy. In such circumstances, the dividend policy tends to be intuitive. Therefore, to make it scientific, it is desirable that undertakings base it on business tenets as well as on legal foundations. In deciding about dividends, managers are expected to take policy decisions pertaining to :

(a) The optimum amount of dividend to be paid;
(b) Varying dividend level; and
(c) Varying Dividend Payout.

It is in the interest of both corporations and shareholders that the dividend rate established should be maintained as far as possible. If the ploughback of profits yields heavy returns in the form of dividends and capital appreciation, the enlightened shareholders will feel contented.

Contrary to this, if dividend limitations are such that the rate of dividend is permanently pegged down at a low figure, prospects of procuring capital will be seriously jeopardized.

Therefore, in deciding about the dividend policy, the following factors should be given due consideration :

(a) The relation of dividends to earnings;
(b) Contractual and legal considerations;
(c) Liquidity, credit standing and working capital requirements;
(d) Need for expansion;
(e) Alternative reinvestment;
(f) Availability of external capital;
(g) Relative cost of external funds;
(h) Considerations of business cycles;
(i) Future capital requirements;
(j) Past dividend policy and stockholder's relationships;
(k) Stability of dividends;
(l) Target payout ratio;
(m) Ability to pay for services.

Besides these factors, a sound dividend policy is contingent upon:

(a) the accuracy with which the firm's income has been estimated;
(b) the accuracy and reliability of the profit forecast;
(c) the accuracy with which future financial requirements have been assessed.

It should be borne in mind that if the dividend paid out of net income is based on highly subjective factors, it is likely to be questioned more than if it is based on clear-cut data. In a firm, if both profit levels and growth rates are relatively equal, the directors have a logical base for formulating dividend policies.

(iii) Retained Earnings

The net profit of the company is generally shown in the surplus account and is more aptly termed as "earnings retained in the business". It is not desirable on the part of companies to pay dividend out of retained earnings and create a capital deficit. Practically all foresighted managements prefer to show more reserves than the amount paid on dividend account in the current financial year. It is always preferable to have large retained earnings because any operating loss or excess of dividend can be charged against this account without affecting the original capital.

Retained earnings are mostly tied up in the form of buildings, inventories, etc., whereas dividends are required to be paid in the form of cash. Therefore, the management, besides maintaining an adequate reserve, should keep adequate cash to disburse dividends.

CHAPTER 14

SOCIAL RESPONSIBILITIES OF BUSINESS

Introduction

Changing Trends in Social Responsibilities of Business

Dimensions of Social Responsibility

Tools of Social Responsibility of Business

Social Responsibilities Towards Different Groups

INTRODUCTION

The growth of large corporations with their professional managers has changed the nature of society through its effect on competitive forces and the ownership of private property. With their increased power in society, they are forced to concern themselves with the nature of social responsibilities. Management must take decisions involving moral issues and must adapt itself to the social forces that affect it. The idea of social responsibility of business is based upon the concept that business is something more than a purely economic institution.[1]

Business is a citizen, too, and in that sense, it has proportionate responsibilities to go beyond the letter of the law."[2] Stenier says that "Each business has responsibilities in some way commensurate with its power."[3] At another place, he observes, "Corporations exist because society wishes them to fulfil a purpose and when the social purpose changes, so will the activities of the Corporation."[4]

The essence is that business as an entity has certain responsibilities to fulfil towards those who contribute their labour, capital, skill, entrepreneurship, and other intangible materials for the success of business operations. The managers, who are in charge of business, are really the trustees of the business and not its owners, disposing of its products as per their wishes. As trustees, their moral responsibility is to balance the interests of the diverse participants/claimants in the enterprise, whose interests sometimes conflict with those of others. The manager has to satisfy the expectations/demands of the customers, employees, owners/stockholders, other business, the community and the government — all within a framework that is constructive, legal and acceptable to society.

Doctrine/Concept of Social Responsibility

The social responsibility concept is based on the premise that business has greater impact on society than can be measured by profit or loss. As a participant in society, business should contribute to the human and constructive social policies that guide society. The concept of social responsibility is merely a first step towards social effectiveness of business. It is the underlying value which gives businessmen a sound basis for social action. It is the philosophy which justifies business involvement in its social community, but philosophy by itself is incomplete. It must be followed by effective social action. In the words of one observer, "Philosophy without programme is a shadow without substance. Perhaps, one should take, therefore, less of *corporate social responsibilities* and more of *corporate social responses*. The former is too redolent of legalism and the notion of fixed obligations; the latter, more open, permits voluntary and creative undertakings by business on behalf of society's larger needs."[5]

1. Bell Danniel, "The Coming of Post-Industrial Society", *Business & Society Review*, Spirng, 1973, p. 17.
2. Cartun, Walter, P., "Fact and Fiction of Social Responsibility," *S.A.M. Advanced Management Journal*, January, 1973, p. 36.
3. Steiner, George A., "Social Policies for Business," *California Management Review*, Winter, 1972, p. 72.
4. *Ibid.*, p. 18.
5. Walton, Clarence C., "Recreating the City of Man," in a *Call to Social Action*, Beta Gamma Sigma, St. Louis, 1968, p. 17.

If business and society get stuck on the legalism of social responsibility, they will drift into inaction. The ultimate need is business *response* which provides progress towards the desirable end of a more effective society. The desirable end is achieved through a sequence of philosophy, process, and functions. In the area of business and society, the *philosophy* is social responsibility, and the *process* is creative decision-making by business. Creative decisions lead to the function of social action by business, which produces the desirable end of a better society. Social responsibility is only the beginning of the sequence. The fact is that business is a major social institution and as such, it is importantly involved in social values.

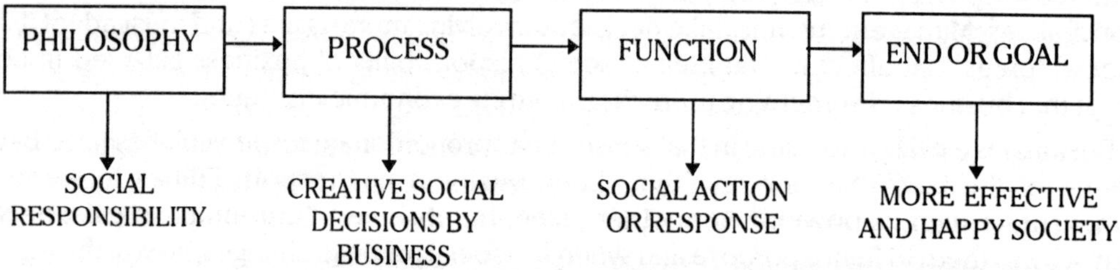

Fig.14.1: A Philosophy of Social Responsibility.

"The idea of social responsibility is that the decision-makers are obliged to take actions which protect and improve the welfare of society as a whole along with their own interests. It builds a better quality of life, thus harmonising organisational actions with society's wants."[6] The idea is that the businessman acts in a manner that will accomplish social benefits along with the traditional economic gains which the firm seeks. His idea is that he becomes concerned with *social outputs* as well as economic outputs, and with the total effect of his economic and institutional actions on society.

Definitions

Between defines the concept as "the obligation of (managers) to pursue those policies, to make those decisions, or to flow those lines of action which are desirable in terms of the objectives and values of our society."[7] He also says that the "Doctrine of social responsibility refers to the idea that voluntary assumption of social responsibility by businessmen is, or might be, a practicable means toward ameliorating economic problems and attaining more fully the economic goals we seek."

Adolf Berle has defined social responsibility as "the manager's responsiveness to public consensus."[8]

Eels and Walton have described social responsibility as: "When people talk about corporate social responsibility, they think in terms of the problems that arise when corporate enterprise casts its shadow on the social scene, and of ethical principle that ought to govern the relationship between the corporation and society. They are concerned with the impact of the corporation on the individual and the possibilities of reconciling big business, big labour, and big government with the values deeply rooted in our form of government."[9]

6. Davis, Keith, and Robert L. Blomstrom, *Business and Society: Environment and Responsibility*, McGraw-Hill Book Company, New York, 1975, pp.6 and 11.
7. Bowen, Howard R., *Social Responsibilities of Businessmen*, Harper and Row Publishers, New York, 1953. p. 6.
8. Berle, Adolph A. *American Economic Republic*, Harcourt Brace & World, New York, 1964, *Ibid.*, p. 8.
9 Eells, Richard and Clarence Walton, *Conceptual Foundations of Business*, Richard D. Irwin, Inc., Homewood, Illinois, 1961, pp. 457-458.

Koontz and O'Donnell have given the definition of social responsibility thus: "The personal obligation of the people as they act in their own interests to assure that the rights and legitimate interests of others are not infringed."[10]

According to Steiner, "Social responsibility is to understand public consensus, to recognise it, and to cooperate in achieving this. Each business has responsibilities in some way commensurate with its power."[11]

Boone and Kurtz have defined social responsibility as "management's consideration of social effects as well as economic effects in its decisions."[12]

From the few definitions quoted above, it may be noted that social responsibility simply means fulfilling the obligations towards the society and the components of business, and improving its economic and social conditions by all possible means. In other words, *the concept of social responsibility assumes that the business has not only economic and legal obligations but also certain other social responsibilities too*, i.e., a businessman man besides taking care of this own interest must also take care of others' interest too, viz., the community members.

Applicability of Social Responsibility

Society wants business as well as all other major institutions to assume significant social responsibility. Social responsibility has become the hallmark of a mature, global civilization. It is necessary in an interdependent world. Consequently, as Drucker has observed; "Under any circumstance, we are moving in the direction of demanding that our institutions take responsibility beyond their performance and beyond their own contribution. We will demand this as well—the university, the hospital, the government agency, the school and even charitable organisations and places of worship."[13]

Rationale of Social Responsibility

The rationale and substance of social responsibility arise from the consequence of one's acts as they might effect the interests of others. The idea of social responsibility recognises that each person is attached to an extended social system on which he or she is party dependent; consequently, certain obligations or social responsibilities arise from this attachment.

Business owes its responsibility towards society, *First*, as a result of the impact of its own operations, which might prove harmful to the community, such as emission of uncontrolled soot from a factory chimney may pollute air or dirty sewage and solid waste material may pollute water.

Second, since it is the society which permits men and women to engage in business, the business in return make contributions to the society, because it is what society demands from it. Elton Mayo rightly remarked that "The modern industrial society faces disintegration because of the breakdown of the social code that formerly disciplined us in effective working together." The businessman's function, according to her, is "to convert men into a modern counterpart of the tribe, clan or guide, in order to save society." Thus, the primary function of the business is "to provide the basis for social order in an industrial society."

10. Koontz, Harold and Cyril O'Donnel, *Management: A Systems and Contingency Analysis of Managerial Functions*, McGraw-Hill Book Company, New York, 1977, p. 93.
11. Steiner, George, "Social Policies for Business," *California Management Review*, Winter, 1972, p. 22.
12. Boone, Louis E. and David. L. Kurtz, *Contemporary Business*, the Dryden Press, Hinsdale, Illinois, 1979, p. 33.
13. Drucker, Peter F., "The Concept of the Corporation," *Business and Society Review*, Autumn, 1972, p. 16.

Third, social responsibility also emanates from social power which corporations possess and develop, say as a result of being potential employers in society; or affecting ecology, minorities and other social problems. If a business has social power, a just relationship demands that business also owns responsibility. If the social responsibility is not effectively discharged, it is just possible that social power may also be lost in the process.

Fourth, business can be viewed as a custodian of a society's resources which it use to accomplish it objectives. Therefore, business has not only to protect the interest of those whom it serves but also of society at large as a wise custodian of the latter's resources. The business operates under a set of cultural strains in the same way that any other person in society does.

Cultural norms are powerful determinants of behaviour; consequently, as society's norms change, as society's norms change, the businessman's behaviour with it also changes. If society moves towards norms of social responsibility as it is now doing, then the businessman is subtly and inevitably guided by these norms. The basic objective of business, which was formerly earning of profit for its own sake," is now undergoing a change. Now the business community has begun to recognise its stake in the well-being of its workers and community. As early as 1930, Alfred North Whitehead, in an address to the Harvard Business School, concluded that business of future must be controlled by a different type of leaders, i.e., "a socially responsible manager." In this way, "the businessman appears to be acting in a socially responsible way even though his first priority is profit."[14] It is now a well-known fact that "profit-earning and customer' satisfaction are no longer the sole and exclusive criteria of business these days."

Fifth, through creative efforts, business can convert the existing environmental ills into a better environment. This concept rationalises that a better society produces environmental conditions more favourable for business operations. The firm which is most responsive to the improvement of the community's quality of life will as a result have a better community in which to conduct its business. Recruitment of labour becomes easier and labour will be of a higher quality. Turnover and absenteeism will be reduced and as a result of social improvements crime will decrease.

Sixth, with problems of society becoming increasingly complex and intractable, business is required to share responsibility of the government to alleviate social problems. Often government's inadequacy in meeting social changes calls for other groups of society —business, voluntary agencies, institutions, charitable organisations, etc. for sharing the government's burden in times of droughts, floods, cyclones, earthquakes, epidemics, and other unforeseen calamities. The enlightened businessmen come forward to fulfil their social responsibility in helping meet the situation.

Seventh, with the passage of time, the era of purely private business for private profits has given place to the new idea that business has a duty to report to the public, whose money it is utilising in order to conduct business itself. Such *Social Audit* gives factual assessment of the things done, and also of the co-operation between labour and management, and the record of their mutual relationship, the economic, social, and educational standard exhibited by the business, and public relations with the consumers.

Eighth, with the emergence of increased public regulation and public ownership of industries, business has been considered as necessary. The equalisation of private and public sectors has, perforce, focused attention to a greater degree on the role of business community in dealing with pressing social problems.

14. Johnson, Harold J. *Business in Contemporary Society: Framework and Issues*, Workdsworth Publishing Co., Belmont, 1971, p. 76.

Ninth, the Great Depression of the thirties and the severe economic crisis in later years, when business was subject to severe criticism/attacks and was blamed for the economic ills in society (such as the supply of fake and spurious goods, poor quality, failure to give fiar measure, lack of services and courtesy to customers, misleading and immoral advertisements, illegal practices like rack-renting, hoarding, cornering, black marketing, profiteering, breach of trust, malpractices and unfair trade practices, and other sins of omission and commission, etc.,) it wanted to get its image improved in the minds of the public. Hence, business began to undertake activities of social benevolence of its own accord.

Tenth, the principle of trusteeship, as propounded by Andrew Carniger and Mahatma Gandhi, emphasised the fact that "A business must be held in trust legally and morally for the benefit of the people whom the business wants to serve." Most businessmen had now begun to assert that "business enterprise must earn a profit to survive and grow, but none takes the view that the organisation must maximise profits." All agree that management must take the responsibility of balancing the interest of the stockholder with other groups in society. George Morse (the then President of the First National City Bank, New York) said that "Social responsibility is not an attitude that a business adopts in a fit of benevolence, it is instead inseparate from its response to the kind of world we live in." Management must reach a balanced solution within the framework of one unassailable precept, viz., "business is a means to an end for society and must not be an end in itself" and, therefore, *business must act in concert with the broad public interest and serve the objectives of mankind and society*.

Other Factors

(i) Changing societal values have also led to the adoption of this concept. Years ago, the phrase "social responsibility of business" might have meant interest in ethics and charity. Today, it encompasses far more because the manager's personal and social values have also changed. Monsen makes the following observations in this regard: "Values for the businessman set the framework within which he can operate and do business. The boundaries of business are set by the prevailing values of society. For instance, do we allow pollution and, if so, of what kind and how much? Such questions are determined by the prevailing values in the society and become crucial for anyone trying to determine why our society allows certain acts and not others and, thus, why business makes one decision and not another."[15]

The changes taking place in the social values are upsetting the delicate equilibrium in our complex society. "It is clearly a relationship in which social, educational, technological, and other types of changes are closely interwoven. Change increases the disequilibrium among the various elements of society, thereby increasing friction among them. This condition, in turn, requires much large inputs of efforts, resources, and knowledge in order to restore effective harmony in the system."[16]

Peter Drucker has observed that "Our modern civilization is experiencing more than an age of routine change. It is passing through an *Age of Discontinuity* in which change is so severe that it will create whole new institutions and significantly alter existing institutions. The four most significant discontinuity are: [17]

15. Monsen. R. Joseph, *Business and Changing Environment*, McGraw-Hill Book Co., New York, 1973, p. 242.
16. Davis, Keith and Robert L. Blomstrom, *op. cit.*, p. 5.
17. Drucker, Peter, F. *The Age of Discontinuity: Guidelines to Changing Society*, Harper & Row, New York, 1968.

1. Technological innovations, such as the computer and television, which are having major effects not only on business but also on the whole society;
2. Development of the world economy as one market, but without suitable institutions for handling it, with the one exception of the multinational corporation;
3. A pluralistic social system in which social tasks are mostly entrusted to large institutions.
4. Most important of all, a knowledge revolution which has made knowledge the crucial resource of society.

(ii) Another major reason for the involvement of business in the social area is *enlightened self-interest*. This doctrine holds that by helping society as a whole, business is actually serving its own long-term interests. It is a reversal of the much-criticised statement that "what is good for one corporation is good for all". Now the feeling is that "*what is good for the country is good for private companies*". This reasoning has affected enlightened self-interest. Such interest has been extended, in modern times, to encompass social responsibility on a massive scale. Business firms across the country justify huge expenditures on higher education health, and cultural activities on the basis of thus being able to hire and retain talented employees by providing "a good place in which to live". Besides, people who live a good life make not only productive employees but also loyal, satisfied customers.

(iii) Yet another reason is the *social issue of people-oriented* management which means that the management must strive to maintain a people-oriented philosophy of management. The constant pressure of commercia l activity often makes it easier to deal with numbers, organisation charts, inter-office memos, and administrative procedures. Industry should also pay its attention to people. In fact, insensitivity to human needs is a critical problem in nearly all organisations: yet *a humanistic approach to management is always good business.* For example, workers are more productive when they have a sense of participation in the decisions affecting them. *Human resource development has, thus, become a major organisational objective for business*. West German firms have labour representation on management boards. The Swedish automobile manufactures have pioneered the concept of job enrichment for assembly line workers. American companies have substantially upgraded their equal opportunity employment and affirmative action hiring programmes. In India, business firms except a few public and private enterprises, have done very little work in this direction.

CHANGING TRENDS IN SOCIAL RESPONSIBILITIES OF BUSINESS

During the 18th and 19th centuries, there prevailed the system of *laissez faire,* which referred to an exchange economy in which these institutions were operative; private property, free labour, free enterprise, free consumers' choice and ubiquitous competition. Income under it was to be distributed functionally in the sense that the income of each individual was to be received as compensation for the services of whatever land, labour or capital owned. And the government's role was to be restricted to such activities as protection of property rights; national defence; establishment of weights, measures and monetary units,; education; and provision of a few public works as roads and aids to navigation.[18]

18. Bowen, H.R., *Towards Social Economy,* 1948. pp. 246-249.

At that time, certain ethical rules for economic conduct of business were more or less generally accepted, though by no means always followed. The basic moral rules for the businessman in the nineteenth century economy were:

1. To observe the principles of private property;
2. To honour contracts;
3. To refrain from deception and fraud;
4. To be efficient and to promote economic progress;
5. To promote the life, limb and health of the workers and the general public;
6. To compete vigorously and in case of failure of competition, to act with restraint;
7. To accept and respect the economic freedom of consumers, workers and owners; and
8. To have regard for the human rights of workers.

This *free-enterprise creed* holds that the aim of business is and should be to maximise profits. According to Milton Friedman, this creed maintains that the pursuit of self-interest, i.e. maximum profits, is today —as in Adam Smith's day —the only logical or efficient way to run a business. In other words, *it is the only way to preserve a free and economically progressive society.*

Milton Friedman's views are:[19]

"In a free enterprise, private property system, a corporate executive is an employee of the owners of business. He has direct responsibility to his employers. That responsibility is to conduct the business in accordance with their desires, which generally will be to make as much money as possible while conforming to the basic rules of the society. ....In so far as his actions in accord with his 'social responsibility' reduce returns to the shareholders, he is spending their money. In so far as his actions raise the price to customers, he is spending the customers' money. In so far as his actions lower the wages of some employees, he is spending their money"

The willing acceptance of the above moral obligations by businessmen were often dishonoured by them, and, therefore, conflict arose between individual and social interests. These conflicts developed because of the non-fulfilment of the responsibilities by business, who indulged in fraudulent practices, did not provide any protection to workers, due to lack of restraint in imperfectly competitive situations and frequent failure of recognition of human rights. These necessitated government interference and control on business activities.

The result was that the system of "free enterprise creed' began to lose its significance. This decline was assisted by factors such as:[20]

(i) growth of large-scale enterprises and concentration of economic power;
(ii) fluctuating general business activity with recurrent periods of unemployment;
(iii) technological unemployment;
(iv) personal insecurity of people with reference to sickness, old age, and death;
(v) disparities in distribution of income and economic opportunities;
(vi) rapid and wasteful exploitation of the limited natural resources;
(vii) materialistic competitive and invidious standards of consumption;
(viii) frequent disregard for the social costs of economic activity and the social values and rights derived from economic activity.

In the 20th century, the state began to take increasing interest in public welfare. Its sphere of interference became vast and covered practically every facet/area that affected the welfare and well-being of the masses. To mention a few:

(1) to alleviate the problems of poverty and personal insecurity relief, social insurance, and farm price supports were provided on a steadily increasing scale;

19. Friedman, Milton, "Does Business Have a Social Responsibility?" *Bank Administration,* New York, April 1971. pp. 13-14.

20. Bowen, H.R., *Social Responsibilities of Businessmen,* pp. 18-21.

(2) to protect life, and health of workers and of the general public, factory laws, safety codes, housing ordinances, pure-food laws, and public health services were provided;

(3) to improve the status of labour and to prevent strife in labour management relations, trade unions were accorded recognition and their relations with employees were subjected to public supervision;

(4) to equalise the distribution of income and to provide for economic opportunity, provision was made for free public education, graded income and other taxes, social insurance, minimum wage laws, and public housing;

(5) to prevent the wastage of natural resources, conservation measures were enacted; river valley projects were undertaken and the government retained or acquired ownership of vast tracts of land;

(6) to promote productivity and economic development, the government subsidised industries, supported research, and adult and professional education, and imposed import duties;

(7) to overcome the problems of deception, fraud and financial manipulation, laws were enacted;

(8) to combat or control, monopoly, collusion and undue concentration of economic power, regulation of rail-roads and public utility services was instituted; and

(9) to achieve greater stability of economic activity, monetary control and fiscal policies were invoked.

By the middle of the 20th century, a new system of economy came into vogue, *viz., mixed economy,* which pertains to retaining a substantial amount of individual initiative and individual freedom of choice in matters of production, consumption, choice of occupation, and mobility of persons. There are substantial elements of socialism as evidenced by governmental ownership, partnership, regulation, control and planning in spheres of business and industry. These efforts have been made to reconcile the goals of freedom and economic progress with the goals of stability, security, justice and personality development.

This new system or ideology, known as *"the social-responsibility creed,* " holds that free-enterprise and maximum profit philosophy of the 19th centruy is an anachronism. so observe Hartman and others:[21]

"The free-enterprise made more sense in the old days of smaller companies, something closer to free competition, and foolish, tyrannical kings, it makes little sense in today's society where huge corporations play not only a vital enconomic role, but also an important political and social role. These corporations cannot avoid having a major and conspicuous impact on society, which society will either approve or disapprove, permit or prevent."

Bowen has stated that: "Road to economic and social welfare lies not in dogmatic adherence to some closed system, but rather in evolution towards mixed system, *containing* elements of private enterprise, co-operative enterprise, joint and public enterprise; *motivated* partly by social-interest with the latter predominating; *controlled* partly by competition, partly by public regulation; and *distributing income* partly on the basis of market, prices of factors and partly on the basis of needs of persons."[22]

The proponents of the "social responsibility creed", hold that if business wants to retain its autonomy, it must be prepared to assume certain social responsibilities, not just go after maximum profit. Further more , the "free-enterprise creed" confirms itself primarily to narrow economic and technical values, but social responsibility extends thinking to social values as well. It also requires thinking in terms of the whole social system, rather than the narrow interest of a single organisation, group, or person.[23]

21. Hartman, Richard I., T.P. Hogan and John T. Wholihan, *Modern Business Administration,* 1975, p. 35.
22. Bowen H.R., *Social Responsibilities of a Businessman,* p. 39.

Social responsibility does not try to remake people; rather it asks them only that they should consider the broader social system and try to act in a way which benefits others as well as themselves. In this manner, they serve their *self-interest* but not a *self-interest*. Similarly, the benefit of a single organisation may be socially responsible if they serve the broader public interest.

The social responsibilities of modern business have been summed up in these words:[24]

"In business, the earning of profit is something more than an incidence of success..... Success must be sought in business also in excellence of performance; and in business, excellence of performance manifests itself, among other things, in the advancing of methods and processes; in the improvement of products; in more perfect organisation; eliminating friction as well as waste; in bettering the conditions of working men, developing their faculties, and promoting their happiness; and in the establishment of right relations with customers and with the community."[25]

DIMENSIONS OF SOCIAL RESPONSIBILITY

Now it has been clearly recognised that business/management does have important responsibilities to stockholders, customers, employees the public, the government, competitors and to itself. Each of the first five entities has something the enterprise needs and without which it can not exist; capital, patronage, work skills, and a suitable legal framework and social climate. The obligations of managements to these entities are conditions precedent to their assets being made available to the enterprise, in striving to meet their management fundamentally in seeking to serve the enterprise. It is to be noted that *management's first responsibility is to the enterprise itself and that all other responsibilities are limited and subsidiary.*

Business has multiple responsibilities. However, it is impossible to determine, in universal terms, the extent of these responsibilities. By their very nature, social responsibilities of business are fashioned by the nature of the company —including its size, products, and financial resources—the customs and religious traditions , and a host of other norms and standards within which the society operates. The concepts, notions and expressions of social responsibility of a business community in a traditional society are bound to be different from those in a modern industrial society.

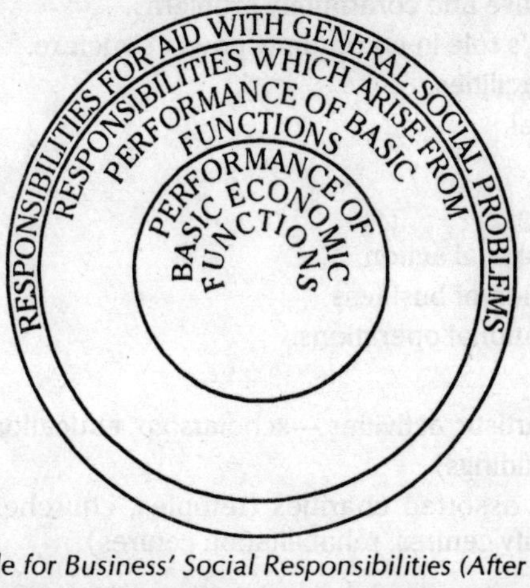

Fig 14.2: A Widening circle for Business' Social Responsibilities (After K.Davis and R.L. Blomstrom).

23. Davis, Keith and R.L., Blomstrom, *op.cit.*, p. 6.
24. Brandeis, L.D. *Business – A Profession*, 1933, pp. 3-5.
25. Votan, Dow, "Genius Becomes Rare: A Comment on the Doctrine of Social Responsibility," Pt II *California Management Review*, Spring, 1973, pp. 16-17.

The areas of social responsibility are expanding. This has been represented by the above diagram. The inner circle represents the traditional responsibility of business for its economic functions. This traditional responsibility has some social implications, such as the need to provide employment and to refrain from restraint of trade, but it is primarily an economic activity The intermediate circle represents the widening area of responsibility that arises directly from the performance of the basic economic functions. These responsibilities have become significant and are represented by such issues as equal employment opportunity, and prevention of pollution from business operations. The outer circle represents an arc that is still not well-defined, but there is a rising public expectation for business to modify its singular pursuit of economic goals and keep society with unsolved general social problems. For example, as a corporate citizen, business should provide significant assistance for solving such problems of the community as prevention of urban decay and training of the unemployed, employment of the handicapped or minority groups.

Keith and Blomstrom have given a list of areas of social responsibility of business. This is by no means exhaustive but only an illustrative one.[26]

AREAS OF SOCIAL RESPONSIBILITY OF BUSINESS

1. *Economy and Environmental Quality*
    - Cleaning up of existing pollution.
    - Design of processes to prevent pollution
    - Aesthetic improvements.
    - Noise control.
    - Dispersion of industry
    - Control of land use
    - Required recycling (of waste material).
2. *Consumerism*
    - Truth in lending, in advertising, and in all business activities.
    - Product warranty and service (after-sales).
    - Control of harmful Products.
3. *Community Needs*
    - Use of business expertise and community problems.
    - Reduction of business's role in community power structure.
    - Aid with health-care facilities.
    - Aid with urban renewal.
4. *Governmental Relations*
    - Restriction on lobbying.
    - Control of business political action.
    - Extensive new regulation of business.
    - Restrictions on international operations.
5. *Business Giving*
    - Financial support for artistic activities —scholarship, educational.
    - Gifts to education (buildings)
    - Financial support for assorted charities (temples, churches, homes for aged persons, orphanages, community centres, rehabilitation centres).

26. Keith, D. and R.L. Blomstrom, *op. cit.*, pp. 8-10.

6. *Minorities and Disadvantaged Persons*
    - Training of hard-core unemployed.
    - Equal employment opportunity and quotas for minority employment.
    - Operation of programmes for alcoholic and drug addicts.
    - Employment of persons with prison records.
    - Building of plants and offices in minority areas.
    - Purchasing from minority businessmen.
    - Retraining of workers displaced by technology.
7. *Labour Relations*
    - Improvement of occupational health and safety.
    - Prohibition of "export of jobs" through operations in nations with low labour costs.
    - Provision of day-care centres for children of working mothers.
    - Expansion of employee rights
    - Control of pensions.
    - Impatience with authoritarian structures, demand for participation.
8. *Stockholder Relations*
    - Opening of Board of Directors to public members representing various interest groups.
    - Prohibition of operations in nations with "racist" or "colonial" governments.
    - Improvement of financial disclosure.
    - Disclosure of activities affecting the environment and social issues.
9. *Economic Activities*
    - Control of agglomerates.
    - Break-up of giant industry
    - Restriction of patent use

Assumption of Social Responsibilities

It should be noted that it is not enough to spell out the social responsibility of business (S.R). To ensure that these do not merely remain on paper, measures have to be evolved to enforce their acceptance by business. The very spirit of the concept of S.R.envisages voluntary action rather than enforcement through more government controls over the activities of the business. In the long run, a deeper understanding of the relationships between the manager, the corporation, and the society is the most effective means to a satisfactory resolution of the challenges posed by this concept.

A good number of business and other types of organisation in India and elsewhere have worked in the area of S.R. They have been concerned about these, mainly for three reasons:

1. They have been *forced* to be concerned;
2. They have been *persuaded* to be concerned;
3. They have been *voluntarily interested*.[27]

27. Hadley Arthur T., *Standards of Public Morality*, Macmillan Co., New York, 1912, p. 96.

TOOLS OF SOCIAL RESPONSIBILITY OF BUSINESS

Smooth relationship and understanding can be developed between the business and the community through the development of communication media or tools which may be the press, trained and educated men and women, local meetings and the social audit.

1. Reliable Means of Communication

In order to establish a smooth liaison and understanding between business and community, there must be a reliable means of communication. This is provided by a free and vigorous press, which is essential if the company is to discharge its responsibilities. It is through the press that good relationship is developed between the business and the people. Regular and periodic representation of facts, figures, and statistics through press is a great asset for the business as much as its image in the public eye is brightened. That is why businessmen hold frequent press conferences to explain their points of view and present facts to the press and are prepared to hear its reactions.

2. Trained and Educated Men and Women

The company needs trained and educated men and women to carry on its business. As a citizen, the company has no right to damage the amenities/property of the community. The presence of bad effluents, smoky chimneys, ugly buildings, heaps of solid waste emitting bad odour, insanitary slums, and polluted atmosphere is an indication of the fact that the business is quite negligent of its moral duty towards the community. To improve the situation regarding proper siting of industry and housing colonies, the company must work through consultation of the locality, rather than build and own these without having such prior discussions. The company should allow its workers time off for civic duties and for assisting the technical and other educational programmes.

3. Public Meetings

Public meetings serve a very useful purpose in as much as they apprise the community of what a company has done, what it proposes to do and whether its objectives have been accomplished. Such local meetings should be regular and annually held and open to the representatives of consumers, workers and the community besides those of the shareholders. At such meetings, the chairman gives the report on the general position of the business, the price of its products, their quality and standards, future prospects for their improvement, conditions of employment, prospects of expansion and growth, relation between business and the community and the activities that business has undertaken for the benefit of the community.

4. Social Audit

This is an important tool by which factual assessment of the work done and of the social performance of business is done. The objective of social audit is to find out whether any cooperation and mutual relationship exist between labour and management, and whether the business has fulfilled its economic, social and other responsibilities and maintained its predetermined standard and status; what is the nature of public relations with the customers etc. social audit must be compulsory for all companies.

SOCIAL RESPONSIBILITIES TOWARDS DIFFERENT GROUPS

In the west the concept came as something totally novel, but for India it was not so. For, in the olden days, whenever there was a famine, the leading businessmen of the area would literally throw open their godowns and their treasure chests to provide food and other aid to the needy. The history of every region is replete with stories of the magnificent manner in which businessmen rose to the occasion in times of calamity. Even in ordinary times, it was the businessmen who looked after the welfare of the destitute, the goshalas, the pinjrapoles, wells, and ponds, wherever water was difficult to get; *pathshalas* for the needy students and *dharmashalas* for the travellers during the course of their journey. Therefore, for the Indians to accept social responsibility is no more than re-dedicating themselves to the cherished values of their ancestors in the field of business. Gandhiji reminded us of these values when he propounded the Theory of Trusteeship.

The abiding truth of our heritage could be stated thus:

"Today the owners of capital and wealth have no absolute right over their economic assets for personal gains; they have to use these assets for the good of society as a whole; this is the basic function and the only justification of ownership of wealth."

One of the most distressing developments of modern times is the abdication of its social responsibility by the business community which is tacitly accepted that it is the function of the government to look after social welfare. But if they want to continue in the competitive world, they will have to accept social welfare as a basic ingredient of economic growth and their survival.

Since the middle of this century, a good number of business and other types of organisation in India have worked in the area of social responsibility. Originally, business participation was governed or motivated by considerations such as improving the corporate image of the organisation; seeking favours and concessions from the government ; government and social pressures for assistance during natural calamities; improving industrial relations etc.

An international seminar on "The social Responsibilities of Business," held at the India International Centre, New Delhi, between the 15th and the 20th March, 1965, at its conclusion issued a *Declaration,* which defined "Social responsibilities of business as responsibility to customers, workers, shareholders, and the community;" and emphasised that "in a modern industrial society, business occupies a meaningful and significant place in national life."

This declaration also emphasised certain main features of Social Responsibility (S.R.) of Business, Viz.,

1. In addition to making a fair and adequate return on capital, business must be just and humane, as well as efficient and dynamic. The modern business has manifold responsibilities: (a) to itself, (b) to its customers; (c) employees; (d) owners, shareholders and partners, (e) community, and (f) the state. *The task of management is to reconcile and harmonise these separate and sometimes conflicting responsibilities*.

2. The S.R. of Business can best be assumed in an atmosphere of freedom with the least possible restraint on healthy competition. Concentration and monopoly have to be watched and guarded, and wherever necessary, dispersed.

3. Every business has an overriding responsibility to make the fullest possible use of its resources, both human and capital. *Management has the responsibility to provide security of*

employment with fair wages and equal opportunity for personal growth and advancement within the business, which is a requirement of justice, and means of securing efficient management.

4. It highlights the respective roles of the enterprises, the shareholders, the workers, the customers, the management and the community. The responsibility of management is to fulfil the fair first needs of these claimants, besides, providing consumer satisfaction.

5. It laid emphasis on the reciprocal duties between business and the community, through laying down of practical measures like reliable means of communication, better eduction of the citizens about civil responsibilities, local meetings and social audit.

On the basis of the above seminar report, we may put down the social responsibilities of Business, in the Indian context in Table. 14.1.

We discuss, in the paragraphs that follow, the S.R. of business towards these different groups. Fig 14.3 presents business's social responsibilities towards different groups.

Business Firm's Responsibilities

Towards Owners/Share-holders
- Fair Dividend
- Solvent and Efficient Business
- Optimum use of Resources
- Planned Growth
- Effective Communication

Towards Employees
- Meaningful Work
- Job Satisfaction
- Fair Salaries & Benefits
- Best Quality of Worklife
- Succession Planning and Development

Towards Customers
- Fair price
- Superior Quality
- Superior Service
- Superior Product Design
- Quick and Complete Information

Towards Government
- Payment of Taxes, Custom Duties etc.
- Abide by the Laws
- Observe the Policies
- Maintain Law & Security

Towards Society
- Employment Without Discrimination
- Employment to Disadvantaged Persons
- Community Welfare Services
- Business Morality
- Maintaining Pollution-free Environment
- Maintaining Ecological Balance

Towards Inter–Business
- Fair Competition
- Cooperation for Sharing of Scarce Resources and Facilities
- Collaboration for Maximisation of Business Efficiency

Fig. 14.3 : Business's Social Responsibilities Towards Different Groups.

Towards Consumers/Customers

Consumers satisfaction is the ultimate aim of all economic activity. This includes that: (a) the goods must meet the needs of the consumers of different classes, tastes, and purchasing power; (b) the goods must be reasonably priced, be of a dependable quality and of sufficient variety; (c) the sale of such goods must be followed by service to ensure advice guidance and maintenance; (d) there should be a fair and widespread distribution of goods and services among all the sections of consumers and community; and (e) that there should be prevention of concentration of goods in the hands of a limited number of producers or purchasers or groups.[28]

28. *Report of the Study Group of the Calcutta Seminar on Social Responsibilities of Business,* Oxford & I.B.H. Publishing Co, New Delhi, 1969, p. 22.

TABLE 14.1 SOCIAL RESPONSIBILITIES OF BUSINESS

Towards Consumers & Community	Employees	Owners & Inter-Business
1. Goods must meet the requirements of different classes, tastes and purchasing power.	1. *Promote a sprit of cooperative endeavour* between employees and employers through participation in decision-making and in improving production and administration.	1. To provide a fair return or dividend on the capital invested.
2. Goods must be *reasonably priced,* must be of *dependable quality* and of *sufficient variety.*	2. *To pay fair and reasonable wages* to labour and *fair salaries* to staff members.	2. Give fair and impartial treatment to all.
3. Provision of after-sales, service/advice, guidance and maintenance.	3. *To develop and adopt a progressive labour policy* based on recognition of genuine trade union rights; settlement of disputes and conciliation; to create a sense of belongingness to the business, and improving human qualities of labour by education, training, living conditions, housing, leisure and amenities.	3. Devloping healthy co-operative business relationship between different businesses.
4. A fair widespread distribution of goods and services among all sections of consumers and community.	4. To provide reasonable and just work conditions.	4. Avoidance of such unfair practices as price-rigging, undercutting, patronage, unfair canvassing and unethical advertisements.
5. Provision of free competition and prevention of concentration of goods in the hands of a limited number of producers or purchasers or groups.	5. To recognise labourer as a "human being" and respect his dignity, and preserve his individual liberty.	5. Control of monopoly practices.
6. Present a "good image" in the minds of the public for honesty and integrity of character.	6. Provide facilities for joint consultation and collective bargaining.	
7. Advertising policy should be based on moral/ethical principles. It should not mislead by false, misleading and exaggerated advertisements.	7. Help development of proper leadership from among the employees.	
8. Support to educational, charitable and other programmes for the benefit of the community.	8. Guarantee religious, social and political freedom to workers to take part in the civic activities.	
9. Social accountability to consumers and public regarding the business conditions.	9. To develop promotion policies to encourage the workers to develop his talent/energy/capacity to the maximum extent.	
10. Avoidance of social and moral dangers of "high spots" and "Social tensions."		
11. Prevention of slum development improvement of housing conditions, elimination of crimes in industrial areas, and meeting the heavy costs of pollution and waste disposal.		
12. Business should lead a life of justice and have a progressive outlook.		
13. Other types of training to the existing employees and the unemployeds.		
The State		
1. To behave like a law-abiding citizen.		
2. To pay its dues and taxes to the state fully and honestly.		
3. Impartiality towards political affairs, i.e., to abstain from direct political involvement; and not to support political parties.		
4. To follow honest trade practices, and avoide activities leading to restraint of trade.		
5. To try not to corrupt public servants for selfish ends.		
6. To sell commodities and services without adulteration.		

In other words, business owes to itself the primary obligation to give a fair and square deal to its customers and consumers. They should be charged a fair and reasonable price which should be well within their reach. The supply of goods should be of uniform standard and of reasonably good quality. The distribution of goods must be widespread as to be within the easy reach of the consumer. No business should directly or indirectly indulge in profiteering, hoarding or creating artificial scarcity. Business should not mislead the consumer and community by false, misleading and exaggerated advertisements, because obscene advertisements are demoralising and a danger to public morals.

Consumer satisfaction is the ultimate aim of all economic activity. But adulteration of goods, poor quality, failure to give fair measure, lack of service and courtesy to the customer, misleading and dishonest advertising, are all examples of a violation by business enterprise of its obligations towards the consumers of its products.

Therefore, free competition must be allowed to operate and should be encouraged by anti monopoly legislation. Where certain monopolies are accepted as unavoidable or in public interest, the price of their toleration has to include the government's right to impose any controls that may be needed to check undue monopoly power. Legislation is required to prevent deception and fraud being practised on consumers, and where essential goods are in short supply, their fair distribution should be ensured.

Moreover, internal accountability to consumers should be extended. The Memorandum of Association of public limited companies and state enterprises should embody a specific declaration of these wider responsibilities of management. The management should encourage the establishment of the Consumers' Advisory Councils/Committees so that these bodies could represent the grievances of consumers to management.

The consumers themselves have social responsibilities to their fellow-consumers. If they passively submit to exploitation, they help to lower the standards of service and of management. Equally, they are a support to consumers' associations which, by investigation and reporting on the comparative prices and quality of products, can assist them in making a more informed choice of their purchases.

Towards Employees

It is the basic responsibility of the enterprise to produce wealth and also to provide opportunities for meaningful work. The management should develop its administration in such a way as to promote a spirit of cooperative endeavour between employers and employees. There should be a sense of participation between capital, on the one hand, and labour and skill, on the other, in their objective toward prosperity and progress.[29] The cooperation of workers can be won by creating conditions in which workers are enabled to put forward their best efforts in the common task as free men. This means recognition; (i) of the workers' right to a fair wage; ii) of the right to participate in decisions affecting their working life; (iii) to membership of trade union; (iv) to collective bargaining; and (v) of the right to strike.

The workers should be helped by education and training and other means to throw up their own leadership. Management should give workers opportunity to develop their capabilities through training, education and enjoyment of freedom to the greatest possible extent. Management should develop among workers a sense of belongingness to the business and provide them with healthy living conditions, cheap houses, leisure and amenities, profit-sharing and efficient system of communication.

29. *Ibid.*, p. 46.

The business or a plant is a community and justice should be its rule. This means there should be a company code of conduct with a recognised procedure for settling grievances which result in improved performance. The code should guarantee the religious, political, and social independence of the workers and make reasonable provision for them to take part in civic activities which benefit the community.

The image of business should be improved in the eyes of the workers so that persons of high calibre and capacity could be drawn to it. Routine monotony and boredom should be broken by job enrichment and job enlargement programmes. Finally, industrial peace and new techniques of professional management must be ensured within the precincts of the industry itself.[30]

Likewise, workers should realize their moral duty to do a good day's job for a good day's salary, to cooperate in increasing productivity, to come forward with suggestions and to participate in discharging their responsibility to the life of the plant and the community.

Towards Owners, Shareholders or Stockholders

Management's first duty is to see that enterprise is stable, enterprising and actively engaged in accomplishing its objectives. It would then be capable of providing those who commit their capital to it with such a fair and adequate reward for risk taken as permits the company to attract the necessary capital from the market. This capital is raised by the owners (proprietors, retailers, wholesalers, sole-traders) owning business, its property and looking after its management; the *share of stockholders* who contribute to the shares and debentures of the company or the partners (if there are any).

The expectations of these three types of owners are:

(i) a fair and reasonable return on the capital invested by them;

(ii) a part in profit, if the Memorandum so specifies, in the shape of profit-sharing or bonus payment schemes;

(iii) Political and economic security for investment through stable government, good law and order situation and stable tax policies and fiscal measures.

(iv) Knowledge about the working of the enterprise, its periodical progress report, so that they may be satisfied that their capital has been faithfully and usefully employed;

(v) a fair amount of dividend or retained earnings; and

(vi) Profiteering, blackmarketing, cornering of supplies, unfair trade practices are curbed and legally prohibited.

The shareholders also have their obligations. Shareholders in the General Meetings should question the Directors on the accounts and discuss policy matters and make their representation more effective through their associations. They can thus ensure that the company is pursuing a dynamic policy and that sufficient profit is laid aside for innovation and expansion. They should play a constructive role in encouraging the directors to pursue a responsible policy towards the company, and its obligations to the community, employees, and customers, upon which, in the long run, the company's reputation and future prospects depend.

Towards Inter-Business

The social responsibilities of business include a healthy co-operative business relationship between different business. Businessmen must resist unfair and unethical competition and avoid unfair interference in their rival's business such as price-rigging, undercutting, patronage,

30. *Ibid.*, pp. 141-142.

unfair canvassing, supply of substandard goods, application of undue financial , legal and political pressure; spreading false rumours/statements about the rival's products, creating labour troubles for the competitors' industry or launching a boycott campaign of their products, employing unethical advertisements, and controlling the supply of particular goods/services produced by them only so that an artificial scarcity is created in the market, giving rise to monopolistic conditions, artificial high prices as per quality of goods, etc.,

Destructive competition is always harmful, or it destroys confidence in business and introduces chaos instead of order and discipline. Therefore, the correct solution is not retaliation but the development of true ideas among the business community and to secure such legal regulation as is necessary to protect businessmen. A good businessman should adopt fair means to meet his rival's competition. This may be by adopting better designs, good advertisements, quick and safe delivery with after-sales service, reasonable price, etc.,

It is needless to say that unfair competition enters with extortion, bribery, kickbacks and granting of discriminatory advertising allowances or brokerage fees, and these should be avoided at all costs.

Towards the State

The social responsibilities of business towards the state (government) demands that:

(i) he will be a law-abiding citizen;
(ii) he will pay his dues and taxes to the state fully and honestly;
(iii) he will not corrupt public servants and the democratic process for his selfish ends;
(iv) he will not purchase political support by unfair means;
(v) he will strive fairly and honestly to stimulate economic growth even by making reasonable sacrifices on occasions of national need;
(vi) he will participate in the public life of the country in helping to make policies, fair legislation and working on advisory bodies
(vii) he will sell his goods, commodities and services without adulteration at fair and reasonable prices; and
(viii) he will maintain fair trade practices and refrain from activities like restraint of trade and will not take recourse to hoarding, cornering, and profiteering and other such unfair practices.[31]

The government has also some obligations towards business, such as to provide:

(i) a clean, prompt and efficient administration;
(ii) intelligent, practical laws, easily understood and easily applied;
(iii) reasonable political and social stability without frequent changes in legislative administrative and fiscal policies;
(iv) law and order ensuring safety of life, property and continuing business;
(v) a dynamic framework for rapid economic growth (infrastructure, legal aid);
(vi) rule of law;
(vii) holding of scales evenly between groups and sections in society;
(viii) political and social stability where business can grow and develop;
(ix) reasonable legislation for protecting units of business against monopoly; and
(x) healthy atmosphere to industrial peace.

31. *Ibid.*, p. 100.

Unfortunately, both have failed to fulfil their reciprocal obligations because of the following caused:

(a) Economic-Political and Organisational Factors

(i) breach of law by employers;
(ii) monopolism/groupism among all sectors;
(iii) business's apathy to change for lack of time and unwillingness;
(iv) ideological and methodical conflicts and differences between different states;
(v) existence of price-cutting, malpractices, and unfair trade practices;
(vi) division of management and labour into two warring groups, one endeavouring to win over the other;
(vii) technological changes, rationalisation, modernisation, leading to false notion of mass employment among labour.

(b) Government Administrative Factors

(i) discriminatory authority vested in government officials;
(ii) excessive political bias in the formulation of targets, policies and procedures without regard to basic economic laws;
(iii) loose, short-lived unco-ordinated administrative structure;
(iv) multiplicity and complexity of laws;
(v) frequent changes in laws and policies;
(vi) absence of integrated economy linking the private – public, large – medium, small and tiny sectors;
(vii) administrative delays and red-tapism; and
(viii) Unstable law and order situation.

What is, therefore, needed is that government should adopt progressive legal and tax policies, and to look to their strict observance; reduction in tax burden; careful planning, keeping in view the economic principle; strict supervision of and penalty for defaulters; easily understandable laws which are not frequently changed.

Towards the Community

The business owes a great irresponsibility to the community in various directions. Some of the major areas where business can and does contribute towards community welfare as a part of its social responsibility are:

1. *In the field of Industry:* Industry/business can help rural areas by introducing "self help' and 'earn-while-you-learn" programmes. Initially, such programmes may be labour intensive in areas like carpentry, pottery, spinning, weaving, agro-based industry, farming, dairy farming, poultry and pig rearing, storage, etc., so that increasing employment could be provided in rural areas. For this purpose, identification of areas needing improvement, facilities, skill requirements, financial assistance may be surveyed by business experts.

2. *In the field of Agriculture:* As a social responsibility, a large business house can play an important role in agricultural development, to provide full-time employment to the vast unemployed rural labour force. For this purpose, the business should get the survey done by its experts in the field of climate, soil conditions, breeding of livestock facilities for irrigation and water supply and actual supply of fertilizers seeds, pesticides, expertise, and finances. Non-agricultural activities seeking linkage with the agricultural sector and the industrialised sector can also be developed.

3. *Housing Facilities*: The social responsibility of business in this sphere is great, specially because a major proportion of the rural population is doomed to diseases, squalid existence in hopelessly ill-planned and filthy houses. Business can, therefore, play its role in changing house-building practices, extending loans and financial - aid facilities, providing material and manpower support. In the urban areas, slum clearance schemes, one or two room tenements with facilities for sanitation should be provided in labour colonies.

4. *Transportation:* Business and other agencies can help the government by undertaking studies and programmes of technical and financial assistance for the development of cheap public transport and distribution systems through improved journey planning and traffic regulation, increased operational efficiency and utilisation of road capacity , improved systems and procedures of granting licenses, more rational and scientific estimates for vehicle fleet size and manpower for different modes of transport, improved maintenance and replacement policy for the spares, and structural changes in urban and rural layouts.

5. *Health and Education:* Business organisations have their responsibility towards improvement of the quality of the people of the community. They can and should be engaged in works like providing water sources for drinking and bathing, improving sewage disposal system, cleaning dirty areas of the solid waste, reducing pollution (caused by soot of chimneys, and too crowded construction of industrial units, disposal of waste water and other residues; noise, etc.), improving sanitary facilities (through construction of underground drains, cleaning of existing foul water and waste-carrying open drains, improving roads by filling pits and giving them a regular slope, provision of public urinals, latrines and bathrooms and maintaining their cleanliness). Such measures would reduce preventible and water-borne diseases. They can also distribute free medicines, nutritious food to school-going children and pregnant mothers, the aged and the sick Holding of open camps for operation of minor ailments, eye diseases, family planning (vasectomy or tubectomy) can also be arranged by them. The explosion in population can be held in check by making available cheap contraceptives and advice for their use.

The problems responsible for ill-health in the rural areas need solution, for they result from lack of health education, unhealthy environment, unclean habits of living, poverty, poor diet, and the social culture. These problems can be solved through medical help, and the help of social workers. Besides, rural education could provide individuals with knowledge and skills to enable them to manage their families, to participate in cultural and economic life and to sharpen problem-solving capabilities.

6. *Industrial Aid to Education in Urban Areas: Progressive* individual businessmen and individual business houses (such as Birlas, Tatas, Modis, Ruias,, Lalbhais, Shreerams and others) are running or supporting schools, colleges and technical/professional educational institutions. In fact, it is a part of modern social responsibility of business that it should support educational programmes, more particularly technical education. In some cases, they help by lending the services of their specialists (as visiting experts) and giving financial help.

The National Industrial Conference Board of America in its Report on "Industrial. Aid to Education" has suggested five different forms of educational aid which business can render to the community;

(i) cash contribution to educational institutions :
(ii) scholarship and loans to undergraduate students;
(iii) contribution of material and equipments to educational institutions;
(iv) teaching aids for students and teachers; and
(v) contribution of company manpower.

7. *Social Audit On Factual Assessment:* This should be done by trained and professional personnel to show the social performance of business. The term "social audit" generally means a comprehensive evaluation of the way a company discharges all its responsibilities to shareholders, customers, employees, community and the govern*ment.* A social audit should generally adopt a four-step process, *viz*;

(a) firm must *itemise* all the activities that have a potential social impact;
(b) the *circumstances* leading to these actions or activities must be explained;
(c) some evaluation of the performance must be conducted; and
(d) the company must examine the relationship between the goals of the firm and those of society to see how the programme relate to one another.

In brief, it may be said that "business must accept responsibility to the society and its various constituents as a trustee for the goods and services that it produces, consumes, saves and reinvests. Such responsibilities extend beyond the business to the lives of the people and the community and as such they should endeavour to:

(a) play their proper role in civil affairs within the goals of the business;
(b) promote amenities and help, create better living conditions;
(c) help in making people law-abiding and improving legislation and administration in municipal and industrial affairs; and
(d) set up socially desirable standards of living, themselves avoiding ostentatious, wasteful expenditure, and improvident display in weddings, festivities and parties."[32]

We give below one example of social responsibilities as being fulfilled by the Indian business community:

Tata Steel – in the Service of the Community[33]

The Articles of Association of the TISCO state: "The Company shall have among its objectives, the promotion and growth of material economy through increased productivity, effective utilisation of material and manpower resources and continued application of modern scientific and managerial methods in keeping with the national aspirations. The company shall be mindful of its social and moral responsibilities to the consumers, employees shareholders, society and the local community."

The objective of the House of Tatas has been to "give the individual a sense of self-respect, opportunities for self-expression and to ensure his willing cooperation in the welfare of the community". To fulfil these objectives and to meet the growing challenges of human development as a whole, the TISCO launched in 1958 an urban community development project known as the Community Development and Local Welfare, through a department set up under the same name. The underlying philosophy of the programme was: "help those who help themselves."

Basic Features of Community Development and Social Welfare Programme

Under this programme, residents of each neighbourhood (mohalla) are involved. It now covers 2 lakh persons through 13 community centres as against 8,000 persons through one centre (Sonari) in 1958.

32. *Ibid.,* p. 132.
33. Largely based on Verma, R.K. "Tata Steel – In the Service of the Community," *Personnel Today,* Vol. 4 No. 2, July - September, 1983, pp. 7-14.

The main features of this programme are:

1. It is meant for the benefit of the entire community, irrespective of the fact whether one is an employee or not.

2. Its aim is to solve problems like illiteracy, population growth, improper utilisation of leisure hours, family budgeting, proper maintenance of community utility items.

3. Self-reliance and voluntary community participation are the guiding principles of every scheme under the programme.

4. It covers both the urban centres (9) and rural centres (4).

5. To carry out the programme, three voluntary committees, besides the community committees, also function. These are (a) *Sevadal Volunteers*, to work as neighbourhood guides (persons of the age group 24 and above); (b) Mahila Sevadal (Women volunteers), of girls of 14 years and above; and (c) *Yuvakdal* (persons of the age group 15-24 years). The members of all these three Sevadals are given training in first-aid, fire-fighting, vaccination, etc.

Activities under the Programme

Various programmes are being carried on under the Scheme, such as:

(i) Running of 200 Kishore Kendras (adolescent centres) and music and dance classes, sewing and knitting classes, adult literacy class, and shorthand and typewriting classes.

(ii) Organising Mahila Vikas Mela, picnics, grow more vegetable competitions and cultural programmes.

(iii) Arranging family planning (special vasectomy and tubectomy) and leprosy camps.

(iv) Encouraging small savings.

(v) "Shramdan work"—Construction of 4 Km long roads, 4 drinking water works, 3 irrigation works, and running 4 community centre-cum-schools.

(vi) Supply of nutritious food to about 1,700 children.

(vii) Running hobby classes in electrical and mechanical fittings, tinsmithy and carpentry, masonry, and training automobile workers, so as to help persons to take up some gainful employment.

(viii) Maintaining a creche for 40 children at 2 places.

Tata Steel Rural Development Scheme

In 1979, another scheme, the *Tata Steel Development Society* (TSRDS), was launched with the primary objective of helping the poor villagers to increase their earnings.

Under this programme, much attention is given to the improvement of agriculture and an all-round development of the village life. For this:

(a) Farmers are given training in modern agricultural practices —improved varieties of seeds, fertilizers and pesticides are supplied at subsidised rates;

(b) Intensive efforts are made to popularise multi-cropping by providing irrigation and technical advice on cash crops and vegetables ;

(c) Providing ancillary occupations like dairy, poultry, and pig-rearing and necessary inputs, such as fodder and free veterinary care;

(d) Encouraging village industries like basket-making, carpet weaving, horticulture and social forestry;

(e) Providing medical and health care, family planning services, education of children, adult literacy supply of clean drinking water, communication facilities between the villagers and the city: helping in having a gobar -gas plant, a tube-well, etc.:

(f) Construction of a residential colony of 32 houses for the tribals in 1981; and another colony of 13 houses in 1983:

(g) Developing and helping in setting up cooperative societies for poultry, bidi-making, pottery and ceramics and weaving;

(h) Building schools and colleges for tribal students, granting them scholarships, and arranging training for them to enable them to get admission to technical and professional courses.

Other Welfare Works

— Tatas have developed "Keenan" stadium for cricket, and Ahuja Statium for badminton.

— Assistance in cash and kind is extended to various organisations to pursue social, cultural, religious and recreational activities.

— Taking care of and showing concern for people, afflicted by , natural calamities and epidemics anywhere (as meeting expenses for eradication of smallpox in Bihar; flood and drought menace in Bihar and Orissa; and cyclone-caused losses in Andhra Pradesh by forming Relief and Rehabilitation Committees, raising funds and helping people in the shape of building homes , distributing food-packets and medicines, and supply other needs of the affected people.

— Giving donations to deserving institutions engaged in various fields of activities all over the country, e.g., providing medical aid of a special nature for certain ailments (like treatment of T.B.,. leprosy, eye diseases, and cancer); rehabilitation of the handicapped, mentally retarded, the dumb, the destitute and those handicapped by loss of some vital limb.

— Running a Blood Bank in Jamshedpur; and starting a Cancer Detection Clinic at the Tata Main hospital, a cobalt therapy unit and a cancer hospital.

— Giving generous monetary help and management know-how for opening a "Naturopathy Centre" at Jamshedpur.

According to the Social Audit Committee composed of three independent experts in different fields set up by the Tatas, "The social performance of the company is of a high order and in its magnitude, is perhaps unequalled in India".

CHAPTER 15

SOCIAL ACCOUNTING AND SOCIAL AUDIT

Social Accounting
Social Audit
Conclusion

SOCIAL ACCOUNTING

Introduction

Business firms cannot function in isolation. They perform their activities as a part of the society. Activities of the business affect significantly the employees, customers and the society. Business firms produce goods and services for the society. They provide the employment to the human resources of the country, exploit the mineral resources and make use of various natural resources. In fact, society provides various facilities and benefits to the business firms. The society provides infrastructure facilities, required finance, and other inputs to the business. The business cannot operate and succeed without the facilities provided by the society. Survival and development of business and society are co-extensive. Business is responsible towards the society as it draws the facilities, benefits and inputs from the latter.

There is a growing demand for reports on activities which reflect the contribution of an enterprise to the society. It is viewed that accounting must deal with measurement and communication of the performance of an enterprise in all spheres of activities. The concepts like 'total performance measurement and socio-economic accounting have gained performance in the recent years.

Corporate social reporting is an act of reporting by a business firm about its social activities having a bearing on such issues on ecology, environment, working conditions and quality of life of the society at large. Social reporting is in contrast to the normal legal financial reporting to shareholders. Different phrases are used to devote social reporting. They are social accounting, social economic accounting, report on corporate social policies, social responsibility accounting, social information system and social responsible accounting.

Definitions

According to Elliot, social responsibility accounting, is a systematic assessment of and reporting on those parts of a company's activities that have a social impact, social responsibility accounting, describes the impact of corporate dimensions on environment pollution, the consumption of non-renewable resources and ecological factors; on the rights of individual and groups; on the maintenance of public services; on the public safety, on health and education and many other such social concerns."[1]

Ralph Eates defines the term social accounting as, "the measurement and reporting, internal and external, of information concerning the impact of an entity and its activities on the society." He views social accounting as an independent discipline which is to measure and report the activities of a business firm affecting the society[2].

Ramnathan defines the term social accounting as, "the process of selecting firm level performance variables, measures and measurement procedures, systematically developing

1. Elliot Robert K, "Social Accounting and Corporate Decision – Making", Management Controls, January 1975, p. 3.
2. Ralph Eates, "Corporate Social Accounting", John Wiley & Sons, New York, 1973, p. 4.

information useful for evaluating the firm's social performance to social groups concerned, both within and outside the firm"[3].

Lee Brummet emphasises the need for total performance measurement. According to him, the total performance of a company is a function of human resource contribution, public contribution, environmental contribution and product or service contribution.

Contribution of Business to Society : The contributions of the business to the society consists of:

(i) Human resource contribution including organisational activities having impact on the people who make up the resources,

(ii) Public contributions include financial and human resource support for public programmes, equal opportunity, training and employment of disadvantaged persons etc.

(iii) Environmental contribution should deal with the environmental aspects of utilising the production facilities and resources, the production process and the product including recycling and other positive environmental activities.

(iv) Product or service contribution in terms of product safety, durability, utility, maintainability, customer satisfaction honesty in advertising, innovation etc.

In essence, social accounting is identification, measurement, recording and reporting of corporate activities which may permit informed decision making with respect to social activities of the firm having direct or indirect effect on the very fabric of the society at large.[4]

Approaches to Social Accounting :

Accountants have tried to report corporate social functions on the basis of social cost concept derived from economics and sociology. Different approaches of social accounting as suggested by David F. Fetyko include :

(i) the inventory approach whereby company's social objectives are prepared;

(ii) cost or outlay approach whereby the expenditure incurred on each activity is disclosed;

(iii) the programme management approach, whereby in addition to the above two disclosures a statement regarding compliance with the objectives, activity - wise or otherwise is recorded, and

(iv) the benefit cost approach, whereby the real worth, i.e., the benefit of the expenditure is indicated.[5]

Three Schools of Thought

Three different schools of thought have been developed by the accountants, economists and behavioural scientists regarding measurement and reporting of corporate social responsibilities.

They are (i) integral welfare theoretical approach, (ii) social indicator concept and (iii) goal accounting and reporting.

(i) ***Integral Welfare – Theoretical Approach :*** This approach advocates the preparation of a social report comprising social profit and loss statement and a social balance sheet. (see exhibit 15.1) The problems involved in this approach are measurement and evaluation.

3. Kava S. Seri V. Ramanathan, "Theory of Corporate Social Accounting.", *Accounting Review*, July 1976, p. 516.
4. P.K. Ghosh, G.C. Maheswari and R.N. Goyale, "Studies in Accounting Theory", Wiley Eastern Ltd., New Delhi, 1990, p. 468.
5. Dutta Amarnath, 'The Corporate Indentity Crisis", *Business India*, Feb. 16-March 1, 1981, p. 26.

(ii) ***Social Indicator Approach :*** This approach refers to the development of social indicators at the firm's level and to the measurement of firm's contribution to overall quantity of life in various areas. These are five areas in which corporate social objectives may be found and where corporate social activities may be measured and reported. They are (a) net income contribution, (b) human resource contribution, (c) public contribution, (d) environmental contribution and (e) product or service contribution.

(a) *Net Income Contribution* : Every business firm has a fundamental right of making profit. Business firm should earn enough profit to pay dividend to shareholders, meet the capital requirements for expansion and/or diversification.

(b) *Human Resource Contribution* : Corporate activities in the area of human resource include : human resource planning, job design, job analysis, recruitment, selection, training, development, morale building, wage and salary levels, fringe benefits, employee welfare, career planning and development, employee attitudes, job satisfaction, relations with trade unions, collective bargaining, workers participation in management, job safety, promotions, transfers etc. Accountants have developed the technique of human resource accounting in order to measure/identify the contribution of human resources to the organisation. Human resource accounting (HRA) involves (i) determination of value of individuals to the organisation, (ii) determination of the reliable and valid measures of cost and value (iii) design of operational system for these measures and (iv) determination of the effects on the decision makers. The concepts of human resource accounting is still in the formative stage.

Exhibit 15.1: Corporate Social Accounting Framework :
The Integral Welfare-Theoretical Approach

Social Costs	*Social Benefits*
I. *Producers' Surplus for:*	I. *Consumers' Surplus for:*
1. Labour Performance	1. Product A
2. Fixed Assets	2. Product B
3. Materials	3. Product C
4. Capital	4. Product D
5. Entreprenurial performance	
6. Performances paid in advance	
II. *Value of Negative External Effects on:*	II. *Value of Positive External Effects on:*
1. Employees	1. Employees
2. Population	2. Population
3. Companies	3. Companies
4. Public Entities	4. Public Entities
III. *Net Social Benefits*	III. *Net Social Costs*

(*Source* : P. Eichhorn, Gesellschftsbezogene Unternehmensrechnung, 1974, p. 94).

(c) *Public Contribution* : Important public contributions include creation of jobs, provision of employment, development of local services like education, health, transportation, roads, drinking water, training for disadvantaged persons, flood and drought relief measures etc. No effort has been made in this area to quantify and report the corporate contributions except incorporating these items in the chairman's report.

(d) *Environmental Contribution* : Corporate social objectives have been located in the abatement of negative external social effects of industrial production, use of resources, production process leading to water, air, and noise pollution and the despoilation of environment and also the use of irreplaceable resources at the cost of future generations. It is viewed that there is no single way to the accountants to approach in this matter.[6]

(e) *Product or service Contribution* : This area relates to the qualitative aspects of the business firm's product or service. The qualitative aspects include : Utility, durability safety, serviceability, customer satisfaction, accurateness in information, advertising, completeness and clarity in labelling and packaging. Exhibit 15.2. exemplifies this approach for the area of business–consumer relations.

(iii) ***Goal Accounting and Reporting :*** Company's formulate mission objectives and goals in terms of economic and social. The aspects of social goals can be divided into

(a) the selection of social goals and (b) reporting and assessment of company's performance according to these goals.

Exhibit 15.2 : Concepts of Corporate Social Reporting
The Social Indicator Approach

Classification of indicators in the field	Objective Indicators			
Instruments of the market - behaviour of the firm	1 Price worthiness of the product	2 Properties of the product	3 Market - situation	4 Subjective indicators
1 Transaction - policies (Price, Conditions)	11 Price-develop-ment profitability of the product	12 Price-consequ-ences of additional product features	13 Competing prices, conditions and market-shares	14 Readiness to pay off actual and potential clients, evaluation of conditions
2 Product-policy	21 Share of the R & D–Costs: – For the product – Fundamental Research	22 Factual proper-ties: –Technical life span – Technical performance – Security – Pollution – Health	23 Properties of the directly competing products and functional alternatives	24 Attitudes, opinions about utility of use, additional utilities and social life span, "brand loyalty".
3 Distribution-policy	31 Share of the distribution costs (The structure of profit)	32 Dependence of the products properties on distribution	33 Terms of delivery attainability of sales points	34 Evaluation of the market treatment
4 Communications policy	41 Share of the advertising cost – For the product – Per Channel	42 Divergence between the published and the actual properties	43 Availability and seizure of external "neutral" communications channels	44 Number of evaluation of discerned alternatives: assessment of the credibility of the sources of information and the nee pressures

Source : Picot, Betriebswirtschaftliche Umweltbeziehungen and Unwoltinformationen, 1977, p. 219.

6. P. K. Ghosh, G.C. Maheswari and R.N. Goyale, *op. cit.*, p. 474.

SOCIAL AUDIT

Evolution of the Concept of Social Audit

The social audit, which is an approach for monitoring, appraising and measuring the social performance of business, is a relatively new development. Kreps may be regarded as the founding-father of the idea. He wrote a monograph on the measurement of social performance, in which he summarised his findings in 72 industries, covering a 20-year period (1919-38). He included among these measurements:[7] (1) employment; (2) production; (3) consumer effort commanded (what have consumers been compelled to surrender in exchange for what they get?); (4) consumer funds absorbed (what has happened to the stream of dollars which the industry has collected from the public and its customers in the exchange for services rendered); (5) pay rolls; and (6) dividends and interest.

Kreps indicated that his measurements do not constitute an exhaustive audit, for they give no indication of such vitally important facts as percentage of capacity operated, investment outlet provided, opportunity for new entrants, stability of operations, fullness of use of patents, modernisation and the like.[8]

The second stage in the development came when Howard Bowen conducted an independent appraisal every five years by a group of auditors, whose report was considered as an evaluation of the firm's work. Bowen suggested eight areas for appraisal:[9] (1) prices, (2) wages, (3) research and development, (4) advertising, (5) public relations, (6) human relations, (7) community relations, and (8) employment stabilisation.

Bowen's version was more related to the modern version of the audit than Krep's approach, but did not contain any specific applications of the social audit.

To Sethi actually goes the credit of using social audit in the right perspective, in the 1970s, When he stated:[10] "At the risk of oversimplification, we might say that the purpose of the social audit is to help break down the broad term 'social responsibility of business' into identifiable components and to develop scales that can measure these components".

Concept of Social Audit

It may be noted that though social audits have now been undertaken in a number of countries, such as the U.S.A., the U.K., Japan and India (by the Tata Iron & Steel Company, Jamshedpur) and some other Western countries, the subject has not yet attained the status of a science. There is no agreement, not to say of unanimity, among its proponents, particularly as to its basic principles or its true objectives. It is only a child of the last decade during which there has been a growing concern with the environment and problems of pollution, consumer protection, worker's safety equal employment opportunity, etc that have come to the fore as a result of a high degree of industrialisation.[11]

7. Kreps, Theodore, J. : *Measurement of the Social Performance of Business: An Investigation of Concentration of Economic Power*, USA Govt. Printing Press, Washington, 1940, pp. 3-4.
8. *Ibid.*, p. 5
9. Howard, R. Bowen, *Social Responsibilities of Business*, Harper & Row, New York, 1953, p. 155.
10. Sethi, Prakash, S., "Getting a Handle on the Social Audit," *Business and Society Review*, No. 4 Winter, 1972-73, p. 33
11. Tata Iron & Steel Company, Research Department, *Report of the Social Audit Committee*, Bombay, August, 1980, p. 2.

The term "social audit" has been interpreted differently by different people. To some it means the public disclosure of a company's social performance, to others, it means internal evaluation of a company's social responsibility performance and to some others social audit is a comprehensive evaluation of the way a company discharges all its responsibilities to shareholders, customers, employees, and to the wider community.

Melvin Aushen remarks that "The social audit is an idea whose time has come but which is not ready to be taken off the drawing board and put to work.[12]

Bowen and Fenn take it to mean: "A commitment to systematic assessment of and reporting on some meaningful, definable domain of a company's activities that have social impact".[13]

Clark C. Abt says that "A social audit should, as far as possible, be approximated to an ordinary commercial audit and this should be based on a 'social balance sheet' with a 'credit' side and a 'debit' side. He calls them 'inputs' and 'outputs' or 'costs' and 'benefits' so far as social balance sheet is concerned ...... The basic purpose of a business corporation is to maximise the *financial return earned* on its financial investment plus the amount of *social return* on its social investment."[14]

According to the Sachar Committee, there are pointers in this direction.

Keeping the opinions of the experts in view, we may define a social audit thus :

It is a systematic study and evaluation of an organisation's social performance, as distinguished from its economic performance.

In other words, it is concerned with possible influences on the "social quality of life" instead of "economic quality of life" The social audit leads to a "*social performance*" or "*social audit*" report for management and outsiders. This social performance refers to organisational activities that affect the general welfare of the society. It emphasises total needs of the whole community and the whole society. It this context, social audit is "the disclosure of the facts regarding performance of a company's activities relating to social responsibility which it has carried out, in the previous year, for the benefit of the various constituents like shareholders, creditors, workers and the community.[15]

It will be noted that definitions cited above represent different points of view. Considerable differences of opinion exist over what topics should be covered by such an audit; what criteria should be employed for measurement; by whom the audit should be done–by internal or external auditors and whether the results of audit should be for internal management use only or it should have a wide circulation among those whose interest are vitally affected. Accordingly, work is still in progress by many individuals who are making efforts to assist business firms in adopting a suitable system of social audit. In the USA the audits of ARA services,[16] Abt Associates,[17] Arthur

12. Quoted in *Social Audit Committee Report*, p. 3.
13. *Ibid.*, p. 3.
14. *Ibid.*, p.3.
15. *Ibid*, p. 3
16. Richman, Barry, "New Paths of Corporate Social Responsibility," *California Management Review*, Spring, 1973, pp. 20-36.
17. Butcher, Bernard, L, "The Programme Management Approach to the Corporate Social Audit," *California Management Review*, Fall, 1973, pp. 11-16.

Little,[18] George Steiner,[19] Carrol and Beiler[20] Dilly and Weygandt[21] and Fetyko[22] and in India the Social Audit Committee, the observations of Eils and Waltan may be noted. They said: "When people talk about corporate social audit, they are thinking in terms of the problems that arise when corporate enterprise casts its shadow on the social scene, and of ethical principles that ought to govern the relationships between the corporation and society. They are concerned with the impact of the corporate on the individual and the possibilities of reconciling big business, big labour, and big government with the values deeply rooted in our form of government."[23]

Social audit is a systematic view. It tends to focus on general humanistic values while reducing traditional economic and technical values to sub-systems within the larger social system. It is concerned with the human meaning of events.[24]

The concept of social audit (or social accountability, or public responsibility, or social objectives or business morality) implies that audit must fulfil the economic and social needs of the community. It starts from the principle that in a democracy the decision-makers are accountable for the use of their powers and, therefore, the managers are required to prepare a "socio-economic operating statement" which may be juxtaposed with the statement on profits and loss.

Objectives of Social Audit

Because of the differing views about social audits, they have multiplied motives, which include satisfying the corporate conscience, increasing the wisdom of social programmes, improving public relations and enhancing the credibility of the business. The particular issues are (i) minority employment, (ii) pollution/environment, (iii) working conditions, (iv) community relations, (v) philanthropic contributions, and (vi) consumerism issues.[25]

Goyder has set the ultimate objectives in the following four *principal objects* of the responsible company.[26]

1. The extension, development and improvement of the company's business and the building up of its financial independence.
2. The payment of fair and regular dividends to the shareholders.
3. The payment of fair wages under the best possible conditions to the workers.
4. The reduction of prices to consumers.

18. Baner, Raymond, A, "The Corporate Social Audit, Getting on the Learning Curve", *California Management Review*, *Ibid.*, pp. 5-10.
19. Steiner, George A., *Summary Results of Survey of Developing Efforts to Measure the Social Performance of Business*, Committee for Economic Development, New York, 1973. Government of India Report of the High-Powered Expert Committee on Companies and MRTP Act, New Delhi, 1978, p. 95.
20. Carrol, Archie, B, and George, W. Beiler, "Landmarks in the Evolution of the Social Audit", *Academy of Management Journal*, Sept., 1975, pp. 596-598.
21. Dilley, Steven, C and Jerry J. Weygandt, "Measuring Social Responsibility: An Empirical Test," *Journal of Accountancy*, Sept., 1973, p. 63.
22. Fetyko, David, F, "The Company Social Audit," *Management Accounting*, April, 1975.
23. Eells, Richard and Clarence Walton. *Conceptual Foundations of Business*, Richard D. Irwin, Homewood, 1961, pp. 457-458.
24. Davis, Keith and Robert L. Blomstrom, *Business and Society: Environment and Responsibility*, McGraw-Hill Book Co., New York, 3rd edition, 1975, p. 51.
25. Carrol, Archie, B and George W. Beiler, "Landmarks in the Evolution of the Social Audit", *Academy of Management Journal*, Sept., 1975, pp. 597-98.
26. Goyder, George, *The Future of Private Enterprise: A Study in Responsibility*, Basil Blackwell, Oxford, 1951, p. 110.

To these, the following four secondary objectives have also been added.[27]

1. The provision of a bonus for the workers.
2. To assist in promoting the amenities of the locality.
3. To assist in developing the industry of which the firm is a member.
4. To promote education, research and development in the techniques of industry or any other purpose approved by the directors and members in a general meeting.

From these objectives, it may be inferred that social audit is really the extension of the principle of public disclosure to which the corporation are subject.

Need for Social Audit

The need for social accountability arises because there is a tendency on the part of the business to use its power indifferently, irresponsibly or in an anti-social way. In this regard, the following observations may be noted:

"A new democracy in industrial economy should be developed, because in the words of the late President Wilson (of USA) on New Freedom: (i) the present organisation of business is made for big fellows and not meant for the little fellows, (ii) that it is meant to exclude those who are at the bottom; and (iii) that it is meant to shut out beginners, to prevent new entries in the race, to prevent building up of competitive enterprises that would interfere with monopolies which great trusts have built up."

Prof. Robert A. Dahl has gone as far as to say that a major business corporation could be responsible for death, injury or disease (for example, through poor product design of quality control or through lack of plant safety, excessive pollution, etc). It may deprive people of their livelihood, well-being or effective personal freedom through decision making on hiring and firing, discrimination, investment or plant location. A major corporation may also influence control and even coerce individuals or groups and sometimes, nations (for example, by advertising, promotions and propaganda and by a wide variety borderline or more patently illegal business practices). Hence, the need for wide disclosure becomes imminent.[28].

Prof. Galbraith has emphasised the social obligation of business towards society as under[29]

"The firm is required, with increasingly technical products and processes, increasing capital, a lengthened gestation period and increasingly large and complex organisation, to control or seek to control the social environment in which it functions or any part which impinges upon it. It must plan not only its own operations; it must also, to the extent possible, plan the behaviour of the people and the State as these affect it. This is a matter not of ambition but of necessity."

In the Annual Address at the Harvard Business School Alumini Association in June 1948, Clarance Francis (Chairman of General Food Corporation, USA), made the following observations echoing the popular sentiments relating to social audit and social responsibility:

"Today, most managements, in fact, operate as trustees in recognition of the claims of employees, investors, consumers and government. The task is to keep these forces in balance and to see that each gets a fair share of the industry's rewards and the activities of the corporation are brought to the knowledge of all parties concerned."

George Goyder rightly points out that: "Industry in the twentieth century can no longer be regarded as a private arrangement for enriching shareholders. It has become a joint enterprise

27. *Ibid.*, p. 111.
28. Chapman, Charles C., *The Development of American Business and Banking Thought.*
29. Galbraith, J.K., *Economics and the Public Purpose.*

in which workers, management, consumers, the local government and trade union officials all play a part. If the system which we know by the name private enterprise is to continue, some way must be found to embrace many interests which go to make up industry in a common purpose....If the corporation has to function effectively, it has to be accountable to the public at large and that private property should be used for the common good.[30]

The Sachar Committee in India has observed as under.[31]

"In the development of corporate ethics, a stage has been reached where the question of social responsibility of business to the community can no longer be scoffed at or taken lightly on the plea that corporations are performing a social purpose in the development of the country. It can only be judged by the test of social responsiveness shown by them to the needs of the community. The company must behave and function as a responsible member of the society like any other individual. It cannot shun moral values nor can it ignore actual compulsions. The real need is for some focus of accountability on the part of the management not being limited to shareholders alone. In modern times, the objective of business has to be the proper utilisation of resources for the benefit of others. A profit is still a necessary part of the total picture but it is not the primary purpose...The company must accept its obligation to be socially responsible and to work for the larger benefit of the community."

The Sachar Committee has, therefore, suggested that: (a) a provision should be made in the Companies Act to the effect that every company, along with its directors' report, shall also give a social report which will indicate and quantify in as clear and precise terms as possible the various activities relating to the social responsibility aspects which have been carried out by the company in the previous year; and (b) it is possible that a company may be required to alter its memorandum with respect to the objects of the company so as to carry out its activities as obligations to the concept of social responsibility.

Thus, social audit need be adopted by every corporation to apprise its shareholders, investors, customers, government and the community of the social activities and financial results of its working. Such information should be disclosed, as mentioned by the National Association of Accountants' Committee on Accounting for Corporate Social Performance in Canada, for four major categories as below:

(1) *Community Involvement* : Socially-oriented activities that are primarily of benefit to the general public. Examples include : general corporate philanthropy, housing construction and financing, health services, volunteer activities among employees, food programmes and community planning and improvement.

(2) *Human Resources* : Social performance directed to the well-being of employees. Categories in this area include employment practices, training programmes, job enrichment, working conditions, promotion policies and employee benefits.

(3) *Physical Resources and Environmental Contributions* : Activities directed towards alleviating or preventing environmental deterioration (pollution). This category includes the adherence to the law and going beyond it in areas such as air quality, water quality. Also included is the conservation of scarce resources and the disposal of solid waste.

(4) *Production or Service Contribution* : Concerned with the impact of the company's product or service on society. This includes consumerism, product quality, packaging, advertising, warranty provisions and product safety.

30. Goyder, George, *The Future of Private Enterprise: A Study in Responsibility*, 1951, p. 1.
31. G.O.I., *Report of the High-Powered Committee on Companies and MRTP Acts*, 1978, p. 95-110.

In India, the companies in general and the public sector undertakings in particular should make disclosure of information for the use of people outside the enterprise, which include: (i) financial institutions and creditors (who are interested in financial position, fund-flow and debt-paying capacity of the enterprise); (ii) shareholders, academic institutions and consultants (who are interested in quantitative and qualitative information regarding proper utilisation of resources transferred to the concern); (iii) the government (for knowing about financial and statistical information for planning and operating of those enterprises and initiating and administering financial and economic policies and programmes at state and national levels; (iv) trade unions, political leaders (require information for broad labour policy decisions, for collective bargaining and negotiations, labour welfare activities, human resource development, etc); and (v) environmentalists (who need information regarding air and water pollutions, ecological imbalances, depletion of resources and conservation of energy)[32].

Disclosure of information should be thus financial and non-financial.

Financial Information

This includes the disclosure of financial position of the firm, the form of balance sheet, profit and loss accounts, special accounts, audit reports. Such information is mainly disclosed in quantitative form, such as income and expenditure of the company, sources and uses of funds, details about assets and liabilities, working capital, new capital investment, outstanding, distribution of earnings, interest, taxes paid, liquidity position and incentives. Financial information reveals the true position of a company regarding its liquidity and bankruptcy.

Model Social Audit is presented in Exhibit. 15.3

Non-Financial Information

This includes information relating to social performance, human resources, marketing activities, business environment, production, etc. Such information may be disclosed in quantitative and qualitative terms, but the disclosure of social responsibility is generally expressed in quantitative terms. The purpose of such disclosure of information is to influence profitability in the long run and to build the company's image.

Information on social performance generally includes various activities regarding employee welfare, community work and involvement, social and cultural programmes, role of company in solving social problems of the area, programmes dealing with training and developing human resources, etc. Social programmes are specified in annual reports.

Information on human resources includes expenditure on recruitment, selection, training and development of employees, facilities for self-development in organisation, special provision for development of hard-core unemployed persons, sponsoring executives for delivering lectures in universities, educational institutions, and for foreign training. Such information is disclosed in the Directors' Report and the Chairman's speech.

Information on marketing includes sales figures product-wise and plant-wise, cash and credit sales, pricing and impact of competition on pricing, product innovations and development, quality of product, advertising and promotional efforts for distribution of the products, selling

32. Singh, D.R., "Performance of Public Sector Enterprises in India – An Evaluation of Information Disclosure in their Annual Reports", in Kaushik, S.L. and Pradeep Sahni (Ed), *Public Administration in India: Emerging Trends,* Kitab Mahal, Allahabad, 1984, p. 284.

commission, travelling expenditure of marketing personnel, etc. Such information is disclosed in the Directors' report, Chairman's statement or in advertisements, etc.

Environment information includes information about the political, economic, socio-cultural and technological environment, especially on such items as inflation, unemployment, impact of changes on taxes, changes in legal requirements of business activities, strikes and lockouts in the company and its impact, general labour relations, welfare activities, contribution and participation in company, in community development, technological development, pollution control measures, use of indigenous raw materials and efforts at conservation of natural and human resources. The disclosure of information finds place in the annual reports and chairman's speech.

Special Features of Social Audit

Thus it will be noted that social audit includes any activity which has a significant social impact, such as activities affecting environmental quality, equal employment opportunity, consumerism, community needs, labour relations, shareholder relations, economic activities, and fixing responsibility within the firm for social performance.

Social audit can determine only what an organisation is *doing* in social areas, but not the "amount of social good that results from these activities." *It is a process of audit rather than an audit of results*. Social audits are so nebulous that they are difficult to measure, and generally accepted social norms are almost not-existent. Raymond Bener observes.[33]

"If there is single technical flaw in the audits that have been attempted, it is the relative absence of norms whereby to judge performance. Granted, many norms are hard to come by: What, for example, would be a good norm against which to judge a company's performance with minority suppliers or community relations? Circumstances vary so much from company to company that it may be a long time before we can come up with any criteria for judgement beyond honest efforts."

Social results are difficult to audit because most of them occur outside an organisation and so a firm has no way to secure data from these outside sources. Even when data are available, cases are so complex that a firm has no way to know how much of the results its actions have caused. However, though results cannot be proved, an audit of what is being done can be considered desirable because it shows how much effort has been made by the business in areas deemed beneficial to community.

Social audit can be made by internal auditors, outside consultants or a combination of the two. Bowen has suggested whoever is selected for doing social audit should be; (a) oriented toward the social point of view, (b) conversant with business practices and problems, and (c) technically trained in such fields as law, economics, sociology, personnel, government, philosophy and theology.

If an internal auditor is appointed, he is familiar with the business but this judgement may be biased because of his loyalty to the company. An outside auditor has an independent view, but he lacks familiarity with organisational activities and he may, therefore, overlook significant data. But the report produced by him more credibility among the public. Hence, social audit should be made by an outside auditor for internal use only and that it should be made only every five years.

Social audits use both quantitative and qualitative data. Quantitative data are generally preferred because they are precise and convincing but in the field of social philosophy and

33. Baner, Raymond, A. "The Corporate Social Audit: Where Does It Stand Today?" *Personnel*, July-August, 1973, pp. 16-17.

human values, they prove misleading, for they represent only a part of the total picture. The firms, therefore, normally use as much quantitative data as possible, whichever is found suitable for communication, and this is then supplemented by qualitative data.

Benefits of Social Audit

Some of the major benefits that accrue from social audit are :

1. It supplies data for comparison with policies and standards so that a management determines how well the organisation is living upto its objectives. "Just as a spaceship in flight must know where it is in order to correct its flight and reach its objective, a business must know where it is in relations to its objectives."

2. It encourages greater concern for social performance throughout the organisation. In the process of audit, preparation of reports and responding to evaluations, employees become more aware of social implications of their actions, and corporate social objectives are more strongly reinforced in all the areas of the organisation.

3. It provides data for comparing effectiveness of different types of programmes, which will give management useful inputs for establishing better programmes.

4. It provides cost data on social programmes so that management can relate the data to budgets, available resources, company objectives, and projected benefits of programmes.

5. It provides information for effective response to external claimants that make demands on the organisation. The press, the public and others want to know what a business is doing areas of their special interest, and a business needs to respond as effectively as possible. *The social audit shows a business where it is vulnerable to public pressures and where its strengths lie*.

Bowen has offered these benefits for the social audit, which are still valid.[34]

(i) It would provide a recognised method for bringing the social point of view to the attention of management;

(ii) The appraisal of individual corporations would be made by persons outside the company who would have more detached and disinterested view of its activities than the company employees:

(iii) The creation of a specialised group of social auditors would give an impetus to the consideration and development of recognised standards for corporate practice;

(iv) The fact that the report on audit would be made to the company and not to the public would make possible complete frankness and at the same time, make the scheme more acceptable to businessmen.

Approaches to Social Audit

Dilley and Weygandt have suggested four general approaches towards social audit:[35].

1. *The inventory approach*, under which a list of all the company's social activities is prepared.

2. *The cost or outlay approach* in which the amount spent on each activity is disclosed.

3. *The programme management approach*, in which in addition to the above approaches, a statement is made as to whether or not the company met its objectives for each activity.

34. Bowen, Howard, R., *op. cit.*, p. 156.

35. Dilley, David C. and Jerry J. Weygandt, "Measuring Social Responsibility: An Empirical Test". *Journal of Accountancy*, 1973, p. 63.

4. *The cost-benefit approach*, under which the benefits of each expenditure, i.e., the real worth, is indicated.

The least informative of these approaches is the inventory approach, but the current practice adopted by most firms is to use this approach. The most informative approach is the cost-benefit approach, but the benefits achieved cannot be measured accurately. Some companies also use the two other approaches. But, a good approach would be to attempt a social audit report based on cost or outlay approach.

The results of social audit may be gauged by looking into the following issues :

(i) What has been the overall approach of the company in its day-to-day conduct of business? Has it been merely actuated by the motive of maximising its profit or it has also kept in view the aspect of service to society?

(ii) Is the company harnessing the natural resources at its command with due care to ensure that the interest of both present and future generations are safeguarded. For example, a coal mine can be worked in a manner that the owners or the lease-holders derive the maximum profits in a short span but in the process make the mine unworkable for future.

(iii) Whether the organisation is helping in advancing efficiency and productivity in society in general?

Exhibit 15.3 : Model Social Audit

			1971	*1970*
	Social benefits and costs of staff			
1.	**Social benefits to staff:**		$	$
	Health insurance, sick leave		93,492	57,271
	Career advancement		345,886	173,994.
	Company school and tuition reimbursement		6,896	—
	Vacation, holidays, recreation		207,565	163,988
	Food service, child care, parking		57,722	51,292
	Quality of life (Space and its quality)		61,002	70,551
	Total Benefits to Staff	(a)	772,563	517,096
2.	**Social costs to staff:**			
	Layoffs and involuntary terminations		9,560	7,500
	Overtime worked but not paid		654,000	474,000
	Inequality of opportunity		—	3,600
	Total costs of staff	(b)	663,560	4,85,160
	Net social income to staff	(c) = (a – b)	109,003	31,936
3.	**Social benefits to community:**			
	Local taxes paid		38,952	31,091
	Environment improvements		10,100	8,367
	Local tax worth of net jobs created		20,480	15,750
	Total benefits to community	(d)	69,532	55,208
	Social costs to community			
	Local taxes consumed in service	(e)	55,700	34,400
	Net social benefit to community :	(f) = (d – e)	13,832	20,808

4. **Social benefits and costs to general public :**			
Social benefits to general public			
Federal taxes		165.800	—
States taxes paid		59,500	9,830
Contribution to knowledge (publications etc)		10,100	8,300
Federal State tax worth of net jobs created		69,800	34,800
Total benefits to public	(g)	305,200	52,930
Social costs to general public :		$	$
Federal services consumed		83,000	77,000
State Services consumed		31,100	23,500
Total costs to general public	(h)	114,100	100,500
Net social income (cost) to general public (i) = (g – h)		191,100	(47,570)
Net social income (cost) to staff, community and public	(j) = (c+f+i)	313,935	5,174
5. Social benefits and cost to clients			
Social benefits to clients			
Added value to previous contracts to clients		22,337,500	12,870,000
Social costs to clients			
Contract revenues as opportunity costs		4,572,459	3,254,541
		17,765,041	9,615,459

Source : Abt Associates Inc., Annual Report and Social Audit, 1971.

(iv) Whether the company is planning its affairs in such a manner that it is able to provide dignity of labour, eradicate unemployment and employ persons according to their abilities and aptitudes.

(v) Whether the organisation, in the matter of recruitment, promotion and diversification, is following a policy of discrimination on grounds of race, religion, political views, social status, sex etc. Has it been able to, by its policies, counteract such discrimination by others?

(vi) Are the company's policies encouraging talents in the field of its activity or in ancillary and related fields of work?

(vii) Whether the working conditions are safe, healthy, and conducive to the development of health and personality of its employees?

(viii) Whether the organisation is motivated by a desire for the well-being of its employees? Has it been taking steps by way of providing insurance, old-age pensions and other retirement and consequential benefits?

(ix) Whether the undertaking is developing an urge amongst its employees to do research and development work and encourage them for new inventions and devices?

(x) Whether the organisation is respecting the rights of labour to organise and have collective bargaining?

(xi) What is the policy of the corporation in the matter of prices, wages and profits and is it progressive in its approach?

(xiii) Whether the corporation is honest in its dealings with persons who come in contact with it and does not resort to such practices as adulteration, cheating and producing substandard goods?

(xiii) Whether it is taking due care to avoid pollution?

(xiv) Whether it is taking due care of consumers and does not indulge in various monopolistic restrictive and unfair trade practices?

(xv) Whether it is catering to consumers' satisfaction and is paying due attention to consumers' grievances?

(xvi) Whether it is taking due care and precaution in the marketing of goods which are hazardous to health or life.

(xvii) Whether it is taking precaution not to indulge in fraudulent, deceitful and grossly misleading information in advertising and in other trade activities.

(xviii) Whether the public finances obtained from banks and other financial institutions are being properly utilised.

(xix) That the auditors should warn the government and the shareholders about the true state of affairs of companies.

(xx) That the auditors should raise warning signals of any impending sickness in the industry.

CONCLUSION

In sum, a social audit is a systematic study and evaluation of an organisation's social performance as distinguished from its economic performance. It is essential for a firm's internal decision-making and for external social reporting. It mostly deals with what an organisation is doing rather than what gain results from these social activities. It provides data for comparison with standards, for comparison of different types of programmes, cost-benefit comparisons, etc. It is expressed in both quantitative and qualitative terms.

A four-step process may be recommended for engaging in a social audit. *First*, a firm must itemise all the activities that have a potential social impact. *Second,* the circumstances leading to these actions or activities must be explained. *Third*, some evaluation of the programmes must be conducted. *Finally*, the corporation must examine the relationship between the goals of the firm and those of society to see how the programmes relate to each other.

Social Audit in India

In India, the TISCO has been the first company to set up a Social Audit Committee for conducting social audit of its work under the chairmanship of Justice S.P. Kotwal, and Prof. Rajni Kothari and Prof. P.G. Mavalankar as members. This Committee was entrusted with the task of "examining and reporting whether, and the extent to which, the TISCO has fulfilled the objectives contained in Clause 3A of its Articles of Association regarding its social and moral responsibilities to the consumers, employees, shareholders, and the local community." The Committee opined, "On an examination of all aspects, the company has fulfilled its obligations to all concerned."

CHAPTER 16

BUSINESS ETHICS

- Introduction
- Principles of Business Ethics
- Ethics in Practice
- Unethical Practices
- Indian Managers and Business Ethics

INTRODUCTION

The word "ethics" is derived from the Greek word "ethos", which refers to character. Webster defines "ethics" as "The discipline dealing with that which is good and bad and with moral duty and obligations."

The term "ethical" is defined by the Webster's dictionary as conforming to professional standard of conduct. What is lawful need not necessarily be ethical as "law is generally concerned only with the minimum regulation necessary for public order while ethics examines both the *individual* and the *social* good in all dimensions."[1]

Baumhart has given the following definitions: *Ethical* : concerning principles of human conduct; according to common usage, the following terms are more or less synonymous with ethical: *moral, good, right, just, honest. "Ethical standards*: principles or ideals of human conduct."[2]

In general, ethics deals more with good than with evil. An action is right or moral, in the view of a given school of thought if it is consistent with a principle verified to the satisfaction of its adherents. Immorality is an action inconsistent with these principles. Obviously, the same action may be moral or immoral, depending upon the school of moral thought to which one subscribes. Again, what is moral in our society may be immoral in another.

Business Ethics

To some, it is very surprising that there should be a term called "business ethics". They agree that what is sauce for the goose is sauce for the gander, that the norms of conduct that apply to common men should also apply to the businessmen. But the businessman's ethics merit special attention because of their specific problems and opportunities, unlike those faced by the society in general. The basic ethical standards are universal, the difference lies in the application of ethical principles to business situations. The actions of businessmen in these situations "their objects, intentions, circumstances, outcome of these actions, and the right or wrong of it, is the domain the business ethic."[3]

The business community forms such a large part of society that "ethics of businessmen" or "business ethics" are of social importance. This business ethics, we may define as: "*Businessman's integrity so far as his conduct or behaviour is concerned in all fields of business as well as towards the society and other businesses*."

"Business ethics" deals with morality in the business environment. It involves moral judgements, based on the understanding of the norms of society. Ethics extends beyond the legal question and involves goodness or badness of an act. Therefore, an action may be legally right but ethically wrong. For example, in a small village, a trader may charge a high price for his product; and legally he may be entitled to do so but morally, this is not fair.

Business morality is the application of moral principles to business problems. Business practices, therefore, become moral and fair or immoral and unfair if they are consistent or

1. Garrett, Thomas M., *Business Ethics*, Times of India Press, Mumbai, 1970.
2. Baumhart, R., *Ethics in Business*, Holt, Reinhart and Winston, New York, 1968, p.10.
3. Baumhart, R., *op. cit.*, p.15.

inconsistent with a particular moral theory. "Morals" refer to any generally accepted customs of conduct and right living in a society.

Garrett has defined "ethics" and "business ethics" thus:

"Ethics is the science of judging specifically human ends and the relationship of means of those ends. In some way, it is also the art of controlling means so that they will serve specifically human needs."[4] From this point of view, ethics involves the use of any human knowledge whatsoever which has something to tell us about the relations between men or about the suitability of the available instruments. As an art, it involves techniques of judging and decision-making as well as the tools of social control and personal development. Ethics is or should be involved in all human activities.

"Business ethics is concerned primarily with the relationship of business goals and techniques to specific human needs."[5] It studies the impact of acts on the good of the individual, the firm, the business community and the society as a whole. *Business ethics, in other words, studies the special obligations which a man and a citizen accepts when he becomes a part of the world of commerce.*[6]

Business system is a means, not an end. It is neither a sacred cow, nor an ultimate value. It is a tool to be re-evaluated in terms of the goals it is supposed to serve. The system itself is controlled by firms and the firms by individuals. Men must do the evaluating and make the changes necessary to bring the system more closely into line with the changing needs of men and society of which they are a part.

Need for Business Ethics

The need for business ethics, i.e., for a set of generally accepted standards of personal conduct, is evident throughout the world. The legislative representatives establish statues and administrative laws in critical areas of inter-personal conduct where the safety and personal welfare of the people can be vitally affected by unethical practices. For furthering ethical practices in business community and professional people, the concept of Professional Codes or Codes of Conduct have also assumed great importance.

These have been and are being developed by the trade associations concerned with these broad objectives:

(i) publication of a Code of Ethics is likely to improve the confidence of customers, clients, employees, etc., in the quality of service they may expect;

(ii) business codes govern the inter-relationships of the members. Business cannot be carried on, in its present complexity, without trust in the ethical standards of vendors and suppliers, of financiers and of government agencies;

(iii) the interest of all those who deal with business – the stock-holders, employees, customers, competitors, dealers and suppliers, and the local community – need be protected from the unethical and dubious ways of dealing and exploitation.

(iv) the consumer's right can be saved and served well only when there is some type of moral binding on the business community: (a) the consumer has the right to be informed; (b) he has the right to safety; (c) he has the right to choose; and (d) he has the right to be heard.

4. Garrett, Thomas M., *Business Ethics*, The Times of India Press, Mumbai, 1970, p. 4.
5. *Ibid.*, p. 4.
6. *Ibid.*, p. 5.

(v) business today is confronted with major groups of social issues: (a) people-oriented management; (b) ecology and environmental protection; (c) consumerism; and (d) the energy crisis and resource utilisation and development. These issues being inter-related, need that business should feel some obligation for meeting these issues.

What Affects Business Ethics?

The business executive working as a professional manager has to decide what is ethical or unethical. Many factors influence this decision. In part, what is ethical is based on:

(a) *The individual's personal code of behaviour*. The personal Code of Behaviour is the result of the complex environment that influences one's life.

(b) *The ethical standards imposed on a manager by his superiors* also influence him in his decisions as to the morality of behaviour. If the superior condones unethical activities such as padding expenses accounts, the subordinate is encouraged to look upon this activity as an acceptable practice.

(c) *The policies of the company* also influence the determination of ethical conduct. Standards of behaviour in an industry are often influenced greatly by the dominant firms in that industry. The authors of the company policy obviously have an effect that is decisive. Garrett puts this idea when he says: "The best protection is the example presented by the conduct of top management and the atmosphere it creates, when leaders are scrupulous, the employees know what is considered right. When example is supported by explicit policy, the followers have a clear idea of how to translate the example of leaders into action. When policy is enforced and enforcement reinforced, the employees know that 'honesty is the best policy in this company".[7]

(d) *The ethical climate of a country*. If, it is poor, then only giant corporations and large undertakings can stand competition and be viable; a small concern is apt to go bankrupt, since business is concerned with employment of a large number of persons, it has the obligation to see that it adheres to an ethical atmosphere. However, considerable differences occur among managers as to what is ethical or unethical; and business truly lacks a Code of Ethics.

Coverage of Business Ethics

In order that the business system functions successfully, brings benefits to the people and the society and survives the economic and ideological conflicts, it must do the following:[8]

1. It must produce vast quantities of goods and services; but the Gross Net Product is not the end in itself, but it is a means to an end, which is satisfaction of the human needs.

2. Business leaders are allocators of scarce resources, they must realise their moral duties in this respect, and must function as allocators wisely and morally.

3. They have a responsibility for product selectivity. They have a moral duty to produce goods and services contributive to the well-being of man.

As Eells has said: "Responsible product selectively may mean the exclusion of product lines that promise large returns but would require the use of capital for socially dubious purposes. A company may choose among alternatives, none of which will result in socially deleterious products and services, but some of which may contribute more substantially to the upbuilding of the kind of community the responsible executive wants to see."[9]

7. Garrett, Thomas, M.S.J. *Ethics in Business*, Sheed and Word, New York, 1963, p. 84.
8. Hagen, Willis W. "Ethics in Business", *Advanced Management Journal*, April 1965, pp. 14-20.
9. Eells, Richard, *The Meaning of Modern Business*, Columbia University Press, New York, 1990, pp. 230-231.

4. The business must make an equitable distribution to each individual contributor of the greatest quantity of material things exchanged for his contribution of services and property to the system; i.e., *the management must play a judicial role in balancing the claims of all groups and individuals* — even of society as a whole —*for their contribution toward the product of the economy*.

5. The business must be able to work within the broad concept of moral ideals, i.e., as Peter Drucker has said, "It must give status and function to the individual, and it must give him justice of equal opportunities. This does not mean that the economic purpose of the corporation's efficient production is to be subordinated to its social function, or that the fulfilment of society's basic beliefs is to be subordinated to the profit and survival interest of the individual business. The corporation can only function as the representative social institution of our society if it can fulfil its social functions in a manner which strengthens it as an efficient producer, and *vice versa*. But, as the representative social institution of our society, the corporation, in addition to being an economic tool, is a political and social body; its social function as a community is as important as its economic function as an efficient producer".[10]

6. The corporation must be concerned not only with its responsibilities to suppliers of capital, but to the suppliers of services, to the suppliers of trained manpower (education institute), to the supplier of police and fire protection, and of sanitary facilities and, in general, of local environment in which the business can operate (the community), and to the suppliers of almost endless factors that merge into its product and enable its continued existence. This it must do in its own interest and to retain the area of decision-making in its management.

Henry Ford II has very aptly said: "If we are to preserve the good name of our respective companies, our corporate executives must keep their own house in order. If and when they fail to do so, the house cleaning job will certainly be put in the less friendly hands. We now run a serious risk of having codes with sharp teeth imposed on business by the legislature. Because such codes would further restrict the areas of free business action and decision, we must, in our various companies and industries, see to the establishment of our own formal principles of ethical practice, plus the effective means of self-policing those principles."[11]

7. The business, like all good citizens, is not only expected to "making a living" for itself, but also to contribute to the community and to society. A good citizen concerns himself with social and public matters and cannot live in isolation, so also the corporation cannot do less if it hopes to retain an image of respectability in society.

8. The firm should exist, from the individual point of view, to supply income, power, prestige, creative satisfaction or a combination of these to those who work for or with it. In other words, the manager is obliged to run the firm as efficiently as possible within the limits set by the basic ethics.[12]

PRINCIPLES OF BUSINESS ETHICS

There are certain basic principles of business ethics which may be stated as below:

1. *Human value grows with the increase in size of business to which it applies*. Therefore, the importance and dignity of human labour has not only to be acknowledged and accepted but practically applied to.

10. Drucker, Peter F., *Concept of the Corporation*, Beacon Press, Boston, 1962, p.140.
11. Ford II, Henry, "Business Ethics and Law," *Management Review*, August, 1961, Vol. 50, No. 8, pp. 54-55.
12. Garrett, Thomas, M., *op. cit.*, p. 25.

2. *The purpose of all economic activity is to meet consumer needs and to contribute to the well-being of the community;* for "*business is not an end in itself but is only a means to achieve an end.*" The end is man himself and the individual. Therefore, business has to contribute to man's material happiness and to his mental, moral and spiritual growth.

3. "*Service first and profit next*" is the motto which business should follow in practice; for this is based on the "Theory of Trusteeship", which according to Gandhiji expresses the inherent responsibility of a business enterprise towards its consumers, workers, shareholders, and the community and the mutual responsibilities of these to one another. In other words, "*business must be held in trust legally and morally for the benefit of the people whom the business wants to serve.*" This is why the present business now has adopted the view of serving the community.

4. *Business must be just and humane as well as efficient and dynamic*. Modern business has manifold responsibilities, *viz.*, to itself, to its customers, workers, shareholders, community and the state; and the task of management is to "*reconcile and harmonise these separate and sometimes conflicting responsibilities.*"

5. The social role of business can best be assumed in an atmosphere of freedom into the least possible restraint on healthy and open competition; and absence of undesirable restrictions or interference from the government. As such "*concentration and monopoly* have to be watched *and guarded and, wherever necessary, dispersed.*"

6. *Every business has an overriding obligation to make the fullest* and best possible use of its inputs – material and human – so that the output produced aids in removing poverty and people's distress and raises their standard of living.

The late American President Woodrow Wilson had laid down four important principles for the proper conduct of business, viz.,

(i) "*The rule of publicity*: Let the people know what it is going to do. Suspicion, false conjecture, and misunderstanding arise out the secretiveness.

(ii) *The rule of equivalent price*: Let the public receive goods and services fully equivalent to the money paid.

(iii) *The rule of conscience in business* : To emphasise that the rules of business games must be of a higher order than those of an ordinary game, sustained by moral judgement of honourable men; and

(iv) *The rule of spirit of service* : To see that the things you do for the public and get money for it is the best thing of that kind that can be done."

ETHICS IN PRACTICE

Ethics Regarding Employees

The ethics of hiring and firing are governed by the dignity of the workers, by the contractual relation and by the purpose of the firm.

The ethics of hiring is governed by the norm of efficiency or the ability and willingness to serve the social good of the company and the public. Job specifications are defined by managers to which the general culture, voice, diction, poise, etc. are relevant. If hiring is done on the basis of job specifications, there is no discrimination; but if it is done on caprice or prejudice, *it is irrational and unethical.*

Firing or dismissal of the employee is based upon certain obligations to the employees, such as: (a) *It must be done only for a just cause*, such as mechanisation, reduction in output, violation of discipline or conduct harmful to other workers, old age, frequent illness, negligence, and prolonged absenteeism which is harmful to other business or other workers. The whim of the employer, his personal political convictions, and the annoying mannerism of an employee are not just cause. (b) *It must also appear just* if the potentially harmful effects of dismissal are to be mitigated, i.e., it is not made arbitrarily and this reinforces the confidence of the workers. (c) *It must mitigate the harmful effects of dismissal*, such as giving adequate notice, arranging for retraining or reallocation of workers etc.

Similarly, in promotion and transfers also, justice should be followed.

Ethics regarding wages and working conditions demands fairness and justice from the employees. Wages must be related to the contribution to the firm, to the market for both labour and products, to the competitive position of the company and to the power of the unions as well as the needs of workers and their families. If any of these factors is ignored, great harm may result. These can be decided through a mutual agreement, which is reasonable and reached without fraud, passion, power or undue pressure or ignorance.

Stabilisation of work and employment is another demand of the employee, for he fears insecurity as much as he fears poverty; and automation, the growth of seasonal industries, and plant re-allocation threaten security. Therefore, before resorting to these, the employers should make the necessary agreements with the worker's unions.

Ethics demands that a worker should not be treated as a "thing". Neither should he or his family be exposed to physical, psychological or natural harm without a proportionate reason. To disregard safety in these areas is to disregard the good of a human being and even the simplest ethical principle, "*safety is ethically important*".

Good ethics and good business require that reasonable methods be taken for the protection of the worker and the firm. New workers need to be informed of the ethical pitfalls connected with their jobs. A watchful eye should be kept lest workers should be exploited. "There are individuals who use a place of business to sell tickets for fraudulent lotteries, there are occasional supervisors who use their staff as a part of an informal harem. There are scoundrels who coerce the staff to co-operate in all sorts of unethical practices under the threat of false denunciation and subsequent dismissal." Such situations need protection of the employees.

Ethics Regarding Information Secrecy

When some information becomes more and more vital to business, *secrecy becomes a major ethical concern*. A secret is a knowledge which a person has a right and/or an obligation to keep hidden. These obligatory secrets always involve situations in which revelation of the knowledge would cause serious harm or the violation of a contract. These secrets may be *natural, promised*, and *professional*.

The *natural secret* involves knowledge of something which by its nature will cause harm if revealed. Unless there is a proportionate reason, the secret should not be disclosed. The *promised secret* involves a natural secret, the obligation to keep it arises from the contract or promise by which one binds itself. These may be revealed when silence will cause more harm than good. *The professional secret* involves not only the above two types of secrets but also the reputation of a group, whose services are necessary for society (doctors, lawyers, accountants, etc). Only for a very serious reason, such secret may be revealed.

Secrets revealed must be made in such a way as to minimise harm; to protect the revealer from a proportionate harm, but not to gain some advantage to which he has no right; it can be revealed by action as well as by word or gesture.

Non-obligatory secrets may be revealed if the person possessing such secrets so wishes.

The employer has an obligation to keep secret a great deal of information about the employee, regarding his health reports, psychological and psychiatric tests, secret investigations of the employee's credit and activities, etc. *Such information must be used ethically*, i.e., not made public without the employee's permission, or else the employer may be guilty of violation of privacy.

Ethics and Honesty

It is unethical to have double standards in business, because it only encourages dishonesty. Dishonest personnel should be dealt with strictly. Ethics demands to condemn them, since, allowed to continue, it disrupts the working of business and exposes innocent persons to unnecessary losses.

Ethics regarding expense accounts demands that if a flat expense allowance has been allowed to an employee, he need not make an accounting. Other expenses reasonably incurred must be reimbursed; but these must be satisfactorily accounted for.

Theft of company's property or temptation to steal can be reduced, if a worker is paid regularly and reasonably.

Ethics Regarding Buyers

The seller must respect the rights of the buyers and users of his products; should recognise them as "human beings" rather than as "enemies or sheep to be shorn" for making a profit. Therefore, there must be a fair sales contract based upon a free agreement. *The seller is unethical* whenever he deliberately *uses* fraud or *power,* or *creates* ignorance and passion in order to gain an advantage. "*Fraud*" exists when there is a deliberate attempt to deceive someone about a material fact. "*Lying*" exists whenever one speaks against his own mind in circumstances where the other has a reasonable expectation of the truth, whether the matter be serious or not. Sound ethics condemns *not only the intent to deceive but also the risking or permitting of deception without a proportionate reason*. Therefore, the greater the danger to deceive and the larger the number of persons who may be harmed, the greater is the obligation to give warnings, to control sale and use, to remedy the defects in the product. These require the seller to disclose latent material defects to the buyer if there is to be a valid contract. The buyer has the right to be "informed", to "safety", to "be compensated", etc.

Ethics of Business Relationship

Relations with competitors should be governed by basic ethics and the rules of fair play rather than by the ethics of self-defence and warfare. Unethical competition turns rivalry into a ruthless battle. Such competition is often done in many ways, e.g., (i) harming a competitor by interfering with his production and distribution; (ii) encouraging labour disputes and work stoppages as well as boycotts of a competitor's products; (iii) hiring away of key employees; or use of market power to move the competitor's products out of the market; (iv) extorting, bribing and the granting of discriminatory advertising allowances or brokerage fees; (v) price-cutting; (vi) Making disparaging statements about the competitor's products or quality; etc.

What is needed is that an ethical businessman must resist the temptation of retaliating against the rival, for such unethical attacks destroys confidence in business and introduces chaos in place of order; and substitutes tricks for real competence and leads to a weakening of all human ideals. The correct solution is to secure through combined efforts such regulations as are necessary to protect honest businessmen.

UNETHICAL PRACTICES

Foremost among the types of unethical practices that have developed in business is that of "buyers business, using baits such as bribes, grafts, the entertainment of buyers by providing call girls or presenting them expensive gifts". *Corruption and unethical practices go together and exist side by side*, as would be clear from the following:

"Even after an order has been passed by a higher authority, the order was not communicated to the applicant until he has paid illegal gratification to the subordinate concerned."

"Corruption is encouraged because business cannot wait and has to be kept going as an existing concern while government red-tape takes time."

"The advance of technology and science is contributing to the emergence of a mass society with a large rank and file and a small controlling elite, encouraging the growth of monopolies, the rise of managerial class often amorphous and anonymous, and that of intricate institutional mechanisms."

Bribe has to be given because:

(i) other competitors blantantly do so and purchase the decisions;

(ii) graft is demanded in return for information or business rendered;

(iii) entertainment of personnel (official or influential customers) to procure favours is necessary by providing call girls or making all arrangements in a posh hotel;

(iv) payment of regular kick-back money to various government officials, particularly central excise, customs, inspection, income-tax officials and many others;

(v) in case of government tenders, the situation often arises of undercutting of prices and lowering prices after tenders are opened; and for buying items from the lowest quoted firms, regardless of qualitative assessment;

(vi) of getting promotions of certain individuals to higher posts who do not deserve to be promoted, or transfers to a place of one's choice, especially in public sector industries;

(vii) giving costly presents to attract deposits for a bank and investment company; or getting business for an insurance company; offering employment to sons and daughters or relatives, and thereby attracting deposits of public sector corporations and companies;

(viii) taking advantage of the scarcity situation and putting up the price of articles with a view to making larger margins and thereby ignoring social obligations to the community. The contractors and suppliers, etc. give bribes to engineers and accountants of the P.W.D., Irrigation or Construction Departments;

(ix) demanding payment of any sort for the execution (or non-execution) of acts which one is obliged to perform or to omit under the terms of his work of contract, i.e., *extortion*, which includes all the evils of bribery plus the violation of the salesman's right to fair and equal treatment.

INDIAN MANAGERS AND BUSINESS ETHICS

A survey undertaken by Prof. Monappa of 115 business executives, attending the middle and senior management programme of the I.I.M., Ahmedabad and belonging to different industries, ages, educational standards, religious affiliations and income groups, has revealed some notable results regarding Indian managers' attitude towards "Business Ethics", The findings are reproduced below.[13]. A new realisation has dawned upon businessmen about their responsibilities towards the employees, shareholders, etc.

"A majority of business managers believe in good ethics; various circumstances like unnatural competition, company policy and a plethora of rules and regulations often prevent the mangers from putting this belief into practice.

- The problems that caused managers the greatest concern were those which involved 'buying business' using gifts, bribes, personal favours, etc. Personal problems also caused anxiety, but mostly due to a conflict of the head and heart when emotions came in the way of responsible decision-making.
- Most managers do take time in making a decision to consider the ethical implications.
- Managers reiterated the importance of company policy in influencing ethical action. A man's personal code of conduct was given only a second place.
- The influence of supervisors, through whom the company policy is most often transmitted, was considered important in influencing ethical action.
- Dishonest methods used by competitors and the unethical climate in the industry were often cited as deterrents to the honest transaction of business.
- Corruption and greed of government officials, red-tapism, nepotism, and suffocating regulations were considered obstacles to ethical business behaviour.
- The attitudes and reactions of the older business managers to situations demonstrated a greater ethical awareness than those of younger ones.
- The size of the company, by and large, had no discernible influence on ethical decision-making.
- Managers were dissatisfied with the idea that profits should be the only guidelines for a businessman in decision-making.
- Formal education and training did not seem to have stimulated the desire to act honestly.
- The ethical attitudes of those who belonged to a religion which was more organised were no better than those in whose religion there is no much scope for guidance.
- Certain areas (construction, engineering, research and development, banking, investment and insurance) seemed more prone to encouraging unethical practices than others.
- A majority of the managers welcomed the idea of a code of conduct and felt it would help to improve the ethical climate in the country.
- Managers felt that the management of each company (i.e., self-regulation) would be the authority best suited to enforce the code."

13. Monappa, Arun, *Ethical Attitudes of Indian Managers*, All-India Management Association, New Delhi, 1977, pp.11-12.

Indian Ethos vis-a-vis Management Thought

True holistic and comprehensive principles of management philosophy could not be developed by Western management principles. Indian ancient wisdom provides value-based holistic approach. Unity and harmony among the following factors should be developed under holism. They are : spirit and science, values and skills, subject and object, left-brain skills and right brain skills, subjective and objective, management of self and management of other people, man and machine, economic development, human and ecological development, Profit motive and service to the society, individual benefit and public benefit, internal development and external development and quality of life and quantity of life.

Business was created by society as an instrument of wealth for welfare to attain socially desirable or needed goals under Indian ethos and insight. These goals should be achieved through ethically worthy means (i.e., value-driven means and value-driven goals) resulting in a generation of healthy, wholesome individuals who carry human and ethical values and positive impulses in their community.

The management acquires new principles if the business adopts value oriented holistic approach. Indian ethos desire individuals to emerge as important, positive, wholesome, harmonious individuals with a sense of growing towards their total fulfilment. Then managers would create a healthy, wholesome, harmonious and happy community. The Indian wisdom emphasises on the concepts like sacrificing individual desires in favour of social benefits, preferring long-term benefits over short term gains, sharing in joy and a sense of cosmic harmony. Business is regarded as a means for evolution of human society towards its own perfection. Exhibit 1 presents the Western and Indian approaches to organisation and management theory.

Indian insight can bring about synthesis through holistic approach. Two broad modifications were introduced in traditional theory *viz.*, i) behavioural science emphasised on psycho-social system and human aspects of management and ii) management science emphasised on the economic technical system and qualification, mathematical models and the application of computer technology. Behavioural sciences have a humanistic approach while management sciences and traditional schools of management emphasise on mechanistic or classical design (see Exhibit 2). The systems approach integrates classical school, behavioural sciences, management science and decision making school of management thought.[14]

Indian Ethos in Management : The following are some of the Indian ethos relevant to management.

1. All work is an opportunity for doing good to the world and thus gaining materially and spiritually in our lives.
2. Strength and inspiration for excelling in work comes from Divine.
3. He who works with calm and even mind achieves the most.
4. As we think, so we succeed, so we become. Attention to means ensures the end.
5. By mutual cooperation, respect and fellow feeling all of us will enjoy the highest good both material and spiritual.[15]

14. S.A. Sherlekar, *Ethics in Management,* Himalaya Publishing House, Mumbai. 1998, pp. 93-95.
15. *Ibid.*, p. 49.

Exhibit 16.1 : Western and Indian Approaches to Organisation and Management

Traditional Western Approach	*Modern Western Approach*	*Indian Approach*
Taylor Scientific Management (Efficient Task Performance) Weber Bureaucratic Model (Authority and Structure) Fayol Administrative or process Management Theory (Universal Management Principles).	Mayo (Hawthrone Studies) Human Relations Maslow, MacGregor, etc.; Behavioural Sciences (Psychological, cultural and sociological issues) Quantitative decision-making Management Sciences (OP) (Economic-technical Rationality)	Views on organisation as: 1. Open, adaptive system in a broader environment. 2. Goal oriented; including 3. A technical sub-system 4. A structural sub-system 5. A psycho-social subsystem and co-ordinated by 6. A managerial system. (Socio-economic and technological system)
1900-1930	1930-1960	1960-onwards

Source : S.A. Sherlekar, *op. cit.*, p. 95.

Exhibit 16.2 : Classical Versus Humanistic Designs

Mechanistic or Classical Design	*Organic or Humanistic Design*
1. Closed systems view of organisations– all variables under management control – static environment.	1. Open and adaptable systems view of organisation existing in a dynamic environment.
2. Full division of work leading to job specialisation and standardisation.	2. Moderate division of work leading to job enlargement, job enrichment.
3. Higher degree of centralisation.	3. Higher degree of decentralisation.
4. Authority and command leading to bureaucratic, authoritarian and autocratic management.	4. Authority, subject to acceptance from subordinates, leading to democratic participative management – decisions by concensus.
5. Tight hierarchical structure with chain of command, and management by command.	5. Loose project organisation and management by consultation and participation.
6. Vertical communication downward more dominant.	6. Multidirectional and free communication, Inter/Intra Network.
7. Negative environment for development of human resources due to limited decentralisation.	7. Positive environment for development of human resources due to adequate decentralisation.
8. Organisation could satisfy only maintenance of economic needs.	8. Ample scope for motivation needs-higher level wants.
9. Relatively tight and close control over subordinates.	9. Increasing reliance on management by objectives (self-control).

10. Rigid policies, procedures, rules and methods – leading to mechanistic organisation.	10. Flexible policies, procedures, methods leading to humanistic and flexible organisation.
11. Formal organisation dominating due to autocratic approach.	11. Integration of formal and informal organisation due to democratic approach.
12. Threatening and performance oriented job environment.	12. Supportive and development oriented job environment.
13. Production centred approach of management.	13. Customer-employee oriented management approach.
14. Theory X approach of leadership.	14. Theory Y approach of leadership.

Source : *Ibid.*, pp. 95-96.

Business ethics depend on ethics of the people, culture of the country, traditions and behaviour of the people. In fact, the culture, traditions and behaviour of Western countries vary significantly from those of Eastern countries and particularly India. The business and managerial ethics of Western countries and Eastern countries particularly India are presented in Exhibit 16.3.

Business and managerial ethics are not static and standard. They go on changing over the period. The changes in business and managerial ethics being significant changes in management concepts and definitions of various terms. In fact some terms or concepts become irrelevant after some time. The changes in the management concepts due to changes in business ethics are presented in Exhibit. 16.4

Managerial Effectiveness

Managers in recent times realised that their job is to produce performers rather than producing results. The top management is visionary. They see the future of the company for the next 20 to 50 years. Managers translate the vision into projects, and they produce performers who are self motivated, self committed and self directed.

Modern managers activities include :

(i) They set the examples for others and for the future managers rather than mere instructing their subordinates.

(ii) They empower their subordinates rather than leading. In other words, they transmit their skills, knowledge, abilities and expertise to their subordinates in addition to delegating their authority to the subordinates.

(iii) Managers are creative rather than mechanistic. In other words, managers always would like to have new methods, new approaches and innovative aspects rather than repeating the old methods and performing the old activities.

(iv) Modern managers are more responsible or accountable to their jobs or duties rather than exercising the power like bureaucrats. Exhibit 16.5 presents new mind set of managers.

Fig 16.1 Presents the activities of the modern managers.

Modern managers approaches towards skills include :

(i) open style rather than rigidity (ii) intuition rather than intellectual (iii) managing self in addition to managing others (iv) viewing intangible factors in addition to tangible factors (v) unifying the total organisation and viewing it as one system rather than breaking it and viewing only a part of it [16]. The approach of the modern managers regarding skills is presented in fig 16.2

Exhibit 16.3 : Business and Managerial Ethics in Western and Eastern Countries and India.

Items	*In Western Countries*	*In Eastern Countries and India.*
1. Belief	Production, Productivity, profit *at any cost.*	Material gain, with belief in achieving human and social welfare also.
2. Guidance	Management guided by mind only, led away by ego and desire. Soul-less management.	Management by consciousness, power beyond mind *i.e.,* soul. Interiorised Management.
3. Emphasis	Worker development, Management of others, Profit maximisation, Human being given only lip sympathy.	Development of Man Integrated Growth Harmony, Happiness and Health, Management of Self.
4. Tools	5 Ms as Resources – men, money, materials, machines, markets. Science & Technology, Information for decision making.	Men, Machines, Materials and Methods as Conscious Partners – all having consciousness whether manifested or dormant. Information and intuition for decisions Ethics and values combined with skills.
5. Problem-solving	Conflict resolution by negotiation, compromise, arbitration liquidation of differences only for a temporary period. No reference to higher consciousness.	Conflicts resolution through integration and synthesis on stressing superordinate common goals so that enduring harmony and unity is assured. Self-introspection, stepping back aids for solution.
6. Decision making	Brain-storming (Round the table approach).	Brain-stilling (Room of silence).
7. Development process	Physical, Vital and Mental only. Soul or Spirit ignored. Material development only even at the cost of man and nature.	Integrated Development, Whole-man approach, breath-control and meditation emphasised. Human Enrichment and Total quality.
8. Approach	External Behaviour Mental, Material, Selfish only, Soulless.	Noble Attitudes, Inner guidance, Team spirit, Total Harmony, Global good.

Source : S.A. Sherlekar, *Ethics in Management,* Himalaya Publishing House, 1998, p.45.

16. *Ibid.,* pp. 48-49.

Exhibit 16.4 : Changes in Management concepts due to changes in Business Ethics

Term	*Previous Concept*	*Changed Concept*
1. Management	Gettings things done.	Helping other people to produce extraordinary results.
2. Productivity	Related to plant capacity.	Related to men's capability.
3. Planning	Management by results.	Management by strategy.
4. Effective supervision	Concern for task and not for people.	Produce performers. Help the subordinates to develop leadership quality.
5. Motivation of People	Maslow's theory of needs with some modifications.	Emphasis on self-motivation by subordinates to have creative joy and autonomy.
6. Resources	Reliance almost on external resources.	Reliance almost on internal resources.
7. Health of the Company.	Balance Sheet and Profit/Loss A/C money-oriented.	People oriented performance, environment friendly. Private Public benefit.
8. Profitability	In terms of money. Social costs	In terms of good public image. not included in Balance Sheet. Social costs internalised. Trust of customers and society.
9. Hygiene factor	Attention only on job enrichment.	Primary emphasis on mind enrichment.
10. Rights and duties	Emphasis on taking not on giving. Rights become primary. Duties become subsidiary.	Emphasis on giving - taking. Duties given great importance and Rights assume secondary value.
11. Marketing	Keen competition to capture and retain demand; market driven economy.	Through co-operation by playing complementary role. Social awareness in marketing.
12. System	Set of inter-related elements working as a whole. Hard-ware aspect. More emphasis on quantity and objective aspect.	Pattern of particular response expressed through organisational functioning. Software aspect. Equal emphasis on quality/quantity with emphasis on subjective aspect.
13. Structure	Hierarchical.	Organic evolution, autonomous.
14. Growth	Ultimately dependent on turnover of goods.	Co-ordinating private and public benefit.
15. Job satisfaction	Hygiene factor. Creativity ignored.	Through innovation uniqueness, extraordinary result, trouble shooting.
16. Training	Functional skills not value oriented and holistic.	Value oriented. Holistic approach and equal emphasis on both (values/skills).
17. Man-Machine Equation	Machine dominates man as human being receives lip	Man behind the machine given due regard. Healthy

	sympathy.	philosophy of life. Emotional stability.
18. Man Placement	As per qualifications and experiences.	More stress on natural inclination and character.
19. Quality	Product quality by I.S.O., TQM., Q.C., Human value, quality plays minor role. We have crises of Value, Adulteration is widespread.	Human quality, values, character, mind enrichment, whole-man approach. Mind and matter are given *equal* treatment.

Source : *Ibid.*, pp. 46-47.

Exhibit 16.5 : New Mind set of the Managers due to change in Business Ethics

Previous Mind Set	*New Mind Set*
1. Produce results	1. Produce performers.
2. Organise men, materials, machines and money.	2. Mobilise men and sound out other readiness.
3. Plan, set goals, prepare schedules, checklists.	3. Obtain agreement and commitment on means and ends.
4. Motivate, praise, reprimand, punish, push people.	4. Inspire, empower, celebrate success, mourn failure, draw people.
5. Check, control, report at the command post.	5. Set personal example; visible, accessible on the move.
6. Co-ordinate, requisition, convene meetings.	6. Facilitate, show ways to overcome obstacles, take part in informal gatherings.
7. Instruct, issue notices, order, demand compliance.	7. Make queries, sound out ideas,encourage suggestions.
8. Manage other I-centred.	8. Manage yourself. Other-centred not egoistic.

Source : *Ibid.*, p. 47.

The Approach

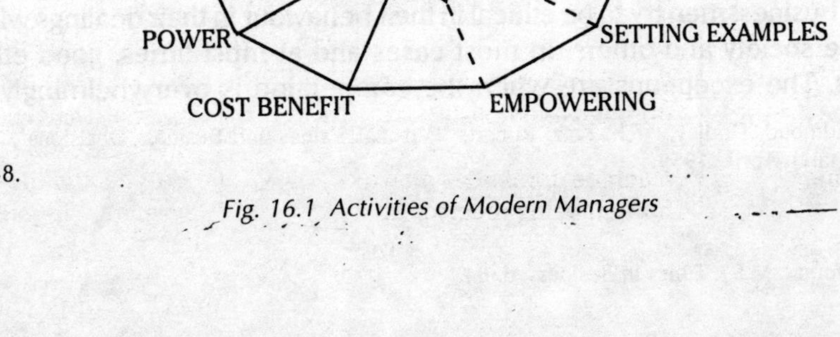

Source: Ibid; p. 48.

Fig. 16.1 Activities of Modern Managers

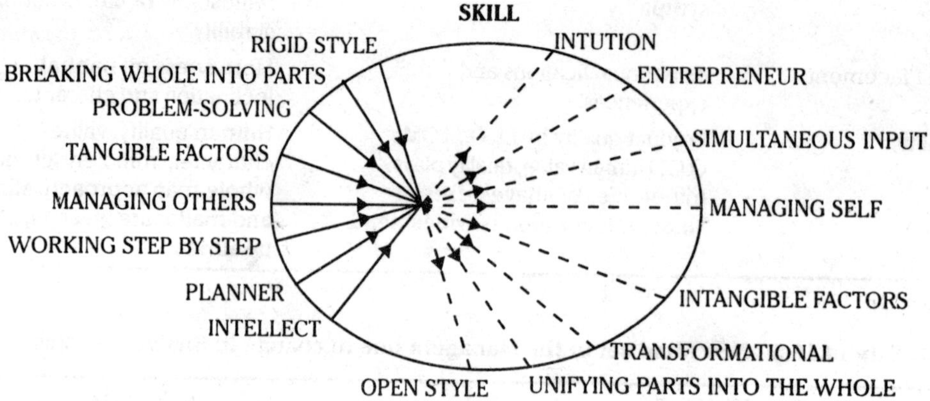

Source: Ibid;

Fig. 16.2 Modern Manager's Approach Regardig Skills

Good Ethics is Good Business

The most common belief is that "good ethics is good business" for it wins laurels in the long run. This has been supported by Learned, Dooley and Katz, who observed: "The businessman's reasons for supporting this saying is due to the fact that: (i) a business man that behaves ethically induces others to behave ethically towards it; (ii) ethical behaviour is a form of insurance against retaliatory acts; and (iii) a good man who steadfastly tries to be ethical... somehow always overtakes his immoral or amoral counterpart".[17] The last one means that "the unethical man preoccupied with deception cannot match the pure creative zeal of the honest individual whose energies are freed for maximum productivity and creativity".[18] But these authors conclude that "The view that good ethics is good business is not a fully adequate or satisfying guide for action.[19]

Similarly, Garrett has observed that good ethics may be a contributing factor to good business, but it cannot be regarded an infallible guide. He observes: "In all frankness, one must admit that it is not easy to be honest any more. In the first place, the honest man must often pay a price for his virtue. In the second place, it has become increasingly difficult to decide what is honest and what is 'dishonest'. This results not only from a general confusion about morals, but from loss of the old rules of thumb that worked fifty years ago but just do not seem to apply today. Even the professional moralist can have difficulties in this field for the simple reason that the facts are hard to come by. Certainly, we may feel uneasy about a certain way of acting, but it is really dishonest."[20]

Garrett reinforces the idea that "Much of the dishonesty is lured by incompetence, cowardice and myopeia. In the world of business, one tends to give rise to the other." Most managers are concerned with short-term results, and very often, it is the consideration of the immediate future that gives rise to the role conflict. It they think of the long-term advantages and do the job competently, there would be less need for them to resort to unethical acts.

So, many businessmen try to be ethical in their behaviour in their dealings with competitors, employees, the society and others. In most cases and at most times, good ethics can mean good business. The exceptions are when the competition is overwhelmingly influenced by

17. Learned, Edmond, Dooley, Arch, Katz, Robert, "Personal Values and Business Decisions", *Harvard Business Review*, March-April, 1959.
18. *Ibid.*
19. *Ibid.*
20. Garrett, Thomas. M.S.J. *Ethics in Business*, p. 64.

unhealthy practices and there are threats of violence, possibly putting the individual concerned out of business or out of job."[21]

Code of Business Ethics

A code, like a law, provides guidelines, since the limits of ethical conduct are situational. The manager knows that this is the accepted limit. A code could be formulated for a whole industry, or a company or a unit or for various units in a single company. Formulation of industry code is a delicate task and might prove as difficult as its enforcement. Executives from different industries should, therefore, use all their knowledge and experience to formulate the code. Depending on the choice of the enforcing authority (i.e., the Management Associations), the members chosen should form a part of those involved in drawing up the code, to understand the tenets laid down and its implications, so that no ambiguity arises at the time of its implementation. In helping to formulate the code, the government representatives and politicians should also be involved so that more restraint is put on the part of the members and the officials in trying to cut corners, knowing that there will be quick censure in the case of violation of the code. The politician and government officials and those in power should realise that they cannot continue to behave unethically, using power for narrow political ends and still expect the business community to act with grace and with exemplary moral standards. Mutual faith and truth has to be there. Code once drafted will not and cannot last forever. It will need frequent modifications in order that it does not become redundant and is thus rendered useless. Further, if the code imposes impossible conditions to implement or adopt, it will often be ignored. Therefore, the reality of the situation should be kept in view, besides the ethical aspects. The code cannot expect to bring about an ideal situation; but if it is to be functional, it should be compatible with regulations based on generally-accepted ideas of truthfulness and honesty; and as far as possible, it should be practicable.

Business Codes of Conduct

All business must meet certain standards of law and minimum cultural standards. All are influenced by the general cultural milieu of their time. These conduct standards may be expressed in meetings, bulletins, company magazines, employee statements, policy management, etc. They are generally in a written form.

To understand business conduct, Walton has classified them into six models.[22]

1. *The Austere Model*. It gives almost exclusive emphasis on ownership interest and profit objects.

2. *The Household Model*. Following the concept of an extended family, the model emphasises employee jobs, benefits and paternalism.

3. *The Vendor Model*. In this model, consumer interests, tastes and rights dominate the organisation.

4. *The Investment Model*. This model focuses on the organisation as an entity and thus on long-term profits and survival. In the name of enlightened self-interest, it gives some recognition to social investments along with economic ones.

5. *The Civic Model*. Its slogan is corporate citizenship. It goes beyond imposed obligations, accepts social responsibility and make a positive commitment to social needs.

21. Monappa, Arun, *op. cit.*, p. 37.
22. Walton, Clarence C, *Corporate Social Responsibilities*, Wordsworth Co., Belmont, 1967, pp. 122-141.

6. *The Creative Model.* This model encourages the organisation to become a creative instrument, serving the cause of an advanced civilization with a better quality of life. The organisation's people perform in the manner of artists, building their own creative ideas into institution's actions, leading it towards new contribution not originally formulated.

The above six models may be thought of as points on a continuum from low to high social responsibility. Regardless of the model adopted by an organisation, one of its most important jobs is to establish and blend its value together so that they become a consistent, effective system that is known and accepted by the fair primary claimant groups–investors, employees, customers and society (including government). The system must be strong enough to withstand changes by patisan pressure groups but flexible enough to move with the changing society.

Exhibit 16.6 presents Indian Ethos vis-a-vis management thought. Exhibit 16.7 presents 'our credo'

Below we give a specimen of a short code of conduct for a business:

BUSINESS CONDUCT

Since its establishment, our company (say Sarvodaya) has been and continues to be dedicated to the following principles of business conduct.

Article 1

To Maintain–

Human dignity and self-respect of the individual by supporting a sound and equitable programme of human relations and by providing the opportunity for self-expression and personal growth.

Article 2

To Earn–

A fair profit to make possible the economic stability and growth of the company and to provide a just return on the investment of stockholders.

Article 3

To Merit–

The respect and confidence of our customers, suppliers and competitors by maintaining the highest standards of product quality and service at fair prices.

Article 4

To Support–

Worthwhile community programmes and to encourage employees to participate in important community affairs.

Article 5

To Fulfil–

Our responsibility to society and government by conducting the business in a manner that will earn trust and confidence.

Article 6

To Require–

That our employees refrain from actions which constitute a conflict of interest.

Article 7

To Perpetuate–

Our priceless heritage of complete integrity in the conduct of our operations.

Exhibit 16.6 : Fair Business Practices

A workshop on "Manufacturers and Fair Business Practices–Problems and Prospects" held in November, 1983, made the following recommendations*.

Manufacturers should ensure:

— Protection of consumer interest and their rights to information, to choose and to be heard.
— Equitable distribution at times of shortages.
— Best manufacturing practices and strive for zero defects in their products.
— Quality inspection and assurance of raw materials and packaging materials and finished products.
— Uniform price on identical quantities and fair returns to distributive trade.
— Proper information of products/services to the buyers.
— Honest advertising.
— Prompt after-sales service.
— Quality, fair price and value for money to consumers.
— Adequate steps against adulteration and short weights and measures.
— Supply of spares in time.
— Fair business practices and self-regulation in self-interest and in the interest of consumers.
— More and more manufacturers should voluntarily seek certification marks like "I.S.I." and "Agmark" for their products.
— Manufacturers must communicate their problems and difficulties, and provide all the relevant information about price changes, shortages etc., to the consumers through mass media and thus try to win the confidence to the consumers.
— Maximum retail prices should be marked on all packaged commodities whether covered under Packaged Commodities Order or not.
— In all territories, make available with the dealers, price lists, preferably containing as many details about local taxes extra as is possible.
— Hold consumers's meets at least once a year and distributors' meets periodically to understand and sort out each other's problems and difficulties in an atmosphere of trust and goodwill.
— Product ingredients in a descending order of their proportion and manufacturing as well as expiry dates must be mentioned on all edible items' including bread.
— Manufacturing and expiry dates must also be mentioned on cosmetics.
— Should withdraw defective goods and avoid tie-in-sales.
— Should also establish Consumers Affairs Cells in their organisations for receiving consumers' complaints and their prompt redressal.
— Retail prices, wherever possible, should be mentioned in the advertisements.
— Instructions to users as to safety measures and other relevant product information must be provided to every consumer.

* Quoted in *Kimat* Vol., 12 No. 11 and 12, December, 1983, Consumer Guidance Society of India, Mumbai, p. 12.

Exhibit 16.7: Our Credo

We believe that *our first responsibility is* to the Doctors, Nurses and Hospitals, Mothers and all others *who use our products.*

Our products must always be of the highest quality. We must constantly strive to reduce the cost of these products. Our orders must be promptly and accurately filed. Our dealers must make a fair profit.

Our second responsibility is to those who work with us, the men who work in our plants and offices.

They must have a sense of *security in their jobs.*

Wages must be fair and adequate.

Management must fix reasonable working hours and maintain healthy and clean working conditions.

Employees should have an *organised system for suggestions and complaints.*

Supervisors and Department Heads must be *qualified and fair-minded.*

There must be opportunity for advancement – for those qualified.

And each person must be considered on individual standing on his own dignity and merit.

* * *

Our third responsibility is to our management.

Our executives must be persons of talent, education experience and ability.

They must be persons of common sense and full understanding.

* * *

Our fourth responsibility is to the communities in which we live.

We must be good citizens, support good works and charity and bear our fair share of taxes.

We must maintain in good order the property we are privileged to use.

We must participate in the promotion of civic improvement, health, education and good government.

And acquaint the community with out activities.

* * *

Our fifth and last responsibility is to our stockholders.

Business must make a sound profit.

Reserves must be created, research must be carried on.

Adventurous programmes developed, and mistakes paid for.

Adverse times must be provided for, adequate taxes paid, new machines purchased, new plants built, new products launched, and new sales plans developed.

We must experiment with new ideas.

When these things have been done, the stockholders should receive a fair return.

We are determined with the help of God's grace to fulfil these obligations to the best of our ability.

CHAPTER 17

CORPORATE STRATEGY: FUNCTIONS AND IMPORTANCE

- **The Concept of Strategy**
- **Strategic Management**
- **Need for Strategic Management**
- **The Strategists**

Today no company in India commands a greater respect for its growth, profitability, turnover and return on investment as the Reliance. The phenomenal growth of Vimal in the textile sector in general and corporate sector in particular can be largely attributed to its dynamic and pragmatic strategies. The success story of Reliance reveals one major single difference between a successful and unsuccessful enterprise in their basic strategic framework. So before elaborating upon the importance of the issue, it would be very much desirable to know what is meant by strategy.

THE CONCEPT OF STRATEGY

In the context of business organizations to explore the concept of strategy, many scholars have advanced a variety of explanations. Tilles has conceptualized strategy as a set of goals and major policies of an organization.[1] This definition embraces the basic objectives of organizations and the major means that will be deployed in attaining those objectives. Another definition has succinctly termed strategy as "the basic goals and objectives of an organisation, the major programmes of action chosen to reach those goals and objectives and the major pattern of resource allocation used to relate the organization to its environment."[2] Chandler also remarked that strategy is ".......the determination of the basic long-term goals and objectives of an enterprise and the adoption of courses of action and allocation of resources necessary for carrying out these goals." Scott has taken a comprehensive view of the approach to the study of strategy by remarking that a long-range strategy is designed to provide information about a company's basic direction and purpose, information which will guide all its operational activities.[3] In fact, it includes the objectives and sub-plans of the organization and action plan for the achievement of those objectives in a highly turbulent and competitive environment. It considers not only the end but also the means.

Ansoff has given a more dynamic definition of the concept of strategy. According to him, a strategy is one which (1) provides a broad concept of a firm's business; (2) sets forth specific guidelines by which the firm can conduct its research and (3) supplements the firm's objectives with decisions which narrow the firm's selection process to the most attractive opportunities.[4] In the said definition, an attempt has been made to separate strategy from objectives. However, in practice, they are both complementary in operation. A more practical definition of strategy has been proposed by Glueck which states that "it is a unified comprehensive and integrated plan relating to the strategic advantages of the firm to the challenges of the environment. It is designed to ensure that the basic objectives of the enterprise are achieved."[5]

One of the well-known definitions of strategy has been advocated by Professor Kenneth Andrews (of Harvard Business School) which states that a strategy is "the pattern of major objectives, purposes or goals and essential policies and plans for achieving those goals stated in

1. Tilles, S., "How to Evaluate Corporate Strategy." *Harvard Business Review*, July Aug. 1963, p.112.
2. Chandler, A.D.Jr., *Strategy and Structure*. The M.I.T. Press, Cambridge, Mass, 1962, p.13.
3. Ansoff, H.I. *Corporate Strategy*, McGraw-Hill Book Company, 1965, p.104.
4. Scott, B.W., "Long-Rang Planning in American Industry", American Management Association, New York, 1965, p. 16.
5. Glueck, W.E., *Business Policy and Strategic Management*, McGraw-Hill, International Student Edition, 1980, p. 9.

such a way as to define what business the company is in or is to be in and the kind of company it is or is to be." Accordingly, all organizational strategies revolve around a specific programme of actions that are capable of facing competition as well as fulfilling organizational objectives so as to utilise the firm's resources effectively and economically. The managers can delve into the company's strategy by trying to find answers to questions like:

- What business are we in or do we want to be in?
- Whether we continue in the same business or shift to another one?
- Whether our profit margin is desirable?
- Whether present policies are conducive to growth and development?
- Whether the company has given adequate attention to threats and opportunities?
- What profit margin the company is expecting after five years?

It is difficult to find correct or near-correct answers to these questions. But even the rough estimates about them are quite helpful in arriving at some definite conclusions which can help the top management in the formulation of some definite action plan for efficiently meeting the opportunities and threats.

A strategy is basically concerned with optimizing goal attainment in the wake of environmental uncertainties by a rational utilization of company's resources. Hence it can be conveniently compared with the design of a military action, as before launching a major attack on enemy, the key military personnel makes a thorough appraisal of the strengths and weaknesses of the enemy. Here, at the very first instance, not all the resources are deployed but a sufficient buffer is built to meet a counter attack or to launch a fresh one. Likewise in business too, a firm does not deploy all its resources in the initial stages but utilizes them as per the needs of the situation.

However, firms are expected to follow more dynamic and radical strategies in comparison with the military because at a time the former are confronted by more than one competitor having a large number of strategic alternatives. Besides this, they are also expected to oblige a host of publics like employees, customers, community, trade unions and government who quite often make a host of conflicting demands on the enterprise, tempting management to deploy a set of strategies to exploit its resources so that the optimum level of effectiveness could be attained. By providing unified guidelines to decision-making, strategies enable the manager to offset uncertainty and exploit possible opportunities to a certain extent.

Effective strategies provide a theme and *raison d'etre* to the internal organization and network of policies to deal with the external environment. In fact, the strategic design adopted by a firm in terms of choice of market segments, product planning, promotional activities, pricing policies, etc. are usually at the core of enterprise's success.

STRATEGIC MANAGEMENT

In the management literature of the early 80's perhaps no other aspect of management is much talked about or debated on as the strategic management is. In fact, the growing complexity of business and the changing complexion of environment have made it the focal point of attention in as much as it is increasingly realized that success of business is linked with its strategic management.

Up to the late seventies, terms like "long-range planning" and "strategic planning" were largely deployed to explain the enterprise's overall approach to deal with both internal and external contingencies. But the said words semantically connote rather a narrow meaning of the terms. Contrary to it, strategic management is a more broader concept; it embraces the overall managerial process to optimize the enterprise effectiveness.

Strategic management embraces a set of decisions, actions and interactions which help in designing an effective strategic net-work to facilitate the accomplishment of enterprise mission. In other words, it can be stated that strategic management emphasizes innovative strategic programme, looks for changes in programme, identifies the potential for changes and makes critical appraisal of programme of attaining enterprise mission.

At this juncture, it is very much desirable to distinguish between what Ansoff and Steiner called "Strategic Management" and "Operational Management". From the strict managerial point of view, there is a substantial difference between these two types of management with regard to the thought process, attitudes, level of importance and the skill required to carry out the task. Strategic management is basically concerned with the top management, aimed at formulating broad policies for the working of organization whereas operational management is the exclusive prerogative of the functional executives. Therefore, the process of strategic management is more complex, circuitous and continuous and requires more foresight, dynamism and intellect on the part of strategists. The process of strategic management basically embraces the following steps:

(i) *Analysis and Diagnosis of the problem*: This process involves crystallization of the problem through adequate environmental scanning. This calls for the preparation of an environment profile, so that accordingly threats and opportunities could be best exploited in the interest of the organization.

(ii) *Selection of Suitable Strategy*: It is aimed at generating and screening alternative strategies for determining the most profitable one.

(iii) *Implementation*: This phase is concerned with creating an adequate organizational climate for the execution of strategy.

(iv) *Evaluation:* This process aims at eliciting necessary information about the working of strategy. In other words, it tries to create and maintain a suitable information system for assessing the effectiveness of strategy.

All the above four steps of strategic management are discussed in the subsequent chapters.

NEED FOR STRATEGIC MANAGEMENT

Anybody who is concerned or bothered about the overall functioning of an enterprise must know the importance of strategic management. A lot has been said and written about it. Here we are crystallizing some of the important thoughts.

(i) *To Keep Pace with Changing Environment*: As discussed in the chapter on Business Environment, modern corporations are operating in a highly dynamic environment, which is ever-changing, constraining and uncertain. They are in a continuous flux of threats and opportunities. Therefore, the most pressing problem of a modern organization is to find out the ways for its survival in a highly volatile and turbulent environment. In such circumstances to keep business going, strategic management is the need of the hour, as by exploring opportunities and minimizing threats, it helps the business to achieve an optimum level of efficiency. Most of the leading American corporations and a few Indian business houses today have utilized strategic management in profitably exploiting business opportunities.

(ii) *To Boost Employees' Efficiency:* It is a common observation that employees carry out their tasks effectively if they have a clear role perception. The firms embracing strategic management, as a rule, clearly define what to do, when to do, how to do and who is to do it. As such the employees are in a position to carry out their tasks effectively. In fact, strategic management by gearing up employees' efficiency makes things to happen which would not otherwise take place.

(iii) *To Furnish a Strong Base For Unified Decision Making*: As strategic management focuses on the determination of the major organizational objectives, by "identifying the things to be achieved," it furnishes a strong base for unified decision-making. Consequently, not only the enterprise, but its various sub-units are also immensely benefited.

THE STRATEGISTS

The success of strategic management is intimately linked with the competence of the strategist, as he owes the responsibility of defining the firm's objectives, laying down strategies for matching its product line(s) to the different market segment(s) by a rational utilization of the company's resources. Strategic management can be practised by the following group of persons, namely:

1. Top managerial personnel;
2. Board of directors who reviews the company's working;
3. Executives of corporate planning department who assist the top management in the formulation and execution of strategies;
4. Management consultants who are called upon by management to give their co-operation in strategic management.

CHAPTER 18

STRATEGIC DECISION MAKING

INTRODUCTION

Managers in the business world, often fail to make a decision in right time and allow the opportunities be grabbed by the competitors and the problems remain or magnify and culminate into a crisis. Decisions should be taken in right time and implemented after problems have been thoroughly analysed. Decision-making means to come to a conclusion and implement it. Decision-making is defined as "the selection based on some criteria of one behaviour alternative from two or more possible alternatives."[1] The need for decision making arises only when there are two or more alternative solutions for a problem.

Values and Alternatives

To select one solution from the available alternatives, each alternative should be evaluated in terms of probable outcomes in comparison with other alternative solutions. The comparison should be based on values in terms of financial, social, psychological, technological and political. These values are conflicting with each other and make the decision-making process a critical one. Concentrating on the important facets of the problem will help in reducing the conflict. However, taking strategic decisions is much more complicated task.

Types of Decision

Decisions are classified into routine and strategic or programmed and non-programmed decisions. Routine or programmed decisions are taken by an established or systematic procedure. The decision-maker, in general, knows the situation in routine or programmable decisions. Managerial decisions covered by policies, procedures, and rules are taken by following established guidelines.

Strategic or non-programmed decisions have little or no precedent. They are relatively structured and generally require a more creative approach. The decision-maker must develop a procedure to be followed. Generally, it is difficult to make non-programmed decisions compared to programmed decisions.[2]

Traditional Process of Decision-Making

Decision-making process involves identification of the problems, searching the environment for conditions requiring a decision, developing and analysing possible alternatives selecting the best alternative solution and execute the solution to achieve the objectives/goals or solve the problem.

The steps involved in the process of decision-making are:

(i) Identification of problem(s) to be solved or determination of objectives to be achieved.
(ii) Searching the environment for conditions requiring a decision.
(iii) Developing the possible alternative solutions.
(iv) Analysing each alternative solution in terms of its ability to solve the problem or to achieve the determined objectives.

1. Charles H. Kepner and Benjamin B. Tregoe, *"The Rational Manager"*, McGraw–Hill, New York, 1965, p. 40.
2. George Prime, *"Putting the other Half of the Brain to Work,"* Training, November 1978, pp. 58–59.

(v) Selecting the best alternative solution.

(vi) Executing the solution to solve the problem or to achieve the objectives.

Earnest B. Archer, proposed a nine-phase decision process. The phases are:

Phase 1: Monitor the decision environment.

Phase 2: Define the decision problem or situation.

Phase 3: Specify decisions objectives.

Phase 4: Diagnose the decision problem or situation.

Phase 5: Develop alternative solutions or courses of action.

Phase 6: Establishing the methodology or criteria for appraising alternatives.

Phase 7: Appraise alternative solutions or courses of action.

Phase 8: Choose the best alternative solution or course of action.

Phase 9: Implement the best alternative solution or course of action.[3]

Strategic Decision

Most part of the strategic management is done through strategic decision-making. Strategic decision-making is not only crucial but also critical and complex. Strategic decisions are made by the top level management and by the strategists whereas the operational decisions are made by the managers at lower levels. Strategic decisions are related to the contribution to the organisational objectives and goals significantly. They determine the direction and destination of the organisation.

CHARACTERISTICS OF STRATEGIC DECISIONS

The characters of strategy and strategic decisions are as follows:[4]

1. Strategic decisions are likely to be concerned with the scope of an organisation's activities. The activities vary from company to company. Some companies activities are limited to one product whereas some other organisation's activities include a wide range of products/services. The range of organisational activities are fundamental to strategic decisions.

2. Strategy is to do with the matching of the activities of an organisation to the internal and external environment in which it operates. In fact, strategies are formulated, evaluated and the best among the alternatives based on the environmental threats and opportunity — analysis (ETOP) and strength weakness, opportunities – and threats (SWOT) analysis.

3. Strategy is also to do with the matching of organisation's activities to its resource capability. Strategy analysis and choice is based not only on the opportunities and threats of the environment but also on the resource base of the organisation. The resource base includes financial, human, material and informational resources.

4. Strategic decisions have major resource implications for an organisation: Basically, the organisation, while formulating a strategy, should be based on the available resources. The organisations, then, search for the opportunities provided by the environment which would match with the resource base to a greater extent.

3. George R. Terry and Stephen G. Franklin, "*Principles of Management*," All India Traveller Book Seller, Delhi, 1987, pp. 76-80.

4. Gerry Johnson and Keven Scholes, "*Exploring Corporate Strategy*," Prentice Hall of India, New Delhi, 1993, pp. 5-10.

5. Strategic decisions affect operational decisions, strategic decisions are the basis for formulating and making operational decisions. The changes in strategic decisions bring corresponding changes in operational decisions.

6. The strategies of organisation will also be affected by the values and expectations of the strategic decision-makers in addition to the environmental forces and resources base, for example, the managing director, general managers and other strategists have the power to formulate strategies. The values and expectations of these strategists affect the nature and magnitude of the strategies.

7. Strategic decisions are likely to affect the long–term direction of the company. Strategies are formulated to achieve the company's mission and objectives which determine the long run direction of the company.

Patterns of Strategy Development

Strategy is concerned with the long–term and future decisions . The organisations formulates, analyses, selects, and implement a strategy. Later, the organisations follow-up, evaluate and improve the strategy in view of the competitor's attack and/or counter attack. Thus, the strategic development is a continuous process rather than a momentum upspring. The different forms of strategy development include,

(i) Incremental strategy development (ii) Intended and realised strategies (iii) Emergent, opportunistic and imposed strategies.

(i) Incremental Strategy Development

Organisations, mostly change infrequently and strategies are formed gradually or through piece meal change. During these periods some strategies are changed, some are remained constant, some are unchanged. During the periods of flux, strategies change but not in a very clear direction. The strategic moves include: product launch, service addition, acquisition, divestment, domestic expansion, overseas expansion etc.

(ii) Intended and Realised Strategies

It is viewed that, strategy is developed by managers in an intended, planned fashion. It is also viewed that strategy is formulated in terms of resource allocation, structure etc. The strategy then comes about or is realised in actuality. Thus, the strategy is conceived of as a deliberate, systematic process.

(iii) Emergent, Opportunistic and Imposed Strategies

Strategies always may not be formulated based on plans and intentions. The strategy which is formulated based on the organisational direction, and is developed over the time is called emergent strategy. The strategy which is formulated to utilise the opportunities offered by the environment and to utilise the strengths of the organisation is called opportunistic strategy. The strategy which is formulated due to the environmental threats and the weaknesses of the organisation is called imposed strategy. The strategies like divestment, retrenchment, cost cut are the examples of imposed strategy. Fig. 18.1 shows the pattern of strategy development.

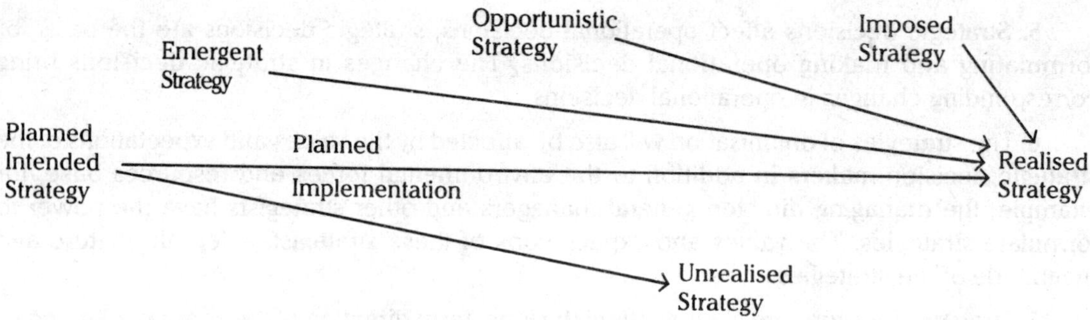

Fig. 18.1 Pattern of Strategy Development.

Views of Strategic Development: The different views of strategic development include:

(i) the natural selection view
(ii) the planning view
(iii) the logical incremental view
(iv) the cultural view
(v) the political view and
(vi) the visionary view.

(i) The Natural Selection View

The natural selection view states that the organisations cannot influence the environment and they respond to the change in the environment. Strategies developed under such circumstances are similar to national selection. Changes in organisation structure, organisation process and systems would also take place in response to the environmental variations. Manager's strategic choice in such organisations, is limited.

(ii) The Planning View

The strategic decision making is viewed as a systematic planning process. This planning process comprises of (a) setting of objectives, goals, procedures, programmes and tactics, (b) analysing internal environmental factors in order to know the strengths and weaknesses of the organisation, (c) analysing the external environment to know the organisational opportunities and threats, (d) formulating all possible strategic alternatives (e) evaluating these alternatives (f) selecting the alternative which suits the best to the organisation's strengths and weaknesses and environment's opportunities and threats, (g) planning and implementing the best solution.

Limitations: This view suffers from the following limitations:

(a) This view does not take into consideration the behavioural aspects of the people who make the strategies and implement them.

(b) Strategies are formulated and implemented by the corporate planning staff of the company. Therefore, the middle level and lower level managers are not involved in the process.

(c) The employees, contribute only to a part of the strategic plan and they do not understand the total process.

(d) The strategy, in this view is thought as a plan.

(iii) The Logical Incremental View

Lindbloom views that strategic choice against present and future objectives would be difficult. He suggests that selecting the best strategy among the alternatives would be possible by comparing the alternatives with one another. He viewed this strategy building through 'successive limited comparisions.[5] Quinn labelled the same situation as 'logical incrementalism.'[6] Quinn meant that managers try to formulate effective strategies in an evolutionary process. He also suggests that different decisions should not be seen as entirely separate. Since the different parts or sub-systems of the organisation interplay with each other, every manager should know the activities of the other managers. It helps them to learn from each other and to evaluate the strategies from multi-directions. Fig. 18.2 shows the notional incremental change.

(iv) The Cultural View

Though the environment influences all the organisations similarly, they respond to the environment differently. This is due to the fact that cultures of the organisations vary from one another significantly. Organisational culture is concerned with the basic assumptions and beliefs that are shared by the members of the organisation. The organisational culture often plays an important role in the strategy development.

(v) The Political View

Organisations are not only economic and social entities, but also political entities. These are powerful internal and external interest groups which influence the resource allocation, strategic decisions etc. Strategies also emerge through a process of bargaining, negotiations and the trading off of political interests.

(vi) The Visionary View

Visionary view of strategic management is concerned with the intuitive capacities of the executive who make strategic decisions. These executives relate more naturally to the identification of new possibilities, new patterns and ideas rather than in-depth search for cause and effect and the system or science of management. They see the new ways of management and working. These managers have more capacities to envisage rather than plan the future of the organisation. These manager make the strategies based on their intuition and their patterns and ideas.

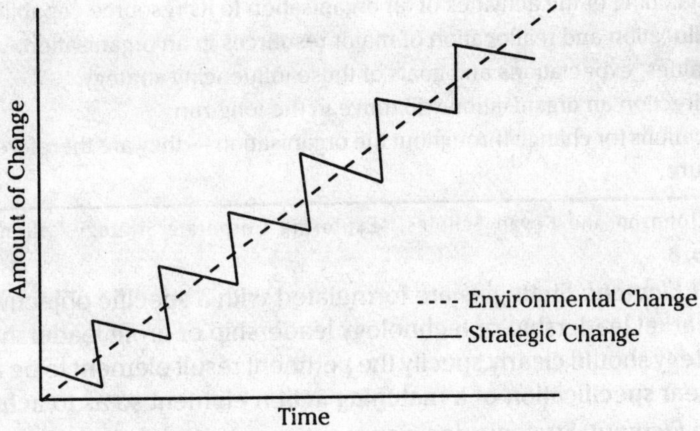

Fig. 18.2 Incremental Change.

5. Lindbloom, "The Science of Mudding Through" *Public Administration Review,'* Vol. 19, 1959.
6. J.B. Quinn, "Strategies for change," *Irwin*, 1980.

The characteristics of strategic decisions, in summary include:

(i) The strategic decision is a major one which affects either the total organisation or the major part of the organisation.

(ii) Even though, operational decisions also contribute towards the achievement of organisational objectives, contribution of strategic decision towards the achievement of organisational objectives is phenomenal and direct. In fact, strategic decisions determine the destiny of the organisation.

(iii) Strategic decisions may introduce change in the organisational policies, practices businesses, customers, product mix, human resource policies, financing sources etc.

(iv) Strategic decision requires interweaving a number of factors, requires development of alternatives in view of increasing environmental demands.

(v) Strategic decision-making, requires trade-offs between conflicting factors, (See Exhibit 18.1)

Elements of Strategic Decisions

The basic elements of strategic decisions are: (i) achievement of objective or desired result through the implementation of the decision, result element, (ii) a course of action or plan indicating the work to be done in order to achieve the objective — the action element, and (iii) inculcating the character of commitment among the employees responsible for implementation of strategic decision — the commitment element.

Exhibit 18.1 : The Characteristics of Strategic Decisions

- Strategic decisions are concerned with:
- The scope of an organisation's activities.
- The matching of an organisation's activities to its environment.
- The matching of the activities of an organisation to its resource capability.
- The allocation and reallocation of major resources in an organisation.
- The values, expectations and goals of those influencing strategy.
- The direction an organisation will move in the long-run.
- Implications for change throughout the organisation — they are therefore likely to be complex in nature.

Source: Gerry Johnson and Kevan Scholes, "Exploring Corporate Strategy," Prentice-Hall, New York, 1988, p. 8.

(i) *Result Element:* Strategies are formulated with a specific objective of either grabbing the market leadership or technology leadership or profit leadership. Completeness of a strategy should clearly specify the pertinent result element to be achieved. It requires the clear specification of a matching action element so as to achieve objectives.

(ii) *Action Element*: Strategic decision is action oriented. A decision may be interpreted as the intervening variable which may ultimately lead to the end-result variables. The action element of strategic decision clearly states what work must be done, how, by whom and when in order to achieve the results.

(iii) *Commitment Element:* Commitment element is most important to put the strategy into action and achieve the results. Commitment element includes commitment of financial

7. George R. Terry and Stephen G. Franklin, *op, cit.*, pp. 79–85.

resources, top management commitment, commitment of executives and employees. Further, specific time period for commitment of resources should also be indicated.[8]

APPROACHES TO STRATEGIC DECISION-MAKING

Different theories have suggested different approaches of decision-making. These approaches are discussed hereunder:

The Intuitive-Emotional Approach

Decision-maker takes decisions based on intuition which is characterised by the use of hunches, inner feelings or the 'gut-feeling' of the decision-maker. Decision-maker who makes decisions based on intuition, practices management exclusively as an art. This decision-maker prefers habit or experience, relative thinking, and instinct using the unconscious cognitive process. The decision-maker takes into account a number of alternatives into consideration, but simultaneously jumps one step in analysis and search to another and back again.[9]

Most of the managers suddenly become emotional and nothing can change their minds. George Odiorne has stated the following emotional factors which can adversely affect decision-makers:

1. They fasten on the big lie stick with it.
2. They are attracted to scandalous issue and heighten their significance.
3. They press every fact into a normal pattern.
4. They overlook everything except the immediately useful.
5. They have an affinity for romantic stories and find such information more significant than any other kind including hard evidence.[10]

This type of emotional attachments are possible and can lead to poor decisions.

The intuitive decision-maker is normally an activist, fast mover, incisely questions situations and finds unique solutions to difficult problems. Some theorists prescribe intuitive approach of decision-making.

The supporters of intuition or judgement point out that in many cases, judgement may lead to better decisions than optimising techniques. They also argue that analytical models are only tools to help the decision-maker to refine judgement.

The opponents of this approach argue that:

(i) It does not effectively use all the tools available to modern decision-makers and
(ii) The rational approach ensures that adequate attention is given to consequences of decisions before big mistakes are committed.[11]

8. L.M. Prasad, *"Business Policy and Strategy,"* Paramount Publishers, Surat, 1985, pp. 33-34.
9. Lawrence R. Jauch and William F. Glueck, *op. cit.*, p. 21.
10. Georges S. Odiorne, *"Management and the Activity Trap,"* Harper & Row, New York, 1974, pp. 128–129 and George S. Odiorne, *"The Change Resisters,"* Prentice Hall, Englewood Cliffs, 1981, pp. 15–25.
11. Lawrence R. Jauch and William F. Glueck, *op. cit.*, p. 21.

Considering the views of both supporters and opponents of this approach, it is suggested that the managers who wish to improve their intuition might try to:

(i) Becoming more involved by filling their minds with facts and experiences in the areas where their future decisions will be made;

(ii) Practicing intuitive decision-making and keeping a score on how well such decisions turned out;

(iii) Developing an awareness that hunches can help in decision-making.[12]

(iv) Becoming aware of biases and allow for them. Undiscovered biases do the most damage, and

(v) Seek out independent opinions. It is always good to seek the opinion of some person who has no vested interest in the decision.[13]

The Rational-Analytical Approach

In the rational-analytical approach, the decision-maker, is intelligent and rational. The decision-maker makes the choice, in full awareness of all available feasible alternatives, to maximise advantages. The decision-maker considers all alternatives as well as consequences of all possible choices, orders these consequences in the light of a fixed scale of preferences, and chooses the alternative that procures the maximum gain.[14]

The rational approval to decision-making includes the following steps:

(i) Recognise the need for a decision;

(ii) Establish, rank and weigh criteria,

(iii) Gather available information and data;

(iv) Identify possible alternatives;

(v) Evaluate each alternative with respect to all criteria; and

(vi) Select the best alternative.

Assumption of Rational Approach

The rational approach is based on the concept of 'economic man'. This concept views that people behave rationally and that their behaviour is based on the following assumptions:

(i) People have clearly defined criteria, and the relative weights which they assign to these criteria are stable:

(ii) People have knowledge of all relevant alternatives;

(iii) People have the ability to evaluate each alternative with respect to all the criteria and arrive at an overall rating for each alternative;

(iv) People have the self-discipline to choose the alternative which rates the highest (they will not manipulate the system).[15]

Criticism

Rational-analytical approach is the oldest theory. It prescribes a rational, conscious, systematic and analytical approach. This has been criticised because:

12. George R. Terry and Stephen G. Franklin, *op. cit.*, p. 94.
13. George S. Odiorne, "Management and the Activity Trap," *op, cit.*, pp. 142–144.
14. Lawrence R. Jaunch and William F. Glueck, *op. cit.*, p. 20.
15. Leslie W. Rue and Lloyd L. Byars, *op. cit.*, p. 97.

(i) The decision-maker is often not a unique actor but part of a multiparty decision situation;

(ii) Decision-makers are not rational enough or informed enough to consider all alternatives or know all the consequences. And information is costly;

(iii) Decision-makers take decisions with more than a maximisation of objectives in mind. They tend to, "satisfies" i.e., make a decision expected to yield a satisfactory, as opposed to an "optimal" outcome. Besides, the objective may change;[16]

(iv) Decision-maker makes decisions based on limited knowledge or less perfect information;

(v) The most difficult stage in the decision process may be the evaluation or the prediction of customers for the various alternatives;

(vi) The problem is the temptation to manipulate the information and choose a favoured; but not necessarily the best alternative. This temptation may come from within the decision-maker or it may be created by external forces.[17]

A Satisficing Approach

As discussed earlier, "economic man" assumptions are generally unrealistic. Herbert Simon developed the principle of bounded rationality. This principle states that: "the capacity of the human mind for formulating and solving complex problems is very small compared with the size of the problems whose solution is required for objectively rational behaviour — or even for a reasonable approximation to such objective rationality."[18]

The principle of bounded rationality states that there are definite limits to human rationality. Based on the principle of bounded rationality. Herbert Simon proposed a decision theory of the "administrative man." The assumptions of the theory are:

1. A person's knowledge of alternatives and criteria is limited.
2. People act on the basis of a simplified, ill-structured, mental abstraction of the real world; this abstraction is influenced by personal perceptions, biases, and so on and so forth.
3. People do not attempt to optimise but will take the first alternative which satisfies their current level of aspiration. This is called satisficing.
4. An individual's level of aspiration concerning a decision fluctuates upward and downward depending on the values of most recently found alternatives.

These assumptions explain that limits exist to human rationality. Therefore, an individual must take decisions based on limited and incomplete knowledge. In view of this, the individual decision-maker cannot optimise but only satisfice.

Optimising means choosing the best possible alternative. Satisficing means choosing the first alternative that meets the decision-maker's minimum standard of satisfaction. Minimum standard of satisfaction i.e., criteria, for aspiration depends on the current level of aspiration. Level of aspiration refers to the level of performance that a person expects to attain and it is determined by the person's prior success and failures.[19]

16. Lawrence R. Jauch and William F. Glueck, *op. cit.*, p. 21
17. Lesile W. Rue and Llyod L. Byars, *op. cit.*, p. 98.
18. Herbert A. Simon, *"Model of Man,"* John Wiley & Sons, New York, 1957, p. 198.
19. Leslie W. Rue and Lloyd L. Byars, *op. cit.*, p. 99.

Satisfying approach to decision-making is presented in Figure.18.3. If the decision maker is satisfied that an acceptable alternative has been found, it is selected otherwise, the decision-maker searches for an additional alternative.

The value of best previous alternative and current level of aspiration influence the value of alternative found. This, in turn, indicates whether or not the decision-maker is satisfied with best alternative found so far? If the decision-maker is satisfied with the best alternative found, he selects that alternative as decision. Otherwise, he searches for additional alternatives and continues the process. The value of best previous alternative and current level of aspiration are influenced by the value of new alternative found. In fact, it is mutual impact.

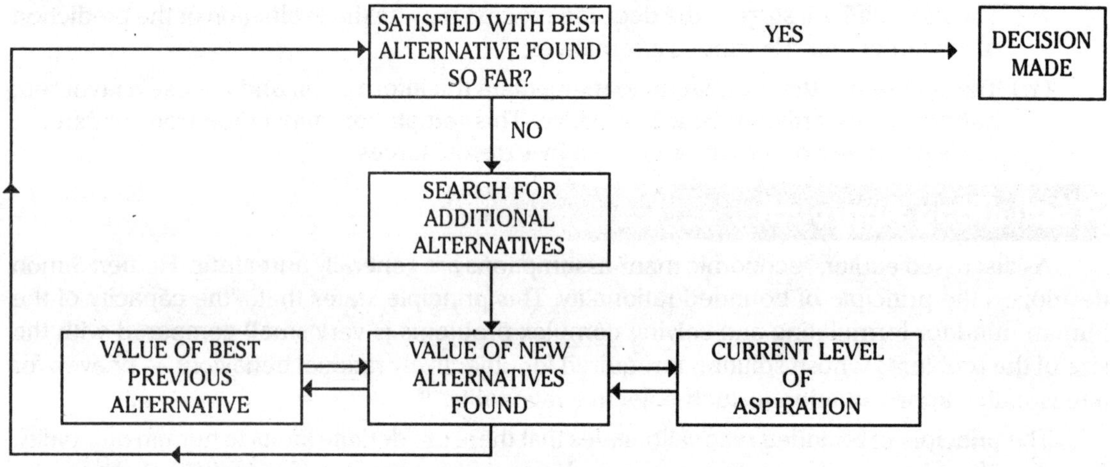

Fig. 18.3 : Model of Satisficing Approach

Source: Adapted from James G. March and Herbert A. Simon, *"Organisations,"* John Wiley & Sons, New York, 1958, p. 49.

Political-Behavioural Approach

Normally decisions made by organisations affect a variety of people and organisations. Hence, another view suggests that the corporations must consider all the people and organisations in making decisions. Corporations interact with a variety of stakeholders as the corporation and its stakeholders are mutually dependent on each other.

The employees exchange their human resources for fair salaries, benefits and harmonious industrial and human relations. Customers exchange their money for qualitative products and courteous services. Shareholders exchange their money for high rate of dividend and safety of their capital. Government provides security and protection and in turn expects payment of taxes regularly. Financial institutions exchange their finance for high rate of interest, security of principal amount and regular payment of interest. Suppliers of inputs expects fair terms of trade and continuous business. Competitors exchange information through chamber of commerce, trade and industry for mutual existence and development. The dealers expects continuous business. Thus, a stake holder is an individual or organisation who can affect or is affected by the decision-making and achievement of organisational purpose and objective.

As stated, every stake holder gives something to the corporation and expects something in return. Similarly, the corporation also gives something to its stakeholders and expects in return. The corporation can have more power, if it maintains favourable relations with the stakeholders compared to other corporations. More powerful stakeholders have better terms of exchange and, therefore, have more influence on decisions. In fact, the corporations depend on such powerful stakeholders.

The stakeholders, influence the decisions of the corporation depending upon their strength. If the labour unions are strong and have strong political affiliation, they can influence the managerial decisions. In fact, such union get even their unreasonable demands met by the management. Similarly, if the number of shareholders is relatively less, they can influence the decision regarding payment of high rate of dividend versus high reserves. Powerful dealers influence the corporation regarding the terms and conditions of trade.

In view of these factors, corporation do a juggling act to meet the demands of various stakeholders. The corporation should balance through political compromise the competiting demands of different stakeholders in making decisions. This process helps for a coalition of interests that will support the decision.

This is a descriptive theory suggesting a decision-making within the alternatives available. Decisions are made through mutual negotiations and consultation among all the stakeholders who affect and/or are affected by the decision. The negotiations/consultations are based on the rule of the power sharing game between the organisation and the stakeholders.

A synthesis: The decision-maker being a human being is a mix of the rational and the emotional. Environment is a mixture of analysable and chaotic change and pressures. Therefore, decisions are made in a typically human way, using the rational, conscious analysis and intuitive, unconscious 'gut feeling' in light of political realities. Blending of these prescriptive and descriptive approaches helps to understand how decision-makers operate.[20]

PROCESS OF STRATEGIC DECISION-MAKING

Though, we have studied, logical incrementalism, different approaches to strategic decision-making, the research suggests us to understand the process of decision-making which actually takes place in organisations and give rise to strategic decisions.[21] There are five steps in the process of strategic decision-making. (Fig.18.4) They are:

(i) Problem Awareness;
(ii) Problem Diagnosis;
(iii) The development of Solutions;
(iv) The Selection of a Solution; and
(v) Implementation of the Solution.

Problem Awareness

Mostly individual employees identify the problems in various areas. Individuals when they get a 'gut feeling' that something is wrong, they identify the problem. The awareness of a strategic problem mostly occurs to employees at grass-root level like sales people, machine operators,

20. Lawrence R. Jauch and William F. Glueck, *op. cit.*, pp. 22-23.
21. Gerry Johnson, *"Strategic Change and the Management Process,"* Basil Blackwell, 1987.

finance assistants, human resource assistants etc. This awareness is likely to develop through a period of 'incubations' in which managers sense various stimuli that confirm and define a developing picture of a problem.[22] Norburn and Grinyer call this stimuli as 'signals' or 'ear twitchers' and are of three types.[23]

(a) Internal performance measurements like level of turnover or profit performance.
(b) Customer reaction particularly to the quality and price of the products and/or services.
(c) Changes in the environment, particularly in terms of competitive action, technological change and economic conditions.

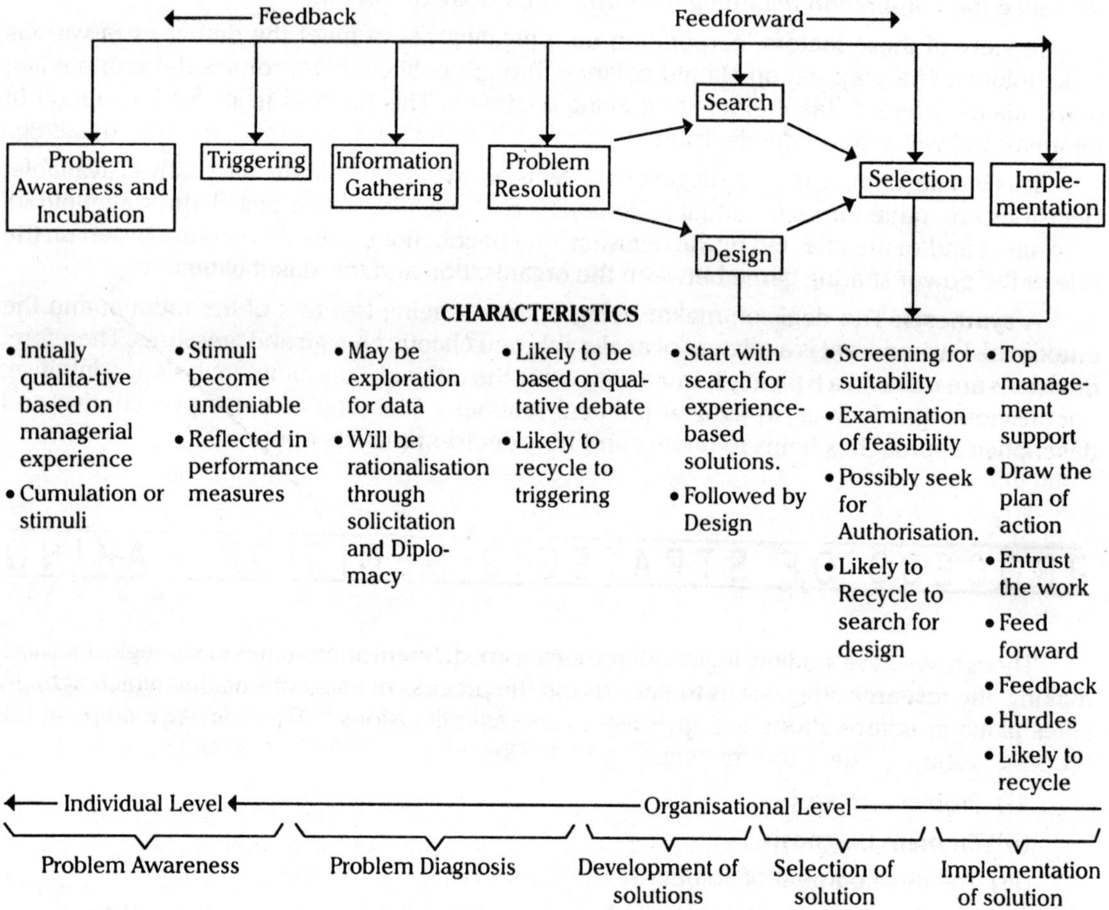

Fig. 18.4 Model of the Strategic Decision Process

Source: Modified version from : Gerry Johnson and Kevan Scholes, "Exploring Corporate Strategy," Prentice-Hall, New York, 1988, p. 32.

These three factors together provide a picture of the deviation of an organisation's circumstances from the planned or expected one. This can be the deviation from a normal trading pattern.

22. M.A. Lyles, "Formulation Strategic Problems: Empirical Analysis and Model Development," *Strategic Management Journal*, Vol.2, 1981, pp. 61-75.
23. D. Norburn and P. Grinyer, "Directors Without Direction," *General Management*, Vol.1, No. 2, 1973–4.

The accumulation of stimuli will clearly indicate the existence of the problem in the organisation. This 'triggering point,' will soon be highlighted by the formal information system in the form of decline in sales, profit, and increase in the rejection level in the production department.

Successful business performance depends upon the ability of management in sensing its environment.[24] Therefore, managers should respond when the problem is identified by the individual employees at the bottom level.

Problem Diagnosis

After the individual employees are aware of the problem and it is informed to the managers, managers will gather the information and define the problem.

Information, may be gathered in the following ways:

(i) Information may be explored to determine the facts of the problem in detail. Such information may be gathered on a verbal and informal basis.[25]

(ii) Rationalise the information and stimuli relevant to the problem so as to clarify the situation.

(iii) Act diplomatically to establish what peer groups or those political support for individual views of the problem.

Try to define the problem through debates and discussions and also get organisational view of consensus on the problem to be solved. The problem, then may take a clear shape by interweaving managerial experience of the executives and political process in the organisations. Some executives, may not accept to proceed or define the problem and ask for additional information or the triggering of a different problem owing to different managerial experience and different views in view of social and political process. In such a situation, the process reverts back to the stage of triggering.

The Development Solutions

After the problem is diagnosed clearly, the tendency of managers is that of searching for ready-made solutions. They do this process: *(i)* through memory search in which the managers seek for known, existing or attempted solutions, or *(ii)* passive search which entails waiting for possible solutions to be offered. If the managers fail in these two searches, they search for the past experiences of themselves and other managers. If they fail to find a solution even through this method, they attempt to designing solutions.

They start designing or developing solutions through a vague idea, gradually improve it, refine it by recycling it through selection routes back into problem identification or through further searches. This process of developing solutions takes place, through discussions, debates, consultations and brain storming sessions and by sharing management wisdom and experience. This can take place both in the form of structured and unstructured team works. The solutions once developed are to be refined until they are developed to the stage of perfection within the available human and other resources of the organisation.

The Selection of a Solution

After the alternative solutions are developed, the solutions have to be formally evaluated based on their inherent strengths and weaknesses and also based on the environmental threats

24. J.B. Quinn, "Strategy for Change," Irwin, 1980 and D. Miller and Friesen, "Archetypes of Strategy Formulation," *Management Science*, Vol. 24, No. 9, 1978.
25. Gerry Johnson and Keven Scholes, op. cit., pp. 31–37.

and opportunities for implementation. These solutions are to be ranked on the basis of their weight in terms of strengths and opportunities after eliminating the non-viable solutions in view of their weaknesses and environmental threats for implementation.

After the formal evaluation and ranking is completed, the managers tend to re-evaluate the solutions based on the managerial judgement followed by political bargaining as the formal evaluation is not the predominant criterion for assessing the feasibility in practice. Therefore the techniques for evaluation of solutions also include social and political process. Quinn suggests that, successful managers actively adopt consultation/bargaining process in order to challenge prevailing strategic inclinations and generate information from other parts of the organisation. The solutions may also be referred to the senior level to seek authorisation.[26]

David Hickson and his colleagues in their study identified three broad types of decision-making processes. They are:

(i) Sporadic processes characterised by many delays and impediments, many sources of influence and information on decision, and therefore, protracted personal interactions and informal negotiation. This type of process exists mostly in public sector organisations.

(ii) Fluid processes in which there are fewer delays and sources of influence, and more formal channels of communication which takes rather less time.

(iii) Constricted process in which information sources are more readily available and decisions can be taken within groups who or by individuals without extensive reference to others in the organisation. This might be the case in a business with a dominant chief executive or where there is an issue which relates primarily to one part of an organisation.[27]

The managers should keep in mind, the various processes discussed above while selecting the solution for implementation. If the managers fail to arrive at a consensus, the process may be recycled to search for new design.

Implementation of the Decision

Implementation of the selected solution is a part of the decision-making process as the process may be required to be recycled due to impediments in the process of implementation. The managers should secure the support of the top management for allocation of resources, time etc. regarding the implementation of the decision. A detailed programme of action specifying the minute details of action, people who will execute it, when it will be implemented, who will provide all necessary resources, how it will be implemented and who will coordinate the work. Employees concerned will be entrusted with the work and relevant information should be fed to them before hand. The managers should also ensure for getting the information back about the progress of implementation. If the decision cannot be implemented due to major hurdles in the implementation process, the process may be recycled for the possible modification. Steps to be a good decision-maker are presented in Exhibit 18.2. It will help in taking qualitative decisions.

We have come across with the concepts of negotiations, consultations and information sharing while diagnosing the problem, development of solutions and selection of a solution.

26. David Hickson, et.al., *"Top Decisions: Strategic Decision–making in Organisation,"* Basil Blackwell, 1986.
27. Frederick C. Miner, Jr., *"Group versus Individual Decision–making: An Investigation of Performance Measures, Decision Strategies and Process Losses/Gains,"* Organisational Behaviour and Human Performance, 33, February 1984, pp. 112–124.

Negotiation, consultations and information sharing will become easy through group decision-making. In fact, strategic decision-making can be effective through group decision making. Fig. 18.5 presents another model of the strategic decision-making process.

Exhibit 18.2 : Steps to be an Effective Strategic Decision-Maker
1. Be alert to signals indicating the need for a decision. 2. Make quite uninterrupted time for thinking and reflecting about things to be decided. 3. Set priorities for different decisions. 4. Separate yourself from the problem and solution. How would another person decide the issue? 5. Ask whether the contemplated decision seems honourable and right. 6. Ask whether you will think well of yourself when you review what has resulted from your decision. 7. Have a backing decision, just in case. 8. Take adequate time to reach a decision-making over the subject serves as a defence against impulsive decisions. In contrast, don't delve into so many aspects that confusion prevails and no defensive action is taken.

Source: George R. Terry and Stephen G. Franklin, "Principles of Management," All India Traveller Bookseller, Delhi, 1987, p. 116.

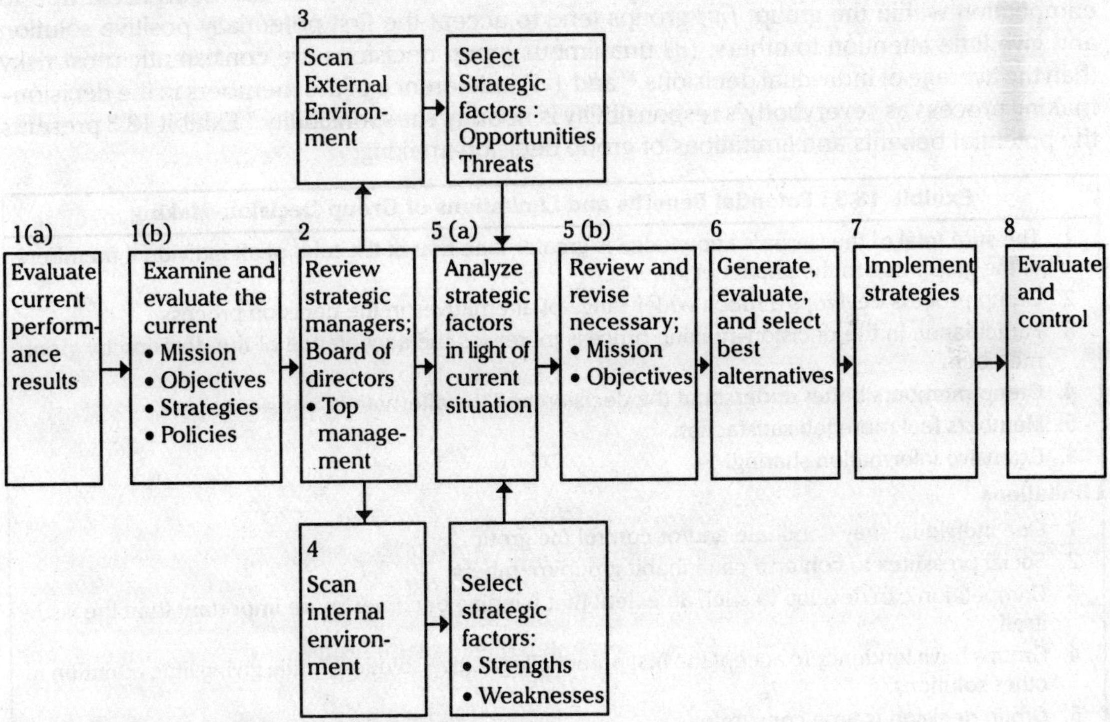

Note: Steps 1 through 6 are strategy formulation.
Step 7 is strategy implementation.
Step 8 is evaluation and control.

Fig. 18.5 Strategic Decision-making Process

Source: Thomas L. Wheeler and J. David Hunger, "Strategic Management and Business Policy," Addison-Wesley Publishing Company, Reading, 1986, p. 27.

Group Decision-making

Most of the managers have the opportunity to make use of the expertise of their subordinates. As we know, two brains are better than one. Group performance in many cases is better than that of the average member of the group.[28] Groups can also be successfully used to develop innovative and creative solutions to problems. Groups are best suitable for strategic decision–making. However, groups take longer time to solve the problems than does the average member of the group[29]. Thus, group decision–making is best suitable when the quality of the decision is more important than the speed.

Potential Benefits of Group Decision–Making

Group decision–making is normally superior to individual decision–making as: (i) the sum total of the group's knowledge and skill are greater, (ii) the group has a much wider range of alternatives in the decision process, (iii) the impact of synergy. (iv) it facilitates and enhances acceptance of the decision by group members–particularly in strategic issues.

Limitations

However, there are certain limitations of group decision–making. They are: *(i)* one person may dominate or control the entire process of group decision–making, *(ii)* the social pressure of conformity, *(iii)* winning an issue becomes more important than the issue itself, due to competition within the group, *(iv)* groups tend to accept the first potentially positive solution and give little attention to others, *(v)* unanimous group decisions are consistently most risky than the average of individual decisions,[30] and (vi) indifference of the members in the decision–making process as "everybody's responsibility is nobody's responsibility." Exhibit 18.3 presents the potential benefits and limitations of group decision–making.

Exhibit 18.3 : Potential Benefits and Limitations of Group Decision–Making

1. The sum total of the Group's knowledge is greater than that of the total of all individual members of the group due to the impact of synergy.
2. Group process develops a much wider range of alternatives in the decision process.
3. Participation in the decision–making process increases the acceptance of the decision by group members.
4. Group members better understand the decision and the alternatives considered.
5. Members feel more job satisfaction.
6. Extensive information sharing.

Limitations

1. One individual may dominate and/or control the group.
2. Social pressures to conform can inhabit group members.
3. Competition can develop to such an extent that winning becomes more important than the issue itself.
4. Groups have tendency to accept the first potentially positive solution, while giving little attention to other solutions.
5. Group decision is time consuming.

28. M.E. Shaw, "A Comparison of Individuals and Small Groups in National Solution of Complex Problems," *American Journal of Psychology*, July 1932, pp. 491–504.
29. N. Kogan and N. Wallach, "Risk Taking as a Function of the Situation, the Person and the Group," in *New Directions of Psychology*, Vol. 3, G. Mardler (Ed.), Holt, Rihehart & Winston, New York, 1967.
30. Lawrence R. Jauch and Willam F. Glueck, *op. cit.*, p. 24.

6. Group decision is costly.
7. Group decision sometimes result in indecision.
8. Argumentation stifles creativity.
9. Game playing among members.

Source: Modified Version: Lesile W. Rue and Lloyd L. Byas, "Management", Richard D. Irwin Inc., Homewood, 1986, p. 106.

Group decision–making is best suitable for strategic decision as quality is more important than speed in case of strategic decisions.

STRATEGIC MANAGEMENT AND STRATEGIC DECISIONS

Strategic decisions includes setting up of objectives of the corporation, sub–objectives for the strategic business units and various functional strategic areas. It also includes formulation of purpose, goals, procedures and programmes. Over a period of time, these objectives, purpose, goals etc. have to be reviewed and reformulated. Further, strategies are formulated for the organisation, SBU level units and functional areas. Thus, decisions are made of strategic nature continuously in strategic management. It is a continuous process. Thus, most of the strategic management is done through making strategic decisions.

As we have discussed earlier, various factors like political, behavioural facts, value orientation of individuals, social and economic factors play a vital role in the decision–making process. Though the techniques of decision–making help in evaluating alternative solutions political influences and intuition play a role in the selection of a solution. Behavioural and political factors become particularly critical in the implementation stage. In fact, political factors also influence the problem of identification phase.

Strategic Decisions: Evolutionary or Revolutionary

Another issue is that strategic change is evolutionary or revolutionary. As discussed earlier under the incrementalisation, strategy setting is evolutionary. Quinn describes how 10 large companies arrived at their most important strategic changes. He suggests that formal rational planning often becomes a substitute for control instead of process for stimulating innovation and entrepreneurship. According to him, incremental process be consciously used to integrate the psychological, political, economic and informational needs of organisations in setting strategy, According to Mintzberg, strategy is a pattern in a stream of decisions. It implies that, strategic decisions are often made piecemeal and outcomes may be unintended. Thus, the strategy may be changed in an evolutionary manner without executives even realising it.[31]

However, there would be hidden costs and inconveniences in incremental changes and evolutionary approach or strategic decision–making. Piecemeal approaches to strategic decision–making may result in internal disharmonies and delays in the project implementation. Strategy change is often viewed as necessarily revolutionary in order to achieve internal and external consistency.

31. *Ibid.*, p. 40.

The need for strategic change can be explained through gap analysisis. Strategic gap analysis is presented in Fig. 18.6.

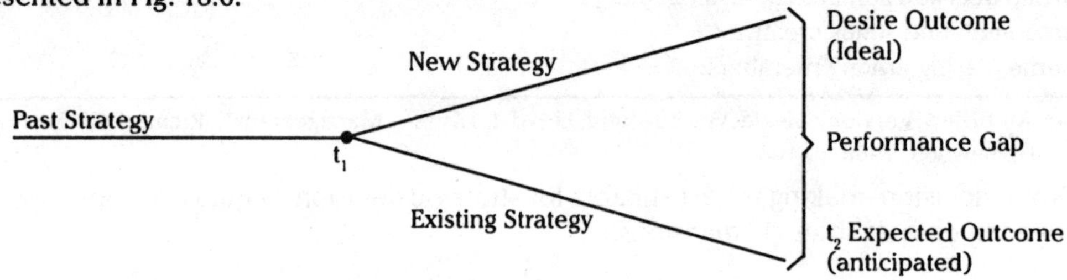

Fig. 18.6 Strategic Gap Analysis

Source: Lawrence R. Jauch and William F. Glueck, "Business Policy and Strategic Management," McGraw–Hill Book Company, New York, 1988, p. 24.

The past strategy leads to the formulation of a new strategy to accomplish a set of desired outcomes. At a given time (t_1), a formal strategic evaluation is made to know the performance of strategic implementation. Normally, proposal for a new activity or change in the strategy will be submitted for consideration. The proposal will be considered keeping in view, the gap between the expected outcomes of continuing with the existing strategy in future (t_2) and the desired outcomes from making a change for the future (t_2) with the proposed new strategy.

A number of conditions will lead to this gap, the changes in objectives, lead to the change in desired outcomes and perceived need for change. The external environmental scanning may result in change in the expected outcome. The internal environmental analysis reveals the firms strengths and weaknesses. Further, continuing past policies may suggest that they will no longer lead to expected outcomes or better way may be found to accomplish the desired outcomes. Hence, an 'incremental' project proposal might trigger a more comprehensive process of strategic thinking, which may lead to revolutionary change.

The conditions that are to be external at this stage to make a change or accept a proposal are: (i) The gap must be perceived to be significant, (ii) the decision–maker must be motivated to reduce the gap, and (iii) the decision–maker must believe that the gap can be reduced. The desired level of outcomes can be attained by implementing the change and implementing the overall process effectively. However, the desired level of outcomes are to be modified accordingly, depending upon the external environmental factors, implementation level of the change, and closeness of the outcomes to the realistic situation.

The strategic decision–maker, therefore is expected to take several factors into consideration, evaluate the process from time to time, scan the environment most dynamically and choose between the incrementalism of revolutionary approach depending upon the strategic issue while making strategic decision and implementing it.

CHAPTER 19

THE STRATEGIST

THE STRATEGIST

"No business can do everything. Even if it has the money, it will never have enough good people. It has to set priorities. The worst thing to do is a little bit of everything. This makes sure that nothing is being accomplished. It is better to pick the wrong priority than none at all".

PETER F. DRUCKER

INTRODUCTION

We have discussed in Chapter 1 strategy, strategy management and business policy. As we have analysed, the areas of business policy and strategic management are concerned with the organisation's philosophy, long range planning and organisation's future direction. Thus, a description of business policy and strategic management involves the use of various terms and concepts that have a variety of meanings and interpretations. Some of the terms are used interchangeably with strategic management. They are: business policy, corporate policy, long-range planning, strategy and policy formulation.

DEFINITIONS OF TERMS RELATED TO STRATEGIC MANAGEMENT

We shall now, define various terms and concepts related to business policy and strategic Management.

Organisational Philosophy

"An organisational philosophy establishes the values, beliefs and guidelines for the manner in which the organisation is going to conduct its business.[1]" It establishes the relationship between the organisation and its shareholders, employees, customers, suppliers of raw materials, dealers, government and the society at large.

A philosophy of an organisation is normally a rather permanent statement that is usually articulated by the chief executive officer. Any organisation in order to survive and achieve success must have a sound set of beliefs on which it premises all its policies and actions.[2]

Mission

Organisations normally perform some function which is valued by society as they are part and parcel of the society. Some functions are valued more highly than others depending upon

1. Lloyd L. Byars, "Strategic Management", Harper & Row, Publishers, New York, 1987, p. 9.
2. *Ibid.*

the requirements of the society. Of course, these priorities change over time. Thus, the organisation's function, to meet the social requirements for their long run survival and legitimate existence. Organisations which make a net contribution to society are likely to be called "legitimate". These organisations are likely to be allowed to survive over the long term.

Organisations define the basic reason for their existence in terms of a mission statement. Mission of a business provides a statement to insiders and outsiders of what the company stands for – its purpose,[3] image and character. Thus, mission statement provides a link between the societal requirements and organisational business.

Business Definition

Part of the mission statement is the definition of the business. A good business definition will include a statement of product, markets and functions. It should meet a certain criteria; it should be as precise as possible and indicate major components of strategy (products, markets, human resources and finance)[4]. It should also indicate how the mission is to be accomplished.

Purpose

The management of an organisation should have a purpose or purposes that the company should achieve in the long run. Normally, the fundamental activity of the company is its purpose. "Its purpose must lie outside the business itself. In fact, it must lie in society since business is an organ of society. There is only one valid definition of business purpose to create a customer."[5]

Objectives

Objectives are the ends towards which activity is aimed. They also represent end towards which organizing, staffing, leading and controlling are aimed. The strategic business units also formulate objectives and they are related to the objectives of the firm and contribute to the firm's objectives.[6] The strategic managers should be aware of the objectives of the firm, strategic business units and departments while formulating the strategies.

Policies

Policies are general statements or understandings which guide or channel thinking and action in strategic decision-making. Policies delimit an area within which a decision is to be taken and assure that the decisions will be consistent with and contribute to objectives.[7] They tend to predecide issues, avoid repeated analysis and provide a unified structure to other types of plans. This process enables the managers to delegate authority while evaluating and controlling strategies. Policy statements, often contain the words to ensure, to follow, to maintain, to promote, to be, to accept and the like. Policies are formulated for each and every level of the organisation.

Procedures

"A procedure is a series of related steps or tasks expressed in chronological order to achieve a specific purpose. Procedures define in step-by-step fashion, the methods by and through which

3. Lawrence R. Jauch and William F. Glueck, *op. cit.*, pp. 57-58.
4. *Ibid.*, pp. 59-60.
5. Peter F. Drucker, *op. cit.*, p. 61.
6. Harold Koontz, Cyril O'Donnel and Heinz Weihrich, "Management," McGraw-Hill International Book Company, Auckland, 1983, p. 162.
7. *Ibid.*, p. 164.

policies are achieved." However, allowance is provided for flexibility and deviation. The strategic managers are expected to know the procedures of the firm and various departments as they help him in the process of strategy implementation.

Rules

Rules are the guidelines that require that specific and definite actions be taken or not taken in a given situation. Thus, no allowance is provided for flexibility and deviations in the rules. Rules are, thus, related to procedure, in that they guide action. However, it doesn't specify time limit. Procedure can be seen as a sequence of rules. However, a rule may or may not be a part of procedure. Strategic managers should carefully understand the rules at various levels of the organisation while implementing the strategies.

Programmes

Programmes are a complex of goals, policies, procedures, rules, task assignments, steps to be taken, resources to be employed and other elements necessary to perform a predetermined action. Programmes are supported by necessary capital and operating budgets. Many sub-programmes may be formulated based on the master programme. For example US $ a billion construction programme by Kenangam Enterprises Ltd., of Korea in Eritrea is a master programme and the sub-programmes formulated based on this master programme are: Sembel Housing Programme in Asmara, Power Project Construction Programme in Masawa, programme of construction of new buildings for University of Asmara., programme of construction of international airports in six cities, etc.

Goal

Goal is precise is expressed in clear and specific terms. The goal for the objective of increase in the rate of profitability may be stated as increase in the percentage of profit on the equity capital from 15 to 18.

Strategy

A strategy is a unified, comprehensive and integrated plan that relates to the strategic advantages of the firm to the challenges of the environment. It is designed to ensure that the basic objectives of the enterprise are achieved through proper execution by the organisation.

Tactics

To be effective, strategies must be put into practice. Detailed programmes on the basis of strategies are to be formulated to put the strategies into practice. These detailed programmes are known as tactics. Tactics are the action programmes through which strategies are executed. Strategies must be supported by effective tactics.

Organisational, decision varies from a broad master strategy at one end and minute tactics at the other. The strategists should have a clear understanding about the differences between strategy and tactics. Exhibit19.1 presents Strategy versus Tactics.

Exhibit 19.1 : Strategy Vs Tactics

Strategy	*Tactics*
1. **Level of Conduct** : Strategy is developed at the top level of the management and relates relates exclusively to decisions in the province of these levels.	Tactics are employed at and relate to lower levels of management.
2. **Regularity** : The formulation of strategy is both continuous and irregular. The process is continuous, but the timing of decision is irregular for it depends upon and is triggered by the appearance of opportunities, new ideas, management initiative, crisis and other non-routine stimuli.	Tactics are determined, for many companies, on a periodic cycle with a fixed time schedule, such as the annual budget process.
3. **Subjective Value** : Strategic decision-making is more heavily weighted with subjective values.	Tactical decision-making is less weighted with subjective values.
4. **Range of Alternatives** : The total possible range of alternatives from which a management must choose is far greater in strategy.	The total possible range of alternatives from which a management must choose is less in tactics.
5. **Uncertainty** : Uncertainty is usually much greater in both formulation and implementation of the strategy. It is difficult to assess the risks in strategy.	It is usually less in tactics. Risks are more easily assessed in tactics.
6. **Nature of Problems** : Strategic problems are generally unstructured and tend to be one of a kind.	Tactical problems are more structural and often repetitive in nature.
7. **Information Needs** : Strategy formulation requires large amounts of information desired from and relating to areas of knowledge outside the corporation. Most of the relevant data needed relate to the future are difficult to get with accuracy and are tailored to each problem.	Tactical informational needs, rely more heavily on internally generated data. Particularly from accounting system, and involve a higher proportionate use of historical information.
8. **Time Horizons** : Strategies, especially when successful, are intended to, and do, last for long periods of time. However, sometimes, the time dimension is very short.	Tactics cover a shorter duration and are more uniform for all parts of an operating programme.
9. **Reference** : Strategy is original in the sense that it is the source or origin for the development of tactics.	Tactics are formulated within and in pursuit of strategies.
10. **Detail** : Strategies are usually broad and with few details.	Tactics have many details.
11. **Type of Personnel Involved in Formulation** : Strategies are mostly formulated by top management and its staff.	Tactics are formulated by lower-level executives.
12. **Ease of Evaluation** : It is difficult to evaluate strategies. It takes a number of years to evaluate strategy.	It is easy to evalute tactics. Tactical results are quickly evident and much more easily identified with specific actions.
13. **Point of View** : Strategies are formulated from a corporate point of view.	Tactics are developed principally from a functional point of view.
14. **Importance** : Strategies are of highest importance to an organisation.	Tactics are relatively less important.

Source: Modified version from : George A. Steiner, John B. Niner and Edmund R. Gray, "Management Policy and Strategy." Macmillan Publishing Company, New York, 1986. pp. 13-14.

Budget

A budget is a statement of expected results expressed in numeric terms. Hence, it is referred to as "numerised programme." Budgets are expressed in financial terms, mandays/man hours terms, units of products, machine hours, etc. Different kinds of budgets include: expense budget, capital expenditure budget, sales budget, cash budget, working capital budget and the like.

Budgetary planning is accurate, detailed and clear. Budgets may be variable budgets and flexible budgets.

THE STRATEGIST

Introduction

It is general view that the general manager in an organisation is the main ingredient in understanding the process of strategy formation. One should not take such a narrow view of the strategist. Anyone in the organisation who controls key or precedent setting actions can be called a strategist. It is also viewed that the strategist can be a collection of people. However, the senior general managers are key candidates for such a role as their perspective is broader than any of their subordinates.

1. The Tasks of a Manager

Mintzbery challenges the traditional view that the managers plan, organise, direct and control. The point is that these words are too vague to understand the reality of managerial work.

Research studies stated that, "managers work at an unrelating pace, and their activities are characterised by brevity, variety, and discontinuity and that they are strongly oriented to action and dislike reflective activities."[8] In addition, managerial task, "involves performing a number of regular duties including ritual and ceremonial, negotiations, and processing of soft information that links the organisation with its environment," Further it is stated that, "the manager's programmes — to schedule time, process information, make decisions and so on – remain locked deep inside their brains."[9] Hence, management specialist has concentrated his efforts on the specialised functions of the organisations, where he could more easily analyse the procedure and quality the relevant information. This is due to the increasing pressure on his job from the customers, subordinates with more democratic norms, demands from the government and increasing influences from outsiders.

2. Roles of a Manager

Managers perform different roles as shown in Figure 19.1. As can be seen from the figure, formal authority gives rise to three informational roles. The two sets of roles enable the manager to play the four decisional roles.

Interpersonal Role

The important interpersonal roles of strategists are:

8. Henry Mintzberg, "The Managers' Job" in James Brain Quinn, Henry Mintzberg and Robert M.James (Eds), *op. cit.*, p. 23.
9. *Ibid.*, pp. 25-26.

Figurehead Role: Managers perform the duties of a ceremonial nature as head of the organisation or strategic business unit or department. Duties of interpersonal roles include routine, involving little serious communication and less important decisions. However, they are important for the smooth functioning of an organisation or department.

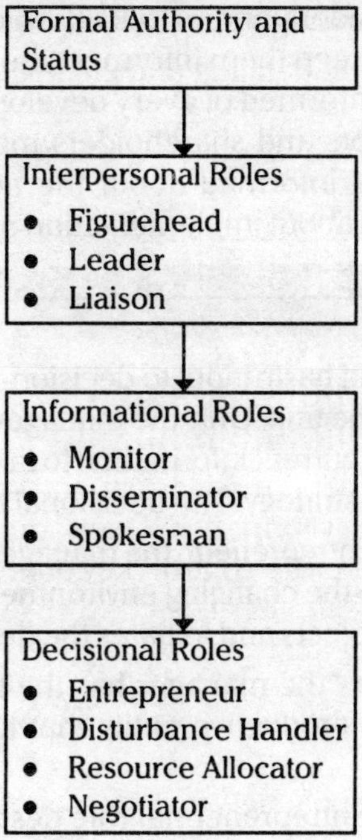

Source : Henry Mintzberg, "The Manager's Job", in James Brain Quinn, Henry Mintzberg and Robert M.James, "The Strategy, Process", Prentice-Hall, New Jersey, 1988, p. 27.

Fig. 19.1. Roles of Manager.

Leader Role: The manager, as in charge of the organisation/department, coordinates the work of others and leads his subordinates. Formal authority provides greater potential power to exercise and get the things done.

Liaison Role: As the leader of the organisation or unit, the manager has to perform the functions of motivation, communication, encouraging team spirit and the like. Further, he has to coordinate the activities of all his subordinates, which involves the activity of liaison.[10]

Informational Role

Manager emerges as the nerve centre of his organisation/department in view of his interpersonal links with his subordinates, peers, superiors and outsiders. Therefore, the manager has to play the information role effectively to let the information flow continuously from one corner to the other corner.

The information roles of a manager include:

Monitor Role: As a result of the network of contacts, the manager gets the information by scanning his environment, subordinates, peers and superiors. Managers, mostly collect information in verbal form often as gossip, hearsay, speculation and through grapevine channels.

10. *Ibid.*, pp. 27-29.

Disseminator Role: Manager disseminates the information, he collects from different sources and through various means. He passes some of the privileged information directly to his subordinates, who otherwise have no access to it. The manager will play an important role in disseminating the information to his subordinates, when they don't have contact with one another.

Spokesman Role: Some insiders and/or outsiders control the unit/department or the organisation. The manager has to keep them informed about the developments in his unit. The manager has to keep his superior informed of every development in his unit, who in turn inform the insiders and outsiders. Directors and shareholders must be informed about the financial performance, customers must be informed about the new product developments, quality maintenance, government officials about implementation of law etc.

Decisional Roles

Information is an important and basic input to decision-making. The managers play a crucial role in decision-making system of the unit. Only the manager can commit the department to new course of action and he has full and current information to take set of the decisions that determine the department's or organisational strategy. The decisional roles of the manager are:

Entrepreneurial Role: As an entrepreneur, the manager is a creator and innovator. He seeks to improve his department, adapt to the changing environmental factors. The manager would like to have new ideas, initiates new projects and initiates the developmental projects.

According to Peter F. Drucker, "the manager has the task of creating a true whole that is larger than the sum of its parts, a productive entity that turns out more than the sum of the resources put into it."[11]

Disturbance Handler Role: Entrepreneurial role describes the manager as the voluntary initiator of change, the disturbance handler role presents the manager as the involuntarily responding to pressures. Pressures of the situation are severe and highly demand the attention of the manager and as such the manager cannot ignore the situation. For example, worker strike, declining sales, bankruptcy of a major customer etc.

The manager should have enough time in handling disturbance carefully, skilfully and effectively.

Resource Allocator Role: The most important resource that a manager allocates to his subordinates is his time. The manager should have an open-door policy and allow the subordinates to express their opinions and share their experiences. This process helps both the manager and his subordinates in making effective decisions. In addition, the manager should empower his subordinates by delegating his authority and power.

Negotiator Role: Managers spend considerable time in the task of negotiations. He negotiates with the subordinates for improved commitment and loyalty, with the peers for cooperation, coordination and integrations, with workers and their unions regarding conditions of employment, commitment, productivity, with the government about providing facilities for business expansion etc.

These negotiations are integral part of the manager's job for only he has authority to commit organisational resources and has nerve centre of information.[12]

11. Peter F. Drucker, "The Practice of Management," 1954, pp. 341-342.
12. Henry Mintzberg, *op. cit.*, pp. 30-31.

Though the different roles of a manager are discussed separately for convenience, they are, infact inseparable. The manager has to perform these roles simultaneously by integrating one with the another. Thus, the major role of the manager is integrating all the roles while playing managerial role or performing his tasks. In fact, the manager cannot play any one role isolating the other roles. As a strategist, the manager has to integrate all the roles in decision-making and performing his tasks.

THE GENERAL MANAGEMENT FUNCTION

Introduction

Though, there are different sub–systems in an organisation like human resource sub–system, marketing sub–system, finance sub–system and production/operations sub–system, organisation as a whole is a single system. The responsibility for the management of this single system rests upon general management. General management includes the board of directors, chief executive officers, entrepreneurs, SBU executives, zonal/area managers, consultants, functional heads, middle level executives and junior level/lower level executives. The strategists perform various general management functions at the policy and executive level. Exhibit 19.2 presents the principal general management functions. Exhibit 19.3 present the strategic management responsibilities of General Managers.

Exhibit 19.2 : Principal General Management Functions
Setting Objectives
Monitoring the Environment
Establishing Strategies
Obtaining Resources
Allocating Resources
Developing Plans and Budgets
Approving Plans and Budgets
Performance Review of the Organisation
Employment of Officers
Coordinating the work of the Board of Directors and Executives
Providing Expert help and Consultancy
Representing the Firm to Outside Parties
Utilising Outside Contacts to the Benefits of the Firm
Utilising Outside Consultants and Experts
Human Resource Development
Managing Operations.

Source: Modified version from Melvin J. Stanford, "Management Policy," Prentice-Hall, Inc., Englewood Cliffs, 1983, p.18.

Exhibit 19.3 : Strategic Management Responsibilities of General Managers
1. **Establishing the Mission** – deciding on the business or businesses that the company or division should engage in and other fundamentals that will guide and characterise the business, such as continuous growth. A mission is usually enduring and timeless.
2. **Formulating a Company Philosophy** – establishing the beliefs, values, attitudes and unwritten guidelines and add up to, "the way we do things around here."
3. **Establishing Policies** – deciding on plans of action to guide the performance of all major activities in carrying out strategy in accordance with company philosophy.
4. **Setting Objectives** – deciding on achievement targets within a defined time range. Objectives are narrower in scope than the mission and are designed to aid in making operational plans for carrying out strategy.
5. **Developing Strategy** – developing concepts, ideas and plans for achieving objectives successfully and meeting and beating the competition. Strategic planning is part of the total planning process that includes management and operation planning.
6. **Planning the Organisation Structure** – developing the plan of organisation and the activities that help people work together to perform activities in according with strategy, philosophy and policies.
7. **Providing Personnel** – recruiting, selecting and developing people to fill the positions in the organisation plan.
8. **Establishing Procedures** – determining and prescribing how all important and recurrent activities will be carried out.
9. **Providing Facilities** – providing the plant, equipment, and other physical facilities required to carry on the business.
10. **Providing Capital** – making sure the business has the money, and credit needed for working capital and physical facilities.
11. **Setting Standards** – establishing measures of performance that will enable the business to best achieve its long term objectives successfully.
12. **Establishing Management Programmes and Operational Plans** – Developing programmes and plans governing activities and the use of resources that, when carried out in accordance with established strategy, policies, procedures and standards, will enable people to achieve particular objectives. These are phases of total planning process, which includes strategic planning.
13. **Providing Control Information** – supplying facts and figures to help people follow the strategy, policies, procedures and programmes, to keep alert to forces at work inside and outside the business; to measure overall company performance against established plans and standards.
14. **Activating People** – Commanding and motivating people to act in accordance with philosophy, policies, procedures and standards in carrying out the plans of the company.

Source: Marvin Bower, "The Will to Manage Corporate Success Through Programmed Management," McGraw-Hill, New York, 1966, pp. 17-18.

We can understand from the functions presented in the Exhibit 19.1 that the general managers of an organisation are executives at the pinnacle of the enterprise or strategic business units who are responsible for the survival and the effective functioning of the corporation.[13] As stated earlier, these general managers range from board of directors to junior executives in an organisation.

Skills of General Managers: General managers need a variety of skills as they are expected to do a variety of functions and perform different roles we have studied earlier in this chapter.

13. Lawrence R. Jauch and William F. Glueck, *op. cit.*, p. 47.

Top level managers are required to have more emphasis on conceptual skills, with relatively less emphasis on human relations skills and low requirement for technical skills. In contrast, lower level managers are assumed to require more emphasis on technical skills and less emphasis on conceptual skills. The middle level managers are expected to have more of human relations skills and moderate degree of conceptual and technical skills as can be seen from Exhibit 19.4.

Exhibit 19.4 : Degree of Skill Requirement for the General Managers at Different Levels

General Management Level	*Degree of Skill Requirement*		
	Conceptual Skills	*Human Relations Skills*	*Technical Skills*
Top Level Managers	High	Moderate	Low
Middle Level Managers	Moderate	High	Moderate
Lower Level Managers	Low	Moderate	High

What Does General Manager Do ?: The general manager is an entrepreneur, strategist, organisation builder, leader and chief implementor. General managers integrate various activities, roles, functions and areas in the process of achieving organisational objectives. According to Harvard Business School, a general manager requires, "Judgement, courage, empathy, the ability to articulate and persuade."

The research studies found that the general managers perform activities differently compared to what theorists say they should do. (Exhibit 19.5) The general managers must simultaneously handle several different activities. Responsibilities and activities of general management are shared by board of directors and executives at top level, middle level and lower level. However, crucial decisions are referred to the shareholders.

Exhibit 19.5 : A Contrast of Theory and Research on the General Manager's Activities

Areas	*The Research says that the General Managers actually do*	*The Theorists say that the General Managers should do*
1. Time allocations	Avoid spending great amounts of time on one issue.	Spend concentrated time to get results.
2. Time horizons	Seek activities that are currently, preferring "hot" information.	Formulate effective strategies that require consideration of major current future trends.
3. Information sources	Prefer verbal sources and avoid documented information.	Formulate effective strategies that require thorough environmental and organisational analysis.
4. Planning process	Discuss strategy in meetings, but such work is fragmented and lacks focus.	Formulate effective strategies that require commitment, focus and concentrated efforts.
5. Basic purposes	Have work that is fragmented with no concentration of effort or pattern of activities.	Have as basic purpose, that of establishing organisational goals and developing the strategies needed to achieve them.

Main Source : C.W. Hofer and C.N. Toftoy, "How CEUs Set Strategic Decision for Their Organisation." Paper Presented at the Ácademy of Management Meeting, 1984.

Shareholders and Strategic Management

The shareholders are the owners of the company. But it is not possible for them to manage their company as they are: *(i)* mainly occupied in various activities, *(ii)* large in number, *(iii)* scattered throughout the length and breadth of the country and *(iv)* not expected to have managerial skills. Hence, they elect the directors to act as their representatives and manage the company. The role of the shareholders is limited to certain statutory requirements of the Companies Act, 1956. However, very crucial strategic decisions are to be taken by the shareholders in their meetings. The representative of the shareholders, i.e., the board of directors share the responsibilities and activities of management with the executives at different levels.

The Board of Directors and Strategic Management

Board of directors represents the shareholders of the company. Mostly, the directors are elected by the shareholders and they in turn elect the Managing Director. The ultimate authority of the Joint Stock Company, lies with the board of directors. However, the authority of the board is subject to the limitations imposed by the Memorandum of Association, Articles of Association of the company and there relevant provisions of the Companies Act, 1956.

The functions and responsibilities of the board of directors differ based on the board composition and its relationship with the company regarding its management. Some directors on the board are appointed by the government to look after its interests. Some directors are appointed by the financial institutions like Industrial Finance Corporation of India, Industrial Development Bank of India, Industrial Credit and Investment Corporation of India and State Financial Corporations which provide long-term loans and advances to the company, to safeguard their interest. Some experts are also appointed on the board to offer their expertise to the company. Some companies emphasise only on legal aspects of board functions. However, many companies today emphasise on management aspects of board functions also.

Responsibilities of Board of Directors

The responsibilities and duties of the board of directors are:

Trusteeship: The board of directors act as trustees to the property and welfare of the company. Hence, the board must use the company's property for the long-run gain of the company, but not for their personal use.

Formulation of Mission, Objection and Policies: Board of directors must see the long run view and have long run perspective of the company. The board formulates, reviews and reformulates the company's mission, objectives and policies which forms the basis for strategy formulation and implementation.

Designing Organisational Structure: The board designs the structure of the organisation based on the objectives, policies, environmental factors, degree of competition, role of quality, expectations of employees etc.

Selection of Top Executives: The board should assume the responsibility of screening and selecting the top executives who can formulate and implement the strategies. Chief executives are key personnel in the process of strategy implementation.

Financial Sanctions: The important financial decisions like sanctioning of finances to various projects, reserves, distribution of profit to shareholders and repayment of loans and advances etc., are taken by the board. Further, the board reviews the financial performance of the company from time to time and reformulates the financial policies.

Feed forward and Feedback: The board has to obtain information from the external environmental factors and feed that information forward to various key points in the company in order to prevent possible hurdles and mistakes in the process of achieving organisational goals. Further, the board also obtains the information from internal sources of the organisation, and feeds it forward to prevent possible failures in decision-making by the top level executives.

The board also feeds the information back to the executives regarding their failures in decision-making with a view to avoid the reocurrence of such mistakes. Thus, feedback of information helps the board to check and control the activities as board has the ultimate responsibility for the success of the company.

Link between the Company and External Environment: The board acts a vital and continuous link between the company and external environment like government, other companies, social and economic institutions etc.

Legal Functions: The board of directors also perform certain legal functions required as per the Companies Act 1956 like criminal liabilities.

Exhibit 19.6 presents legal functions of the boards.

Formal and Information Functions: In fact, the board has to direct and lead the executives. The directing function has both formal and informal components.[14] The board, formally reviews and screens the executive decisions and informally directs the activities in view of environmental factors. In general, the board directs, guides and controls the top executives in formulating, implementing, evaluating and controlling objectives, policies and strategies.

In Practice: Mace, in his research, found that the board of directors actually –

1. Serve as source of advice and counsel;
2. Offer some sort of discipline, value; and
3. Act in crisis situations,[15] instead of performing (as per the concepts) of –
    1. Selecting top executives;
    2. Determining policy;
    3. Measuring results;
    4. Asking discerning questions.

Exhibit 19.6 : Legal Functions of the Board of Directors

I. Duty of Loyalty

A. Avoiding conflicts of Interest

B. Fairness

C. Corporate Opportunity (ahead of personal)

D. Confidentiality

II. Duty of Care

A. A director shall perform his duties as a director in good faith, in a manner he reasonably believes to be in the best interest of the corporation, and with such case as an ordinarily prudent person in a like position would use under similar circumstances.

B. Attention
1. Attention at meetings
2. Reliance on management and professional information
3. Delegation (to management to operate the business)

C. Decision-Making – exercise reasonable business judgement.

Main Source : Modified version from : Corporate Director's Guidebook, 1976.

14. S.K. Bhattacharya and N. Venkataraman, "Managing Business Enterprises –Strategies, Structure and Systems." Vikas Publishing House, New Delhi, 1983, pp. 168-169.
15. Myles L. Mace, "Directors: Myth and Reality," Harvard Business School, Boston, 1971, pp. 10-71.

The charter of duties and responsibilities for board of directors as suggested by Mace, are shown in Exhibit 19.7.

Exhibit 19.7 : The Charter of Duties and Responsibilities of Board of Directors
1. Responsibilities To Shareholders. Monitoring: *(a)* Return on Investment *(b)* Security of Investment *(c)* Dividend Policy *(d)* Social Accountabilities 2. Select and elect CEO (usually the president) and delegate to him all the duties to manage the company not specifically reserved to the board. 3. Evaluate the performance of the CEOs and division presidents for performance and compensation. 4. Evaluate performance of CEOs and division presidents quarterly in comparison with competitors. 5. Review and approve major corporate objectives, policies, budgets and strategies as initiated by the CEO. In reviewing the strategic plan, confirm its directors, or propose changes of direction. 6. Monitor, review and appraise management: *(a)* Provide for orderly succession of CEOs *(b)* Duties and limits of CEOs *(c)* Selection of outside legal counsel *(d)* Select all officers *(e)* Compensation of officers *(f)* Advise Managing Directors and others. 8. Monitor, review and approve employee relations. 9. Monitor company's performance. 10. Management of the board. 11. Compliance with all laws affecting the business.

Source: Modified from: Myles L. Mace, "Designing a plan for the Ideal Board," *Harvard Business Review*, November-December 1976, pp. 21-22.

Changes in Boards: Changes in boards were forecasted and are as follows:

1. Boards will shrink in size – become working boards.
2. Boards will meet less often instead board committees will meet quite often.
3. Proportion of outside nominated and/or appointed members will increase.
4. Age of directors will remain constant.
5. Executive searches for directors – more diversified experience.
6. Less emphasis on stature and more on experience, competence and commitment of directors.
7. Appraisal of directors based on quality and extent of contribution to the firm.
8. Directors will demand sufficient time and information to make decisions and will exercise power to change the company's course when considered necessary.
9. More scrutiny of possible conflicts of interest.
10. Increase compensation of directors, based on increased time and talent commitment.[16]

16. "The Changing Board," Directors and Boards, Winter 1979, pp. 50-51. and 57. Quoted in Melvin J. Stanford, "Management Policy," Prentice-Hall Inc., Englewood Cliffs, 1983, p. 22.

International Scenario : A research study conducted by Jeremy Bacon and James K. Brown on, "The Board of Directors: Perspectives and Practices in Nine Countries," shows that the director's responsibilities are about the same in all the nine countries surveyed. They are:

1. Long-range corporate objectives.
2. Corporate strategies or long range plans for meeting objectives.
3. Allocation of major resources.
4. Major financial decisions.
5. Mergers, acquisitions, divestments.
6. Top Management Performance Appraisal.

Smaller Company Boards

Normally, the responsibilities of board of directors in small size companies vary from those of larger companies. However, certain responsibilities of the boards in small and large companies are common. They are compliance with legal requirements, formulation, evaluation and reformulation of objectives, policies and strategies etc. The need for outside help can be critical in small companies. Kumar Jain pointed out important means that outside directors can help small companies. They are:

- As a consultant
- Helping handle government regulations
- Public relationships
- Mediating conflicts between management and investors and regarding objectives, strategy, executive appointment and dismissal and decisions about assets and financial matters
- planning and other areas.

Role of Board in Strategic Management

Board of directors of many companies, in recent times, have actively engaged themselves in strategy formulation. Added to this, with the appointment of outsiders as directors in the boards, more boards are involved with linking strategy with the consequent corporate action (Fig.19.2). These boards are supporting new strategies, mobilising resources, protecting the organisation from outside threats and linking the company with powerful outsiders.[17]

Boards actively involve themselves in formulating vital strategies like mergers, acquisition, takeover, expansion, diversification, backward and forward linkages, etc., evaluation of corporate strategy and performance, advising, guiding and directing the chief executives in strategic management, feeding the data and information back and forward to the top level executives in strategy formulation and implementation.

Thus, the board of directors plays a crucial role in formulation, implementation, evaluation and reformulation of strategies. Strategic management styles are summarised and presented in Figure 19.3. The board of directors constitute various committees to help in policy making. The responsibilities of these committees are presented in Fig. 19.4.

The Chief Executive Officer and Strategic Management

The Chief Executive Officer (CEO) is designated as the Managing Director, or President or General Manager or Chairman or Executive Director. The CEO is the person responsible for the

17. S.Kumar Jain, "Look to Outsiders to Strengthen Small Business Boards," *Harvard Business Review*, July-August 1980, pp. 162-170. Quoted in *Ibid.*, p. 25.

functioning of the entire organisation. He cannot really delegate all his or her strategic responsibilities to anyone else, despite the fact that the board of directors and other officers can play a major role in this process.[18]

Effect of Gresham's Law of Planning: The CEO is normally involved in day-to-day and routine activities and consequently is left with a little time for broader and important considerations. As such, the CEO is always faced with the effects of Gresham's Law of Planning, which states that, "Routine drives out creativity." A top priority requirement of the CEO is to allocate time for strategic responsibilities.[19]

The CEO is expected to play a crucial and multiple roles in formulating and implementing mission, objectives, policies and strategies. His multiple roles include: organisation builder, organisation leader, sharing success, executive selection, and path to the top.

CEO as Organisation Builder: The CEO has the responsibility for organisation building through organisational change. Organisational building strategies depend on the market opportunities, expansion and diversification. Organisational changes should be made gradually and regularly and assignment of responsibilities for the organisation should be permanent, not situational.[20] People resist change due to: (i) parochial self-interest, (ii) misunderstanding and lack of trust, (iii) different assessments, (iv) low tolerance for change. The CEO can deal with the resistance through

(i) Education and communication,
(ii) Participation and involvement,
(iii) Facilitation and support
(iv) Negotiation and agreement,
(v) Manipulation and cooperation,
(vi) Explicit and implicit coercion.[21]

CEO as Organisation Leader: The CEO must have a base for leadership. A leader must have support from both within and outside the organisation, in addition to personal skills. A leader must have the skill of "motivation to manage," which includes:

Degree of Involvement in Strategic Management

Low (Passive)					High (Active)
Phantom	*Rubber Stamp*	*Minimal Review*	*Normal Participation*	*Active Participation*	*Catalyst*
Never knows what to do; if anything; no degree of involvement.	Permits officers to make all decisions. It votes as the officers recommend on action issues.	Formally reviews selected issues that officers bring to its attention.	Involved to a limited degree in the performance or review of selected key decisions, indicators or programmes of management.	Approves questions, and makes final decisions on mission, strategy, policies and objectives. Has active board committees. Performs fiscal and management audits.	Takes the leading role in establishing and modifying the mission. Objectives, strategy and policies. It has a very active strategy committee.

Source: Thomas L. Wheelen and J. David Hunger, "Strategic Management and Business Policy," Addison- Wesley Publishing Company, Reading, 1986, p. 57.

Fig. 19.2 Degree of Involvement of Board of Directors in Strategic Management.

18. Melvin J. Stanford, *op. cit.*, p. 27.
19. *Ibid.*
20. Shea Smitth III and John E. Walsh, Jr., "Strategies in Business," John Wiley, New York, 1978, p. 184
21. John P. Kotter and Leonard A. Schlesinger, " Choosing Strategies for Change," *Harvard Business Review*, March-April 1979, pp. 106-114.

(i) favourable attitude towards those in positions of authority, such as supervisors
(ii) desire to engage in competition, especially with peers
(iii) desire to assist oneself and take charge
(iv) desire to exercise power and authority over others, particularly subordinates
(v) desire to behave in a distinctive and different way, which involves standing out from the crowd.
(vi) sense of responsibility in carrying out the numerous routine duties associated with managerial work.[22]

Degree of Involvement by Top Management	Low	High
High	Entrepreneurship Management	Partnership Management
Low	Chaos Management	Marionette Management

Fig. 19.3 Strategic Management Styles.

Source : Thomas L. Wheelen and J. David Hunger, *op. cit.*, p. 71.

Executive Committee

1. To act within specified bounds for the board of directors between board meetings.
2. To serve as a "sounding board" for ideas of the CEO before they are presented to the full board.
3. To monitor, extended negotiations.
4. To oversee activities not specific delegated to other committees.

Audit Committee

1. To assure that company policies and practices are within the bounds of accepted conduct.
2. To select (or recommend) auditors and determine the scope of audits.
3. To review financial reports to gain full insight into the company's current and future financial condition.
4. To review internal accounting procedures.
5. To assure the integrity of the company's operations.

Compensation Committee

1. To assure that compensation (including stock options, benefits, bonuses, and salaries) will attract, hold and motivate key personnel.
2. To see that compensation and benefit plans throughout the organisation are competitive, equitable, and well executed.
3. To oversee the development and implementation of human resource plans.

Financial Committee

1. To review and advise the board on the financial structure and needs of the organisation.
2. To recommend to management and the board the timing and types of financing needed (both long and short-term).

22. John B. Miner, "The Human Constraint: The Coming Shortage of Managerial Talent", Bureau of National Affairs, Washington D.C., 1974.

3. To assist top management in establishing good working relationships with the financial community.
4. To provide advise about various investment, expenditure, and funding alternatives.

Nominating Committee

1. To recommend candidates for membership on the board.
2. To recommend candidates for managerial or officer positions in the company.
3. To advise management on human resource planning.

Source: Adapted from J.K. Louden, *The Director* (New York: AMACOM, 1982), Chapter 7.

Fig. 19.4 : Responsibilities of Board Committees

Success Sharing by CEO

Monitoring, sponsoring and helping others along the road to success, is an important activity of CEO. The CEO has to help the others both within and outside their organisation along the road to success in various ways like training, coaching, assisting, informing, writing letters of recommendations etc. Managers at higher levels spend more time in monitoring or sponsoring the subordinates.[23]

Executive Qualities of CEO

Personalities of successful CEOs tend to vary considerably, but they also have some commonalities. The qualities of CEOs are:

(i) Knowing the strengths and spend most of their time in performing those activities in which they are strong.
(ii) Know how to manage their time.[24]
(iii) Satisfy the board of directors and shareholders.
(iv) *Intuitor*: A creative, artistic person who deals well with ideas, theories and innovations.
(v) *Thinker*: Highly, organised and efficient with a mind like a calculator.
(vi) *Feeler*: Sentimental, loyal and "true blue"; thrives on personal relationships.
(vii) *Sensor*: Restless, driving "doer", a frequently impatient, tireless competitor.
(viii) Motivated by power and ability to make things happen.
(ix) Comfortable with a wide range of people, but prefers casual associates.
(x) A high energy level.
(xi) Immune to stress-related diseases.[25]

Personality Dimensions for Selection of CEO

Harry Levinson, suggested some dimensions of personality as a basis for selection of Chief Executive Officer. These criteria are:

(i) Capacity to abstract, to conceptualise, to organise and to integrate different data into a coherent frame of reference.

23. Gerard R. Roche, "Much Ado About Mentors," *Harvard Business Review*, January- February, 1979, pp. 14-28.
24. Peter F. Drucker, "How the Effective Does It," *Fortune*, February, 1967.
25. Bill Sloan, "Life at the Top," *Dallas*, September, 1979, pp. 15-19.

(ii) Tolerance for ambiguity, can stand confusion until things become clear.
(iii) Intelligence, has to capacity only to abstract but also to be practical.
(iv) Judgement, knows when to act.
(v) Authority, has the feeling that he or she belongs in the boss's role.
(vi) Activity, takes a vigorous orientation to problems and needs of the organisation.
(vii) Achievement, oriented toward organisation's success rather than personal aggrandisement.
(viii) Sensitivity, able to perceive subtleties of others' feelings.
(ix) Involvement, sees oneself as a participating member of an organisation.
(x) Maturity, has good relationship with authority figures.
(xi) Interdependence, accepts appropriate dependency needs of others as well as of him or himself.
(xii) Articulateness, makes a good impression.
(xiii) Stamina, has physical as well as mental energy.
(xiv) Adaptability, manages stress well.
(xv) Sense of humour, does not take self too seriously.
(xvi) Vision, is clear about progression of his or her own life and career, as well as where the organisation should go.
(xvii) Perserverance, able to stick to a task and see it through regardless of the difficulties encountered.
(xviii) Personal organisation, has good sense of time.
(xix) Integrity, has a well-established value system which has been tested in various ways in the past.
(xx) Social responsibility, appreciates the need to assume leadership with respect to that responsibility.[26]

Role of CEO in Strategic Management

Among all the strategists, the Chief Executive Officer (CEO) is the key person in strategic management. He is the link between the board and top level executives of the organisation. Being the top most general manager of the organisation, he integrates different functional areas of management and visualises the total organisation. He also foresees the external environmental factors and their impact on the business. He organises the whole data, ideas and information and conceptualises them.

The CEO looks forward based on his past experience and ability to understand the future changes. He evaluates the present mission, objectives, policies and strategies against the future probable changes and reformulates them, if necessary. Further, he formulates new objectives, policies and strategies as and when grand changes in the environment like economic liberalisations and technological advancements take place.

The CEO provides information and data to the board regarding strategy formulation. He provides the observations of strategy evaluation to the board and advises it either to continue the present strategy or to reformulate it or formulate a new strategy.

26. Harry Levinson, "Criteria for Choosing Chief Executives," *Harvard Business Review*, July - August 1980, pp. 114-118.

The CEO provides data regarding external environment to the senior mangers, guides and helps them in formulating, implementing and evaluating and reformulating strategies at strategic business units are based on the corporate strategies.

Entrepreneurs and Strategic Management

"Entrepreneurs are individuals who start a business from scratch."[27] Many entrepreneurs start a business like this. "The entrepreneur always searches for change, responds to it and exploits it as an opportunity."[28] The qualities of an entrepreneur include:

(i) Zeal to do something new.
(ii) Enthusiasm, idealism, sense of purpose.
(iii) Independence of thought and action.
(iv) Having creative and innovative ideas.
(v) As initiators, they motivate others to follow or imitate them.
(vi) Proactive rather than reactive in actions.

The entrepreneur is the chief strategist in an entrepreneurial firm. By virtue of his qualities discussed above, the entrepreneur formulates creative objectives and novel strategies and thereby exploits the markets. As he is proactive in actions, he initiates the change and creates the opportunities for himself and reaps the fruits. Then he acts as a guide and path finder to others. Thus, the entrepreneur, controls and moulds the external environmental factors to his favour through his innovative strategies.

The entrepreneur inspires his subordinates in strategy formulation, implementation and evaluation. He closely participates along with the subordinates in strategy reformulation. Strategic management is just like a play to the entrepreneurs and he makes it a play to his subordinates also.

The entrepreneur will face problems, if he expands the organisation into a large one. He has to meet the challenges of competition, appointing competent managers who should be more intelligent and can see the future beyond the entrepreneur's vision. It would be very difficult to the entrepreneurs to recruit the executives with these qualities. Hence, it would be appropriate to the entrepreneurs, to consider this limitation while formulating expansion and diversification strategies.

Chief of the Family Operated Firm and Strategic Management

A family operated firm is a business whose major ownership, management and control is by a family and most of the key executives are family members. The chief of the family (or Karta of the family) is the main strategist. The chief strategist of the family must consider the preferences of the family members who are active in the management of the firm and/or family. Normally, the family members render full support to the chief and do not interfere in normal activities of the business. Therefore, the family chief formulates the strategies like entrepreneurs.[29] Women

27. Lawrence R. Jauch and William F. Glueck, *op. cit.*, p. 52.
28. Peter F. Drucker, "Innovation and Entrepreneurship," William Heinemann, London, 1985, p. 25.
29. Lawrence R. Jauch and William F. Glueck, *op. cit.*, p. 54.

are also starting family business, in recent times. The chief of the business takes the strategic decision by involving the other members of the family in the process. In fact, he encourages and develops other members in strategic management.

The family operating business also will have certain limitations in expanding the business into a large one, as entrepreneur's business, though, it may not be of the same magnitude. Hence, the chief of the family business should also consider this limitation while formulating expansion and diversification strategies.

Strategic Business Unit – Level Strategists

The diversified businesses, multi-product, multi-service, multi-divisionalised firms are organised into Strategic Business Units (SBUs). The head of each SBU is its chief executive. If the company is structured based on the modern principles of organisation like, autonomy, freedom, responsibility and empowerment, corporate strategists encourage the SBU level Chief executives in formulating their strategies.

SBU chief executives, play a vital role in strategic management at their level as the chief executive at corporate level. The SBU level chief executive performs the roles similar to those of Managing Director and attempts to achieve the best results in their business units within the facilities and resources provided, autonomy and freedom sanctioned and under the overall guidelines of the corporate objectives and policies.

Intrapreneurship: With a view to avail the benefits of entrepreneurship, the corporate world started providing the entrepreneurial climate in their SBUs. In other words, the SBU chief executive is given freedom and autonomy to develop new ventures, to have vision like entrepreneur etc. This concept is often described as "intrapreneurship."

With the increase in operations, production of new varieties of goods and/or rendering services, need for developing new ventures, the SBU manager is encouraged to start new ventures, or the SBU itself may be a new venture established within the present corporation. For example, Sparkle India Ltd., provided autonomy to its tungsten divisional head to formulate and implement his own strategies and play the role like an entrepreneur. The chief of this SBU empowered his employees and developed them into an autonomous team which could work without the chief.

SBU chief, under these circumstances, plays the role of entrepreneur and strategist. SBU chiefs may have to be replaced when the entrepreneurial activities are completed as with independent entrepreneurs.[30] This situation was more evident in Sparkle's India Ltd's tungsten wire division.

Corporate-Level Planners and Strategic Management

Corporate level planners are the supporting staff to the strategists. The large business firms provide the planning staff to their chief executives who are busy with their prime responsibilities. The planners are specialist staff with skills in strategic management techniques, process, analysis etc. In addition, the planning staff are also trained in various strategic management techniques.

The planning staff prepare the entire ground work for strategic decision-making, implementation, evaluation and reformulation of strategies. Their activities include:

(i) Collection of data and information about (a) external environmental factors, (b) internal strengths and weaknesses and (c) results of the present strategies.

30. *Ibid.*, p. 55.

(ii) Competitor's strategies, their performance, and their proposals for new strategies,
(iii) Identification of new business opportunities and future threats to the existing businesses.
(iv) Performing and maintaining environmental scanning.
(v) Analysing strategy performance.
(vi) Development of the new strategies based on environmental scanning, business opportunities, strategy performance and competitor's strategies.
(vii) Performing of the analysis of strengths, weaknesses, opportunities and threats of each alternative strategy.
(viii) Rank the alternative strategies.
(ix) Conducting research and special studies relating to strategic decision-making and strategic management.
(x) Communicating the alternative strategies, research results etc. to the strategists.
(xi) Providing administrative support to the strategists for formulation and implementation of strategies, and
(xii) Performing any other related work entrusted to them by the strategists like expert advice, suggestions and monitoring.

Perform a Staff Function: Thus, planning staff performs a staff function but not a line function as in case of human resource specialists. These are the rare chances of performing strategic management function by the planning staff, but those chances lead to conflict between the planning staff and the line managers who perform the strategic management functions as that of line and staff conflicts between human resource department (in the staff relationship) and line managers. Hence, it is concluded that, corporate planning staff performs staff function in almost all the situations with regard to strategic management.

Senior Managers and Strategic Management

Senior mangers include second line mangers at the corporate office, divisional office, zonal office, SBUs, functional heads etc. These managers also play due role in strategic management process. Most of the companies constitute the committee for strategy formulation, implementation and evaluation. The committees are constituted with the senior managers as members.

The senior managers perform various functions of strategic management like environmental scanning, finding out business opportunities, formulation of alternative strategies, performing SWOT analysis, examining the strategies, participating in the decision-making process along with other members of the committees.

Middle-Level Managers and Strategic Management

Middle level managers include immediate subordinates to the heads of various functional managers like production manager, marketing manager, finance manager and human resource manager. These managers mostly are executives and therefore, they mostly actively participate in implementation of functional strategies. However, they help the functional heads in formulating functional strategies like production strategy and marketing strategy. They collect the data and information, scan the relevant environment, identify the opportunities, develop the alternative strategies. Perform SWOT analysis relating to functional strategies and participate in strategic decision-making process along with the functional head. These middle-level managers get the required on-the-job training to become functional strategists in the future. Thus, he performs the job of strategic implementation, learns the skill for the future strategist for the organisation and helps the functional head in strategic management.

Lower-Level Executives and Strategic Management

Lower-level executives are the junior managers or managers at the bottom level of the managerial hierarchy. These managers normally take routine decisions which are just repetitive. As far as strategic decisions are concerned, lower-level executives mostly play the role of corporate planning staff. They collect data and information, classify them, tabulate them and present them to the middle-level executives. They also play their role in strategic implementation. They implement the orders of the middle-level executives and mostly perform the work at grass-root level and supervise the work performed by their subordinates. However, they can offer new ideas and suggestions to the top management regarding business opportunities. They also communicate the new concepts of strategic management to the middle-level management, they have learned in their business schools in the recent past.

This process provides the company to share the ideas of the young blood and the lower-level executives get the opportunity of learning practical issues of strategic management and equip talents necessary to formulate and implement strategies.

Consultants and Strategic Management

All organisations may not be large enough to employ strategists owing to economic reasons and also continuous need for the services of the strategists. Consultancy firms have formed to help such organisations. Consultancy services are provided by consultancy companies, individual professionalists and academicians.

Many consultants offer consultancy services in the area of strategic management. They provide consultancy service in the form of designing and helping to implement a formal strategic management system for an enterprise.[31] Other services include: conducting research studies or a part of strategic management process, advising them regarding formulation, implementation and control of strategies. Some of the consultancy firms after providing continuous service to the company, become the chief strategist of the firm.

Consultants provide services on technical matters, evaluate projects and trends affecting the business. Consultants primarily advise the chief strategist of the company as the corporate planning staff and other executives of a large company.

Large-size consultancy firms with their wide network and specialist employees provide a variety strategic management functions to the company. They are: *(i)* collection of data and information, *(ii)* studying the business opportunities, *(iii)* environmental scanning, *(iv)* identifying the strengths and weaknesses of the client firm, *(v)* formulation of alternative strategies, *(vi)* performing SWOT analysis for each strategy, *(vii)* advising the strategist about the strategy formulation, *(viii)* helping the company in implementing the strategy, *(ix)* assisting the company in strategy evaluation, *(x)* guiding the company in reformulation of strategies.

The family owned companies, small companies and companies with high-competition will benefit from the skills, expertise knowledge and varied talents of the consultancy firms. These firms get balanced advise at low cost.

31. *Ibid.*, p. 57.

Thus, consultants provide expertise, balanced and varied services at low cost like corporate planning staff. In other words consultants also perform staff function. The chief strategist of the company, after giving due consideration to the advice of the consultants, formulates the strategy.

STRATEGIC PLANNING AND THE GENERAL MANAGER

The formal strategic planning process supports the strategic management process. It may be highly formalised and include many organisational members, or it may be far less formal approach limited to a few. The terms strategic planning, strategy formulation and strategic management are often used interchangeably. However, some view strategic planning differently. The strategic planning process is a rational model that assumes a certain degree of consensus among decision-makers. Strategic planning is a more pervasive, encompassing activity that also incorporates other organisational realities. The prerequisite for useful strategic planning system is the availability of necessary relevant information. A well-conceived strategic planning process will employ mechanisms to clarify they key assumptions upon which managers will make decisions.

A strategic planning system is a stuctured – that is designed – process that organises and coordinates the activities of the managers who do the planning. An effective planning system requires 'situational design' – it must take into account the specifics of a particular situation, especially the dimensions of size and diversity.

Strategic planning involves allocation of resources to programmed activities calculated to achieve a set of business goals in a dynamic, competitive environment. Strategic management, on the other hand, treats strategic thinking as a pervasive aspect of running a business and regards strategic planning as an instrument around which all other control systems – budgeting, formation, compensation, organisation – can be integrated.[32] This independency usually comes to light when a business has trouble in implementing the results of a freestanding strategic planning process. Exhibit 19.8 presents topics and responses in the evaluation of strategic planning systems in multibusiness companies. Exhibit 19.9 depicts the principles of strategic planning.

Managerial Tasks and Management Control

Managers at all levels from the managing director to the supervisor at the shop floor perform the tasks of strategic planning and management control. These tasks include:

(i) Appraising the external environment in order to be aware of opportunities in the light of the market competition, customers' wants, companies' strengths and weaknesses.
(ii) Formulation of objectives or goals. Where we want to be and what we want to accomplish and when.
(iii) Considering strategic planning premises. In what environment – internal or external – will our strategic plans operate.
(iv) Identify Alternatives. What are the most promising alternatives to accomplishing our objectives?
(v) Compare alternatives in light of goals sought. Which alternative will give us the best chance of meeting our goals at the lowest cost and highest profit?

32. Daniel H, Gray, "Uses and Misues of Strategic Planning," *Harvard Business Review*, January-February, 1986.

(vi) Choose an alternative. Selecting the course of action we will pursue.

(vii) Formulating supporting plans. Such as plans to: buy equipment, buy materials, hire and train workers, develop new product.

(viii) Numerise plans by making budgets. Develop such budgets as volume and price of sales, operating expenses necessary for plans and expenditure for capital equipment.

It is necessary for management to adopt certain assumption or premises – particularly with regard to external factors – that serve as a background for the planning function. One major premise of this type involves public policy and the relationship of government to business, prospective economic conditions, fashion trends, competitive developments and population trends must also be considered in any attempt at intelligent planning.

Managerial tasks also include (i) Establishing standards of performance of implementation of strategic planning, (ii) Measurement of actual performance, (iii) Comparison of actual performance against standards, (iv) Identification of deviations, (v) Analysis of causes of deviation, (vi) Programme of corrective action, (vi) Achievement of desired performance.

Organisation for Strategic Planning

All managers irrespective of their levels, perform the function of strategic planning. However, the magnitude and the scope vary from one level to the another level in the organisational hierarchy. As a basic function, strategic planning is an inherent part of each manager's duties. A distinction can, however be made between the line managers and staff managers. Line managers perform the major part of the strategic planning, whereas the staff managers provide information and assist the line managers in the process.

Exhibit 19.8 : Topics and Responses in the Evaluation of Strategic Planning Systems in Multi-business Companies

Topic	*Response*
Source of greatest frustration or disappointment.	Implementation difficulties.
Other areas of major concern.	Skills of line managers. Adequacy of information.
Rating of current planning system on a Scale 1 to 10, from worst to best.	56 percent in 6-7-8 range. Mode: 7 Mean: 5.5
Nature of planning output	General direction or thrust for strategic action.
Locus of planning responsibility.	Line managers; 78 percent.
Relation to budget process.	Planning first, budgeting afterward: 55 percent.
Sources of market information.	In-house: 80 percent.
Number of strategic business units (SBUs).	Range from 6 to 48.
Basis of unit definition.	Product lines: 57 percent.
Relation of SBUs to profit centres.	Coincide: 51 percent.
How unit goals and objectives are set.	Top-down: 33 percent.
Who owns an SBU's cash flow.	Corporation: 83 percent.
Unit strategy development process.	Interdepartmental group give-and-take: 34 percent.
Linkage of planning to other controls.	More to budgets than anything else: 42 percent.
Impact of strategic planning on organisational	Structure often adapted to support

structure.	strategy: 70 percent.
Relationship of executive bonuses to strategic performance.	Financial results only: 60 percent. Financial and strategic mix: 22 percent.
Authority of groups or divisions over SBU planning.	Not significant: 68 percent. Controlling: 32 percent.
Corporate resource allocation process when resource requests exceed resources available.	Perceived as unfair: 49 percent. Perceived as fair: 37 percent.

Source: Daniel H. Gray, "Uses and Misuses of Strategic Planning," *Harvard Business Review*, Jan-Feb, 1986.

Top management, by virtue of their responsibility, closeness to the information, formulate the strategic plan for the total organisation. Middle level and functional managers formulate the strategic plans for their respective strategic business units and departments. Broad management participation is also necessary for genuine acceptance of adopted plans otherwise, a line manager is inclined to blame the plan, if difficulty is experienced or to ignore it as much as possible. Top management leadership is also essential if effective and comprehensive strategic planning is to be achieved.

Exhibit 19.9 : Some Principles for Strategic Planning

- Strategic planning is a line management function for which training in strategic analysis and participative skills is usually necessary.
- Strategic business units need to be defined so that one executive can control the key variables essential to the execution of his or her strategic business plan.
- A unit's concept of the business must above all be formulated from the outside in so that it can most effectively engage the dynamics of its strategic environment.
- Action plans for achieving business objectives are the key to implementing and monitoring strategy. They require extensive lower-level participation and special leadership skills. Action plans are complete when underlying assumptions, allocation of responsibilities, time and resource requirements, risks, and likely responses have been made explicit.
- Participative strategy development, a prerequisite for successful strategy execution, often requires cultural change at the upper levels of corporations and their business units.
- The strategic planning system and other control systems designed to guide managerial and organisational behaviour must be integrated in a consistent whole if business strategies are to be executed well.
- Productivity improvement programmes are best treated as aspects of strategic business plans since productivity takes on significantly different meanings as the strategic balance between marketing and production shifts.
- Well-managed organisations must be both centralised and decentralized – centralised so that strategies and control systems can be integrated and decentralised so that units in each strategic environment can act and be treated with appropriate differentiation.
- Over time, good strategic planning, once considered a separate activity, becomes a mindset, a style and a set of techniques for running a business – not something more to do but a better way of doing what has always had to be done.

Source : Daniel H. Gray, "Uses and Misuses of Strategic Planning, *Harvard Business Review*, Jan-Feb. 1986.

The Planning Staff: Many corporations have established planning offices called, "Planning Coordinators," "Directors of Plannings," etc., to provide leadership in strategic planning. Strategic planning is not an activity that must be squeezed into an already busy operating schedule for such staff offices. The direct involvement of line managers, including the chief executive, is essential for successful planning. Work of the planning staff supplements, rather than replaces, planning by other managers. The major role of the planning staff is overall coordination of the total planning effort.

Contributions of the Subordinates to Strategic Planning

The top management, performs the function of planning. In addition, strategic plans should also be formulated by the managers at strategic business units level and functional level. The middle level and lower level managers formulates specific plans related to their divisions and departments, within the framework of the organisation's strategic plan. Involvement of line managers in planning requires careful formulation of the planning process to provide for their inputs. Unless the process is structured properly, the pressure of the work or other factors may cause the process to break down. Managers should encourage the subordinates to contribute to the planning by way of submitting proposals. Suggestions or criticisms on the draft plans and participating in the planning committees.

Role of the Chief Executives

The Chief Executive Officer (CEO) is normally involved in day-to-day and routine activities of the business and consequently is left with a little time for broader and important considerations. However, a top priority requirement of the CEO is to allocate time and his resource for strategic planning. The CEO has the responsibility for organisation building through organisational change, leading the organisation as its leader, disseminates information etc. The roles of the CEO as figurehead, leader, liaison, monitor, disseminator, spokesman entrepreneur, disturbance handler and resource allocator are depicted in Exhibit 19.10

Exhibit 19.10 : Key Roles of CEOs

Henry Mintzberg concluded that the job of a top manager contains ten interrelated roles. The importance of each role and the amount of time demanded by each probably varies from one job to another. These roles are as follows:

Figurehead	:	Acts as legal and symbolic head; performs obligatory social, ceremonial, or legal duties (hosts retirement dinners, luncheons for employees, and plant dedications; attends civic affairs; signs contracts behalf of firm).
Leader	:	Motivates, develops, and guides subordinates: oversees staffing, training, and associated activities (introduces Management By Objectives [MBO], develops a challenging work climate, provides a sense of direction, acts as a role model).
Laison	:	Maintains a network of contracts and information sources outside top management in order to obtain information and assistance (meets with key people from the task environment, meets formally and informally with corporate division managers and the CEOs of other firms).
Monitor	:	Seeks and obtains information in order to understand the corporation and its environments; acts as nerve

		centre for the corporation (reviews status reports from vice-presidents, reviews key indicators of corporate performance, scans *Wall Street Journal* and key trade journals, joins select clubs and societies).
Disseminator	:	Transmits information to the rest of the top management team and other key people in the corporation (chairs staff meetings, transmits policy letters, communicates five-year plans).
Spokesman	:	Transmits information to key groups and people in the task environment (prepares annual report to stockholders, talks to the Chamber of Commerce, states corporate policy to the media, participates in advertising campaigns, speaks before congressional committees).
Entrepreneur	:	Searches the corporation and its environment for projects to improve products, processes, procedures, and structures; then supervises the design and implementation of these projects (introduces cost reduction programmes, makes plant trips to divisions, changes forecasting system, brings in subcontract work to level the work load, reorganises the corporation).
Disturbance Handler	:	Takes corrective action in times of disturbance or crisis (personally talks with key creditors, interest groups, congressional committees, union leaders; establishes investigative committees; revises objectives, strategies, and policies).
Resource Allocator	:	Allocates corporate resources by making and/or approving decisions (reviews budgets, revises programme, scheduling, intiates strategic planning, plans personnel load, sets objectives).
Negotiator	:	Represents the corporation in negotiating important agreements; may speak directly with key representatives of groups in the task environment or work through a negotiator; negotiates disagreements within the corporation by working with conflicting division heads (works with labour negotiator; resolves disputes, negotiates with creditors, suppliers and creditors).

Source : H. Mintzberg, "The Nature of Managerial Work," Harper & Row, New York, 1973, pp. 54-94.

Long Range Planning

The basic question in considering any sort of long-range planning is: Why should a firm attempt to look into the future? These are three basic reasons: (i) The first reason for looking into a future in a systematic way to understand the future implications of present decisions, (ii) The second reason for looking into the future in a systematic way is in a sense the observe to the first. As well as considering the future implications of present decisions, it is necessary to examine the present implication of future events, (iii) The third reason for looking into the future in a systematic way is to provide such motivation and such a mechanism.

National, Regional and Corporate Plans

Macro-economic plan at the national level indicates the trends in income, prices, population, production, distribution etc. National level plans indicate the total production of all industries in the country, demand for the production, price level etc. Industry-wise plan indicate the production level of a particular level of a particular industry, distribution of production, price level etc. Regional plans indicate the level of production, price levels of different products in the region. The total of all regions would be the national level estimates. Thus, the regional plans are the basis for the national plan. Corporate plans indicate the level of employment, investment, production, price and different kinds of investment. Estimates of all the corporations functioning in a particular region form the basis for estimates of the region. Thus, the corporate plan is the basis for regional plans and national plan.

CHAPTER 20

ENVIRONMENTAL ANALYSIS

INTRODUCTION

Andrews defines the environment of a company as the pattern of all external influences that affect its life and development.[1]

A company's environment consists of factors and forces that are external to the business management function of the firm and that impinge on the management's ability to develop and maintain successful transactions with its customers.[2]

The environment of business may be defined as "the aggregate of all conditions, events and influences that surround and affect it."[3] This environment is broad and constantly changing; but a single business firm's environment is usually narrower in scope than the total environment of a business.

We define business environment as *those aspects of the surroundings of business enterprise which affect or influence its operations and determine its effectiveness*.

Thus, everything that surrounds and affects business inevitably becomes a part of its environment: the natural surroundings, the history of these surroundings, the economic condition, the political-legal system, cultural patterns and society as a whole. The company environment is always changing, constraining, and uncertain. The environment is in continual flux, spinning off new *Opportunities* and new *Threats*, i.e., E = O and T. This environment is always capable of producing major shocks and surprises, which Drucker has called as "An Age is Discontinuity" and Toffler as "The Future Shock." To be successful, the business firm must be constantly alert to environment changes. According to Hicks, "The firm can (1) adjust to the environment, or (2) if it has the ability, change the environment."[4]

The business firm co-operates with its environment, from which it receives the necessary "resources" and "opportunities" for its existence, future growth and survival. A business needs land and raw materials, it needs people to work, and it needs capital. All these resources come from the environment. In turn, the business must supply satisfactory "returns" to the environment. These returns are usually in the form of goods and services.

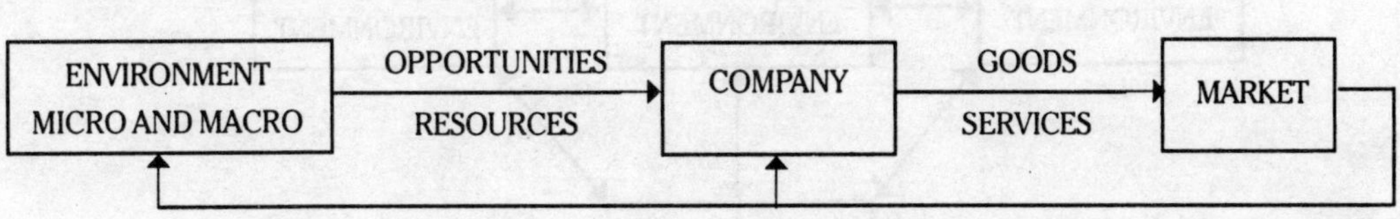

Fig. 20.1: The Business Firm's interaction with its Environment.

Although it is easy to speak of a firm's environment as consisting of different elements, the environment is subtly more complicated. Each component/element overlaps and influences

1. Andrews, Kenneth R., *The Concept of Corporate Strategy*, D.B. Taraporewala & Sons Co. Pvt. Ltd., Mumbai, 1972.
2. Kalter, Philip, *Principles of Marketing,* Prentice-Hall of India, Pvt. Ltd., New Delhi, Second Ed., 1983, p. 84.
3. Davis, Keith, *The Challenge of Business*, McGraw-Hill Book Co., New York, 1975, p. 43.
4. Hicks, Herbert G., *The Management of Organisation: A System and Human Resources Approach*, McGraw-Hill Book Co., New York, 2nd ed., 1972, p. 65.

others. For a better understanding of its different constituents, the firm's environment may be broadly into two categories:

(a) *The micro-environment*, which consists of factors in the firm's immediate environment that affect its ability to serve its customers, viz., the company, market channel, firms, customers, markets, competitors, and public; and

(b) *The macro-environment*, which consists of the larger societal forces that affect all the factors in the company's micro-environment, viz., the demographic, economic, natural, political, social and cultural and technological forces. These two constituents are shown in Fig. 20.2 and 20.3 below.

Importance of the Study of Business Environment

A study of the firm's environment by the business executive is of vital importance for more than one reasons.

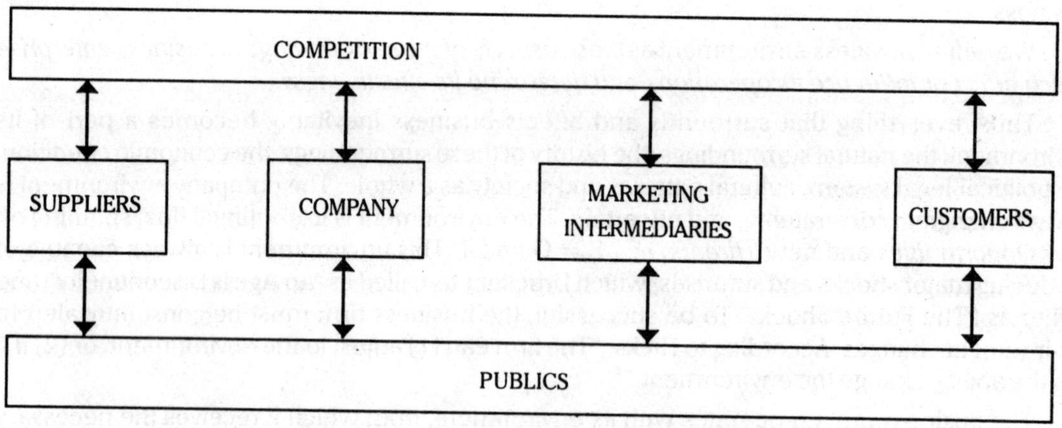

Fig. 20.2: Micro-Environment of the Company.

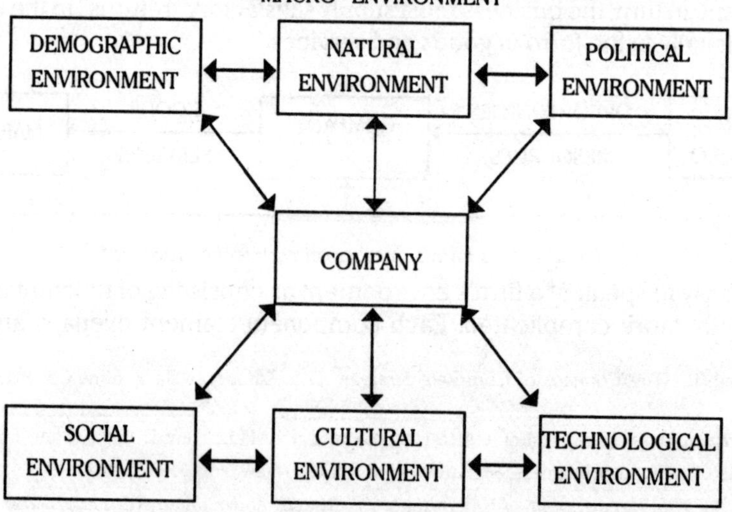

Fig. 20.3: Macro-Environment of the Company.

First, information about environment is necessary for the successful conduct of business.

Secondly, environment opens up fresh avenues for the expansion of new entrepreneurial operations. When environment is favourable, new ideas, schemes and ventures may be put into action, and advantage taken of the resources supplied by the environment.

Thirdly, an acquisition of knowledge about the changing environment will keep the businessmen dynamic in their approach which helps the firm to avoid ecological strains and stresses and to maintain harmony with the environment.

Fourthly, businessmen in a modern democratic set-up must earn popular support and improve its image which is possible when they not only study the environment consisting of all external conditions and influences affecting the life and development of an organism, but also strive to make the environment hospitable to the growth of business and business dimensions.

Finally, with the study of the nature and character of control over the enterprise by the environment, the business executives try to adjust to the conditions prevailing and thus influence the environment in order to make it congenial to business.[5]

Dr. Agarwala has observed that "the penalty of environmental disregard is heavy. It not only reduces profit margins and makes opportunities for expansion slip, but it also arouses social hostility and makes social environment growingly inhospitable to business operations."[6]

KEY FACTORS OF ENVIRONMENT

There is a close relationship between a business firm and its surrounding environment. This environment is multi-dimensional and often complex in nature and basically includes six elements– natural, economic, social and cultural, political, and legal, and technological. In the Indian context, governmental regulations play an important part in influencing the activities of large organisations, if not all organisations.

The Business's Micro-environment

Every business's primary goal is to conduct itself profitably, i.e., to supply goods and services needed by different sections of the society. The business executive is required to distribute the internal work among different personnel function-wise. However, its success will be affected by the firm's philosophy and functions followed by it, the consumers or customers, the suppliers, the intermediary channel, the public and the competitors.

1. *Company*: The working of the entire company is divided into functional areas. For example, the marketing executives work closely with other departments. Financial executives are concerned with arranging of funds to meet the firm's objectives, the allocation of the funds for different product manufacture, and marketing activities, and the R and D; executives focus on the technical problems of designing safe and attractive products and spare parts. All these executives work in unison with each other for accomplishing the objectives of the company.

5. Tandon, B.C., *Environment and Entrepreneur*, Chugh Publications, Allahabad, 1975, p. 2.
6. Motilal Nehru Institute of Business Administration, *Quarterly Journal of Management Development*, Allahabad, Cochin Conference Number, Sept. 1971, p. 3.

2. *Suppliers*: These are firms and individuals who provide resources needed by the company to produce the particular goods and services. They also supply labour, equipment, fuel, power, and other factors of production to carry on its economic activity. Development in suppliers' environment can have a substantial impact on the company's business and marketing operations. Therefore, its executives must keep themselves abreast of the price trends of the key inputs. Rising supply costs may force a price increase that will reduce the company's forecasted sales. Further, shortages of essential supplies may badly affect the production schedule, and the company may fail to fulfil its promises to customers, which might damage its goodwill, if the situation continues for long.

3. *Marketing Intermediaries*: These are firms that help the company in promoting, selling and distributing its goods and services to the final buyers. They include middlemen, physical distribution firms (such as warehouses, transportation firms), marketing service agencies (such as marketing research firms, advertising agencies, media firms), and the financial intermediaries (like banks, credit institutions, insurance and other financing institutions). The business executives have to keep good relations with all these for the successful operation of business.

4. *Customers*: The company needs to study its customers' markets closely. Such markets may be of five types, viz., (i) *individuals and households* that buy goods for personal consumption; (ii) *producers and organisations*, who purchase these for the production process in order to make profits or achieve other objectives; (iii) *retailers* who buy in order to resell to make profit; (iv) *Government agencies*, who buy goods and services either to produce public services or transfer these goods to others who need them; and (v) *international buyers*, foreign consumers, producers, resellers and governments.

5. *Competitors*: Every company faces a wide range of competitors, such as *desire competitors*, i.e., immediate desires that the consumer might want to satisfy; *generic competitors*; the different ways in which the buyers can satisfy a particular desire; *form competitors*. i.e., product forms that can satisfy the buyers' particular desire; and *brand competitors*, i.e., the brands that can satisfy the same desire.

6. *Public*: "A public is any group that has an actual or potential interest in or impact on an organisation's ability to achieve its objectives." A public can help or hurt a company's efforts to serve its market. Every company is usually surrounded by seven types of public, viz.,

(i) *financial publics* which affect the company's ability to obtain funds. Banks, investment houses, stockbroker's firms and stockholders are the examples;
(ii) *media publics* that carry news, features and editorial opinion, specifically, newspapers, magazines, radio and television;
(iii) *government public;*
(iv) *customer organisations;*
(v) *local public* such as neighbourhood or community residents and community organisations;
(vi) *general public*, its attitude towards the company's products and activities; and
(vii) *internal public*, including blue-collar and white-collar workers, managers, boards of directors, etc.

7. *Types of Ownership*: Modern business is generally conducted by three different types of ownership. The *first is the sole proprietorship* which is owned by one individual. The *second* is a *partnership*, which consists of two or more individuals who combine their resources, energy and ideas to start a business; and *third*, a *corporation*, which is made up of a number of individuals who share ownership.

The above constituents of the micro-environment of a firm operate in a larger macro-environment of forces that shape opportunities and pose threats to the company. These forces represent "uncontrollables" which the company must monitor and respond to.

The Macro-environment of Business

The six basic environments of business are: natural, demographic, economic, social and cultural, political and legal, and technological. These environments interact and depend on one another. Therefore, business must consider not only its total environment but also each of these environments. Each environment provides some resources to business and each expects satisfactory returns.

1. Natural or Ecological Environment

This environment consists of air, land, water and all natural resources found on the surface of the earth and in its bowels. Much of the success of business in the future will depend upon how it responds to the problem of depletion of natural resources. With the rapid growth in population and industrialisation, large quantities of water began to be needed for domestic and industrial purpose, transportation and production of energy and power. Industries were, therefore, generally located near waterways and close to places where other natural resources could be available in plenty. These resources began to be used carelessly, leading to their depletion and the destruction of the natural environment, which resulted in pollution of land, water and even air, by misuse of land resources, dumping of industrial waste in water courses and emission of soot from factory chimneys. Individuals and businessmen, for immediate gain, ruthlessly exploited the rich resources without caring for their preservation.

Kenneth Boulding has pointed out that "Planet earth was like a spaceship in danger of running out of fuel if it failed to recycle its materials." Meadowes raised concern about the adequacy of natural resources to sustain economic growth.[7] Rachel Carson pointed out that "The environment damage to water, earth and air caused by industrial activity of mankind is harmful for future generations."[8]

The growing consciousness and the blame put on the activities of businessmen, and the changing values towards the use of natural resources for community's good led business to adopt new standards. In some case, government through legislation and local pressure forced business to control the misuse of resources, and control its air and water pollution as well as its waste-disposal processes. Now, most business firms are meeting the challenges of environmental pollution and its diseconomies. However, the cost of pollution control being very high, business alone cannot meet the total expenditure, the public and the government must also pay for it.

The need of the time, therefore, is that businessmen should be aware of the threats and opportunities with four trends in the environment: impending shortages, increased cost of energy, increased levels of pollution, and government intervention in natural resource management. The earth's materials consist of the infinite, the finite renewable resources. An infinite resource, like air and solar energy, poses no immediate problem, although environmentalists have warned for a ban of certain propellents used in aerosal cans because of their potential damage to the ozone layer of air. Water shortage in most of the countries has been a serious problem. But finite renewable

7. Meadows, Donella H. and Dennis, L. Meadowes, Jorgen Randers and William W. Behrens, *The Limits to Growth*, New American Library, New York, 1972, p. 41.
8. Carsen, Rachel, *Silent Spring*, Houghton Mifflin, Boston, 1962.

resources, such as forests and food, have to be used wisely. The paper and board making mills, saw mills, those preparing other wooden furniture, etc., must look to reforestation of the denuded areas in order to protect the soil, and ensure a regular supply of conifers and hard woods. Even food supply can be a major problem in that the quantity of arable land is relatively limited and moreover, the urban areas are constantly encroaching upon the farmland. Finite non-renewable resources, such as oil, coal and precious minerals – lead, zinc, copper, manganese ore etc. – are in short supply and they pose a serious problem for the future. One author has cautioned a warning: "... it would appear at present that the quantities of platinum, gold, zinc and lead are not sufficient to meet demands., Silver, tin, and uranium may be in short supply even at higher prices by the turn of the century. By the year 2050, several more minerals may be exhausted if the current rate of consumption continues. Their conservation and finding new alternatives is, therefore, a must."[9]

The main source of energy is coal and oil. But oil has created the most serious problem for future economic growth. The major industrial countries of the world are heavily dependent on oil, and until cost-effective substitute forms of energy can be developed, oil will continue to dominate the world's political and economic picture. High price of oil and its non-availability in many countries has led to a frantic search for alternative forms of energy. Efforts are on the way to search for practical means to harness solar, nuclear, wind and tidal power for energy purposes.

Rapid industrialisation has inevitably damaged the quality of the natural environment. The disposal of nuclear and chemical wastes, the large quantities of mercury, petroleum in the ocean and DDT and other chemical pollutants in the soil and food supply, and the littering of the environment with other waste material have created a severe problem of air and water pollution, for which public consciousness compels many business firms to develop pollution control devices, and search for alternative ways to produce and package goods that do not cause environmental damage.[10]

2. Demographic Environment

This is of vital importance to businessmen because "people make up markets", and people means population in its various dimensions – growth, age, sex, educational standard, etc. Population growth means growing human needs that business has to meet. It means growing markets if there is sufficient purchasing power. It there is insufficient purchasing power, it means recession and vigorous attacks against business institutions. Population is increasing at rates varying from 1.5 to 2.5 percent. In some countries, it is even below 1% and in some others about 3%. According to changes in age composition of the population, business production has to be adjusted; further, a shift in population is mostly visible from rural to urban areas and this trend also affects the business significantly so far as employment and construction activities are concerned. Sex distribution also affects occupational distribution, and the female sex needs more household or outside home occupations which the business should provide without making sex discrimination.

3. Economic Environment

There is a close relationship between a business firm and the economic environment around it. Economic environment is of multidimensional nature and includes the structure of the economy; the agricultural, industrial, fiscal, tax, transport and trade policies of the country; the growth and

9. *First Annual Report of the Council on Environment Quality*, Government Printing Press, Washington, 1070, p. 158.
10. Henion, Karl E, *Ecological Marketing*, Grid Publishers, Ohio, 1976.

pattern of national income, its distribution, *per capita* income, etc,; inflationary pressures and the disposable personal income; availability and prices of needed capital goods; expectations and demands of various publics served by the business firms; forces of competition; the quality of liquid capital (cash) and social overhead capital (i.e., infrastructure) to keep the functioning of business effectively.

Economic environment affects directly the business enterprises. The general conditions of economic environment govern the firm's ability to remain viable. In prosperity, labour and other resources may be scarce; and in depressions, many businesses may find it difficult just to survive.

Some factors can bring about changes in the economic environment. By changing monetary and fiscal policies, the government affects business. For example, to control the money supply, the Reserve Bank of India may decide to raise the rates at which member can borrow. The member banks, in turn, raise their interest rates to any one borrowing money. The business firm then may find its resources limited for the time being. This restraint on business is exercised from time to time.

Also the customers of the firm may change their tastes concerning the products of the firm. Such changes may be initiated by changes in other environment. For example, changes in natural environment have influenced preferences of some car-owners, they now demand diesel or low-pollution automobiles. By making contraceptives available, the firms producing these have been able to shape the habits and customs of their customers.

The 1976 Industrial Policy of the government has placed certain restrictions on undertakings belonging to larger industrial houses and the existing policy of reservation for the small-scale sector continued. In respect of agro-industries, particularly undertakings processing sugarcane, jute, cotton, groundnuts, etc., preference has been given to the co-operative sector.

Since economic environment affects directly the business firms, the managers must keep a careful watch on changes in the economic environment both within and without the country and their possible impact on business. Economic conditions change continuously, and they fluctuate frequently; they require tactical and even strategic responses. However, it must be emphasised that while economic environment has its own significance, economic insights yield only partial results for decisions which must be made by managers and government planners. No doubt, the problems of product techniques, sales promotion and worker motivation relate to economic considerations, yet they also involve problems of education, sociology, psychology, cultural anthropology, law, political science and other similar disciplines.

4. Political-Legal Environment

Economic environment within any nation is closely linked with its political and legal systems, because the latter invariably are explictly or implicitly built on ideologies and values which relate to both economic and social goals.

Political-legal environment is the background of laws on regulations within which business conducts its affairs. This environment is made up of government agencies, laws and pressure groups that influence and constrain various organisations and individuals in society. This environment provides opportunities, poses challenges and creates problems for the businessmen. In this environment, government strongly interacts with business. Governments at three levels–local, state and centre–exert varying amounts of influence over business. Any change in the political environment may bring about radical changes in laws governing the natural and international affairs of the administration of existing laws and implementation of new ones. Hence, political and legal environment generally go together; and it is difficult to draw any clear-cut demarcation line between them.

The government plays at least *four roles* as it interacts with business. It is most influential as a regulator, as a supplier, as a competitor and as a customer – the last three ones often overlap.

As a *regulator*, the government performs both supportive and restrictive functions, by enacting legislation to regulate the conduct of the business, e.g., through Monopoly Restrictive Trade Practices Act, it supports the rights of small firms to compete in market place and, at the same time, restricts some large firms that seek to dominate the market. Other regulations affect product quality, prices charged for them, and the manner of advertising them, besides governing conditions and hours of work, minimum wages, social security provisions. The government also regulates business firms through taxation.

Thus, the main reasons for enacting legislation are: (i) to protect firms from each other "by defining and preventing unfair competition"; (ii) to protect consumers from unfair business practices; and (iii) to protect the larger interests of society against unbridled business behaviour.

As a *supplier*, government owns and supplies land and natural resources needed by business.

As a *competitor*, it produces goods and services that compete in the market place with those produced by private firms. e.g., the government competes as electricity producer, shipbuilder, construction and communication owners.

As a *customer*, it buys goods and services of the private business.

The business executive needs a good working knowledge of the major natural laws protecting competition, consumers, and the larger interest of society, for "ignorance of law is no excuse". *Secondly*, since the existing laws are changed from time to time, and new laws are enacted frequently, keeping in view the needs of the society, managers are expected to keep themselves posted with the latest developments in the laws of the country for the continued growth and survival of their business. Observed Prof. Agarwal, "A business manager should know (a) something about the country's legal system; (b) at least the names of various laws which govern business activities and their subject-matter; and (c) a working knowledge of the basic business laws governing factories, taxation, and companies. But this is not all he needs to know. He should pick up the rest as he goes about his executive duties; experience is a great teacher and has always been so."[11] Knowledge of basic laws is a must, because business has to work on those lines.

TABLE 20.1: MILESTONES IN INDIAN LEGISLATION.

I. Affecting Consumer (i.e., Consumer Protection)

1. Prevention of Food Adulteration Act, 1954.
2. Prevention of Food Rules, 1954.
3. Essential Commodities Act, 1955.
4. Weights and Measures Act, 1958.
5. Dangerous Drugs Act, 1930.
6. Drugs and Cosmetics Act, 1940.
7. Trade and Merchandise Act, 1958.
8. Packaged Commodities Order, 1975.
9. Fruit Products Order, 1955.
10. Drugs and Magic Remedies (Objectionable Advertisements) Act, 1954.
11. Price Control Regulations.
12. Household Electrical Appliances (Quality Control) Order, 1976.

11. Agarwal, A.N., *The Emerging Dimensions of Indian Management,* Asia Publishing House, Mumbai, 1970, pp. 166-167.

II. Affecting Private Business:

1. Indian Companies Act, 1956.
2. The Monopolies and Restrictive Trade Practices Act, 1969, as amended in 1984.
3. Industries (Development and Regulation) Act, 1951.
4. The Capital Issue Act, 1947.
5. Import and Exports (Control) Acts, 1947.
6. The Securities Contracts Regulation Act, 1957.
7. The Foreign Exchange Regulation Act, 1973.
8. Income Tax Act, 1961.
9. Forward Contracts (Regulation) Act, 1952.

III. Affecting Employers/Employees:

1. The Factories Act, 1948.
2. The Workmen's Compensation Act, 1923.
3. The Trade Unions Act, 1926.
4. The Payments of Wages Act, 1936.
5. The Industrial Disputes Act, 1947.
6. The Industrial (Employment) Standing Orders Act, 1946.
7. The Minimum Wages Act, 1948.
8. The Employee's State Insurance Act, 1948.
9. The Employees Provident Fund Act, 1952.
10. The Bonus Act, 1965.

Business managers should also understand the working of the political system because a political change may mean changes in relationship between the government and specific firms. Some firms may gain, others may suffer as new people take over, new favourites are chosen, and new ideologies are introduced. Alliances have often to be made with political personalities or groups. But such alliances often seriously affect the fortunes of many businesses, as they become completely subject to the whims of the politicians.

There are two opinions whether or not business should have relationship with politics. The traditional view is that businessmen should not align themselves with any political party or officials and political bosses. Their views and attitudes should be that of a non-partisan. But the modern view is that businessmen should keep themselves in touch with political process and they should take a keen interest in the political affairs of the local, state and central governments. Businessmen should have their representatives on various bodies at all levels of policy-making and plan formation. They should provide the government with persons who are experienced administrators.

5. Social and Cultural Environments

Of all the environments basic to business, perhaps the social and cultural environment has the greatest impact on its policy and action. This is the environment that most seriously poses a challenge to business. "*Social environment*" may be described as "the environment of society as a whole – of everyone involved". "*Cultural environment*" is "an aggregate of all sub-cultures, each with different concepts and benefits."

Both these environments influence the welfare of a business concern in the long run. We have an ever-changing society. New demands are created and old ones lost in due course. A business firm is called upon to make necessary adjustments in its production and marketing plans to fulfil these new social demands.

There are three kinds of social environment: (i) *Changes in our life styles and social values*, such as the changing rate of women from housewife to that of working-women; emphasis on quality of goods rather than on its quantity; greater reliance on government for different types of welfare services for the community; greater preference for leisure time activities; change in taste from that for alcoholic drinks to *marijuana, hashish, cocaine* or orange and other fruit juices; greater liking for "ponytail" hair than for waist-length plait among young girls; preference for "midies", "jeans" and "maxies" in place of saris; disco–dancing in place of going to temples or mosques, etc.

(ii) *Major social problems*, e.g., greater concern for pollution of the environment–air, water-noise, land etc., demand for socially–responsible marketing – "consumer-orientation" rather than "market–orientation;" need for safety in occupations and products used; elimination of unemployment; training and hiring of minority groups; the creation of child-welfare and health centres, health care for the aged; advertising credibility; and stabilisation of economic conditions–these are a few of the needs of society that require the fullest help of business.

(iii) *Growing consumerism*, indicating consumers' dissatisfaction, on a large scale, with unfair trade practices. Consumerism is becoming increasingly important to the marketing decision process. Advocates of consumerism insist that business should prove its social responsibility by taking direct and immediate action in many areas.

Business has attempted to fulfil its social role in several ways, some assumed voluntarily, and some imposed by legislation. But these "returns" by business are said to be more scratching the surface, so far as the realisation of the societies' objectives is concerned, i.e, what has been done is not enough, more needs to be done in this respect. Cultural forces constitute cultural environment. Dr. Edward Taylor defines culture as "That complex whole which includes knowledge, belief, art, morals, law, custom, and other capabilities and habits acquired by mass as a member of society". People grow up under a particular culture, in which a given society holds many beliefs and values. These have a high degree of persistence and are passed on from parents to children and are reinforced by the society's institutions like schools, business, government and religious institutions. These values change rather slowly but they do produce various constraints-factors which must be taken as "given" for a majority of business firms operating in the country.

As is said, "traditions and values die hard." For example, in India, every auspicious act–from sowing and harvesting to opening of a new business or celebrating some religious or social ceremony o laying the foundation of a building or project, roofing a house, or even starting a journey for business or some special purpose may be undertaken only on some special days and at a particular time or hour after consulting the priest or the astrologer, or only after an offering to God has been made. For Americans, time is money; for Asians, it has no meaning. In certain Latin American countries, greasing of the palm of officials to get work done is not unethical as is known in the USA and North European countries. In India, this is now more readily given and accepted without regard to any moral scruples.

A number of social beliefs have emerged that are of significance to the business manager. Among the most important of these are:[12]

1. the belief that there are opportunities of various kinds for people who are willing and able to work to take advantage of them;
2. a faith in business and respect for business-owners and leaders;

12. Koontz, Harold, and Cyril O'Donnel: *Management: A System and Contingency Analysis of Managerial Functions*, McGraw-Hill Kogakusha Ltd., Tokyo, 1976. p. 84.

3. a belief in competition and competitiveness in all aspects of life, particularly in business;
4. a respect for individual regardless of race, religion or creed;
5. a respect for authority arising from ownership of property, expert knowledge and elected political position;
6. a belief in logical processes, science and technology; and
7. a belief in the importance of change, of experimentation to find better ways of doing things.

In India, tradition, custom and social values have largely moulded the attitudes and beliefs of the people. Here family traditions, which are mostly non-economic, play an important part in shaping the institutions and social organisation and in determining the low level of income of the family. Management here is generally in the hands of the traditional heads of the family. The people have developed with the passage of time some beliefs such as:

1. simple living and high thinking;
2. caste-ridden society and untouchability as a taboo.
3. business and property, in a joint family often passes on from father to the eldest heir in the family;
4. a faith that work done after consultation with a priest generally results in success;
5. a faith that fortune is determined by Destiny and is not the outcome of labour alone;
6. a belief that business should be conducted on ethical and moral grounds.

Now the cultural values are changing and showing the following trends:

Other-centeredness	⟶	self-fulfilment
Postponed gratification	⟶	immediate gratification
Hard work	⟶	easy life
Formal relationships	⟶	informal relationships
Religious orientation	⟶	secular orientation

A business manager who moves from one social or cultural group to another must take into account the facts about cultural environment and consciously respond to them, according to the needs of the local place, using suitable techniques.

Socially-conscious businessmen financially support and encourage; (i) fine arts projects as civic theatres, operas, art shows and galleries, and music nights; (ii) sports events–matches and tournaments; (iii) communication media through advertising; (iv) helping education through donations to educational and professional institutions and universities for building, for teaching programmes, for scholarships, equipments and books, and even offer 'chairs" for specialised subjects.

6. Technological Environment

The most dramatic force shaping people's destiny is technology–the accumulated technical knowledge and capital of a country. Technology includes inventions, innovations and affects the way the resources of the economy are converted into output. Technology mainly influences the ways of doing things that a man designs, produces, distributes or sells goods and services, managerial practices and organisation structure. Rapid technological developments have been referred to as "Revolution" by Koontz and O'Donnel.[13] In order to survive, a business executive

13. Koontz, Harold and Cyril O'Donnel, *op. cit.*, p. 80.

must keep abreast of the technology applicable to techniques of production of goods and services and their distribution.

Spectacular advances in technology have been made in the last three years and more advances are yet under way. Observes Dr. Kotler: "Many of today's products were not available even one hundred years ago. Abrahim Lincoln did not know of automobiles, aeroplanes, phonographs, radio or the electric light. Woodrow Wilson did not know of television, aerosal cans, home freezers, automatic dishwashers, room air-conditioners, antibiotics, or electric computers. Franklin Roosevelt did not know of Xerography, synthetic detergents, tape recorders, birth control pills or earth satellites. And John Kennedy did not know of personal computers, digital wrist-watches, video-recorders or word processors."[14]

During the last three decades, technology has worked wonders and released life-saving penicillin and other sulfa-drugs and antibiotics, open-heart and plastic surgery, replacement of eyes, and birth control pills. At the same time, it has released such horrors as the nuclear bomb, nerve gas, the submachine gun. It has released such mixed blessing as the automobile, television, electron microscope, night-vision instruments, kidney and heart transplant operations, inoculations for polio, synthetic fibres, etc.

Koontz and O'Donnell have listed the following categories of technological changes:[15]

1. Increased ability to master time and distance for movement of freight and passengers; railroads, automobiles, and trucks, aeroplanes, space vehicles.
2. Increased ability to generate, store, transport and distribute energy: electricity, nuclear power and laser.
3. Increased ability to design new materials and change the properties of others so that they better serve needs: steel alloys, synthetic fibres, plastic, new drugs.
4. Mechanisation and automation of physical processes.
5. Mechanisation and automation of certain mental processes: the computer.
6. Extension of human ability to sense things: radar, the electron microscope, night-vision instrument.
7. Increased understanding of individual and group behaviour and how to deal with it: psychological bases of motivation, group behaviour patterns, improved management techniques.
8. Increased understanding of diseases and their treatment: inoculation of polio, kidney transplants, antibiotic treatment of infections, etc.

Prof. Kahn and Wiener have termed the new developments in technology as "Innovation", "Revolution" or "Break-through". They have listed one hundred areas where technology has worked wonders during the last thirty years: 25 of which they call "unambiguous examples of progress", another 25, they call areas which are "clearly controversial"; and the last 50 items are referred to as "almost certain" and "very significant innovations."[16] These are the lists given in *Exhibit 2* at the end of this chapter.

14. Kotler, Philip, *Principles of Marketing*, Prentice-Hall of India Pvt. Ltd., New Delhi, 1983, p. 105.
15. Konntz, Horold and Cyril O'Donnel, *op. cit.*, pp. 80-81.
16. Kahn, H and A. J. Wiener, "The Next 33 Years: A Framework for Speculation," in Ansoff, H. Igor (Ed), *Business Strategy*, Penguin Books Ltd., Harmondsworth, Middlesex, England, 1983, pp. 82-88.

Scientists today are working on new technologies that will revolutionise our products and production processes. The most exciting work is being done in bio-technology, solid-state electronics, robotics, and material service.[17] Besides these the new fields of innovation are:[18]

1. Practical solar energy
2. Cancer cures.
3. Chemical control of mental health.
4. Desalinisation of sea water.
5. Commercial space shuttle.
6. Lung and liver cures.
7. Household robots to do cooking and cleaning.
8. Human clones.
9. Non-fattening, fasting nutritious foods.
10. Happiness pills,
11. Electric cars.
12. Electronic anaesthetic for pain killing.
13. Totally safe and effective contraceptives.
14. Small flying cars.
15. Three dimensional television.
16. Space colonies.

Toffler sees an accelerative thrust in the invention, exploitation, and diffusion of new technologies. More ideas are being worked upon; the time lag between new ideas and their successful implementation is decreasing rapidly; and the time between introduction and peak production is shortening considerably.[19]

Again elsewhere, Toffler forecasts the emergence of the "*electronic cottage*" as a new way in which work and play will be organised in society. This will reduce the amount of auto pollution, bring the family closer together as a work unit, and create more home-centered entertainment and activity; and it will have a substantial impact of the consumption pattern of the people. Further, the introduction of word-processing typewriters, telecopiers, personal computers, and audio and video-links makes it possible for many people to do their work at home instead of travelling to and from office, which are located 30 to 50 kms away.[20]

Some basic facts about technology may be noted that:

(a) every new technology is a force for "creative destruction". Transistors hurt the vacuum-tube industry, Xerography hurts carbon-paper business, the auto hurts the railroads, the television hurts the movies, and the synthetic fibres hurt cotton textiles;

(b) the discovery of many new technologies affect the economy's growth. For example, much investment is made over time for different transport media–the railroads and autos, or the radio and the television – because when one innovation replaces the old media, there is a time lag in between which the economy can stagnate;

(c) each new technology creates major long-run consequences that are not always foreseeable. For example, the contraceptive pill or contraceptives led to smaller families, more

17. Gaber, Dennis, *Innovations: Scientific, Technological and Social*, Oxford University Press, London, 1970.
18. Panat, Charles, *Breakthroughs*, Houghton Mifflin, Boston, 1980.
19. Toffler, Alvin, *The Future Shock*, Bantom, New York, 1970, pp. 25-30.
20. Toffler, Alvin, *The Third Wave*, Bantom, New York, 1980.

working women, and larger discretionary incomes resulting in higher expenditure on standard of living;

(d) more and more money is being spent on Research and Development activities, especially in the field of missiles, electrical equipment, chemicals and allied products, automobiles, textiles, etc., with a view to improving the quality of the goods produced and reducing the cost of production.

However, technological changes are not easily accepted by all, especially those who see these as threatening nature, privacy, simplicity and even the human race. But one's attitude towards technology depends on whether one is more impressed by its beneficial or abusive results. The business executives need to understand the changing technological environment and how new technologies can serve best the interest of human beings. They need to work in close collaboration with R & D scientists to encourage more market-oriented research. But, at the same time, they must be alert to put a check on the harmful effects of technology.

7. International Environment

The home or domestic environment of every business firm in a country is also influenced by the relationships it has with other countries in the form of trade treaties, or cultural ties. These relationships give rise to what is known as "*international environment*". Many forces/factors build up this environment, such as foreign policy; international treaties (unilateral or bilateral); defence policy, foreign exchange and foreign capital policy, etc., besides numerous enactments which might directly or indirectly affect business dealings and consumer interest.

International environment never remains static but it always changes with changes in the structure of the governments and their policies. The most important factor of international environment is the form of "*Multinational Corporations*". These are concerns whose ownership is scattered over more than one country. The two important features are: (i) They do business in two or more countries in such volume that their well-being and growth rests in more than one countries in such volume that their well-being and growth rests in more than one countries; (ii) they have centralised managerial and financial controls. A multinational is usually in the form of a big "*holding company*" with a number of operating subsidiary companies, each subsidiary located in one country. Decisions are taken by the multinationals on the basis of multinational alternatives.

The foreign subsidiary is concerned with these environmental conditions:

(a) the domestic and international environment of both the "parent" company's country and of the host country in which it operates its business;
(b) investment climate available in the host country;
(c) policies of the host country regarding profit remission, exchange control, import and export restrictions;
(d) patterns of international trade;
(e) balance of payments trends;
(f) national and political ideologies of the host country.
(g) attitude towards foreign firms and foreigners; and
(h) special legal enactments and rules for foreign business.

Any neglect of these and other factors may endanger the very survival of these subsidiary companies.

The multinationals have, therefore, to take cautious actions and give due consideration before opening business in foreign countries. The present trend is now, instead of opening and conducting business through subsidiary holding companies, multinationals undertake to complete a project from the beginning to maturity and hand it over to a private or public sector enterprise when it is ripe for operation, i.e., "turn key" and the new enterprise starts operation. For example, a complete installation of a textile unit or a petroleum refinery or fertilizer plant or hydro-electric power station is set up in a foreign country and handed over to the private or public sector enterprise in that country as per the contract, which may be on the basis of "open tender" or on the basis of "cost-plus-fee for services".

INTERACTION OF ENVIRONMENTAL FACTORS

Environmental factors interact with each other. But business also has its influence on these factors in so far as it selects the environment within which it will operate and then continually attempts to shape the environment to accomplish its objectives. In the paragraphs that follow, we shall see how environmental factors interact with each other.

Interaction between Natural Economic Environment

During the last two decades, there has been a growing concern over the deterioration of the natural environment, as evident from the water and air pollution, ruthless cutting down of forests, creation of radio-active materials, oil spills on the ocean and cases of poisoning of human beings and animals and plant life. Traditionally, Nature has been viewed as available for human exploitation; resources to be used for the betterment of human living, etc. Now, however, from the point of future concern, steps are being advocated for bringing about a balance between Nature and human activities. This obviously raises major issues about economic, materialistic and social progress of the present and future generations. In fact, every industrialised society is facing problems of environmental deterioration and, hence the need for conservation and better utilisation of scarce resources for greater industrialisation and improvement in quality of life. To meet environmental issues squarely, re-evaluation of priorities and concepts is the need of the hour; for this, development of new ideologies, legal and structural management and management skills will be needed.

Interaction between Historical Environment and Economic Environment

These two environments are interdependent. The present economic environment of business can be treated as a legacy of its past environment. Every business has a history, and every historical phenomenon has a lesson. As such the present reflects the past and the present problems can be handled in terms of past experience. For example, the economic environment of business in India is the outcome of the colonial rule which it had for quite long. But the past history, as a storehouse of information and lessons, has guidelines for present economic policy decisions. The implementation of the past six Five-Year Plans can provide the right direction to the Seventh Plan on the basis of which, again, future planning may be done.

Interaction between Social-Cultural Environment and Economic Environment

The social attitude towards business and management determines how many people would enter business. If business is regarded as respectable occupation, commerce and industry will develop rapidly and professional managers will emerge to manage modern business houses. If there is a conflict between labour and management, instead of cooperation, a repressive economic system may be needed to cope with industrial unrest. If, on the other hand, the aim of industry is the attainment of the highest productivity, the workers will be given more incentives to increase production than aiming at maximisation of profits.

The cultural environment–educational facilities–may foster economic development.

Interaction between Political-Legal Environment and Economic Development

Direct relationship exists between political and economic environment. With political stability, business activities prosper and new activities develop; but if there is political instability, the business definitely suffers–money market investments shrink, installation of new enterprises is held in check and profits dwindle. The economic policy of the state determines whether private or public enterprise should be developed. The state of political environment decides the pattern of economic legislation, and the state of economic environment decides the continuity or discontinuity of a particular political administration.

It will, thus, be noted that there is a "linkage" between the business's environment and its internal sub-systems—the technology used in the transformation process, the relationships among people doing various tests, and the managerial functions.

CONCLUSION

From the foregoing discussion, it will be noted that environment and business are interrelated. The various environments affect each other in a "give and take" manner. If a firm produces a certain product or service that is acceptance to one of the environments, the environment rewards the firm by continuing to supply resources to it. Contrarily, if the firm's production or service is not acceptable, the inputs by the different environments may be stopped or reduced or restricted to an extent.

Business is also influential in shaping the total environment in which it works. It offers much to its environment. It gives to the environment and also receives from the environment. In other words, it may be said that business and its environment are mutually dependent. Their relation is a symbiotic one, benefit to both. Moreover, a change in one perforce becomes a challenge to the other–to adapt itself and go ahead.

Exhibit 1 : Key Environmental Factors (Adapted from Dymsza)[1]

1. Economic factors	2. Social & Cultural Factors	3. Political & Legal Factors
(i) Population and its distribution by age-groups; population density; annual percentage of working population; agricultural population; urban population.	(i) Literacy and educational levels. (ii) Business, economic, technical, and other specialised education available. (iii) Language and cultural characteristics.	(i) Types of political and economic systems, political philosophy, national ideology. (ii) Major political parties, their policies.
(ii) Level of economic development and industrialization.	(iv) Class structure and mobility.	(iii) Stability of government: (a) Changes in political parties. (b) Changes in governments.
(iii) Gross national product, gross domestic product, or national income in real terms and also	(v) Religion, racial, and national characteristics. (vi) Degree of urbanization.	(iv) Assessment of nationalism and its possible impact on business of foreign company.

per capita basis in recent years and projections over future planning period. (iv) Distribution of personal income. (v) Measures of price stability and inflation, wholesale price index numbers, consumer price index, other price indices. (vi) Supply of labour, wage rates, balance of payments equilibrium or disequilibrium, level of international monetary reserves, and balance of payment policies. (vii) Trends in exchange rates, currency stability, evaluation of possibilities of depreciation of currency. (viii) Tariffs, quantitative restrictions, export controls, exchange controls, state trading, and other entry. barriers to foreign trade. (ix) Monetary, fiscal and other policies. (x) Exchange controls and other restrictions on capital movements, repatriation of capital and remission of earnings.	(vii) Rate of social change.	(v) Favourable political aspects; (a) Tax and other concessions to encourage foreign investment. (b) Credit and other guarantees. (vi) Anti-trust laws and rules of competition. (vii) Protection of patents, trade marks brand names and other industrial property rights.

4. Competitive Factors	5. Government Laws, Regulations, and Policies of Home Country.	6. Technological Factors
(i) Analysis of industrial structure: (a) definition, size, scope of industry. (b) Value, quantity, and growth rates of domestic production, imports, exports. (c) Technological state of industry. Product life-cycle and rate of product development. (d) Degree of market saturation and maturity. (ii) Analysis of major competitors: (a) Identification of principal competitors at home and abroad. (b) Their types of operation manufacturing, licensing, exporting, importing and various combinations. (c) Channels of distribution and sales organisation.	(i) Monetary and fiscal policies and their effect on price tends, interest rates, economic growth and stability. (ii) Balance of payment policies. (iii) Commerical policies, especially tariffs, import restrictions. (iv) Tax policies. (v) Monopolies and Restrictive Trade Practices Act, Foreign Enterprise Regulation Act. (vi) Export controls and other restrictions on trade with some countries. (vii) Industrial licensing and other government policies.	(i) Technological factors and their influence on business.

(d) Advertising and promotion.
(e) Pricing, branding policies.
(f) Productivity and efficiency in manufacturing.
(g) Financial strength and effectiveness.
(h) Effectiveness of personnel, labour union policies, and general management.

(iii) Performance differentials of company with major competitors:
(a) Rate of growth of sales.
(b) Market penetration of other products and market development.
(c) Product-mix.
(d) Distribution channels and sales organisation.
(e) Servicing, credit, delivery.
(f) Advertising and other promotional programmes and brand establishment.
(g) Pricing policies.
(h) Profitability and rate of return on sale and investment.

(iv) Plans and major programmes of competition and potential competition:
(a) Marketing.
(b) Production.
(c) Personnel.
(d) Finance.
(e) General Management.

1. Dymsza, William, A, *Multinational Business Strategy*, McGraw-Hill Book Company. New York, 1972, pp. 83-85 and 94-95.

Exhibit 2 : One Hundred Technical Innovations Likely in the Next 33 years.

1. Multiple applications of lasers and masers for sensing, measuring, communicating, cutting, heating, welding, power transmission, illumination, destructive (defensive), and other purposes.
2. Extremely high-strength or high-temperature structural materials.
3. New or improved super-performance fabrics (papers, fibres, and plastics).
4. New airborne materials for equipment and appliances (plastics, glasses, alloys, ceramics, intermetallics, and cermets).
5. New airborne vehicles (ground-effect machines, super helicopters, giant supersonic jets).
6. Extensive commercial application of shaped charges.
7. More reliable and large range forecasting.
8. Intensive or extensive expansion of tropical agriculture and forestry.
9. New sources of power for fixed installations (e.g.., magneto-hydro-dynamics, thermionic, and thermoelectric, radioactive).

10. New sources of power for ground transportation (storage-battery, fuel-cell propulsion or support by electromagnetic fields, jet engines, turbines).
11. Extensive and intensive worldwide use of high altitude cameras for mapping, prospecting census, land-use and geological investigations.
12. New methods of water transportation (large submarines, flexible and special purpose "container" ships, more extensive use of large automated single-purpose bulk cargo ships).
13. Major reduction in hereditary and congenital defects.
14. Extensive use of cyborg techniques (mechanical aids or substitutes for human organs, sense, limbs).
15. New techniques for preserving or improving the environments.
16. Relatively effective appetite and weight control.
17. New techniques in education.
18. New improved plants and animals.
19. Human "hibernation" for short periods (hours or days) for medical purposes.
20. Inexpensive "one of a kind" design and procurement through use of computerised analysis and automated production.
21. Controlled super-effective relaxation and steep.
22. More sophisticated architectural engineering (geodesic domes, thin shells, pressurised skins, esoteric materials).
23. New or improved use of the oceans/mining, extraction of minerals, controlled "farming", source of energy.
24. Three-dimensional photography, illustrations, movies and television.
25. Automated or more mechanised housekeeping and home maintenance.
26. Widespread use of nuclear reaction for power.
27. Use of nuclear explosives for excavation and mining, generation of power, creation of high-temperature/high-pressure environments, or for a source of neutrons or other radiation.
28. General use of automation and cybernation in management and production.
29. Extensive and intensive centralisation of current and past personal and business information in high speed data processing.
30. Other new and possibly pervasive techniques for surveillance, monitoring, and control of individuals and organisations.
31. Some control of weather or climate.
32. Other (permanent or temporary) changes or experiments with the overall environment (such as generation of nitrogen in the air).
33. New and more reliable "educational" and propaganda techniques for affecting human behaviour–public and private.
34. Practical use of direct electronic communication units and stimulation of brain.
35. Human hibernation for relatively extensive periods (months to years).
36. Cheap and widely available or excessively destructive war weapons and weapon systems.
37. New and relatively effective counter–insurgency techniques.
38. New kinds of very cheap, convenient, and reliable birth control techniques.
39. New, more varied, and more reliable drugs for control of fatigue, relaxation, alertness, mood, personality, perceptions and fantasies.
40. Capability to choose the sex of unborn children.
41. Improved capability to change sex.

42. Other genetic control or influence over the "basic constitution" of an individual.
43. New techniques in the education of children.
44. General and substantial increase in life expectancy, postponement of ageing, and limited rejuvenation.
45. Generally acceptable and competitive synthetic foods and beverages (carbohydrates, fats, proteins, enzymes, vitamins, coffee, tea, cocoa, liquor).
46. "High quality" medical care for underdeveloped areas (for example, use of referral hospitals, broad-spectrum antibiotics, artificial blood plasma).
47. Design and extensive use of responsive and super-controlled environments for private and public use (for pleasurable, educational and vocational purposes).
48. "Non-harmful" methods of "over-indulging".
49. Simple techniques for extensive and permanent cosmetological changes (features, figures, perhaps complexion, skin colour, even physique).
50. More extensive use of transplantation of human organs.
51. Permanent manned satellite and lunar installations–inter-planetary travel.
52. Application of space life systems or similar techniques to terrestrial installations.
53. Permanent inhabited under-sea installations and perhaps even colonies.
54. Automated grocery and departmental stores.
55. Extensive use of robots and machines "slaved" to humanity.
56. New use of underground and tunnels for private and public transportation.
57. Automated universal (real time) credit, audit and banking systems.
58. Chemical methods for improved memory and learning.
59. Greater use of underground buildings.
60. New and improved materials and equipment for buildings and interiors (variable transmission glass, heating and cooling) to thermo-electric effect, electro-luminescent and phosporescent lighting).
61. Widespread use of cryogenics.
62. Improved chemical control of some metal illnesses and some aspects of senility,
63. Mechanical and chemical methods for improving human analytical ability more or less directly.
64. Inexpensive and rapid techniques for making tunnels and underground cavities, in earth or rock.
65. Major improvements in earth moving and construction equipment generally.
66. New techniques for keeping physically fit or acquiring physical skills.
67. Commercial extraction of oil from shale.
68. Recoverable boosters for economic space launching.
69. Industrial flying platforms.
70. Simple inexpensive video recording and playing.
71. Inexpensive high-capacity, worldwide regional and local (home and business) communication (using satellites, lasers, light pipes).
72. Practical large-scale desalination.
73. Pervasive business use of computers for the storage, processing and retreival of information.
74. Space defense system.
75. Practical home and business use of "wired" video communication for both telephone and television (possibility including retreival of tapped material from libraries or other sources) and rapid transmission and reception of fascimiles (possibly including news, library material, commercial announcements, instantaneous mail delivery (other print-outs).
76. Shared-time computers generally available to home and business on a metered basis.

77. General availability of inexpensive transuranic and other esoteric elements.
78. Other widespread use of computers for intellectual and professional assistance (translation, teaching, library research, medical diagonsis, traffic control, crime detection, computation, design analysis. etc., to some degree, as a general intellectual collaboration).
79. Inexpensive and reasonably effective ground-based ballistic missile defense.
80. Very low-cost buildings for home and business use.
81. Personal "papers" (i.e, two-way pocket phones) and other personal electronic equipment for communication, computing and data-processing.
82. Direct broadcasts from satellites to home receivers.
83. Inexpensive, long-lasting, very small battery-operated television receivers.
84. Home computers to "run" the household and communicate with the outside world.
85. Maintenance-free, long-life electronic and other equipment.
86. Home education via video and computerised and programmed learning.
87. Programmed dreams.
88. Inexpensive, rapid, high-quality black and white reproduction, followed by coloured, highly detailed photography reproduction.
89. Widespread use of improved fluid amplifiers.
90. Conference television (both closed-circuit and public communication system).
91. Flexible penology without necessarily using prisons (by use of modern methods of surveillance, monitoring and control).
92. Common use of individual power source of lights, appliances and machines.
93. Inexpensive worldwide transportation of humans and cargo.
94. Inexpensive road-free transportation.
95. New methods of teaching language rapidly.
96. Extensive genetic control of plants and animals.
97. New biological and chemical methods to identify, trace, incapacitate, or annoy people or for police use.
98. New and possibly very simply methods for lethal biological and chemical warfare.
99. Artificial moons and other methods of lighting large areas at night.
100. Extensive use of "biological process" in the extraction and processing of minerals.

CHAPTER 21

ANALYSIS OF ORGANISATIONAL RESOURCES

INTRODUCTION

External environmental analysis provides an understanding about the opportunities provided and threats posed by the environment. Traditional methods of strategy formulation over emphasised the external environment as the lead-edge of strategy formulation. But, the strategy formulation would be effective, if it takes organisational resource base and capabilities, in addition to external environmental analysis.

THE PERFORMANCE GAP ANALYSIS

As discussed in chapter 3, the past strategy leads to the formulation of new strategy to achieve desired objectives. The environment factors should be taken into consideration in projecting the future performance under the current strategy. A performance gap exists, when projected performance cannot be achieved under the current strategy. The reasons for the gap are : the inappropriateness of current strategy to the changing environmental factors, inappropriateness of the current strategy in view of the changes in internal environment or resources, improper implementation of current strategy. Fig. 21.1 presents performance gap.

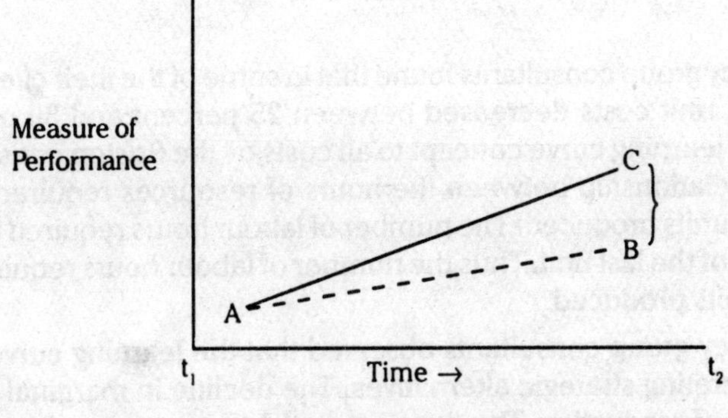

Fig. 21.1 The Performance Gap.

AB : Performance trajectory from following current strategy in forecasted environment conditions.
C : Target
CB : Strategic gap – projected short fall in performance on relevant measure.

Adjusting Current Strategy

Performance gap can be bridged by more careful implementation of the current strategy. Adjusting the internal resources based on the needs of the current strategy can also help to close the performance gap. If the change in operations help to bridge the gap, the strategist should concentrate on those strategic change is more difficult. Hence, efforts must be taken to improve resources, increase efficience, performance, competitive position and market share by improving margins without provoking competitors. Improving margins is also possible by cutting the cost when the sales are just below or just above the break-even point. If the, company is much below the break-even point, drastic measures like asset reduction/divestment may be necessary as shown in fig 21.2

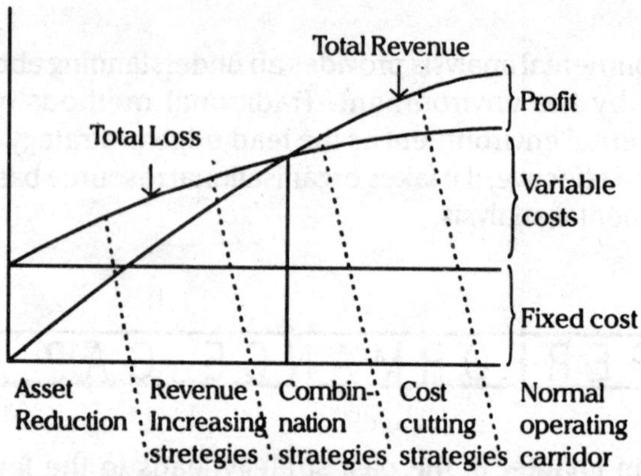

Fig. 21.2 Break Even Point and Divestment Strategy.

If, the gap exists due to the external environmental changes, the strategist has to change the strategy.

LEARNING/EXPERIENCE/TECHNOLOGY CURVES

The Boston consultancy group consultants found that in some of the their clients, every time when production doubled, unit costs decreased between 25 percent and 30 percent. This is based on the application of learning curve concept to all costs by the Boston consultancy group. The learning curve is the relationship between the hours of resources required to produce a product and the number of units produced. The number of labour hours required to produce the first unit is greater than that of the last unit. Thus the number of labour hours required to produce declines as a function of units produced.

The Boston consultancy group consultants observed that the learning curve relationship/ effect can be used for generating strategic alternatives. The decline in marginal cost helps the company to reduce the cost of production. The company with largest market share can enjoy the advantage of lowest marginal cost. The company produces most and sells most by reducing the cost to the lowest level. Thus the market share is the focus. The lowest cost helps the company to increase the market share further than its competitors. Competitors can not challenge the company owing to the impossibility of matching cumulative experience.

These are certain limitations to the effect of learning curve they are:

(i) Costs do not automatically decline with experience

(ii) Competitors may also employ the strategy of price cut which affect all the producers,

(iii) Customers may select the substitutes when the prices are increased. Consequently anticipated margins may disappear.

Learning/experience curve is an useful tool in developing strategic alternatives. However it cannot be used as the only analytical tool. Exhibit 21.1 presents and experience curve

Exhibit 21.1 : Experience curve

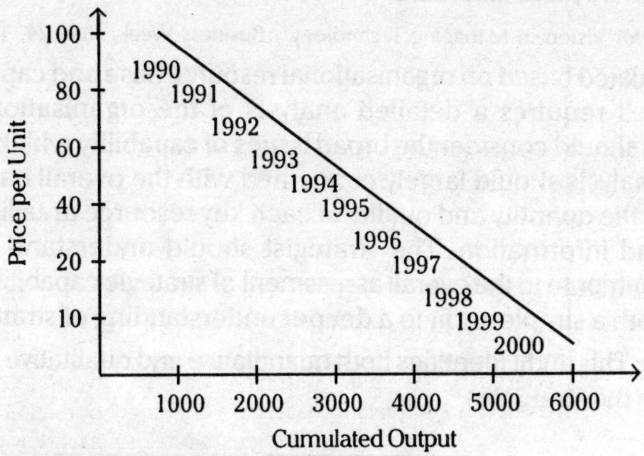

Technology Curve

Extension of learning/experience curve is technology curve. This curve plots the life cycle of technology. This curve is based on the idea that each technology has a limit or points of diminishing returns. Common danger signals appear when the limit is being approached: The relationship between the investment of man-hours and product. Performance is presented in the technology, curve. Considerable R & D efforts are necessary to achive small gains during the early days of technology development. At the later stages small efforts result in large gains. The returns begin to diminish at some point. Large efforts are necessary to get small gains in performance at this stage. These factors are volunerable to the development of substitution of another product technology Exhibit 21.2 presents technology S curves. Organisations should not depend on single technology and they should alert themselves to the danger signals as they indicate the limits of the current technology. The strategist should shift to the substitute technologies when these signals occur. Further, the strategist should resort to product development and diversification strategies in order to reduce the dependence on particular products.

Exhibit 21.2 : Technology S Curves

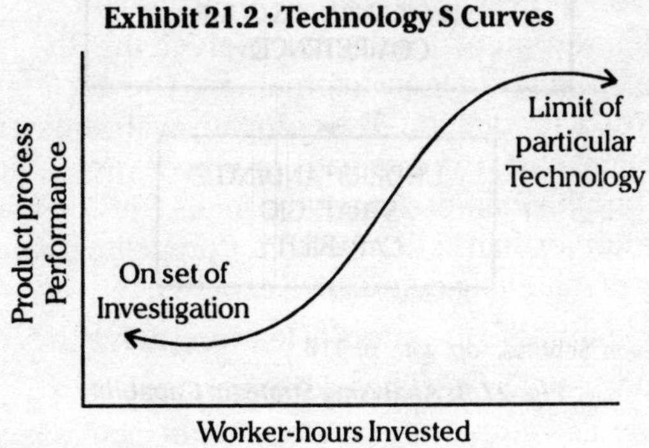

Signs of Approaching Limits

- R & D Productivity is Declining
- Most progress is in process rather than product

- R & D staff not getting along well
- Creativity seems to be lagging
- Small competitors are getting shares
- Small competitors are more innovative.

Source : R. N. Foster, "A Call for Vision in Managing Technology", Business Week, May 24, 1982, p. 26.

The Strategies formulated based on organisational resource base and capabilities will exploit the core competencies. It requires a detailed analysis of the organisational resources and capabilities. This analysis should consider the broad issues of capability which are relevant to the total organisation. The analysis should largely concerned with the overall balance of resources and mix of activities, and the quantity and quality of each key resource area like finance, human resource, technology and information. The strategist should understand how the different resources analyses will contribute to the overall assessment of strategic capability. Fig. 21.3 provides the process of moving from a simple audit to a deeper understanding of strategic capability.

The Resource Audit: This audit identifies both quantitative and qualitative resources available and necessary to achieve the strategies.

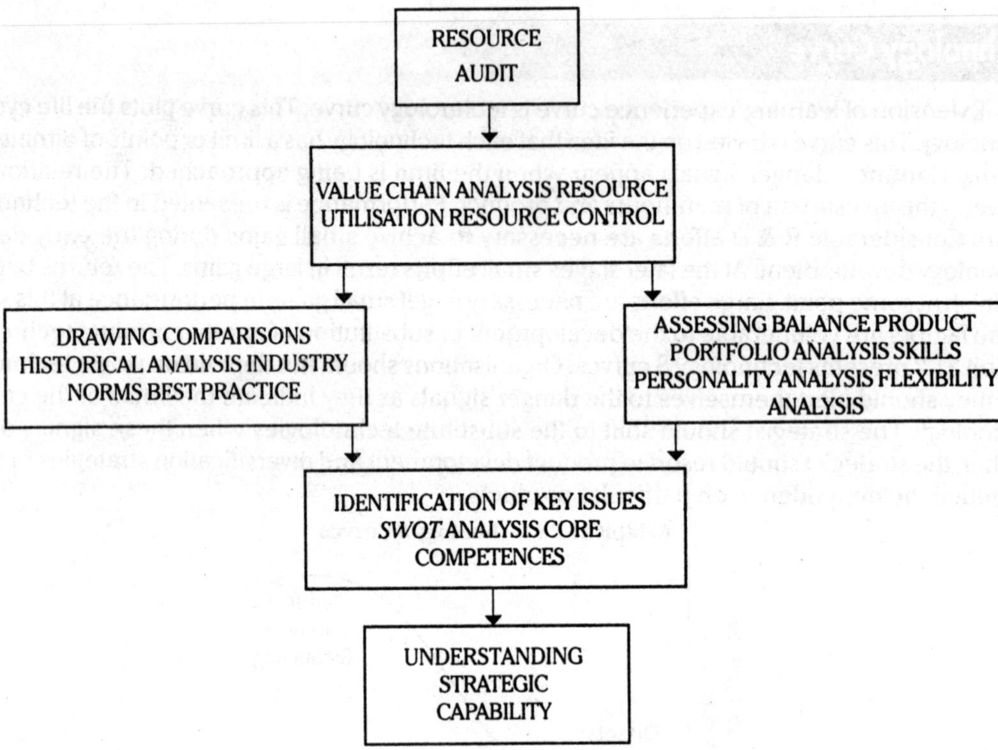

Source : Gerry Johnson and Keven Scholes, *op. cit.*, p. 118.

Fig. 21.3: Analysing Strategic Capability

RESOURCE AUDIT

Strategic capability can be better understood through resource audit. Resource audit helps to understand the strengths or weaknesses of the resource base. In other words, the quality of resources available to implement the strategy can be known though resource audit. The resource base includes physical resources, human resources, financial resources and intangibles.

Physical Resources : The audit of the physical resources includes listing of physical resources like machines, building, equipment etc, their age, condition of work, life span, capabilities, location etc.

Human Resources : Human resource audit includes assessing, verifying and listing out the number of employers, their skill inventory, age inventory, qualification-wise inventory, knowledge wise inventory and capability-wise inventory.

Financial Resource : Financial resource audit includes analysis and listing out sources and uses of financial resources, capital structure, working capital, accounts receivables, control of debtors and creditors, relationship among shareholders, bankers, debenture holders etc.

Intangibles : The resource audit exercise should not forget the intangibles. Intangibles have value like goodwill. Goodwill plays vital role in service-oriented organisations, retail organisations etc. Good will is represented by the brand image, customer loyalty, congenial contacts and relations, public image about the firm, quality and reliable service etc.

The resource audit should take into considerations all resources necessary for the implementation of the strategy. The audit should not restrict to the legally recognised assets. The audit should also consider the resources/assets outside the organisation. These assets include networks, contacts with the customers, dealers, suppliers etc.

The audit should also point out the organisation's distinctive capabilities in addition to the resources necessary for strategy implementation.

VALUE-CHAIN ANALYSIS

Value chain analysis links the organisational resources with the purpose of the strategy. This analysis deals with utilisation of resources, control of resources and linking the resources and strategy.

Value is the amount buyers are willing to pay for what a firm provides them creating the value for buyers that exceeds the cost of manufacturing and marketing is the goal of any business unit generic strategy. The total revenue reflects the value. Micheal E. Porter points out that a firms value chain is an important determinant of competitive advantage.

Value chain analysis was originally used as an accounting analysis to improve the profitability by observing the areas where cost reductions can be made and/or value creation can be improved. Indentifying building blocks and assessing the value added from each were linked to an analysis of an organisation's competitive advantage by Micheal E. Porter. The value chain displays total value consists of value activities and margin. These are two types of value activities viz., primary activities and support activities (see Fig. 21.4).

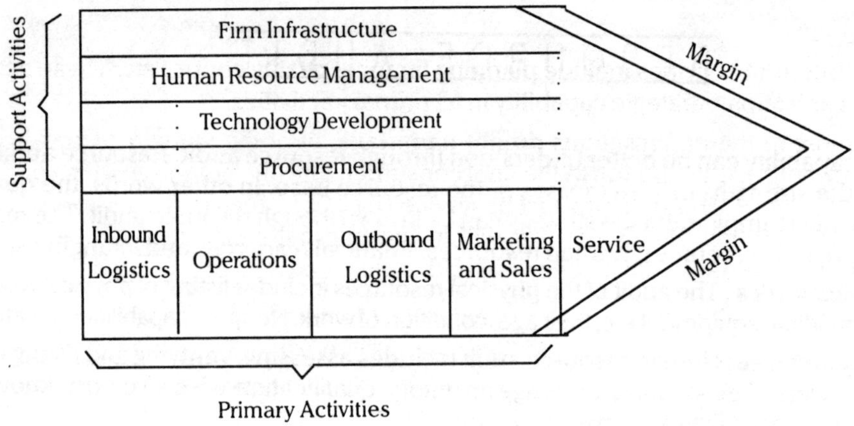

Source: Michael E. Porter, Competitive Advantage, Free Press, 1985.

Fig. 21.4, The Value Chain.

Primary activities include: (i) inbound logistics (ii) operations, (iii) outbound logistics (iv) marketing and sales and (iv) services.

(i) Inbound Logistics: These are the activities concerned with receiving, storing and distributing the inputs to the product/service. Materials handling, stock control and transportation are some of the functions involved in this activity.

(ii) Operations: Inputs are converted into output by the production/operations. These activities include machining, assembling, testing, packaging and delivering.

(iii) Outbound logistics : These activities include collection of finished products, storing them, and distribute it to the customers.

(iv) Marketing and Sales : Demand for the product/service is created by creating awareness among the consumers/users and make them to buy it. The activities include: Promotional programmes, sales administration, delivering the product etc.

(v) Service covers pre-sales and post sales service to satisfy the customer and enhance the value of product/service.

Identifying Support Activities

Each of these groups of primary activities is linked to support activities. Support activities are divided into four areas. They are procurement, technology development, human resource management, and firm infrastructure.

(i) Procurement: This activity involves procurement of all kinds of inputs including services. These activities are related to the entire value chain and supports every activity.

(ii) Technology Development : Technology activities are concerned with the product, manufacturing process and all other value activities. Technology development involves a variety of discrete activities. Many of these activities are performed within the R & D Department while others are performed outside the R & D department.

Human Resource Management

HRM activities cut across the entire value chain. Hence this area is particularly significant. These activities include: employment, training, development, rewarding, industrial and human relations, employee empowered etc.

Infrastructure

Firm infrastructural activities include planning finance, quality control etc. These activities are vital to an organisations strategic capability in all primary activities.

Normally most of the organisations do not undertake all of the value activities from the product design through to distribution to the final consumer. Any one organisation is a part of the wider value system which creates a product or service (fig 21.5). Much of the value is created in the supply and distribution chains not just within the internal position of the organisation. Therefore, the total process should be analysed and understood.

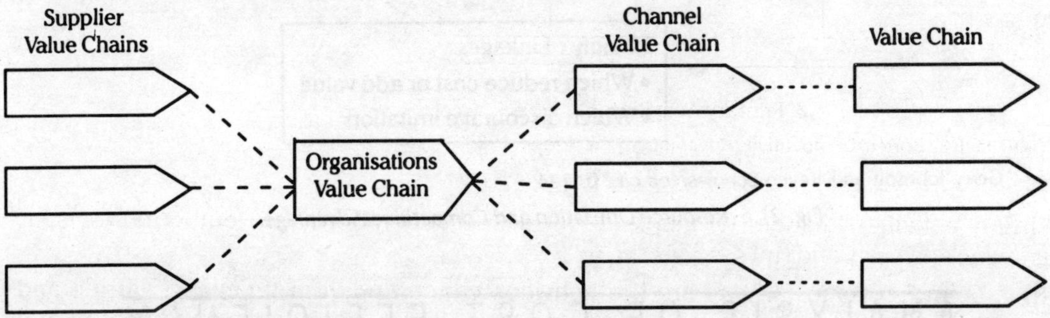

Source: Michael E. Porter, *op. cit.,*

Fig. 21.5 The Value System.

Value Chain and Internal Analysis

Value chain helps to analyse the company's present and potential strengths and weaknesses. The strategist can identify key internal factors for further examination as potential sources of competitive advantage.

Resource Utilisation

Value activities and linkages among machines, materials, men and markets are sources of competitive advantage for companies. Therefore organisational resource utilisation analysis can be undertaken and linked to competitive advantage. (fig 21.6).

Organisation

Organisation may be disintegrated into the various value activities. Important value activities which critically underpin the organisations competitive position. Low cost of inputs, low cost of operations, low cost of distribution can give the firm competitive advantage in fixing the lowest possible price. Value must be assessed or perceived from the point of view of the final consumer or user. The factors which sustain the competitive position are to be identified. These factors are called cost drivers or value drivers. The linkages among value activities, between suppliers, organisation and customers will enable the competitive advantage to continue. The close link between the primary activities and supportive activities is the basis of competitive advantage. Similarly external linkages to value activities in supplier organisations is also source of competitive advantage.

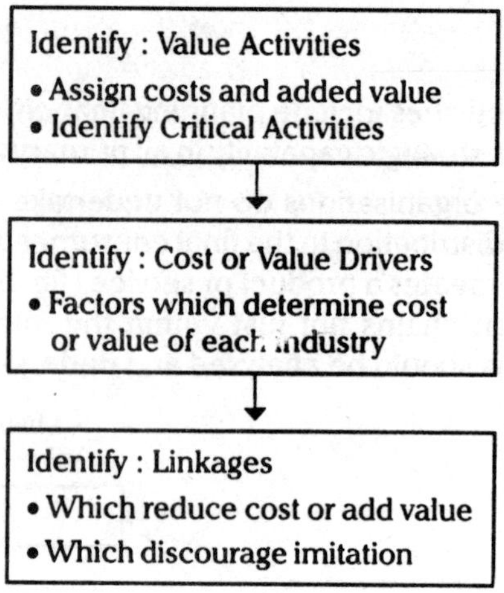

Source : Gerry Johnson and Keven Scholes, *op.cit.*, p. 124.

Fig. 21.6 Resource Utilisation and Competitive Advantage.

ANALYSIS OF COST EFFICIENCY

Cost efficiency can be achieved through several means. They include: large scale economies, lowering the supply costs, achieving high efficiency in production design and process and getting perfection through experience.

Analysis Effectiveness

Matching the organisation's product/ services to identified needs of the client results in effectiveness. Client needs include product attributes, service expectations and price sensitivity. Organisation's capability factors include product features, services performance and communication with clients.

Control of Resources

Proper control of resources is another factor which helps to assess the company's strategic capability. Efficient control of resources helps for value addition and cost minimisation.

Financial Analysis

Financial capability and performance influence the strategic capability of an organisation. The major stockholders concerned with the financial capability are the shareholders, bankers, financial institutions, suppliers of inputs and employees.

COMPARATIVE ANALYSIS

Different basis of comparison include: historical analysis, comparison with industry norms and best practice analysis. The company compares the present level of deployment of resources with the previous years figures. Under the industry comparison norms, the resources level of a company is compared with similar factors analysed for the industry. The historical analysis and industry norms analysis suffer from shortcomings. Hence, the best practice analysis is developed.

The best practice analysis establishes benchmarks of performance related to the best practice. Different types of best practices include competitor analysis based on the best practices of the key competitors, bench marking, and base budget reviews.

ASSESSING THE BALANCE OF RESOURCES

Balancing the organisational resources as whole is important and complementary. Portfolio analysis, balancing of skills/personalities and flexibility analysis help to assess the balance of resources.

Portfolio analysis is valuable in assessing the contribution of the balance of activities to the strategic capability of the organisation. Balance of skills needed to run the business efficiently are essential to an organisation. Financial, material and human resources are necessary to run the business efficiently. Balance of human resources include skills, knowledge, personalities, leadership styles etc. Organisation's resources should be flexible and adaptable in order to cope up with the changing environmental situations. Therefore, another issue is the assessment of the extent to which an organisations resources are flexible and adaptable. This assessment can be done with help of flexibility analysis. This analysis should assess the extent to which flexibility is balanced with the uncertainty faced by the organisation.

Identification of Key Issues

Identification of key issues arising from previous analyses is the major task at this stage. An useful and efficient analysis of organisation's strengths, weaknesses, opportunities and threats can be made at this stage. The resource analysis then can be useful basis to judge the future courses of action. The important assessments are SWOT analysis and core competences. SWOT analysis can be powerful if it incorporates a comparison with competitors. Core competences those areas which give the firm an edge over the competitors.

CHAPTER 22

SELECTION OF STRATEGIC ALTERNATIVES

INTRODUCTION

For any strategist, it is a million dollar question to know the types of strategies that are effective for his business.

If he has a clear perception of the major strategies to be used, their nature, relative contribution to organisational goals, It is relatively easy for him to prepare the blueprint for various sub-strategies to be used in different sub-units or departments.

Obviously, there is a logic in the fact that the success of a business is tied in with effective strategies.

Small firms where the business in a low key and which do not experience cutthroat competition, can survive with one or two strategies; but the larger firms as a rule will have to use a variety of strategies to survive, develop and grow in a highly dynamic and hostile environment.

So, to begin with, it is necessary for a strategist to know the type of strategies which may be profitably deployed.

Glueck[1] has identified the following types of strategies:

(i) Stable Growth Strategy;
(ii) Growth Strategy;
(iii) Retrenchment Strategy;
(iv) Combination Strategy.

STABLE GROWTH STRATEGY

The stable growth strategy is desirable for a firm which has a smooth sailing and where environment is not excessively hostile. This type of strategy is followed by a firm when:

(i) There is no deviation from the existing strategy, that is, no drastic change is expected in the goals or objectives of the enterprise;
(ii) It goes on serving customers in similar product or service sectors as mentioned in the business charter;
(iii) The environment is relatively stable or not much change is expected in it.

In such strategies, a *status quo* is maintained with regard to decisions in different functional areas of management. Only a few major functional changes are made in the product line, prices, channels of distribution, etc. By adopting this strategy, a company concentrates on the resources which it enjoys, or rapidly develops a meaningful competitive advantage in a given market situation. The various sub-strategies of the stable growth strategy include:

1. Glueck, William F., *Business Policy and Strategic Management*, McGraw-Hill International, Student Edition, 1980.

TABLE 1
STRATEGIC ALTERNATIVES

Grand Strategy	*Variation in Grand Strategy/Sub-Strategy*	*Frequency of Use*	*Effectiveness*
Stable Growth	1. Incremental growth	Most frequent strategy	1. Successful when environment is changing and firm is successful.
	2. Profit		2. Successful when industry is mature.
slowly	3. Stable growth as a pause	—	3. Successful if environment is slowly changing.
	4. Sustainable growth	—	4. Succesful if resources are depleting
Growth	1. Internal growth	Second most frequent strategy	
early in	(a) Single product/service or product/service line		1. Successful if life cycle
	(b) Diversification		
	(1) Concentric diversification		
	(2) Conglomerate diversification		
	2. External growth		2. Mixed success
	(a) Single product/service or product/service line		
	(b) Diversification		
	(1) Concentric diversification		
	(2) Conglomerate diversification		
	3. External growth (joint venture)		3. Mixed success
	4. Vertical integration		4. Usually not very successful
	5. Grow to sell out		5. Mixed success
Retrenchment/Turn Around	1. Turn around		1. Mixed success
	2. Divestment		2. Mixed success
	3. Liquidation or sell out		3. Last resort strategy.
	4. Captive company		4. Mixed success
Combination periods	1. Combine two or more grand strategies simultaneously	1. Used mainly by large firms	1. Successful in of economic transition (recession recovery)
periods	2. Combine two or more grand strategies in sequence.	2. Used more often than retrenchment.	2. Successful in of change in main product/service life cycle.

Source: William F. Glueck: *Business Policy and Strategic Management*, McGraw-Hill International, Student Edition, 1980, p. 203.

(i) Incremental growth strategy;

(ii) Profit strategy;

(iii) Stable growth as a pause strategy;

(iv) Sustainable growth strategy.

INCREMENTAL GROWTH STRATEGY

A short account of various sub-strategies is given here.

An enterprise adopting the incremental growth strategy sets itself those objectives which are more or less similar to those which were accomplished earlier. These objectives usually represent the industry average, though the incremental growth strategy is less profitable than the other growth strategies, but it is adopted because of the following reasons:

(a) When a firm has smooth sailing or perceives itself to be a successful one. In this case, the management knows the factors which are responsible for the present state of affairs. That is why it sticks to the present strategy.

(b) It has been observed that risky ventures, stemming from new product the new investment decisions, often fail. Therefore, the management prefers to shun these strategies and tries to stick to less risky strategies. As a result, the incremental strategy is adopted.

(c) It is both convenient and comfortable to follow this type of strategy because there is no disruption in the routine activities of the organization.

The firms following this strategy usually concentrate on one product or service line, and grow slowly and incrementally by entering new territories, taking up new product lines, etc. Many companies have profitably employed this strategy. A few instances are given here:

(a) Lakme has concentrated on cosmetics and is doing well.

(b) Amul has concentrated its business on milk and allied products, and is doing well.

(c) Hindustan motors is competing well in the automobile market.

Profit Strategies

When the objective of a firm is to generate cash immediately for itself or the stockholder, profit (or harvesting) strategies are followed. Herein, if necessary, the firm forgoes its market share to generate the cash. It has been noted that a harvesting strategy will work if many or most of these conditions exist:

(a) The unit's product is in a stable or declining market.

(b) The unit does not promote the sales stability or prestige of the firm;

(c) The unit's market share is small, and it would be very costly to increase it;

(d) The unit does not contribute a large percentage to total sales;

(e) The corporation has better use for its funds;

(f) Sales will decline less rapidly than the reduction in corporate support.

Harrigan and Porter[2] describe profit strategy as the end-game strategy. They have noted that some firms have successfully profitted from careful management by the sale of products which most firms felt were obsolete. For instance, two sick mills (namely, Mahalaxmi Mills and Edward Mills of Rajasthan after being taken over by N.T.C.) are now progressing well.

Harrigan and Porter have referred to the functional strategies used by the successful endgame players. There are:

(a) Dominate market share;

(b) Hold market share;

2. Harrigan, Kathryn and Porter, Micheal, "A Framework for Looking at End Game Strategies," *Proceedings of Academy of Management*, August 1978, p.14.

(c) Shrink selectively;
(d) Milk the investment
(e) Divest now.

Growth as a Pause Strategy

Firms following this strategy reduce their level of growth to attain a stable level. In doing so, they focus attention on their resources and operations to attain a higher level of efficiency. This strategy is largely deployed when strategists feel that a higher level of growth is both inefficient and unmanageable, or when the firm requires a breathing spell to stabilize itself before embarking on a new mission.

A sustainable growth strategy is defined as an increase (or decrease) in the system's productive capacity, with commensurate increases (or decreases) in its external environment's carrying capacity.[3] This type of strategy is largely adopted when the managers feel that the external conditions – resource availability, technology and others – are not conductive to the efficient working of the strategy.

Growth Strategies

In the present environment dilemma, "grow or perish" has become the central theme of strategy formulation. The drive for growth among managers is so deep-rooted that it has become a prime motivating force in boosting the efficiency of business. A firm pursues the growth strategy under the following conditions:

(a) For those industries which are operating in a highly competitive market short-term success means long-run growth. Therefore, growth is necessary for survival.
(b) When the company focuses, its strategic decision on major functional performance areas;
(c) When it significantly increases the level of its objectives.
(d) When it is believed that growth is linked with effectiveness of the organization.

Here important growth strategies are discussed.

Internal Growth by Increasing Sales of the Single Product Service Line

In this strategy, the firm increases its level of objective achievement rather than what is extrapolated against past performance by increasing the sales and profit of its present product or service line. By doing so, the firm increases its market-share profit at a much faster pace than it experienced in the past. It is a most successful strategy for a firm which is striving for rapid growth. This may be achieved in the following ways:

(a) By expanding sales through increasing primary demand and encouraging new uses for its present product or service;
(b) Expanding sales of product/service to different income groups;
(c) Expanding sales of product/service by adopting a differential pricing strategy;
(d) Expanding sales of different market segments by producing goods/services which cater to different purposes, purses and personalities.

3. Kefalas, A.G., "The Case for a Sustainable Growth Strategy," p. 252, in William F. Glueck, *Business Policy and Strategy Management*, McGraw-Hill International, Student Edition, 1980.

A few examples of the firms which have profitably used the internal growth strategy are:

(a) Bakeman's home products have expanded the sales of its products by geographically expanding its area of operations.

(b) The Oberio group of hotels has grown by establishing hotels not only in India but abroad as well, and thereby earning the title of ownership of a worldwide chain of hotels.

INTERNAL GROWTH BY DIVERSIFICATION

A diversification strategy is one by which the firm attains a growth level with the addition of new products/service internally to the existing product/service line. The diversification is of two types:

(i) Synergistic diversification

(ii) Conglomerate diversification

Synergistic Diversification

In the synergistic diversification, new products/services are sold in new markets, when the resources required for producing or marketing the new line are highly compatible with the existing resources. The synergy may result from the commonalities in production facilities, R & D facilities, sales force skill or in particular management skill (such as ability to handle a large advertising budget).

Conglomerate Diversification

In the conglomerate diversification strategy products/services are added to the existing line which is not significantly related to the present product/service in technology production process and R & D facilities. Godrej and DCM groups follow this strategy. How a company can grow may be best explained by the example of the T.T.K. group. It started its business in 1958 as the manufacturer of Woodward's gripe water. Later on, it shifted to ethical products in association with Kalichemie A.G. of West Germany and then to packaging materials. It has done well in coloured condom (Fiesta) market also; the Fryum (ready-to-fry food) has won a good market. The group has already entered on the production of capsule machinery and capsules, and now intends to embark on I.V.R. (Intra vaginal ring).

Factors Influencing Diversification

There are a number of factors which tempt a firm to diversify internally and externally. A few of these important factors have been listed here.

(i) When the management feels that its product/service line is approaching a declining phase, to stabilise diversification becomes imminent to stabilise earnings.

(ii) When an industry experiences excessive competition even though it has a smooth sailing, diversification acts as a cushion against any financial calamity.

(iii) A firm may diversify to achieve a high level of growth.

(iv) The benefits arising out of synergy can also be had by diversification.

(v) A firm may diversify by merger to acquire technical expertise for increasing its market share or preventing a takeover.

Ansoff[4] has developed a mechanism for analysing diversificatiion decisions. This has been shown in Exhibit 1.

Exhibit 1 : Ansoff's Diversification Matrix

	New products	
New Missions	Related technology	Unrelated Technology
Firm its own customer	Vertical integration	
Same type of product	Horizontal integration	
Similar type of product	Marketing and technology concentric diversification	Marketing related concentric diversification
New type of product	Technology related concentric diversification	Marketing related concentric diversification

Ansoff's diversification matrix helps the strategist to consider the various possible strategies which may be profitability exploited in a given marketing environment. This type of strategy is widely utilised by firms operating in a quite hostile environment. Chandler and Dames have noted that, for years in Europe, Japan and the United States, the diversification strategy was more popular than the single product/service line strategy.

EXTERNAL GROWTH BY MERGER AND JOINT VENTURES

An external growth strategy is one by which a firm increases its level of objective achievement through mergers and joint ventures.

A merger is that process by which two or more firms, acquire the assets and liabilities of the other in exchange of stock, or cash, or both. It can be two type, namely, concentric and conglomerate.

(i) *Concentric Merger*: A concentric merger is one in which two or more firms, which are related by the production process, technology and markets, combine.

(ii) *Conglomerate Merger*: A conglomerate merger involves the combination of two or more firms not closely related by technology, production process or markets.

Factors Affecting Merger

Many reasons tempt a firm to go in for a merger. A few important reasons have been listed below:

(i) To attain a high degree of efficiency and profitability especially when there is synergy between two firms.

4. Ansoff, H.T., *Corporate Strategy*, McGraw-Hill, New York, 1965, p. 132.

(ii) To increase the growth rate of the firm more rapidly than can be brought about by an internal growth strategy;
(iii) To stabilise the firm's earnings by acquiring another firm whose sales and earnings are at its peak;
(iv) To diversify the product line when it has attained the growth stage.
(v) To acquire additional resources quickly, such a advanced technology, machinery, and expertise;
(vi) To minimise competition by buying out the competitors.

Joint Venture

It can take any shape, and can take place between two or more firms of the same country or between the firms operating in different countries. As they are formed with a different purpose and have a different rate of success, they have been discussed here independently.

Joint Ventures Within National Boundaries

This type of venture takes place between two or more firms operating in the same country. That is, there can be a participation between the private sector and Government or between two or more private undertakings. Such types of ventures are usually created to:

(i) Minimize the risk of the new venture;
(ii) Introduce new technology;
(iii) Mobilise techno-managerial resources;
(iv) Accelerate economic growth.

For instance, the Government of India has entered into collaboration with the private sector in many spheres. A few notable examples are the Cochin Refineries, Madras Refineries, and Gujarat State Fertiliser Company.

Joint Ventures Across National Borders

When two or more different enterprises of different companies agree to create a new organisational entity, the joint venture across national borders comes into being.

According to Freiken, the following factors account for these agreements:

(i) Joint ventures save financial outlays for both parties, thus lowering cost;
(ii) Joint ventures increase sales, thus allowing for important production cost savings;
(iii) Joint ventures provide speedy channel acceptance, and this reduces marketing costs;
(iv) Joint ventures ensure the independence of both companies;
(v) Joint ventures provide the foreign country with a "front row seat" in the new country. This means that the locals interpret the industrial language and the customers of the country.

It also reduces the fear of the nationalistic concerns of "foreign takeover".

In our country, ever since independence, to speed up the tempo of industrialisation, foreign collaborations were accepted in varying degrees under different regimes. With the recent liberalization of economic policies, a spate of joint agreements have been signed. Consequently, the emphasis is now on multilateralism. In the recent past, important agreements have been entered in the field of electronics, automobiles, drugs and pharmaceuticals, textile and farm machinery, and engineering industry.

A few of foreign joint ventures include:

- Hindustan Motors has entered into collaboration with Caterpillar Company of U.S.A for the production of its entire range of earth-moving machines and tractor engines.
- The Standard Motors Products of India Ltd has entered into collaboration with the Austin Rover group for the production of the luxury motor car, Standard 2000.
- A few other notable collaborations in the automobile industry includes Mahindra & Mahindra with Peugeot Automobiles, France, Bajaj Tempo Ltd, with Daimler Benz A.G. of West Germany, TELCO with Mercedes Benz, DCM with Toyota, Premier with Nissan Motor Co., and Maruti with Suzuki.

Researchers like Ansoff et al, Birley Stancil, Chandler, Thompson and Rosenbloom have remarked that, for a successful merger, there must be effective planning. The firm which chooses to acquire other company must in advance decide whether it wants to follow a concentric or a conglomerate approach. Information pertaining to products, customers, market structure, and the future prospect of industry should therefore be gathered.

Willard Rockwell, Jr., who has been personally involved in a number of mergers, has given "ten commandments" for the acquiring company, which are:

Must Factors

(i) Pinpoint and spell out the merger objectives, especially the earning objectives.
(ii) Specify substantial gain for the stockholders of both the companies.
(iii) Be able to convince yourself that the acquired company's management is, or else can be made to be, competent.
(iv) Certify the existence of important dovetailing resources; but do not expect perfection.
(v) Spark the merger programme with the chief executive's involvement.
(vi) Clearly define the business you are in (for example, bicycle or transportation).
(vii) Take a depth-sounding strength, weaknesses and other key performance factors – the target acquisition company's and your own.
(viii) Create a climate of mutual trust, anticipate problems and discuss them early with other company.
(ix) Do not let "caveman" advances jeopardise the courtship. Do not threaten the management that is to be acquired.

The most important of these rules, make people your number one.

Vertical Integration

Vertical integration is a growth strategy characterised by entering (or leaving) one or more stages in the process of the manufacture and distribution of goods and services. It may be brought about in two ways:

(i) By backward integration
(ii) By forward integration

Backward Integration Strategies

It involves the supply of some of the firm's inputs or requirements. A few instances of this type of integration are given below:

- The Gujarat Milk Marketing Federation (the Amul industry) collects milk from a variety of sources, which is then utilised in the production of milk, butter and allied products.
- The I.D.P.L. entered a backward integration by starting to produce the raw materials necessary for the production of certain drugs.
- Most of the people involved in the publishing trade integrate backwardly, taking care of operations like proof reading, editing, binding, jacket design, etc.

Forward Integration

It involves entering into the business of finishing, distributing or selling some of the firm's present output. A few instances of this type of integration are:

- A few years ago, a number of textile manufacturers entered into this type of integration by selling their goods through chain stores.
- The Indian Oil Corporation can integrate forwardly if it decides to sell all its petrol output through its own service station.

Every business is involved in one or more types of the vertical integration strategy. A few firms should position by performing limited economic functions: others take a quite comprehensive view by embracing the whole chain of sequential occurrences, including the processing of raw materials and production, and subsequent operations which cover the marketing of goods and services as well. Efforts have been made to establish why firms follow a vertical integration strategy. It has been noted that not only mere technical complexity but the volume of business, too, tempts an industry to go in for vertical integration. Thompson has noted that firms with long-linked technology are more effective if they grow through vertical integration. So if a firm feels that it can derive advantages from a vertical integration, it adopts this policy after a proper scanning of the environmental variables and the availability of resources.

RETRENCHMENT STRATEGY

A retrenchment strategy involves the pruning or curtailment of the operations of the business so as to achieve a higher level of efficiency. However, this sort of strategy is used by undertakings only in exceptional cases. The following situations warrant the deployment of this strategy:

(i) The current level of performance is far below its past achievements;

(ii) The management aims to wipe out the previous deficit;

(iii) It seeks to serve the public by offering some products/services but finds it necessary to slice out certain products/services.

The important ingredients of this grand strategy include the following sub-strategies.

Turn Around Strategy

This strategy aims at improving the efficiency of the firm by turning around its resources. This can be brought about by reducing assets, achieving cost reduction and increasing revenues.

Divestment Strategy

A divestment strategy calls for the sale or liquidation of a sub-unit or a major part of undertaking to tide over a crisis. The divestment generally takes place for the following reasons:

- An unfavourable market environment
- Declining market share and negative sales growth;
- Unprofitable mergers;
- S & T changes which requires the firm to invest more resources than it has the capacity to invest.

The divestment may also be brought about in the following ways:

- If the sub-unit, is viable, it may be segregated from the parent unit, and the later one sold;
- The sub-unit may be sold to an independent buyer;
- The sub-unit may be liquidated and its assets be sold.

The divestment decision is a very crucial one for the management. Therefore, it should be taken after giving due consideration to the many complex issues involved in it; otherwise the very existence of the company may be jeopardised.

Liquidation Strategies

A liquidation strategy involves the winding up of the business by selling it off or closing down its operations. It is the least popular strategy and is adopted in exceptionally rare circumstances, such as:

(i) When bankruptcy is inevitable.
(ii) The various instrumentals will be better off with the liquidated results than by continuing the firm at a loss.

Captive Company Strategy

The company is said to follow a captive strategy when more than 75 per cent of the production/services are sold to a single customer. A company normally follows this captive strategy:

(i) When it is unable or unwilling to strengthen its marketing or other functions;
(ii) When the company can maximise its profit by using this strategy.

The best example of captive strategy is that of the marketing policies or ordnance factories which sell out their entire production to the government.

When these policies are adopted, the captive dictates the terms pertaining to product design, production control, and quality control. Moreover, it negotiates the price of goods.

Here, as the success of the business is intimately limited with one single customer, the management has to develop a long-term relationship with it so that it may prosper and be hedged against probable losses.

Combination Strategy

This type of strategy involves the blending of different types of strategies for the company or its sub-units. Normally, deployment of this strategy is based on the premise that a company should have "different strategies for different environmental situations."

Where a combination strategy is followed, the management uses different strategies for different sub-units or for different phases in time. The possible combinations may be as follows:

(i) Stable growth in some sub-units while retrenchment in others.

(ii) Stable growth in some sub-units while growth in others;

(iii) Retrenchment in some sub-units and growth in others.

As a result of resource constrains and lack of managerial expertise, it is not a possible for a small undertaking to enjoy this privilege. It has been noted that multi-branch, multi-product enterprises can reap the benefit of this policy.

CHAPTER 23

TOTAL QUALITY MANAGEMENT

- Meaning and Definition
- Principles and Core Concepts of TQM
- Steps to Implement TQM
- Methods of Consultation for TQM
- Organisation Structure and TQM
- ISO 9000 and TQM

MEANING AND DEFINITION

The two key elements of total quality movement are:

(i) Eliminating of waste and errors in the production process and in the process of rendering services.

(ii) Refocussing of the entire organisations towards their customers. Every in the organisations has a role to play in producing qualitative products, whether the customers are internal or external. The most important concern is the quality. The firms those neglect the customers, in the competitive world will have to hand over their customers to the competitors.

Total quality is defined as the conformance to the customers needs and expectations. Total quality movement makes the customer the arbiter of what needs to be done.

Total Quality is defined as, ".... a people-focused management system that aims at continual increase in customer satisfaction at continually lower cost. TQ is a total system approach (not a separate area or programme), and an integral part of high level strategy. It works horizontally across functions and departments, involving all employees, top to bottom, and extends backwards and forwards to include the supply chain and customer chain"

Total Quality Management (TQM) is a continuous process of improvement for individuals, groups of people and total organisation. Unlike other methods, TQM is the concentrated focus on continuous improvement. TQM is about changing the way things are done within the organisation's life time. People, must know what to do, how to do it, have the right methods to do it, and be able to measure the improvement of the process and the current level of achievement in order to improve the process.

Joseph Juran believes that there are no short cuts to quality. Quality does not happen suddenly and it must be planned. He believes that 80% of total quality problems are the fault of poor management.

Therefore, Juran suggests that:

(a) Establish specific goals to be attained.
(b) Establish plans to attain the goals.
(c) Assign clear responsibilities for meeting the goals
(d) Rewards should be based on the results achieved.

W. Edwards outlines 14 points of action to be taken to maintain total quality. They are:

(a) Create constancy of purpose for improvement of product and service. Redesign the manufacturing system accordingly (Fig. 23.1)
(b) Adopt the new philosophy – a transformation of the style of management.
(c) Cease dependence on mass inspection
(d) End the practice of awarding business on price tag alone.
(e) Constantly and forever improve the system of production and service.
(f) Institute modern methods of training on the job
(g) Institute modern methods of supervision to help people and machines do a better job.
(h) Drive out fear from the organisation.

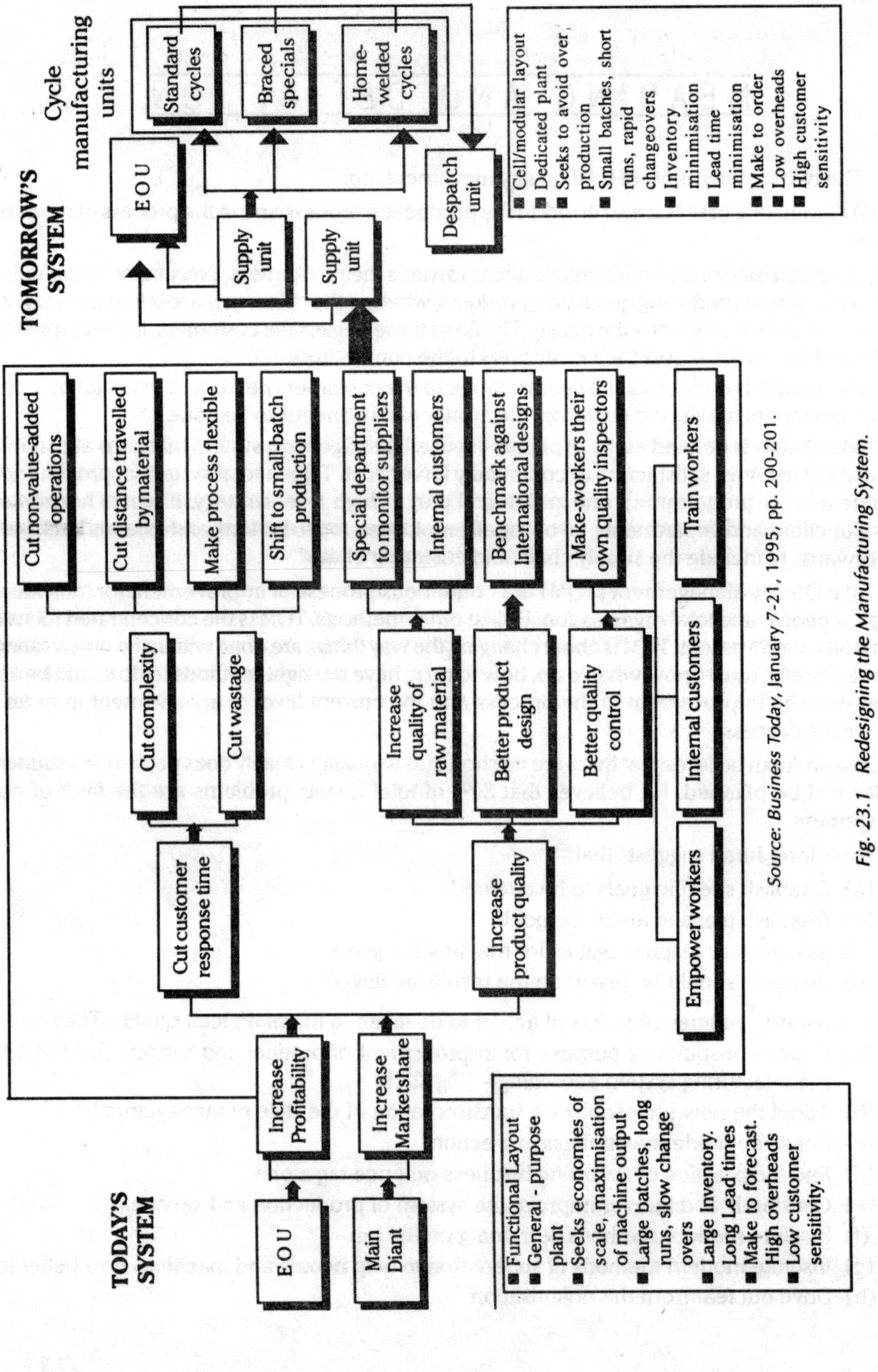

Source: *Business Today*, January 7-21, 1995, pp. 200-201.

Fig. 23.1 Redesigning the Manufacturing System.

(i) Break down barriers between departments.
(j) Eliminate slogans and exhortations asking for zero defects.
(k) Eliminate work standards based on numerical quotas.
(l) Remove the barriers to pride workmanship
(m) Institute a vigorous programme of education and training.
(n) Create a structure in the organisation which allows everyone to work towards the transformation.

Philips B. Cross by states these are four absolutes quality management. They are:

(a) The definition of quality is conformance to requirements
(b) The system to be used is prevention
(c) The performance standard is zero defects
(d) Measurement is based on the cost of quality.

PRINCIPLES AND CORE CONCEPTS OF TQM

Total Quality Management encompasses a set of four principles and eight core concepts as shown below:

Principles of TQM	*Core Concepts of TQM*
1. Delight the customer	(a) Customer satisfaction
	(b) Internal customers are real
2. Management by fact	(a) All work is process
	(b) Measurement
3. People-based management	(a) Team work
	(b) People make quality
4. Continuous improvement	(a) Continuous improvement cycle
	(b) Prevention

1. *Delight the Customer:* The focus is on the external customer. Delight means being best at what really important to the customer. Making the continuous changes to satisfy the customer is an integral part of TQM.
2. *Management by Fact*: The management should know the quality of the product or service that the customer is presently using. This quality level is used as bench mark to improve it further. Management gathers the facts about the present level and provides this information to the employees at all levels to make the decisions based on the facts. These facts are an essential aspect of continuous improvement.
3. *People-based Management*: The management should make the employees understand what to do, how to do it, get the feedback about their performance. The people should also be encouraged to assume responsibility for the quality of their work. People can be more committed to the customer satisfaction, if they are involved more. The quality is heavily influenced by the continuous involvement of the people rather than by the systems, standards and technology.

4. *Total Quality Management is a Continuous Process* : It is a management and a long-term process. It is not a short-term programme based on goals or targets or a programme or a project. TQM is a continuous improvement based on the incremental change.

Core Concepts for Improvement

Customer Satisfaction: Companies should understand the importance of the external customer as the external customers is the main source of income. Companies should identify the changing needs of the customers from time to time, find out the factors which satisfy them and which cause grief to them. Companies should enhance the satisfying factors and reduce the factors those cause grief.

Internal Customers and Real: Internal customers are as important as external customers as they continuously influence the quality maintenance. They also influence speed, efficiency, perfectness and cost. All work is process:

All Work is a Business Process: Business process is a "combination of methods, materials, manpower and machines that taken together produce a product or service."

Measurement

Measurement of present level of quality is more important in order to determine the future quality level. Internal quality measurement of product are: (a) Breach of promise, (b) Performance to standard, (c) Reject level, (d) Accidents, (e) Process in control, (f) Yields scarp, (g) Time cost due to availability raw materials, (h) Number of changes to works order, (i) Cost of quality.

Team Work: People work together in teams to accomplish the most difficult goals. People work in teams to maintain and improve the quality. Team work enables the people to work from a cross-functional approach.

People Make Quality: Mostly organisational efforts influence the quality. Organisational efforts the individuals and teams in the organisation to commit to the quality.

Continuous Improvement Cycle

Identifying the present level of quality standards, establishing the customer needs, establishing the ways and means to produce the product or render service to meet the customer needs, measuring the success and improving the quality continuously are the parts of the continuous improvement cycle.

Prevention

Preventing the failures to occur is the central system of total quality management. Foreseeing the possible failures and take steps in advance to prevent them from occurrence. Feeding information forward helps to prevent the failures. This process helps for the creation of the culture for continuous improvement. Fig. 23.2 pyramid model for TQM.

Methods of Total Quality Management

Gopal K. Kanji and Mike Asher outlines 100 methods of Total Quality Management Exhibit 23.1 presents the methods of TQM.

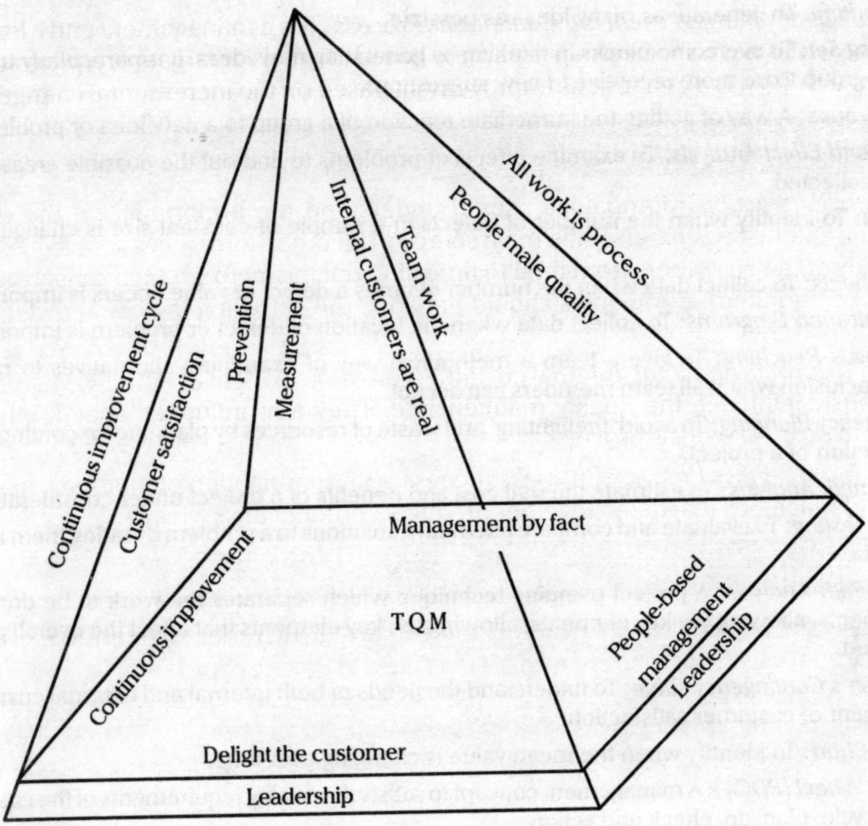

Fig. 23.2: Pyramid Model of TQM.

Source: Kanji and Asher, 1993.

Exhibit 23.1 : Methods of Total Quality Management

Acceptable Quality Level (AQL): To provide a structure of sampling plans, risks and inspection strategies to ensure that the customer receives the quality that the supplier has contracted to deliver.

Affinity Diagram: To organize large amounts of data in groups according to some form of natural affinity.

Arrow Diagram: To show the time required for solving a problem and which items can be done in parallel.

Bar Charts: To display discrete data collected by checksheets so that patterns can be discovered.

Basic Statistics: The mean, median, mode, range and standard deviation are ways of summarizing and describing large volumes of data. The first three are measures of location, the last two are measures of spread.

Benchmarking: To identify and fill gaps in performance by putting in place best practice, thereby establishing superior performance.

Box and Whisker Plots: To provide a simple way of drawing the basic shape of the distribution of a set of data.

Brainstorming: To generate as many ideas as possible without assessing their value.

Brainwriting: To generate as many ideas as possible.

Breaking Set: To overcome blocks in thinking by generating new ideas. It is particularly useful in prompting a group to be more receptive to new suggestions.

Buzz Groups: A way of getting the immediate reaction of a group to a new idea or problem.

Cause and Effect Analysis: To examine effects or problems to find out the possible areas where data can be collected.

C Chart: To identify when the number of defects in a sample of constant size is changing over time.

Checksheets: To collect data when the number of times a defect or value occurs is important.

Concentration Diagrams: To collect data when the location of defect or problem is important.

Consensus Reaching: To give a team a methodical way of examining alternatives to reach a collective conclusion which all team members can accept.

Contingency Planning: To avoid 'firefighting' and waste of resources by planning for contingencies in the completion of a project.

Cost-benefit Analysis: To estimate the real cost and benefits of a project under consideration.

Criteria Testing: To evaluate and compare alternative solutions to a problem by rating them against a list of criteria.

Critical Path Analysis: A project planning technique which separates the work to be done into discrete elements, allowing the key elements, allowing the key elements that affect the overall project to be identified.

Customer's Contingency Table: To understand the needs of both internal and external customers for the fulfilment of customer satisfaction.

Cusum Chart: To identify when the mean value is changing over time.

Deming Wheel (PDCA): A management concept to satisfy the quality requirements of the customer by using the cycle: plan, do, check and action.

Departmental Cost of Quality: To provide a financial measure of the quality performance of an organisation.

Departmental Purpose Analysis (DPA): To review the internal customer-supplier relationship.

Domainal Mapping: To assist in the identification of internal customers and their needs.

Dot Plots: A simple graphic device which presents observations as dots on a horizontal scale.

Error Proofing (pokayoke): To design an operation in such a way that specific errors are prevented from causing major problems to the customer.

Evolutionary Operation (EVOP): A sequential experimental procedure for collecting information during on-line production to improve a process without disturbing output.

Failure Mode and Effect Analysis (FMEA): To assist in the foolproofing of a design or a process.

Fault Tree Analysis: To perform a quantitative as well as qualitative analysis of a complex system.

Flowcharts: To generate a picture of how work gets done by linking together all the steps taken in a process.

Force Analysis: To identify external and internal forces at work when developing a contingency plan.

Force Field Analysis: Allows you to identify those forces that both help and hinder you in closing the gap between where you are now and where you want to be.

Gannt Charts: For planning the steps necessary to implement quality improvement.

Geometric Moving Average: To identify trends in small changes in the process mean. The geometric moving average is sometimes called the exponentially weighted moving average (EWMA).

Histograms: To display continuous data collected by checksheets so that any patterns can be discovered.

Hoshin Kanri (quality policy development): To delight the customer through the manufacturing and servicing process by implementing the quality goals of the organization.

Idea Writing: To bring all participants into groupwork.

Imagineering: To assist a company to identify areas of opportunity by concentrating on the ideal outcome then working back from it.

Improve Internal Process (IIP) Plan: To provide the structure to develop work plan details for a task using various factors, such as measurable, responsible resources, times and previous task owners.

Is/is not Matrix: To identify patterns in observed characteristics by a structured form of stratification.

ISO 9000: To demonstrate to yourself, your customers and an independent assessment body that you have a effective quality management system in place.

Just In Time (JIT): To deliver the raw materials or components to the production line to arrive just in time when they are needed.

Kaizen: A Japanese term meaning 'change for the better', the concept implies a continuous improvement in all company functions at all levels.

Lateral Thinking: A way of transferring from one frame of reference to another, enabling you to break down barriers which inhibit creative thought.

List Reduction: To reduce a list of ideas to one of manageable size.

Matrix Data Analysis: To provide a picture of numerical data from matrix diagram in an efficient way.

Matrix Diagram: To provide information about the relationship and importance of task and method elements of the subject.

Mind Mapping: A way of generating and recording ideas individually rather than in a group. Mind mapping makes use of work associations, encouraging you to follow your own thought patterns, wherever they lead, It also provides a written record of the ideas generated.

Minute Analysis: To estimate the survival period of a particular product unit under certain conditions, using a simulated experimental environmental.

Morphological Forced Connections: To generate new ideas or ways of approaching problems. It combines lists of attributes and forces new connections between them, so triggering new options.

Moving Average: To identify trends in data when short-term variation or cyclical patterns are confusing the longer-term picture.

Multi-vary Charts: To show the dispersion in a process over the short and long-term, using a graphic control chart.

Multi-voting: To select the most popular or important items from a list.

Mystery Shopping: A technique involving looking at your business from the outside and measuring the efficiency of your own key processes from the customer's viewpoint.

Nominal Group Technique: A way of generating ideas from a group and identifying the level of support within the group for those ideas.

NP Chart: To identify when the number of defective items in a sample of constant size is changing over time.

Objective Ranking: Helps to place your current activity in perspective and enable you to understand the purpose of your efforts.

Opportunity Analysis: Offers the opportunity to evaluate quickly a long list options against desired goals and available resources.

Paired Comparisons: To help a group to quantify the preferences of its members.

Parameter Design: To determine which factors are important in the manufacturing process and to find the optimum set of working conditions.

Pareto Analysis: To separate the most important causes of a problem from the many trivial. Also, to identify the most important problems for a team to work on.

Paynter Charts: To displays information over time in a way that allows changes in patterns of failure to be discovered. Paynter charts will show when one failure mode takes over from another in terms of importance or when the overall failure rate is changing over time.

P Chart: To identify when the percentage data, pie charts are an effective means of showing the relative size of the individual parts to the total.

Potential Problem Analysis (PPA): To examine plans to identify what can go wrong with them, so that preventive action can be taken.

Problem Prevention Plan: To anticipate what can go wrong and plan to prevent problems.

Process Analysis: Enables a group to look for opportunities to improve processes. It can also be used to identify standards and measures for critical parts of processes.

Process Capability: To demonstrate whether a process is capable of meeting a specification and to calculate an index to show this capability.

Process Cost of Quality: To provide a financial measure of the quality performance of an organization.

Process Decision Programme Chart: To focus on possible sequences to help lead to a desirable result and contingency planning.

Programme Evaluation and Review (PER) Technique: To establish a planning technique for complex and multi-level projects.

Quality Circles: A special type of small group activity which forms a vehicle for the development of individuals.

Quality Functions Development (QFD): A technique or disciple for optimizing process of developing and producing new products on the basis of customer need.

Relation Diagram: To illustrate the relationship between problems and ideas in complex situations. Also to identify meaningful categories from a mass of ideas when relationships are difficult to determine.

Reliability: To find the cause of failures and try to eliminate them and to reduce the effects or consequences of failure.

Rich Picture: To allow a group to capture all ideas developed without judgement or analysis, in a pictorial form that allows the strength of the ideas to be recorded.

Robust Design (off-line quality control): To achieve the proper functioning of a component even when affected by interfering factors, whether external, internal or manufacturing variation.

Sampling A Method by which a Small Number of Items (the sample): is drawn from a larger number of items (the population) in order to draw a conclusion about the population based upon information from the sample.

Scatter Diagrams: To allow the relationship between cause and effect to be established.

Snowballing: Sometimes called 'pyramiding', snowballing is a technique for gathering information or ideas.

Solution Effect Analysis: To examine solutions to problems to find out whether there are any detrimental consequences and to plan the implementation of the solution.

Spider Web Diagrams: To show performance against a target when several criteria are being set.

Statistical Process Control (SPC): To identify when processes are changing over time.

Stem and Leaf Diagram: To present raw data and to show their distribution visually.

Stratification: To assist in the definition of a problem by identifying where it does and does not occur.

Suggestion Schemes: To generate ideas for improvement.

System Design: To apply special scientific and engineering knowledge to produce a basic functional prototype model, having surveyed the relevant technology, manufacturing environment and customer need.

Taguchi Methods: A technique for the optimization of products or processes, Taguchi involves a two-stage experimental design that gives the benefits of robustness and efficiency with the minimum number of experiments.

Tally Charts: To collect data when the value of a defect or problem is important.

Teamwork: To organize activity which requires a number of people to collaborate and work together for a common goal.

Tolerance Design: To find out by the experiment where the variability in a process (product) occurs and where adjustments can be made.

Total Productive Maintenance: To help a process which aims at making the most effective and efficient use of existing production structures.

Tree Diagrams: To identify the tasks and methods needed to solve a problem and reach a goal.

U Chart: To identify when the number of defects in a sample of variable size is changing over time.

Why-how Charting: When thinking in both abstract and concrete terms, and needing to move between the two, why-how charting enables a goal to be translated into action.

Xmoving Range (x-MR) Chart: To identify when a value is changing over time.

X-R Chart: To identify when the mean value or range in a sample of constant size is changing over time.

Zero Defects: To allow teams to experience the success involved in meeting over more demanding targets without demotivating them by not achieving absolute success at once.

Source: Gopal K. Kanji and Mike Asher, *100 Methods for Total Quality Management,* Response Books, New Delhi, 1996, pp. 13-19.

STEPS TO IMPLEMENT TOTAL QUALITY

The following steps help to implement total quality Fig 23.3 presents how Modi-Xerox implements TQM:

1. **Monitoring and Evaluation**: Manager has to lay greater emphasis on the checking of results. For example, changes in the current management information system may be initiated so as to produce checkable results on quality and quantity. Quality aspects should be integrated into the way in which success is judged.

2. **Briefing Quality**: Employees at all levels are to be educated in order to have clear idea through face-to-face communication or through team briefing. Regular quality briefings will make a significant contribution to overall improvement. Briefing must be conducted by the immediate boss with an emphasis on local achievements, difficulties and targets.

3. **Consultation**: Consultation about the work should be improved as consultation by experts will improve quality and methods of work. Consultation improves the sense of belongingness and has a psychological impact in helping people in making valuable contributions. It provides an opportunity to the employees to concentrate on customer needs. Consultation may be informal or formal through the methods like quality circles and suggestion schemes.

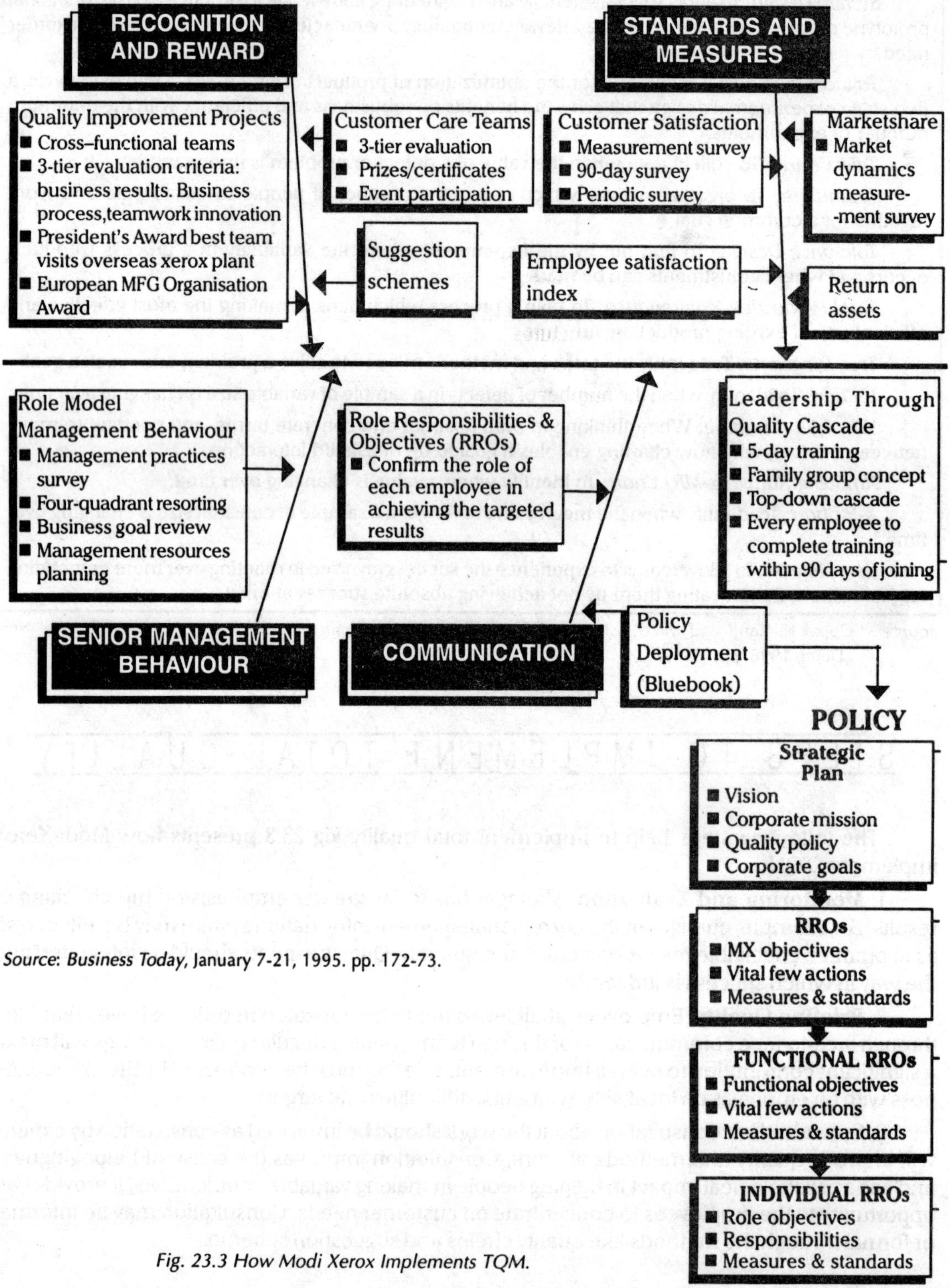

Source: *Business Today*, January 7-21, 1995. pp. 172-73.

Fig. 23.3 How Modi Xerox Implements TQM.

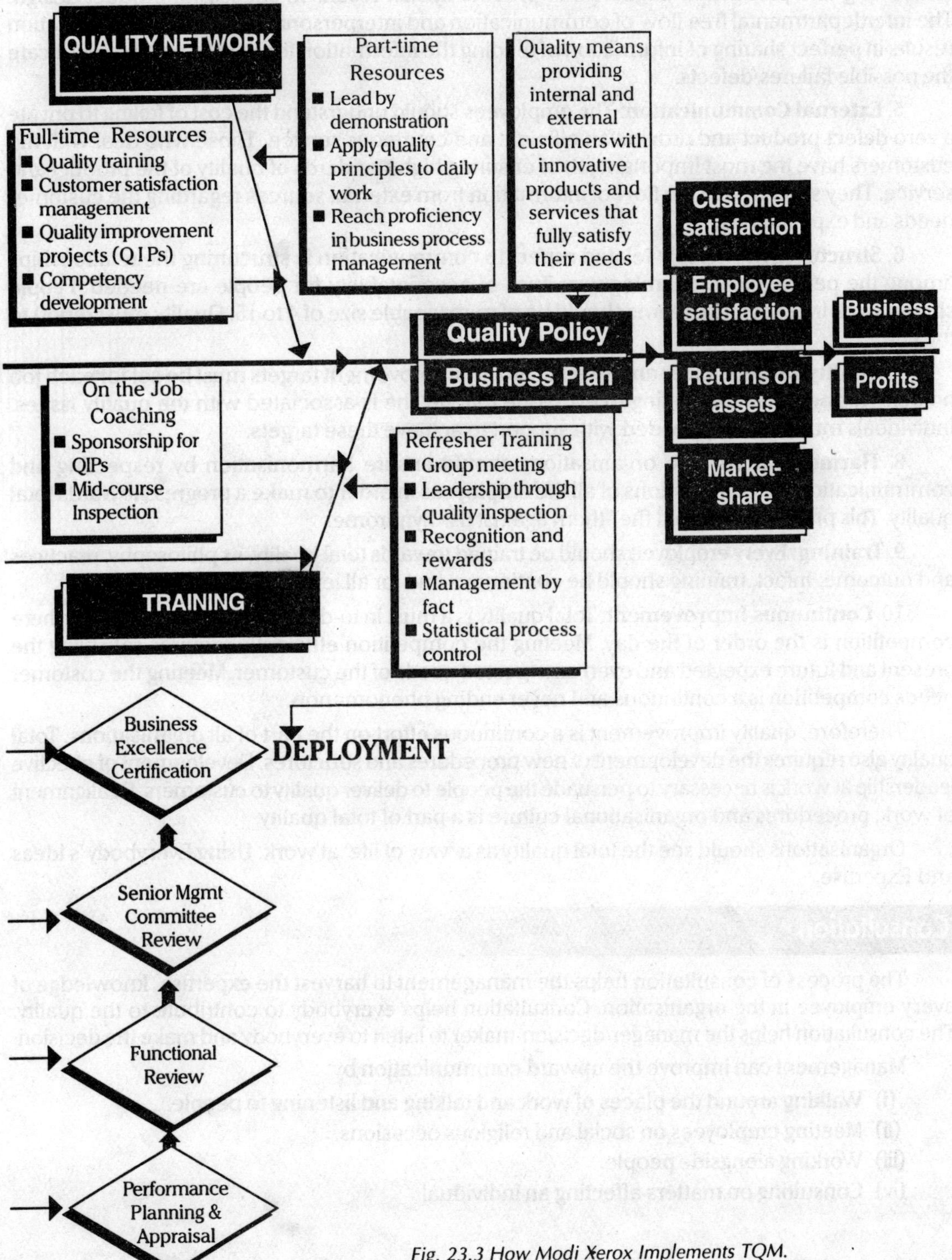

Fig. 23.3 How Modi Xerox Implements TQM.

4. **Lateral Communication**: An early involvement of specialists in marketing, designers, accounting and production engineers in product design results in successful product design. The interdepartmental free flow of communication and interpersonal free-flow communication results in perfect sharing of information of feeding the information forward in order to eradicate the possible failures/defects.

5. **External Communication**: The employees should understand the cost of failing to private a zero defect product and provide an efficient and courteous service. Those who deal with the customers have the most important job of ensuring high standards of quality of the product and service. They should have the flow of information from external sources regarding the customer needs and expectations.

6. **Structure**: The closely related aspect to communication is structuring the relationships among the people clear, unambiguous lines of accountability for people are needed. People should work in teams. The teams should be of manageable size of 4 to 15. Quality must report to the line.

7. **Quality Targets**: Clear and specific quality improvement targets must be set for each job holder. This act gives the feeling to everyone that he/she is associated with the quality issues. Individuals must also be provided with support to achieve these targets.

8. **Harmonisation**: The organisations should ensure harmonisation by respecting and communicating the contributions of all the employees in order to make a progress towards total quality. This practice will avoid the "them against us" Syndrome.

9. **Training**: Every employee should be trained towards total quality, its philosophy, practices and outcome. Infact, training should be continuous and for all levels of employees.

10. **Continuous Improvement**: Total quality is a must in to-day's economic scenario, where competition is the order of the day. Meeting the competition efficiently requires satisfying the present and future expected and even unexpected needs of the customer. Meeting the customer needs competition is a continuous and never ending phenomenon.

Therefore, quality improvement is a continuous effort on the part of all organisations. Total quality also requires the development of new procedures and structures. Development of effective leadership at work is necessary to persuade the people to deliver quality to customers. Realignment of work, procedures and organisational culture is a part of total quality.

Organisations should see the total quality as a 'way of life' at work. Using Everybody's Ideas and Expertise.

Consultation

The process of consultation helps the management to harvest the expertise, knowledge of every employee in the organisation. Consultation helps everybody to contribute to the quality. The consultation helps the manager/decision-maker to listen to everybody and make the decision.

Management can improve the upward communication by:

(i) Walking around the places of work and talking and listening to people.
(ii) Meeting employees on social and religious occasions.
(iii) Working alongside people.
(iv) Consulting on matters affecting an individual.

(v) Listening views reported up through the management chain.

(vi) Meeting with trade unions in consultative/negotiating committees.

METHODS OF CONSULTATION FOR TOTAL QUALITY

The purpose of consultation is to involve all the employees in the decision making process in order to improve quality. The different methods of consultation are quality circles, suggestion schemes, inter-department task forces and small teams.

Exhibit 23.2 : Different Approaches to Problem Solving

	Quality Improvement Team	Corrective Action Team	Task Force	Quality Circle
Definition	A cross-functional team identifying opportunities for improving quality in the process of providing a product or service.	A functional team to resolve a specific quality issue in one section/department.	Across-functional team assiting the planning and implementation of a major change.	A functional team selecting their own work related issues to analyse and solve.
Membership	Selected or volunteer members from internal customers/suppliers departments.	Selected members from the one section/ department.	Selected or volunteer members from departments affected. covering a range of disciplines and grades.	Volunteers from one section/department.
Leadership	Line management.	Line management.	Senior management.	First line supervisoror elected leader from volunteer members.
Activity	Ongoing.	One-off.	One-off.	Ongoing.

Source: Jeremy Thorn *"Managing for Total Quality"* p. 22.

Quality Teams: Different kinds of quality teams include task force, Corrective Action Teams, quality circles quality improvement teams etc. These teams are mostly cross functional. Exhibit 23.2 presents different approaches to problem solving Exhibit 23.3 presents setting up of quality teams.

Top Team Workshop

A top team workshop using an external facilitator, the divisional, technical, commercial, marketing, quality assurance and production managers consider the basic issues facing the business.

The role of the facilitator is crucial for the success of the workshop. The team in the workshop will concentrate its collective mind on the issues involved. Exhibit 23.4 presents Total Quality Control.

Exhibit 23.3 : Setting up Quality Teams

What sort of teams are needed and how to set them up.

- process oriented teams–cross–functional
- high impact process teams–repetitive, customer interface.
- business focused–aimed at improved business results.
- customer focused–aimed at improved customer satisfaction.

Key Attributes :

- they work a team with a common mission
- process owner/sponsor named and responsibility/accountability accepted
- empowered team–capacity to act
- experts in the process
- skilled in quality tools
- statistical/analytical support
- facilitator
- consultant/trainer
- management inspection, coaching, counselling, role modelling.

Team Problem Solving at Texas Instruments

Effectiveness Teams :

- voluntary participation
- team selects problem
- usually local problem
- permanent
- team presentation on project completion
- trained in problem solving and interpersonal techniques.
- participation and development emphasis
- 52 teams active

Quality Improvement Teams :

- management appointed
- problem assigned by manager
- usually cross-functional
- team reassigned on completion
- milestones feedback to quality steering team
- trained in problem solving techniques
- problem solving process emphasis
- 44 teams active.

The Benefits of using Teams are :

- create an environment of participation
- establish broad based problem solving ability
- encourage synergy
- provide recognition for quality project activity
- obtain maximum benefit from human resources
- standardise team activity
- overlay team activity on organisational structure.

Source: Ibid., pp. 24-25.

Exhibit 23.4 : Total quality culture problem solving process

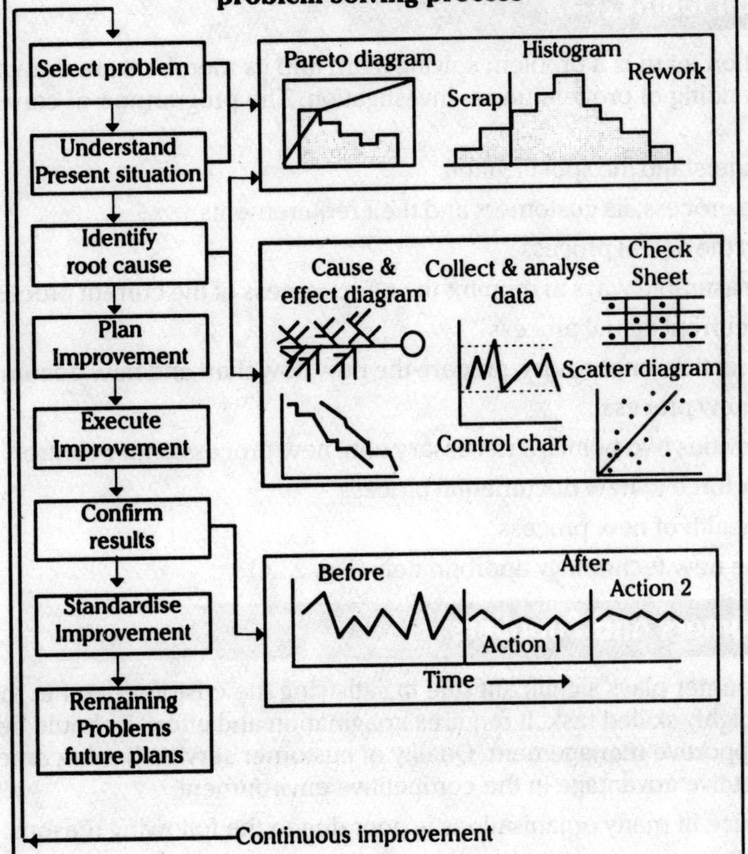

Source: Ibid., p.24.

Rolling Workshop

The top management after sharing their expertise and discussing various issues, invite the middle level managers into the workshop. The top management briefs the middle level management the nature of the problem and the broad strategy agreed upon. An external consultant facilitates the workshop.

Corrective Action Teams

Corrective action team is a problem solving team and its members are drawn from those with a full understanding of process under investigation. The programme of corrective action team include:

(a) clearly understand the specification
(b) define the process, its customers and their requirements
(c) flow chart the actual process
(d) define measurable ways to monitor the effectiveness of the current process
(e) measure current actual process
(f) make correction if necessary, prepare the new flowchart and new documents
(g) measure new process
(h) repeat previous two points, if necessary until new process under control
(i) train work force to new documental process
(j) monitor health of new process.
(k) Absorb the new technology appropriately (Fig. 23.4)

Service to Customers and Suppliers

Service to customer plays significant role in satisfying the customer and in the system of total quality. It is a highly skilled task. It requires imagination and effort. It should be backed up by effective and supportive management. Quality of customer service has become a vital part of providing competitive advantage in the competitive environment.

Customer service in many organisations is poor due to the following reasons.

(i) absence of commitment
(ii) lack of confidence and or knowledge
(iii) lack of internal communication
(iv) absence of care for staff
(v) lack of cooperation from staff of the employers are treated by colleagues harmoniously, they extend their cooperation the quality of service provided by one member of staff to another affects the quality of service given to an external customer. Fig. 23.5 presents how Mukhand focuses on the customer

Improving Customer Care

Manager should improve the existing levels and dimensions of customer service. Managers should know that rendering qualitative customer service is a skill and it can be learned, developed

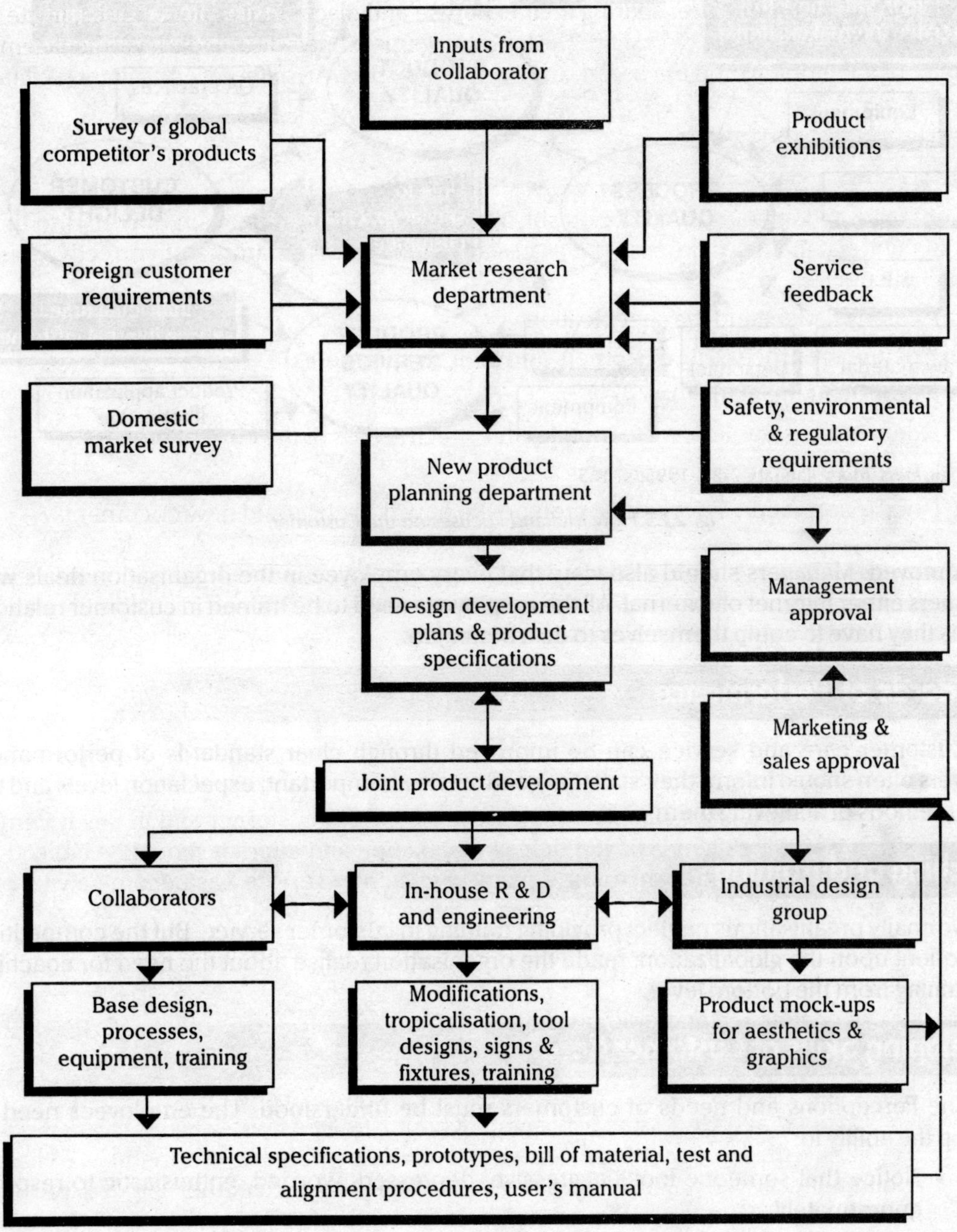

Source: Business Today, op. cit., p. 184.

Fig. 23.4 How BPL Handles Technology Absorption

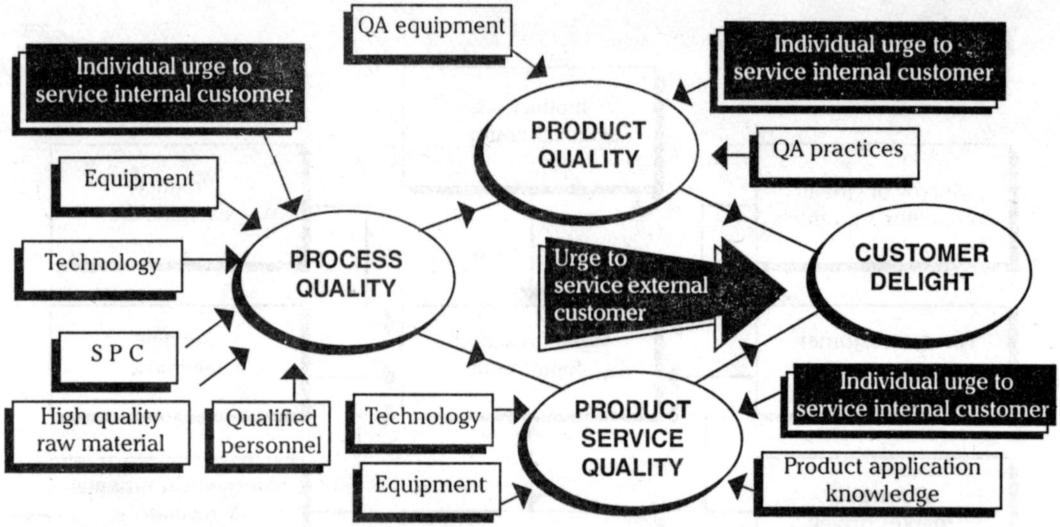

Source: *Business Today*, January 7-21, 1995, p. 165

Fig. 23.5 How Mukand Focuses on the Customer.

and improved. Managers should also view that every employee in the organisation deals with customers either internet or external. All the employees need to be trained in customer relations skills as they have to equip themselves to do a better job.

Standards of Performance

Customer care and service can be improved through clear standards of performance. Managers often should inform their staff that good service is important, expectation levels and the ways/ methods of achieving them.

Coaching and Training

Normally organisations neglect providing training in customer service. But the competition consequent upon the globalization, made the organisation realise about the need for coaching and training from the bottom level.

Developing Skills of Customer Care

The Perceptions and needs of customers must be understood. The employees need to develop the ability to:

- Notice that someone looks aggressive, depressed, worried, enthusiastic to respond appropriately.
- Listen, which is not just a matter of hearing but also of picking up handling complaints:

Complaints handing is a critical skill. It should be developed to make a positive contribution to the organisation. Improvements in the quality of goods/service will reduce the incidence of complaints. Total Quality Management should concern with treating the customers and improving the skills and attitudes of staff to render qualitative customer service.

Internal Customer Service

Effective external customer service to a greater extends depends upon the effective internal customer service.

But the services to internal customers suffers from the following limitations

(i) Many employees fail to perceive the colleagues as customers.

(ii) Interdepartmental prejudices and differences cause unnecessary friction and delay. This in turn impairs the internal customer service.

The management should create teams and team culture in order to minimise interdepartmental conflicts (Fig.23.6). All the employees in the organisation must be persuaded that they have supplier–client relationship with other members (Fig. 23.7). Under the internal customer approach, everything that is done is part of a process. Everyone has a customer i.e., the next person in the chain. The responsibility of every employee as a supplier is to research customer needs and continously improve to achieve satisfaction. Every employee, as an internal customer should ensure that his supplier fully and accurately understands his needs/requirements

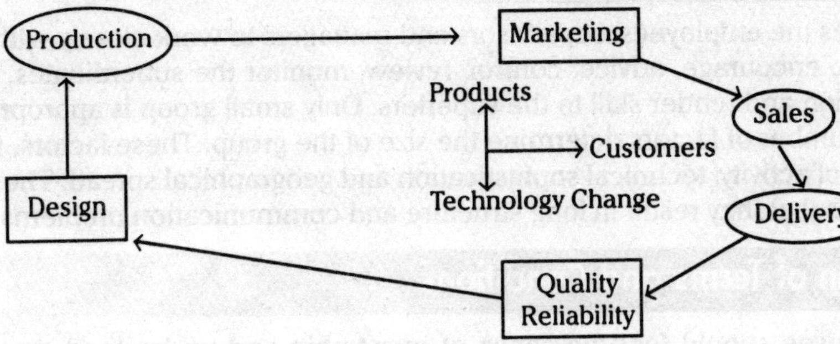

Fig. 23.6 Team Culture for Total Quality Management.

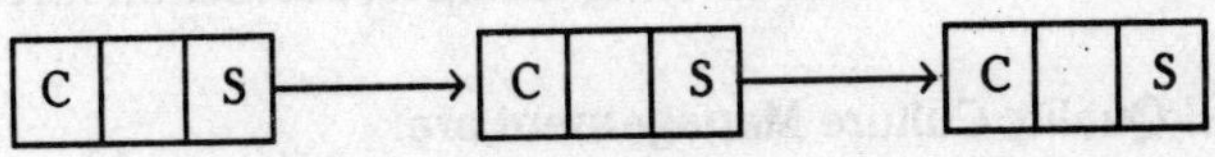

Fig. 23.7 : Internal Customer Approach.

ORGANISATIONAL STRUCTURE AND TQM

The organisational structure should follow the TQM strategy. The structure should be appropriate to the requirements of the total quality. The following aspects should be taken care of in order to have an appropriate structure.

(i) The organisational structure should be unambiguous so that employees understand their roles and responsibilities clearly.

(ii) People should work in small and identifiable teams.

(iii) Managers should be accountable for both quantity and quality.

(iv) The organisational policies should be humanised to a greater extent. Irrational differences in treatment between/among levels of staff should be avoided.

(v) Structure to a greater extent should relate to customer needs.

Clarity of Structure

Structure is not completely clear in many organisations. Further the existence of one-to-one relationship also complicates things.

The following two factors need to be considered in building a structure.

(i) Decide which is the 'think line' reporting relationship. It should identify who is principally accountable for the quantity and quality of work of individuals. Possible contradictions and conflicting priorities should be avoided.

(ii) Prepare an accountability chart which can present the people listening to their bosses and their accountability.

Size of Teams

TQM requires the employees, supervisors and managers to work closely with each other. The purpose is to encourage, advice, control, review, monitor the subordinates, provide rich and apt information and render skill to the superiors. Only small group is appropriate to serve the purpose. A number of factors determine the size of the group. These factors, for example, include diversity of activity, technical sophistication and geographical spread. The limitation of the small teams is that they result in long structure and communication problems.

Harmonisation of Terms and Conditions

Every employee should feel the sense of ownership and understand the value of his contribution to make TQM effective. However, employees in some departments cannot feel these things in TQM. They are the members of catering facilities, protection force, car parking, health facilities etc.

Principles of Total Quality Culture Management are:

- Single Status terms
- First name terms
- Open Communication
- Employee Involvement
- Results-based Performance Appraisal system.
- Emphasising continuous improvement
- Individual Accountability
- Strong Team work
- Competitive compensation package
- Employ and develop essential skills
- Positive Response to change.

Individuals and TQM

The success of the TQM depends on the contribution of the individual employees. The areas important for action are

(i) specification of action and priorities to individuals.
(ii) providing advice and encouragement on the job to the individual employees.
(iii) provide training to the individual employees to meet the challenges of rapidly changing technology. Exhibit 23.5 presents making total quality work.

Exhibit 23.5 : Making Quality Work

Role of the Manager

Managing Work Processes

Use information...
- Hard Data
- Soft Data
- Experimental Data

Apply the 7 Basic Quality Tools...
- Histograms
- Scatter Diagrams
- Fishbone (Cause and Effect) Diagrams
- Control Charts
- Pareto Charts
- Checksheets
- Graphs

to achieve...

Continous work process improvement

Empowering Work Teams

Establish and maintain a proper work environment by...
- Focusing objectives
- Providing stable work processes
- Ensuring opportunity for continuous learning
- Coaching, counselling, teaching
- Building trust
- Facilitating empowerment, communication, and change
- Providing Recognition and Reward

to achieve...

Employee satisfaction/motivation.

Business Results

Source : Ibid., p. 42.

Leadership and Total Quality

Leadership plays a significant role in the maintenance of total quality in addition to other behavioural issues. The other behavioural issues include organisation's life, relationship with surrounding community etc. The community include customers, suppliers, employees etc.[1]

The leader should consider several factors in ensuring total quantity. The factors those need to be consider by the leader are presented in Exhibit 23.6. Fig. 23.8 presents how to promote quality leadership.

1. Jeremy Thorn, *"Managing for Total Quality"*, University Press.

Exhibit 23.6 : Factors Need to be Considered by the Leader

- Focusing the whole organisation on the customer by launching Total Quality and reminding People about it on numerous occasions.
- Gaining senior management commitment to Total Quality – really effective initiative require commitment starting at the top.
- Introducing new business processes and/or manufacturing systems.
- Using statistical process control to target and eliminate faults.
- Training staff to improve their customer care.
- Listening to other organisation's experience getting a network of contacts.
- Designing systems to deliver quality to the customer more effectively, for instance, restructuring so that a group of staff cover all functions relating to a group of customers.
- Establishing a checkable system for briefing quality progress so that it is certain that everyone is aware of progress on a regular basis.
- Training briefers to put their message across clearly and simple and making sure they each keep a file of local quality facts.
- Introducing or improving suggestion schemes.
- Introducing visual information on quality, for example wall charts.
- Mounting a poster campaign on quality.
- Displaying your Quality Policy Publicly.
- Introducing or improving quality circles or similar specific consultative exercise.
- Establishing inter-departmental improvement teams.
- Defining standards of internal service delivery gaining clear understandings between internal customers and suppliers.
- Establishing regular systems for internal liaison.
- Ensuring the structure is clear and unambiguous; even if people have project and departmental responsibilities making sure they know who the 'thick line' boss is.
- Ensuring that quality reports to the line and that line managers' standards refer to both quality and quantity.
- Making sure people are working in small, manageable teams.
- Setting regular quality improvement targets for each individual.
- Regular coaching-making sure all managers and supervisors have appropriate coaching skills.
- Increasing investment in training, particularly in the skills than will help to involve everyone in the Total Quality movement.
- Developing management information systems that measure both quality and quantity.
- Walking the job, talking to each individual about their work and its contribution.
- Regular monitoring and evaluation.
- Encouraging people to admit mistakes - not admitting should earn disfavour, not mistakes themselves.
- Looking at community involvement and environmental policies–try to purse quality in all aspects of the organisation's life.
- Targeting a reduction in the number of external suppliers – agreeing clear standards with those remaining.
- Actively seek direct customer feedback.
- TAKE SOME ACTION NOW

To survive we must compete on quality as well as price. There is, therefore, no option but to pursue Total Quality.

Source: Ibid., pp. 46-48.

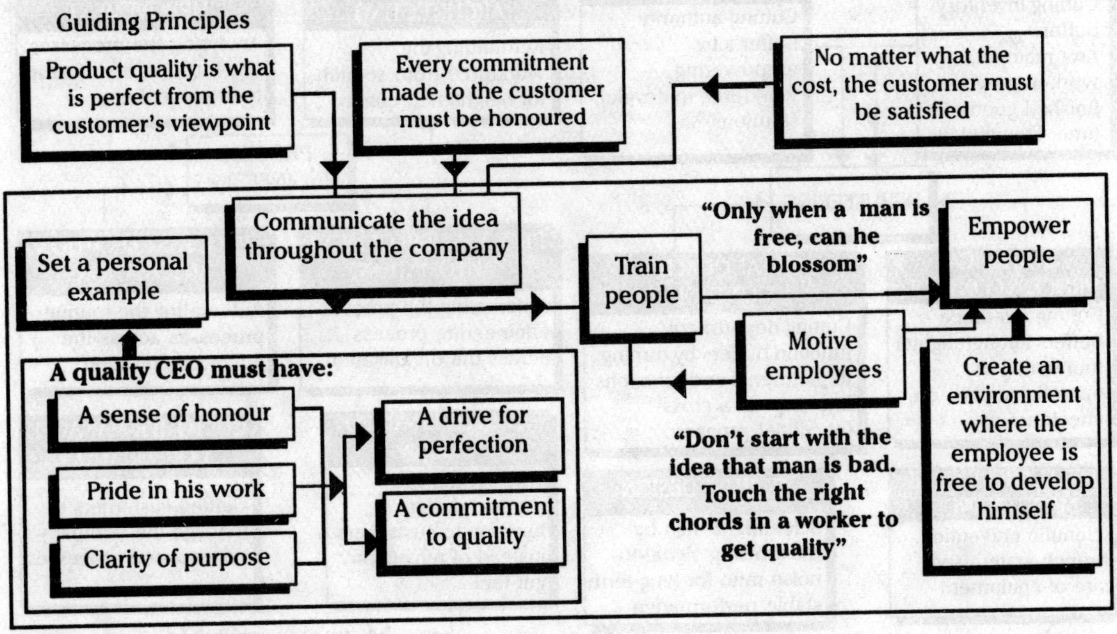

Source: Ibid., pp. 148-149.

Fig. 23.8: How PMT Promotes Quality Leadership.

APPROACHES TO TQM

There are different approaches to TQM. These approaches refund the business on a flow basis, with customers directing the content of the flow and competitors, the process capabilities. These approaches to total TQM include: Just in time, statistical process control, Total preventive maintenance, Statistical and Management Tools, Automation Development, Quality function development, Quality circles, Total Quality control, Robust design, High Technology Circles, New Technology Development, Policy deployment, Process architecting, Process deployment automation, Customer-aided design, Kansei engineering, Cognitive quality of worklife, Social democratic quality, Process improvement, Process execution automation, Customers managed corporation, Middle-up-down management, Metacognitive organisation, Democratic scientific management. Fig 23.8 presents the 24 major approaches to TQM.

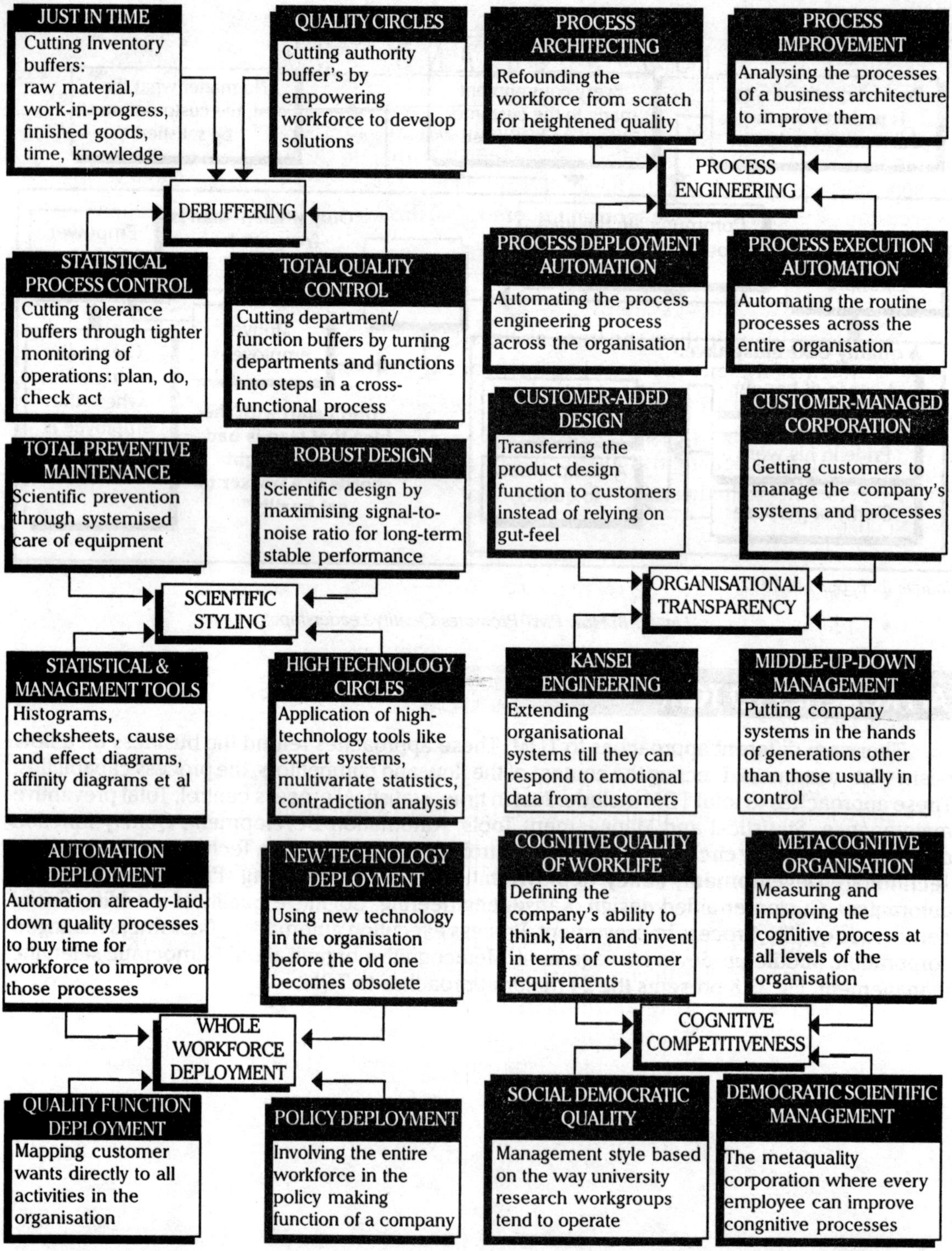

Source: Ibid., pp. 72-73.

Fig.23.9: The 24 Major Approaches to TQM.

ISO-9000 AND TQM

Over the last a few years, acquiring a certificate of quality from the International organisation for standardisation (ISO) has virtually become India's corporate sector's ultimate status symbol. ISO-9000 standard defines only the basic elements of the systems needed to ensure that products meet customer needs. ISO-9000 series-numbered 9000 through 9004. The elements stipulated by ISO include:

- Effective Quality systems
- Valid Measurement systems
- Product Identification and trace ability systems
- Systems for the creation and maintenance of records
- Product-handling, packaging and delivery systems
- Inspection and Testing Systems
- Systems for dealing with non-confirming items
- Personnel training systems.

ISO-9000

- Is a set of written standards laying down a quality systems
- Defines the basic elements of the systems through documentation
- Creates are quality system rooted in customer's requirements
- Ensures uniform systems that are universally recognised
- Creates the discipline required for a total quality process.

How ISO-9000 Leads to TQM

- ISO-9000 standards complement TQM's emphasis on the human element
- ISO-9000 helps the companies to assess their quality requirements
- ISO-9000 translates quality concepts into achievable targets
- ISO-9000 provides an opportunity to create and improve quality systems
- ISO-9000 helps spread the message of quality across the organisation.

ISO-9000 helps:

- the companies that market their products in the European Common Market
- Vendors supplying to companies that demand ISO-9000 certification
- Companies whose competitors are certified or are seeking ISO-9000 certification
- Companies with geographically-scattered facilities and global operations
- Companies whose transuational parents are seeking ISO-9000 certification.[2]

2. *Business Today*, January 7-21, 1995, pp. 99-101.

CHAPTER 24

BUSINESS PROCESS RE-ENGINEERING AND ENTERPRISE RESOURCE PLANNING

Introduction

Need for Redefining the Management Concepts

What is Business Process Re-engineering (BPRE) ?

BPRE- A Grand Strategy

Enterprise Resource Planning (ERP)

INTRODUCTION

Liberalisation, Privatisation and Globalization of business across the globe brought revolutionary changes. The significant among them is competition based on the customer service, price, quality, product design and information. The increasing competition among firms made various management practices obsolete.

Further, as we step into the information age at the turn of millennium, pardigms are shifting in a fundamental way in the area of enterprise management. It is true that different concepts / models / theories / principles at some point of time reach its limit. This manifests itself in the fact that more and more interactions emerge that it can no longer explain.

NEED FOR REDEFINING THE MANAGEMENT CONCEPTS

It had been accepted widely that Fayol's principles of management were applicable universally. But, to-day's private corporations observe that employee has more than one superior under team management. In fact every member of the team is a leader depending upon the situation. Further, the orders or information can flow from multi–dimensional sources. Thus the principles of unity of command and scalar chain have limited relevance in to-day's competitive business firms.

Adam Smith broke work down into specialised tasks. F. W. Taylor in his scientific management emphasises on division of labour and specialisation. But, the modern corporations prefer the employees with multi-skills. In fact, the concept of empowerment goes hand-in-hand with generalisation. The modern organisations also desire to recruit the candidates with multi-cultural, skill, job and organisational background as they believe in the emerging view that the 'rolling stone gathers mass'.

Corporate structures which until now have been predominately hierarchical in accordance with the F.W. Taylor's model are no longer a match for the dynamism of global markets. Function oriented hierarchical organisations require rigid information flows and they lead to long lead times for internal and external orders. Further, it results in coordination problems at each interface point. This organisational principle was designed for relatively stable environmental conditions. Change is no longer slow and evolutionary. Instead it is rapid and revolutionary. The change is also from an industrial society to an information society. Customer requirements and expectations of the quality of products and level of services are also taking a new direction. Further, the corporations proact to design new products /services and provide the information in view of the competition.

Most of the organisation follow the principles, structures and management concepts laid down more than two centuries ago. Michael Hammer and James champy in their book on "Re-engineering the corporation" opined that the time has come to retire those principles and to adopt a new set. They suggest that the to-day's organisations should forget these old principles and concepts and give up the structures. The organisations should re-engineer their business process in order to improve their efficiency and meet the competition effectively.

What is business process ?

Business enterprises foresee / forecast the needs of the customers and then standardise these needs. Firms design the products based on these standardised needs, estimate the raw materials, parts, finance, human resources, technology, machinery and equipments, tools etc, procure them, convert the inputs into output, appoint the market intermediaries, supply the products / services to the customers through these intermediaries, provide pre-sales and post-sales service. In addition, the firms solicit the customer opinions / grievances for the modification of products / services and the process. The various infrastructural facilities like transportation, banking, insurance, and ware-housing, help to complete these activities smoothly and at a fast rate. This process of conversion of inputs into output and meeting the customer needs is called business process.

WHAT IS BUSINESS PROCESS RE-ENGINEERING?

Business process re-engineering (BPRE) or business re-engineering has become the millennium's buzzword in management and industry circles. Business process re-engineering has become a most efficient grand strategy for the industry leaders to keep up their competitive position for the followers to attack the leaders. The BPRE concept is meant to be used as a strategic instrument for maintaining an enterprise competitiveness. BPRE is for the 21st century what strategy was for 1970's, quality for 1980's, empowerment and service for 1990's.

Michael Hammer and James Champy define the term re-engineering as. "The fundamental rethinking and radical redesign of business processes to achieve dramatic improvements in critical, contemporary measures of performance, such as cost, quality, service and speed."[1]

The word fundamental in the definition indicates that the business people in doing re-engineering must ask the basic questions like.

- Why do we do what we do ?
- Why do we do it the way we do ?
- How can we do the present work more efficiently ?

Answering these questions helps the company in determining what must it do ? and how should it do it ? Nothing is taken for granted in re-engineering.

Radical redesign means changing from the roots but not superficial level. Radical redesign in re-engineering refers to "disregarding all existing structures and procedures." and developing the new methods of doing the work. Re-engineering is "business reinvention". The word dramatic in the definition refers to "achieving quantum leaps in performance".[2]

The present managers are oriented towards tasks, jobs, functions, departments and structures but not processes. But the manager under re-engineering should be oriented towards

1. Michael Hammer and James Champy, "Re-engineering the Corporation - A Manifesto for Business Revolutions", Nicholas Brealey Publishing, London, 1993, p. 32.
2. *Ibid.*, p. 33.

business process. Business process is defined by Michael Hammer and James Champy as "a collection of activities that takes one or more kinds of input and creates an output that is of value to the customer".[3]

The present system of doing the things in most of the enterprises is based on the Adam Smith's notion of breaking the total work into simplest tasks and assigning each task to a specialist in order to get the advantage of division of labour and specialisation. Therefore, managers concentrate on the individual tasks lose sight of the larger objective. The larger objective would be delivering the goods to the customers who ordered them.

Business process re-engineering, thus, can be thought of as the task of combining the business tasks jobs, functions, departments and structures into a coherent business process. The business process should contain primarily tasks, functions, jobs and departments that taken together and create value for the customer. The business process is a sequence of activities that require input of one or more different pieces of detailed information, material or other resources and that creates a value for the customer.

Hammer and Champy view that Business Process Re-engineering is not possible in a small steps. According to their version an enterprise should give up their old principles overboard, unlearn the present concepts, dismantle the existing structures and work out a new concept and a new enterprise model that is oriented towards business process. The goal of business process reengineering is to bring improvements in orders of magnitudes. They are not simple improvements in departments that are pursued, but quantum leaps for the enterprise. This requires the destruction of the old and the creation of the new.

What is not Re-engineering

Michael Hammer and James Champy view that re-engineering is not just change in the business. According to them reengineering is NOT :

- Downsizing of the organisation business
- Restructuring the organisation business
- Automation or technology upgradation
- Software Engineering
- Reorganising or changing the structure from tall to flat or vice-versa.
- Delayering
- Quality improvement
- Total Quality Management (TQM) / Total Quality and Productivity Management (TQPM).
- Continues incremental and slow improvements. Japanese call it Kaizen.[4]

Hammer and Champy basically view that re-engineering is about REVERSING the industrial revolution. Re-engineering rejects the concepts like division of labour, economies of scale, hierarchical control and the like.

Characteristics of Re-engineering

Re-engineering varies from one business to another. However, Michael Hammer and James Champy observed some common characters in the re-engineering process of their client firms.

3. *Ibid.*, p. 35
4. *Ibid.*, pp. 47-49.

These Common Characters Include

- Several jobs are combined into one : The feature of re-engineered process is absence of an assembly line. The formely distinct tasks / jobs are combined and compressed into one. The jobs are combined mostly based on the customer needs / preferences.
- Integrating the jobs / process reduce the errors, misunderstandings, eliminate the delays and reworking, and administration overheads.
- Workers make decisions as they are required to do so. Jobs are combined not only horizontally but also vertically. In other words jobs are compressed based on job enlargement and job enrichment. Vertical integration incorporates the tasks of decision making in the top ladders of the hierarchy. In addition, the workers in the re-engineering are empowered. The empowered workers are motivated and self determined to make decision. Decision-making is part of the work of the workers.
- Compressing the work both horizontally and vertically reduces delays, overhead costs and better customer response and satisfaction.
- The steps in the process are performed in a natural order straight-line sequence is avoided in the re-engineering. Activities are performed not in artificial order but in natural order. This process is termed as 'delinearising' which allows performing of many jobs simultaneously. This process reduces the process time and thereby delay.

Processes have Multiple Versions

At present business produce customised or standard products. The business standardises the needs of the customers, designs the product, procures standard inputs, converts the inputs into output in the line process. The ultimate product may not exactly suit the needs of the customer. Therefore, the customer has to compromise his needs / preferences and satisfy himself / herself with the product available in the market. The best example is that the customer has to satisfy himself either with '8' size or '9' size shoe, if his foot measurements are in between these two. It is also true in case of ready made garments.

The re-engineered process aims at producing the products based on the exclusive needs preferences of each individual customer. Thus, under re-engineering process, customerised products or customer based products are produced. Therefore processes have multiple versions. For example, the shoes are manufactured based on the exact measurements of the two feet of the customer and customer preferences.

Recently one Japanese automobile company announced that it would deliver the car within two days by manufacturing it based on the exact preferences and designs of the customer. Work is performed by those people who are at the helm of affairs.

Traditionally tasks were performed based on division of labour and specialisation. Consequently tasks are decentralised and entrusted to the people who specialise in it. For example, purchases for various departments are done by the purchase department of the company rather than by the job holder. This causes the problems like delay, non suitability of the material purchase etc.

Under the re-engineering the job holder / employees at the helm of affairs perform all the related activities. For example the employee purchases all inputs necessary, design the product/ service, produce the product or perform the service and makes all decisions relating to his work.

Minimisation of Checks and Control

Normally the companies under maturity stage employ more checks and controls. But traditionally most of the companies were organised based on the bureaucratic structures. Bureaucratic structures are characterised by the checks and controls. Too many checks kill the credivity and innovation. They reduce employee motivation.

Re-engineered process empowers employees and expands the job both horizontally and vertically. These factors require freedom and autonomy to the employees. Hence the business process re-engineering reduces checks and controls.

Minimisation of Reconciliation : Under the re-engineered approach all the related work is done at point by a single work. In this process the coordination and reconciliation are automatically done. As such, the activities and process of reconciliation are minimised in the re-engineering process.

Single Point of Contact for the Customer

Point of contacts are several in traditional organisations. For example a dissatisfied customer of a television has to contact the marketing department, production department and finance department. But under a re-engineered company, it would be enough to the customer to contact only one employee. For example a customer of a television contacts the company regarding the failure of the product in a re-engineered business. The employee who receives the complaint studies the functioning of the television and analyses the problem from multiple angles like product quality, inputs quality, performance, finance, marketing etc. He makes the decision whether to reset the product, or to pay the price back to the customer or to replace the television. The customer's grievance is redressed only with a single point of contact. Thus, under the reengineered process, single point of contact is enough regarding the multiple angles of the work.

Centralisation and Decentralisation are two in One

Traditional business firms preferred centralisation of organisational activities and decision-making whereas the modern organisations prefer decentralisation. Both centralisation and decentralisation have their advantages and disadvantages. Under the re-engineered business, different units of the business perform all the activities of the entire organisation and serve all the needs of the customer. Hence, each unit is autonomous and can function independently without depending on other units. This is true even in case of jobs. Thus the jobs are also independent and autonomous. As such, the organisations under re-engineered process are decentralised. But the information technology connects all the independent and autonomous jobs and units of the re-engineered business through wires and satellite links. These links provide the business the characters of a centralised organisation like coordination, conciliation and reconciliation, decision-making with the knowledge of the top etc. the decentralised business with the help of information technology, even the business units / jobs are located physically across the globe acquires the characters of a centralised organisation. Thus the advantages of centralisation and decentralisation are combined in the re-engineered business.

Radical Shifts

As mentioned earlier, business process re-engineering brings radical changes. Some of these changes include :

- Line process will disappear
- Functional departments will be insignificant
- Employees plan and execute their work not based on the direction of their bosses or supervisors but based on the requirements and wellbeing of their customers.
- Business units / work units are structured based on process teams but not on functional departments. The process teams, restructure their work by dividing the work in tasks and allot to the members of the team. However, all the members are expected to perform all the activities, if needed, though they have allotted duties as in case of sport teams.
- As indicated earlier, job changes from a single task / a few tasks to multidimensional work.
- In view of the multidimensional work, workers with multiskills rather than single specialised skill are preferred for employment.
- The need for multiskilling workers, employees are trained in various skills and job knowledge.
- Management tends to believe that the workers of the organisation should be masters of all trades rather than master of one only.
- Traditionally workers were placed under 'child ego' and controlled and checked. But under the re-engineed process workers are placed under 'Adult ego' and empowered.
- Employees are continuously educated not only with regard to job activities, organisational activities, external environmental factors, technical skills, human relations skills and conceptual skills.
- Employees compensation package under re-engineered process depends on employee performance.
- Employees promotion to the next higher level is based on their ability and competence in performing the next higher level job rather their level of performance on the present job.
- Organisation structures should be based on the flat and team structures rather than on the tall structures.
- Managers are mostly expected to be the leaders.[5]

BPRE– A GRAND STRATEGY

Liberalisation, Privatisation and Globalisation across the globe resulted in mounting competition among the business firms. Added to this the increase in investment and number of business firms made the competition serve. The increasing competition made the firms to formulate the new strategies to win the new customers and retain the existing customers.

BPRE is an effective strategy compared to other strategies. Retaining the existing customers is easy in the re-engineered process as it serves the customer most efficiently. The contact point is single. As mentioned earlier, the employee solves all the problems of the customer, meets different needs of the customer.

5. *Ibid*, pp. 51-79.

Re-engineered business can attract the new customers as they produce customerised products in contrast to the customised products. Customers need not sacrifice / compromise their needs / preferences / conveniences. Hence, the customers prefer the products / services of the re-engineered businesses.

Re-engineered business helps for product / service innovation, product development etc. as products are manufactured based on the convenience, preference of each and every customer. In other words products are produced based on the customerisation. Customerisation also include price, quality, delivery and the like.

Thus, BPRE can be a grand strategy of the company as it radically changes the total organisation for the efficient and effective functioning of the company to achieve the corporate objectives.

ENTERPRISE RESOURCES PLANNING (ERP)

Where does the Enterprise Resource Planning fit in the so called radical redesign ? Harnessing the organisational resources by the use of information technology to achieve the dramatic improvements in the critical areas of performance or the measure of success like cost, quality, service and speed is what the Enterprise Resource Planning is all about. In other words ERP is the grearing up of the use of organisational resources with the help of information technology. The purpose is to drastically improve the organisational performance in the critical areas. The goal of the BPRE is to design business processes in such a way that they meet the market induced demands for increased flexibility and quality as well as the reduced run time and costs.

ERP is the buzzword of global corporate world. Corporations change their directions and revitalise their structures. They change their strategies to reduce their turnaround time, reduce cycle times, improve profit margin, enhance the quality, optimisation of inventories etc., ERP emerges as a leading solution provider and integrates people who share common tasks and enables the organisation to enhance free flow of accurate and timely information avoiding inconsistencies in corporate decision on making.[6]

As these powerful ready-made, off-the-shelf information systems become available. More demands are placed on the users of these systems. The increase in scope and complexity brought about by the implementation of integrated business processes increases the importance of criteria such as comprehensibility, correctness, user friendliness, reliability, flexibility documentation and maintainability. When designing business processes, enterprises must decide whether to develop the application software themselves or build on solutions available in the market. Often, custom software has the problems of being too error-prone, insufficient consideration of the users' requirements, lack of reuse of software components etc. For this reason there has been a trend in business towards implementing integrated standard software like SAP R/3, BAAN, J.D. Ewards, Oracle Financial, Peoplesoft to name a few.. One of the main goals of using standard software is to reduce the costs for personnel, software development, training and maintenance. The need to replace exiting Data Processing System in favour of integrated standard software has steadily

6. Diana Rajendran, "ERP-A Dynamic IT Management Tool," *Indian Management*, November 1998, p. 59.

increased over the past few years. The costs for example to develop and maintain a software system tailored for an enterprise have risen more than the costs for a comparable standard solution from a software supplier.

Integrated standard software offers a generic problem solution. Integrated standard software supports several operational application areas, such as sales, materials, management, production, financial accounting, controlling and human resource management. The individual areas are implemented as applications and these access a common logical database. This allows business processes to be performed in an integrated manner across departmental boundaries and automated to the highest degree possible.

New Horizons : Alliances on Virtual Basis

Current information and communication technology enables enterprises to join together to form virtual corporations. The cooperation is temporary and may involve independent companies, vendors and customers who work on a project together. The extensive use of telecommunication systems is the fundamental thing that differentiates virtual corporations from traditional joint ventures. In contrast to other forms of cooperation, there is no underlying group contract, and there is no need to found a new company. A virtual corporation, therefore has the advantage that is so important in competition : flexibility, because it can build small teams of experts depending on the market situation and customer requirements. These teams combine the problem specific core competencies of the individual participants. This know-how includes more than just a command of product technology and process technology. Core competencies are enterprise specific, they provide problem solutions that are superior relative to the competition and that can be applied in more than one business area. The special thing about them is that only their combination in a dynamic network can trigger their synergical effect. It is rare that all of the capabilities required to execute a project in a way that appropriately addresses its requirements are available in a single enterprise : the result is a need to link complementary core competencies. Currently you find this employed in the software project implementation and in particular in ERP implementation.

ERP Applications [7]

- Software links different departments /units/branch offices and it enables the employees, customers, dealers and the like to have access to the information to match his / her needs.
- Plant management software packages help to reduce the down time of a plant / machine.
- ERP packages provide the top management visibility to formulate appropriate production plans and achieve the objectives most efficiently with the available resources.
- Supply chain Management software uses sophisticated modelling techniques and business rules. It helps the companies in planning, sourcing, producing and delivering products in most cost effective and integrated approach. SCM is part of ERP and these two work together for total solutions.
- ERP enables the effectiveness of HRD of the organisation.

7. *Ibid.*, pp. 59-60.

Implementation of ERP Grand Strategy

ERP is a grand strategy for the overall development of the business. ERP grand strategy may be implemented as follows :

- Formulation of right strategy keeping the business compulsions in mind.
- Choose the right ERP system and modules appropriate to the business compulsions, rules and regulations.
- Formulate ERP budgets keeping in mind the significant factors which were underestimated or ignored.
- Keep ERP implementation project under feed forward, feedback and other control measures.[8]

ERP and Indian Experience

- Mahindra and Mahindra is expected to complete its ERP implementation by April 1999.
- HLL started its ERP implementation during 1997.
- Cadbury India's Mumbai headquarters in March, 1997 was linked with 26 depots, six factories and cocoa sourcing unit in Kerala. [9]

8. Rajesh Haldipur, "ERP Software-Look Before You Leap" *Indian Management*, November 1998, p. 69.
9. Diana Rajendran, *op. cit.*, p. 62.

CHAPTER 25

E-COMMERCE AND POLICY IMPLICATIONS

INTRODUCTION

Information is recognized as an important resource. A wide variety of information needs of a business are organized into what is called management information system (MIS). A management information system consists of inter connected subsystems. They provide the information necessary to stay competitive. Accounting information system is the most important subsystem because it plays the key role of managing the flow of economic data to all parts of a business. As an information system it collects and communicates economic information about a business enterprise or other entity to a wide variety user whose decisions and actions are related to the activity. All this is made possible by the use of computers. The computer is an electronic tool that is used to collect, organize, analyse, interpret and communicate vast amounts of information with great speed. Accountants were among the earliest and most enthusiastic users of computers, and today they use microcomputers in all aspects of their work.

An accountant sitting in front of a small table opening a large bound book and writing with a fountain pen or a ball pen is an anachronism nowadays. A modern accountant sits in a revolving chair, in front of a computer monitor and a keyboard, logs himself in and keeps himself responding to beeps is a reality. A conventional accountant has no place in the present set up is a fact. Accounts are not maintained in books but in chips, measured not in words but in bytes, written not in ink but with stylus inside the computer on motherboard, secured not by lock and key but by the use of passwords and ciphers.

The use of computers increased the pace of business, globalization increased competition, Electronic Data Interchange (EDI) facilitated the speedy, secured and accurate transfer of documents across the globe and emergence of E-commerce blurred the boundaries of sovereign states. Increase in the pace of the business and competition both at home and abroad, a need to preserve the quality and thereby profitability is felt strongly today. Computers make possible a paperless working system. If computer of a businessman or a manufacturer is linked up with those of his customers and suppliers all the transactions can be done electronically. All these and a few other developments have brought a phenomenal change in the accounting education, profession and practice towards which accounting teachers, professionals and practitioners cannot afford to turn a blind eye and deaf ear.

E-COMMERCE — MEANING

To understand better the impact of E-commerce and Internet on accounting education, profession and practice it is necessary to understand the meaning of the E-commerce and related concepts better.

Prashant Jain defined **Electronic Commerce (E-commerce or EC)** as "the exchange of business information using electronic formats, including **Electronic Mail (e-mail), Electronic Bulletin Board (EBBs)** and **Electronic Funds Transfer (EFT), E-commerce Technologies** are designed to replace traditional paper-based work with faster, more efficient and reliable communications between computers." He further stated that "**e-commerce** is the process of two or more parties making business transactions via computer and some type of network e.g. a direct connection or the Internet.

This includes business-to-business transactions, online retail, and the digitalization of the financial industry. Some experts and leading '**Netropreneurs**' even argue the **e-commerce** includes all the steps that occur in any business cycle, such as placing ads, completing invoices, and providing customer support. The term **e-commerce**, often used interchangeably with IBM's coined term e-business, covers a lot of ground and refers to all these areas."

As per the Microsoft Computer Dictionary Electronic Commerce is a "commercial activity that takes place by means of connected computers. Electronic commerce can occur between a user and a vendor through an online information service, the Internet, or a BBS, or between vendor and customer computers through electronic data interchange (EDI)." IBM has used the term e-business for e-commerce.

Electronic Data Interchange is "a set of standards for controlling the transfer of business documents, such as purchase orders and invoices, between computers. The goal of EDI is the elimination of paper work and increased response time." (MS Computer Dictionary, p. 169) **EDI** facilitates transfer of business documents stored in structured formats–through mutually agreed messaging protocols–from one computer application to another. Thus EDI is a tool for business-to-business communication. E-commerce, on the other hand, is a concept reflective of the infrastructure and technology available for conducting business using the electronic media.

Through **EDI** and **E-commerce**

(a) orders from the customers can be analysed and executed without any delay,

(b) orders can be raised to reflect both demand and stock availability.

(c) instructions can be sent to distributors in parallel to ensure faster deliveries,

(d) carriage by road, rail, sea or air can be booked simultaneously and

(e) customs clearance can be obtained even before the goods arrive.

All this can be done without any paperwork.

E-mail is "the exchange of text message and computer files over a communications network such as a local area network or the Internet, usually between computers or terminals." It is also defined as "an electronic text message" (MS Computer Dictionary, p. 173).

Internet is "the world wide collection of networks and gateways that use the TCP/IP suit of protocols to communicate with one another. At the heart of the Internet is a backbone of highspeed data communication lines between major modes or host computers, consisting of thousands of commercial, government, educational and other computer systems, that route data and messages. One or more Internet nodes can go off line without endangering the Internet as a whole or causing communications on the Internet to stop."

ADVANTAGES OF E-COMMERCE

Provides with Easy Shopping

Shopping on the Internet provides with a fascinating experience. In traditional shopping a busy customer has to travel all the way to a local store to purchase things. If he is not satisfied goes to another shop and so on. In the process he will be wasting lot of time and energy. A busy person finds it difficult to go in search of a product of his liking. On the other hand a potential customer can turn to web, browse different shops and place orders for a variety of articles without wasting his precious time and energy.

Saves Operating Costs by Eliminating Human Intervention in Order Processing

E-commerce saves operating costs by eliminating human intervention in order processing. It is profoundly influencing the structure of business supply chains. For example, Chrysler Corp., by linking to its suppliers through a Web-based network, reportedly saved more than $1 billion in cost of materials in 1997. By 2000, Chrysler's estimated annual average savings would amount to $2 billion. (Subramanyam, 1998, p. 49)

Higher Degree of Personalisation in Serving the Customer is Possible

Higher degree of personalization is made possible by E-commerce. In the past, business designed a product with a mass market as a target. Now, using the reach, the information and processing power available, suppliers can have a more comprehensive knowledge of their clientele. They can use this knowledge to customize their products/services. As customization grows, suppliers can differentiate their brands as much on an understanding of the customer as on price and quality.

Provides Round the Clock Advantage to the Customer

E-commerce is a round-the-clock advantage for the customer. A virtual stores can be kept open round the clock. It is not possible in the case of a real store.

Allows Fast and Flexible Execution and Response to Market Opportunities

E-commerce allows fast and flexible execution and response to market opportunities. The Web enables a company to introduce a new product, get immediate customer reaction, refine and perfect without heavy investment and with much greater assurance of success.

Customer's Online Buying Habits can be Learned

Companies betting on E-commerce can learn about their customers online buying habits.

DISADVANTAGES OF E-COMMERCE

Inability to Browse a Virtual Store for Merchandise

Web shopping differs from traditional shopping in many ways. One of the most important differences is web shoppers inability to browse a virtual store for merchandise. In a real store the customer can walk through the general area looking for the merchandise required by him before homing in on the exact product he wants to buy. On the other hand an online shopper turns to search tools to locate products. Ideally, he types in a word or phrase and gets back a list of products meeting his needs. The engineers insist on exact and correct spelling, they cannot extrapolate from a simple phrase, and often they come up with bizarre products that are no where near what the customer is looking for. (Chuck Musciano, 1999, p.11)

Customer cannot Look Back and Revive his Choice for Merchandise

In personal inspection one can select or reject the merchandise several times before he finalizes the transaction and makes payment. But in online shopping he cannot do so. He cannot also look back into contents of his basket to decide whether his shopping is complete or not.

Order Checking, Cancellation and Monitoring are not Possible

Many commerce sites do not allow order checking and cancellation. Naturally a customer would like to know whether his order has been executed or not, if not, reason for the same. In addition to that customer may change his mind, items may get lost and cheques may bounce. A good commerce site must allow order revision and monitoring but in practice many commerce sites do not. (Chuck Musciano, 1999, p.11)

Easy Entry into and Exit from Web may not be Possible

Customers who browse the commerce/web sites do not take a fixed route. They enter in some page or the other at random and try to come out early to another product page, home page, check out page or the customer registration page. Many commerce sites are not designed to facilitate such an easy entry and exit (navigation). (Chuck Musciano, 1999, p. 11)

Widens the Gap between Haves and Have-nots

E-commerce may further widen the gap between the haves and have-nots. On-line business transactions required a computer and an internet connection, which have not yet come within the reach of common man. Hence E-commerce and Internet may further marginalise the poorer population groups and countries.

Customer Relations may be in Jeopardy

In E-commerce customer relations may actually be in jeopardy. If the orders not fulfilled quickly customers could become disillusioned and take their business to competitors or back to the off-line world. Obviously, changes must be made before the promise of E-commerce can be fulfilled.

Change in the Organisation Culture is Required

The best challenge for companies involved in electronic commerce is not the technology but it is changing the corporate culture. It requires an organisation to be bold.

INTERNET AND E-COMMERCE IN INDIA

Dewang Mehta, Executive Director, NASSCOM, said, EDI and E-commerce have become extremely essential for the Indian economy. According to a study undertaken by the Indian Market

Research Bureau (IMRB) a mere 30 per cent of business in India which have the means to access the Internet have a Net connection at their premises. A special correspondent of the Hindu reports the development of Internet and E-commerce in India as follows :

(a) Net commerce came to India over the last one year and the impact on all sectors of business is only now becoming apparent. It is expected to become possibly the fastest growing area of IT in the coming months.

(b) For travel companies, whose clientele has a geographical spread across national borders, "going on the Net" makes sound commercial sense. Amadeus, the market leader in CRS saw its terminals in India increase fifty fold in four years, to over 1,500 this year. Galileo, which began operations in India at about the same time, has about 1,200 terminals.

(c) In recent weeks, Indian Airlines jettisoned its creaky old on-line reservation system and moved to a new IBM ES-9000 based network. Air India has joined SITA to put the "Gabriel" CRS on its Unisys mainframe computer. Among the private carriers only Jet Airways subscribes to a CRS-"Sabre".

(d) Indian internet sites like "Indiapavilion" (www.indiapavilion.com) which uses a server in North Carolina and a Chennai-based channel partner, Saigan Connections, or Indiamart (www.indiamart.com) from the Delhi-based Intermesh Systems, now offer Net-based umbrellas which shelter dozens of commercial sites doing brisk business in a mindboggling array of products. Indiamart boasts links to 60,000 Indian companies manufacturers, importers and exporters, service providers and NRI operations.

(e) The high profit presence on Internet of global booksellers like Amazon or Barñes & Noble has encouraged some India-specific book dealers to set up shop on the Net. The U. S. -based India Book House (www.indiabookhouse.com) specializes in books by Indian authors. The Mumbai based India Bookshop (www.indiabookshop.com) set up recently has quickly notched up Rs. 10,000 worth of orders in the opening week. And from Chennai Tulika Books (www.tulikabooks.com) aims for a niche in children books in Indian languages.

(f) The "India on Internet" site from Calcutta (www.allindia.com) is another anchor for interesting commercial and information services: including the largest dealer in jute based products, Aarbur. Today one can buy fresh vegetables in Delhi by leafing through the catalogues at Baba Bazaar and pizzas in Chennai from Pizza Deli.

(g) Assisting smaller business houses, which want to graduate to "e-selling", has now emerged as a new service niche. Three engineer-entrepreneurs, Messsrs. Ninad Pradhan, M. S. Srighar and S. K. Anand, saw an opportunity in the need for Indian language based commercial sites. They are the brains behind Domain Host India—a service which helps small businesses create, maintain and do business from Websites, at costs which could be as low as Rs. 1,500 per month. What's more they offer special font software, which enable the sites to "speak" most Indian languages. Many of their clients share their site (www.indianlanguages.com;www.indiansites.com) but their unique URL (universal resource locator) or site name gives them "virtual sites" of their own.

(h) New players like Satyam Infoway and Manipal Control Data (MCD) focus even more sharply on the world of EDI-Electronic Data Interchange. Satyam has set up its own E-Commerce backbone spanning eight Indian metros. The early clients, to use its expertise include the Cochin Chamber of Commerce, which now enables its members to exchange all import-export documents electronically.

(i) 'Delhi on the Net,' a first ever comprehensive Website on the city of Delhi is now available on the Internet at http://www.ace101.com. It has been launched by **Ace Internet Services**, a consultancy firm. The Website contains comprehensive data of all the hospitals, discotheques, schools, markets, shops, parks, hotels, restaurants, historical places, libraries, cinema halls, etc. located in Delhi. Foreigners and other visitors planning to visit Delhi can get lots of practical tips, and other vital information from this Website. (Information Technology, February 1998, p. 16).

IMPACT ON ACCOUNTING EDUCATION, PROFESSION AND PRACTICE

Rapid strides in technology have changed the way the accounting is done. Today, PC's are an integral part of the account's appendage. Accountant who shuns technology has no place in the present day business environment. Global Internet based trade practices include surfing the net, ordering by e-mail, remitting the money and generating the documents electronically, and copying and transmitting the documents through EDI. Hence an accountant besides accounting knowledge posses the abilities required to use the computers, Internet, e-cash, one or two accounting and ERG packages.

Abilities to use the Computers

Computers are widely used now-a-days in organisation. The electronic computer does not affect accounting principles because they are independent of processing methods, but the enhanced processing capabilities of the computer have improved the capability of organizations to implement advanced management information systems which were not practical while using manual processing methods. Therefore, those involved in the accounting and information system of an organization should understand the capabilities of computers and the changes in data processing potential because of the computer. In organizations using the computers for data processing, the accountants shall be able to understand computer data processing methods and the organization and processing of computer files. The ability to do analysis, to provide meaningful reports and / or to prepare statements depends, to a great extent, on the existence of appropriate files and processing capabilities. The accountants shall also understand quality control for computer processing because the reliance, which should be placed on computer-based records, is dependent on the quality of files and accuracy of processing. Hence it is appropriate for any programme on accountancy to have systems course prior to accounting and auditing courses. For an accountant background in computer programming is also desirable though not essential. However an accountant must be able to us front-end tools. Accounts shall also be aware of computer technology and internal control principles in computer-based applications system. They shall atleast know the fundamentals of data processing systems.

Ability to use Internet

On line trading is possible only through Internet. Hence accountants shall also acquire capabilities necessary to use the Internet. Once accountants learned Dbase to make software the way they wanted it to be. But now the accountants have to learn Tcl/Tk. Tcl/Tk will do for the Internet what Dbase did for databases. With Tcl/Tk one can do whatever he wants directly. He does't require the help of a professional intermediary to create Web pages on the Internet (Vijay Mukhi, Oct. 1996, p. 9).

Ability to use one or more Accounting Packages

Recognizing the need some of the software development companies have released accounting packages. The students and practising accountants have to acquire the capacity to use the accounting packages like WINGS, TALLY, FOCUS, PROFIT, and E. X. NGN– the latest Business Accounting software from TCS.

Ability to use one or More Enterprise Resource Planning Packages

Now-a-days many companies are using enterprise resource planning (ERP) packages like Oracle, Oracle Financials, BaaN, SAAP and People Soft. So the accountants have to be familiar with the use of one or more ERP packages.

Ability to use e-cash

In the second-generation E-commerce transfer of money takes the form of bytes-chains of zeros and ones. These are *Digital Value Units* (DVUs) which can be transferred easily without any loss of time from one computer to another computer at any place in the world with a few keystrokes. Only at the end of the journey it is transformed into cash or coins. Different forms of electronic money are under development. They are increasingly used in E-commerce. Accountants shall acquire the capabilities required to use electronic money of different types. Electronic money can be divided into three general forms. They are (a) Electronic Debit and Credit Systems, (b) Smart Cards and (c) Digital Cash.

(a) Electronic Debit and Credit Systems : Electronic debit and credit systems already exist when a consumer uses an ATM card to pay for merchandise, funds are transferred from his or her account to the merchant's account. Credit cards are used to make payments over the Internet. Software products such as *Intuit* provide an electronic bill payment facility. Electronic debit and credit systems represent new and more convenient means of payment.

(b) Smart Cards : Smart cards are plastic credit cards with an embedded microchip. They are used over transit payment devices. They can be loaded with currency at an ATM counter. This money can then be spent over vending machines, or turnstiles equipped with appropriate devices. A smart card is simply a debit card that does not require a bank approval for each transaction. Banks and other institutions can provide value on smart cards through loans, payments for services, or products. Any immediate transfer of funds between bank accounts is not necessary; units of value can circulate from card-to-card and from user-to-user-without debiting or crediting third-party accounts. By responsing confidence in a creating institution, 'money' can be created on smart cards, and can circulate almost indefinitely before redemption. *Mondex* is an example for a smart card or electronic purse. It can be 'loaded' with electronic money from an *automatic teller machine* (ATM). Money is spent either by swiping the card through a retailer's terminal, or by using a card reader and a personal computer with an Internet connection. An electronic wallet allows an anonymous card-to-card transfer.

(c) **Digital Money**: Electronic money can take a truly digital form (existing as units of value in the form of bytes stored in the memory of a computer), and may or may not be backed up by reserves of real money. This 'money' can be downloaded from an account, supplied as a loan or payment, or bought with a credit card over the Internet. As long as digital cash can be authenticated, and there is confidence in its continued acceptance, it can circulate indefinitely, allowing peer-to-peer payments at will. These conditions pose big 'ifs,' but they are well within the realm of the possible.

Certain advantages can be derived from using the E-cash. They are anonymity, security and divisibility. Anonymity of the transaction can be maintained. Public-key encryption technology and digital signature allow blind transactions. Identity of the payer can be kept secret. It is difficult to tack the transfer of E-cash. It also offers a high security, as it is impossible to alter the value or E-cash. E-cash is almost infinitely divisible. Filters can be set in an electronic purse to screen out E-currencies that are not acceptable.

Ability to Maintain Accounts both in Computer and Computer-free Environment

This is an age of transition. Computers and systems concepts are not completely used by both small and big businesses. Hence accountants shall be able to maintain books of accounts both in computer-free and computer environments.

POLICY IMPLICATIONS AND CONTENTIOUS ISSUES

Financial

E-commerce erases the national boundaries. For the Government tracking the import and export of knowledge goods (software) through Internet is difficult. Calculation and collection of customs duty is a big problem. For this purpose tax laws, procedures and practice may have to be reviewed and revised.

Payment Systems

To facilitate the payment in e-commerce e-cash is being developed. E-cash is also called digicash, cybercash etc. It is called electronic funds transfer system. It is nothing but the usage plastic money. Still several private companies are engaged in research to find out a safe and secured means of transferring money electronically. In electronic funds transfer system only at the end of the transaction transfer of legal tender money comes into the picture. There are several unsettled issues relating to the safety, security and control of the Digital Value Units generated by private companies.

Legalising E-commerce

In e-commerce agreements are entered into through electronic media i.e. orders are sent through e-mail and documents are transmitted through EDI or BBs. Validation of these business contracts requires the passage of new laws by the Government. Otherwise the letters sent by e-mail or through other electronic means may not give the same meaning or may not bind the parties in the same way as the traditional stamped and signed papers do.

Protecting Intellectual Property Rights

Protecting Intellectual Property Rights in the area of E-commerce is another problem. The problem gets magnified because of its international dimension. In the case of creation of web sites to decide what is original is a problem. A web site, can be created by copying pictures, designs and captions from different sources. Can it be called original and protect the rights? As a web site is accessible to people in different countries this problem acquires international dimension.

Privacy

Sometimes availability of data on the Internet may create and increase the problems of certain people. When the Government and private organisations go on line and place information relating to salaries, bonuses, provident funds and retirement data on net, employees fall easy prey to the agents of banking and non-banking financial institutions.

Security

Security, authentication and control are the biggest problems in on the trading, e-mail, EDI and electronic funds transfer. If proper care is not taken the information transmitted from one electronic data processing unit to another electronic data processing unit can be intercepted, accessed and altered unauthorisedly. Encryption, authentication, password controls, firewalls and a range of other techniques and technologies provide security to the users of E-commerce and Internet.

Encryption protects the confidentiality of stored data and electronic communications by making them unreadable, without a decryption key. Strong encryption can be used to protect trade secrets.

Digital signatures permit the users to know who they are communicating with on the Internet. Certification services support the digital signatures. Cryptography facilitates the use of digital signatures and serve to maintain confidentiality. Accelerating the growth of trusted electronic commerce environment requires the Government to develop and manage the infrastructure which supports authentication, integrity and confidentiality.

To support security of Internet and other applications, Intel has provided each PC with 'Processor Serial Number'. When a customer visits a E-commerce site, in programme in the web site will check the processor serial number and if it is genuine or not and then only access will be established. This enhances security of e-business transactions.

Standards

Standards are required to assure reliability, interpretability, ease of use and scalability in areas such as:

(a) electronic transfer of text messages (e-mail).

(b) electronic transfer of documents in structured formats (EDI and BBs).

(c) electronic funds transfer (e-cash).

(d) network technologies.

(e) security (all aspects of confidentiality, authentication, data integrity, public key certificate authorities etc).

(f) electronic copyright management systems.

(g) video and data conferencing and

(h) digital object and data interchange.

Standards are also necessary for products and services from different vendors to work together, for reducing uncertainty in the domestic/global markets and for harmonizing the E-commerce practices. They contribute a lot for the success and growth of E-commerce. Governments or its agencies shall play an important role in developing, legalizing, popularizing and implementing the standards.

CONCLUSION

Twenty-first century is going to become an age of E-commerce and/or E-trade. A large number of competing E-currencies offering anonymity, security, divisibility, liquidity, convenience and swiftness will enter into the market. For a customer selection becomes difficult and for the Government control over the business becomes difficult.

Allover the world the number of companies and countries using EDI and E-commerce are increasing. The E-commerce capable countries are setting deadlines for counties not equipped with similar capabilities. For example Singapore declared that it wouldn't keep trade relations with those countries that do not acquire EDI and E-commerce capabilities by July 1998. Almost 99 per cent of the Fortune 1000 companies have already implemented EDI. It is very difficult to imagine the backward thrust a company or country suffers because of delay in the implementation of EDI and E-commerce. Hence the choice is between E-trade and no trade.

References

1. Anurag Sharma "Policy Issues in E-Commerce", *Software Review,* January 1999, pp. 18-23.
2. A special Correspondent, "Internet Commerce - Burgeoning Opportunities", *Survey of Indian Industry* 1998, The Hindu, Chennai, 1998, p. 111.
3. Balasubramanian, T.N., E-commerce. Is it Working?, *Computers Today,* June 1998, pp. 48-50.
4. Chuck Musiciano, "Are you ready for e-commerce?", *Express Computer,* February 8, 1999, p. 11.
5. *Computer Dictionary,* Microsoft Press, Washington, Third Edition, 1997.
6. George H. Bodnar and William S. Hopwood, *Accounting Information Systems,* Allyn and Bacon, Inc., Boston, 1987.
7. Pattabhi Ram, "Professional Accountant in CIRCA 2000 AD", *The Chartered Accountant,* October 1996, pp. 14-19.
8. Prashant Jain, "Doing Business on the Web", *Software Review,* January 1999, pp. 12-16.
9. Ramesh Menon, "E-Commerce – An Overview", *Software Review,* January 1999, pp. 9-11.

10. Rich Niemiec, "Getting Ready for E-Commerce", *Oracle Magazine,* November/ December 1998, pp. 89-92.
11. Stephen J. Kobrin, "The End of National Markets", *Information Technology,* February 1998, pp. 65-67.
12. "The New World Order", *Information Technology,* July 98, pp. 29-30.
13. Vijay Mukhi, "Tcklets – Internet programming for the common man", *The Chartered Accountant,* October 1998, pp. 8-9.

Glossary

Electronic Data Interchange is "set of standards for controlling the transfer of business documents, such as purchase orders and invoices, between computers. The goal of EDI is the elimination of paper work and increased response time. For EDI to be effective, users must agree on certain standards for formatting and exchanging information, such as the x. 400 protocol", (MS Computer Dictionary, 1997, p. 169).

E-mail is "the exchange of text message and computer files over a communications network such as a local area network or the Internet, usually between computers or terminals". It is also defined as "an electronic text message". (MS Computer Dictionary, 1997, p. 173.)

Internet is "the worldwide collection of networks and gateways that use the TCP/IP suite of protocols to communicate with one another. At the heart of the Internet is a backbone of high-speed data communication lines between major modes or host computers, consisting of thousands of commercial, government, educational, and other computer systems, that route data and messages. One or more internet nodes can go off line without endangering the Internet as a whole or causing communications on the Internet to stop because no single computer or network controls it. The genesis of the Internet was a centralized network called ARPANET created by the Department of Defence in 1969 to facilitate communications in the event of a nuclear attack. Eventually other networks, including BITNET, Usenet, UUCP, and NSFnet, were connected to ARPANET. Currently, the Internet offers a range of services to users such as FTP, e-mail the World Wide Web, Usenet news, Gopher, IRC, telnet, and others." It is also called the Net. (MS Computer Dictionary, 1997, p. 258).

- **Electronic Bulletin Board System (EBBs or BBS)** is a "a computer system equipped with one or more modems or other means of network access that serves as an information and message-passing centre for remote users... Many BBSs allow users to chat online with other users, send e-mail, download and upload files that include freeware and shareware software, and access the Internet. Many software and hardware companies run proprietary BBSs for customers that include sales information, technical support and software upgrades and patches." (MS Computer Dictionary, 1997, p. 46).

Surf: To browse among collections of information on the Internet, in newsgroups, in Gopherspace, and especially on the World Wide Web. As in channel surfing while watching television, users ride the wave of what interests them, jumping from topic to topic or from one Internet site to another. Also called cruise.

Tcl/TK: Acronym for Tool Command Language/Tool Kit. A programming System that includes a scripting language (Tcl) and a graphical user interface toolkit. (Tk). The Tcl language issues commands to interactive programs, such as text editors, debuggers, and shells, which tie together complex data structures into scripts.

TCP/IP: Acronym for Transmission Control Protocol/Internet Protocol. A protocol developed by the Department of Defense for communications between computers. It is built into the UNIX system and has become the de facto standard for data transmission over networks, including the Internet.

Scripting language: A simple programming language designed to perform special or limited tasks, sometimes associated with a particular application or function. An example of a scripting language is Perl.

Corba: Corba the common object request broker architecture implies the use of 'objects' which, in this context, are small standardised components that can be stored in one place and called over a network for execution from other applications. The advantages are that the other applications become leaner and their creation becomes considerably more efficient. Since Microsoft has also acceded to harmonise future developments in its own COM (common object model) and DCOM (distributed COM) to Corba, virtually the entire computing world has agreed to use a common layer for data interchange.

Contributed by Dr. P. B. Appa Rao, Professor and Head, Department of Commerce, Sri Krishnadevaraya University, Anantapur.

CHAPTER 26

MULTINATIONAL CORPORATIONS

DEFINITION

A multinational corporation/company is an organisation doing business in more than one country. These companies have sales offices and/or manufacturing facilities in many countries. A multinational corporation (MNC) engages in various activities like exporting, importing, manufacturing in different countries. MNCs have worldwide involvement and a global perspective in its management and decision-making,[1]

(i) MNCs consider opportunities throughout the globe though they do the business in a few countries.

(ii) MNCs invest considerable portion of their assets internationally.

(iii) MNCs engage in international production and operate plants in a number of countries.

(iv) MNCs take managerial decisions based on a global perspective. The international operations are integrated into the corporations overall business.[2]

MNCs are huge industrial/business organisations. They extend their industrial/marketing operations though a network of branches or their Majority owned Foreign Affiliates. MNCs produce the products in one or a few countries and sell them in most of the countries. Transactional corporations produce the products in each country based on the specific needs of the customers of that country and market these Transactionals mostly uses the inputs of the host country where it operates unlike a multinational company.

Large Corporations having investment and business in a number of countries, known by various names such as Multinational Corporations. International Corporations and global corporations (or firms, company or enterprises) have become a very powerful driving force in the world's economy

As ILO Report Observes, "the essential nature of the multinational enterprises lies in the fact that its managerial headquarters are located in one country (referred for convenience as the 'home country') while the enterprise carries out operations in a number of other countries as well ('host-countries). Obviously, what is meant is a Corporation that controls production facilities in more than one country, such facilities having been acquired through the process of foreign-direct investment. Firms that participate in international business, however large they may be, solely by exporting or by hunting technology are not Multinational enterprises."[3]

Distinction between MNC, INC, and GC.

International company: A company with manufacturing, investment (or service operation) in atleast one foreign country may be regarded as an international corporation.

Multinational company: MNCs are usually organised around a national headquaters, from which international control is exercised. Still they have a national identity, even though their

1. Dymsza, p.5.
2. Thomas L. Wheelen and J. David Hunger, *op.cit.*, pp. 263-64.
3. ILO Report.

subsidiaries may not always come to allow that identity to obtrude in the markets they serve. (Unilever, Royal Duch, Shelt)

Global Corporation: Global Corporation is one which views the entire world as a single, homogeneous market which should be catered to by globally standardised products.

FACTORS CONTRIBUTED FOR THE GROWTH OF MNCs

MNCs exercise massive control over world economy. Several factors contributed for the growth of MNCs.

The important among them are:

(i) *Expansion of Market Territory:* The growth of the various economies along with the growth of GDP, and percapita income resulted in the rise in the living standards. These factors contributed for the expansion of market territory. Added to this, the large operations of the MNCs build the image, which contributed for the expansion of market territory.

(ii) *Market Superiorities:* MNCs enjoy a number of market superiorities over the domestic companies. They include (a) Availability of more reliable and up-to-data data and information. (b) they enjoy market reputation, (c) They face less difficulties in marketing the products. (d) They adopt more effective advertising and sales promotion techniques, (e) they enjoy quick transportation and warehousing facilities.

Financial Superiorities: MNCs enjoy financial superiorities over national companies, in addition to market superiorities.

They are : (i) Huge financial resources at the disposal of the MNCs. These resources and be used for turning the environment and circumstances in their favour. (ii) They can use the funds more effectively and economically as the excess funds from one country can be used to meet the requirements in other countries. (iii) They have easy access to external capital markets (iv) They can mobilise different types of resources of high quality easily, (v) They can have the access to international banks and financial institutions.

Technological Superiorities: MNCs are allowed, if not invited by the developing countries mostly due to the technological backwardness of these countries. Infact, MNCs are rich in advanced technology. They develop the technology through continuous research and development. The rich financial and other resources of the MNCs enable them to invest on R and D and develop the advanced technology.

The developing economies regard the transfer of the technology from the MNCs as an useful account due to the following reasons:

(i) Industrialisation is backward indeveloping countries and the resources available in developing countries are insufficient to develop the technology and thereby industrialisation.

(ii) Developing countries are rich in mineral and natural resources. They are unable to exploit them fully due to paucity of financial resources and low level technology.

(iii) Local manpower, materials, capital etc cannot be optimally utilised by the developing countries on their own. Therefore, MNCs are invited by the developing countries to help them in exploiting and exploiting the resources.

(iv) Developing countries would be required to import raw materials, capital equipment, technology etc on their own. This in turn needs heavy foreign exchange resources. Developing countries which suffer from paucity of foreign exchange resources invite MNCs in this regard.

(v) Developing countries, though they produce goods and services on their own by importing technology and materials, they fail in marketing the products due to severe competition. This inability of developing countries, force them to invite MNCs.

Product Innovation: MNCs by virtue of their wide spread operations in many countries, collect information regarding customers taste and preferences. Further, the MNCs with their strong R & D departments, invent the new products and develop the existing products. Developing countries suffer from limitations in this regard. Therefore, they invite MNCs to their countries.

Control Over MNCs

The difference agencies in India control the MNCs. These agencies include: (i) the Ministry of company Affairs (ii) the Reserve Bank of India (iii) the Ministry of Industrial Development and (iv) the Ministry of Finance. These agencies normally do not work in coordination. Hence, control of MNCs may not be efficient. In view of this, the Government of India imposed certain regulations to control MNCs. These include:

(i) Some industries were not allowed to import technology where the products are not essential and where domestic capacity was adequate

(ii) The maximum rate of royalty was imposed on technology, imports for those industries which were allowed to import technology.

(iii) Import of foreign capital was allowed but sometimes were made by administrative decisions.

(iv) Permissible period of agreement was reduced from 10 years to 5 years.

(v) Exports and other marketing restrictions were not allowed.

MERITS AND DEMERITS OF MNCs

As the preface to the ILO report on Multinational enterprises and social policy observes, "for some, the multinational companies are an invaluable dynamic force and instruments for wider distribution of capital technology and employment; for others, they are monsters which our present institutions, national or international cannot adequately control, a law to the selves with no reasonable concept, the public interest or social policy can accept"[4]

The important arguments in favour of the MNCs:

It is claimed that MNCs help the host countries in the following ways:

1. MNC's help increase the investment level and thereby the income and employment in the host country.
2. The MNC's have become vehicles for transfer technology especially to developing countries.

4. *Ibid.,*

3. They also kindle a management revolution in the host countries through professional management and employment of highly sophisticated management techniques.
4. The MNCs enable the host countries to increase their exports and decrease their input requirements.
5. They work to equalise the cost of factors of production around the world.
6. MNCs provide an efficient means of integrating national economies.
7. The enormous resources of the multinational enterprises enable them to have very efficient research and development system. Thus, they make a commendable contribution to inventions and innovations.
8. MNCs also stipulate domestic enterprises because to support their own operations, the MNCs may encourage and assist domestic suppliers.
9. MNCs help increase competition and break domestic monopolies.

Demerits: MNCs have, however, been subject to a number of criticisms, like

1. As Leonard Gomes points out, the MNCs technology is designed for world-wide profit maximisation, not the development needs of poor countries, in particular employment needs and relative factor scarcities in these countries.
2. Through their power and flexibility, MNCs can evade or undermine national economic autonomy and control, and their activities may be inimical to national interests of particular countries.
3. MNCs can have unfavourable effect on the Balance of Payment of a country. For instance, the coca-cola, until 1978, had remitted abroad nearly Rs 6 crores on an initial investment of Rs. 6.6 lakhs in India.
4. MNCs may destroy competition and acquire monopoly powers.
5. The tremendous power of the global corporations poses the risks that they may threaten the sovereignty of the nations in which they do business.
6. MNCs retard growth of employment in the home-country.
7. The transactional corporation cause fast dept depletion of some of the non-renewable natural resources in the host country.
8. The transfer pricing enables MNCs to avoid taxes by manipulating prices on intra-company transactions

Payment of Dividends and Royalty: A large sum of money flows to the foreign countries in terms of payments towards profits, dividends and royalty.

Distortion of Economic Structure: MNCs invest in those sectors which earn high rate of profit, exploit the material etc. Further MNCs suppresses domestic entrepreneurship, extension of oligopolistic practices like unnecessary product differentiation, heavy advertising, exploitation of customers etc. MNCs supply/transfer out-dated or absolute technology and products. MNCs meet the requirements of high-middle income groups, rich income groups, double-income with no kids (DINKS) groups and Double Income with single child (DISC) groups

Political Interference: It is criticised that the MNCs through their financial and other resource strengths influence the decision making process of the governments of developing countries. MNCs do not transfer the advanced technology to the third world countries. MNCs suddenly withdraw their capital from the developing countries inorder to destabilise the governments. Hence the governments of developing countries hesitate to allow MNCs to operate in their countries. In view of these political activities of the MNCs governments of the developing countries restrict the activities of the MNCs.

5. Francis chemlam. *"International Business"* op. cit., pp. 155-156

Technology Transfer not Necessarily Conducive to Development

The MNCs do not engage in R & D activities relevant to the developing countries. Their R & D efforts are relevant to advanced home countries. The MNCs transfer the technology developed in advanced countries to the developing countries though it is not conductive to their development. The transfer of such technology is determental to the economic development of the development countries.

ORGANISATION DESIGN AND STRUCTURE OF MNCs

Designing Organisational Structure

Organisations are economic and social entities in which a number of persons perform multifarious tasks in order to attain common goals. Organisations are effective instruments in that they help individuals accomplish personal objectives that they (persons) cannot achieve alone. According to Argyris, organisations are usually formed to satisfy objectives, "that can best be met collectively.

Organisation is only a means to an end. It takes certain inputs from the environment and converts them into specified outputs desired by the society. Organisation design deals with structural aspects of organisations: it aims at analysing roles and relationships so that collective effort can be explicitly organised to achieve specific ends. The design process leads to development of an organisation structure consisting of units and positions. There are relationships involving exercise of authority and exchange of information between these units and positions. Thus, organisation design may lead to the definition and description of a more or less formal structure. Organisation design is "the process of systematic and logical grouping of activities, delegation of authority and responsibility and establishing working relationships that will enable both the company and employee to realise their mutual objectives".

Steps in Designing Organisational Structure

The first step in organisation design is analysis of present and future circumstances and environmental factors. The next stage deals with detailed planning and implementation. Organisation analysis is the basis for organisation design and is the process of defining aims, objectives, activities and structure of an enterprise. Organisation analysis includes an analysis of the following aspects:

1. External environment – economic, political, legal etc.
2. Overall aims and purpose of the enterprise – survival, growth, profit maximisation, wealth maximisation etc.
3. Objectives – specific aims or targets to be achieved.
4. Activities – assessment of work being done and what needs to be done if the company is to achieve its objectivities.
5. Decisions to be taken across horizontal and vertical dimensions.
6. Relationships – from the view point of communications.

7. Organisation structure – includes grouping of activities, span of management, management levels etc.
8. Job structure – job design, job analysis, job description, job specification etc.
9. Organisation climate – working atmosphere of the enterprise. It includes team work and co-operation, commitment, communications, creativity, conflict resolution, participation, confidence and trust.
10. Management style – includes *laissez-faire*, democratic, benevolent-autocratic.
11. Human resource – includes availability of human resources marked by skill, knowledge, commitment, aptitude etc.

Organisations of MNCs can be designed based on two options. Vertical/tall organisations and horizontal/flat organisations.

Vertical/Tall Organisations

Vertical/tall organisations refer to increase in the length of the organisation's hierarchy chain of command. The hierarchical chain of command represents the company's authority – accountability relationship between superiors and subordinates. Authority and responsibility flows from the top to the bottom through all the levels of the hierarchy. Accountability flow from the lowest level to the highest level. Employees at each level should report to their superior, who in turn should report to his boss. Thus, the activities are reported to the top. Authority is more centralised in tall organisation.

Horizontal/Flat Organisations

Horizontal/flat organisations refer to an increase in breadth of an organisation's structure. The increasing bio-professionalisation and multi-professionalisation and wide acceptance for empowerment allowed even the large business firms to reduce the number of hierarchical levels of their organisations. Consequently, large sized firms also started adopting horizontal/flat organisation by delayering. In fact, this structure is well suited for the small size business firms.

Authority is more decentralised in relatively flat structures. Manager with broad span of control must grant more authority to his subordinates. Decisions are more likely to be made by the employees who are at the helm of affairs and more familiar with the situations and ground realities. Organisational activities are mostly performed informally. Professional managers are treated as real professionalists.

Approaches to Organisation Structure of MNCs

There are five approaches to structure the organisation. They are (1) Product organisation structure, (2) Geographical organisation structure, (3) Decentralised business divisions, (4) Strategic business units, and (5) Matrix organisational structure.

Product Organisation Structure

Activities are divided on the basis of individual products, product line, service and are grouped into departments in product organisation structure. All important functions viz., marketing, production, finance and human resource are contained within each department. This type of organisation structure overcomes many of the major limitations of functional organisational structure. Fig. 26.1 presents the product organisation structure.

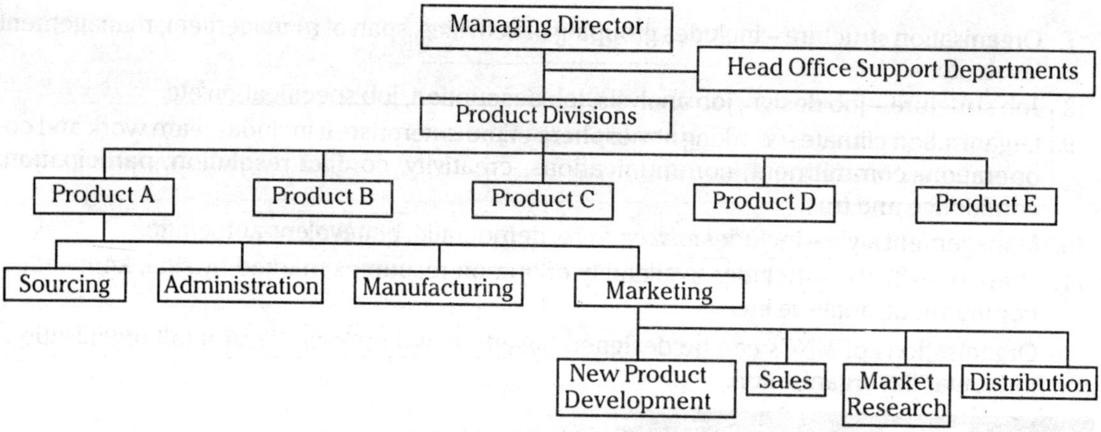

Fig. 26.1 Product Organisational Structure

Advantages: (i) The product organisation structure is more appropriate than the functional form of organisation for firms producing multiple products. (ii) Coordination among functional areas like product design, producing, distributing, marketing is effective as all functions are performed in each department. (iii) Since, each department is independent, most of the decisions can be made at departmental level without involving the top management in this process. It will result in fast decisions, enhancement of organisational competency to compete in rapidly changing environment. (iv) Responsibility and accountability for market share, sales, profit/loss is clearly fixed. Thus, either the credit for the success or blame for the failure of a product can be clearly attributed to a particular department. This advantage cannot present in case of functional organisation structure.

Disadvantages: Product organisational structure is also not free from limitations: (i) One of the major limitation is that unnecessary duplication of equipment and personnel among various departments. This results in loss of specialisation. (ii) Each department will have production, marketing, human resource, finance managers, secretarial and support staff, computers and testing equipment. As such specialised personnel and equipment cannot be procured. (iii) Some decisions like pay, promotion, product quality, design and pricing strategy may be inconsistent between departments. (iv) Interdepartmental conflicts arise regarding sharing of common resources, allocation of common and overhead expenses etc.

Geographical Organisation Structure

The activities or functions are grouped into departments based on the activities performed in the geographical areas/regions. Each geographical unit includes all functions required to produce and market the products in a particular geographical area. Figure 26.2 presents a geographical organisation structure. Multinational organisations, enterprises operating in diverse geographic markets or serving an expansive geographic area are organised based on the geographic structure. This structure is also used by chain stores, power companies, restaurant chains, dairy products, banking companies, insurance companies etc.

Advantages: The advantages of this type of organisational structure are: (i) Products and services are better designed to the climatic and cultural needs of specific geographical regions. (ii) A geographical structure allows a firm to respond to the technical needs of different international areas. (iii) Producing and distributing products in different national or global locations may give the organisation to better serve the consumer needs of various nations. (iv) This organisation structure enables a company to adapt to varying legal systems. (v) It also allow firms pinpoint the responsibility for profits or losses.

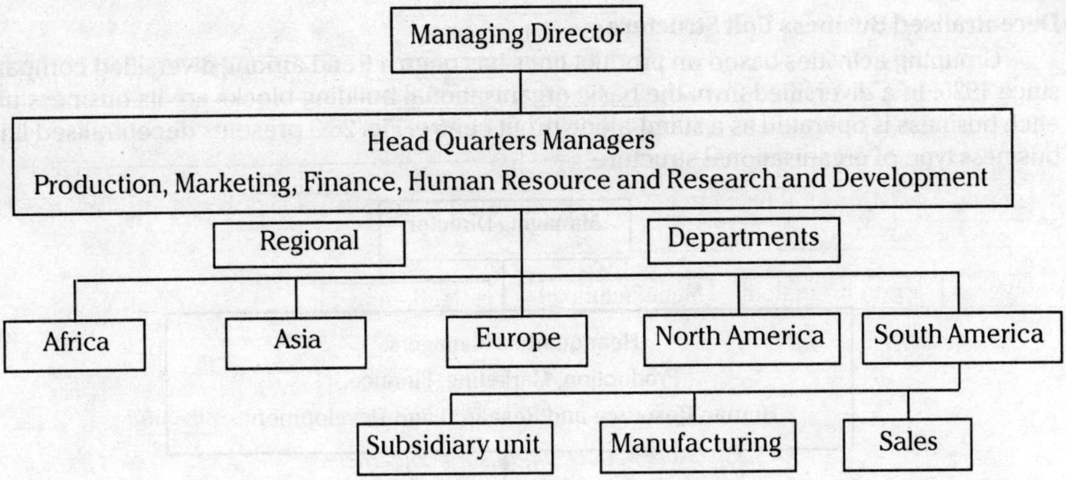

Fig. 26.2 Geographical Organisation Structure

Disadvantages: This organisational structure is also not free from limitations. The limitations of this structure are similar to those of product structure. (ii) Often more functional personnel are required. The firm cannot appoint specialists unlike in functional structure due to duplication of personnel. (ii) There would be duplication of equipment and facilities. (iii) Coordination of company-wide activities would be difficult. (iv) There would be a problem of imposing degree of uniformity and diversity. (v) It is difficult to maintain consistent company image or reputation. (vi) This structure adds another layer of management to run geographic units. Advantages and disadvantages are presented in Exhibit 26.1.

Exhibit 26.1: Strategic Advantages and Disadvantages of Geographical Organisation Structure

Advantages	*Disadvantages*
• Allows tailoring of strategy to needs of each geographical market. • Delegates profit/loss responsibility to lowest strategic level. • Improves functional coordination within the target market. • Takes advantages of economies of local operations. • Area units make an excellent training ground for higher level general managers. • Clarifies profit/loss accountability. • Result in good functional coordination.	• Poses a problem of how much geographic uniformity headquarters should impose versus how much geographic diversity should be allowed. • Greater difficulty in maintaining consistent company image/reputation from area to area when area managers exercise much strategic freedom. • Adds another layer of management to run the geographic units. • Can result in duplication of staff services at headquarters and regional levels, creating a relative cost disadvantage. • Results in inconsistent decisions from one region to another region. • Results in duplication of equipment and personnel. • Encourages dysfunctional competition for resources. • Results in loss of specialisation. • Emphasises regional rather than company goals.

Source: Thompson and Strickland, *op. cit.*, p. 226 and Joe. G. Thomas, *op. cit.*, p. 267.

Decentralised Business Unit Structure

Grouping activities based on product lines has been a trend among diversified companies since 1920. In a diversified firm, the basic organisational building blocks are its business units, each business is operated as a stand-alone profit centre. Fig. 26.3 presents decentralised line of business type of organisational structure.

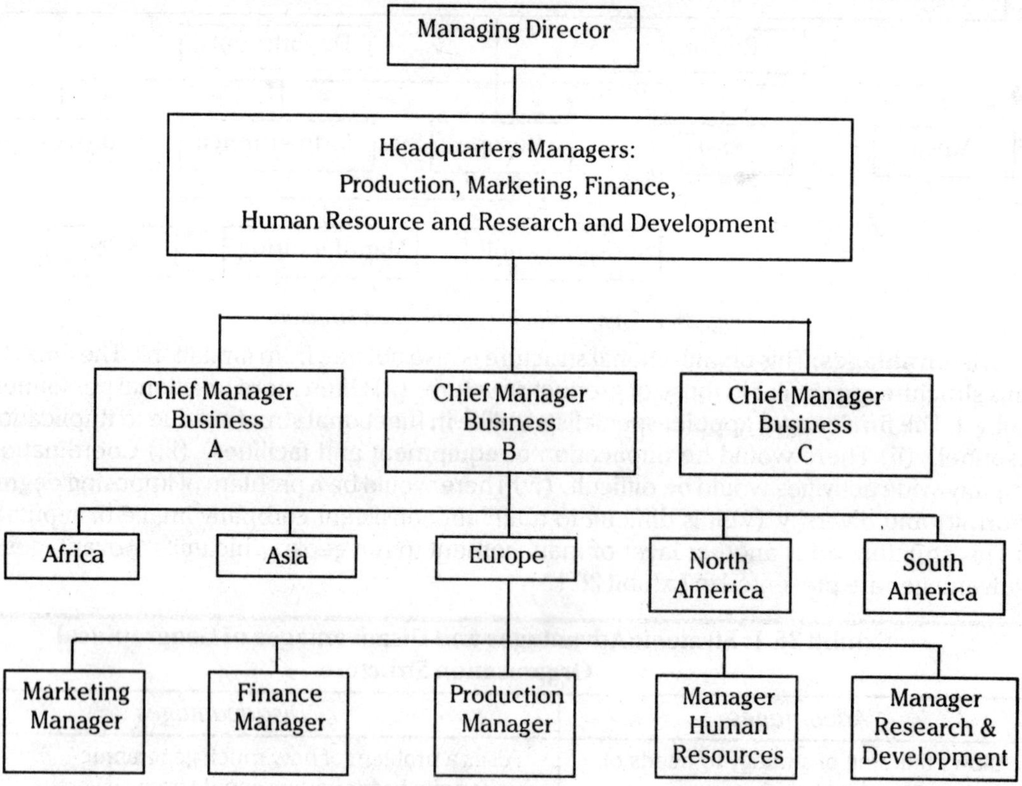

Fig. 26.3 Decentralised Line of Business Type of Organisation Structure

Strategic Advantages: Functional structure and geographic structure are standard organisational building blocks in a single business firm. But, in multibusiness firms, the business are diversified. (i) Diversification is generally managed by decentralised decision-making and delegating authority and responsibility to a manager at each business unit. (ii) Each business unit should be managed by an enterpreneurially oriented general manager who is delegated with authority to formulate and execute business strategies. (iii) Each business unit operates as a stand-alone profit centre. Each business unit is structured on the basis of either functional structure or geographic structure depending upon strategy, key activities and operating requirements.

Strategic Disadvantages: The disadvantages are: (i) The major problem of this type of organisation is absence of mechanism for coordinating related activities across business units. (ii) General manager incharge of each business unit functions independently. It makes coordination a complicated task. Therefore corporate headquarters must devise some internal mechanism for achieving strategic coordination and to capture strategic benefits. Coordination can be achieved by developing corporate R & D department, corporate sales force, sales force of closely related businesses, merging the order processing and shipping functions of businesses with common customers and consolidating the production of related parts.

Strategic Business Unit Structure

A single chief executive cannot control a number of decentralised units of a broadly diversified company. The business can be effectively controlled, if the related businesses are grouped into strategic units and the efficient and senior executive is delegated with the authority and responsibility for its management. The senior executive will in turn report the matter to the chief executive. This arrangement will improve strategic planning and implementation, though it adds one layer in the organisational hierarchy. Top management coordinates the interests of the diversified business units.

A strategic business unit is a grouping of business subsidiaries based on some important strategic elements common to each. The common or related elements could be an overlapping set of competitors, a closely related strategic mission, a common need to compete globally, an ability to accomplish integrated strategic planning, common key success factors and technologically related growth opportunities. Fig. 26.4 presents SBU type of organisation structure.

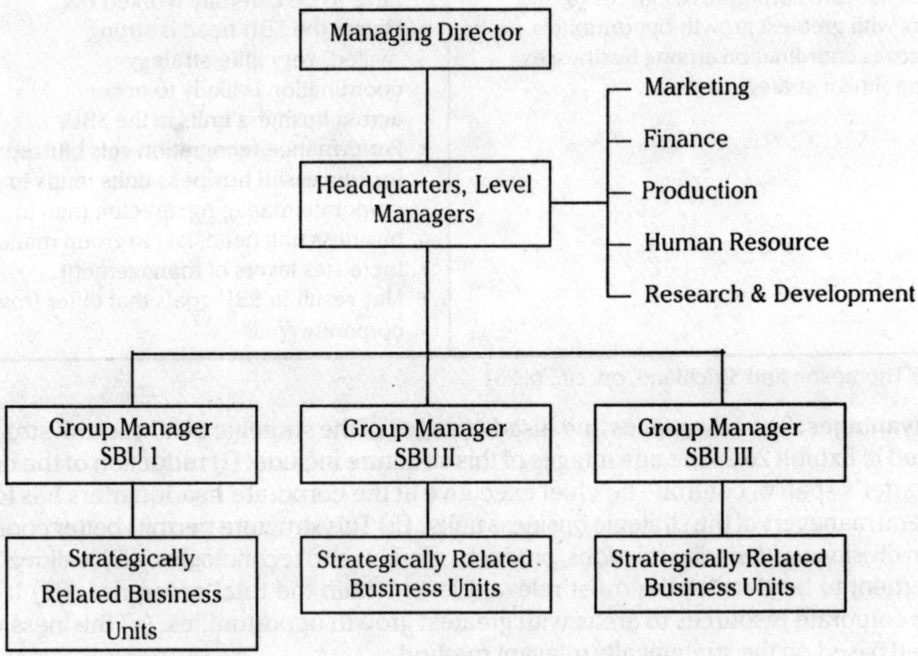

Fig. 26.4 Strategic Business Unit Type of Organisation Structure

Exhibit 26.2 : Advantages and Disadvantages of Strategic Business Unit (SBU) Type of Organisation Structure

Advantages	*Disadvantages*
• Provides a strategically relevant way to organise the business-unit portfolio of a broadly diversified company. • Facilitates the coordination of related activities within an SBU, thus helping to capture the benefits of strategic fit in the SBU. • Promotes more cohesiveness among the new initiatives of separate but related businesses. • Allows strategic planning to be done at the most relevant level within the total enterprise. • Makes the task of strategic review by top executives more objective and more effective. • Helps allocate corporate resources to areas with greatest growth opportunities. • Improves coordination among businesses facing similar strategic issues.	• It is easy for the definition and grouping of business into SBUs to be so arbitrary that the SBU serves no other purpose than administrative convenience. • If the criteria for defining SBUs are rationalisations and have little to do with the nitty-gritty of strategy coordination, then the groupings lose real strategic significance. • The SBUs can still be myopic in charting their future direction. • Adds another layer to top management. • The roles and authority of the managing director, general manager, SBU level managers have to be carefully worked out. • Unless the SBU head is strong willed, very little strategy coordination is likely to occur across business units in the SBU. • Performance recognition gets blurred; credit for successful business units tends to go to corporate managing director, then to business unit head, last to group manager. • Increases layers of management. • May result in SBU goals that differ from corporate goals.

Source: Thompson and Strickland, *op. cit.*, p. 231.

Advantages: The advantages and disadvantages of the strategic business unit structure are presented in Exhibit 26.2. The advantages of this structure include: (i) reduction of the corporate headquarter's span of control. The chief executive at the corporate headquarters has to control the general managers of the strategic business units. (ii) This structure permits better coordination between divisions with similar missions, products, markets and technologies. (iii) It allows strategic management to be done at the most relevant level within the total enterprise. (iv) It helps to allocate corporate resources to areas with greatest growth opportunities. (v) Business units are organised based on the strategically relevant method.

Disadvantages: The strategic business unit structure also has certain disadvantages. (i) The first disadvantages is that corporate headquarters becomes more distant from the division. (ii) conflicts between/among the strategic business unit managers for greater share of corporate resources can become dysfunctional. (iii) Corporate portfolio analysis becomes complicated one in this structure.

Matrix Organisation Structure

Organisational structure discussed earlier have possessed a single chain of command. In other words, employees in those structures reports to only one manager. But, the organisation structure possesses a dual chain of command. Both functional and project managers exercise authority over organisational activities, in matrix structure. Thus, personnel in this structure have two superiors *viz.*, a project manager and the manager of the functional department at the headquarters level. Fig. 26.5 presents the matrix organisational structure.

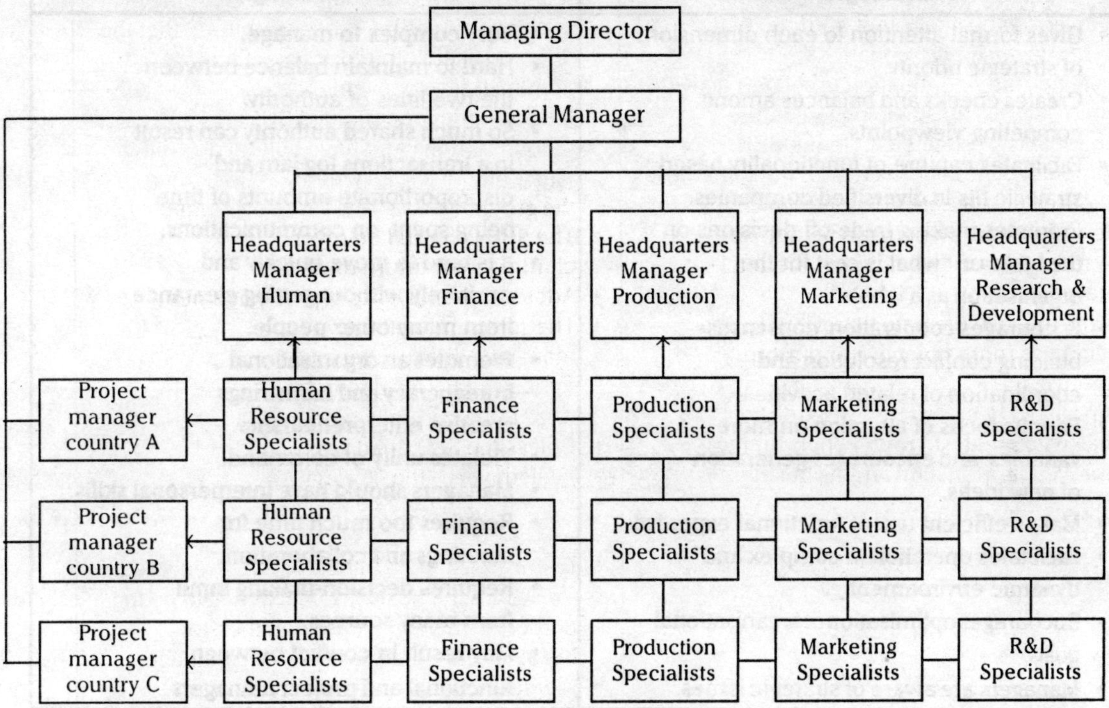

Fig. 26.5 Matrix Organisation Structure

A matrix organisational structure is appropriate when:

(i) Management attention must be focused on two or more key issues (technical issues, consumer needs, functional efficiency).

(ii) Large amounts of diverse information need to be processed.

(iii) Problem solving is complex (environmental uncertainty, interdependence among organisational units, complex products or technology).

(iv) Economies of scale require the sharing of human resource expertise to achieve high performance.

Advantages: The matrix structure is commonly used in the firms whose technological change is rapid. The advantages of matrix structure include: (i) the company can have the advantages of both project type of organisational structure and functional organisation structure. (ii) Functional personnel are paid for their services whenever, they are used by project managers. This practice enables the management to reduce the cost. (iii) This structure has considerable flexibility. The personnel can be transferred from one project to the other depending upon the need of the project. (iv) The lower level functional employees are highly motivated and satisfied with their job as they are involved in decision making. (vi) Each project manager is incharge of a unit. Therefore, he can be developed as a general manager through performing general management functions.

Exhibit 26.3 presents the strategic advantages and strategic disadvantages of matrix organisational structure.

Exhibit 26.3 Advantages and Disadvantages of Matrix Organisation Structure

Advantages	*Disadvantages*
• Gives formal attention to each dimension of strategic priority. • Creates checks and balances among competing viewpoints. • Facilitates capture of functionality based strategic fits in diversified companies. • Promotes making trade-off decisions on the basis of, "what is best for the organisation as a whole". • Encourages cooperation, consensus-building conflict resolution and coordination of related activities. • Permits focus of attention on more variables and encourages generation of new ideas. • Makes efficient use of functional expertise. • Facilitates operation in complex and dynamic environment. • Encourages optimisation oforganisational goals. • Managers are aware of strategic issues.	• Very complex to manage. • Hard to maintain balance between the two lines of authority. • So much shared authority can result in a transactions log jam and disproportionate amounts of time being spent on communications. • It is hard to move quickly and decisively without getting clearance from many other people. • Promotes an organisational bureaucracy and hamstrings creative enterpreneurship. • Violates unity of command. • Managers should have interpersonal skills. • Requires too much time for meetings and collaboration. • Requires decision-making input from many sources. • May result in conflict between functional and project managers.

Source: Thompson and Strickland, *op. cit.*, p.232 and Joe G. Thomas *op.cit.*, p.269.

Disadvantages: The significant disadvantages of matrix organisational structure include: (i) Greater administrative costs associated with its operation. Personnel spend much of their time in meetings and exchanging of information to coordinate functional areas with projects. (ii) In view of the two forms associated in this structure, they are characterised by conflicts. The most critical conflict is between functional managers and project managers. (iii) Functional employees experience stress by working in matrix structure. Reporting to two bosses, creates role ambiguity and role conflict. Some companies reverted their organisational structures back to traditional structures from matrix structures due to these problems.

Relationship between Headquarters and Subsidiaries

The MNC can directly manage, if the number of subsidiaries are a few. If the number of subsidiaries are more in number, it has to make a permanent structural relationship between itself and its subsidiaries. This is because, the MNC supplies various resources and inputs to its subsidiaries and also receives inputs from the subsidiaries. In addition, the activities between the MNC and subsidiaries need to be coordinated and controlled. In fact, the information technology provided on line facility to coordinate and control the activities.

The different aspects of relationships between the Headquarters and subsidiaries include:

- Information sharing
- Resource sharing
- Decisions flows
- Coordination of activities
- Control of operations
- Strategy formulation.

- **Information sharing:** MNC headquarters share the information with subsidiaries. Information flows both directions. Headquarters receives the information from the subsidiaries regarding their markets, demand, customer preferences, finances, product designs, country environment, daily sales, financial positions etc. Similarly the subsidiaries get the information from the MNC headquarters regarding the approvals, employment of people etc.

- **Resource sharing:** MNC headquarters and subsidiaries share various type of resources among them like financial, human, material, and technology.

- **Decisions flows:** Decisions made by the MNC headquarters flow to various subsidiaries for information and implementation. Similarly, subsidiaries inform the decisions made by them to the headquarters for approval and to other subsidiaries for information.

- **Coordination of activities:** MNC headquarters balances the production, demand for it, human resources, supply and demand for finances and any other inputs among the subsidiaries. Similarly, MNC coordinates the activities of subsidiaries and external stakeholders like suppliers of inputs, bankers, market intermediaries, Governments of various foreign countries, custom officials etc.

- **Control of operations:** MNC headquarters control the operations of its subsidiaries based on the customer needs, competitors positions, Government policies, rules and regulations of various countries, terms dictated by suppliers of materials and financial institutions.

- **Strategy formulation:** MNC headquarters help the subsidiaries to formulate the strategies for their countries. It further formulates global strategy. It directs and guides MNCs in implementing, evaluating and controlling strategies.

MNCs IN INDIA

Most of the MNCs in India had originally entered the Indian Market during the colonial era. They grew fast with state patronage. During the post independence era, the actual number of MNCs; who entered was small. The entry was generally made through collaboration with Indian big business. For instance, Bajaj Tempo and Telco joined hands with Dailmee Benz of West Germany; Cynamid, Ciba and Ciba-Geigy jointly established new undertakings with Lalbhai House; Birlas became the spokesmen of Kaisers and Ford. Sarabhai Murguppa Chattair, Naidu, Thapars, Kirloskars and other houses also joined to promote large private sector companies in collaboration with MNCs. With Political, administrative and business contracts of local minority partners MNCs could make a successful bold entry on the Indian source.

At the end of 1990, there were 469 foreign companies in India. In addition, there are many Indian Companies with foreign equity participation. Several Indian Outfits of MNC's like Pond's Johnson and Johnson, Lipton, Brookebond, Colgate-Palmolive etc., are in low technology consumer goods sector. Hindustan Lever, while popular in low tech consumer sector, has diversified into a high technology and export oriented sectors. Ponds has diversified into thermometers and Leather upper mushrooms entirely for exports (Ponds, Brooke Bond, Lipton and HLL come under the multinational Umbrella of Unilever). ITC (Indian Tobacco Company formerly Imperial Tobacco Company) has diversified into areas like hotel, paper boards and edible oils. There are MNCs like Siemens which are in high technology are as:

There are several MNCs; in the pharmaceutical industry, like Glaxo, Bayer, Sandoz and Hoechst MNCs like Marubeni and Nissholwan confine to foreign trade. Table 26.1 presents the number of top 500 MNCs operating in India and their country of origin.

TABLE 26.1: TOP 500 MNCS OPERATING IN INDIA AND THEIR COUNTRY OF ORIGIN.

Country		*No. of MNCs*	*Country*		*No. of MNCs*
USA	–	157	Netherlands	–	7
Japan	–	119	India	–	6
UK	–	43	Finland	–	6
Germany	–	33	Belgium	–	4
France	–	32	South Africa	–	4
Sweden	–	14	Spain	–	4
South Korea	–	13	Norway	–	3
Switzerland	–	10	Turkey	–	3
Australia	–	9	Mexico	–	2
Canada	–	9	Britain/Netherlands	–	2
Italy	–	7	Others		13
			Total		500

Table 26.2 presents the top 10 MNCs operating in India and market captured by them.

TABLE 26.2 : TOP MNCS AND MARKET CAPTURED BY THEM

Name of MNC in India	*Particulars*	*Ranks*	*Market Captured*
			(Rs Million)
1. HLL	Unilever	5	91675.80
2. ITC	British–American tobacco	6	91116.50
3. Tata-Dailmer Benz (Tata-Mercedes Benz)	Germany	11	67020.80
4. Colgate Palmolive (India) Ltd	Colgate Palmolive –US	13	58381.50
5. Brooke Bond Lipton India Ltd	Broke Bond Liebag of London –Unilever	14	52668.30
6. ICICI	Joint Venture J.P. Morgan (40% ES)	19	45061.90
7. Castrol India Ltd	Associate of Castrol UK	23	34155.10
8. Ranbaxy Laboratories	Joint Venture with Ehihilly & Co-(USA)	29	28094.00
9. Nestle India Ltd	Nestle Alimentana Switzerland	33	25892.00
10. Sterlite Industries (India) Ltd	Technical Collaboration with Esses group, a division of United Techno–logies – USA	34	23306.90
11. Motor Industries Co., Ltd	German multinational	36	21490.90
12. Siemens	Germany	49	17760.30
13. Ponds (India) Ltd	Chese borough Ponds	50	16953.50
14. Philips (India) Ltd	Netherland based	51	15623.40

Operation of MNCs in India.

How have the MNCs been viewed in India?

At the policy level there is no distinction between an enterprise that is MNC or one which is a small entity with parents abroad. At the first stage, the policy regarding MNC, is the same as for the foreign private capital in India. However, large foreign companies and dominant firms (in a product) are covered by the MRTD commission as indeed is true for even the wholly owned Indian corporate sector. The specific policies regarding foreign companies in India can be said to be the ones under the Foreign Exchange Regulation Act, 1973 (FERA).

Debate on the Role of Multinational Corporation in world development in general and the developing countries like India, in particular, continues to be an intense one, let us discuss it specifically with respect to India.

BOX 26.1 FACETS OF OVERSEAS INVESTMENT

TWO RECENT REPORTS concerning global movements of funds have major implications for India. The first deals with foreign direct investment (FDI) which since the Nineties have spectacularly personified the globalisation of the economies. According to UNCTAD's preliminary estimate, at a global level, cross-border FDIs during 1998 jumped by 39 per cent over the previous year to reach $644 billion. The second report issued by SEBI is more focussed on India. It says the foreign institutional investors – another distinct category of overseas investors – who have recently been channelling large amounts into the country's stock markets, took their aggregate investments past the $9.5-billion mark. That has been the highest level of FII investment, ever since they are permitted to invest in the Indian exchanges from September 1992 onwards. Both these developments need to be understood in their correct perspective.

Of specific relevance to India are two major dimensions to the global fund transfers: the desirability of one form, say FDI, over portfolio transfers. Second, to see whether any policy level initiates can be modified to tap these funds for the benefit of the economy. As a general rule, FDI flows are stable than portfolio funds. The direct investors are prepared to look at the long-term and often build fixed assets to produce goods and services. Moreover, before investing, they are guided by the growth potential and the structural characteristics of the recipient country. The size of the market and the attaintment of other efficiencies are key motivations for the direct investor. From the standpoint of the host country FDI flows are stabler than the investments that go into stocks. Evidently, it is far easier to liquidate stock market holdings and exit from a country than to dispose of plant and machinery. The FII investment may not be unrelated to the corporate performance of the recipient country but is definitely influenced by the ephemeral behaviour of its financial markets. This has grave implications for India in the context of the current border problems.

Evidently – and especially for India – there cannot be a watertight categorisation of the different types of inflows. Nor should policy ever countenance discouraging one or the other. Both FDI and FII are necessary, perhaps inevitable in the current globalizing context and, to a large extent, complement each other. Yet if the issue is not one involving an "either-or" answer, the time is about right to judge the efficacy of these fund flows in a larger context. The FIIs' large investments are welcome but the flip side of the resultant stock market behaviour has been the observation that overseas funds–handled by half a dozen or so managers alone–overwhelmingly dominate the Indian markets.

As for direct investments, the bulk of last year's increase has been caused by the proliferation of big ticket deals involving mergers and acquisitions (M & As). The M & As have become very common in the developed world and, in most cases, bypass the developing ones in the matter of transferring capital. There are a number of factors which underpin the further progress of the M & As at the global level. For India, which along with other developing countries actually received less of direct investment last year, the challenge is two-fold: to understand the implications of these large deals outside but having a substantial indirect impact on the domestic industry. And to keep attracting fresh overseas investment in greenfield projects. That has been the preferred and orthodox route all these years. Simultaneously there has to be an awareness of the ramifications of the mergers outside. Policy-level responses covering legal and regulatory aspects might become necessary soon.

Source : The Hindu, Dated July 2, 1999.

Firstly, a multinational corporation is a private organisation in the world production. Since MNCs are private organisation, the primary objectives of these corporations has to be profit maximisation. MNCs cannot be expected to function on considerations which are non-profitable. Since MNCs are in private business none should live under any illusion that their operations would ever be directed for welfare of humanity at large as that MNCs are instruments of world development. Additionally, MNCs are not only private business organisations, those are also impersonal organisations. MNCs therefore constitute a system and not private business organisations alone. The key elements of this system are:

1. Profit Maximization Objective

MNC's are engaged in economic activities spread over a number of countries. The overall objective of MNC's is to maximize profits at the global level and not that each of its subsidiary or associate company should attempt to maximize profits. In India there has been political sensitivity on high profits made by MNC's. The MNC's therefore, had to think in terms of showing lower profits for Indian Business. For this, the mechanism used to help another subsidiary of their located else where to make high profits. In substance, excessive profits made by have to be transferred from one country to another. The most convenient and common practice of this has been to impact raw materials and machines from the parent company or any other foreign associate at a conveniently higher price MNC's can also transfer the high profits through exports at prices that were below the actual cost of production. The MRTP commission had shown that philips has exported its production at below the actual cost of production. In India IBM is also known to have indulged in this practice.

2. International Net Work of Marketing

Apart from providing subsides on exports to MNC's most of the developing countries are developing a perception that since MNC's do control the international network of marketing, a real break through in exports can only be achieved with the co-operation of MNC's India is no exception. The latest industrial policy statement of the GOI has thrown an open invitation to foreign private capital for establishment of units which would be expert oriented exclusively.

3. Diversification Policy

It is only in this frame work that one would be able to appreciate the entry of ITC in luxury hotels and chloride India in shrimp export trade undertaking diversified economic activities is in the logic of MNC's and large business organisation., curiously enough the push for diversification in India has been government prompted. Naturally, one does wonder if the government policy was formulated from the view point of national interest as from the stand point of MNC's and other private large business Groups. One can already see that the largest number of companies taking advantage of the diversification policy have been the MNC's and Indian large undertakings.

4. Location of Central Control Offices

MNC's having the objective of profit maximisation cannot confine to one country. Given the choice of determining their own country parentage MNC's would naturally decide to opt for baring their central control offices at location which provide them the maximum global advantage. Unilever, though a company born in Holland, took up British percentage for operations in the erst while British colonies. MNC's can carry a label of "Under developed world".

For instance, USSR used to never favour obtaining consumer goods from undeveloped capital markets. India has been provided with a special status. There is a rupee agreement and Indian exports received a preferéntial treatment from USSR and other socialistic countries. If one examines as to who are the main suppliers of goods to USSR one would find these include Bata, HL and Nestles (even when it is canalised through the India Coffee Brand). For MNC's India is a good platform for extending their operations in the third world.

5. Achieving Public Acceptability

One of the most important, nonetheless interesting too, part of the operations of MNC's is that MNC's, being conscious of hesitations which host country population may have towards foreign companies, adopt various techniques to achieve public acceptability. For instance,

Mulchandani Electronics and Indian Tobacco Company may be more acceptable to Indian Government (for operating of Licenses, etc) than murphy as Imperial Tobacco Company. To a large Hindu population/products of Brindeben (a Lipton Unilever Company) and of Tribeni (British-American Tobacco) would be more acceptable. Such choices are deliberately made by MNCs. On the publicity front too, MNC's do their best to project themselves as if there were wholly identified with Indian Economy. Of late many of the foreign managed companies have started claiming themselves to have acquired Indian Nationality. This became that due to dilution of equity holdings many of the foreign companies are no more foreign subsidiaries but there has been no change in business reality. [Technically, this became, possible with adoption of FERA by GoI and it is true] But, as a MNC in India would be Indian and in Britain British. For the sake of business interests any one nationality can be sacrificed.

6. Existence of Modern and Sophisticated Technology with them

It is a fact that MNC's are large private organisational and their overall objective is to maximise global profits. And yet another aspect of the reality is that in a number of areas the modern and sophisticated technology and know how only exists with them. Not only that MNC's posses highly sophisticated technology these corporation also enjoy monopolistic control over the capitalists world's distribution system and have vast financial resources at their command. Thus, a country like India had to depend on one as the other MNC if it decides to have latest technologies in production. The only operational Question is if MNCs should be allowed to invest in India and bring technology with them as MNCs should be allowed to have technical collaborations with public sectors organisation as private business.

7. Business and Not Social Service

MNC's are in business and not in social service. These corporation believe in the superiority of free market economies. For profits to maximized MNC's here to allocate new investments according to market demand. In India, since there are acute inequalities in ownership of wealth and incomes a small section of population can afford high standards of living. The MNCs under the situation, take full advantage of the unequal society and have mainly attempted to cater to the needs of this section. MNCs do not produce cheap cloth; these do however produce commodities to grap the market of upper and high middle class, leaving the rest to local markets.

8. MNCs and Process of Planned Economic Development in India

How do MNCs fit in the process of planned economic development of India? This is one of the most important issues of debate and of crucial significance. MNCs believe in allowing investable resources to be allocated, in response to market demand. On the other hand, planning exercises are directed to control market investments and ensure that social needs of the country. These are opposed to each other.

The about features of MNCs should help us to understand that these do not come only as manufacturing a trade enterprises, their entry and expansion has implication on various national aspects. It is unfortunate that while we in India are quite sensitive to anything concerning our national honour and Political Independence, yet we do very little to meet challenges from within the fast growing section of the economy which shall never identify itself with India's national economic interests.

Generally we have a feeling that MNCs and foreign brands will have a run away success and domestic firms will not be able to survive their competition it is not right. The Double Cola has not been a success in India. Parle appeared to be very much worried about the entry of Pepsi and did everything to prevent its entry. But, when the competition become a reality, it faced it heed on and the parle brands outselled the Pepsi's. In the soft drink concentrate market, while juice of the Kothari–General Roads (MNC) combined failed, the product of the small firm, Nirma Industries, has become a grand success. Asian paints which had its beginning as a small unit has become the unrivalled industry leader, the Nirma story is well known.

THE INDIANISATION OF TRANSNATIONAL

Transnational corporations operating in India have been trying to win over the country's one billion customers. It is now clear that the long-accepted law of globalisation. One world, one strategy does not hold once India's borders are crossed. Squeezing profits out of new markets like India with old products, sunset technologies, global corporate centre will not work.

As C.K. Prahlad and Ken Lieberthal put it, "the needs of global competitiveness have ensured that the old ways of doing business will not suffice." Hence, the Indianisation of the transnational is becoming evident. Global Corporations are deviating from their international methodologies developing their strategies for local markets. The Ford Motor Company announced that its next car, the Ikon, has been designed exclusively for India. LG Electronics is using purely the Indian brand names like sampoorna, for its TV Sets. Coca-Cola has redesigned its distribution-crates and trucks for safe delivery through India's rough roads. Electrolux is working on a made-for-India refrigerator designed to serve just three basic purposes viz., chill drinking water, keep cooked food afresh and withstand long power cuts.

Indianise a Global Company

Some of the Transactionals are as flexible as Indian Companies. According to Arun Maira, the flexibility depends on how much diversity a transnational can accommodate and how many of its global standards it needs to maintain. Two major strategies are available to a global company viz., (i) following a rigid globally-erect template and (ii) clean-slate localisation. Some transnationals Indianise in some areas and pick-up global practices in other areas. The Global companies to be successful should follow this strategy. Benckiser failed to impress Indian customers with its Jovan and Coty Healthcare cosmetics. Coca-Cola failed in impressing the Indian customers through its global advertising compaigns : Fig. 26.6 presents how to Indianise a global company.

However, some companies are successful in Indianising themselves by bringing deviations. Exhibit 26.4 presents how transnationals Indianised for success.

Exhibit. 26.4: How Transnationals Indianised For Success.

	global strategy template	**deviation for India**
PEPSI Company	Maintain uniform brand image	Indianised positioning and ads.
	Control country budgets strictly	Had a free hand on Investments
	Depute managers from head-office	Operated through local managers
	Enter markets on own terms	Agreed to speed up entry.

	global strategy template	deviation for India
REEBOK	Build brand around sports	Picked new positioning
	Sell the same products globally	Developing exclusive products
	Focus on selects segments of market	Widened appeal to all segments
	Maintain control over distribution	Operated via multi-brand stores.
HYUNDAI	**global strategy template**	**deviation for India**
	Enter markets at the premium end	Entered with a small car
	Stay only with imports	Indigenised manufacturing
	Emphasise Korean engineering	Used local stars for endorsements
	Draw on global business models	Developed a new business model

Source: *Business Today*, July 7, 1999, p. 66.

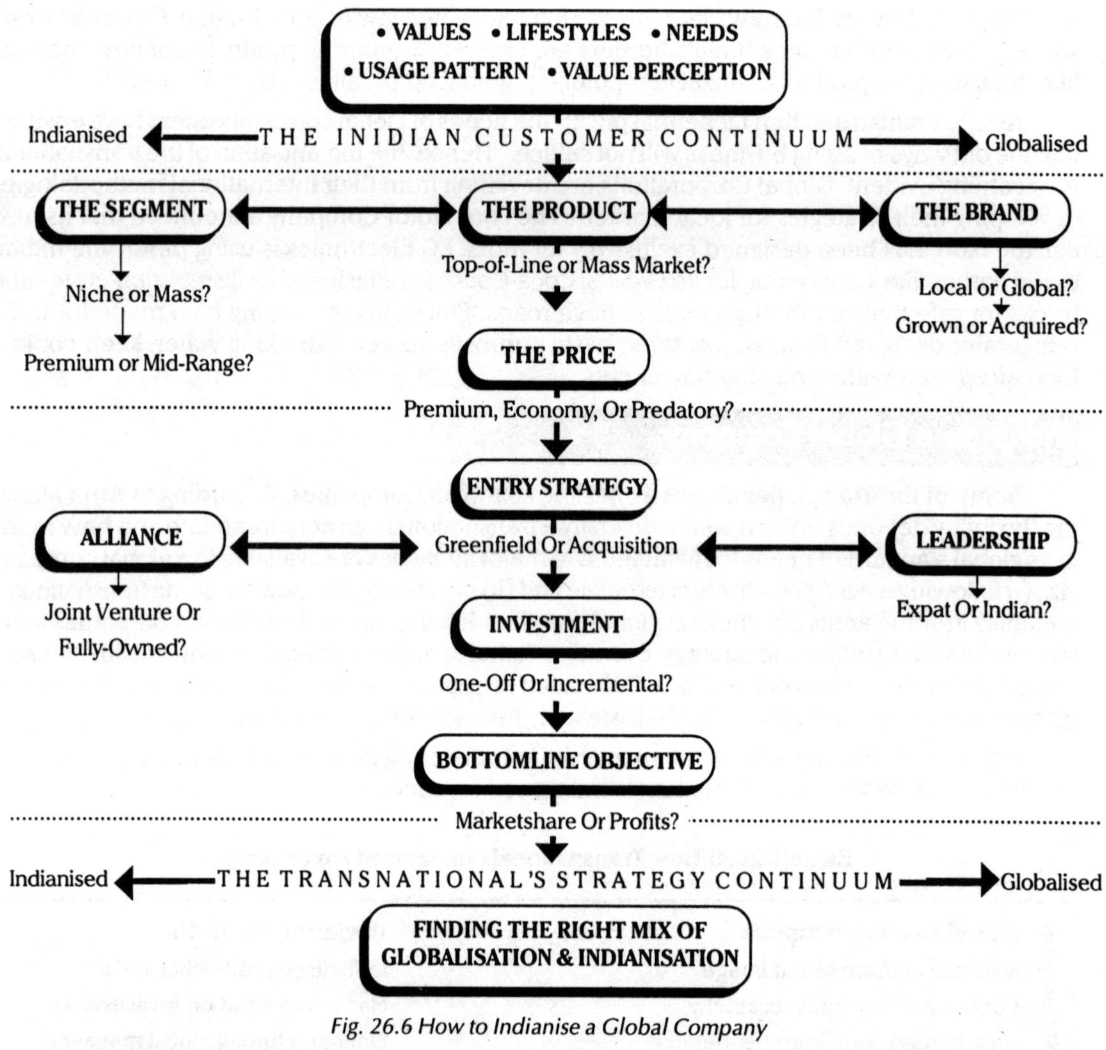

Fig. 26.6 How to Indianise a Global Company

Source: *Business Today*, July 7, 1999, p. 65.

CHAPTER 27

STRATEGY FORMULATION

- **Introduction**
- **Process of Strategy Formulation**
- **Choosing a Strategy**
- **Managerial Attitude to Risk**
- **Power Politics in Organisation**

INTRODUCTION

"Man's beginnings were described in the Bible in terms of conscious planning and grand strategy. The opposing theory developed by Darwin suggested that no such grand design existed, but the environmental forces gradually shaped man's evolution. The disagreement between the Biblical and Darwinian theorists is paralleled on a more mundane level in strategy making. There are those who envision grand calculated designs for the corporate entity and there are those who cite current practice to argue that organizational strategy evolved is shaped less by man than by his environment."[1] In most complex modern organizations, strategy formulation is largely the outcome of environmental threats and opportunities because the environment in which an organization functions is hostile to it. The management is, therefore, constrained to design a strategy which best suits the environment at a given time.

The organizational strategy is the core element on the basis of which all major policy decisions are taken and subsequent strategies are formulated. Therefore, as far as possible, the strategy chosen must be unambiguous and practicable.

Major strategic decisions are required to be made within the various functional areas of management, such as finance, purchase, production, personnel and marketing. However, the detailing of such activities in terms of the managerial function (i.e., planning, organization, motivation, controlling and co-ordination) is a quite uphill task, for uncontrollable factors are often a stumbling block in their formation. A strategic formulation therefore calls for a through scanning of such variables with a view to minimizing uncertainty.

Charles Hofer has made some startling statements on the strategic choice.[2] He observes that:

(i) Different types of challenges lead to different strategies;

(ii) When environmental opportunities are large and/or when there are excess resources, firms try to increase the scope of their operations;

(iii) When conditions different from the previous conditions develop, firms retrench staff and make changes in functional strategies or choose conglomerate diversification;

(iv) The most frequent strategies are developed for new products for existing markets and for increased penetration of existing products in the existing markets;

(v) The least frequent strategies used are forward vertical integration and internal diversification.

Strategy development is a crucial task, and calls for the undivided attention of the top management. To make the process effective, it enlists the assistance of line and staff personnel in arriving at the most profitable alternative. The "strategic planning process" is different from routine planning, for it calls for a rigorous analysis of the problem so that more promising strategies may be developed.

1. Mintzberg, Henry, "The Science of Strategic Making," in *Industrial Management Review*, Vol. 8, 1967, pp. 71–81.
2. Hofer, Charles, "Some Preliminary Research on patterns of Strategic Behaviour", in *Proceedings Academy of Management* (1973).

Strategic Development and Definition of Business

One of the major factors which has to be examined at the beginning of strategy formulation is the definition of *business* itself. For a small firm, it is relatively easy to define business in terms of the volume of sales, return on investment, gross profit, etc. However, a majority of medium-size and large-scale firms have multiple businesses. For instance, the TTK group is engaged in many business, each of which has different objectives. Similarly, Hindustan Lever has such a wide range of business — (it manufactures and markets such as toilet soap, detergent, washing powder and vegetable ghee) that it is difficult to define it and its objectives. By and large, companies having multiple businesses consider only the specifications of corporate objectives in terms of growth rates, whereas others aim at a high rate of profitability, a high rate of return. Some concentrate on corporate excellence, whatever may be the objectives of the business. While considering strategic formulation, the strategist should seek to answer the following questions:

(i) What is our business? What should it be? What should it be like in 5 years from now? In 10 years from now?

(ii) Should we stay in the same business or businesses?

(iii) Should we get out of this business entirely or a part of it by merging, liquidating or selling it?

(iv) Should we do a more efficient or effective job in the business we are in, in a slimmed down way?

(v) Should we try to grow in this business by increasing our present business or acquiring similar other business?

(vi) Should we try to grow primarily in other businesses?

(vii) Should we opt for alternative (iii) and (v).

If the answer to question (i) is in the affirmative, the choice is a stable growth strategy, (ii) If it is in the negative, and alternative (iii) or (iv) is accepted, the strategy is retrenchment. Alternatives (v) and (vi) are called "growth strategies" and alternative (vii) is called a *combination strategy*.[3]

Though a variety of alternative choices are often suggested, it is difficult to develop an effective strategy because it has to be radically different from that of others in two respects:

(i) It should follow a course of action which is more pragmatic and which has more favourable consequences than those of the competitors;

(ii) Such action should be initiated as will not be beneficial to the competitors if they copy it.

A successful strategy derives its efficacy from the differences between competitors with consequential differences in their own behaviour. Strategy development therefore consists of conceiving of ways and means of emphasizing the differences *vis-a-vis* the competitors. In designing the strategy, the following crucial elements must be given adequate consideration.

(i) The objectives of the business and its current level of performance should be clearly defined.

(ii) A proper environmental forecasting must be made, with special reference to those elements which are critical to success of the industry.

(iii) In the light of environmental forecasting, it should be determined whether the objectives of the business will remain the same or requires a revision.

3. Glueck, W. F. *Business Policy and Strategic Management*, McGraw Hill International Book Company, 1980, p. 199.

(iv) The strengths and weaknesses of a firm's strategy must be evaluated in comparison with those of the competitors. The appraisal should be with reference to market share, return on investment, cost, employee commitment, corporate image, etc.

(v) The major differences between firm's strategy and that of its competitors should be scientifically evaluated.

(vi) Major policies and strategies should be designed in such a way that the firm has an edge over its competitors.

PROCESS OF STRATEGY FORMULATION

Strategy formulation is basically a decision–making activity. It covers all those steps which are essential in the process of decision–making. The various steps involved in strategy formulation include:

(i) Assessment of present strategy;
(ii) Definition of the problem;
(iii) Discovering the strategic or core element;
(iv) Determination of alternatives;
(v) Evaluation of alternatives;
(vi) Choosing a strategy.

These have been briefly discussed in the paragraphs that follow.

Assessment of Present Strategy

One of the foremost steps in the formulation of a strategy is a thorough assessment of the present strategy. It aims at finding the weaknesses and stregths of a firm's present strategy *vis-a-vis* that of the competitors. In cases where a firm follows a definite strategy, the process of appraisal is relatively easy in comparison with that of firms which do not follow a definite strategy or adopt a loosely defined one. However, at any stage of the performance of the company and of executive behaviour, some idea can be had of the strategy of the firm.

Strategic assessment is of paramount importance in the sense that it assists in the identification of the problem and subsequently the determination of alternative strategies.

Definition of Problem

Strategic assessment, at the very outset, reveals the efficiency of a strategy or otherwise. Quite often, it has been noted that even the most effectively drawn strategy suffers from one or another limitation. This step therefore involves the observation of the phenomenon surrounding the problem — opinions, symptoms and facts. Observation may take the form of a casual glance or an indepth study of the problem. The capable strategist should be sensitive to problems. He should be sure that he has identified the real problem and not just a symptom or symptoms of the problem. Once the problem has been identified, the management must undertake the process of environmental scanning in relating to its strategy. This would enable the strategies to determine whether the present environment is conducive to current as well as future strategies, or whether some changes are expected in it. Accordingly, strategies can be amended or recast to suit the environment in which they are expected to be implemented.

Discovering the Strategic or Core Element

The mere identification of the problem is not enough; it is necessary to discover the variables and constraints which are at the root of the problem. Many difficulties are experienced in identifying the core elements affecting the choice of a particular strategy. In most cases, it is rather difficult to isolate precisely the strategic element either because of its complexity or because of unforeseen circumstances. In such cases, strategic alternatives are based on a mere guess or a hunch, with the result that strategies may prove ineffective in operation.

Determination of Alternatives

Once the strategic elements have been identified, the management should develop alternative courses of action or tentative solutions to solve the problem. In this context, it is worthwhile to note that there is hardly any problem for which an alternative does not exist. However, the crucial problem is to find the most profitable alternative. To generate effective alternatives, consideration should be given to the firm's resources and its competitive strength. Managerial philosophy, values, and sense of social responsibility also deserve consideration. While making decisions, managers should therefore give due weightage to both the qualitative and quantitative variables to overcome uncertainty. Many strategists often develop alternatives which are expressed in terms of the O.R. model. These are largely computer-oriented. For the final solution, this step involves invention, analysis, imagination and discovery. It is, in this, primarily a creative activity. In fact, ideas are generated about a plausible prediction of an event.

While determining the alternatives, the various pros and cons of a particular course of action should be properly weighed. For instance, an electronic firm feels that a change in strategy is required because the market share and R.O.I. statistics are not promising. In this situation, the plausible alternatives available for a firm are:

* To enter a new business;
* To merge with any other company;
* To import modern technology to overcome the competition;
* To pursue aggressive sales policies;
* To undertake extensive R & D activities.

When any one of these or some of these alternatives are accepted, a number of minor decisions bearing on a specific alternative are required to be taken. Suppose the firm wants to enter a new business. The question that then arises is: How will the new venture be financed? Will a new technology be required; and if so, how will it be arranged for? Is there any need for changing the organizational step-up; if so, how will it be brought about? And the like.

In this process, several models may be developed, if different approaches look promising for a final solution. As each model is developed, the deficiency may become apparent. If it fails to diagnose the problem, it should be abandoned.

Evaluation of Alternatives

Once the number of alternative models or tentative solutions have been narrowed, the remaining ones have to be evaluated in order to select the optimum one. At this stage, the management considers the impact of various factors on the choice of the strategy. The alternatives should be compared in terms of:

- Degree of risk;
- Relative efficiency in solving a problem;
- The degree to which each matches the company's resources and competence;
- The relative degree of competitive advantage;
- The extent to which they satisfy the management's preferences.

In the light of these factors, the straight should assign ranks to different alternatives. To determine the hierarchy of alternatives in terms of predetermined criteria, a number of qualitative and quantitative techniques exist. But to make the strategy objective, sound and logical, emphasis is often placed on mathematical models.

If a given alternative fits the operational research model, the evaluation is relatively easy. But if the mathematical relationships of the model are too complex for any standard OR model, a custom–made model may be required. No matter how much factual information and scientific analysis are used in the evaluation of strategic alternative, the actual selection of the strategy depends on the situational variables, preferences and value systems of the strategist.

CHOOSING A STRATEGY

The selection of strategy involves a selection from among alternative strategies of the strategy which best meets the enterprise objectives. The choice involves a consideration of alternative factors, their evaluation with reference to objective criteria, and the choice itself. In other words, it may be stated that the strategic choice process aims at the selection of an appropriate alternative which is the best bet for the organization. Mintzberg *et al* refers to this as the "selection phase" of decision–making.

The effectiveness of the strategic choice depends on the choice process itself. From the managerial point of view, there are two factors on which the effectiveness of choice rests. These are:

(i) The strategist's perception of different possible alternatives;
(ii) The strategist's ability to discriminate between the potency of various alternatives.

These elements would direct the manager to the most effective alternative if due attention is given to the firm's past and current strategies, and their future goals, and the anticipated environment in which the firm is likely to operate. This will impel the manager to develop an objective strategic statement, which will reveal the company policies relating to investment, earnings, market share, sales volume, etc. *vis–a–vis* those of the competitors. It will assist the management not only in designing its current strategy but will furnish a strong base for its evaluation and redesigning.

To arrive at the final choice, the various alternative strategies for which mathematical models have been prepared should be verified experimentally. An experiment is often conducted on a limited scale; but verification embrances most or all of the target population. This step is necessary because the reaction of competitors, test marketing and other comparable factors observed in the limited sample, tested experimentally, may not hold good for the entire population. So it must be translated into a set of operating procedures capable of being understood, applied and tested by those who are responsible for their use. The major and minor changes should then be incorporated and implemented.

Establishment of Proper Controls

Once the strategy has been implemented the next step in strategy formulation involves control of that strategy. A solution derived from the model remains effective as long as the strategy yields the desired results. If it goes off the track, the variables pertaining to the strategy would also change. The importance of the change depends on its comparison with that of the present strategy. To establish control over the solution, it is necessary to design an effective monitoring system, so that a timely feed–back may be made available to personnel at the various management levels. A continuous monitoring through feedback provides means for modifying the strategy in obedience to the external–internal environment change over time. If changes are necessary, the strategist should go back to the first step.

The aforesaid steps are seldom conducted in a sequential manner because there is usually a constant interplay between the various steps in the process. For instance, an exact and precise formulation of a problem is never possible unless the alternatives are properly screened. However, these steps offer us a conceptual framework for dealing with strategic formulations.

Factors Affecting Strategic Choice

Strategic choice decisions in organizations are largely monitored by such factors as the following

(i) Goals of the enterprise;
(ii) Managerial experience of past strategies;
(iii) Managerial attitude towards risk;
(iv) Managerial perception of dependency on external environment;
(v) Power politics in organization.

Goals of Enterprise

The strategy which an enteprise adopts is based on its goals. So if it sets short–term goals for itself, it is desirable to follow a strategy which pays off in a relatively short span of time. For instance, the strategies which yield a quick return on investment, achieve higher sales, etc., are more beneficial so far as short–term goals are concerned. If long–term profitability is desired, the strategy of stable growth, innovative marketing, long–range profit planning is more rewarding.

Managerial Awareness of Past Strategies

This factor influences to a considerable extent the strategic choice, for past strategies furnish a basis for new strategies. There has been some research which support this point of view. The classical work of Henry Mintzberg[4] in which he examined the strategic choices of the manufacture and marketing of Volkswagen from 1934 to 1969 and of the U.S. Government over its Vietnam policies from 1950 to 1968, showed that past strategic choices strongly governed later strategic choices. Specifically it was observed that:

4. Mintzberg, H. *et al.*, "The Structure of Unstructured Decision Process," *in Administrative Science Quarterly*, Vol. 21, pp. 246–275.

(i) The present strategy evolved from the past strategy developed by a powerful leader. This unique and tightly integrated strategy (a Gestalt strategy) was major influence on later strategic choices;

(ii) The strategy becomes programmed and bureaucratic when momentum keeps it going. Mintzberg called it a "Push–Pull Phenomenon." The original decision–maker pushes the strategy; the lower level management pulls it along;

(iii) When this strategy begins to fail because of changing conditions, the enteprise grafts new strategies onto the old and only later gropes for a new strategy.

As the environment changes, the enterprise begins to consider seriously the questions of retrenchment or growth strategies previously suggested by a new executive who was ignored at the time. Miles and Snow[5] have given the typology of a firm's past strategies on active and passive dimensions. They studied the text book publishing companies, electronic and food processing industries, and voluntary hospitals. In strategic terms, firms were designated as defenders (passive), analyzers and prospectors (active) and reactors (signifying unstable strategic postures). The author also noted that it was very difficult for a firm to move away from its present strategies if the executive did not change.

Staw,[6] in his research finding, noted that if a strategist was personally involved in a decision, he was likely to divert increasingly larger resources to the fullfilment of his commitments. This explains why the management replaces the top executive to bring about a drastic change in its grand strategy when the results have been unfavourable for a reasonably long period.

MANAGERIAL ATTITUDE TO RISK

The risk-taking attitude or ability of the manager is a critical factor in strategic choice. The managerial attitude to risk may fluctuate between a high degree of risk and no risk, with an intermediate one of a moderate risk. The different attitudes to risk and strategic choices are shown in the Exhibit 1.

Whatever may be the strategist's attitude to risk before he has made any choice, a thorough scanning of the external environment and an adequate appraisal of internal environment should be made so that the advantages offered by a risky strategy may be fully exploited.

Exhibit 1

Attitude To Risk and Strategic Choice

Attitude to Risk	*Probable Strategic Choice*
(1) Risk is necessary for survival and growth	High risk strategies are accepted
(2) Risk is essential for existence, but only calculated risk is desirable	Moderately risky strategies are adapted
(3) Risk is disastrous for business	Risky projects are never ventured on.

5. Miles, R.E. and Snow, G.C., *Organisational Strategy, Structure and Process*, McGraw Hill Book Company, New York, 1978.

6. Staw, B.M., "Keep Deep in the Big Muddy: A Study of Escalating Commitment of Chosen Course of Action," in *Organizational Behaviour And Human Performance*, Vol. 16, No. 1, June 1976, pp. 27-44.

POWER POLITICS IN ORGANISATION

To a certain extent, the power equation and politics in an organization play a significant role in the design of a strategic choice. The man at the top in the organization often designs a power game in such a fashion that he attains whatever is desired through the people at work. All successful strategists often lay down one effective alternative and see to it that it is unanimously approved. But if he fails to synchronize group efforts, cliques may develop and the strategy choice will be tossed between the *pro* and *anti* groups. Sometimes personalities are involved in the strategic choice. In such cases, the whims and fancies of the boss play a major role in the selection or rejection of a strategic proposal. In this state of affairs, if something goes wrong, the blame is shifted to those who stand outside the power group.

Mintzberg *et al*[7] have done some interesting work in examining the problems of power politics and strategic choices. They have concluded that there are three ways in which strategic choices are made, namely, judgement, bargaining and analysis. They noted that where authority was centralized, the time pressure was great and there was little scope for selection from among the alternatives. In such cases, on the basis of past strategies, experienced judgements were made. The bargaining method is used when the power of decision making is decentralized. A group of people make a decision with conflicting objectives. However, the process is objective. The analysis technique is adopted by relatively large corporations, for it places a premium on data analysis and mathematical modelling. Guth,[8] in his study of a billion–dollar US corporation, noted that decisions were significantly influenced by the interpersonal relations and power relations of the top managers.

In sum, it may be deduced that if the strategist is powerful he can easily find ways of attaining his objectives, while an executive, with a low-power profile, struggles hard to attain his own.

Influence of Subordinates on Strategic Choice

Strategic choices are largely determined by top managers. However the choices suggested by subordinates delimit their freedom in strategic choice, to a considerable extent. Bower,[9] in his study, found that executives at different levels affected the process in such a way that, at the time of final choice, it was difficult to consider all the possible alternatives. Guth's[10] finding, too, offers some insights into the strategic choice decisions when lower level managers or corporate planning staff also participate in strategy formulation. He observed that:

(i) If others participate, the strategic choice actually made will differ somewhat from the top strategist's formulation;

(ii) If others participate, their views are likely to be influenced by parochial considerations and the objectives of their sub–units.

The formulation of an effective strategy calls for joint decision making, which facilitates the process of arriving at the most practicable strategy and furnishes motivational impetus to

7. Minitzberg *et. al., op. Cit.*, p. 247
8. Guth, William "Towards A Social System of Corporate Strategy," *in Journal of Business*, Vol. 49, No.3, July 1976, pp. 374–388.
9. Bower, Joseph, *Managing the Resource Allocation Process*, Harvard Business School, Boston.
10. Guth, *op. Cit.*, p. 376.

subordinates. Whatever has been described here is just the tip of the iceberg. In fact, the strategic choice involves a thorough scanning of the environment in which the firm operates and forecasts the direction and extent of strategic trends and the position of the firm in the total environmental setting. It involves an adequate assessment of the resources which are at the disposal of the firm and are necessary for organizational action in terms of goal attainment. Besides tangible resources, it includes such intangible resources as human assets, their values, skill and attitudes. More specifically, it calls for an understanding of the dynamics of formal and informal organizations.

In the final analysis, one has to choose the best course of action. The elaborate process of decision–making has to be carefully monitored in all effective task–oriented organizations. Senior executives or a group of executives are entrusted with the responsibility of choosing the best course of action.

CHAPTER 28

STRATEGY IMPLEMENTATION

INTRODUCTION

Strategic implementation is one of the crucial aspects of strategic management in the sense that if it is not properly implemented, the whole strategic planning will be aborted, producing serious handicaps in organizational working and, at times, chaos or even the death of an enterprise. Therefore, great care should be taken in the implementation of the strategy so that, with minimum effort, the desired results may be obtained.

In this context, it must be borne in mind that the mere development of a dynamic and efficient strategy is not enough in itself for an enterprise to attain its mission. To keep the strategy operative and useful, the strategist should see to it that it is properly implemented inside and outside the organization. Basically, strategy implementation involves the communication of strategic objectives to various units, departments and sections, so that resources may be allocated, functional policies and organizational structure may be developed, besides nurturing a climate of support for the grand strategy. In putting strategy to work, the prime function of the strategist is to develop medium and short–range plans so as to facilitate the accomplishment of the grand strategy. The task of implementation calls of a complete stock–taking of top managemnet skills and capabilities, besides those of other personnel who are to contribute substantially to the implementation of the strategy. Though the list of functions related to strategic implementation goes up to twenty or so, the function of planning tends to dominate the scene. This is so because of the fact that strategic implementation and allied activities spurt from planning. In the words of Barnard, the strategic development functions of executives cover the "developing and maintaining a system of communication, promoting and securing the personnel services that constitute the material of organization, and formulating and defining the purpose of the organization."[1]

The implementation phase is so important and vital for the success of the organization that every strategist should know its nature, its process and dynamics in the context of the overall strategic framework and the goals of the enterprise.

Implementation generally takes place in a cascade–like fashion. Initially, the grand strategies are decided at the top corporate level and communicated to different units which, in turn, choose their specific strategy for which their various departments or sections are to strive.

In the strategic implementation, the management has to concentrate on the following three dimensions, namely:

(i) Functional Policy Implementation;
(ii) Organizational Implementation;
(iii) Leadership Implementation.

In order to carry out his job effectively, the analyst or leader must understand the complexity and gravity of the issue with which he is confronted. This understanding calls for greater emphasis on functional decisions, especially on the production, finance, personnel and the marketing management functions. It enables them to sharpen their skills for the effective utilization of the company's resources.

1. Barnard, Chester I., *The Function of Executive*, Harvard University Press, 1938, p. 215.

FUNCTIONAL POLICY IMPLEMENTATION

As the business becomes more complex and comeptitve, formulation of coherent and pragmatic strategies becomes imperative in order to facilitate goal attainment. The functional strategies to be adopted can only be effective when they support the main strategy and are in harmony with it. But quite often it is found that the top management without going into details of very many delicate and intricate problems of functional departments, decides a strategy and pass it down. This not only results in failure but breeds dissatisfaction among organizational participants. Therefore it is necessary for management to take care of various functional problems before designing any strategy.

The operationalization of the functional policies involves two processes — resources deployment and development. It has been observed that a proper implementation of functional policies can make or mar the future of an organization.

Woot et al, in their study of 168 Belgian firms, noted that a firm's success was contigent on a proper implementation of policies. They observe that:

(a) Profitability depends on a proper balancing of resources and policies among the various functional areas of management.

(b) Profitability is contingent on an effective implementation of product policies.

In the light of these facts, the top management, the sub–unit and departmental head should be employed to reinforce the strategic choice.

Resource Development

It is an important sub-aspect of the implementation of strategy, for no strategy can be effectively implemented unless there is an adequate resource allocation among the different units/departments of an undertaking. It requires the top management to decide as to how and in what quantity resources would be allocated among the different units or departments, and what will be the criteria for doing so.

In the recent past, a host of companies have allocated heavy capital expenditure on the diversification of projects. If that is their growth strategy, action must be taken to see to it that they yield the desired results. But if a strategist defines a strategy and does not allocate resources (both human and non-human), the strategy will be merely a paper strategy which will cause a considerable amount of frustration among functional executives. If a strategist believes that the product life cycle of a firm should influence its budgeting, the balance sheet and income statements should look differently at different times depending on the condition of the product life cycle.

Development of Policies

The development of functional policies is yet another important aspect of the implementation phase. It enables subordinate managers to know:

(i) What, when, who and how of a particular plan;

(ii) What will be the outcome of the plan.

The policies are a guide to managerial action which makes strategy one of the key elements in the development of policies. It should be ensured that policies are compatible, workable and praticable, and that they contribute optimally to the effective working of the strategy. This can be brought about by a manager when he takes into consideration how, when, and where the strategy is prepared and under what circumstances its redesigning becomes imminent. For instance, the company intends to diversify. The policy–makers must them decide about what to diversify, how to diversify, and how diverisification will be financed; and what policy changes are required in the area of production, personnel and marketing.

Policy–making varies with the type of product/service for sale, size of business, and style of management, etc. The major functional areas for which policies are required to be formulated include:

(i) Finance/Accounting
(ii) Personnel
(iii) Production and Operational Management
(iv) Marketing
(v) Research and Development

Accordingly, decisions are required to be taken for the implementation of the policies framed for the different functional areas of management. If the firm's objective is development and growth, the policies followed will be:

(i) Financial / Accounting Policies

The important financial policy decisions stemming from the growth objectives and requiring adequate implementation include:

- From where will the company get the required amount of funds to grow: will it mobilise them externally or internally?
- If interanlly, how and to what extent will the reserves and surplus be utilized?
- If externally, how? From where? And in what quantity?
- If both the sources are used, what will be their ratio?
- What will be the ratio of growth rate to cash flow?
- What will be the expected pay-back period?
- What capital structure policy is required to be followed?
- How much cash and other assets should the company keep in hand?

The answers to these questions can be had from the prevailing financial status of the company and its overall strategy.

(ii) Personnel Policy Implementation

The major personnel policy decisions on whose implementation the success of the different functional policies and of the grand strategy depends, include:

- Do we have an adequate work force to carry out our plans?
- Do we require more hands? If so, how many and of what quality?
- How will their training and development be brought about?
- Is the compensation plan just and fair?

- Are motivational policies tied to strategic objectives?

(iii) Production/Operation Policies

The important production/operation policies needing implemnetation include:

- Whether the deployment of new technology is imminent, if so how its implementation will be brought about.
- Can the firm handle the additional business with present facilities, i.e., the number of shifts, equipment and personnel, etc.? If not, how the desired level can be attained.
- What is the optimum level of productivity a firm should seek to attain?
- Is the present level of inventory desirable?

(iv) Marketing Policies

The crucial marketing policies which call for implementation decisions cover the following areas:

- Which of the product line is required to be expanded or contracted, and to what extent?
- Which channel(s) will be used to market the new product line?
- How will the promotion of new products be brought about?
- Should the company lay greater emphasis on advertising, personal selling or other forms of promotion?
- How will price and non–price competition be countered?
- Do we have an adequate sales force to push the sale of our products?

(v) Research and Development Policies

The following are the important research and development policy decisions which call for adequate implementation:

- Are our present R & D policies yielding the desired results, or do they call for changes to meet the current requirements?
- What new projects are necessary to support growth?
- How much should the company spend on R & D?
- Can the company afford a rush investment on R & D programmes?

When managers have implemented the various functional strategic choices, the process of policy implementation is ended.

To optimize goal effectiveness, it is necessary to define the time frame of a strategy. There are certain policies which can be easily designed and implemented (for instance, the recruitment of *badli* workers, the training of supervisory personnel). In contrast to these, there are policies which take a long time before they yield results (such as product planning and development, R & D).

If strategists develop contingency planning, then for each functional area, contingent strategies. must be developed. Implementation programmes may then be designed.

Techniques of Functional Policy Implementation

An effective implementation of policies requires the development of an elborate mechanism of control and follow–up. There are a number of tools which can be used to learn whether there is any deviation from strategic plans; and if so, how it may be elimated. These tools includes MBO and PERT. For instance, in MBO, objectives are determined before the strategic planning process is initiated. Then these objectives are interpreted in terms of strategic choices; and, finally, each sub–unit, or department, develops a strategic plan on the basis of the strategic choices made. In this way, the growth strategy by internal development is operationalized as shown (See Exhibit 1). This is the first breakdown. Subsequent breakdowns are required at different levels of management.

Exhibit 1

Performance Plan for a Branch Manager

(1) Increase overall profit by 4 percent.

(2) Branch sale growth of 10 percent. Sales of cosmetics to be increased by 4 percent, pharmaceuticals by 2 percent and consumer goods by 6 percent.

(3) Reduce operating costs by 2 percent

- Lower overtime by 2 percent
- Lower inventory level by 3 percent.
- Lower training and development cost by 1 percent.

(4) Reduce financial cost by 3 percent.

- Improve the cost management position.
- Ensure speedy collection of receivables.

At any point of time, the effective implementation of a strategy depends on vigorous follow–up plans and procedures in operation at all levels of the enterprise. It calls for an effective information system and an appropriate control mechanism so that the relevant information may be gathered from the organizational environment.

ORGANISATIONAL STRUCTURE AND STRATEGY IMPLEMENTATION

One of the major elements of the impelmentation of strategy is the organization of resources within and outside the enterprise. It is basically concerned with determining how far the organizational structure which has been adopted facilitates the implementation of the strategy. At any point of time, the strategist must seek to answer the question: Do we have the right type of organizational structure for the execution of our strategies? In fact, the structure may be defined as the design of an organization by which the enterprise is administered. The design, whether formally or informally defined, has two aspects. It includes, first, the lines of authority and commnication between the different administrative offices and officers; and, second, the information and data that flow through these lines of communication and authority. Such lines and data are essential to ensure effective co–cordination, apprasal, and planning, which are necessary in implementing the basic goals and policies and in knitting together the total resources of the enterprise.[2]

Chandler has placed emphasis on the organizational structure and its inter–relation with strategy. The organizational structure, by establishing the authority relationship and lines of communication among different levels, tells the strategists what is to be done, how it is to be done, what information is needed and at what level. As indicated earlier, strategy formulation, implementation and evaluation are inter–related phases, with the strategy preceding the structure. Therefore, the structure should be in conformity with strategic objectives. It goes without saying that a strategy would rarely succeed without an adequate organizational design. The organizational

2. Chandler, J. Alfred D., *Strategy and Structure,* The M.I.T. Press, Cambridge, Massachusetts, 1962, p. 16.

history is full of examples which underscore the fact that, in a variety of business undertakings, well-conceived strategic plans are thwarted by a poor organizational design. This proposition has been supported by a variety of researchers. For instance, Chandler[3] noted that when a firm adopted a strategy of diversification, it had to change its design.

Allen[4] observes that a variety of organizational problems stem from the management's inability and unwillingness to adopt a proper organizational design after strategic changes have been introduced. This calls for designing the right type of organizational structure for the effective execution of strategy. While deisigning the organization structure, the strategist should not only bank upon "principles" or the best way of organizating the design they should determine which structure is the most propriate in terms of goal attainment. The manager must realize that the

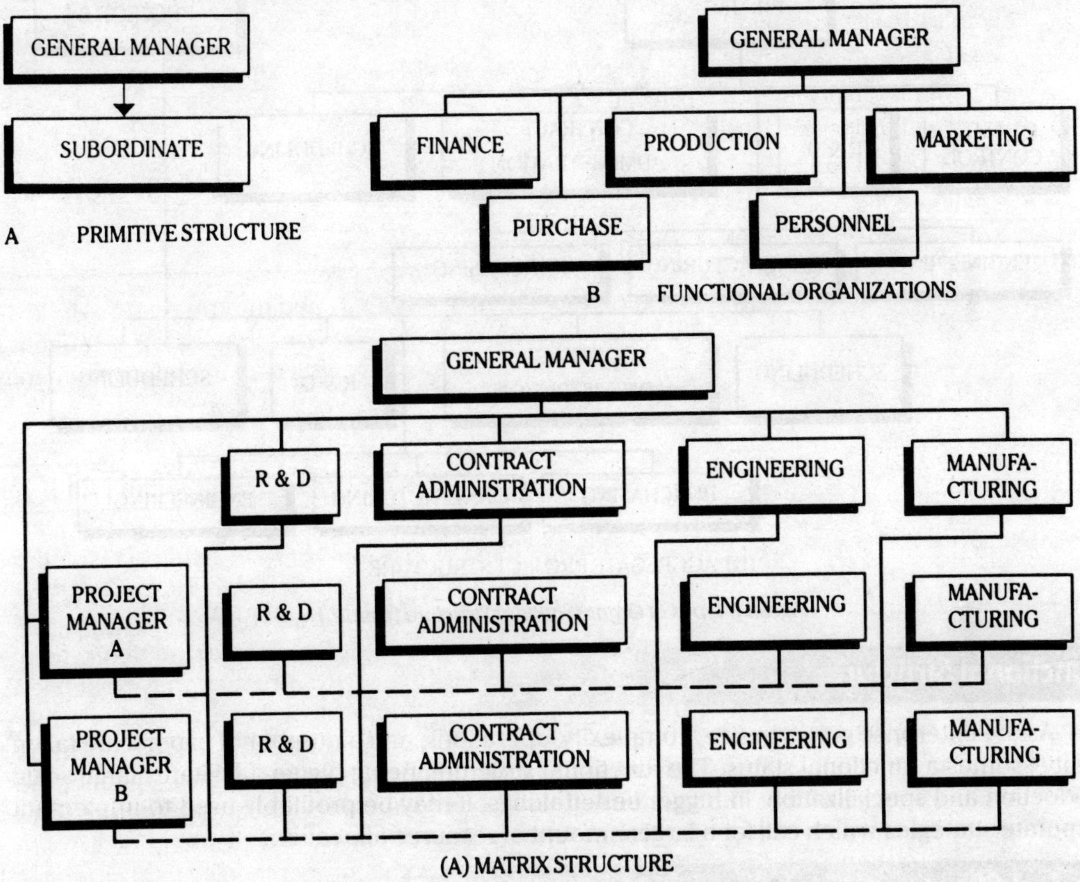

Fig. 28.1 : Types of Organizational Structures

achievement of objectives calls for a deep appreciation of the entire range of organizational and administrative activities which are the core of strategic implementation. The ways in which various implementation activities are deployed depends on the structure of the organization. A well concei ved design facilitates resource allocation, and gains the support of organizational

3. *Ibid.*
4. Allen, Stephen, "Organizational Choice and General Management: Influence Net-work in Divisionalized Companies," in the *Academy of Management Journal*, Vol. 21, No. 3, 1978, pp. 341–365.

participants for the objectives and policies of the enterprise. As the different strategies call for different structures, it is necessary to throw some light on the different types of available structures. Fig. 28.1 illustrates the different categories of the available structures. When an organization is relatively small in a size, it does not use an advanced technology, for the nature of the business is not complex or diversified. In such cases, one-man-one-boss type of organization structure is quite suitable.

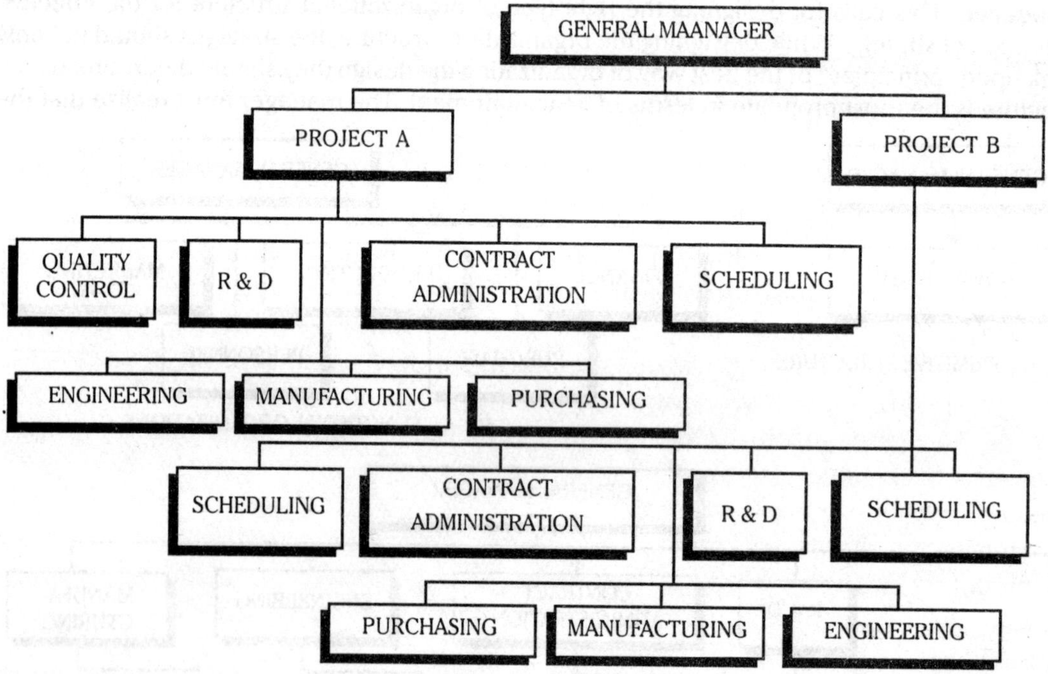

(B) AGGREGATE PROJECT STRUCTURE

Fig. 28.1 Types of Organizational Structure (Contd.)

Functional Structure

As the enterprise grows in size, complexity, operations, and a number of experts are taken on, it assumes a functional status. The functional structure, being bigger, facilitates large scale production and specialization. In bigger undertakings, it may be profitably used to implement corporate strategies which call for a larger amount of resource allocation.

Project Structure

When an organization has more than one project on hand and pursues more than one strategy, then, to implement these strategies, it may enlist the help of different project structures. This type of structure is normally followed when the management decides to focus greater talent and more resources for a given period on a specific project goal. The structure for this purpose facilitates an adequate utilization of resources, maximize co-ordination of sub-units and increase response to changes in the environment.

Matrix Structure

A matrix structure emerges when a project organization is superimposed on a functional one. Here the functional departmental heads have a line authority over the specialists in their departments. The specialists look after the projects. This sort of structure enables the management to reap the benefits of optimum utilization of human and non–human resources. At the same time, it facilitates specialization and low cost of production.

Which Organizational Form is Desirable?

The quest for the most "appropriate" structure for attaining effectiveness is business has tempted management theorists to pour out vast literature on the subject. But there is no consensus among the experts on this issue.

As every organization has its own personality, identity, mission, environment structure and problems, it is quite difficult to identify a deisgn which may be universally applied to all types of enterprises. The best organizational structure is one which fits into the organization's size, nature, volatility, complexity, personal characterstics and its surroundings. But in spite of these facts, some generalization may be made. First, when the business is conducted on a small scale and the object is to maximize profit in the short run, a one–man–one–boss organizational structure is very suitable. In general, the functional structure works well in a relatively stable environment where the compnay enjoys a fairly good market share and does not experience any immediate environmental threat. The project and matrix structure may be profitably exploited by a large multi–product enterprise operating in a highly changing and turbulent environment.

Reorganization

It has become a favourable pre–occupation of some strategists to talk of reorganization for effective implementation of the strategy. It is increasingly believed that when major strategic implementation issues are involved it is always desirable to reorganize the enterprise. The conditions which warrants such reorganization include:

- Excessive diversification of product.
- Rapid growth leading to problems of co–ordination and control.
- High degree of environment uncertainty and cut–throat competition.
- Spread of activities in several different locations. While venturing on new avenues the strategists must seek to answer the following questions:
  - What are its strengths and weaknesses? What are its capabilities in terms of technology, system and people?
  - Where does it stands today in terms of certain major management characteristics?
  - Is the organization climate conductive to re-organization?
  - Will the changed structure facilitate the accomplishment of objectives?

If the answer to these questions is affirmative, then reorganization should be resorted to, after proper environmental scanning both internal and external to organization. However, all the times and in all the cases it is not cure for all organizational ills. Chandler in his study of four American giants (namely, General Motors, Dupont, Standard Oil and Sears Roebuck) of a period of one century found that whenever the restructing was resorted to deal with interal and external crisis, it failed.

LEADERSHIP IMPLEMENTATION

The effective implementation of a strategy is contingent on the type of leadership available in the organization, for the leader is primarily responsible for designing the organizational blueprints, determining policies, laying down the work procedure and nuturing a proper climate for the attainment of predetermined goals.

Barnard has identified four areas of leadership behaviour as the "determination of objectives, the manipulation of means, the control of the instrumentality of action, and the stimulation of co-ordinated action."[5] These tasks are in conformity with the various steps involved in the development and implementation of a strategy.

An important dimension of leadership implementation is related to ensuring that the right strategies are chosen in the right proportion for the firm and its various subunits. The pressing problems of leadership implementation raise the following questions:

(i) Are leaders of the right quality chosen for the implementation of strategy?
(ii) Which leadership style is the most effective?
(iii) How can the desired leadership behaviour be achieved through adequate motivation?

Leadership Qualities

One of the important dimensions of leadership implementation is the need for ensuring that the right type of leadership is made available for the implementation of the right type of strategy. While dealing with this issue, the management must seek to answer the following questions:

(i) Who are currently occupying key leadership positions?
(ii) Do they possess the right characteristics for the implementation of the strategy?

So far as an answer to the first question is concerned, it has been noted that, in a variety of cases, the chief executive, the unit/departmental head or even the individual manager may not be an ideal one in all respects of strategic management. In fact, a strategist must have many qualities of head and heart. A few of these qualities are:

(i) Education and ability:
(ii) Skill and experience:
(iii) Analytical and decision-making ability; and
(iv) Interpersonal skill.

It is impossible for a manager to acquire all these qualities. Therefore, it is the duty of the top management to see to it that the managerial personnel generally possesses the necessary qualities required for effective implementation.

5. Barnard, Chester I., *Organization and Management*, pp. 85-91.

However, in most cases, the strategist must possess a certain quality if at all he wants to be effective. For instance, the production manager of a firm using high technology must possess the required technical expertise and ability. Similarly, a general manager or chief executive should possess a high degree of conceptual and human relations skill. When strategies are changed or revised, the manager must make sure that the people who are to implement these strategies must possess the right type of expertise, ability, qualifications, personality, etc. If these are lacking, then they had better be trained or replaced. The major obstacles in strategic implementation must be identified and properly assessed.

Leadership Style

The term *leadership style* refers to behavioural pattern employed by a leader to integrate organizational and personal interests in the pursuit of some goal or objective. The type of leadership style available in an organization has a great deal to do with the implementation of strategies.

In management literature, different researchers have identified different styles. For instance, Lewin *et al*[6] have recognized three distinct types of leadership dimension – authoritarian, democratic and *laissez faire*. Stogdill and Coon[7] are of the view that consideration and initiating structure are important dimensions of leadership. Likert[8] has laid empahsis on employee–oriented supervision. Blake and Martin[9] hold the opinion that task accomplishment and personal relationship are important dimensions of leadership. Reddin[10] has noted the essence of leadership lies in task behaviour, relationship behaviour and effectiveness.

Khandwalla[11] has done extensive research in the relationship between management style, the nature of environment and effectiveness. He has found that there are basically seven styles (see Chart 1). He has specified the characteristics of the style along five dimensions.

(i) **Risk Taking**: Willingness to make high–risk, high–return decisions.

(ii) **Technology**: Degree of commitmne to planning, employment of technically qualified persons, and pratice of management science techniques.

(iii) **Organicity**: Degree of loose and flexible organizational structuring; low organicity is mechanistic in tightly structured organizations.

(iv) **Participation:** High participation implies extensive participation of those other than the top management in key positions.

(v) **Coercion**: High coercion means extensive use of fear and domination by top managers as a management technique.

Further Khandwalla has characterised the environment along the following dimensions:

(1) Degree of Turbulence of Volatility: Fast changeability and un-predictability.

(2) Degree of Hostility: Hostile environments are highly risky and overwhelming.

6. Lewin K., Lippit, R. and White, R.K., "Pattern of Aggressive Behaviour in Experimentally Created Climate," in *Journal of Social Psychology*, 1939, Vol. 10, pp. 171–199.
7. Stogdill, R.M. and Coon, A.E. (Ed.), *Leader Behaviour: Its Description and Measurement*, Bureau of Business Research, Ohio State University, Columbus, Ohio, 1957, pp. 98–99.
8. Likert, R., *New Pattern in Management*, McGraw Hill Book Company, New York, 1961.
9. Blake, R. and Martin, J.S., *The Management Grid*, Gult Publishing, Houston, Texas, 1961.
10. Reddin, W.J. Managerial Effectiveness, McGraw Hill Book Company, New York, 1970.
11. Khandwalla, Pradip, "Viable and Effective Organization Design of Firms," in the *Academy of Management Journal*, Vol. 16, No. 3, (September 1973), pp. 481–495.

(3) Degree of Heterogeneity: This refers to diversity of markets and types of consumers.

(4) Degree of Restrictiveness: Restrictiveness means many economic legal, social and political constriants.

(5) Degree of Technological Sophistication: With complex technologies, R & D is necessary for survival.

Khandwalla notes that when the management style matches the strategic choice (firm's environment), firms tend to be more effective. However, the leadership style that an individual selects should depend on the situation in which he finds himself, the type of strategy to be managed, and the general environmental variables.

Reinforcement of Managerial Motivation Through Adequate Incentives

The mere adoption of a suitable leadership style is not enough. Adequate steps must be taken for the reinforcement of favourable styles through adequate motivation. If people are not properly motivated, they will lose interest in the job, and job satisfaction would decline. The reinforcement of desirable leadership behaviour is contigent upon the available motivational climate which, of course, varies with the type of organization, strategists, turbulence in environment, etc. For instance, job enrichment, challenging work and promotion, etc., can be good reinforcers of favourable leadership behaviour.

Chart I

Seven Styles of Top Management

	Risk Taking	Techno-cracy	Organicity	Partici-pation	Coercion
1. Entrepreneurial Style	High	Moderate to Low	Moderate to High	Moderate to Low	Variable high in innovation, resisting organization otherwise.
2. Neo-Scientific Management Style	Variable	High	Moderate to Low	High	Moderate to low
3. Quasi-Scientific Style	Variable	High	Moderate to Low	Moderate to Low	Moderate to High
4. Mudding-through Style	Moderate to Low	Low	Moderate to High	Moderate to Low	Moderate to High
5. Conservating Style	Low	Moderate to Low	Moderate to Low	Moderate to Low	Variable
6. Democratic Style	Moderate to Low	Moderate to Low	Moderate to High	High	Variable high if there are factions; low otherwise
7. Middle-of-the-road Style	Moderate	Moderate	Moderate	Moderate to Low	Moderate to Low

Source : Khadwalla, Pradip : *Some Top Management Styles, thei r context and performance, Organisation and Administrative Science*, Vol. 7, No. 4 (Winter 1976/1977), p. 27.

CHAPTER 29

STRATEGIC EVALUATION

- Introduction
- The Evaluation Process
- Criteria for Evaluation
- Problems in Designing Evaluative Criteria
- Considering Change in Strategy

INTRODUCTION

As a business operates in a quite dynamic and hostile environment, there is no surety that the corporate strategy, which has been adopted will yield the desired results. Therefore, to attain the enterprise objectives, a regular evaluation of the strategy is necessary before a course of action can be designed which is the most appropriate for the success of business. This strategic evaluation would enable managers to compare the performance of the strategy against pre-determined targets. For most of the executives, strategy evaluation is simply an appraisal of "how well" the business is doing in terms of the goals which have already been laid down, whether it is a question of profitability, sales volume, rate of return or even the projection of the corporate image. If the answers to these parameters are affirmative, it is said that the strategy is effective and efficient. But, unfortunately this is not so, for there are a number of factors which determine the current performance of a strategy but which are not even easy to assess or detect. So by the time *opportunities* or *threats* arise it is often too late for the management to remould the strategy so that it may meet the crises which have developed.

From this discussion, it is obvious that strategy evaluation aims at scanning those critical factors which govern the destiny of the business rather than at the assessment evaluation of the classical parameters of the short-term health of the business. In this context, the role of the strategist is like that of a physician, who, while examining a patient, evaluates the symptom and makes the most effective diagnosis. An appropriate diagnosis results from an analysis and choice of strategic management. The diagnosis leads to the implementation process. If the diagnosis fails, the analysis method is adopted again (a new strategy is chosen) to deal with the ailment. As physicians do not leave the patient at the mercy of the gods, so the strategist goes on evaluating/testing his strategy again and again and designing and redesigning the most appropriate course of action till the best results are achieved.

Strategy Evaluation – Some Issues

Strategic evaluation involves the consideration of the following issues:

(i) Whether the objectives of the enterprise are appropriate and attainable with given resources;

(ii) Whether major policies and strategies are in line with corporate objectives;

(iii) Whether the results obtained from the evaluation confirm or negative the assumptions from which strategy flows.

Obtaining reliable and accurate information pertaining to these issues is quite an uphill task, for it calls for a reasonable store of situation-based knowledge, foresight on the part of executives, besides up-to-date and efficient management information system. But in spite of all these, it is not so easy to determine why strategies do not yield the desired results. This may be so because:

(i) Strategy is basically concerned with the selection of enterprise objectives and goals. Most of the grey-haired executives find it easier to set the goals and work towards their attainment; but cannot lay down objective standards for their evaluation;

(ii) Each enterprise has a unique set of strategies. For instance, one enterprise may adopt the strategy of heavy under-cutting to face competition; another may stick to the strategy of selling quality goods to boost its corporate image. Neither of the strategies is "right" or "wrong" in any absolute sense; both may be right or wrong, depending upon the firm in question. Therefore, strategic evaluation should be based on the situation of the firm's environment and not on the "so-called" best way.

(iii) However rigorous the evaluation, it only reflects the past effectiveness of a strategy, because by the time the data on the operational working of the strategy are available, the environment may have changed substantially.

THE EVALUATION PROCESS

While dealing with the evaluation process, the management has to determine the level at which strategies will be evaluated. Normally, strategies are evaluated both at the corporate and the unit levels; but if the management at the unit level does not appraise the strategy, the corporate level executive may intervene. In any organisation, executives evaluate the overall corporate strategy on the whole besides monitoring the unit level and the sub-unit level strategies. The evaluation process requires;

(i) The incentive to evaluate;
(ii) A feedback system to provide data on evaluation;
(iii) Criteria for evaluation.

The Incentive to Evaluate

To make the evaluation effective, it is desirable on the part of the management to link it with the performance of the executive.

The executives who have experienced failure are exceptionally cautious in designing and evaluating strategies; they take every precaution to see to it that deviations are promptly reported. But it is equally disastrous for those who have not experienced any failure. People with a rewarding or happy experience take things for granted, with the result that, in a crisis they have a hard time. Failure reminds us that there is a need for evaluating strategy on a continuing basis. If we look at political history, we would find that failure results largely from the unwillingness of rulers to evaluate their strategies, whether it is the strategy of a Hitler or that of the US relation to the Vietnam war. The motivation to evaluate a strategy arises on the policy of the management to link it with performance. If the reward is related to performance, executives will be strongly motivated to evaluate strategies. But in most cases, this is not so, for even people who have shown poor performance are given a raise. Quite often, those at the top make recommendations for their own promotion. In such cases, it is very difficult, for them to appraise the performance of their subordinates. Therefore, unless the person at the top himself takes some concrete decision, nothing can be expected from others.

Feedback for Evaluation

The basic requirement of an effective evaluation is the availability of quantified information on the different aspects of a strategy. This can be made possible by an effective management information system and honest complete and quick reporting of the results of the strategy at all levels. If the management has adequate information about the working of the strategy, it can take firm action to reinforce its success.

CRITERIA FOR EVALUATION

One of the basic tenets of science is that a theory can never be provided to be absolutely effective. It can, however, be declared to be absolutely ineffective if it fails to stand up to scientific testing. Similarly, it is very difficult to demonstrate or test that a given strategy is effective or that it will yield the desired results. Though one cannot figure out its flaws or serious handicaps in absolute terms, scientific criteria may, to some extent, enable the management to assess the working of the strategy against the targets that have been laid down.

There are as many criteria as the authors on the subject. Here, a few popular criteria have been quoted. Rumelt[1] has suggested the following criteria for the evaluation of a strategy:

(i) *Consistency:* The strategy must not present mutually inconsistent objectives and policies.

(ii) *Consonance:* The strategy must represent an adaptive response to extend environment and to the critical changes occurring within it.

(iii) *Advantage:* The strategy must provide for the creation and/or maintenance of a competitive advantage in the selected areas of activity.

(iv) *Feasibility:* The strategy must neither over-tax available resources nor create unsolvable problems. These are qualitative criteria which can be profitably deployed after the implementation is complete.

Seymour Tiles[2] has given us a list of criteria to evaluate a strategy soon after the implementation phase is over. These are:

(i) *Internal Consistency:* Does the policy implementation of the strategy fit into the integrated pattern of the organization?

(ii) *Consistency with the Environment:* Are policies in conformity with the present environmental status?

(iii) *Appropriateness of given Enterprise resources:* Does the implementation of the strategy facilitate the most economical use of scare resources?

(iv) *Acceptability of Degree of Risk:* In the given attitude of the management towards risk, to what extent is strategy capable of eliminating risk, or making it possible for the management to bear it?

(v) *Appropriateness of Time Horizon:* Does the strategic implementation give due cognizance to the time horizon?

(vi) *Workability:* Does it achieve the enterprise goal?

Stonier noted those factors which are important for the success of a strategy and calls for a rigorous evaluation.[3] He says:

(i) Attract and maintain high quality top management.

(ii) Develop future managers for domestic operations.

1. Rumelt, Richard, "Evaluation of Strategy" "Theory of Models," in Dan Schendel and Charles Hofer (eds.), *Strategic Management: A New View of Business Policy and Planning,* Boston, Little Brown, 1979.
2. *Tilles, Seymour "How to Evaluate Corporate Strategy," in Harvard Business Review, Vol. 41, No. 4, 1963,* pp. 112-121.
3. Stenier, George, *Strategic Factors in Business Success,* Financial Executive Research Foundation, 1969.

(iii) Motivate sufficient managerial drive for profits.
(iv) Ensure better judgement, creativity and imagination in decision-making at the top management level.
(v) Perceive new needs and opportunities for products.
(vi) Develop a better long-range planning programme.
(vii) Improve service to customers.
(viii) Provide a competitive return to stockholders.
(ix) Minimize the value of stockholder investment.
(x) Develop the willingness to take risks with commensurate returns in what appears to be excellent new business opportunities to achieve growth objectives.

Stenier emphasised that, among the different executives of different companies, there is little disagreement on the criteria to be used for evaluation purposes. However, he insists that the crucial aspects of strategy which need evaluation are:

(i) Management quality and development;
(ii) Environmental analysis and diagnosis, especially of marketing;
(iii) Financial return.

Hofer[4] after reviewing the shortcomings of the many criteria, has given a different evaluation yardstick. He has proposed three measures (shown in Exhibit 1) for strategic evaluation:

Exhibit 1: Hofer's Measure of Organisational Performance

Performance Characteristics	*Some Traditional Measures*	*Proposed New Measures*
Growth	Dollar Sales, Unit Sales, Dollar Assets	Value Added+
Efficiency	Gross Margin, Net Profits;	ROVA*
Asset Utilization	Net Profits/Dollar Sales ROI, Return on Equity, Earning per share.	ROVA/ROI

+ Value added – dollar sales – cost of raw materials and purchased parts

$$* \text{ ROVA – Return on Value Added} = \frac{\text{Net Profit Before Tax} \times 100}{\text{Value}}$$

In attempting to evaluate the effectiveness of its corporate strategy, a firm should determine how well it has done in comparison to its competitors with respect to such factors as:

- Net Profit
- Return Per Share
- Return on Equity
- Return on Investment
- Cost of Production and Efficiency
- Market Share
- Sales Growth
- Adaptiveness
- Employee Satisfaction
- Productivity.

4. Hofer, Charles, *ROVA: A New Measure for Assessing Organisational Effectiveness*, Graduate School of Business, New York University, 1979. Mimeograph.

This is a short but certainly not exhaustive list of criteria for the evaluation of strategies. In fact, the quest for a universally acceptable criterion has tempted management experts and practising managers to deploy a variety of criteria to suit their whims and fancies. Consequently, we have a pile of idiosyncratic criteria for the measurement of the effectiveness of strategies.

PROBLEMS IN DESIGNING EVALUATIVE CRITERIA

Due to the lack of a universally acceptable criterion, a great many difficulties have been encountered in the evaluation of strategies. In this connection, Steer has remarked: "The absence of consistency makes it very difficult to operationalize the concept for the practice of management. If agreement cannot be reached as to what actually constitute the evaluative criteria, it is logical to assume that considerable difficulty would be encountered in any attempt to assess the relative effectiveness or ineffectiveness of a given organization or set of organizations[5]. The common problems associated with designing of a universally acceptable criterion are:[6]

(i) Construct Validity Problem: Most of the research findings indicate that neither the construct for organizational effectiveness is valid nor is there any valid construct for which valid criteria have yet to be developed.

(ii) Criteria of Stability Problem: Most of the criteria used for the evaluation of a strategy, whether based on a conceptual or empirical foundation, deploy those parameters which are relatively unstable over time. That is, criteria used to evaluate the strategy of an organization at one time may turn out to be invalid or misleading at other times, even if used for or by the same organization.

(iii) Time Perspective Problem: Though some criteria are based on time dimensions, most of the time they fail to depict the true happenings.

(iv) Multiple Criteria Problem: Most of the evaluate criteria for attaining comprehensiveness integrate several elements into a unifying framework. But it has been obvious that such criteria are in conflict with each other.

(v) Measurement Precision Problems: Quite often, it is assumed that different criteria for evaluating a strategy can be precisely quantified. However, quantification is often difficult because of the complexity and magnitude of problems.

(vi) Generality Problem: Though a variety of criteria exist for the evaluation of a strategy, they cannot be widely applied to similar or different types of organization.

(vii) Theoretical Relevance Problem: Quite often, questions are raised about the theoretical relevance of various criteria employed in the evaluation of corporate strategies. It is, therefore, open to question whether they are of real value in assessing the worth of strategies. If a yardstick fails to assist us in understanding the working of strategies, they have little value from the theoretical point of view.

Apart from the problems cited in the foregoing paragraphs, the fact remains that the type of criteria to be deployed that are qualitative or quantative has been a point of controversy. For some executives, quantative criteria are of paramount importance because they directly indicate the

5. Steer, R.M., *Organisational Effectiveness: A Behavioural View*, Good Year Publishing, Ins., New York, 1973, p. 43.
6. *Ibid.*, pp. 54-57.

efficiency of an enterprise in straight numerical terms. But qualitative criteria are of equal importance. Therefore, neither qualitative nor quantative criteria will alone make evaluation effective. A combination of both is necessary for an effective evaluation of an enterprise, which is only possible when a valid criterion, encompassing the various issues, is designed, apart from those which are applicable to particular forms of organization.

CONSIDERING CHANGE IN STRATEGY

However scientific, objective, and practical a strategy, and however rigorously it is implemented, it has been often noted that the management fails to attain its objectives. The factors which are beyond the control of the management are a stumbling block in the working of the strategy. Therefore, to keep business going, it is necessary for managers to modify or remould the strategy in accordance with the needs of the situation. The change in strategy follows from the effectiveness of the evaluation system which pinpoints problems, weaknesses, strengths and opportunities. In other words, we may say that evaluation should give a manager a deep insight into the various aspects of a strategy so that a strong base may be created for a change in strategy or sub-strategy.

The changes in strategy become necessary for a variety of reasons, among which the most pressing and obvious one is to correct the deviations which are most apparent. These deviations arise whenever there is any change in the external or internal environment of an organisation. However, when changes in various external environments, viz., S & T economic, social political and legal, take place, the business is faced both with *threats* and *opportunities* which call for an adequate management of the situation that has arisen. It has been noted that changes in the S & T environment are more drastic than others, and therefore call for greater management attention. Though not equally pressing, it is equally important to sense the changes in internal environment, especially those relating to the financial resources, the production system, human resources, managerial attitude, etc.

Whenever any deviation from stated strategies is observed, the manager should consider the desirability of a change in strategy.

Leading American corporations like Xenx, IBM, NCR, AT & T and many others have, by changing their strategies, been immensely benefited. Also, a few Indian corporations like Reliance, Godrej, Lakme have benefited from changes in their strategies.

While redesigning the strategy, the strategist should see to it that it is so designed as to be appropriate or, more importantly, as to yield the best possible results in the future. Though it is quite difficult to predict the future, an assessment of tomorrow's environment is essential if the strategy is to be effective and efficient. This is only possible when the manager behaves like a futurologist, and regularly monitors the changing environment.

CHAPTER 30

MANAGING STRATEGIC CHANGE

Introduction

Diagnosing Stategic Change Needs

Resistance to Change

Styles of Managing Stategic Change

Communicating Change

INTRODUCTION

"Most of us fear change. Even when our minds say change is normal, our stomachs quiver at that prospect. But for strategists and managers today, there is no choice, but change." **Robert Waterman, Jr.**

Only 'Change' is permanent. It does mean that everything, except change, changes. Change is the law of nature. It is a necessary way of life in most organisations for their survival and growth. Organisations have to mould themselves continuously to meet new demands and face new challenges and situations. The term 'Change' implies the creation of imbalances in the existent pattern or situation. Adjustment among people, technology and structural set up is established when an organisation operates for a long time. Change requires the organisations to make new adjustments in the environment.

Understanding Types of Strategic Changes

The major and drastic changes are often termed as strategic changes. Change could be both reactive and pro-active. A pro-active change has necessarily to be planned to attempt to prepare for anticipated future environmental changes. In fact, organisations, sometimes changes even external environment in order to introduce strategic change. A reactive change may be an automatic response or planned response to change taking place in the environment.

Strategic Change Management and Unfreezing

Unfreezing: Unfreezing is the first stage in the change process. In fact, unfreezing creates the need for change. Substantial shifts results from unfreezing. The process of substantial changes through challenge, information building and experimentation is shown in Fig. 30.1

The dissatisfied customers and other stockholders of the company communicate the rumours and signals regarding price, quality, and the like. These signals indicate the need for change. The signals may be ill-defined but felt need for change. This step contributes for further strategic drift. This stage of unfreezing leads to a situation of flux or crisis in the organisation.

This crisis leads to identification or surface the problems through discussions, arguments and brain storming.

The sessions of debate or brain storming give rise and is fed by information building. Executives would like to defend their positions. Information building is viewed as meaningful as it makes sense in this process. The information building process helps the individuals and groups to have conflicting and new information. The conflicting information challenges the fundamental assumptions and gives rise to new strategic options. These new strategic options would be tested through experimentation. If these new options are successful, this would lead to the emergence of a new paradigm.

Always, the process of the emergence of a new pardigm or strategies may not be successful. Therefore, the managers dealing with the new paradigm or facing the challenges/disturbances need a 'safety net' for the future. Some times they may revert to the old. In both the cases refreezing process starts. This helps for consolidating a changed paradigm. There may be pressures to confirm to the old ones. However, these pressures may be minimised by having strong stimulus for change.

The Nature of Strategic Change

The major and drastic changes are often termed as strategic changes. Strategy is a continuous process and therefore, the strategic development of organisations is also a continuous process. "There is a tendency towards 'momentum' of strategy; once an organisation has adopted a particular strategy then it tends to develop from that strategy within rather than changing its direction."[1] Thus, drastic and sudden changes in strategy in the organisation are not common.

Global changes bring the changes in the nation, corporate world, and the organisation. The effect of this change on the organisation is gradual, incremental and piecemeal. In other words, all the strategies of an organisation do not get changed over a night. Some of the strategies remain as they are, some of them are changed slightly and step by step improvement, other new strategies are formed gradually, some old strategies are dropped out gradually. Some times some strategies are unchanged and continuity is maintained. Sometimes i.e., periods of flux, some strategies change without any clear direction.

Strategic change, thus, is not sudden and dramatic. During the process of continuity, minor improvements or deletions in a strategy take place. These minor changes over a period culminate into a significant change in the gradual process over a period, this process brings a significant shift in strategy.

These little changes continuously make a lot of sense to the organisation. If, there were major changes in the external environment and consequently significant and sudden shifts in strategy, many organisations cannot manage the change. For example, most of the small industries in the country collapsed and some of the large-scale industries turned into sick units due to severe competition from multinational corporations, transnational corporations and joint ventures consequent upon the opening up of the Indian economy to the rest of the globe suddenly.

As the sudden shift in the strategy may lead to collapse of the company, strategies need more fundamental change or adopting to global strategies. Sudden changes in environment are infrequent, if environment changes gradually, then the organisation can have incremental strategies.

Strategies always need not be formulated as intended or planned fashion. There may be emergent strategies that come about or realised without the explicit intention of managers but which result from flow of more operational, day to day decision-making. Some of the intended strategies may be unrealised strategies. It does not mean that all the intended strategies are unrealised strategies.

The strategist should find out to what extent the organisation will have to change in order to succeed in the strategic implementation. Different kinds of strategies require different change in the business process, nature and size. For example a stability strategy affects the present business and organisation to the least extent. Similarly, a new pricing strategy affects only people in the marketing department and brings a few changes in the day-to-day business operations. In fact, the joint venture strategy brings radical changes in the organisation viz., replacing the existing organisational structure, introducing a more flexible, cross-functional organisational structure based on team building, new production process, technology, new markets and market practices, dropping existing products and adding new productsand/or services.

Strategic change can be a continuum varying from no variation in strategy to a complete and radical change in the project procedure, organisational mission, objectives and organisational structure. Samuel C. Certo and Paul Peter divide strategic change into five discrete stages. They are stable strategy, routine strategy change limited strategy change radical strategy change, and organisational redirection. Exhibit 30.1 presents levels of strategic change.

Exhibit 30.1: Levels of Strategic Change

Strategic Change	*Industry*	*Organisation*	*Products*	*Market Appeal*
Stable Strategy	same	same	same	same
Routine Strategy Change	same	same	same	new
Limited Strategy Change	same	same	new	new
Radical Strategy Change	same	new	new	new
Organisational Redirection	new	new	new	new

Source: Samuel C. Certo and J. Paul Peter, *op. cit.*, p. 113.

The implementation process of strategy involves many people, tasks, business units and products when it moves from stable strategy to organisational redirection. The implementation process becomes more complex when it moves towards organisational direction.

Stable Strategy

Stable strategy is continuation of stability in all aspects of the business. Therefore, mostly, it requires continuation of strategy from the previous planning period. It requires running of the business and performing the same tasks with the same skills. Successful implementation of stability strategy requires monitoring the activities to ensure that the objectives are achieved. The learning from previous experiences (experiences curve effects) will help to achieve the objectives effectively.

Routine Strategy Change

In the routine strategy change, a firm seeks to attract customers, by making normal, predicted adjustments in the methods. The strategy changes include: Changing advertising appeals, update packaging, using different pricing tactics, change the distributors, distributing channels and methods, adding gifts etc. Managers should integrate and coordinate the activities with various agencies and intermediaries in order to implement the strategies successfully. Similarly, the strategists should also coordinate the activities within the company. For example, the strategy of price reduction will enhance the demand for the product. Hence, the strategist should coordinate the activities of marketing department and production department to increase production, capacities of distribution channels and distributors. This strategy does not require major efforts and major changes for its successful implementation.

Limited Strategy Change: This strategy involves offering new products to new markets within the same general products class. Products are new, though they belong to the same general class. Hence, the managers have to perform many new activities. These activities include: designing the new products, procurement of new kinds of inputs, new machinery, producing new products, arranging new market intermediaries (if necessary), new market channels and the like.

Radical Strategy Change: This strategy involves a major shift for the firm. The radical strategy change is necessary, when the firm adopts the strategies like merger and acquisitions in the same basic industry. These strategies create complex problems in integrating the two firms into one firm. These complex problems include: restructuring the organisation, organisational change, change the organisational culture, change in the positions of key personnel, change in the distributors and distributing channels etc.

Organisational Redirection

This strategy involves mergers and acquisitions of firms in different industries. The magnitude of strategic change depends on the degree of variation of the nature of industries and the degree of centralisation of the new firm. Another form of organisational redirection involves when a firm leaves one industry and enters a new one. For example, a firm enters the hot drinks industry by leaving the soft drinks industry.

DIAGNOSING STRATEGIC CHANGE NEEDS

At this juncture, the organisation has to consider the internal and external environmental factors, future of the change process, competitors analysis etc. in order to assess the type and degree of appropriate change. This can be done by assessing the required incremental change and by indentifying the specific barriers to the change.

1. Detecting Strategic Drift

Incremental strategic change is less disruptive than transformational change. It is significant to know the situation when incremental change has given rise to strategic drift and when more fundamental change may be required. Determining the stage of strategic drift is mostly a matter of managerial judgement. Some of the symptoms of strategic drifts are:

- A highly homogeneous organisational culture in terms of beliefs, values, assumptions about the organisation, similar symbols and stories, little toleration for challenges, etc.
- Existence of power blockage blocks to resist change. Existence of groups, leaders or powerful individuals who resist change.
- Organisations with little focus to its external environment particularly to its markets. This includes absence of relevant information about markets, customers, price. etc.
- Declining relative performance. This includes trailing behind the competitors or decline in sales, profits, customer loyalty etc.

2. Indentifying Barriers to Strategic Change

Barriers to strategic change are natural. But, it is essential to identify these barriers in order to develop levers and mechanisms to reduce the impact of the barriers. This process helps for the successful implementation of the change.

Mostly employees resist to change due to fear of reduction in employment, demotion, increase in workload/exert new energies, the need for acquiring new skills, social adjustment, cultural changes etc. Managers also resist change due to increase in responsibilities, stress and tension, a feeling of uncertainty regarding the success of the change.

ORGANISATIONAL SYMPTOMS'	STAGES	PRESSURES FOR CONFORMITY
* Rumours and signals.	**Unfreezing mechanisms** ↓	* Early signals made sense of within paradigm
* Questions and challenges * 'Felt need' for change	**Organisational anticipation** ↓	* Political pressures not to 'rock the boat'
* Competing views of causes of problems and remedies	**Organisation flux** ↓	
* Information collection	**Information building** ↓	* Information made sense of within paradigm
* Political 'testing' of support		
* New ideas tested out	**Experimentation** ↓	* Resistance to new ideas
	Refreezing (the signalling of confirmation of change)	

Fig. 30.1 : Substantial changes through challenge, information building and experimentation

Organisations would like to retain the present culture. The routines, control systems, organisation structures, symbols, power or dependence relationships are therefore, change blockages.

Identification of the blockages or resistance to strategic changes help to develop a mechanism to overcome these blockages and implement change successfully.

Systems view of Incremental Change.

Lindblom suggested that rational planning models of strategic choice were unrealistic. According to him, managers cannot consider all possible strategic options in terms of all possible futures and evaluate these against pre-set, unambiguous objectives. This is because of the complex nature of organisation and the environmental dynamics. This task is further complicated in the organisations which have conflicting views, values and power bases. Alternative strategies are evaluated by comparing the strengths, weaknesses and the possibilities of implementation against each other. The strategy which would give the best outcome will be chosen. Lindblom called this strategy building through 'successive limited comparisons'.

Quinn studied nine major multinational businesses and concluded that the management process could best be described as logical incrementalism. By this he meant the following:

1. Managers develop the organisation through evolutionary approach. By doing so, they develop a strong, secure and flexible core business.
2. Effective managers accept uncertainty in external environment as it is unavoidable. They scan the environment continuously and become sensitive to the environmental changes. They adopt small-scale steps in strategy to test the uncertainties.
3. Managers encourage experimentation in the organisation. The experimentation is done as a team work by both top level management and lower level management. Specific objectives are not formulated due to its effect on experimentation.
4. According to managers, this process results in significant benefits. Quality of information for decision-making is improved due to continual testing and gradual strategy implementation. This continuous process develops commitment to change among employers.

Thus, implementation of strategy is the continual testing of the suitability of s atrategy to the circumstances of that organisation. Logical incremental view of strategic management process is presented in Exhibit. 30.2

Quinn argues that, "Good managers are aware of this process, and they consciously intervene in it. They use it to improve the information available for decisions and to build the psychological identification essential to successful strategies... Properly managed, it is a conscious, purposeful, pro-active, executive practice." Quinn also suggests that the various decisions in the incremental process should be seen as a continuous process as the subsystems in a total system. As shown in Figure 30.2, strategy formulation is a process through which the organisation keeps itself in line with the change in the environment. The other strategic models are : Liner, adaptive and interpretive (Exhibit 30.2)

Exhibit 30.2 : A Logical Incrementalist View of Strategic Management

Managers often see their jobs as managing adoptively; continually changing strategy to keep in line with the environment, whilst maintaining efficiently and keeping stockholders happy. Managers say:

1. We tend to test a number of different approaches on a small-scale with only limited or local company identification. If, we approach works, we will test it further and amplify its use; if another bombs, we try to keep it from being used again... then along comes another issue and we start all over again. Gradually, the successful approaches merge into a pattern of actions that becomes our strategy.
2. We begin wide-ranging discussion with people inside and outside the corporation. From these a pattern eventually emerges. It is like fitting together a jigsaw puzzle. At first, the vague outline of an approach appears like the sail of a ship in a puzzle. Then suddenly, the rest of the puzzle becomes quite clear. You wonder why you did not see it all along.
3. We had no particularly entrenched ideas as to where we were... So there was an infinite amount of flexibility. One thing we decided was that we wanted to keep this appeal–it might not bring us an enormous leap forward, but as long as we can keep adjusting our merchandise mix and image satisfactorily, we can keep a fair share of the market.
4. The real strength of the company is to able to follow these peripheral excursions into whatever...one has to keep thrusting in these directions; they are little tentacles going out, testing the water.

5. We haven't stood still in the past and I can't see with our present set up that we shall stand still in the future; but what I really mean is that it is a path of evolution rather than revolution. Some companies get a successful formula and stick to that rigidly because that is what they know. We hopefully have changed gradually and that is what I think we should do. We are always looking for fresh openings without going off at a tangent.

Source: I.B. Quinn, "Strategies for Change", Irwin, 1980 and G. Johnson, "Strategic Change and the Management Process," Basil Blackwell, 1987.

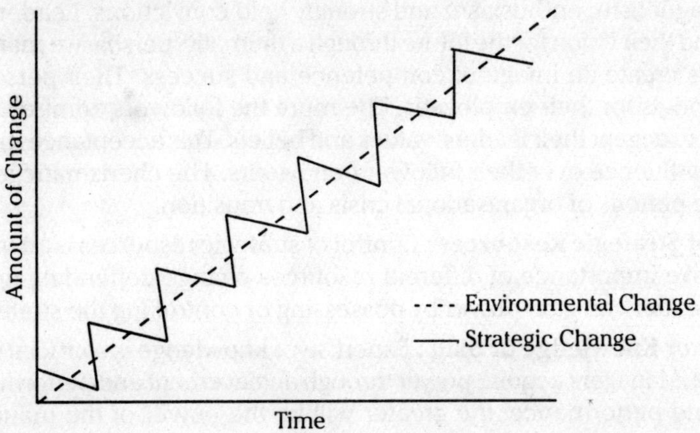

Source: G. Johnson, "Strategic Change and Management Process," Basil Blackwell, 1987.

Fig. 30.2: Incremental change of the strategy in response to Environmental change

Sources of Power :

The sources of power can be divided into two categories viz., (i) internal sources, and (ii) sources for external stakeholders as shown below.

SOURCES OF POWER

Internal Sources	*Sources for External Stakeholders*
1. Hierarchy (Formal Power)	1. Control of strategic resources (Ex : Materials, Men, Money)
2. Influence or Charisma (Informal power)	2. Involvement in strategic implementation (Ex : Distribution outlets, franchise, licenses etc.)
3. Control of strategic Resources	3. Possession of knowledge (Ex: skills)
4. Possession of knowledge/skills.	4. Through internal links (Ex. Informal influcence)
5. Control of environment (Ex: Negotiation skills)	
6. Involvement in strategic Implementation (Ex. Exercising discretion)	

Source : Gerry Johnson and Kevan Scholes, *op. cit.*, p. 134

Internal Sources of Power

***(i)* Hierarchy :** Hierarchical positions in the organisational structure provide formal authority to the managers at higher levels. The managers with more formal authority influence the policy formulation and implementation extensively. Managers should use this power along with other types of power to make their influence efficient.

***(ii)* Influence/Charisma :** Influence is an important source of power. This arises from personal qualities like charisma of the leader. Charisma is the leader's ability to influence others through his/her personal magnetism, enthusiasm and strongly held convictions. Leaders communicate these convictions and their vision for the future through a dramatic, persuasive manner of speaking. Charismatic leaders create an image of competence and success. Their personal magnetism make them role models for their employees. The more the followers admire their leaders, the more likely they are to accept their leaders' values and beliefs. This acceptance makes the leaders to exert significant influence over their follower behaviours. The charismatic leaders are more powerful during the periods of organisational crisis and transition.

***(iii)* Control of Strategic Resources** : Control of strategic resources is an important source of power. The relative importance of different resources change depending upon the strategy and situation. The leader can gain power by possessing or controlling the strategic resources.

***(iv)* Expertise or Knowledge or Skill :** Expertise or knowledge is a crucial source of power for top management. Managers acquire power through achievement and performance. The better the achievement and performance, the greater will be the power of the managers. Expertise refers to a manager's ability to influence the behaviour of others. The subordinate follow the managers as they believe that their managers have command and knowledge of the problems.

***(v)* Control of the Environment :** Normally events in the company and company's internal environment affect the company's performance. Some groups or individual employees have more influence over events and company's internal environmental factors. This can be a source of power within the company. Marketing and finance managers can control the important internal environmental factors. Therefore, they play a dominant role in the strategic management whereas the human resource manager and production manager take a back seat.

***(vi)* Exercising Discretion :** Exercising discretion is a most significant source of power within an organisation. Individuals due to the nature and level of their jobs, derive power. These individual employees occupy different positions in the organisation. Strategy is to be implemented by a number of individuals across the organisation. These individuals use the power so derived in the process of strategy implementation.

Sources for External Stakeholders

So for, we have discussed the sources of power for the internal groups. Now, we discuss the sources of power for external stakeholders.

***(i)* Resource Dependence :** Almost all external stakeholders like banks, financial companies, suppliers of raw materials etc. derive power as the company depends on them for resources. The short term survival of the company is mostly dependent on any one of these stakeholders.

***(ii)* Involvement in Implementation :** The importance has been shifted from manufacturing to the distribution. The distribution agencies have the power of knowledge about consumer's tastes and preferences. In fact distribution agencies determine or influence the type of product to be produced. Thus the distribution agencies derive power by involving in the implementation process.

***(iii)* Expertise :** The agencies having specialised skill or expertise that is demanded by the company derive the power for their expertise knowledge.

***(iv)* Internal Links:** Internal links can provide a way for external stakeholders to influence the company's strategy. Highly authritarian organisation normally does not provide inter links and give chance to external stakeholders to influence the strategic management process.

Methods of Assessing Power

It is rather very difficult to assess the power of internal individuals or groups and external stakeholders. Preffer suggests that the best way of assessing the power is to depend on indicators of power.

Indicators within organisations: There are four indicators of power within organisations. They are:

***(i)* The status of the Individual or Group:** The position of the individual in the organisatinoal hierarchy, and the job grade work as an indicator to assess the power. The reputation of individual or group compared to others can also be used to assess the power.

***(ii)* The claim on Resouces :** The claim of the individual or group for resources in terms of share in budget, number of employees etc. can be used to measure the power. The resources of the least powerful group normally are eroded by the more powerful group.

Managing the Strategic Change Process

The term 'Organisational Change' implies the creation of imbalances in the existent pattern or situation. Adjustment among people, technology and structural set up is established when an organisation operates for a long time. People adjust with their jobs, working conditions, colleagues, superiors etc. Similarly, an organisation establishes relationship in the external environment. Change requires individuals and organisations to make new adjustments. Complexity and fear of adjustment give rise to resistance and problem of change. Human resource is an important factor in the adjustments among individuals as well as between the organisation and environment, as an organisation is mostly composed of people. Individual members can resist either individually or in group.

Change could be both reactive and proactive. A pro-active change has necessarily to be planned to attempt to prepare for anticipated future challenges. A reactive change may be an automatic response or a planned response to change taking place in the environment.

Types of Changes

Changes can be broadly divided into: *(i)* Work change; and *(ii)* Organisational change. Work change includes changes in machinery, working hours, methods of work, job enlargement and enrichment, job-redesign or re-engineering. Change may also be in the working hours like morning shifts, evening shifts, operation of the organisation on Sundays/Holidays.

Changes relating to organisation include change in employees due to transfers, promotion, retrenchment, lay-off, restructuring or organisation, introduction of new products or services, imposition of regulation, changes in organisational goals or objectives etc.

Reasons for Change

Changes in organisations are a must, whether brought about deliberately or unwillingly. The reasons for change are categorised as follows: Changes in business conditions, changes in Managerial Personnel, Deficiency in existing Organisational Patterns, Technological and Psychological reasons, Government Policy, size of the organisation etc.

Response to Change

Work change does not produce direct adjustment. Instead it operates through each employee's attitude to produce a response that is conditioned by feelings towards the change. People often show this attachment to the group by receiving it in some uniform response to the change, though they individually interpret the change differently. This response makes possible some illogical action like mass walk-outs when obviously only a few people actually want to. A group develops responses in response to its members' conflicting attitudes towards change. Therefore, each pressure encourages counter pressure within the group. The net result is a self-correction mechanism to restore balance wherever change threatens. Thus, people act to establish a steady state of need fulfilment and to protect themselves from disturbances of that balance.

Every change is likely to have some cost as well as bring additional benefits to the organisations. Organisations introduce change when the benefits (additional benefits derived due to change) are relatively more than the cost (additional cost incurred due to change). Cost and benefits are not only economic but also social, psychological environmental etc.

RESISTANCE TO CHANGE

The basic problem in the management to change is the study of causes of resistance to change. Despite the fact that change is a persistent phenomenon, it is a common experience that employees resist change whether in the context of their pattern of life or in the context of their situation in the organisation. The best example is resistance of employees to computerisation. Change of any type requires readjustment. Man always fears the unknown, and a change represents the unknown.

Reasons for Resistance

Some of the important reasons for resistance to change are as follows:

(a) Economic Reasons: Economic reasons for resistance are classified into three groups. They are:

1. *Fear of Reduction in Employment:* Due to the change in technology, methods of work, quantity or quality of work etc. This fear leads to resistance to change on the part of people. Opposition to automation is an example to it.
2. *Fear to Demotion:* Employees may fear that they may be demoted if they do not possess the new skills required for their jobs, after the introduction of change. Hence, they prefer 'status quo'.
3. *Fear of Workload:* Change in work technology and methods may lead to the fear that workload will be increased while there will not be any corresponding increase in their salaries and benefits. This feeling creates resistance to change.

(b) Personal Reasons: Personal reasons for resistance are also divided into three classes. They are:

1. *Need for Training:* If change in technology and work organisation necessitates training and re-leaning on the part of employees, it may lead to resistance, as all do not like to go for refresher and retraining courses off and on.

2. *Boredom and Monotony*: If the proposed change is expected to lead to greater specialisation resulting in boredom and monotony, it may also be resisted by employees.
3. *No participation in change* : Some employees resist any change as they are critical of the situation and they are not being given any part in decision-making process for change. When they do not understand fully the implications of change, they resist it.

(c) Social Reasons: Social reasons for resistance are also classified into three groups. They are:

1. *Need for New Social Adjustment:* And organisational change requires new social adjustment with the group, work situation and new boss etc. All individuals are not ready to accept this challenge. Some people refuse transfers and promotions for this reason only, as they will have to break their present social ties.
2. *Taking Change as Imposed from Outside:* Some employees take any change as imposed from outside upon time.
3. *Other Considerations:* Some employees may consider that every change brought about is for the benefit of the organisation only and not for them, their fellow workers or even the general public. Hence, they resist the change.

Resistance from the Side of Managers

It is not a common fact that change is always resisted by the employees only. Managers also resist change sometimes. Any change sets in new responsibilities and imposes new tension, stress and strains over them is normally resisted by managers The feeling of uncertainty, whether they will be able to handle new circumstances successfully or not, motivates them to resist.

Approaches to Organisational Change

Management is said to be an agent of change. It means that management has to introduce change successfully in its organisation. It has to overcome the resistance and make it a successful venture. The management must realise that resistance to change is basically a human problem, though on surface, it may appear to be related to the technical aspect of change. So, it must be tackled in a human and social manner. Management has to take the following steps to implement the change successfully.

1. *Participation of Employees:* Before introducing any change, the employees should be fully consulted and they must be made a party to any such decision. The meaning and purpose of the change must be fully communicated to those who will be affected by it. Enough time should be allowed for discussion, and pros and cons of the change should be explained, in detail, to employees.

2. *Planning for Change:* Before implementing any change the management should plan for it. Employees should get an opportunity to participate both in planning the change and installing it. This will help the group of the affected employees to recognise the need for change and thus prepare them fore receiving it without any fear.

3. *Protecting Employees' Interests:* Management should ensure that employees are protected from economic loss, loss in status or personal dignity. If those things are protected, the degree of resistance to change will be at the lowest ebb.

4. *Group Dynamics:* Group dynamics refers to the everchanging interactions and adjustments in the mutual perceptions and relationships among members of the groups. Such group interactions are the most powerful instruments which facilitate or inhabit adaptation to change. Adaptation is a team activity which requires conformity to the new group norms, moves, traditions and work patterns. If these could be activity articulated by management the result are likely to be more successful and able.

5. *Cautions and Slow Introduction:* The management should not introduce any change suddenly and abruptly. It must be an objective for the management to build the organisation an awareness of change and an ability to forecast it, and also to instruct an attitude of welcoming change. Change must be introduced in sequential parts if possible, the results must be reviewed, and required adjustments must be made in it.

6. *Positive Motion:* The management should use the policy of positive motivation to counteract negative resistance. It should be the attempt of the management to make the job easier and less exerting. The management should impact proper training to its employees in new techniques and work knowledge etc. The leadership styles should also be supportive and human oriented. This policy will also bring down the resistance to change.

7. *Sharing the Benefits of Change:* Any change whether technical, social or economic will be least resisted by the employees if the management permits the employees to share benefits which arise out of the change. So, the management must see that employees are not only assured of it, they are given due advantage of it as well.

8. *Training and Development:* Management should plan for change. Based on the change plan, the job should be redesigned. Management should train the employees before-hand and prepare the employees to invite change. Normally trained and developed employees will not resist change as they cannot keep quiet with enriched skill and knowledge.

9. *Career Planning and Development:* Organisation on the basis of change plans and redesigned jobs should plan for careers of employees, possibilities to move the employees to the higher levels and develop them. The developed employees for future careers demand the management to implement change.

10. *Organisation Development:* Organisation development aims at moulding and development of employees in the psychological and behavioural areas with a view to achieve organisational effectiveness. Employees with enriched behaviours welcome the change.

Principles of Change

Management should also follow the undermentioned principles of change;

(1) Understanding the change itself, its purpose, its benefits and then making them understood to the employees.

(2) Estimating the reasons for the possible resistance to change and preparing to allay their fears.

(3) Mindful of channels of authority.

(4) Preparedness for all the questions and criticism.

(5) Listening to the suggestions and criticism of employees and incorporating them in the scheme as far as possible.

(6) Creating interest in them, convincing them and preparing them.

(7) Keeping in touch with the process of change.

Planning and Implementing Change

Management is often called a 'change agent' as its role is to initiate the change, and help make it work successfully. Employees support is most essential in implementing the change successfully as they are at the helm of affairs, though the management is an agent of change. Change is typically viewed as the required three steps, viz., unfreezing, changing and re-freezing. Unfreezing mean that old ideas and practices need to be cast aside so that new ones can be learnt. Change is the step in which the new ideas and practices are learnt so that an employee can think and perform in new ways. Refreezing means that what has been learnt is integrated into actual practice.

Implementation is the institutionalisation and internalisation of a change after it has been accepted by an organisation and a decision has been taken to accept and make it part of the on-going activity. Implementation may be seen as multidimensional process. The end result of implementation is the institutionalisation and stabilisation of change. Institutionalisation is making the change permanent part of organisation and internalisation means stabilisation of the change. The implementation process should start with planning. The three important stages of implementation of change process (see Fig. 30.3) are: *(i)* Monitoring the change; *(ii)* Taking action in relation to the change; and *(iii)* Making necessary adjustments in the programme accepted for implementation.

Planning: The main objective of planning, is to have an overall understanding of the nature of implementation. Planning process refers to determining in advance the entire process of implementation of change phasing. Planning may be focused on phasing. Phasing may be either temporal (in terms of time) or spatial (in terms of various units or the locations of the organisation).

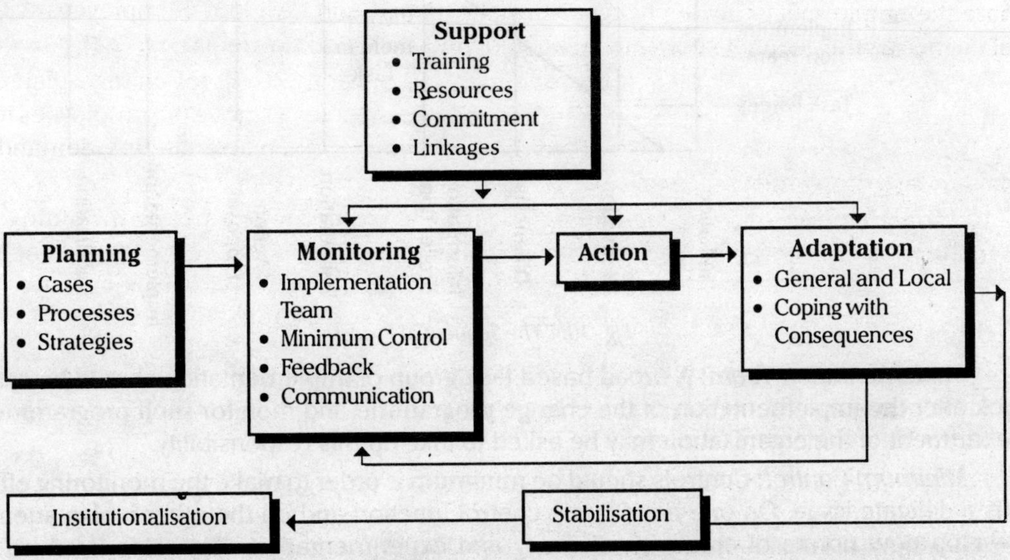

Fig. 30.3 The Model of Implementation of Change in an Organisation.

Processes: Various processes involved in implementation should be decided in advance. Various stages of the process include: initiation, motivation, diagnosis, information collection, deliberation, action proposal, implementation and stabilisation (see Fig.30.4). Attention should be paid to the process of collaboration, increasing the capability of the organisation to face the problems of change, establishing the norms and values.

Strategies: Management should formulate various strategies for implementation. These strategies should focus on taking outsider's help, change agent, designing permanent organisational structures, unit/location of the organisation to be selected for initial process, openness with the environment etc.

Monitoring: It is the process of "routine periodic measurement of programme inputs, activities and outputs undertaken during programme implementation. Monitoring is normally concerned with the procurement, delivery and utilisation of programme resources, adherence to work schedules or progress made in the production of outputs." Monitoring is essential to make implementation effective. Monitoring/control is to ensure that a plan proceeds according to the original design. A broader group of people should be involved in monitoring function. An independent team without having interest in change may be entrusted with the task. This team may have a continuous status.

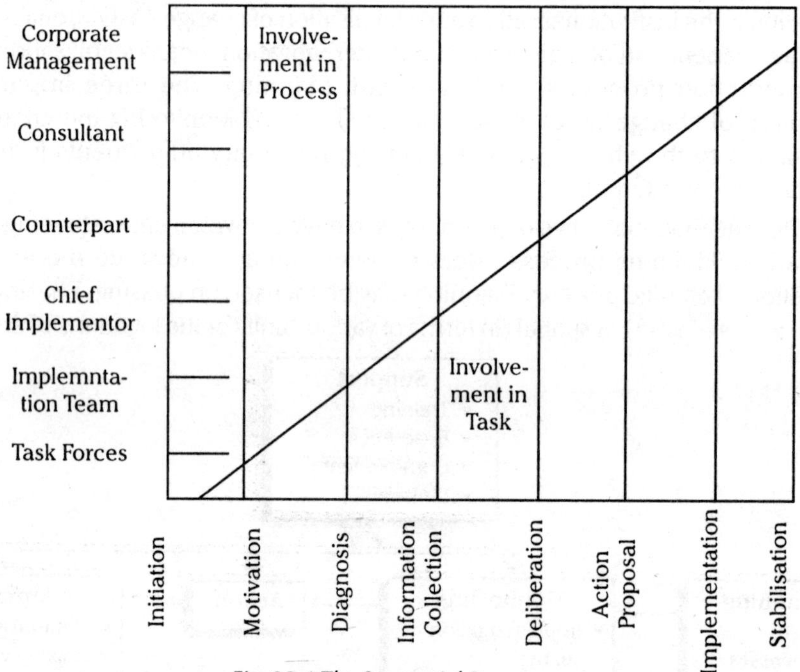

Fig. 30.4 The Sequential Process.

Implementation Team: A broad based task group of implementation should be set–up to look after the implementation of the change programme and monitor such programme. HRD department of the organisation may be asked to take up this responsibility.

Minimum Control: Controls should be minimum is order to make the monitoring effective. It is a delicate issue. On one hand it is a control function and on the other it also attempts to develop new norms of creativity, diversity and experimentation. Key roles involved in the implementation process are task force, implementation team, chief implement or counterpart consultant and corporate management. These roles at various stages of process are depicted in Fig. 30.4.

Review and Feedback: Implementation requires reviewing various process and provide feedback. It involves getting data information and experiences and providing feedback to the people on how they are implementing compared to the design and plans.

Dissemination of Information: The data, information and experiences collected in the various units/processes of the organisation may be provided to all the parties of change implementation with a view to reinforce a sense of success amongst various people.

Action: Action covers all the minute details of what is to be implemented at different stages. This process involves various phases and steps for people and various group tasks in relation to change programme.

Adaptation: Adaptation is the combination of two main criteria of effectiveness of implementation. Adaptation may be both general in the sense the some modifications may be made in the original plan and some may be developed at later stage.

Support: Various types of support from all concerned will be required for the implementation of change. Main agencies which render the necessary support are:

Human Resource Development: Effective implementation of change requires new and varied technical, managerial and behavioural skills and knowledge. Human Resource Development department can contribute for the enhancement of these skills through training, executive development and organisation development programmes.

Resources: Implementation requires support in the form of various fields like financial, human resources, technological etc.

Linkages: Support may also be required in terms of building linkages both with external experts, various external agencies and internal departments. Linkage among departments, implementation teams, line management and top management is essential.

To Management Commitment: The most important aspect of support essential for implementing change is the support and commitment to top management. Top management should involve itself in the process of change implementation, encourage the implementation team, provide all types of resources.

Management has to get the support from employees through the following means: *(a)* Encouraging and using group force: *(b)* Development of leadership for change; *(c)* Encouraging participation and sharing views; *(d)* Maintenance of employees security; *(e)* Effective communication; *(f)* Participation and working with the unions; *(g)* Working with the total system of the organisation which requires adopting useful and necessary changes; *(h)* Changing by evolution but not by revolution: (*i*) Adopting the change with adequate attention to human relations: (j) Identifying and taking care of post change problems.

Sources of Power

The sources of power can be divided into two categories viz., *(i)* internal sources, and *(ii)* sources for external stockholder as shown in Fig 30.5.

Sources of Power

Internal Sources	*Sources for External Stakeholders*
1. Hierarchy (Formal Power)	1. Control of strategic resources (Ex: Materials, Men, Money)
2. Influence or Charisma (Informal power)	2. Involvement in strategic implementation (Ex: Distribution outlets, franchise, licenses etc).
3. Control of strategic resources	3. Possession of knowledge (Ex: skills)
4. Possession of knowledge/skills.	4. Through internal links (Ex: Informal influence)
5. Control of environment (Ex: Negotiation skills)	
6. Involvement in strategic implementation. (Ex: Exercising discretion)	

Source: Gerry Johnson and Kevan Scholes, *op. cit.*, p. 134.

Fig. 30.5 Sources of Power

STYLES OF MANAGING STRATEGIC CHANGE

There are a number of management styles appropriate for managing strategic change efficiently. They include:

***(i)* Education and Communication:** Employer resist change or create blocks when the employees are not well informed the decision of strategic change. Managements should educate and inform the employees regarding the change. Small group briefing sessions, discussion sessions and debate sessions. In addition, management should communicate the idea and programme of change to all employees in order to have clarity.

***(ii)* Participation:** Employee participation in the process of strategic change decision making helps the organisation to educate the employees, to solicit the employee ideas, experiences and to create a feeling of ownership and belongingness among the employees. Further, it helps to formulate teams or task forces to implement change. Employee participation makes the strategic change implementation successful. Further, it increases the quality of strategic decisions.

***(iii)* Intervention Approach:** Under this approach change agent delegates the authority of idea generation, data collection, detailed programming etc., to the organisational employees. He keeps the authority of coordination and control with himself/herself.

***(iv)* Manipulation:** When change is essential and drastic accompanied by possible opposition by employees and managers, top management has to manipulate the internal environment and organisational behaviour of the company. The manipulation helps to modify the conditions into a favourable situation for implementation of strategic change.

***(v)* Coercion or Edict:** If management fails to get the cooperation of employees for strategic change by all means, then the management imposes change through coercion or edict. Management imposes change through issuing directives or orders. Further, if the change situation is urgent, management uses the style of coercion or edict. Similarly, this style is more appropriate, when the employees have divided opinions on strategic change.

Exhibit – 30.3 Presents the different stratics of managing strategic change.

Changes in Organisational Routines

Routines' are the institutionalised ways of doing the activities in an organisation. These are the well established practices and people are habituated to the routines. The people resist to change the ways of doing the things as they need different skills and knowledge.

Managers normally fail to estimate the power of the 'routines' and take them for granted as and when strategies are changed. In other words, managers view that, routines will be automatically changed as and when new strategies are implemented. But, the employees resist to change the routines which causes either delay in implementing the strategy or failing in implementing the strategy. Therefore, managers must estimate the power of routines and their probable hindrance on strategy before implementing it. It will help the managers to take steps to modify the routines to the strategy requirements.

Exhibit 30.3: Strategies to Manage Resistance to Changes

Styles	*Commonly used Situations*	*Advantages*	*Drawbacks*
Education+ Communication	Where there is a lack of information or inaccurate information and analysis.	Once persuaded people will often help with the implementation of the change.	Can be very time consuming if lots of people are involved.
Participation+ Involvement	Where the initiators do not have all the information they need to design the change and where others have considerable power to resist.	People who participate will be committed to implementing change and any relevant infomation they have will be Integrated into the change plan.	Can be very time consuming if participators design an inappropriate change.
Facilitation+ Support	Where people are resisting because of adjustment problems.	No other approach works as well with adjustment problems.	Can be time consuming. expensive, and still fail.
Negotiation+ Agreement	Where someone or some group will clearly lose out in a change and where that group has considerable power to resist.	Sometime it is a relatively easy way to avoid major resistance.	Can be too expensive in many cases if it alerts others to negotiate for compliance.
Manipulation+ Co-operation	Where other tactics will not work or are too expensive.	It can be a relatively quick and inexpensive solution to resistance problems.	Can lead to future problems if people feel manipulated.
Explicit+Implicit coercion	Where speed is essential and the change initiators possess considerable power.	It is speedy and can overcome any kind of resistance.	Can be risky if it leaves people angry at the initiators.

Source: "Choosing Strategic for Change" by Kotter & Schlesinger, March–April 1979, *Harvard Business Review*.

Symbolic Activity in Managing Strategic Change

Strategic change activities are not only overt and formal in nature, they are also symbolic. The symbolic aspects of organisations include logos, offices, cars, titles, type of language and terminology commonly used etc. The other cultural factors include routine ways of doing the things, the rituals such as training programmes, promotions, performance appraisal, stories told by the insiders and outsiders, control systems and reward systems and the power structures. (See. Exhibit 30.4)

Behaviour of the change agents is one form of symbol in relation to strategic change. The important factor that affects change implementation is the language used by the change agents.

Managers should understand the symbols those affect the strategic change implementation process and take steps to mould these symbols in a suitable form.

Political Processes

Political activity is quite normal in organisations. Political activity prevails wherever there is human element. Managers should understand the political process while formulating and implementing strategic change. The understanding and appropriate moulding of political process helps for implementing change successfully. However, it creates blockages in general. Therefore, managers should be sensitive to the political dimensions in order to reduce the blockages and to turn the political dimensions favourable to strategic change implementation.

Power

Power, from the view point of strategic management is extent to which individuals or groups are able to persuade, induce or coerce others into following certain courses of actions. A clear distinction should be made between the authority and power in assessing the impact of power on strategic change implementation.

Exhibit 30.4 : Types of Rite (ritual) and their Roles in Culture Change

Types of rite	*Social Consequences*	*Role in Promoting Consolidating Culture Change*	*Examples*
Rites of passage roles	Facilitate transition roles and statues that are new for them	Consolidate ways people of people into social new recruits Promote new ways of social interaction	Induction of carry out social
Rites of degradation	Dissolve social identities and their attendant power	Provide public acknowledgements that problems exist Defend group boundaries by redefining who belongs and who does not Reaffirm social importance and value of role involved	Firing and replacing top executives
Rites of enhancement	Enhance social identities and their attendant power	Spread good news about the organisation Provide public recognition of individuals for their accomplishments and motivate others to similar efforts	Award ceremonies at company conferences

		Emphasise social value of performance of social roles	
Rites of Renewal	Refurbish social structures and improve the ways they function	Reassure members that something is being done about problems Focus attention on some problems and away from others Legitimate systems of power and authority	Problem-centred/ project task forces Appointments of consultants on specified projects
Rites of integration	Encourage and revive shared feelings that bind people together and keep them committed to a social system	Permit venting of emotion and temporary loosening of various norms Reassert and reaffirm, by contrast, moral rightness of usual norms	Office Christmas parties
Rites of Conflict reduction	Reduce conflict and aggression	Re-establish equilibrium in disturbed social relations Compartmentalise conflict and its disruptive effects	Internal appeal systems Union–management Committees

Source: Adapted from H.M. Trice and J.M. Beyer, "Using six organisational rites to change culture; in R.H. Kilman *et al.* (eds), *Gaining Control of the Corporate Culture*, Jossey Bass, 1985, pp. 374 – 375.

Problems: Change and political activities are quite normal and they are unavoidable. There are several problems in managing political systems. The managers face problems in identifying political groups and their potentiality in implementing the change successfully. After identifying the potential groups, the manager should identify himself/herself with the group and involve in the group activities. This process helps the managers, to get the cooperation in implementing the change.

Another problems is that the managers may not have enough power to influence the major power groups. The next problem is that changing the *status quo* needs a lot of influence on the existing values, beliefs and attitudes of the people, which the manager may not have. The change agents may also face the political manoeuvers of other managers who resist the change. Exhibit 30.5. presents countermoves to change.

COMMUNICATING CHANGE

Strategic change is significant and drastic as it affects the entire or most part of the organisation and employees. Normally the employees, whether they are affected by the change or not would like to know the plans and programmes of change as they view the company is their own. Further, some employees feel insulted or alienated if they are not informed about the change. Most of the employees emotionally contribute their resources willingly, if they are consulted or informed about the change.

In fact, the organisation can enhance the quality of the strategic decisions by involving and storming the brains of the employees. Group decision making rather than individual decision making is more appropriate for strategic change decision-making Group decision making is possible by involving the employees through communication. Hence, the organisations should communicate the change to the employees. This process helps the organisation to overcome employees resistance to change and to solicit the willing cooperation of all employees.

Change Tactics

Change is most essential in the competitive environment. The change decision should be appropriate to bear its fruits. However, changes is resisted by the employees and managers. Therefore managements should use tactics to implement change successfully.

The change tactics include:

- Use group decision making process as it storms the brains and results in the most efficient decision through synergy.
- Shared Rewards: Employees-affected by change can be secured by providing the opportunity of sharing the rewards among themselves.
- Cooperation from Trade Unions. Support and cooperation from trade unions is essential for implementing change. These can be secured by communicating, consulting and involving the trade unions in change process.
- Concern for Employees: When change affects the employees significantly, the management should exhibit its concern for employees.

Role In Change Process

Managers at different levels in the organisational hierarchy play their roles in the change process in managing change. The important among them are change agent, middle level managers, other organisational members, external stakeholders and outsiders.

(i) Change Agent: The change agent may be from within the organisation or from outside the organisation. The Chief Executive of the company or the top level managers normally would be change agents from within the company. These change agents continuously observe the external environment and conceptualise the environmental and changes. He foresees the change requirements and possible changes based on the environmental opportunities. Further, he plays active role in identifying the areas for change and motivates the middle level managers to carry out the change process.

(ii) Middle Level Managers: Middle level managers help the Chief Executive / Top Level managers in identifying the change areas. They formulate detailed programme of change, prepare detailed strategies and tactics, guide and help the lower level operational managers in implemnetation of change.

(iii) Other Organisational Members: Other organisational members include mostly junior level / operational level managers. These mangers help the middle level managers in formulating strategic change, detailed programmes and tactics. Further, they play active role in formulating detailed programmes and in implementing strategic change programmes.

(iv) External Stakeholders: External stakeholders include suppliers, financial institutions, creditors, customers and competitors. These members are not directly involved themselves in the strategic change. But, management take the interests of these members very much in formulating change. Further, management consults those stakeholders regarding change. Thus, these stakeholders acts as consultants and advisors to the management regarding strategic change.

(v) Out Siders: Outsiders are mostly general public. They play the role of creation of the image regarding the organisation, strategic change and its input on organisational performance.

Leadership and Change Agency

Many large companies appoint the consultants as change agents to implement strategic changes. It is essential to understand the characteristics of a change agent.

(i) *Clarity of Direction of Charge Agent*: It is to be analysed and understood that whether the change agents has clear direction in terms of vision, mission and objectives of strategic change.

(ii) *Significance of the Context*: The change agent should have a clear idea of the type of the change required. Opportunities for change and threats of change. The change agent should have the ability to encash the opportunities by implementing the change and to reduce the threats.

(iii) *Appropriate Management Style*: The change agent should identify the type of the change circumstances, management style appropriate to it. The agent should adopt that appropriate style rather than imposing his own style which would be inappropriate to the circumstances.

(iv) *Political and Symbolic Processes*: The change agent should understand the existing political and symbolic systems in the organisation. He has to perceive the most appropriate systems for efficient change implementation. Then he has to find the ways and means to change the political and symbolic processes as desired.

(v) *Endowed Authority*: Change agents normally do not exercise the formal authority to influence the people's values in implementing change. Rather, they relate the change around the value system of the people supporting the change in an organisation.

(vi) *Personal Traits of the Change Agents*: The successful change agents possess the skills of supervision, team building, team playing, self-analytical, listening, self-learning, constructive restlessness, concentration for long hours. Self-directed and self-confident.

Exhibit 30.5 : Countermoves to Change

* *Divert resources*. Split budget across other projects, give key staff other priorities/other assignments.
* *Exploit inertia*. Request everyone to wait until a key player takes action, read a report, or make an appropriate response; suggest the results from another project should be assessed first.
* *Keep goals vague and complex*. It is harder to initiate appropriate action if aims are multidimensional and specified in generalised, grandiose or abstract terms.
* *Encourage and exploit lack of organisational awareness*. Insist that 'we can deal with the people issues later', knowing this will delay or kill the project.
* *Establish clear direction and object-tives.* Goal clarity enables action to *proceed* more effectively than ambiguity and complexity, which can slow down action.
* *Establish simple, phased programming*. For the same reasons as having clear goals.
* *Adopt a fixer- facilitor-negotiator role*. Resistance to change can rarely be overcome by reason alone, and the exercise of these interpersonal skills is required.
* *Seek and respond to resistance*.
Take a proactive approach to resistance in order to overcome, mitigate or block it; appeal/refer to high values/standards or powerful authorities, warn them off; use

* *'Great idea – let's do it properly.'* Involve so many representatives or experts that there will be so many different views and conflicting interests it will delay decisions or require meaningless compromise.
* *Dissipate energies.* Conduct surveys, collect data, prepare analysis, write reports, make overseas trips, hold special meetings.............
* *Reduce the change agent's influence and credibility.* Spread damaging rumours, particularly among the change agent's friends and supporters.
* *Keep a low profile.* Do not openly declare resistance to change because that gives those driving change a clear target to aim for.

influential intermediaries; infiltrate meetings and supporters; wait them out or wear them down.

* *Rely on face to face.* Personal Influence and persuasion is usually more effective in winning and sustaining support than the impersonal memo or report.
* *Exploit a crisis.* People will often respond more positively to a crisis which they understand and face collectively than to personal attempts to change behaviour.
* *Co-opt support early.* Build coalitions and recruit backers; of prior importance to the building of teams: co opting opponents may also be tactically useful.
* *The meaningful steering committee/ task force/project team.* Include in its membership key players in the organisation who carry 'weight', authority and respect.

Source: Adapted from D. Buchanan and D. Boddy, *The Expertise of the Change Agent: Public performance and backstage activity*. Prentice Hall, 1992. pp. 78-79.

Characteristics of a Change Agent

(i) The change agent should be creative and visionary about the future.
(ii) The change agent must be insightful and action-oriented.
(iii) He should have credibility in carrying the people with the change.
(iv) He should have efficient communicating skills in addition to have willingness to communicating all issues to the organisational employees.
(v) He should have focus and clarity of strategic change in order to avoid ambiguity and complexity.
(vi) He should have the ability to maintain the organisational performance while adapting the strategic change.

Exhibit – 30.6 Presents key competencies of change agents

Exhibit 30.6 : Key Components of Change Agents

Goals

1. Sensitivity to changes in key personnel, top management perceptions and market conditions, and to the way in which these impact on the goals of the project in hand.
2. Clarity in specifying goals, in defining the achievable.
3. Flexibility in responding to changes without the control of the project manager, perhaps requiring major shifts in project goals and management styles, and risk taking.

Roles

4. Team-building abilities, to bring together key stakeholders and establish effective working groups, and clearly to define and delegate respective responsibilities.

5. Networking skills in establishing and maintaining appropriate contacts within and outside the organisation.
6. Tolerance of ambiguity, to be able to function comfortably, patiently and effectively in an uncertain environment.

Communication

7. Communication skills to transmit effectively to colleagues and subordinates the need for changes in project goals and in individual tasks and responsibilities.
8. Inter-personal skills, across the range, including selection, listening, collecting appropriate information, identifying the concerns of others and managing meetings.
9. Personal enthusiasm, in expressing plans and ideas.
10. Stimulating motivation and commitment in others involved.

Negotiation

11. Selling plans and ideas to others, by creating a desirable and challenging vision of the future.
12. Negotiating with key players for resources, or for changes in procedures, and to resolve conflict.

Managing up

13. Political awareness, in identifying potential coalitions and balancing conflicting goals and perceptions.
14. Influencing skills, to gain commitment to project plans and ideas from potential sceptics and resisters.
15. Helicopter perspectives, to stand back from the immediate project and take a broader view of priorities.

Source: Adapted from D. Buchanan and D. Boddy, *The Expertise of the Change Agent: Public Performance and Backstage Activity*, Prentice Hall, 1992, pp. 92-93.

Summary of the Findings of A Study

Pettigrew and whipp conducted a study of firms which managed change successfully. According to them, the organisations which managed change successfully demonstrated the following five characteristics.

(i) ***Environmental Appraisal***: The organisations which managed change successfully are most of open learning systems. They are more sensitive to the environmental changes. Managers set their role very close to environmental changes. External orientation is the part of the organisational culture. The orientation of the organisational structure is on the external environment rather than internal environment.

(ii) ***Leading Change***: Leadership and management for change depends upon the organisational content and the change requirements. The change agent has to set the context in terms of culture and capabilities of the organisation. The change agent has to change his styles of leadership and management according to the contextual requirements of the change.

(iii) ***Linking Strategic and Operational Change***: The change agents could successfully link strategic change with operational change of the organisations which implemented change successfully. This linkage process emphasises on translating strategic change into detailed resource plans, critical success factors, key tasks, control processes, communication network, organisational culture etc.

The change is continual and day by day rather than transformational or dramatic. If the organisation has not been changing continually and arrives a point of dramatic change, then it would be difficult to link strategic change with operational change.

(iv) *Strategic Human Resources Management*: Human resources are the premier assets of any organisations. In fact, they are responsible for the successful implementation of strategic change. Human resource management has been placed at strategic level by many of the modern organisations.

The organisations should formulate human resource policies of the higher order. And they should integrate the human resource policies with their strategies from time to time. The organisations should take their missions, objectives and strategies, as basis in formulating human resource policies and in performing various HRM functions like selection, training, development, compensation, human relations etc. In fact, these functions should not be treated or performed from the operational point of view.

The developed human resources from the strategic view point mostly enable the successful implementation of strategic change.

(v) *Coherence in Managing Strategic Change*: The successful implementation of strategic change needs integrate or coherent various aspects and activities across the organisations. These should be consistency between strategic objectives and intended strategies. Environment provides opportunities and pose challenges. The strategies should be formulated in the direction of environmental opportunities rather than threats. Strategies should also take into consideration the interests of customers, suppliers and financiers.

The strategies should be economically viable, financially feasible, managerially and socially appropriate. The ultimate purpose of the strategy is to achieve competitive advantage and excel in alround performance.

(vi) *Pull all the Threads Together*: Many successful organisations believe that clarity in the strategic direction and the relevance to the external environment is more important. Organisations should continuously sense the forces around them, the direction of the forces, modify the forces towards the organisational direction, if possible and if not set the organisation, learn and adopt based on the requirements of the forces. The learning and adaptation should be by integrating all the functional areas and functions of the management of the company. This process needs pulling all the threads together from multidirections.

CHAPTER 31

STRATEGIC MANAGEMENT IN NON-PROFIT ORGAINSATIONS

Introduction

Categories of Non-Profit Organisations

Mission, Objectives and Goals

Strategy Formulation and Implementation

Popular Strategies of Non-Profit Organisations

Strategy Evaluation and Control

Measures to Control the Constraints

INTRODUCTION

Traditionally, studies in strategic management have dealt with profit making business organisations engaged in manufacturing and/or service. They neglected the non–profit organisations. The basic concepts of strategic management discussed in the earlier chapters are applicable to profit and non–profit organisations. All organisations formulate the MOST *i.e.*, Mission, Objectives, Strategies and Tactics. In fact, they analyse their environments— internal and external, formulate strategies, analyse and select the appropriate strategies, implement the strategies and evaluate and control the strategies. However, there are distinct differences between profit and non–profit organisations.

CATEGORIES OF NON-PROFIT ORGANISATION

Non–profit organisations can be basically classified into two groups viz., *(i)* private non–profit organisations, and *(ii)* public non–profit organisations. Significant differences among profit organisations and non–profit private organisations are presented in Exhibit 31.1.

Exhibit 31.1: Differences between Profit and Non–Profit/Private Organisations

	Profit Organisations	*Non–profit/Private Organisations*
Ownership	Private	Private
Funding	Sales revenue	Membership fee, contributions from public and/or private sources, sale of products or services
Types	Single proprietorship, partnership, corporation	Floated by members
Activities	Production and/or Marketing of goods and/or services	Educational, charitable, social service, Health service, foundation, cultural, religious, and recreational
Main objective	Profit maximization	Service maximization

Significant differences between business and non–profit government organisations are presented in Exhibit 31.2.

Though the public organisations like central government, state governments and local governments are also included under non–profit organisations, typically the term non–profit includes private non–profit organisations such as hospitals, private universities, private colleges, recreational societies etc. Public utilities like transportation corporation, water supply corporations, dairy corporations are in a grey area somewhere between profit and non–profit organisations. Non–profit organisations assumes importance as the society particularly the low–income people depend on these organisations. Further, they provide services, which cannot be provided by the profit–making organisations.

Types of Non–Profit Organisations

The different types of non–profit organisations include:

(i) Private educational institutions like private universities, colleges, and schools,
(ii) Charities,
(iii) Social service organisations.
(iv) Health service organisations like Sri Venkateshwara Institute of Medical Sciences.
(v) Foundations.
(vi) Cultural organisations.
(vii) Religions organisations like Tirumala–Tirupati Devasthanams and Shirdi Sai Samsthanams.
(viii) Social organisations.

Exhibit 31.2: Significant Differences between Business and Public (Government) Organisations

	Business	*Public Non–Profit Organisations*
Main Objective	Profit	Public service
Economic Objectives	Profit required bankruptcy possible	No profit required bankruptcy unlikely
Structure	Frequently decentralised into profit centres	Usually a centralised bureaucracy
Accountable to	Shareholders	Representative of the people
Control of Strategy	Management	Representatives of the people
Scope of Activity	Unlimited, no monopoly	Limited, State monopoly·
Major Sources of Funds	Shareholders, banks, financial companies	Government Taxation

Source: A. Waldansky, "The Politics of Budgetary process," Little Brown and Company, Boston, 1964.

Importance of Sources of Revenue

The sources of revenue is one of the important factors which differentiates the profit organisations and non-profit organisations. The profit organisations mainly depend upon the revenue of sales of goods and/or services. Their sources of income is the customer who buys and uses the product and/or service, and who pays for it when received. Profit results when the revenue is more than the costs of producing and distributing the product. Profit is the main measure of the corporation's effectiveness.

The non–profit organisations depends on membership dues, assessments, donations, funding from sponsor agencies, subscriptions to the periodicals published by the organisations. Thus, revenue for these organisations comes from a variety of sources.

Strategic Issues in Non-profit Organisations

Strategic management is applicable for both profit–making organisations and non–profit organisations. Now, we discuss various issues of strategic management concerning to non–profit organisations. These issues include: formulation of mission, goals and objectives, environmental analysis, strategy formulation and implementation and strategic control.

MISSION, OBJECTIVES AND GOALS

Even, non–profit organisation should have mission, objectives, and goals.

Mission

Formulation of well defined mission is important to non–profit organisations to have a clear direction. In fact, the major non–profit organisations formulate mission. According to Peter F. Drucker, "the best non–profits devote a great deal of thought to defining their organisation's mission."[1]

The non– profit organisations while formulating the mission should consider the questions like: What is our business? Or what are our activities? Who is the customer? Or who are our clients? What does our customer (or client) consider the value? As Hesselbein explained, "more than any one thing, that made the difference. Because when you are clear about your mission, corporate goals and operating objectives flow from it."[2]

As an example, the mission statement of one non–profit medical institute is:

"Our mission shall be the promotion of human knowledge within the field of the basic sciences (principally in the field of medical research and medical education) and the effective application thereof for the benefit of mankind."[3]

The mission statement of a management educational institute is:

The establishment of a full–fledged management institute as an international centre of excellence for education, research and consultancy in all the areas of management.

Objectives and Goals

The non–profit organisations based on their mission statement, should formulate objectives and goals. But many non–profit organisations fail in this regard. Profit organisations can easily measure their production, sales, turnover, profits, market share etc. But the non–profit organisations cannot have such clear goals. The reasons for the absence of clarity in goals are:

(i) Many goals of the non–profit organisations are value-laden.

(ii) Non–profit goals often involve important trade-offs.

(iii) Goals often be deliberately vague, broad and general like. "Protect our environment," or "provide high quality education."

Goals in non–profit organisations are often vague because leadership is subject to frequent changes and it leads to change in direction.

Goals many sometimes not reflect the needs of the organisation's customers/clients as much as they reflect the wishes of the organisations' financial donors. Some non–profit organisations, may not turn down substantial donations, if the donors insists that the funds be used for a purpose other than the basic mission of the organisation. In view of these observations, though it

1. Peter F. Drucker, "What Business can Learn from Non–profits," Harvard Business Review, Vol. 67, No. 4, 1989, p. 89.
2. Brayne, "Profiting from the Non-profits," p.72.
3. The Annual Report of the Howard Hughes Medical Institute 1989.

is difficult to formulate goals compared to that in business firms, non–profit organisations should formulate goals. Formulation of objectives and goals will help the organisation to have a clear direction.

The non–profit organisations may formulate objectives and goals by considering the interests of all the stakeholders. They should bring balance among the conflicting interests of different stakeholders. The organisations can define specific, if not quantifiable objectives and goals. Methods of determining cost–benefit ratios and standards are essential. The standards like expenditure per client, norms for defining à deserving client may be determined. Such standards act as a surrogate performance measure when profit figures are not applicable.[4]

The goals of the non–profit health organisation include:

(i) Community services like health, educational and environmental protection.
(ii) A centre for prevention of ill health, community problems.
(iii) Educational for the community regarding health, sanitation, cleanliness, consumerism etc.
(iv) Training and education of volunteers who will carry out the mission of the organisation like instructors, medical practitioners, religious priests etc.
(v) Providing facilities for physicians, teachers etc.

Determining the goals of a temple or church is equally perplexing. The goal to provide: *(i)* worship facilities, *(ii)* religious education, *(iii)* evangelical effort, *(iv)* missionary effort, (v) opportunities for members to fulfil social and psychological needs,*(vi)* fund raising for charitable organisations, *(vii)* contribution to the identification and solution of societal problems.[5] *(viii)* contribution to the development of educational and health facilities like Sri Satya Sai Central Trust, *(ix)* revival of the ruined temples like Tirumala Tirupati Devasthanams. Exhibit 31.3 shows the objectives and goals of a management institute.

Exhibit 31.3. Objectives and Goals of a Management Institute

Objectives:

To pursue the stated mission, the Institute strives to achieve the following objectives.

(i) To train young students, add the value, develop their competency and inculcate professionalism among them in order to prepare appropriate managers and entrepreneurs for Eritrean economy.
(ii) To undertake research studies with a view to provide inputs to the policy makers of the Government, and business.
(iii) To organize management development and training programmes with a view to equip practicing managers with latest skills and techniques of management profession.
(iv) To organize seminars and conferences in order to disseminate the advanced managerial knowledge to the practicing managers.
(v) To provide consultancy services with a view to solve the managerial and operational problems of Eritrean business.
(vi) To undertake any related activities to pursue the mission.

4. P.D. Harvey and J.D. Synder, "Charities Need a Bottom Line Too," Harvard Business Review, Vol. 65, no. 1, 1987, pp. 14–22.
5. David E. Hussey, "Corporate Planning for a church," Long Range Planning, April 1974, p. 63.

Strategies:

To achieve the above mentioned objectives, the following strategies are formulated.

(i) Strengthening teaching facilities like curriculum revision, preparation of qualitative course material and teaching aids.

(ii) Human resource development. It includes the development of junior staff through Ph.D., programmes of linkage Universities.

(iii) Secondment of senior faculty.

(iv) Support the library in the process of procurement of books and journals.

Goals:

Our goals during 1997–98 Academic year are:

(i) Educate the students towards their M.B.A., degree with conceptual, practical skills and knowledge.

(ii) Modify the curriculum incorporating the courses relevant to Eritrean business.

(iii) Carryout the research studies in the areas of

(a) Human Resource Management and
(b) International marketing.

(iv) Provide Tutorial classes for the government officers who are pursuing Certificate course in Management of the Open University U.K.

(v) Provide consultancy services.

(vi) Organization of National and International Seminars and Conferences:

(vii) Conduct Management Development and Training Programmes.

STRATEGY FORMULATION AND IMPLEMENTATION

Strategy formulation is more or less the same in non–profit organisations compared to that of profit organisations. In general most of the organisations attempt to satisfy specific social needs. The strategies of non–profit organisations complement the strategies and services of governmental agencies. For example, the strategies of Ministry of Health, Government of India and the non–profit health organisations strategies are more or less similar. They include: providing medical and health facilities to the people, development of hospitals and health clinics, development of doctors and para–medical personnel etc. Some non–profit organisations have the distinct strategies. However, they are comparable with the corporate strategies. Exhibit 31.4 shows the growth strategies for churches.

Sometimes, the strategies of non–profit organisations particularly government agencies differ from those of corporate strategies. One of the important reasons for the difference is the presence of greater political constraints upon their strategic choices. Most of the decisions in public organisations are to be approved by the ministers, parliaments or the legislative assemblies. These bodies politicalise the strategic decisions by their public visibility in the press. The rules, regulations, procedures and formalities of public organisations complicate the process of strategy formulation.

Constraints on Strategic Management

Though, there are some common features of the strategic management in profit and non–profit organisations, non–profit organisations are different from profit–making organisations. There are a number of characteristics peculiar to the non–profit organisations that constrain their behaviour and affect their strategic management. Newman and Wallender list the following five constraining characteristics:

Exhibit 31.4: Growth Strategies for Churches

One of the nation's largest churches is Willow–creek Community Church in South Barrington, Illinois, a Chicago suburb. Although the church was founded only in 1974, it now has over thirteen thousand parishioners. Its founder and pastor, Bill Hybels, adopted the growth strategy, based on business fundamentals. He originally went door to door asking people why they did not attend church. From this market research, he began to offer services that catered to the needs of his "customers." For instance, he holds full services on Wednesday evenings because some working parents prefer to spend Sundays with their children. And for those unable to attend any of the services, he provides his sermons on cassette tapes.

Another huge religious institution following a growth strategy is Houston's Second Baptist Church. With a Sunday morning attendance of twelve thousand, the church complex covers 32 acres. In 1984, however, the church was simply a conventional church on a large plot of land. Its incoming pastor, H. Edwin Young, was familiar with the demographics of the area: thousands of young families and single people new to Houston. He sold his vision of a growing church to his congregation and persuaded them to pledge over $ 1 million needed for new physical facilities while the church borrowed over $ 26 million for additional construction costs.

Pastor Young dispatched church members to study office management techniques at Xerox and IBM, parking and people skills at Disney World. He varied religious services to fit particular needs. In addition to the traditional Sunday morning service, there is a Sunday evening service that caters to mostly singles crowd; and on Wednesday nights, separate services are offered, one traditional and one with religious rock music.

Today, computers regulate mood lighting during church services; shuttle buses bring latecomers in from outlying parking decks; parking attendants empty the church's numerous parking lots every Sunday in half an hour; billboards and television ads invite people to visit this "Fellowship of Excitement"; an information desk is staffed with cheerful beginning at 6:00 A.M.; and a restaurant offers two types of menus: "saints" for those who prefer a low–calorie meal and "sinners" for those who desire richer food.

Sources: R.G. Niebuhr, "Megachurches Strive to Be All Things to All Parishioners," *The Wall Street Journal*, 13 May 1991; P.F. Drucker, "What Business Can Learn from Non–profits," *Harvard Business Review* 67, No. 4 (1989): 89.

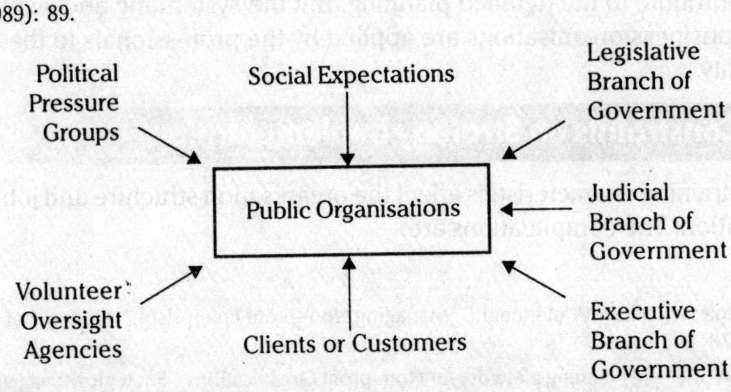

Source : Wright, Pringle and Kroll, *op. cit.*, p. 250.

Fig. 31.1 Stakeholder Constraints on Public Organisation

(i) Service is often intangible and hard to measure. This problem is compounded by the existence of multiple service objectives developed in order to satisfy multiple sponsors.
(ii) Client influence may be weak. Often the organisation has a local monopoly, and payments by customers may be a very small source of funds.
(iii) Strong employee commitment to profession or to a cause may undermine theii allegiance to the organisation employing them.
(iv) Resource contributors — notably fund contributors and government — may intrude upon the organisation's internal Management.[6]

Stakeholder Constraints on Public Organisations are shown in Fig. 31.1.

In view of these constraints, the strategic management process for any given situation will be different in a non–profit organisation than in a profit making organisation.

Impact of Constraints on Strategy Formulation

The above mentioned constraints affect the long–range planning and decision making. The complications arise in strategy formulation are:

***(i)* Goal conflicts interfere with rational planning** : Divergent goals and objectives are likely as the non–profit organisations typically lacks a single and clear–cut goal.[7] Different interests of the sponsors may prevent the management from formulating the goals. The low influence of the clients permits the organisation to have diversified values and goals to occur. This goals conflicting situation interfere with rational planning of the organisation.

***(ii)* An integrated planning focus tends to shift from results to resources**: There is almost no net bottom lines as non–profit organisations tend to provide services that are hard to measure. Therefore, planning is concerned with the resource inputs than the service outcomes.

***(iii)* Ambiguous operating objectives create opportunities for internal politics and goal displacement**: The combination of vague objectives and resource concern give a room for more self interest than the organisational interest. There is a scope to ignore the clients as the organisation concentrates on satisfying the sponsors than the clients. Even the board of the trustees are selected on the basis of their ability to mobilise funds rather than managerial experience. These factors result in goal displacement and creation of politics.

***(iv)* Professionalisation simplifies detailing planning but adds rigidity**: The professional employees contribute to the detailed planning. But the systematic and scientific operations as applicable to business organisations are applied by the professionals to the strategic planning. This adds rigidity.

Impact of Constraints on Strategy Implementation

The constraining characteristics affect the organisation structure and job design of the non–profit organisation. The complications are:

6. W.H. Newman and H.W. Wallender III, "Managing Non–profit Enterprises," Academy of Management Review, January 1978, p. 26.
7. P.C. Nutt, "A Strategic Planning Network for Non–profit Organisations," Strategic Management Journal, January–March, 1984, p. 57.

***(i)* Decentralisation is Complicated:** Decentralisation and delegation of decision–making authority is complicated due to the absence of clear cut goals and hard to measure output i.e., service. Therefore, the decision–making is centralised. Further, the defensive centralisation is necessary to avoid the objections of the sponsors.

***(ii)* Linking pins for External–Internal integration become Important**: As indicated earlier, the non–profit organisations excessively depend upon the external sources for funds particularly the sponsors, and donors. Some employees should act as linking pins between the internal operations and external sponsors. Some organisations employ public relations officers or fund raising officers.

***(iii)* Job Enrichment and Executive Development**: Job enrichment and executive development may be restrained by professionalism. Employment of Professionals at various levels with restrain job enrichment as it is viewed as encroachment into the authority of the next higher level professional.

POPULAR STRATEGIES OF NON-PROFIT ORGANISATIONS

The general objective of non profit organisations is to satisfy an ultimate need of a segment of a general public. The organisation expands its activities, if the revenue is more than the cost. In contrast, the organisations reduces its activities, if the expenses are more than the revenue. Some organisations change their missions in order to attract new sponsors and carry out activities different from the existing ones. But more organisations rejects such donations and they stick to their missions. Such organisations impose pressure on their members to increase membership contributions and enable the organisations to carry out their activities successfully. Three popular strategies are: (1) Strategic piggybacking, (2) interoganisational linking and (3) Linkage with a profit making organisation.

Strategic Piggybacking

The term strategic piggybacking is coined by Nielsen. This term refers to the development of a new activity for the non–profit organisations for the purpose of generating funds needed to make–up the deficits in the budget.[8] The new activity is taken up primarily to subsidise the primary service activities. Further, the new activity may be some what related to the existing activities even, indirectly. Top management invests in new, safe cash cows to fund its current cash–hungry stars, questions marks and stars, in an inverted use of portfolio analysis.[9]

Edward Skloot, President of the New York Consulting firm New Ventures suggests that a non-profit organisation have five resources before beginning a revenue–earning activity.[10] They are:

8. R.P. Nilsen, "SMR Forum: Strategic Piggybacking — A self subsidising strategy for Non–profit Institutions," Sloan Management Review, Summer 1982, pp. 65–69.
9. Thomas L.Wheelen and J. David Hunger, *op. cit.,* p. 304.
10. E. Skloot, "Should Non–profits Go into Business," Harvard Business Review, January–February 1983, pp. 20–26.

(i) Something to sell: The organisation should see whether it can find a market for its goods or services.

(ii) Critical mass of management talent: There must be enough people available to nurture and sustain an income venture over the long haul.

(iii) Trustee support: Trustee may actively or passively resist commercial involvement, if they do not like earned–income ventures.

(iv) Entrepreneurial attitude: Management must be able to combine an interest in innovative ideas with business like practicality.

(v) Venture Capital: Engaging a joint venture with a business organisation can provide necessary funds to initiate the activities as well as marketing and management support.[11]

Inter–Organisational Linkage

A major strategy often employed by non–profit organisations to increase their ability to serve clients efficiently or to acquire resources is developing cooperative ties with other organisations.[12] Non–profit hospitals increasingly use this strategy as a way to cope up with raising costs or declining revenues. Through the cooperation with other hospitals, services can be purchased and provided more efficiently than if done alone.[13]

Linkage with a profit–making Organisation:

The strategy of developing a linkage with a profit making organisation is an effective one as it solves the problems of shortage of funds, marketing of services and management of non–profit organisations. This strategy is more popular in educational institutions in India. Educational Institutions. Particularly business schools adapt this strategy. They get funds, manpower like guest lectures, employment for their graduates etc. This strategy solves the problem of funds throughout the life time (or at least until the financial position of the profit making organisation is sound) of the non profit organisation.

STRATEGY EVALUATION AND CONTROL

Strategic evaluation and control is rather very difficult as the objectives and goals are unclear. For example, the efficiency of hospitals can be measured in a number of ways. They are: *(i)* number of patients treated, *(ii)* number of patients cured, *(iii)* number of medical doctors, *(iv)* number of total staff, *(v)* number of beds etc. These controls may not be effectivey without formulating goals clearly. Similarly the efficiency of educational institutions can also be measured in a number of ways. They are: *(i)* number of and level of courses the institutions is offering, *(ii)* number of and level of staff, *(iii)* number of students registered, *(iv)* number of students successfully completing their courses every year, *(v)* number of students getting placements etc.

11. *Ibid.*, p. 24.
12. K.C. Provan, "Interoganisational Cooperation and Decision Making Autonomy in a Consortium Multihospital System," Academy of Management Review, July 1984, pp. 494–504.
13. Thomas L. Wheelen and J. David Hunger, *op. cit.*, p. 305.

These standards are also not effective unless the goals are clearly stated.

Obviously, control is more difficult, when goals are not clear or when goals are conflicting. Some non–profit organisations have literally no goals.

However, the strategies of non–profit organisations may be evaluated in more aspect. This approach to evaluation in the absence of equatifiable objectives, is being cost–aware and concentrating upon making the operation efficient*i.e.*, to achieve the same output with less input. However, if the organisation does not have objective/goals, the importance of a budget–based organisation is determined by the size of its staff and the size of its budget.[14]

Impact of the Constraints on Evaluation and Control

There are two problems caused by the constraints discussed earlier. They are:

***(i)* Rewards and Penalties have little or no relation to performance**: When the objectives and goals are unclear or conflicting, the results expected are vague. Under such situations, judgement about performance is subjective. Performance is judged either intuitively or on the basis of those small aspects of a job that can be measured. Therefore, the rewards and punishments have little or no relation to performance.

***(ii)* Control the inputs heavily rather than output**: The non–profit organisations may control the inputs heavily rather than output as inputs can be measured than output as stated earlier. Therefore, more emphasis may be laid on controlling costs and expenses.

MEASURES TO CONTROL THE CONSTANTS

The non–profit organisation can deal with the complications arising from the constraints to some extent through the following measures.

***(i)* Select a Dynamic and Forceful Leader**: The leader should be selected based on values to be used in decision–making, enough power to make important choices, be influential to make the others to accept his/her decisions. The leader can formulate appropriate mission, objectives and goals and raise to approach that the decisions are pushed from top to the down. Therefore, the lower level managers should adapt the approaches of 'play it safe,' 'await the guidance' etc.

***(ii)* Develop a Mystique**: The non–profit organisation can be integrated toward efficient goal accomplishment by developing a 'mystique' that dominates the enterprise and attracts the likely sponsors. The shared value about the important mission by the employees and sponsors can serve to motivate unusually high performance and client satisfaction. Once established, the mystique sets the character and values to decision makers and others are expected to follow.[15]

***(iii)* Generate Rules and Regulations:** The non–profit organisations suffer from the absence of objectives and goals and concentrating on the sponsors rather than clients. Hence, the top management should formulate rules and regulations so that the employees will pay enough attention towards the clients.

14. Peter F. Drucker, "Management: Tasks, Responsibilities and Practices," p. 142.
15. W.H. Newman and H.W. Wallender III, op, cit., p. 28.

***(iv)* Appointment of a Strong Board**: Appointment of a strong board of trustees will help the organisation in funds raising, formulation of mission and objectives. Then the employees can concentrate on the clients. The board can concentrate on strategic issues as well as on the operational issues like hiring, directing and developing the budget.[16]

***(v)* Establishment of Performance–based Budgets**: Establishment of performance–based budgets is the fifth approach in dealing with complications of non–profit organisations. This approach is to institute an information system that ties measurable objectives to budget line items. One such system is planning, programming and budgeting system. It includes five steps:

(a) Specify objectives as clearly as possible in quantitative measurable terms.

(b) Analyse the actual output of the non–profit organisation in terms of the stated objectives.

(c) Measure the cost of the particular programme.

(d) Analyse alternatives and search for those that have the greatest effectiveness in achieving the objectives.

(e) Establish the process in a systematic way so that it continues to occur over time.[17]

16. E.H. Fram, "Changing Expectations for Third Sector Executives," Human Resource Management, Fall 1980, p. 9.
17. Keating B.P. and Keating M.O., "Not For Profit," Thomas Horton and Daughters, New Jersey, 1980, pp. 140 –141.

INDEX